WILLIAM
SHAKESPEARE

COMEDIES
VOLUME 1

Shakespeare forged his tremendous art in the crucible of his comic imagination, which throughout his life enveloped and contained his tragic one. His early comedies – with their baroque poetic exuberance, intense theatricality, explosive bursts of humor, and superbly concrete realizations of the dialectics of love – capture as in a chrysalis all that he was to become. They provide a complete inventory of the mind of our greatest writer in the middle of his golden youth.

EVERYMAN,
I WILL GO WITH THEE,
AND BE THY GUIDE,
IN THY MOST NEED
TO GO BY THY SIDE

WILLIAM SHAKESPEARE

Comedies

with an Introduction by Tony Tanner
General Editor – Sylvan Barnet

VOLUME 1

EVERYMAN'S LIBRARY

Alfred A. Knopf New York Toronto .

205

THIS IS A BORZOI BOOK
PUBLISHED BY ALFRED A. KNOPF, INC.

First included in Everyman's Library, 1906

These plays are published by arrangement with New American
Library, a division of Penguin Books USA, Inc.

Book Design by Barbara de Wilde and Carol Devine Carson

COMEDIES

CONTENTS

———

INTRODUCTION

O if it prove,
Tempests are kind, and salt waves fresh in love!
(*Twelfth Night*, III, iv, 395–6)

Where a river meets the sea, there is a strange point at which
the fresh water of the river suddenly gives way to the salt water
of the sea (or, if you are coming in, salt water becomes fresh).
The actual place of the transition may change according to
whether the sea is at the full – in which case it pushes the river
back – or ebbing – when the river runs further out. But, either
way, the transition is relatively sudden – now this, now that;
here salt, here fresh. In this, it differs from the usual gradual-
isms which mark natural changes – the acorn becoming the
tree; the calf becoming the bull; the girl growing up, the man
growing old. Because of this prevailing gradualism, we have
the saying – nature does not make leaps. But it does. Now salt,
now fresh. It seems rather mysterious – but it *is* part of nature.
Natural magic.

Tennyson notes this phenomenon, and used it for his own
purposes in *In Memoriam*:

> There twice a day the Severn fills;
>   And salt sea-water passes by,
>   And hushes half the babbling Wye,
> And makes a silence in the hills.
>
> The Wye is hush'd nor moved along,
>   And hush'd my deepest grief of all,
>   When fill'd with tears that cannot fall,
> I brim with sorrow drowning song.
>
> The tide flows down, the wave again
>   Is vocal in its wooded walls;
>   My deeper anguish also falls,
> And I can speak a little then.

(XIX)

Tennyson is using the natural phenomenon to project – and
perhaps to understand – the fluctuations in his own grief.

xi

Sometimes it is silenced and 'bottled up' and the tears 'cannot fall' – as when the powerful sea blocks the outward flow of the river. But sometimes his grief finds a degree of tearful release and articulation – as when the river is allowed to run out some distance into the ebbing sea. The natural phenomenon provides an analogue – and perhaps, in part, an explanation – for his moods. Now salt; now fresh. Now you cry; now you don't. Shakespeare, as I shall suggest, uses it somewhat differently.

The sea, even more for the Elizabethans than for us, is always a potential place of tempest and shipwreck; of lostness, confusion, and destruction; of chaos, disappearance, and death. By contrast, the river, flowing calmly and containedly between its 'wooded walls', bespeaks the peace, order, and reassuring familiarity of a known and stable land. The paradigmatic movement of Shakespearian comedy is out and away from just such a stable place, onto or into just such a sea-realm (literal or metaphorical), back to a land haven. But there is something unusual and unprepared for about that third movement. It is not just a 'return' – it is a 'catastrophe', which means literally a *sudden* turn (used by Ben Jonson of comedies and tragedies alike). Characters can seem to be in direst extremities and confusion – all at sea, as we say – when lo!, they find themselves in calm, clear, fresh water. So much, I have suggested, may be justified by a strange, natural phenomenon. But for Shakespeare's characters – the lucky and deserving ones – tempests do not just calm down but 'are kind', and they find themselves in 'salt waves fresh in love'. Another element has been added, another perspective opened up; nature is turning benignly, magically, metaphoric. It is not exactly supernatural, but it is as if a mysterious power and force has supervened. Now salt, now fresh *in love*.

In the anonymous letter attached to the second Quarto of *Troilus and Cressida*, the unknown writer asserts (of Shakespeare's work): 'So much and such savored salt of witte is in his Commedies, that they seeme (for their height of pleasure) to be borne in that sea that brought forth *Venus*.' Venus means sex, and sex is 'the height of pleasure', and that, says our enthusiastic friend, is the kind of pleasure we get from Shakespeare's comedies. At first sight, it might seem rather

odd to conflate wit and sex in this way; but a little consideration yields the recognition that he is in the right of it. They
are inextricable in Shakespearian comedy, and – think only of
the erotically suffused sparring of Beatrice and Benedick – our
commentator is probably spot on in suggesting that the two
saltinesses spring from the same source. And the salt waves of
sexual desire (often producing an insatiable thirst) can – it is
another deeply natural mystery – turn into the refreshing,
fresh water of love. Venus is always rising – though, of course,
her native element may wreck and drown you.

The sea, and tempests and shipwrecks, recur in Shakespearian comedy literally from first to last. So much was a
familiar theatrical plot device. Indeed, a French critic writing
in 1641 complained that 'authors make tempest and shipwreck at will', though he did see that 'the sea is the most fitting
scene for great changes, and ... some have called it the theatre
of inconstancy'. More than a thousand years earlier (AD 523),
in the *Consolation of Philosophy* of Boethius, the figure of
Philosophy adopts the role of Fortune and speaks for her:

Must I only be forbidden to use my right? ... The sea hath right
sometime to fawn with calms, and sometime to frown with storm and
waves. And shall the insatiable desire of men tie me to constancy, so
contrary to my custom? This is my force, this is the sport which I
continually use. I turn about my wheel with speed, and take a
pleasure to turn things upside down ...

The sea/Fortune/inconstancy – this is the element man must
move in, and at a basic level it is always a matter of sink or
swim. In *The Two Gentlemen of Verona*, the character all too
aptly named Proteus cries out near the end: 'O heaven, were
man/But constant, he were perfect!' (V, iv, 109–10). But only
heaven is 'perfect'. Here in the sublunary world, we have
forever to struggle in the sea of inconstancy, an inconstancy, as
Shakespeare so often demonstrates, that is both within and
without us. But, even here, it is a matter of more and less – and
to make the point, Shakespeare will present us with heroines of
such constancy as to merit the description 'heavenly true'
(Desdemona, but applicable to many others), affording us at
least glimpses and intimations of a world beyond change.

And, although many of his characters have to undergo

tempest, shipwreck, near drowning, and sea-changes, there is invariably that coming back to a land haven, or some equivalent. The end of Shakespearian comedy (perhaps all comedy) is characterized by at least some of the following 're-' words. I apologize for the list, but it does have some cumulative point: return (which implies a previous dislodgement or flight); restoration (after displacement, exile or usurpation); recognition, which includes clarification and unravelling (after confusion, tangles, darkness); reconstitution and re-assemblage (after a disordering and scattering); remedy (for sickness); release (after constraint, repression); reversion (after inversion, and perhaps perversion); revitalization (of lost energies); replenishment and refreshing (for emptiness and desiccation); recovery (of someone/something missing or lost); reunion (after separation); resolution (of problems and uncertainty); reconciliation (where there was discord and enmity); reordering (of actual or potential chaos); rebirth (after seeming death); renewal (after stagnation); regeneration (superseding blocked generation); and – perhaps – redemption (of sins). I leave the explicitly religious possibility until last for a reason. As Northrop Frye often pointed out, there is a clear parallel between the structure of romantic comedy and the central myth of Christianity: 'The framework of the Christian myth is the comic framework of the Bible, where man loses a peaceable kingdom, staggers through the long nightmare of tyranny and injustice which is human history, and eventually regains his original vision.' Or, in terms of my very simple model – land–sea experience–back (somewhat miraculously) to fresh water and harbour; and Eden–history–Paradise – may be felt, as sequences, to be in some (tenuous or distant) way homologous or isomorphic. There is, indeed, often some feeling, some flickering, some hint, of the supernatural, the supernal, the other-worldly, even the expressly religious at the end of some of Shakespeare's romance comedies (this of course includes the Last Plays). And yet, I shall want to suggest, it is a feeling – an experience – generated from *within* nature. (Venus rising can seemingly attain almost angelic heights.) There are no *trans*cendental (or transcendentalizing) words in my list. The prefix 're-' simply means 'back' or 'again'. Not, that is, 'up' or 'beyond'. Though getting or coming back, and happening or doing again, may not be either simple or easy. More likely it will happen suddenly and strangely. As when the salt wave is, again, fresh.

*

Valentine. She shall be dignified with this high honor –
    To bear my lady's train, lest the base earth
    Should from her vesture chance to steal a kiss,
    And, of so great a favor growing proud,
    Disdain to root the summer-swelling flow'r,
    And make rough winter everlastingly.
              (*The Two Gentlemen of Verona*, II, iv, 157–62)

This preposterous conceit, used by Valentine to claim his lady's superiority over any other woman, is an extreme example of the foolish hyperboles often employed by young men in Shakespeare's comedies in their would-be gallant rhetoric. Quite rightly, Proteus protests – 'What braggardism is this?' But in this bit of absurd 'braggardism', Shakespeare, in his own inscrutable way, has incorporated what is in effect a glance back at the very origins of comedy. One of the most ancient of dreads was that spring might not return, that the 'base earth' would, precisely, 'make rough winter everlastingly'. All the laments and nightmares throughout literature about wastelands and periods of protracted sterility are, in effect, echoes or elaborations of that primal fear. There was, correspondingly, a great joy when the 'summer-swelling' flowers did, after all, duly appear. Many rituals and festivities grew up both to awaken and revive the forces of fertility still sleeping in the 'base earth', and to celebrate the feelings of renewal which accompanied the liberation of energies after the long hibernation of 'rough winter'. Comedy comes out of these seasonal celebrations of nature's periodicity, the alternation of the seasons, the succession of generations. (Hesiod's personification of harvest-bloom and feasting, Thalia, became the muse of Comedy.) These archaic feelings were clearly still fresh and strong in (still primarily rural) Elizabethan England. Here is part of the song announcing Summer's approaching death, in Nashe's *Summer's Last Will and Testament*:

Fair Summer droops, droop men and beasts therefore;
So fair a summer look for never more.
All good things vanish, less than in a day,
Peace, plenty, pleasure, suddenly decay.
  Go not yet away, bright soul of the sad year;
  The earth is hell when thou leav'st to appear.

This pageant (written during the plague years of 1592–4, when Shakespeare was writing his early comedies) contains the famous lines:

Brightness falls from the air,
Queens have died young and fair,
Dust hath clos'd Helen's eye.
I am sick, I must die;
  Lord, have mercy on us.

The threat of 'rough winter everlastingly', the 'hell' which is the absence of summer and the end of the 'summer-swelling flower', that falling from the air of brightness – none of these are forgotten in Shakespeare's comedies which, one way or another, always bear what Henry James called 'the dark smudge of mortality'.

Shakespeare lived through a time when there were increasing attacks – from Puritans and city authorities – on both the great church festivals (vestiges of Catholicism) and rural folk festivals (too pagan and disorderly). The Puritan triumph over festivals was completed in 1644, when they were officially banned. Nevertheless, a great number of festivals persisted throughout Shakespeare's lifetime, such as those marking moments in the agricultural year – Plough Monday, sheep-shearing, rush-bearing, hop-picking, nutting, bringing in the may, harvest-home etc.: in addition there were all kinds of primitive folk dramas related to (elaborations of) festival – mummer plays, Robin Hood plays, morris dances, wooing games, mock battles as between Carnival and Lent, and other pastimes, revels, and pageants: not to mention fairs and wakes, christenings, weddings, and funerals. (It is in these rurally-based games and plays that we find the figure – so important for Shakespeare – of the clown, which then meant simply 'peasant'.) Shakespeare refers to many of these festivals and festival activities in a variety of ways – sometimes alluding to them, sometimes incorporating bits of them in a different context, sometimes elaborating and transforming some of their structural features and principles for the theatre, which was, after all, a kind of festival, albeit a self-conscious one, with the crucial difference from actual festivals that it was completely scripted and controlled (traditional festivals could become anarchic and chaotic, as in the ancient saturnalia or the Lord of Misrule feasts). Shakespeare's interest in (and very likely youthful familiarity with) festivals was searching and profound: in festival and in 'festivity' itself – as an ineradicable human compulsion, need, and desire; as both a social and socializing resource *and* a potential problem (some festivals were *very* disorderly – for instance, brothels and theatres sometimes got pulled down!); as an ambivalent phenomenon which somehow draws on and enacts some of our deepest feelings about the relationship of man and nature. We should not be surprised if some of his comedies turn out to be not only a sort of sophisticated festival themselves, but also dramatic inquiries into the nature of festival. 'Festivals' about festivals, in other words. Or, perhaps better, plays about playing – in every sense.

There are, needless to say, books exclusively on the subject of Elizabethan festival and Shakespeare. The most comprehensive, and one of the very best, is François Laroque's *Shakespeare's Festive World*. He traces festival's roots in an archaic sense of time and the cosmos, and stresses the qualitatively differentiated time of the countryside and the agricultural calendar linked to natural cycles, as opposed to the homogenous, quantitative clock-time of the town. (John Kerrigan says that, with the introduction of the fob-watch into Elizabethan England, 'clock time invaded men's lives'. 'There's no clock in the forest' Orlando reminds Rosalind.) He shows how Shakespeare manages to contrive the coexistence of the cyclical time of festival and the linear time of theatrical representation. Reminding us of the great urban and commercial boom affecting Elizabethan England, he says:

Yet the town/country opposition still lay at the heart of the whole phenomenon of festivity, for even if it was through the towns that festivals were developed, embellished, and enriched, essentially the

xvii

festival was the product of a rural civilization whose seasonal rhythms and magico-religious beliefs were linked with the mysteries of natural fertility. Furthermore, for Shakespeare's contemporaries, the country-side (whether cultivated or fallow or forest), lying *extra muros*, beyond the town walls, was still the object of ancient beliefs and deep-rooted fears. The forest, linked with royal privileges, was the domain of hunting, wildness and the sacred, as is testified by the ballads and legends of Robin Hood, [and] the wealth of iconographic variants on the grotesque theme of the *homo sylvarum* . . .

The forest stands with the sea as a crucial part of the topography of Shakespeare's comedies.

Laroque makes two particularly important points, as I see it, about the two-wayness, and the two-sidedness of festival. Thus: at some times, flowers, plants, etc., were gathered and arranged indoors – 'these were ritual gestures that moved from the outside inwards, betokening a twofold desire: to overstep boundaries and to appropriate nature'. At other times, the town/countryside relationship was reversed, and people headed out to disport themselves in the fields and woods. Again, there was the 'beating of the bounds' during which people toured the parish, and, at certain points, the children were beaten to impress on their memories the boundaries and frontiers of different plots of land, and paths, and so on – a kind of consecration of property. But on May Day and Midsummer Day, people were allowed to 'commit crimes against the vert' – that is, they could steal flowers, timber and trees from forests and parks. 'This provides us with a particularly striking illustration of the ambivalence of the festival: sometimes it served as a solemn ratification of boundaries, points of refer-ence, and dividing lines; at other times it gave a community licence to transgress those boundaries and abolish those divid-ing lines.' Ratifying and transgressing boundaries and dividing lines of all kinds – not least those of gender and rank – are matters at the very centre of Shakespeare's comedies.

Festival is holiday, and holiday is precisely not workday, though it takes place within the awareness of the inevitable and necessary return to the sobrieties and exigencies of the everyday world. It was a (limited) time of liberty and release, an outflowing of energies and vitalities usually held down, or kept in, by awe, deference, and respect (or the police). And some of the energies which started to flow were akin to the juices which went into those swollen summer flowers. Laroque quotes from an interesting anonymous piece called *The Passionate Morrice* (1593), to this effect:

Liking will not be long a dooing; and love that followes is but little, whereby he brings no great harme; but al the mischieefe comes with desire, which swells the affections, and predominates over love and liking; he makes the misrule, and keeps the open Christmas; he desires the sporte, and maintains the pastime, so that, though he be long in comming, and staies but little in his Lordship, yet the remembrance of his jolitie is not forgotten a long time after.

Swelling flowers, swelling affections – there is something inherently tumescent in comedy ('the height of pleasure' at least one spectator found it, remember). And, of course, all (or most) of the mischief – almost anywhere – *does* come from desire – here importantly differentiated from love and liking – which may indeed 'stay but little' in the desirer but can have results 'not forgotten a long time after'. Undoubtedly, there was intoxication and a degree of sexual promiscuity at festival times, though surely not as much as the fevered imaginations of the Puritans pruriently conjured up. (In this connection, see the invaluable *Anatomie of Abuses* by the Puritan Phillip Stubbes, which gives the most vivid, not to say high-temperature, accounts of contemporary festivals that we have.) Here is a characteristically balanced comment by C. L. Barber (whose magisterial *Shakespeare's Festive Comedy* remains the best single book on Shakespearian comedy) on the Misrule festivals: 'The instability of an interregnum is built into the dynamics of misrule: the game at once appropriates and annihilates the mana of authority. In the process, the fear which normally maintains inhibition is temporarily overcome, and the revellers become wanton, swept along on the freed energy normally occupied in holding themselves in check.' To the authorities, revellers might easily become rebels, even revolutionaries, and in their eyes you couldn't always tell a revel from a riot. There is no doubt that some festivals could release forces of destruction, as well as those of procreation. François Laroque is at some pains to remind us 'just how great the ravages caused by festivity can be', as, he maintains, Shakespeare's comedies sometimes reveal. But, more importantly, those comedies are, says Laroque, like 'the upside-down festival world characterized by all the ambiguities and metamorphoses of desire'. In this sense, they certainly are 'borne in that sea that brought forth Venus'.

One last point about festival, which I take from Barber. He quotes one of Phillip Stubbes' descriptions of a Maypole ('stinking idol' – Stubbes) festival which, as Barber points out, serves, perhaps inadvertently, 'to bring out how completely all groups who lived together within the agricultural calendar shared in the response to the season'. Then he quotes this very revealing comment from the Puritan castigator:

I think it convenient for one friend to visit another (at some-times) as opportunity and occasion shall offer itself; but wherefore should the whole town, parish, village, and country keep one and the same day, and make such gluttonous feasts as they do?

As Barber acutely comments – 'clearly Stubbes assumes a world of isolated, busy individuals, each prudently deciding how to make the best use of the time'. The Puritan distrust of pleasure and appetitive excess is familiar; but, as important, is this inability to appreciate the instinct of a community to experience itself *as* a community – the sociality and bonding power of festival. Now think of those crowded last scenes of Shakespeare's comedies, and you realize how important the communalizing, harmonizing, integrating instincts were for him.

Finally, I just want to suggest that perhaps the greatest influence of festival on Shakespeare was on his comic imagination. If ever language went on holiday and enjoyed a carnival time it is in his comedies – in the awareness, always, that holidays have to end.

*

I am transformèd, master, am not I?
(*The Comedy of Errors*, II, ii, 196)

There are three explicit invocations of the name of Ovid in Shakespeare's plays (*The Taming of the Shrew*, *Titus Andronicus*, *As You Like It* – four, if you include 'Ovidius Naso' in *Love's*

Labor's Lost). He names one character 'Proteus', and allows one other – the future Richard III – to boast that he will 'add colors to the chameleon,/ Change shapes with Proteus' (3 *Henry VI*, III, ii, 191–2). Joan de Pucelle is accused by York of giving him a witch-like look 'as if with Circe she would change my shape', while the bemused Duke, confronting the identity confusion in *The Comedy of Errors*, says 'I think you all have drunk of Circe's cup' (V, i, 271). The word 'metamorphis'd' in the same play is given by the OED as the earliest known usage of the word. 'Metamorphosed' occurs twice in *The Two Gentlemen of Verona*, and nowhere else in Shakespeare. All this by way of indicating that the influence on Shakespeare of Ovid's *Metamorphoses* is there from the start (as it was on very many Renaissance writers and artists. To give just one, relevant, contemporary example, the evil shape-shifter Archimago, so crucial in Spenser's *Fairy Queen*, is able to take 'As many forms and shapes in seeming wise,/As ever *Proteus* to himself could make'). The somewhat more pertinent point to note is that all these very *specific* references to Ovid and his main work, occur in Shakespeare's earliest plays. Subsequently, the influence is diffused. Or rather, it is opened out and deepened, as Shakespeare engages in repeated dramatic explorations of the phenomenon of 'transformation' at all levels and in every part of life (the word – and cognates like 'translate' – occur from first to last: more generally, 'change' – word and phenomenon – is everywhere). It is almost as if Shakespeare is 'transforming' specifically Ovidian *Metamorphoses* to get down to the very heart of the mystery of metamorphosis – the metamorphosing drive in nature – itself.[1]

1. Less specific allusions to, and borrowings from, stories in Ovid, are to be found throughout Shakespeare. One way or another, he nods to tales from almost every book of the *Metamorphoses* – in addition to the early references to Proteus and Circe: the Golden Age; Phaeton; Acteon; Narcissus and Echo; Pyramus and Thisbe; Ceres and Proserpina; Arachne and her tapestries; Medea; Baucis and Philomel; Hercules and the shirt of Nessus; Orpheus; Venus and Adonis; Ajax and Ulysses; Hecuba; the philosophy of Pythagoras; and so on. Jonathan Bate gives all the details, and it is his informed opinion that 'approximately 90 per cent' of the mythological references in Shakespeare come, or could come, from Ovid.

John Lyly, an important precursor of Shakespeare, was, according to Jonathan Bate (in his admirable book, *Shakespeare and Ovid*), the first writer to introduce Ovidianism into English drama. His plays abound in Ovidian metamorphoses – see, for example, *Love's Metamorphosis* from the 1580s. Shakespeare allows only one literal metamorphosis – 'O Bottom, thou art changed!' – in his drama, and here (in *A Midsummer Night's Dream*) it takes place in the atmosphere of an archaic form of folk drama which is set in the larger context of his own much more sophisticated play; as if Shakespeare was not only looking back to one of his own drama's crude antecedents, but saying something about Ovidian literalism – and perhaps literalism itself. (Shakespeare put his Ovidianism into his language – which does, at times, become a magic realm of metamorphosis and metaphoric transformations.) And, of course, Bottom's metamorphosis is – unOvidianly – reversible. In Lyly's *Gallathea* (1585), two girls dressed as boys (for self-protective disguise) fall in love. This awkwardness is resolved when the goddess Venus agrees to metamorphose one of them into a boy, saying she has already done it to Iphis, a character in a story in Ovid. A number of girls dress up as boys in Shakespearian comedy – and since they were already boy-actors dressed up as girls, this allows Shakespeare enormous scope for all kinds of receding ironies, from sexual *double entendres* and ambiguities, to searching and unsettling probes into the nature and boundaries of gender identity. These boy-girl-boys may also problematically arouse the desire of a member of their own sex (Viola and Olivia in *Twelfth Night*). But the problems have to work themselves out *in* nature – there are no divinely ordained gender alterations (nor, I would maintain, divinely ordained anything else). All Shakespeare's main comic lovers are transformed by desire in some way – for the better (a love which ennobles and spiritualizes), for the worse (a lust which degrades and bestializes), and Shakespeare is clearly fascinated at all the changes and transformations which can be occasioned and precipitated by aroused desire. But the changes are *within* – psychological, emotional, spiritual. Ovidianism, we may say, is internalized. As the Doctor warns Conrad's Marlow before he sets out for

Africa (in *Heart of Darkness*) – 'the changes take place inside, you know'.

In his famous *Oration on the Dignity of Man* (1486) – a seminal Renaissance declaration – Pico della Mirandola has God say this to Adam:

'We have made thee neither of heaven nor of earth, neither mortal nor immortal, so that with freedom of choice and with honor, as though the maker and molder of thyself, thou mayest fashion thyself in whatever shape thou shalt prefer. Thou shalt have the power to degenerate into the lower forms of life, which are brutish. Thou shalt have the power, out of thy soul's judgment, to be reborn into the higher forms, which are divine.' O supreme generosity of God the Father, O highest and most marvelous felicity of man! To him it is granted to have whatever he chooses, to be whatever he wills ... Who would not admire this our chameleon? Or who could more greatly admire aught else whatever? ... It is man who Asclepius of Athens, arguing from his mutability of character and from his self-transforming nature, on just grounds says was symbolised by Proteus in the mysteries.

It is hard to imagine a more exhilarating, celebratory pre-scription for that stress on 'self-fashioning' which is such an important feature of the Renaissance (see Stephen Green-blatt's *Renaissance Self-Fashioning*). But when 'this our cha-meleon' turns out to be, for example, Richard III, then man's seemingly miraculous self-transforming powers seem less obviously to be a matter for unequivocal delight and self-congratulation. If a man really *can* become anything, then he may easily become nothing, or certainly no one certain stable knowable thing. Richard himself (in his nightmare before Bosworth) ends in a state of terminal identity fragmentation and dispersal. He just doesn't know who he is. Ovid's evoca-tion of an endlessly flowing world, in which 'nothing is permanent' and 'all things are fluent ... wandering through change', opened up all kinds of possibilities of release and emancipation from all manner of restricting, blocking, rigidi-fying forms of constraint and arrest. Flexibility, suppleness, 'fluency', openness and willingness to change, are essential virtues in Shakespearian comedy – indeed, it is just those fixed and fixated figures who, locked up in themselves, cannot and

will not change – Shylock, Malvolio, Jacques – who resist, and
are unapt for, assimilation into the harmonizing reintegrations
of the comedies' conclusions. That aspect of the Ovidian
precedent was all for the good, and invaluable for Renaissance
humanism. (Montaigne, whose first pleasure in books was
'reading the fables of *Ovids* Metamorphosies', and who
revealed himself in his essays to be '*ondoyant et divers*', is another
important influence for Shakespeare. It seems likely that the
only surviving copies of books owned by Shakespeare himself
are an annotated edition of the *Metamorphoses* and a copy of
Montaigne's *Essais*. 'Perhaps too convenient' says Bate.)

But there were distinctly less desirable sides to what Golding
(translator of the *Metamorphoses*), rather nicely called 'Ovid's
dark philosophie of turned shapes'. Ovidian change just goes
on and on – indeed his Pythagoras argues that change itself
provides the only constant principle; there is no Christian
belief in, or hope for and aspiration towards, a realm beyond
or above 'mutability'. A living metaphor for this belief in, or
aspiration for, permanence is marriage, with a related stress on
the importance of the virtue of chastity. Marriage and chastity, of little interest to Ovid, are of supreme importance in
Shakespeare. Then again, there is a lot of very real violence in
Ovid – people are dismembered and raped in good earnest: in
Shakespearian comedy there is often the sinister threat of real
violence, but it is, as Bate says, invariably forestalled, and
those threatening it converted or expelled. William Carroll (in
his very valuable book, *The Metamorphoses of Shakespearian
Comedy*) sums up the ambivalence felt by Renaissance writers,
concerning the metamorphosing power of self-fashioning. Following Mirandola, they celebrated it:

but they also feared this power, not only because it seemed funda-
mentally a chaotic energy, and not only because they might sink
down the scale of being, but also because no matter what the nature
of their transformation – self-controlled or random, higher or lower,
celestial or bestial – man's essential identity is put at risk ... In this
respect, the whole idea of metamorphosis is subversive, for it under-
mines the traditional belief in a stable, fixed, and ordered self upon
which much of western thought, and in particular ethics, rests.

And one final consideration about metamorphoses – they may

be generated from within, and they may be caused by some mysterious outside force: it is one thing for a girl to resolve to simulate a man, or for a prince to determine to prove a villain; and quite another to wake up and find yourself a cockroach – or an ass. But every kind of metamorphosis, all aspects of the phenomenon are brought into focus by Shakespeare's eye which, as we often come to feel, seems to have missed nothing.

*

While at school (as a pupil, or, as one legend has it, briefly as a master), Shakespeare was almost certainly exposed to the 1550 edition of *Andria*, by Donatus, a fourth-century grammarian. It contained, among many other things, a theory of, a formula for, comedy. Thus: 'Comedy ought to be five-parted, the first of which unfolds the argument' (or in another version 'contains either the peril, the anguish, or some trouble'); 'the second completes the same. The third has the increment of turbations and contentions' (or 'brings on the perturbations, and the impediments and despair of the desired thing'); 'the fourth seeks a medicine for the perturbations' (or 'brings a remedy for the impending evil') 'and is a preparation for the catastrophe, which the fifth demands by right for itself'. (See T. W. Baldwin, *Shakespeare's Five-Act Structure*; Martin Herrick, *Comic Theory in the Sixteenth Century*.) As we might expect, Shakespeare was clearly an attentive student. Comedy is related to what Henry James called our 'precious capacity for bewilderment'. Not only do we slip on banana skins, which can be funny enough; but we also get things wrong – hopelessly, sometimes indeed 'catastrophically', wrong, which can be far funnier (and, of course, more serious). And there are times, of course, when we simply don't know what on earth is going on. Donatus stressed that there should always be 'something towards error' (*aliquid ad errorem*') in comedy; and two important Italian plays of the Renaissance (both known to Shakespeare) are the anonymous *Gl'Ingannati* (*The Deceived*) and Ariosto's *Suppositi* (translated as *Supposes* by Gascoigne who explained in a Prologue: 'But understand, this our Suppose is nothing else but a mistaking or imagination of one thing for another'). Deceptions can be intentional tricks;

'supposes' can be innocent misapprehensions. Both contribute to (are essential for) what another grammarian-theorist, Evanthius, called 'the forward progress (or growth) of the confusions (or turmoils)' (*'incrementum processusque turbarum'*). Whether or not Shakespeare needed to learn all this in school may be doubted, but it is absolutely pertinent to his comedies, the first of which was, indeed, a 'Comedy of *Errors*'. And what he certainly did study – and what Donatus and Evanthius are theorizing from – is Roman New Comedy.

This means, effectively, the plays of Plautus (254–184 BC) and Terence (186–159 BC). These are translations, imitations, and adaptations of Athenian New Comedy which, unlike the Old Comedy of Aristophanes with its ironic concern for the myths and conduct of the whole city-state, concentrated on domestic concerns, sexual rivalry, marriage settlements, money-making, household discords and reconciliations. It emphasized the separation of town from country, and its background, instead of farming (Old Comedy), is trade, with a lot of business trips, and related journeying and travelling. The (bourgeois) family is the dominant social unit, and the comedy comes from all those things which can hinder or threaten its smooth running and self-perpetuation – obstructive fathers, shrewish wives, wayward sons, disobedient daughters, all variously aided and abetted, or foiled and thwarted, by clever servants and wily slaves. Identification and misidentification; worries, uncertainties and confusions concerning birth, name, and status; the disguises, trickeries, and dissimulations often required to pursue a prohibited love affair or outwit a tyrannical master – such things are the very meat of New Comedy: not surprisingly perhaps, it made extensive use of twins and doubles, and developed the dramatic technique of the 'double plot' – resources and devices calculated to accelerate the 'forward progress of the confusion'. Shakespeare based his first comedy on a play by Plautus (of which more in due course), and his Roman-Italian borrowings play a decisive role in many of his subsequent comedies. (On this, as on much else, see Leo Salingar's admirable and helpful book, *Shakespeare and the Traditions of Comedy*.)

These Roman plays are visibly contrived, almost ostentatiously artificial, even mechanical and tending towards an almost mathematical abstraction in that they offer the spectacle of problems being set and then solved (they were thus very popular among the law students at the Inns of Court). In this, they are at a far remove from the primitive semi-improvizations of folk games, and even further from the unpredictable frolics of festival. Different again were the rambling medieval romance narratives which informed the popular drama which had been in existence probably from the fifteenth century. These meandering stories characteristically told of chivalric love, painful separation, long-suffering heroines (calumniated queens were very popular), prolonged searchings, and miraculous reunions. The humour of New Comedy tended towards the sharpness of satire; to this, Shakespeare added the sweetness of romance (and, perhaps some intimations of mystery from the miracle plays). He also used the tighter forms of New Comedy to give a more urgent and compact shape to these romances, as well as to harness, contextualize, and control the festive impulse. We should add to these dominant influences on the young Shakespeare – morality and miracle plays and interludes (a pervasive influence on his history plays as well); and courtly entertainments, masques and revels and mythological pageants. (Leo Salingar points out that Shakespeare is much more drawn to the great house and the court in his comedies, than to the bourgeois world of craftsmen, tradesmen and shopkeepers. In almost every concluding scene there is a prince figure – not present in New Comedy – arbitrating, arranging, or just overseeing the appropriate reconciliations and reunions.) One more writer must be mentioned – Boccaccio. Leo Salingar sees him as an absolutely crucial influence, for the following reasons:

The stories transmitted to Shakespeare by Boccaccio and his followers are remarkable, not so much for their air of reporting actualities ... but for their internal balance and rationality, for the authors' skill in propounding a quandary in practical conduct and then showing its resolution by means of an exact system of moral equivalences, an exchange of gifts or actions or speeches which is symmetrical and at least logically satisfying. In Boccaccio such concern with ethical symmetry is a guiding artistic principle ... but it is present in all the stories which interested Shakespeare, and, together with the writers' sober attention to the realities of civic life, must have made the Italians' stories stand out from the other moralistic or ramblingly romantic fiction available to him.

In sum, in Shakespeare's comedies, there is an extraordinary confluence of classical, medieval, renaissance, and folk traditions and influences. With his astonishing assimilatory alchemy, he produced out of this unprecedented synthesis Mozartian miracles still capable of inducing a ravishing delight.

*

One other factor should be taken into consideration as we approach the individual plays. In Shakespeare's childhood, it was still the case that plays and performances of all kinds took place in social spaces not primarily intended for that purpose – the court, great halls and houses, universities, inn-yards; or the church, church-yard, street, market square, and other public places. In 1576 (Shakespeare was twelve), James Burbage built the first permanent playhouse in England, intended solely for the drama. It was called simply the Theatre – as well it might be, since there was no other. Others soon followed, of course – the Swan, the Globe (Shakespeare's main theatre), the Rose, the Fortune, and so on. Shakespeare's lifetime saw quite unparalleled theatrical activity in London, with up to five companies performing plays every day except Sunday; and, it has been reckoned, some two thousand new plays appearing between 1590 and 1642 (when the theatres were closed). The main point here is, that when Shakespeare started writing plays (let's say, around 1588), 'the theatre', a place devoted *exclusively* to dramatic performances and plays, was a new kind of social space which had, as it were, been inserted into the community. Clearly any young playwright was going to be fascinated by the relation of the theatre space to the other social spaces which contained it, and on which it now directly, or indirectly, impinged. Drama was make-believe, but the Theatre was real. How did it react with the other realities around it which, one way or another, it reflected or represented? If Shakespeare puts a play within a play, he is not anticipating Pirandello, but rather exploring the implications and possibilities of a relatively new fact of social life. And another – related – thing. Until some time around the middle of the sixteenth century, the performers in all kinds of plays and performances – aristocratic, religious, popular – were amateurs or part-time players. From around the 1540s, we start to find full-time professional actors. So as well as a new kind of social space, here was a new social being – for a professional actor was a man of no certain rank, no recognized role, no accredited function, dedicated exclusively to simulation and masquerading. Yet he, too, was real. What was the relation between that real man and the role(s) which he assumed? And between the actor and the non-acting spectators? Shakespeare was himself, of course, a professional actor, so we should not be surprised to find him fascinated by such questions, and their dramatic possibilities – leaving us, perhaps, finally not entirely certain where acting starts and stops.

*

THE PLAYS

There is no available certainty, nor complete editorial agreement, concerning either the date of composition of the first four comedies or the sequence in which they were written. There is a general consensus that they were written between 1592 and 1594, and I have retained the sequence preferred by E. K. Chambers.

THE COMEDY OF ERRORS

It is remarkable that Shakespeare's (possibly) first comedy opens with an old man under sentence of death, so that the long shadow of mortality falls over all that follows. The Syracusian Egeon submits, without hope, to the sentence passed on him for having entered Ephesian waters. The Duke of Ephesus, explaining this harsh punishment, speaks of 'enmity and discord' between 'our adverse towns', leading to 'rancorous outrage', 'intestine jars'; and invokes 'law' and 'rigorous statutes' while specifically excluding 'all pity from our threat'ning looks'. He evokes a little world in which all the normal, nourishing 'traffic' between two geographically related places has been blocked – trade replaced by violence, communication by contestation, love by law, and pity by 'penalty'. All the normal life-maintaining, life-enhancing, circulations and modes of meeting and exchange, have gone, somehow, fatally awry. It offers an opening glimpse of a world of sterility, oppugnancy, and death. This is the *start*. It is just such a world that comedy conspires to break up and uncongeal, by restoring the normal channels of communication and relationship to their proper flowings, leading to the re-establishment of a better appreciated amity and concord. That is all to come.

Asked to explain why he has risked coming to Ephesus (given the mortal interdiction on Syracusians), Egeon gives a long narrative account of how he lost his wife and one of his sons in a shipwreck – a common danger for travelling merchants such as he; of how, years later, his remaining son 'became inquisitive /After his brother' and set out in 'quest of him'; of how he, Egeon, grown old, has since spent five years roaming through Asia and Greece searching for him – and, at last, had to try Ephesus. 'I hazarded the loss' he says – loss of family, loss of remaining son, finally loss of life. Hazarding loss is an important willingness, bravery if you like, in the world of comedy, where, it may be said, 'nothing venture, nothing gain' is an operative rule, and losing is often a necessary prelude to finding. Egeon's story – voyage, calamity, loss, quest and so on – is archetypal romance material; but material which, one way and another, Shakespeare will draw on throughout his writing career; for the theme of the broken family – members variously separated, scattered, believed lost – and the ensuing desolation, searching, and final reunion, is one to which he returned time and time again. Egeon stands there, a true figure of pathos – the old patriarch, utterly alone, bereaved, bereft. His life could be ransomed for a 'thousand marks', but since he is friendless in a hostile city, this seems to offer no reprieve. The Duke feels a certain amount of sympathy for him, but stresses that 'we may pity, though not pardon thee'; that he 'may not disannul' the laws; and that the 'passed sentence may not be recalled'. It is still an iron world – inflexible, intransigent, obdurate. But this is still only the first scene; so far, we have romance threatening to end in tragedy. It remains to be seen if, and how, comedy can 'disannul' law.

*

The 'comedy' begins with the next scene, and Shakespeare has based this comedy on the *Menaechmi* by Plautus – during the Renaissance, one of the most popular, and often adapted, Roman plays (and, itself, taken from an ancient Greek play – thus justifying Bullough's observation that 'it is interesting to find Shakespeare, in what may be his first comedy, going back to the classical source of modern drama'). How Shakespeare transforms this source is so important and illuminating with regard to all his comedies (and comedy-romances) that a brief summary of the Plautus play is necessary. The play opens with a soliloquy by 'Peniculus, a Parasite', foregrounding a concern with appetite and greed, riches of the table and the market. The comedy arises from the mistakes and misunderstandings – errors and 'supposes' – which are occasioned by the arrival of one of a pair of identical twin brothers (the Menaechmi of the title) in a town, Epidamnum, where, as the Prologue or Argument explains, 'th'other dwelt inricht, and him so like,/ That Citizens there take him for the same'. The first brother is actively searching for this long-lost second brother, but has, of course, no idea that he has finally arrived in his home town. (This is exactly the root situation Shakespeare takes over.) Act I shows us the wealthy resident brother having a row with his shrew of a wife. Out of patience with her, he resolves to give one of her cloaks to his favourite courtesan (Erotium), with whom he plans to have dinner – and whom he unambiguously prefers ('I never looke upon thee, but I am quite out of love with my wife'). The other, newly arrived, brother appears in Act II, and, to his amazement, is knowingly approached by the courtesan's servant, and then by Erotium herself. He thinks they are mad, but he goes along with them, accepts their hospitality, and pretends to be whoever they think he is. In Act III he is given, mistakenly of course, the cloak his brother had taken from his wife, and then a gold chain is also thrust upon him. Fine by him – 'Do not all the gods conspire to loade mee with good luck?' Not so fine for his brother, who, in Act IV, is taxed by his wife about the cloak, and by Erotium concerning both cloak and gold chain, and ends up by being 'everie way shut out' by both of them. Act V sees the confusion ever more deeply confounded, until pretty well everybody thinks that everybody else is 'starke mad' – and then the twin brothers appear on stage together for the first time, and the source of all the errors is revealed – 'I never saw one man so like an other; water to water, nor milke to milke, is not liker then he is to you' (bear in mind this 'watery' image of similitude). So then follow joyful reunions and happy endings, with the resident Menechmus concluding the play by saying that he would willingly sell his shrewish wife 'but I thinke no bodie will bid money for her'.

The Plautus play is basically a farce, with hilarious misunderstandings proliferating from one root cause – mistaken identity. Now, it is true that the phenomenon of twins or identical siblings (or rather, *almost* identical siblings – it is important that nature does not produce *exactly* interchangeable replicas) touches a deep human nerve. For some reason – think about it – the phenomenon is funny. Pascal noted that 'Two faces that are alike, though neither of them excites laughter in itself, make me laugh when together on account of the likeness.' It must have something to do with the spectacle of *difference* – which makes me *me* – almost disappearing into *sameness* – which would make me indistinguishable from everybody else. But identical twins are not only funny; they are, as folk-tales bear out, slightly uncanny – 'with all the divisible indivisibility that traditionally mysterious relationship implies' (Leah Scragg). Clearly, the phenomenon can raise questions about the nature and stability of identity, and it certainly fascinated Shakespeare. But Plautus really does nothing with it – apart from exploiting its obvious potential for identities mistook. His characters are more like ciphers or types – irascible merchant, bemused stranger, nagging wife, amiable whore, parasitical parasite, and so on. They have no significant inner experience; they do not learn; they do not change. Indeed, nothing really changes: matters get tangled up – then, with sudden facility, straightened out. The mercantile life of the city of Epidamnum goes on as before after barely a ripple.

Shakespeare takes exactly the same root situation, including many of the incidents and details – such as the courtesan and the gold chain; but, with his changes and amplifications, he produces an infinitely richer play. All his changes are, in different ways, significant. He does away with the Parasite – parasitism and self-interested greed is not, here, part of his interest. He reduces the role of the courtesan (there is no comedy in casual adultery for Shakespeare); and, more importantly, greatly enlarges the role of the wife, who, while still shrewish, is also complex, articulate, and sympathetic. (He also gives the wife a sister which, in the event, makes possible the expression of a kind of romantic love completely absent in Plautus.) Indeed, it may be said that, in general, the main characters have an emotional and even moral dimension, an inner life, which is entirely foreign to Plautus' mercenary knock-abouts. An apparently slight structural shift is, perhaps, even more interesting. Plautus starts his play with an emphasis on the resident brother, who has the larger part in the play – the, as it were, foreign brother only arrives in town after the local domestic scene has been set. Shakespeare reverses this. We see the newly arrived, traveller brother first, trying to make sense of a new and strange town; so that, as Harry Levin put it, 'we experience what goes on from the alien's point of view'. Concomitantly, of the two brothers, *he* now has (much) the larger part. And *we* have much more 'strangeness'.

Shakespeare raises the stakes – and multiplies the possibilities for comic confusion – by doubling-up on identical twins, adding the two Dromios as servants of the brothers Antipholus. Whatever else, this gave him a longer play; for, while at 1777 lines it is his shortest, it is in every way larger than the *Menaechmi*. But the more significant amplification is the addition of the framing romance narrative concerning the sad, sentenced Egeon; his lost and sundered family; and its final rediscovery and reunion. There is no trace of this in Plautus, whose play shows no interest at all in the *family* as such. For

Shakespeare, it is to be a central concern. One more change –
and this perhaps the most interesting of all. Shakespeare
changed the city in which the action is set from Epidamnum to
Ephesus. Why?

Not surprisingly, it was Geoffrey Bullough (in his *Sources*)
who first suggested a cogent reason for the move. The name
Epidamnum suggested bad luck to the Romans, and thus
perhaps suitable enough for a place where everything seems to
go wrong. Ephesus was better known to the Elizabethans, as a
great port and the capital of Roman Asia; and – more to the
point – 'renowned for its Temple of Diana and as the place
where St Paul stayed two years (Acts 19)' (Bullough). Acts 19
refers to the 'curious arts' (sorcery, exorcism and so on) which
Paul found were practised in the city when he arrived.
Shakespeare develops the hint. Whereas in the Plautus play,
Messinio warns his master that Epidamnum is 'full of
Ribaulds, Parasites, Drunkard Catchpoles, Cony-Catchers
and Sycophants ... Curtizans', in Shakespeare's play Antipholus of Syracuse says apprehensively:

> They say this town is full of cozenage:
> As nimble jugglers that deceive the eye,
> Dark-working sorcerers that change the mind,
> Soul-killing witches that deform the body
>
> (I, ii, 97–100)

There are no *actual* witches and sorcerers in this Ephesus; it is
still very much a merchants' (and, from what we see, honest
merchants') town. But as the characters grope their way
further and further into the fog of misapprehension, Shakespeare wants them to *feel* that there must be some sorcery and
witchcraft – a kind of weird magic – in the air, as they believe
themselves either being driven, or simply going, mad. They
experience a far deeper sort of mental estrangement and
disorientation than in Plautus, where people simply believe
that other people seem to have gone a bit dotty.

Bullough suggests, convincingly, the relevance of another
Pauline reference. In his Epistle to the Ephesians, Paul writes:
'Wives, submit yourselves unto your own husbands, as unto
the Lord. For the husband is the head of the wife, even as

Christ is the head of the Church ... Husbands, love your wives
... let every one of you in particular so love his wife even as
himself; and the wife see that she reverence her husband'
(5: 22, 25, 33). Paul was concerned about domestic harmony
and unity. In his play, Shakespeare inaugurates what will be a
continuing, vital debate about 'marriage', and the most
appropriate relationship between man and wife, throughout
his work. Indeed, in no play is it more seriously examined than
in *The Comedy of Errors*. And Ephesus was also the place of the
great Temple of Diana. Here again, Shakespeare makes a
crucial change. Instead of a temple and Diana, we have a
priory and an Abbess. That this Abbess turns out to be the
long-lost wife of Egeon and the mother of the Antipholus
brothers serves to contribute decisively to that atmosphere of
wonder, strangeness, and possible improbability with which
Shakespeare chooses to end his play, as the far-flung family is,
seemingly miraculously, reunited. It is a far cry from the rueful
joke about his unsellable wife with which Menechmus concludes the Plautus romp.

The priory and the Abbess do not mean that Shakespeare
has simply Christianized the Roman world of Plautus –
though it is as important for his comedies as it is for his
tragedies that Christianity supervened between the ancient
classical models and his own practice. Antipholus of Syracuse
refers to himself as a Christian, but he comes to Ephesus where
the paganism of the antique Mediterranean world seems to
cohabit with the religion brought there by St Paul. This
enables Shakespeare to draw on, and combine, both pagan
and Christian language to create a far more complex feeling
than would be generated by an orthodox rehearsal and
deployment of the one discourse or the other. Although, as
Gunnar Sorelius has demonstrated, 'Shakespeare uses biblical
language more strikingly in this his most classical comedy than
anywhere else', the pagan world is still vibrantly, resonantly
there. It is a case of simultaneity and fusion rather than any
supplanting conversion – a pagan-Christian perspective offers
much greater depth than either would separately afford. From
the start, Shakespeare is a great includer and amalgamator,
a capacious gatherer-in. (Thus here, he *adds* romance to

comedy; just as he will soon add comedy to history.) An unprecedented richness ensues.

*

The comic part starts with Antipholus of Syracuse, just arrived in Ephesus, handing over his money (a thousand marks – ironically, exactly the sum which would ransom his father, of whose presence in the city Antipholus has, of course, not the slightest idea) to his servant Dromio for safe-keeping. 'Go bear it to the Centaur, where we host' (I, ii, 9) are his first words; and even here there is an anticipatory sign if we care to read it. The centaur was, of course, half man and half horse, posing, among other things, questions about the boundary between the human and the animal – questions which will be raised, in other forms, throughout; for this is, in part, an Ovidian play, with possibilities of metamorphosis very much in the air. (We soon learn that the other Antipholus, of Ephesus, lives at a house called 'the Phoenix', I, ii, 75 – a self-transcending bird, pointing to higher forms; while, when later a group heads off for a good dinner in town, they repair to 'the Tiger' inn – unmistakably all animal. The courtesan, incidentally, lives in a house called 'the Porpentine' – i.e. porcupine – an animal known for its prickles; which is perhaps all that need be said about that bit of nomenclature. Shakespeare is having his fun, but even with these house and inn signs, he is glancing at one of his most serious themes: how far from, near to, the beasts are these people – are *we*?) Dismissing his servant, Dromio, Antipholus S. (for convenience) indicates his immediate intentions: 'I will go lose myself,/And wander up and down to view the city' (I, ii, 31–2). Put like that, it sounds like a simple resolve to go for a random meander in the strange port. But the opening phrase returns with renewed force in his next speech, a short soliloquy which effectively adumbrates the central issues of the play. A departing merchant politely says: 'I commend you to your own content'; and Antipholus:

> He that commends me to mine own content
> Commends me to the thing I cannot get.
> I to the world am like a drop of water

That in the ocean seeks another drop,
Who, falling there to find his fellow forth,
Unseen, inquisitive, confounds himself.
So I, to find a mother and a brother,
In quest of them, unhappy, lose myself.

(I, ii, 33–40)

'Content' – in his separated, isolated state, he cannot be happy: 'content' – he doesn't yet know what is in him, what he contains. It is what, crucially, he has to find out; what the action of the play will reveal to him. Then he likens himself to 'a drop of water'. A drop of water does not, I suppose, have much 'content' (either way), and certainly suggests degree zero identity; but this water drop proves to be the master image of the play. In Plautus, the image also occurs – but simply to stress similitude, apparent indistinguishability. When the two twins are finally on stage together, a witness comments: "I never saw one man so like an other; water to water, nor milke to milke, is not liker than he is to you.' Shakespeare is doing more. Dissolving, melting, various forms of liquefaction – such processes are often invoked by Shakespearian characters to articulate a felt, or feared, loss or blurring of identity; a weakening sense of the separate, independent self. As when Antony confronts his own impending erasure, and compares himself, implicitly, with a cloud which rapidly loses its shape and form and becomes 'indistinct/As water is in water' (*Antony and Cleopatra*, IV, xiv, 9–11). (Ovid is full of figures, admittedly invariably women – Cyane, Byblis, Egeria, who dissolve into rivers, fountains, waters and so on; as Sorelius puts it – 'diminution by dissolution is one of the persistent events in the *Metamorphoses*'.) But Antipholus is also using the metaphor in a positive sense; he has become like a drop in the ocean, *but* in an attempt to 'find his fellow forth' – this is accepting the risks of dissolution in the interests of relationship. The bravery of the drop of water daring the engulfing ocean. It is, exactly, losing to find – and what is to be lost is no less than the self. Now, of course, one of the most famous of Christ's exhortations is: 'For whosoever will save his life shall lose it: and whosoever will lose his life for my sake shall find it' (Matthew 16:25; repeated in slightly different forms in Mark 8:35, and Luke 9:24). It is the basic Christian promise, and produces an ethics which extends from the small self-sacrifices of unselfishness to literal martyrdom. This play is emphatically not a Christian allegory, but that central Christian idea is refracted and diffused throughout. So that when Antipholus says again – 'I [will] lose myself', the repetition has much greater resonance and potential implication than his first use of the word, which merely suggests not knowing one street from another. Both the Antipholus brothers (and the Dromios), like the father and mother before them, will have to lose their selves – experience a loss of identity – in order to find themselves, *and* their necessary, complementing and completing others. And, thereby, a healed and better life. After this soliloquy, the Ephesian Dromio enters to summon Antipholus, incomprehensibly, home to dinner. More worryingly, he denies knowledge of the money which Antipholus is sure he just recently gave him to look after. He is beaten for his pains, and a puzzled Antipholus is left in the beginning of his amazement. The comedy of errors is under way.

However, the next Act shows us Adriana, the wife of Antipholus of Ephesus (E. for convenience), in confidential conversation with her sister, Luciana. Luciana and the conversation itself are very much Shakespeare's addition to Plautus, and the whole scene serves to initiate that prolonged debate about the nature of marriage – the correct behaviour of husbands and wives – which is a serious concern of the play. Adriana is fretful and angry at her husband's unexplained absence, and spiritedly complains that husbands have more 'liberty' than wives. Luciana, unmarried, more demurely and conventionally counsels patience, accepting male superiority, and boundedness and boundaries in general:

> Why, headstrong liberty is lashed with woe.
> There's nothing situate under heaven's eye
> But hath his bound, in earth, in sea, in sky.
> The beasts, the fishes, and the wingèd fowls
> Are their males' subjects, and at their controls ...
> [Men] Of more preeminence than fish and fowls,
> Are masters to their females, and their lords;

Then let your will attend on their accords.

(II, i, 15–25)

Adriana is scornful of this orthodox compliance and 'fool-begged patience', on the reasonable grounds that it is easy for a woman to be meek if she doesn't have a grievance, or, come to that, a husband. Luciana's views are, in part, validated by the play; and for all we know, they might have been, in part, Shakespeare's own. But only in part. For while Shakespeare undoubtedly honours and reveres his Cordelias and Desdemonas, he has a good deal of sympathy with Adriana's 'headlong liberty' even though, or perhaps just because, it all too often procures its own lashing 'woe'. A woe we soon witness, as Adriana succumbs to a fit of anguished melancholy, prompted by feelings of resentment and neglect:

> His company must do his minions grace,
> Whilst I at home starve for a merry look:
> Hath homely age th' alluring beauty took
> From my poor cheek? Then he hath wasted it.
> Are my discourses dull? Barren my wit?
> If voluble and sharp discourse be marred,
> Unkindness blunts it more than marble hard.
> Do their gay vestments his affections bait?
> That's not my fault; he's master of my state.
> What ruins are in me that can be found,
> By him not ruined? Then is he the ground
> Of my defeatures. My decayèd fair
> A sunny look of his would soon repair.
> But, too unruly deer, he breaks the pale,
> And feeds from home; poor I am but his stale.

(II, i, 87–101)

There is perhaps a touch of plangent self-pity there, but Luciana's dismissive, summary criticism – 'Self-harming jealousy!' – is entirely inadequate. The lines are heartfelt, at times even moving, and bespeak a serious conception, based on experience, of the kind of vital symbiotic relationship a marriage can be. Adriana certainly has a case to make.

The seriousness continues when, accompanied by her sister, Adriana goes out into the town looking for her husband. She runs into Antipholus S. whom, of course, she takes to be her own Antipholus E. The man, understandably enough, shows no signs of knowing her. And this occasions a very articulate, and important, lament:

> How comes it now, my husband, O how comes it,
> That thou art then estrangèd from thyself?
> That, undividable, incorporate,
> Am better than thy dear self's better part.
> Ah, do not tear away thyself from me;
> For know, my love, as easy mayst thou fall
> A drop of water in the breaking gulf,
> And take unmingled thence that drop again
> Without addition or diminishing
> As take from me thyself, and not me too.
> How dearly would it touch thee to the quick,
> Shouldst thou but hear I were licentious,
> And that this body, consecrate to thee,
> By ruffian lust should be contaminate!
> Wouldst thou not spit at me, and spurn at me,
> And hurl the name of husband in my face,
> And tear the stained skin off my harlot brow,
> And from my false hand cut the wedding ring,
> And break it with a deep-divorcing vow?
> I know thou canst, and therefore see thou do it.
> I am possessed with an adulterate blot.
> My blood is mingled with the crime of lust;
> For, if we two be one, and thou play false,
> I do digest the poison of thy flesh,
> Being strumpeted by thy contagion.
> Keep then fair league and truce with thy true bed,
> I live distained, thou undishonorèd.

>> (II, ii, 120–47)

Now, there is something comic in the *situation* – a wife addressing a torrent of reproach to a bewildered man who doesn't, as it were, know her from Eve. But the sentiments expressed are of the utmost seriousness (and the verse has a corresponding passionate energy and kinaesthetic power which would not be out of place, I venture to say, in many of Shakespeare's later, greater plays – particularly those which touch on sexual infidelity. This is true of quite a lot of the poetry given to Adriana; as, for example, when, referring to her husband, she asks her sister what she has observed of 'his heart's meteors tilting in his face', IV, ii, 6 – one of those astonishing Shakespeare images which, I find, leave one both speechless and haunted). The drop of water image is there again, you will notice, though with another turn. Once you've let fall a drop of water into the sea, you can't get it out again, at least, not as it was. The theme is the indissolubility of the marriage bond, and one of the texts behind it, again, is Paul's Epistle to the Ephesians: ' . . . a man shall leave his father and mother, and shall be joined unto his wife, *and the two shall be one flesh* ' (5:31 – my italics). The two-in-one-ness achieved, or achievable, in the marriage tie, was a crucial notion for Shakespeare. He writes in 'The Phoenix and the Turtle', at around this time:

> So they loved, as love in twain
> Had the essence but in one;
> Two distincts, division none:
> Number there in love was slain.
>
> . . .
>
> Property was thus appalled,
> That the self was not the same;
> Single nature's double name
> Neither two nor one was called.

I will just say here that the two-in-one-ness of marriage, which somehow preserves difference in unity (which is how number is 'slain'), is, for Shakespeare, the ideal of a true relationship; while the two-in-one-ness suggested by identical twins (it points to a narcissistic effacement of difference – just glanced at in the final scene: 'Methinks you are my glass and not my brother') is very much the wrong model for relating. And the experience that 'the self was not the same' is undergone, has to be undergone, by those figures in Shakespearian comedy who variously emerge from the self to achieve, or rediscover, a true relationship. When Adriana asks Antipholus S. 'how comes it,/ That thou art then estranged from thyself?' she is being much more pertinent, and prescient, than she can possibly know. For that is just what is about to happen to him. *And*, in a different way, to her errant husband as well.

The feeling of self-estrangement, and possible transform-ation, immediately takes hold of this Antipholus and Dromio:

> D.S. I am transformèd, master, am not I?
> A.S. I think thou art in mind, and so am I.
> D.S. Nay, master, both in mind and in my shape.
> A.S. Thou hast thine own form.
> D.S. No, I am an ape.
> A.S. If thou art changed to aught, 'tis to an ass.

> (II, ii, 196–200)

The Ovidian moment, with the Shakespearian difference. They do *not* experience a change in shape and form, but something is happening in their minds. Dromio, as perhaps befits a servant, has a traditional (English) rustic-superstitious explanation for what is happening:

> This is the fairy land. O spite of spites!
> We talk with goblins, owls, and sprites;
> If we obey them not, this will ensue:
> They'll suck our breath, or pinch us black and blue.

> (II, ii, 190–93)

We will encounter fairy land, and a man transformed to an ass, in a later Shakespeare comedy. Here, Antipholus has the more relevant response to this seeming strangeness of being known to women (because of their names) whom they have never seen.

> What, was I married to her in my dream?
> Or sleep I now, and think I hear all this?
> What error drives our eyes and ears amiss?
> Until I know this sure uncertainty,
> I'll entertain the offered fallacy.

> (II, ii, 183–7)

Awake, asleep; sane, mad; right, wrong? – the important point is that, whatever is the case, he is both willing and determined to 'entertain the offered fallacy'. He thus shows himself to be a good candidate for positive metamorphosis. He repeats this resolve when Adriana insists that he comes back to dinner with herself and Luciana:

> Am I in earth, in heaven, or in hell?

Sleeping or waking, mad or well-advised?
Known unto these, and to myself disguised?
I'll say as they say, and persever so,
And in this mist at all adventures go.

(II, ii, 213–17)

It is this resolve to plunge into the 'mist' which is the saving, or
rather the making, of this Antipholus. Mist, like water, like
dream, is an area in which boundaries blur and identities
dissolve – as William Carroll puts it: 'metamorphosis thrives in
unstable regions, and it takes some courage to step into "this
mist"'. He will gain his reward.

Once Adriana has her 'husband', as she thinks, securely
back within the house, she orders the doors to be locked and
no one allowed entrance. This leads to one of the central
scenes of inversion, or subversion, of the play. The local
Antipholus, of E., at last puts in an appearance for the first
time (Act III), and finds that he is barred from his own house,
denied access to his own wife. This is a visible image of the sort
of topsy-turvydom which is beginning to spread outwards
from the initial mistakes of identity – the stranger is within, the
familiar is without; the outsider is inside, the insider outside.
Antipholus E. is, understandably, both angry and bemused.
He is starting *his* experience of self-estrangement, displacement and dislocation, which will take him, as it will his
brother, to the edge of a kind of madness or mania – from
which he too will emerge a new, or renewed, man. (For
Antipholus S. the experience mainly concerns spiritual or
mental strangenesses; for his brother, it is more a matter of a
series of domestic and social goings-wrong.) The comic errors
begin to multiply.

Inside the house, Antipholus S. is suddenly and powerfully
smitten by the sister, Luciana, and thus he addresses her:

Less in your knowledge and your grace you show not
Than our earth's wonder, more than earth divine.
Teach me, dear creature, how to think and speak:
Lay open to my earthly-gross conceit,
Smoth'red in errors, feeble, shallow, weak,
The folded meaning of your words' deceit.
Against my soul's pure truth why labor you

> To make it wander in an unknown field?
> Are you a god, would you create me new?
> Transform me, then, and to your pow'r I'll yield.
>
> (III, ii, 32–40)

This is Ovidianism refracted through Revelation ('And he that sat upon the throne said, Behold, I make all things new', 21:5). The vocabulary is laced with Christian terms – grace, soul – and projects the idea of being purified of the error-prone grossness of man's earthly condition. Just as he calls her 'my sole earth's heaven, and my heaven's claim'. (Note, incidentally, Shakespeare's first use of the word 'folded' – concealed, hidden; it was to become a crucial word for him.) But he also shifts into a pagan key which, perhaps unconsciously, reveals more wariness or ambivalence about Luciana's female attractions.

> O train me not, sweet mermaid, with thy note,
> To drown me in thy sister's flood of tears.
> Sing, siren, for thyself, and I will dote;
> Spread o'er the silver waves thy golden hairs;
> And, as a bed I'll take them, and there lie,
> And, in that glorious supposition, think
> He gains by death that hath such means to die.
> Let Love, being light, be drownèd if she sink!
>
> (III, ii, 45–52)

Perhaps she promises, not redemption but (admittedly delicious) drowning – not a saviour but a siren. (It offers yet another extension of the motif of entering water – to find, or to lose.) By the end of the scene, he has decided to 'trudge, pack, and begone' – flee the possible danger. Luciana (who, of course, thinks he is her brother-in-law and has given him no encouragement) is, he says:

> Possessed with such a gentle sovereign grace,
> Of such enchanting presence and discourse,
> Hath almost made me traitor to myself.
> But, lest myself be guilty to self-wrong,
> I'll stop mine ears against the mermaid's song.
>
> (III, ii, 165–9)

It is, of course, the time-honoured Ulysses strategy, and for

Antipholus, it represents a defensive, self-retractive instinct coming into play. Deciding that 'There's none but witches do inhabit here' (III, ii, 161), he wants to leave Ephesus – get out of the 'mist' as it were. But that will not prove so easy.

In the same scene, Dromio reveals that he, too, has had a disturbing encounter with a strange woman – the 'kitchen wench', called Luce rather than Luciana, and (on account of her kitchen work) 'all grease', not 'grace'. Dromio's account of this encounter offers an amusing parody of the Petrarchan, etherialized discourse of love which we have just heard from his master. Famously, with earthy humour, he describes her very large body in terms of contemporary geography – 'I could find out countries in her' – thus Ireland is 'in her buttocks' and so on. (Curiously, this topographical tour of the female body provides the only occasion, in all his plays, on which Shakespeare refers to 'America'.) It all points to the extremely physical and corporeal element in the relationship between the sexes. Dromio, too, is beginning to feel that sense of self-estrangement which seems to be spreading. 'Do you know me, sir? Am I Dromio? Am I your man? Am I myself?' The important point about his encounter – apart from its amusingness – is that it threatens a *downward* transformation: 'she would have me as a beast – not that, I being a beast, she would have me, but that she, being a very beastly creature, lays claim to me ... She had transformed me to a curtal dog, and made me turn i' th' wheel.' (III, ii, 86–9, 151). Grease, not grace. Metamorphosis can go either way. Revelation *and* Ovid. Remember that the whole play takes place under the signs, as it were, of 'the Centaur' and 'the Phoenix' and 'the Tiger'. Are these people going up – or down? Experiencing a change in the self can be an unnerving – and risky – business.

*

From here on, the confusion becomes worse confounded – or better, from the point of view of comedy. It is comic, as the errors and perplexedness of other people can be (in this play, almost uniquely, the division between complete knowledge for the audience, and total ignorance and obliviousness for the participants, is maintained until about a hundred lines from the end. There is here no plotter or 'practicer' on stage – no Richard III, Don John, Iago, Iachimo; no Rosalind, Portia, Viola, Helena, Hamlet, Oberon, Prospero – mediating between us and the characters). But there are potentially serious results as well. Relationships are threatened, and the sense of individual isolation increased, as assumptions cease to be shareable, and mutuality fades and fails. The trust on which the commerce of the city depends is threatened, as promises are seemingly broken, words not kept, contracts not honoured, goods not delivered, debts not paid. *Apparently*, that is. For this is a world in which appearances become increasingly unreliable. There is the sense of a small community moving towards chaos – and a corresponding increase in the explosions of rage and violence (more of the tiger than the phoenix for a while). The Antipholus brothers move towards a condition of complete paranoia – Antipholus S. becomes convinced that he is in a town of 'fiends' and 'witches'; and Antipholus E. is bundled away and locked up as, as it were, certifiably insane (premonitory shades of the treatment of Malvolio). By the time he has broken free, and the other Antipholus taken refuge in the priory, the turmoil is total. Well might the Duke say – 'I think you all have drunk of Circe's cup' (V, i, 271); and well may Adriana cry out – 'I long to know the truth hereof at large' (IV, iv, 144).

At this point, the 'unfolding' begins; for once the twins are seen *together*, errors are explained, and clarification spreads rapidly. It is a dazzled moment for the onlookers, who seem to be seeing double and begin to wonder which is which, and who is who, and, indeed, what is what? Individual identity itself seems to shimmer unsteadily. Ontology wobbles. The Duke reasons:

> One of these men is genius to the other;
> And so of these, which is the natural man,
> And which the spirit? Who deciphers them?

> (V, i, 333–5)

This is, perhaps, the main question of the play; a question which, in one 'deciphering' way and another, Shakespeare never stopped asking – which, what, finally *is* the 'natural' man; which and what the 'spirit'?

But before all that happens, Shakespeare has reintroduced the romance element, or the frame narrative, and this deserves some comment. There has been, throughout the day of the play, a constant awareness of time (and much bantering about it), as we move inexorably towards five o'clock, the appointed hour for the execution of Egeon. Everything and everyone converges on this place and this time, which occasions the first 'recognition' as Egeon sees what he takes to be his lost son, Antipholus E. But it is the wrong Antipholus who, understandably, does not recognize his father. This provokes a lament of true pathos from the father:

> O, grief hath changed me since you saw me last,
> And careful hours with time's deformèd hand,
> Have written strange defeatures in my face.
> ...
> Now know my voice! O, time's extremity,
> Hast thou so cracked and splitted my poor tongue
> In seven short years, that here my only son
> Knows not my feeble key of untuned cares?
> Though now this grainèd face of mine be hid
> In sap-consuming winter's drizzled snow,
> And all the conduits of my blood froze up,
> Yet hath my night of life some memory;
> My wasting lamps some fading glimmer left

(V, i, 298–301, 308–16)

Time's deforming and 'defeaturing' hand works more slowly than the 'magic' or 'miracle' of metamorphosis. But 'time's extremity' is as powerful a force as there is in Shakespeare's world, and it is a crucial point, both here and in all that is to come, that time can prove to have a *re*forming, a *re*featuring hand, as well. As Egeon soon discovers when the Abbess appears.

The Abbess, just prior to her final appearance, has taken the chance to trick Adriana into confessing her own shrewishness, for which the Abbess blames the 'madness' of Adriana's husband:

> And thereof came it that the man was mad.

xlvii

> The venom clamors of a jealous woman
> Poisons more deadly than a mad dog's tooth.
>
> (V, i, 68–70)

Adriana accepts the way she has been manoeuvred into self-accusation – quite meekly: 'She did betray me to my own reproof' (V, i, 90). But it is an important last touch – bearing in mind Shakespeare and 'shrews' – that her erstwhile critical sister now speaks up in her defence. Thus Luciana:

> She never reprehended him but mildly,
> When he demeaned himself rough, rude, and wildly.
> Why bear you these rebukes and answer not?
>
> (V, i, 87–9)

Adriana may have to curb her tongue a little; but rough, rude Antipholus will have to mend his ways – reform, indeed – to become a proper husband.

And now the Abbess can reclaim *her* husband – old Egeon – along with their two lost sons, who now stand before them. The family is thus magically, 'miraculously' reunited; and what better site for such a wonder than the precincts of the priory or abbey (Temple). (It is interesting that when Antipholus E. now offers to pay the ransom for his father's life, the Duke answers: 'It shall not need; thy father hath his life' (V, i, 391). Such effortless remission was not possible at the start; but in the new atmosphere of mercy and reconciliation, inflexible sentences can melt away – the comedy has finally worked to 'disannul' the law.) The Abbess, Emilia as wife and mother, invites all into the abbey – nobody locked out this time, everybody included in:

> And all that are assembled in this place,
> That by this sympathizèd one day's error
> Have suffered wrong, go, keep us company,
> And we shall make full satisfaction.
> Thirty-three years have I but gone in travail
> Of you, my sons, and till this present hour
> My heavy burden ne'er delivered.
> The Duke, my husband, and my children both,
> And you the calendars of their nativity,
> Go to a gossips' feast, and joy with me

After so long grief such nativity.

(V, i, 397-407)

By now, the Antipholuses and the Dromios have sorted themselves out, identities have been re-secured, names are properly affixed, people are seeing straight again, and on all sides, relationships are being established, reaffirmed, and rediscovered – 'traffic', in every sense, is beginning to flow again between Syracuse and Ephesus. The Abbess summons them all to a new christening, or 'gossips' feast' (gossip, from 'godsibb' – godparent or sponsor at a baptism), to celebrate 'such nativity'. This is not birth, but *re*birth – she says she has been 'in travail' for thirty-three years for this second delivery of her children (the insistence by Antipholus S. at the beginning that 'In Ephesus I am but two hours old', II, ii, 149, unknowingly suggests that this is a place where he might be 'born again'). This is, then, effectively the rebirth and renewal of the whole community. There is nothing of all this in Plautus, and if this is indeed Shakespeare's first comedy, it is truly remarkable how many of the themes and preoccupations of his later work he here, thus early, broached – how promptly, as it were, he staked out his dramatic territory.

*

THE TAMING OF THE SHREW

For she is changed as she had never been. (V, ii, 115)

Adriana could be 'shrewish', though not without provocation – 'My wife is shrewish *when I keep not hours*' admits Antipholus (my italics). But she is shown to be, throughout, a serious and devoted wife, if prone to possessive jealousy. In *The Taming of the Shrew*, Shakespeare gives us a woman who appears to be a total shrew – shrewish all the way down, as they say; seemingly, the most unprepared and unsuitable candidate for marriage and wifely responsibilities (and feelings) that could be imagined. (I might say here that Brian Morris, in his excellent Arden edition, argues that *Shrew* is the earlier play – indeed, perhaps Shakespeare's *first* play. His arguments are quite persuasive, and one thing is undeniable. Adriana is a much more complex, more intellectually and emotionally advanced character than the relatively primitive Kate, who is, it has to be said, not very intelligent; though, importantly, shown to be more 'educable' than her sister.)

'Shrew', as a word, has an interesting history. The word for a mouse-like animal, wrongly thought to be venomous, it was applied to the devil up to the fourteenth century (and is indeed related to an old German word which meant 'devil' – *schrawaz*). It was also used to refer to a malignant person of either sex. By the sixteenth century it was reserved for women (Morris finds the first use in this sense in Chaucer), by which time it meant pretty much what we mean by it today, though it still carried suggestions of something evil and malevolent, if not diabolic. Shrews are, apparently, very aggressive, and go in for 'squeaking matches'; they have a reputation for irascibility and noise – 'a particularly scolding and complaining note' in the words of an expert on shrews, quoted by Morris (for the Romans, it was a 'noise of ill-omen'). Why something as small as the shrew should be used to figure something as, presumably, large as the Devil, one can only speculate. Women, notoriously, have a dread of mice and mice-like creatures, though whether that horror was shared by the dames of sixteenth-century rural Warwickshire, I have no idea. It probably has to do with fast little scurrying, squeaking, things which can get anywhere, and with the combination of smallness and aggression (not unfamiliar from the human realm) with what can apparently be unbearable *noise*. We perhaps need a rural account. Writing in 1607, the Rev. Edward Topsell said of the shrew: 'It is a ravening beast, feigning itself gentle and tame, but, being touched, it biteth deep and poysoneth deadly. It beareth a cruel minde, desiring to hurt anything, neither is there any creature that it loveth, or it loveth him, because it is feared of all.' And Gilbert White, in his matchless *Natural History of Selborne*, writes: 'It is supposed that a shrew mouse is of so baneful and deleterious a nature that, wherever it creeps over a beast, be it horse, cow, or sheep, the suffering animal is afflicted with cruel anguish, and threatened with the loss of the use of the limb.' Shakespeare must have known this country lore. Be that as it may, Kate is

1

called a 'shrew' at least ten times, and 'devil' nearer fifteen, while her noisiness and aggression are constantly remarked and displayed; so there can be little doubt about what type of woman she is meant to be – at least in the eyes of everyone around her. Which might not be the fairest – and certainly not the final – verdict.

There are, effectively, three different worlds represented in the play – all, of course, occupying the same stage space. Here again, from (what might be) the very beginning, we can see Shakespeare pursuing mutually enriching, mutually ironizing, genres and modes. The Induction (a device he never used again) is set, undoubtedly, in his own rural Warwickshire. The main story is rooted in familiar folk-tales and fabliaux concerning the subjugation or taming of an overbearing shrewish wife. (Leah Scragg records that there are over four hundred versions still extant, and she gives as a typical example *A Merry Jest of a Shrewde and Curste Wife, Lapped in Morrelles Skin, for Her Good Behavyour* (*c.* 1550). Morrell is a horse, and his owner kills and flays him so that he can enclose his shrewish wife in the skin, after he has beaten her unconscious. This way, she quickly learns deference and obedience, as who wouldn't. Petruchio employs, on the whole, less violent and subtle methods, and it could be said that his efforts are aimed at releasing Kate from a 'beastly' condition, not returning her to one.) The sub-plot, wonderfully interwoven with the main story, takes us into the sophisticated, complex world of Italian comedy. The specific source was Gascoigne's *Supposes* (1566), which was a version of Ariosto's *I Suppositi* (1509) – a source Shakespeare specifically refers to in his play, a self-conscious acknowledgment of theatrical precedent. Gascoigne explained the title: 'But understand, this our Suppose is nothing else but a mistaking or imagination of one thing for an other. For you shall see the master supposed for a servant, the servant for the master: the freeman for a slave, and the bondslave for a freeman: the stranger for a well known friend, and the familiar for a stranger.' This is the world of Roman New Comedy; a world of misunderstanding – errors – disguise, deception, subterfuge, and intrigue. Just so, Shakespeare's sub-plot is a world of 'counterfeit supposes' (V, i, 115), in which one character, multiplying manufactured identities for plotting purposes says:

> I see no reason but supposed Lucentio
> Must get a father, called 'supposed Vincentio'
>
> (II, i, 400–401)

All this plotting is occasioned by the contest between a number of suitors for the hand of Bianca, Kate's apparently mild and angelic sister. Both plots are about wooing and courtship: but, while Petruchio has recourse to his own kind of 'counterfeiting', his 'blunt' and 'peremptory' approach is in marked contrast to the Italianate intriguing practised by the others. It is also, in part, the contrast between conventions of realism and romance, which runs through the play. Brian Morris comments: 'Contrasts of social and dramatic convention of this kind are the staple of the play's development, and they comment ironically one on the other, refusing to allow any single attitude to love and marriage to go unchallenged.' Where Italian Classical comedy was contextualized by Romance in *The Comedy of Errors*, here it intermingles with folk-tale and rural tradition. Long before Ezra Pound's specific injunction, Shakespeare always 'made it new'.

The Induction is only 282 lines, yet it is one of the richest and most compacted pieces in Shakespeare's comedies. It seems to set up a 'frame' situation, so that we will have a play-within-the-play, but, somehow, somewhy, Shakespeare does not complete the frame. It centres on Sly, the tinker, and involves two scenes. First, a 'rural alehouse', where he gets drunk and falls asleep. A local Lord, returning from hunting 'with his train', decides to 'practice on this drunken man' (another 'practicer' – or director on stage), and arranges for Sly to be transported to his mansion where he will be made to believe, when he wakes up, that 'he is nothing but a mighty lord'. Itinerant actors or players arrive, and the Lord arranges that they shall perform a play, both for 'lord' Sly, and the Lord and his house (and, of course, us). Scene two is set in a bedroom in the Lord's house, where Sly wakes up and is convinced that he is, indeed, an amnesiac lord, and settles down to watch the 'pleasant comedy' which he is told has been arranged for him – on doctors' orders. This play turns out to be *The Taming of the Shrew*. The theme of the beggar transported into luxury can be found in the *Arabian Nights*, and the poor man who wakes up and thinks he is in heaven is another old folkloric subject. But, given this basic motif, it is amazing how many themes and issues Shakespeare touches on, or anticipates, in this relatively short Induction.

I should, perhaps, mention here the existence of a play, published anonymously in 1594, entitled *The Taming of a Shrew* (my underlining). Shakespeare's play only appeared in print in the Folio of 1623, and there have been ongoing arguments – which need not concern us – as to whether *A Shrew* was a 'first shot' by Shakespeare, or – more likely – some kind of inadequate reconstruction of Shakespeare's play by others. I don't think much should be made of the shift between definite and indefinite article (on the lines that Shakespeare was offering *The* definitive article): the plays are very similar in outline, theme, and scenic detail – though *A Shrew* is detectably the cruder play. The important difference concerns Sly, and the framing situation. In Shakespeare's play, Sly slides off into silence and, apart from a moment at the end of the first scene, when he nods off, and wishes it was all over, he is never heard from again. One *can* justify this, and say that, with the disappearance of Sly, the play-within-the-play becomes simply *the* play, scaffolding jettisoned; and we, as audience, are brought one step nearer to the depicted events. That is – rather than looking at X looking at Y (us looking at Sly looking at Kate), we watch Y (Kate) direct (the now irrelevant Sly forgotten). I can see this as a plausible case, and, personally, I am quite happy with the play as we have it. But in *A Shrew*, Sly interrupts the 'play' on four occasions, and, more importantly, the play ends back with him at the alehouse – frame completed. Distinguished editors, from Bullough to Morris, think that, for a variety of reasons, the text we have is defective, and that Shakespeare's play almost certainly included Sly's interruptions, and the completion of the frame back at the alehouse at the end. That ending is certainly potentially important, and I will return to it.

But now let us consider Shakespeare's Induction, just about

twice as long as the one in *A Shrew* – and much more interesting. It opens with the Hostess of the alehouse – the shrew? – fiercely upbraiding the drunken Sly. A note of struggle and discord between the sexes is immediately struck. Then the Lord enters, accompanied by his retinue and dogs – affectionately named (Merriman, Clowder, Silver, Bellman, Echo – not yet time for Lear's Tray, Blanche and Sweetheart). This is very much rural England, and will make the shift to the bourgeois, merchant world of Padua in the 'play' all the more marked. Seeing Sly, drunkenly asleep, the Lord comments: 'O monstrous beast, how like a swine he lies.' He has undergone a downward transformation – humans into beasts (swine if Circe had anything to do with it): it is very much Ovid's world. The Lord decides to 'practice' on him, and simulate an upward transformation – like a magician, or a playwright:

> What think you, if he were conveyed to bed,
> Wrapped in sweet clothes, rings put upon his fingers,
> A most delicious banquet by his bed,
> And brave attendants near him when he wakes –
> Would not the beggar then forget himself?

(37–41)

In the event, the beggar does, finally, *not* forget himself – which may be taken to indicate that some people are unapt for metamorphosis, or that there are limits to the metamorphosing art. This is the case with Sly: it won't be true of Kate. The Lord continues with making the arrangements to carry out his plan. He really *is* like a stage director, specifying the decor, supervising the props and trappings, and, in particular, giving very detailed instructions as to how people are to 'act'. His page, Bartholomew, is to have the crucial role of pretending to be 'lord' Sly's loving wife. This is how he is to do it:

> Tell him from me – as he will win my love –
> He bear himself with honorable action
> Such as he hath observed in noble ladies
> Unto their lords, by them accomplishèd.
> Such duty to the drunkard let him do
> With soft low tongue and lowly courtesy,
> And say, 'What is't your honor will command

Wherein your lady and your humble wife
May show her duty and make known her love?'
And then, with kind embracements, tempting kisses,
And with declining head into his bosom,
Bid him shed tears, as being overjoyed
To see her noble lord restored to health
Who for this seven years hath esteemèd him
No better than a poor and loathsome beggar.
And if the boy have not a woman's gift
To rain a shower of commanded tears,
An onion will do well for such a shift,
Which in a napkin being close conveyed
Shall in despite enforce a watery eye.

(109–128)

Now, of course, this is exactly how a boy playing a part in an
Elizabethan play (by Shakespeare, among others) would be
prepared – dressed up as a woman, and then told how to
simulate the emotional states of a mature woman (not easy,
surely, for a young lad, who no doubt had recourse to the
onion trick and other stratagems). So we may fairly say that
here Shakespeare (a theatre professional, after all) is, effectively, showing himself at work. And a boy into a woman is a
theatrical equivalent of tutoring and changing an unbearable
shrew into just such an obedient, courteous, *quiet*, loving wife
as young Bartholomew is ordered to impersonate. The whole
process of the coming drama of transformation is here antici-
pated, to be this time, of course, managed by Shakespeare
himself. And where the Lord fails – Sly remains the same old
Sly – Shakespeare will succeed. Superior magic. Just watch me
do it – the Induction seems to say.

When Sly wakes up in the Lord's bedroom, and the servants
duly enact their allotted, pampering roles, he thinks they are
mad (as Kate will think Petruchio is). 'What, would you make
me mad? Am I not Christopher Sly ... now by present
profession a tinker? Ask Mariam Hacket, the fat ale-wife of
Wincot.' Wincot was a village near Stratford, so we know that
Shakespeare is, as it were, close to home. In addition to wine
and delicacies, the servants offer him music (but, in time, lutes
will be broken); hunting (Petruchio will take that over); and
paintings:

Dost thou love pictures? We will fetch thee straight
Adonis painted by a running brook
And Cytherea all in sedges hid,
Which seem to move and wanton with her breath
Even as the waving sedges play with wind.
. . .
We'll show thee Io as she was a maid
And how she was beguilèd and suprised,
As lively painted as the deed was done.
. . .
Or Daphne roaming through a thorny wood,
Scratching her legs that one will swear she bleeds,
And at that sight shall sad Apollo weep,
So workmanly the blood and tears are drawn.

(49–60)

This is Ovid plain, or rather Ovid illustrated (it is a good
example of *ekphrasis* – a verbal description of a work of art).
All the examples are from the *Metamorphoses*, and, indeed,
Jonathan Bate is of the opinion that 'what is laid out here is
almost a programme for Shakespeare's subsequent Ovidianism'. (This is continued in the play: Ovid is mentioned by
name in the first scene, line 33 – one of only four times in
Shakespeare; and when Lucentio is smitten by Bianca he says:

O yes, I saw sweet beauty in her face,
Such as the daughter of Agenor had, [i.e. Europa]
That made great Jove to humble him to her hand
When with his knees he kissed the Cretan strond.

(I, i, 167–70)

In Ovid's account, Jove changed himself into a bull; Lucentio,
with less scope, turns himself into a schoolmaster.) Here, there,
and everywhere, metamorphosis of one kind or another (from
change of clothes, roles, identities, to some deep inner change
in the self) is in the air. It might be pointed out that the
Ovidian illustrations do not offer particularly felicitous examples of the results of love – Adonis killed by a boar; Io changed
to a heifer; and bleeding, crying Daphne turned into a laurel.
Ovidian metamorphosis is, invariably, a brutal, and 'brutaliz-
ing', business; Shakespeare wants to find a better way. Sly,
deciding to go along with the 'play' in which he finds himself,

tells his 'wife' to undress and come to bed; he is, he makes clear – 'it stands so' – ready for it. Shakespeare, with his boy-girl figures (not to mention his boy-girl-boy characters), often delights in taking us to the very borders of so-called sexual normality, allowing us to feel the dangerous, exciting edge of imminent and proximate deviance. (Just in case we were feeling complacent and too much at ease in our sexual identities.) Bartholomew makes his excuses; not before, in one last anticipation of a Kate to come, s/he has vowed to Sly – 'I am your wife in all obedience' (107). Then the players – the next lot of players – enter, and Sly and Bartholomew settle down to watch what is rather curiously promised as 'a kind of history' (141 – never be too sure which genre you are in in a Shakespeare play). The alehouse yard becomes a bedroom, which in turn becomes a theatre – fairly seamlessly. The boundaries hardly seem fixed; nor, perhaps, determinable. Is what we are about to see just a continuation of Sly's dream (wherever that started or stopped)? Or is it as real as a row in an alehouse yard? Or stage-stuff to entertain a lord? It doesn't really matter. One way and another, implies Shakespeare, it is all pretty theatrical – like much of life.

So, from Wincot (thereabouts) to Padua, and we are soon among the would-be wooers of Baptista's two daughters. Most of them are bidding for the hand of the apparently perfect and demure, Bianca. I say 'bidding' advisedly; it cannot be missed to what extent courtship is involved with money (riches, property, dowries, contracts, etc.) in this play. Romance – no, *marriage* – is, it seems, if not indistinguishable, then inseparable from finance. We may check at this a little – Baptista very clearly auctioning off Bianca is not perhaps how we see a father's role. Perhaps this is Shakespeare's version of how merchants – or Italians! – view marriage; or perhaps it was for him the merest realism. Which is not to say that he put a cash value on true love: *that*, indeed, is priceless. Make sure you find it – if you can. But it arrives, or is come by, in strange ways; and, as it transpires, the infatuated Petrarchanism of Lucentio's wooing of Bianca is by no means a certain way of securing it. How about Petruchionism?

Where Lucentio appears to be a conventional lover ('I

burn, I pine, I perish' and so on), Petruchio presents himself as
an unashamedly mercenary fortune hunter:

> I come to wive it wealthily in Padua;
> If wealthily, then happily in Padua.
>
> (I, ii, 74–5)

as he makes quite explicit – 'wealth is burthen of my wooing
dance' (I, ii, 67). He is told about Katherine Minola, who as
the elder daughter of Baptista will have a very large dowry (he
wants her off his hands, anyway – she is very much 'for sale');
but he is also warned that she is 'intolerable curst/ And shrewd
and froward' and, adds Hortensio, 'I would not wed her for a
mine of gold' (I, ii, 91). 'Thou know'st not gold's effect' is
Petruchio's cool reply, and he announces his intention to
marry her. The other suitors think that he will not be able to
abide, and prevail over, her 'scolding tongue', but there are
two hints which may alert us to his subsequent course of
action. He dismisses the problem of her shrewish tongue:

> Think you a little din can daunt mine ears?
> Have I not in my time heard lions roar?
> Have I not heard the sea, puffed up with winds,
> Rage like an angry boar chafèd with sweat?
> Have I not heard great ordnance in the field
> And heaven's artillery thunder in the skies?
> Have I not in a pitchèd battle heard
> Loud 'larums, neighing steeds, and trumpets' clang?
> And do you tell me of a woman's tongue ...
>
> (I, ii, 199–207)

The discernible figure behind Petruchio here is Hercules – an
identification made explicit a moment later when Gremio,
referring to Katherine, says 'Yea, leave that labor to great
Hercules' (I, ii, 256). Gunnar Sorelius is the only commentator I know who has pointed to the importance of recognizing
Petruchio as a Hercules figure, but there can be doubt that it is
central. Sorelius points out that in the speech just quoted you
can catch glimpsing references to various of Hercules' labours
– the Nemean lion, the Erimanthian boar, and perhaps his
capture of Troy. And in his ninth labour, Hercules subjugated
the Amazonian, Hippolyte. Hercules was, of course, *the*

culture hero, the master of monsters, the controller of the barbaric; as such, he was regarded as a primary civilizing force. Petruchio's treatment of Kate must be seen at least partially in that light.

But there was another side to Hercules, best known to the Elizabethans through translations of Seneca's *Hercules Furens* (from the play by Euripides). This shows Hercules gone mad, and killing his wife Megara. This should also be remembered when considering Petruchio's treatment of Kate, who indeed, thinks he is 'mad' from the beginning. His violent and disruptive behaviour at his own wedding, biffing the priest and throwing wine over the sexton, indeed suggests a Petruchio *furens* ('Such a mad marriage never was before', III, ii, 182). Likewise, the bizarre, ragged, and desperately slovenly clothes he wears for the wedding, make him 'a very monster in apparel' as well as 'an eyesore to our solemn festival' (III, ii, 70, 101). But, as the shrewd and perceptive Tranio observes: 'He hath some meaning in his mad attire' (III, ii, 124). Or, more generally, there is, as we say, method in his 'madness'. Hercules, the human hero raised to the level of a god, was famous both for his immense powers of control (including self-control), and for his *anger*. Not for nothing do we see Petruchio apparently controlling and commanding time ('It shall be what o'clock I say it is', IV, iii, 193); the planets or heavenly bodies ('this gallant will command the sun', IV, ii, 194; 'It shall be sun or star or what I list', IV, v, 7); and even gender (making Kate address Vincentio as a young girl and then as an old man). But he also shows signs of violent anger. We first see him beating his (insolent) servant; and later he throws dishes, food, clothes about, not to mention roughing up the clergy (though it should be noted he uses no physical violence with Kate, and only threatens to hit her after she has struck him – she clearly believes him!). There is something particularly menacing in absolutely cool anger – lethal wrath contained within total composure. It is, indeed, god-like, and this is what marks Petruchio. Kate moves from being furious, to being bemused and bewildered, to being simply frightened. We hope that there is a succeeding phase – wifely happiness.

The second early clue as to what to expect from Petruchio,

is provided by his servant Grumio, who clearly knows his master well. 'Scolding' will have no effect on Petruchio:

I'll tell you what, sir, and she stand him but a little, he will throw a figure in her face and so disfigure her with it that she shall have no more eyes to see withal than a cat.

(I, ii, 110–15)

Cats are supposed to have very sharp sight (Kate scratches like a cat, as well as 'squeaking' like a shrew), so either Grumio has muddled it up, or – Morris suggests – he is referring to the old saying 'Well might the cat wink when both her eyes were out.' But, whatever his intended meaning, his prediction that Petruchio will 'throw a figure in her face' could hardly be more accurate, whether we think of figures of speech or figures as images. It is just how he will proceed. First, by holding up an image of herself to her which is the exact opposite of what she *is*, but a 'figure' of what he wants her to *become*:

> I find you passing gentle.
> 'Twas told me you were rough and coy and sullen,
> And now I find report a very liar,
> For thou art pleasant, gamesome, passing courteous,
> But slow in speech, yet sweet as springtime flowers.
> Thou canst not frown, thou canst not look askance,
> Nor bite the lip as angry wenches will,
> Nor hast thou pleasure to be cross in talk,
> But thou with mildness entertain'st thy wooers,
> With gentle conference, soft and affable.
> Why does the world report that Kate doth limp?
> O sland'rous world!

(II, i, 236–47)

It must be particularly galling for Kate, who prides herself on her fast, wounding tongue, to be told that she is 'slow in speech', while as for limping – we have just seen her 'flying' after her sister in violent pursuit. Faced with this unrecognizable image in the mirror of Petruchio's speech, Kate is nonplussed, finding her reality helpless against the fictional being Petruchio insists upon. It should be noted, here, that Kate is distinctly 'slow in *thought*': she never tries to analyse what this apparent madman might be up to. Like the animals

– she is shrew, cat, haggard (untamed hawk) – she reacts, but does not reflect. Until, perhaps, after her 'conversion' – or capitulation – after which she is given all the signs of a thinking being.

The other kind of 'figures' he throws in her face are of a different kind – they are enactments, if she could but see it, of aspects of her own nature and behaviour. When he comes to his wedding in that grotesque tattered motley of hopelessly ill-matched and shoddy garments (described at amazing length – it is like an extended portrait of a person in terms of clothes), it is as if he is saying to her, in visible, material signs – this is about how prepared *you* are for marriage, given your dire inner dishevelment. When he makes a messy parody of the wedding, with his loud rudeness, blows, and sop-throwing, he is saying – and *this* is the sort of respect *you* have for the solemn ceremonies of society. And when he throws the food, and pots, and clothes around, and behaves with incomprehensible con-trariness, he is offering a representation, for her benefit, of the kind of domestic chaos which sustainedly 'shrewish' behaviour would bring to the household. And so on, with all his other 'counterfeiting' with her. As one of his servants acutely notes: 'he kills her in her own humor' (IV, i, 174). By distortion and exaggeration, he '*dis*figures' her by throwing her own 'figure' back at her in a rather terrifying form. And, just as Grumio had predicted, Kate is, temporarily, blinded. Petruchio is educating and 'taming' Kate in, as he sees it, the only way in which she will learn. (Perhaps inevitably, and not irrelevantly, all this has also been seen – by Ruth Nevo – as a 'therapeutic psychodrama'.)

Importantly, Petruchio reveals these two strategies to the audience in the only two soliloquies of the play. This makes him one of those Shakespearian 'practicers' who, alone of all the characters, knows just what is going on because, to a large extent, he is, as it were, stage-managing it. (It is notable that he has a far larger part than Kate, whose speaking part is, in fact, rather small.) The soliloquies also align us with him through the privilege of shared knowledge – we know exactly what is really happening, while we watch poor Kate flounder in bemused, uncomprehending ignorance. The first soliloquy is early, in Act II. It announces the first strategy – of offering the contradicting, ideal image:

> Say that she rail, why then I'll tell her plain
> She sings as sweetly as a nightingale.
>
> (II, i, 170–71)

and so on. The later soliloquy, in Act IV when the process is well advanced, outlines the other, more rigorous, part of the process:

> Thus have I politicly begun my reign,
> And 'tis my hope to end successfully.
> My falcon now is sharp and passing empty,
> And till she stoop she must not be full gorged,
> For then she never looks upon her lure.
> Another way I have to man my haggard,
> To make her come and know her keeper's call,
> That is, to watch her as we watch those kites
> That bate and beat and will not be obedient.
>
> (IV, i, 182–90)

Falcon, lure, haggard, kite, keeper – this is Petruchio the hunter, the falconer, the tamer. Kate will 'bate and beat' (flap and flutter) for a little while yet; but she will, finally, 'stoop' – which for a bird means swooping back to the lure (a device used in training to entice a hawk to return from flight); for a woman it means to submit – perhaps in time to conquer, but certainly to obey. Petruchio in fact makes clear his intentions and plans to Kate herself almost as soon as he has met her: 'And will you, nill you, I will marry you' (II, i, 264). Her sometimes frantic 'nilling' will prove impotent before his implacable 'will'. He has the real, Herculean power.

> For I am he am born to tame you, Kate,
> And bring you from a wild Kate to a Kate
> Conformable as other household Kates.
>
> (II, i, 269–71)

At this stage, Kate simply thinks him mad. But the inexorable programme and process has been set in motion. Hercules is beginning his 'labour'.

We might want to pause at that line – 'a Kate/ Conformable

as other household Kates'. Does he *really* want a bleached-out conformist, indistinguishable from a crowd of other domestic drudges, or 'household Kates'? Since he 'bought' her from her father sight-unseen, as it were, we cannot say that he fell in love with her at first sight (as Lucentio does with Bianca). It is possible that his interest is aroused by what he is told about her apparently ungovernable tongue (perhaps scenting a challenge worthy of his taming energies and prowess). Certainly, when Hortensio enters with his 'head broke', Kate having beaten him with her lute, Petruchio warms to her in advance of seeing her:

> Now, by the world, it is a lusty wench!
> I love her ten times more than e'er I did.
> O how I long to have some chat with her!

> (II, i, 160–62)

One feels that the (apparently) totally-tamed Bianca leaves him cold – she is for romance, he is for hunting. There is no mistaking his enjoyment – as well as his determination – as he sets about the unwincing and unflinching struggle to break Kate's spirit. But is there not a paradox here – is he drawn to a wildness of spirit which he then proceeds to stamp out, or at least bring very much to heel? It is, perhaps, the necessary paradox of all education, and this play is very much about 'education'. It is set in Padua, a famous seat of learning, and in the sub-plot, two of Bianca's suitors (Lucentio and Hortensio) gain access to her father's house by posing as teachers for her – of mathematics and music, and languages and philosophy. A good traditional academic syllabus, you might think. Of course they teach her nothing, though this is hardly the fault of these venerable and estimable subjects. More to the point, Bianca *learns* nothing, nothing at all, and at the end of the play shows signs of shortly needing the sort of 'education' to which Kate has been subjected.

For Petruchio is a teacher, as well as a hunter – he is specifically called 'the master' of 'the taming school' (IV, ii, 55–6). In good education, the aim is to encourage the exfoliation of a pupil's best potentialities, to 'lead' him or her 'out'(e-ducare) of ignorance and uninstructed helplessness.

But this also involves a necessary curbing of all kinds of instinctual waywardness, a disciplining of all sorts of temperamental unruliness – otherwise people would be unbearable (perhaps I should say *more* unbearable) and society impossible. To the extent that it hopes to produce citizens, education *could* be said to aim at turning out 'conformists' – though of course there is a positive, productive way of obeying laws and recognizing conventions, as well as more negative, mindless adherence and automatism. Perhaps enough of that. When Kate finally gives up and gives in, conceding Petruchio the Adamic privilege of 'naming' all things ('What you will have it named, even that it is', IV, v, 21), Horatio tells him 'the field is won'. Petruchio answers:

> Well, forward, forward. Thus the bowl should run,
> And not unluckily against the bias.
>
> (IV, v, 24–6)

This is the first time that Shakespeare uses this image from bowls (in which the bowl has a weight on one side so that its natural movement is a curve in one direction). It was to be a very important one and he uses it in subsequent plays, from *Twelfth Night* and *King John* to *Hamlet* and *King Lear*. Its possibilities are obvious: here, Petruchio is maintaining that he has, in effect, *trained* Kate to move in the proper manner, to stop fighting against the way she was meant, and made, to go. Now, it is certainly possible to see a certain amount of what I think is called sexist essentialism in this (it is *natural* for women to be subservient and obedient); and you could say – people have – that what Petruchio gives Kate is a lesson in old-fashioned patriarchy and unreconstructed male dominance. Certainly, such lines as

> I will be master of what is mine own.
> She is my goods, my chattels; she is my house,
> My household stuff, my field, my barn,
> My horse, my ox, my ass, my anything ...
>
> (III, ii, 229–32)

may be thought offensive (though the element of exaggeration is unmistakable – my *barn*? my *anything*?); and making Kate trample her own cap underfoot at the end can be seen as the last stage of enforced abjection and self-abasement. If you don't like the play, you don't – and you will not be in bad company. I don't just mean some (by no means all) feminists: George Bernard Shaw found it 'altogether disgusting to the modern sensibility', and Quiller-Couch thought it 'brutal stuff and tiresome ... positively offensive to any modern civilized man or modern woman'. (Finding this play sexist would go along with finding *Othello* racist, and *The Merchant of Venice* anti-semitic. Quite wrong-headed in my view – but a line which has been argued.) But it *is* possible to see Petruchio as curbing, rather than crushing, Kate; making her into a worthy companion instead of an all-over-the-place wild-cat, beating her head against every convention in sight (the possibility that her father has contributed to this by his manifest favouritism towards Bianca is clearly hinted). Seen this way, he is liberating her from a pointlesss, self-lashing, 'beast-liness' – the Herculean labour. There is certainly no getting round her final long speech in favour of female 'obedience'. It effectively concludes the play and cannot be heard as irony: nor is it contextually undermined by any sort of, as it were, Falstaffian sub-commentary. But the act of *dis*obedience with which the, supposedly, so docile and biddable Bianca starts her marriage (in the final wager), bodes ill for that couple's future felicity – Shakespeare may well have thought it was better to start from financial realism and move towards mutual affection, than to begin with intoxicated romanticism and run into disillusion and discord. And when, at the end, Petruchio says 'Come, Kate, we'll to bed', one cannot but feel that, not to put too fine a point upon it, they will have a better time there than Lucentio and Bianca. Her essential vitality ('a lusty wench') is, we feel, still there, if now reined in and directed. In this, she is a forerunner of Shakespeare's later wonderfully spirited heroines. Bianca leads nowhere.

The main point in all this – apart from the sense of ubiquitous struggle and contest, between sexes, sisters, suitors, generations – is 'change'. The sub-plot is full of changing – of clothes, names, roles; indeed, emphasizing the prevailing note, disguised Lucentio adopts the name Cambio – which is simply the Italian for change, exchange. But none of the changes are radical, or other than momentary improvizations and opportunistic simulations. The transformation of Kate is clearly another, deeper, matter. For, by the end, changed she certainly is. At her final demonstration of tractability and wifely obedience, Lucentio says 'Here is a wonder, if you talk of a wonder', while her father, more interestingly, more ambiguously, says 'For she is changed as she had never been' (V, ii, 106, 115). Changed as *if* she had never been a shrew? Changed as if she had never existed? Changed as she has never been changed before? William Carroll has noted these ambiguities, and sees them as reflecting an indeterminacy and uncertainty about the finality of Kate's transformation – on the grounds, roughly, that if she has changed once, she can change again. I take the point, but I don't think it quite fits with the spirit of the conclusion – though I suppose one can hear a residual, lingering doubt or scepticism in the very last line of the play – ''Tis a wonder, by your leave, she will be tamed so'. I think the multiple possibilities in her father's remark suggest the mysteriousness of a radical transformation of personality, that element of the unfathomable in an apparent identity change. The remark does justice to the *strangeness* of the phenomenon. At one point in her 'treatment', Kate is described as sitting 'as one new-risen from a dream' (IV, i, 180). There is a lot of waking from dreams – literal and metaphoric – in Shakespeare's comedies, and at one extreme it can involve waking to a new self, a new life. The father's remark in *A Shrew* is – 'Oh wonderfull metamorphosis', which, whether or not it is by Shakespeare, points directly (perhaps too directly) to the central action or drama of the play. It is an Ovidian metamorphosis, but with Shakespeare's radical change of that process (metamorphosis metamorphosed). For this is an upward metamorphosis, ending, not like Io, Daphne, and Adonis, in blood, tears, and death, but with a woman woken from shrewishness and turned into a good wife (much better than the other two new wives, one is led to believe). And it is a metamorphosis which, finally, she positively accepts and adopts; thus, says William Carroll, being 'among the first of Shakespeare's characters to embody the necessity of self-willed transformation'.

If the completing of the frame action which is there in *A Shrew* was originally part of Shakespeare's play, then we would see Sly carried on, asleep/drunk, and left in front of the alehouse where the Lord and his men had found him. He is awakened by a Tapster who tells him that he had better get home, where his wife will give him what-for. But Sly, too, has learnt something:

> Will she? I know now how to tame a shrew,
> I dreamt upon it all this night till now,
> And thou hast wakt me out of the best dream
> That ever I had in my life, but Ile to my
> Wife presently and tame her too
> And if she anger me.

Perhaps he will, and perhaps he won't, but as he wakes from his dream, so we must 'wake' from the play. Perhaps we've learned something – and perhaps we haven't, though there is much more to it than the crude apology for patriarchy and phallo-centrism which some have discerned. It is, that is to say, a better 'dream' than that. We will encounter, in a later comedy, another simple, uneducated lower-class figure who wakes up from the best dream he ever had in his life – though, as here, *we* can, wakefully, watch the dream. That will be on midsummer night – when, traditionally, anything can happen. And, more importantly, the 'dreamer' will not be a tinker, but – a weaver.

*

THE TWO GENTLEMEN OF VERONA

> It is the lesser blot, modesty finds,
> Women to change their shapes than men their minds.
>
> (V, iv, 108–9)

In *The Two Gentlemen of Verona* (in whichever order it was written – some editors think that *this* is Shakespeare's first comedy), we move away from the predominantly bourgeois, mercantile atmosphere of the previous two plays, and enter a world of royal courts, 'tilts and tournaments', emperors, kings, princes, and noblemen. It is still Italy, though a rather geographically indeterminate Italy. It opens with the two young gentlemen moving from Verona to Milan, but, as Dr Johnson observed, keeping a very straight face, 'the author conveys his heroes by sea from one inland town to another in the same country'. Speed says 'welcome to Padua', while the Duke of Milan seems to think he is in Verona. It doesn't matter of course, for this is a generic 'Italy' of story and romance, more Boccaccio than atlas. I mention Boccaccio advisedly, since one of his stories almost certainly lies behind what became the most notorious incident in Shakespeare's play. The eighth story of the Tenth Day of *The Decameron* concerns two inseparable male friends – Gisippus and Titus. Gisippus falls in love with a beautiful woman – Sophronia – and they become engaged. Titus, following the principle described by René Girard as 'mimetic desire' (whereby, roughly speaking, people tend to desire what someone else, particularly a close acquaintance, already desires) promptly falls in love with Sophronia as well. At first, he reproaches himself, invoking 'the duty of a true friend'. 'Will you allow yourself to be carried away by the delusions of love, the specious visions of desire? Open your eyes, you fool, and come to your senses' he says to himself. But other internal arguments prevail. 'But then he remembered Sophronia's beauty, and took the opposite viewpoint, rejecting all his previous arguments. And he said to himself: "The laws of Love are more powerful than any others; they even supplant divine laws, let alone those of friendship ... Besides, I am young, and youth is entirely subject to the power of Love. So that wherever Love decides to lead me, I am bound to follow."' This sort of sophism, by which the power of Love is used to justify the betrayal of friendship, recurs in Shakespeare's play. But it is Gisippus' reaction, when Titus confesses his disloyal love, that has – translated into Shakespeare's play – caused the trouble: 'he *instantly* decided that his friend's life meant more to him than Sophronia', and simply hands Sophronia over, as it were, to Titus, saying 'you may rest assured that she shall enter the bridal chamber, not as my wife, but as yours' (my italics).

Boccaccio's tale has its own ensuing complications and resolutions, which are not germane to Shakespeare's play. But Shakespeare has kept that 'instantaneousness' of the renunciation of beloved woman and bestowal of her on a treacherous friend, and it has proved hard to swallow.

Briefly: at the start, in Verona, Valentine mocks his friend Proteus for his single-minded, stay-at-home love for Juliana (he calls it 'sluggardizing'!), saying that he is fancy-free and off to see the world. When he gets to Milan, however, he is enchanted by Silvia, and duly becomes a true 'Valentine' lover: while when Proteus follows his friend to Milan, he turns 'protean'. For he 'instantly' falls in love with Silvia, and forgets Julia. How he treacherously betrays Valentine, who is duly banished by Silvia's father, the Duke (always the prohibiting, obstructing father – as usual, no mothers to be seen), and attempts to seduce Silvia, forms the central action of the play. It all converges on the forest, where Valentine, improbably enough, has become the captain of a band of outlaws, and where Silvia has gone in search of him – followed, for one reason and another, by everybody else. There, Proteus finds Silvia and, failing once again (as he always has) to move her to anything more than contemptuous rejection, resolves to complete his infamy by raping her: 'I'll ... love you 'gainst the nature of love ... I'll force thee yield to my desire' (V, iv, 58–9). Valentine, a spectator throughout, steps forward and arrests the attempt, denouncing his 'treacherous friend': 'I am sorry I must never trust thee more', adding 'the private wound is deepest' (V, iv, 69–71) – not a word about the intent to 'wound' Silvia. What follows, follows very quickly. Proteus apologizes, repents, and asks forgiveness (five lines). Valentine accepts, forgives – and 'instantly' offers to hand over, as it were, Silvia to Proteus:

> Then I am paid;
> And once again I do receive thee honest.
> Who by repentance is not satisfied
> Is nor of heaven nor earth, for these are pleased.
> By penitence th' Eternal's wrath's appeased;
> And, that my love may appear plain and free,

All that was mine in Silvia I give thee.

(V, iv, 77–83)

Silvia is offered by her lover to the man who, *twenty-four* lines
previously (three minutes? two?), tried to rape her. Silvia
herself doesn't say another word for the remainder of the play
– not surprisingly, you may think. But George Eliot described
this moment as 'disgusting'; and Quiller-Couch, who, you feel,
knows a cad when he sees one, harrumphed that 'there are by
this time *no* gentlemen in Verona'. By and large, readers have
been able, despite its psychological implausibility, to just
about accept the immediate forgiveness – for forgiveness
counts as a generosity and a grace, and is god-like. But there's
no doing anything about those last two lines. Either they have
to be explained away (young Shakespeare in thrall to conventions he had not yet mastered); or allowed to stand as a
scandal and disgrace – either as a sign of the playwright's
callowness, or as a whiff of a more barbaric age. Clearly,
Valentine's offer to Proteus is, by any standard and from any
point of view, entirely unacceptable. But, before we retreat to
the Club House with Quiller-Couch, we might ask, what was
Shakespeare – what might he have been – doing?

Commentators often – and rightly – remind us of the
importance of friendship literature, from the Middle Ages to
the seventeenth century. Bullough gives a relevant example
from Lyly's *Endimion* in which Geron says:

for all things (friendship excepted) are subject to fortune: love is but
an eye-worme, which only tickleth the head with hopes, and wishes;
friendship the image of eternitie, in which there is nothing movable,
nothing mischievous.

Proteus, who proves to be totally 'movable' and in whom
there is a very great deal that is 'mischievous', thus becomes a
dark example of the false friend, while Valentine is a perfect
embodiment of the true friend. M. C. Bradbrook insisted that
we should see this play as illustrating the importance and
strength of the Friendship Cult (so that Valentine's offer of
Silvia to Proteus shows the true 'courtly virtue of magnanimity' – not quite the George Eliot reaction). Clearly,

Valentine and Proteus are to be seen as closely linked by a
strong friendship. Thus Valentine on Proteus:

> I knew him as myself; for from our infancy
> We have conversed and spent our hours together
> ...
> And, in a word, for far behind his worth
> Comes all the praises that I now bestow,
> He is complete in feature and in mind
> With all good grace to grace a gentleman.
>
> (II, iv, 61–2, 70–73)

'I knew him as myself' (in Boccaccio's story Gisippus calls
Titus 'my second self') – clearly the bonding is very close.
Indeed, you can see Proteus as, effectively, trying to *become*
Valentine – take over his other self. Valentine goes to Milan,
Proteus follows; Valentine is welcomed into the Duke's
family, Proteus ingratiates himself with the father and treacherously ensures that his friend is sent away; Valentine falls
in love with Silvia, Proteus (instantly) starts making love to
her in his friend's absence. Valentine is, thus, seemingly,
almost totally displaced, replaced. It is not surprising that at
one point he feels he has become 'nothing' – stripped and
deprived of everything that gave him substance, made him
him. Now, this may certainly be seen as an exploration of
'friendship', but, despite the incredible magnanimity of
Valentine's selfless (self-effacing) offer, hardly an unequivocal
celebration of it.

What we have, and arguably more interestingly, is the
beginnings of a study of dishonourable conduct deliberately
chosen, wrong-doing knowingly pursued. After Proteus come,
with all their differences, Richard III, Don John (*Much Ado*),
Bertram (*All's Well*), then Iago, finally Macbeth – Shakespeare's greatest exploration of *conscious* evil. Compared to
Macbeth, Proteus is a rank amateur; but he is perfidious
enough, and points the way. We can follow this in the three
important soliloquies by Proteus (the soliloquy always being
the privilege of the plotters and 'practicers' – both wicked and
benign). In the first (II, iv, 190–213), he examines his instant
desire for Silvia and forgetting of Julia:

> Even as one heat another heat expels,
> Or as one nail by strength drives out another,
> So the remembrance of my former love
> Is by a newer object quite forgotten.

The second soliloquy follows almost immediately, and constitutes a whole scene in itself (II, vi, 1–43). We hear him finding arguments to justify his imminent betrayal of Valentine and infidelity to Julia, invoking the irresistible power of Love – 'Love bade me swear, and Love bids me forswear'. He knows what he owes to Julia and Valentine, but – as he sees it – 'If I keep them, I needs must lose myself'. That this particular 'self' might be better lost, he no longer allows himself to consider. He is resolved:

> I will forget that Julia is alive,
> Rememb'ring that my love to her is dead;
> And Valentine I'll hold an enemy,
> Aiming at Silvia as a sweeter friend.
> I cannot now prove constant to myself,
> Without some treachery used to Valentine.

What *real* constancy is, and might involve, is an important concern of the play. But to maintain that constancy requires 'treachery' is to engage in very special pleading indeed. It is of a piece with the twisted casuistry with which Proteus tries to put a gloss on an indifferent-to-all-other-considerations lust. But he is determined to prove a villain, and immediately sets to work to 'plot this drift'. The third soliloquy (IV, ii, 1–17) shows him continuing in his resolve – 'Already have I been false to Valentine,/ And now I must be as unjust to Thurio.' While not exactly wading in blood like Macbeth, he is getting deeper into infamy, beginning to discover the inexorable law whereby one bad deed invariably requires another, and so on *ad infinitum*. He is also beginning to realize that his plotting and wickedness will have been all to no purpose, since the truly constant Silvia will not be moved. Like Henry James' Madame Merle, he is about to discover that he has been 'vile for nothing'. But by now he cannot stop himself.

As the play is concerned with friendship, so it is very much about love: commitment and disloyalty, pursuit and rejection, love and betrayal, constancy and change – the play resolves around these issues and tensions. A word with which we are becoming familiar, is used here – and only here – twice. Proteus claims to have been 'metamorphized' by Julia (I, i, 66), while quick-thinking Speed tells his slow-witted master, Valentine, that he is 'metamorphized' by Silvia (II, i, 30). Another word which occurs twice in the play is 'chameleon' – subsequently to be used only by Hamlet, and the future Richard III, who manages to call himself 'chameleon' and 'Proteus' in the same sentence (3 *Henry VI*, III, ii, 191–2); which is apt enough since both words refer to versions of the same phenomenon – sudden, self-activated change. 'Metamorphosis' of one kind and another infects the two inter-involved young couples in various ways. Valentine shifts overnight from being a roaming sceptic to being a committed, Petrarchan lover – which may be counted as a positive transformation. Proteus (and remember that the name of the mythic shape-shifting sea-god was used in the Renaissance as a figure of both good transformation – improvement, and bad – degeneration), manifests the worst kind of unstable volatility and disposition to change. Julia could use the *words* of Proteus, and say that she has to 'lose myself' in order to be 'constant to myself' – she changes her clothes, her gender, and her status to be true to her love (dressing up as a page to become Proteus' servant); but their meaning would point all the other way. In her own words, she may change her 'shape' but she never changes her 'mind' – the latter, in this play, is an exclusively male activity. Silvia, once she has committed herself to Valentine, does not change her shape or her mind: she remains an absolutely fixed point of 'constancy' throughout all the various changings and messing about that go on around her. Her father, the Duke, confident that her affections can easily be weaned from the now disgraced Valentine, asserts:

> This weak impress of love is as a figure
> Trenchèd in ice, which with an hour's heat
> Dissolves to water, and doth lose his form.
> A little time will melt her frozen thoughts,
> And worthless Valentine shall be forgot.

(III, ii, 6–10)

COMEDIES

He could not be more wrong. The image is hopelessly misapplied and belongs squarely with Proteus, who has already
confessed out loud (concerning his love for Julia):

> for now my love is thawed,
> Which, like a waxen image 'gainst a fire,
> Bears no impression of the thing it was.

(II, iv, 199–201)

In this play, it is the watery men who are the dissolvers, the
thawers, the melters. The women, once the fires of love have
been ignited within them, burn with a steady, constant flame –
melting waxen men, perhaps, but themselves as firm and fixed
as, following the images, ice. Hot ice.

Proteus, on the other hand, is as changeable as the English
weather, as he unwittingly predicts in one of the most beautiful images in the play (the devil often has the best lines):

> O, how this spring of love resembleth
> The uncertain glory of an April day,
> Which now shows all the beauty of the sun,
> And by and by a cloud takes all away!

(I, iii, 84–7)

This is unmistakably an English, rather than an Italian April.
Proteus thinks he is complaining about being separated from
Julia by his father's orders that he must go to Milan; but, in
fact, he is issuing a weather-forecast about his own coming
behaviour in all matters concerning affairs of the heart. His
subsequent multiple betrayals provoke this stinging rebuke
from faithful Silvia:

> Thou hast no faith left now, unless thou'dst two,
> And that's far worse than none; better have none
> Than plural faith, which is too much by one.
> Thou counterfeit to thy true friend!

(V, iv, 50–53)

Proteus is a counterfeiter all right, and, in matters of love, a
manifest 'pluralist'. But there, Silvia insists, two is 'too much
by one'. Julia makes a similar point in a poignant little scene
when, disguised as a male visitor, she has to listen to the music
with which Proteus is serenading Silvia. She is standing with

lxxiv

the Host of the inn where she is lodging. He likes the music, but Julia uses the occasion to deliver herself of some heartfelt ironies – which of course only s/he can fully appreciate. Thus, she gives her opinion that Proteus 'plays false', his music 'jars', and 'grieves my very heartstrings'. The Host admires the modulations in the music, which allows Julia to utter perhaps the most important line in the play:

> *Host.* Hark, what fine change is in the music!
> *Julia.* Ay, that change is the spite.
> *Host.* You would have them always play but one thing?
> *Julia.* I would always have one play but one thing.
>
> (IV, ii, 66–9)

More arithmetic – and, of course, *we* can follow Julia's point. Music may change, but lovers should not. In matters of love, men ought not to modulate. But, of course, there is an irony here which Shakespeare, so far from wishing to avoid, wants to exploit – and wishes us to enjoy. He is having fun, serious fun if you like, with the comparatively recent phenomenon of professional actors in a full-time theatre. Every actor in his play (whether playing Silvia or Proteus) has already, simply by being in the play, taken on a second part ('too much by one'). In that play, for different reasons, they may then go on to 'play' more than 'one thing' – the actor who played Proteus arguably three or four (Proteus as friend and lover, as scheming betrayer, as penitent, as rueful returned lover), and the Julia actor, in one amazing moment (to which I will return), at least five. They are all, necessarily, 'pluralists'. Of course, one can 'play' the constant lover, and another may change as fitfully and quickly as a chameleon or the weather of an April day. That is understood, and we have no trouble in attending seriously to the spectacle of an actor denouncing histrionic tendencies in another character. But it does raise more far-reaching questions. Can any of us in our, supposedly, non-theatrical waking lives, 'always play but one thing'? More to the point perhaps, *should* we? Repetition is fixity, is rigidity, is stagnation, is – potentially – death. Everything in organic life enjoins the recognition and acceptance of flexibility, adaptability, change. But where then is continuity, fidelity, trust – identity itself? We are back with the problem of distinguishing good and bad metamorphosis, and Shakespeare is clearly deeply interested in the ethical and emotional problems in managing the appropriate, the best, relationship and adjustment between desired constancy and necessary change.

Related matters are raised by the frequent use of the word 'shadow' – which, for the Elizabethans, was one of the synonyms for 'actor'. Let me draw attention to three moments. When Valentine is banished from Milan and Silvia, he feels it as a kind of death – 'To die is to be banished from myself;/And Silvia is myself. Banished from her/Is self from self'. As far as he is concerned:

> She is my essence, and I leave [cease] to be,
> If I be not by her fair influence
> Fostered, illumined, cherished, kept alive.
>
> (III, i, 171–3, 182–4)

All he will be able to do, separated from Silvia, is *think* about her 'And feed upon the shadow of perfection'. When Proteus begs the unresponsive Silvia, at least to give him a picture of herself, he adds:

> For since the substance of your perfect self
> Is else devoted, I am but a shadow,
> And to your shadow will I make true love.
>
> (IV, ii, 121–3)

Poor Julia, who hears this, says in an aside:

> If 'twere a substance, you would, sure, deceive it,
> And make it but a shadow, as I am.
>
> (IV, ii, 124–5)

It is Julia, as Sebastian, who has to carry Silvia's picture to her 'master' Proteus, and, taking hold of it, she says, in soliloquy:

> Come, shadow, come, and take this shadow up,
> For 'tis thy rival. O thou senseless form,
> Thou shalt be worshiped, kissed, loved, and adored!
> And, were there sense in his idolatry,
> My substance should be statue in thy stead.
>
> (IV, iv, 197–201)

I will come back to 'idolatry', but here let us just consider the
play on shadow (and form) and substance (and essence) – and
'perfection' (this word, or its cognates, occurs interestingly
often in Shakespeare; but nowhere as often as it does in this
play). An actor is both a 'shadow' (also a counterfeit image)
and, in as much as he is a corporeal being, 'substance'. Proteus
is, indeed, a double shadow – an actor counterfeiting a
counterfeiter. Valentine and Julia feel that they are 'shadows'
having, as they think, lost their lovers, thus feeling dispossessed
of themselves. In the Platonic perspective, all we mortals
living in a material world can ever see is shadows of the Real,
the Ideal, the truly Substantial, the Essential (and thus all
mimetic art – pictures, statues, plays – offers only secondary
copies of things – shadows of shadows – at one more remove
from the Real). Shakespeare plays with this proposition, and
turns it round – or perhaps, rather, scrambles it. Thus, the
'shadows' Julia and Valentine feel, as it were, ontologically
emptied out by being bereft of their loves – Valentine has a
very powerful image for the feeling:

> O thou that dost inhabit in my breast,
> Leave not the mansion so long tenantless,
> Lest, growing ruinous, the building fall,
> And leave no memory of what it was!
>
> (V, iv, 7–10)

But these shadows turn out to have true 'substance'. While
Silvia is conceived of as being, not a shadow or reflection of the
Real (Plato), but an 'essence' in herself (Plato hyperbolically
set on his head); so that thinking about *her* becomes the
Platonic exercise whereby a human can intuit an essence, a
perfect form. I don't think we should feel we are involved in
some dizzying epistemological regression here – shadows
playing shadows who also carry around other shadows
(pictures). Rather, I think Shakespeare likes the idea of
showing substantial shadows discussing who is shadow and
who substance; in the process, certainly, shaking up our ideas
of where the one realm ends and the other begins – indeed,
perhaps making us wonder to what extent they are, finally,
separable.

'Perfection' points in a Christian as well as a Platonic direction – 'Be ye therefore perfect' is the biblical injunction. This age had seen the idea of the 'parfit', gentle knight (there's supposed to be one in this play – Sir Eglamour), the perfect courtier (such as the gentlemen aspire to be), the perfect prince (which the Duke should be), which, in a sense, all reflect, perhaps derive from, the Christian notion of 'perfection'. Julia thinks that Proteus has this star-like, heavenly perfection:

> But truer stars did govern Proteus' birth.
> His words are bonds, his oaths are oracles;
> His love sincere, his thoughts immaculate;
> His tears pure messengers sent from his heart;
> His heart as far from fraud as heaven from earth.

(II, vii, 74–8)

– exactly wrong in every particular, of course (the idea that love is either blind or has too many eyes runs through the play). And note the word 'immaculate' – literally, without spot. 'Perfection' comes from 'per-facere', done or made throughout – thus entire, whole; and thus, without blemish. But Shakespeare knew very well that to be human is to be maculate – no 'im' about it. At the moment of his sudden repentance, Proteus remorsefully declares:

> O heaven, were man
> But constant, he were perfect! That one error
> Fills him with faults, makes him run through all th' sins;
> Inconstancy falls off ere it begins.

(V, iv, 110–13)

(There is no comment here on the theological doctrine of '*original* sin': these 'sins' are acquired, or 'run through'.) No one with more personal experience of 'inconstancy' than Proteus, and he is shamed by the bravely constant Julia. But the truth holds. We live in change – which need not be, in itself, 'sinful': to some extent, life *is* change and mutability. Perfection, if it exists, belongs, indeed, in 'heaven' with the stars. When Julia excuses her male disguise by saying 'it is the lesser blot ... Women to change their shapes than men their minds', she is acknowledging that we are all, to some extent, blemished, while making the equally important point that some blots are a good deal worse then others. It is an important part of the play that Proteus turns out to be the spottiest of the lot – maculate through and through – while the 'blots' on Julia, such as they are, seem eminently forgivable.

Julia is the most interesting, we might say the most promising (together with Launce), of the characters in the play. She alone gives the impression of experiencing and knowing what she nicely calls 'the inly touch of love' (II, vii, 18), breaking free from stereotype while the others seem to be operating and speaking mainly from conventions (more of that in a moment). She is the first of Shakespeare's women to dress up as a man and, for honourable reasons, venture out into the world thus disguised. In her own way, she is 'losing' her self, or her identity or 'shape', in order to find, or preserve, it – being 'false' to be true. She thus anticipates the vital, brilliant, and determined heroines of the later comedies – such as Portia, Rosalind, Viola. As Proteus' page Sebastian, she is given the painful task of being sent to plead on his behalf to her rival. Shakespeare makes much more of this situation in *Twelfth Night*, but here it does occasion an amazing moment. Silvia knows that Proteus is committed to a woman named Julia, though of course she has no idea that Sebastian is in fact the woman in question. Virtuous and compassionate gentlewoman as she is, she feels sorry for this Julia, and asks Sebastian for details about her – such as, how tall is she? Julia then gives what has to be called an extraordinary performance:

> About my stature: for, at Pentecost,
> When all our pageants of delight were played,
> Our youth got me to play the woman's part,
> And I was trimmed in Madam Julia's gown,
> Which servèd me as fit, by all men's judgments,
> As if the garment had been made for me.
> Therefore I know she is about my height.
> And that time I made her weep agood,
> For I did play a lamentable part.
> Madam, 'twas Ariadne passioning
> For Theseus' perjury and unjust flight,
> Which I so lively acted with my tears

That my poor mistress, movèd therewithal,
Wept bitterly; and would I might be dead
If I in thought felt not her very sorrow!

(IV, iv, 158–72)

This is sending all kinds of signals, not so much to Silvia who of course cannot pick them up, but to the audience, and to herself. And think about it. A boy actor is playing a woman (Julia), who is playing a boy (Sebastian), who describes being dressed up as a woman who is in fact herself, who then plays the part of the mythical female, Ariadne. Curiously enough, it is at this moment of five-levelled artifice, that she comes across to us most convincingly as 'real', the most substantial of shadows – a grieving, abandoned woman who has lost her love.

Pentecost and Ariadne – the Christian and pagan world again in the same sphere. Pentecost is the festival which comes fifty days after Easter and celebrates the descent of the Holy Ghost, which is a reminder, or re-enactment, of God's willing descent into the lower form of a man in order to achieve salvation for humans. Paula Berggren suggests that this glancingly refers to what Julia herself is doing – taking on the inferior status of a male servant to work for the salvation of 'sinful' Proteus. (She relevantly points out that whereas Rosalind, when she puts on male disguise, chooses the rather sexy name Ganymede – the boy loved by Zeus – and enjoys androgynously charming both Phebe and Orlando, Julia chooses the name Sebastian, a Christian martyr, and 'ultimately it is not the sexual but the social ingredient of Julia's disguise that counts'. Also, where Viola–Cesario and Orsino have a complicated, sexually ambiguous relationship when s/he is acting as his servant, the relationship between Proteus and Julia–Sebastian is perfunctory and undeveloped – some forty lines.) 'Ariadne' reinforces this idea of salvation from a pagan perspective. Ariadne, too, is descended from a god (her father was Minos, a son of Zeus by legend), and she sacrifices herself to help Theseus out of the labyrinth, saving him from the Minotaur and securing his liberation. Theseus then, of course, abandoned her for her pains. Slightly differently, Julia is an abandoned woman who nevertheless enters the labyrinth to save Proteus from the bull of lust, rescuing him from damnation, redeeming his 'sins' (?), and liberating his better self. These Christian–pagan allusions are not elaborated, but they are undoubtedly there.

By comparison, the other main characters seem to remain within the romances and conventions which engendered them. The traces, and bits and pieces, of romance are very clear. Sir Eglamour, as described is, indeed, a veritable anthology of the chivalric virtues of knight errantry and courtly love. We have a princess kept in a tower; a planned escape by ladder; a serenading lover; a forlorn and despairing woman pursuing her lost man; a wicked villain and a trusting friend; reluctant partings, happy reunions, generous forgiving. We also have noble, Robin Hood style, outlaws in the forest: this episode is also rather perfunctory and undeveloped, but it is important since it allows Shakespeare a shift from the court into the country (what Northrop Frye called 'the green world'), which anticipates far more important shifts – to places like the Forest of Arden and Prospero's island. Shakespeare is experimenting with all kinds of 'devices' which he will use in later plays.

The lovers themselves – I am excepting Julia – love according to convention. Valentine, in particular, once he falls in love, not only becomes a walking anthology of Petrarchanism, but also a parody of it, particularly as seen by the mordant eye of his servant, Speed ('these follies are within you, and shine through you like the water in an urinal' – see II, i, 17–40). Even Proteus is moved to protest against his 'idolatry' and 'braggardism' (when Silvia says to Proteus 'I am very loath to be your idol, sir', IV, iii, 126, she not only speaks for the two women, but for women in general against that male cult of 'idolizing' women, which is the very reverse of real love, and is more akin to a form of narcissism).

These figures, particularly the 'gentlemen', love by the book. A 'love-book' is mentioned in the first scene, and the love is, in general, a pretty papery matter – it does not strike one as very 'inly', to use Julia's word. There are constant letters, not to mention sonnets and songs, and we have many orders or observations and requests, such as – writers say, bear this letter, peruse this paper, write some lines. Two early scenes underline this involvement with paper and writing. Julia receives a letter from Proteus, and (playing the cruel mistress) ostentatiously tears it up in front of her maid – 'Dare you presume to harbor wanton lines?' Once the maid has left, she scrabbles around on the floor, trying to put some bits together again. Then she starts making love to the reassembled scraps – 'I'll kiss each several paper for amends' (I, ii, 108). Finally, she finds a piece with her name on it, and another piece with his name on it, and, effectively, puts them in bed together to 'couple':

> Thus will I fold them one upon another.
> Now, kiss, embrace, contend, do what you will.
>
> (I, ii, 128–9)

It is an interesting, perhaps rather charming, displacement or substitution. But it has to be said, it is part of the prevailing indirectness of the 'love' in this play. Indeed, the lovers scarcely make love to each other in any unmediated way; instead, we usually hear them talking about their 'love' to someone else, or to themselves (most of the play is duologue or soliloquy). In a scene which follows shortly after, we see Valentine bring Silvia a letter which she has asked him to write on her behalf to a 'secret nameless friend'. She pushes the letter back at him – 'take it for your labor', but Valentine, obtusely, cannot see that the letter is meant for *him*. Speed sees the 'device' immediately:

> Was there ever heard a better,
> That my master, being scribe, to himself should write the letter?
>
> (II, i, 136–7)

He tries to get it into Valentine's head that 'she hath made you write to yourself'. Speed spells it out. Silvia is perhaps too 'modest' to reply directly to Valentine's letters to her:

> Or fearing else some messenger that might her mind discover,
> Herself hath taught her love himself to write unto her lover.
> All this I speak in print, for in print I found it.
>
> (II, i, 163–5)

Valentine still seems not to understand – he really is an extraordinarily slow fellow. But Speed's last cryptic line should resonate throughout the play, and indeed beyond. Written plays, of course, literally 'speak in print'. Speed may simply mean that he is quoting, but his words point also to the fact that the lovers in the play have a tendency to, effectively, 'speak in print'; for, when it comes to words expressing love, 'in print they found them'. To some extent, this must be true for all of us. One of the concerns of the comedies might then be to explore to what extent – and with what effects – 'love' can be *generated* by pre-existing words, books, conventions, forms; and to what extent – and how – a genuine, individual love can discover itself, and express its authenticity, breaking out of, or shining through, the words and conventions which are everywhere in place waiting for it – to shape, deform, distort, deflect, arrest, inflame, perhaps enable, it.

The one character who most conspicuously does *not* 'speak in print', and whom I have deliberately not discussed until now, is of course Proteus' servant, Launce – particularly when he is speaking (soliloquizing) to his dog, Crab. There were comic or 'clownish' servants in Classical comedy, and in Shakespeare's two plays already discussed. Speed is just such another figure, but Launce is something else, something more – and he looks forward to such notable figures as Touchstone and Feste. We first hear him, about to leave for Milan, talking about their leave-takings to (or at) Crab.

I think Crab my dog be the sourest-natured dog that lives. My mother weeping, my father wailing, my sister crying, our maid howling, our cat wringing her hands, and all our house in a great perplexity, yet did not this cruel-hearted cur shed one tear. He is a stone, a very pebble stone, and has no more pity in him than a dog ... Nay, I'll show you the manner of it. This shoe is my father; no, this left shoe is my father. No, no, this left shoe is my mother; nay, that cannot be so neither. Yes, it is so, it is so, it hath the worser sole. This shoe, with the hole in it, is my mother, and this my father; a vengeance on't! There 'tis. Now, sir, this staff is my sister, for, look you, she is as white as a lily, and as small as a wand. This hat is Nan, our maid. I am the dog. No, the dog is himself, and I am the dog. Oh! the dog is me, and I am myself; ay, so, so ... Now the dog all this while sheds not a tear, nor speaks a word; but see how I lay the dust with my tears.

(II, iii, 5–34)

We have, just immediately before this, witnessed a tearless, finally 'dumb' and wordless, parting between Julia and Proteus, and this scene between Launce and Crab marks the start of an increasingly telling parody of (and critical commentary on) that relationship. Proteus will duly turn out to be 'a stone' with 'no more pity in him than a dog'. We shouldn't be too heavy about this, but as we watch Launce's uncertainty about which is the dog and which himself, we can respond to larger, comic implications. You can just never be sure which and who the real 'dogs' are – nor, indeed, when the cats might start wringing their hands! And his confusion over shoes and hats, and which shall play whom, has another resonance – apart from the obvious jokes about holes and soles/souls. I quote a comment by Leonard Barkan:

Shakespeare also defines theater as the transformation of one thing into another ... of a whole set of accoutrements into a family romance (Launce and co.) ... Shakespeare has [here] brought metamorphosis down from Olympus (and its courtly equivalent in contemporary theater) to the level of the Globe groundlings. But it is not merely democracy at work. In the process he has recognized that transformation is a universal feature of his own art, restricting itself neither to monarchs nor to clowns, neither to amateur theatricals nor to kings who see themselves as players – though it is likely to be the clowns who keep us aware that the illusion of metamorphosis is an illusion.

Behind Launce there is Shakespeare saying – give me a shoe and a hat and I'll give you a play.

In a subsequent soliloquy (again, with Crab), Launce laments the recent 'foul' behaviour of his 'cur' – stealing a capon, stinking up the dining room, 'pissing' on 'a gentlewoman's farthingale'. More apt, indirect comment on Proteus' increasingly 'foul' behaviour, of course. But Launce reveals that he has taken the blame for all Crab's mess, and duly, as he has often done before, drawn upon himself all the punishment intended for the miscreant hound (a whipping).

'How many masters would do this for his servant?' (IV, iv, 30). Not, perhaps, *exactly* a Christ-like cry – but very similar to one we hear immediately afterwards from Julia–Sebastian, 'unhappy messenger', ordered to go and woo Silvia on behalf of her beloved Proteus – 'How many women would do such a message?' (IV, iv, 90). We are seeing very clearly who are the *true* selfless, self-sacrificing, servants – and who are the dogs.

Canny, 'clownish', Launce also sees clearly enough what is going on, even if he does express himself mainly to, and through, Crab. 'I am but a fool, look you, and yet I have the wit to think my master is a kind of knave. But that's all one, if he be but one knave' (III, i, 262–4). More arithmetic, but Proteus it not a 'one part' man: just as he is engaging in 'plural faith', so he is sinking into plural knavery. But Launce is in love (he tells us), and, once again unconsciously (perhaps) parodying his betters, he '*pulls out a paper*', which carries a 'cate-log of her condition' (III, i, 273). He keeps it 'in print', we may say. There follows a long, comic exchange with Speed: Speed reads out the 'items' concerning the nameless wench (her, distinctly non-Petrarchan, virtues and vices), allowing Launce to comment on each one. I want to single out one item and response:

Speed. 'Item: She hath more hair than wit, and more fault than hairs, and more wealth than faults.'
Launce. Stop there; I'll have her. She was mine, and not mine, twice or thrice in that last article.

(II, i, 348–51)

In *A Midsummer Night's Dream*, Helena will say: 'And I have found Demetrius like a jewel,/Mine own, and not mine own' (IV, i, 194–5). Mine, and not mine: mine own, and not mine own. Shakespeare is here looking at, and acknowledging, the unavoidable, ineradicable, residual uncertainty at the heart of *all* love relationships – whether Launce and his wench (or his dog), or Helena and her jewel. There is *no* complete possessing of another person: 'mine, and not mine' is as far and as close as you can get. But that is right, too. If you do aim, obsessively, at *complete* possession of a loved one, you are in danger of ending up (in one way or another) like 'Porphyria's Lover', in Robert Browning's monologue of that name. He, you may remember, wants to make sure that the lovely Porphyria is 'mine, mine' – entirely, unchangingly. And he is, insanely, sure that he has found the way to ensure this. He has strangled her.

Launce reminds us that this is a romantic *comedy*. Certainly, Shakespeare is, as Bullough suggests, beginning to look at the possibilities offered by the Renaissance world of romance and story for the lyrical treatment, and the ethical exploration, of love and friendship. But the comic perspective is crucial, and not just because the play ends with the usual marriages and festive reconciliations – 'One feast, one house, one mutual happiness' is the last line – which conventionally conclude comedy. Consider what Shakespeare does to some of the conventions he deploys. Take Sir Eglamour, that supposed paragon from the world of medieval romance, whom Silvia chooses to be her protector when she ventures into the forest in search of Valentine. At the first sight of the outlaws, he runs away with, apparently, impressive speed – and goodbye knightly chivalry. The outlaws themselves are ludicrous – pantomime pirates. Valentine demonstrates some of the absurd excesses in Petrarchan love (Silvia is an honourable lady from within the convention, while Julia moves off into a new seriousness). The Duke of Milan, having shown exemplary courtesy to his guests, collapses into crude rudeness when he discovers Valentine's love for his daughter – 'Go, base intruder! Overweening slave!' There is even something ridiculous in Proteus' wickedness (when Silvia reproaches him for his dastardly advances, she asks – what about your love, Julia? She's dead, says Proteus promptly. And what about your friend Valentine? – er, as a matter of fact, he's dead too. This is lame stuff indeed. Richard III, his near contemporary, could do much better than that, and Iago would have been appalled at the resourceless ineptitude of his feeble precursor). His attempted rape does reveal the latent brutality in conventions of romance, and Launce – the better man – unwittingly (?) shows him up for the dog he is. Perhaps more seriously, Launce shows up the comparative unreality of most of those around him (Julia excepted). I think H. B. Charlton is almost exactly right in his comment on the play – 'Clearly, Shakespeare's first attempt to make romantic comedy had only succeeded so far that it had unexpectedly and inadvertently made romance comic.' Almost – because I am not persuaded of the need for the words 'unexpectedly and inadvertently'. Which brings me back to the opening question concerning Valentine's incredible, or unacceptable, offer of Silvia to the man who has just tried to rape her. I think this is part of Shakespeare's discovering of instabilities, absurdities, unrealities in the conventions he was experimenting with. I should, perhaps, make my general position clear. I hold it as axiomatic that, if we find something (or somone) cruel, unconscionable, intolerable (not to mention admirable, lovable, or laughable), in Shakespeare's plays, then so did Shakespeare. I think the same goes for anything which we find implausible or unacceptable. I have little time for the line that begins – you have to bear in mind that, back then, they felt differently about ... I have no wish to sound like Jan Kott in *Shakespeare Our Contemporary* (though I am not out of sympathy with the implications of the title). I believe we should do all we can to discover the beliefs, values, expectations and so on, of the age Shakespeare lived in. Historicism, old and new, is to be, selectively, welcomed. But if Shakespeare does not appeal to universal feelings, then nothing does. The idea of 'making allowances' for Shakespeare, seems to me some kind of ultimate in benighted presumptuousness. I assume that if we feel something, he felt it too. Shakespeare was certainly learning as he went along, and learning very quickly. But I believe, and thus assume, that he always knew what he was doing. Even if he did not realize quite how extraordinary it all was.

*

LOVE'S LABOR'S LOST

Moth. They have been at a great feast of languages, and stol'n the scraps.
Costard. O, they have lived long on the alms-basket of words. I marvel thy master hath not eaten thee for a word.

(V, i, 39–43)

One way to approach this play is to bear in mind the phenomenon alluded to in the title of Richard F. Jones' deservedly famous book – *The Triumph of the English Language*. Even up to the 1580s, in learned circles, where Latin gave dignity and conferred prestige, it was a matter for debate whether English was suitable for anything but low, everyday matters. Then quite suddenly, towards the end of the 1580s, apologies for the barbarousness of the vulgar tongue gave way to a new (nationalistic) triumphalism concerning the English language (a triumph finally sealed with the translation of the bible). English took over everywhere, in all subjects, and spread, and developed, and proliferated in a way that makes one want to refer to a veritable explosion. Barber says of *Love's Labor's Lost* that it catches something of 'the excitement of the historical moment when English, in the hands of its greatest master, suddenly could do anything'. You also feel, in this play, that Shakespeare is beginning to realize that he can do anything, too.

The Elizabethans, it may be said, were, or became, mad about language. Books about rhetoric (usually drawing on Quintilian) were popular and much studied. Two of the most important were Henry Peacham's *The Garden of Eloquence* (1577), and George Puttenham's *The Arte of English Poesie* (1589), which you may be sure Shakespeare knew. When Holofernes modestly boasts of his 'foolish extravagant spirit, full of forms, figures, shapes, objects, ideas, apprehensions, motions, revolutions' (IV, ii, 66–8), he not only reveals that he has been a good student of Puttenham – he is also a representative voice of the age, even if in comical form. When, in the third line of the play, the King of Navarre expresses the hope that fame will 'grace us in the disgrace of death', we are aware that he is playing on a word (and 'grace', in all its senses, will be an important word, occurring more often here than in any other of Shakespeare's plays). We would be less likely to know that this was called *Polyptoton* ('employment of the same word in various cases' – for the explanation of this, and all other rhetorical terms, see *A Handlist of Rhetorical Terms* by Richard A. Lanham: see also *Shakespeare's Use of the Arts of Language* by Sister Miriam Joseph). When Armado explains that the King would like him to arrange 'some delightful ostentation, or show, or pageant, or antic, or fire-work' (V, i, 112–13); or when he holds forth a paper adding 'which here thou viewest, beholdest, surveyest, or seest' (I, i, 242) – why use one word when you can think of four or five? – we know what's going on, but perhaps don't recognize it for *Pleonasmus* or *Macrologia* ('too full speech ... needless repetition'). When Nathaniel asks Holofernes to 'abrogate scurrility', meaning 'no dirty talk', we probably detect *Euphemismus* ('circumlocution to palliate something unpleasant'); but when Holofernes describes Armado as 'too picked, too spruce, too affected, too odd, as it were, too peregrinate, as I may call it' (V, i, 14–15), could we identify it as *Periergia* ('superfluous elaboration of a point')? And when Armado is amused and says 'thou enforcest laughter ... the heaving of my lungs provokes me to ridiculous smiling' (III, i, 76–8), I think that none of us, alas, could reach for *Bomphiologia* ('when trifling matters be set out with semblaunt and blazing wordes' – Peacham: as Ruth Nevo lamented, why did we ever lose such a useful word!). Shakespeare, and his audience (almost certainly, initially, an educated one – it was perhaps a court entertainment) would have known these rhetorical terms and many more, even if we no longer do.

Not that it matters. We can still recognize pedantry and affectation when we hear it (even if less when we speak it?). Shakespeare's play can be seen as offering a satire, parody, burlesque on all the uses and abuses of rhetoric so painstakingly classified and anatomized in the rhetoric handbooks of the day. But it is also a *celebration* of the energy, and pleasure in language, which generated those uses and abuses – and the books which so compendiously analysed them. When Berowne vows to renounce:

> Taffeta phrases, silken terms precise,
> Three-piled hyperboles, spruce affectation,
> Figures pedantical – these summer flies
> Have blown me full of maggot ostentation:
> I do forswear them ...

(V, ii, 407–11)

his disavowal gives itself the lie by the manifest relish with which the words are chosen and uttered. Nothing like a few taffeta phrases, and some silken terms precise, eh Berowne? Even his vow to aim at plain-speaking comes dashingly dressed in metaphor:

> Henceforth my wooing mind shall be expressed
> In russet yeas and honest kersey noes.

(V, ii, 413–14)

– nice glowing red-brown affirmatives, and good stout woollen negatives. It's rather as if Henry James was trying to promise he would write like Ernest Hemingway! It is all part of the fun, for this *is* a 'great feast of languages', and, as is appropriate at feasts, everyone is, for the most part, having a thoroughly good time – not least, as one feels, Shakespeare himself. If the Princess asks Boyet to open a letter, it is 'you can carve – /Break up this capon' (IV, i, 56–7). Dull is not just illiterate – 'he hath never fed of the dainties that are bred in a book./He hath not eat paper, as it were, he hath not drunk ink' (IV, ii, 24–5). At times, it actually does seem surprising that someone has *not* eaten the tasty, morsel-sized Moth 'for a word'! (He is called a 'flapdragon' – a raisin in brandy; and a 'pigeon-egg' – a delicacy.)

And this is a feast to which everyone is invited – 'Sir, I do invite you too: you shall not say me nay' (IV, ii, 166–7) as Holofernes kindly says to Dull. Indeed, apart from a bout of disgraceful upper-class boorishness (a timeless enough phenomenon – as Henry James said, there is nothing like the bad manners of good society), the people in this play are extremely generous and nice and polite to each other, and some of the courtesy (for instance that of the Princess) is exquisite. There is nothing like the *good* manners of good society, as well. Nobody is left out, excluded, isolated, or alienated; there are no malcontents, killjoys, or spoil-sports – and certainly no villains, plotters, or practicers. For, as it is a feast, so it is a game – and any number can play. 'Away! the gentles are at their game, and we will to our recreation' says Holofernes (IV, ii, 167–8). Like his betters, Costard can think of four words for one, when he explains that he was caught with a wench, damsel, virgin, maid. Even Dull has a go at a joke, and is resolved to join in – 'I'll make one in a dance, or so', he says, and Holofernes cries encouragingly 'To our sport, away!' (V, i, 154–6). And as this is a feast and a game, so it is a dance, a masque, a sport, a play, a pageant – Armado is right; you need at least five words to describe it.

One thing it is not is a drama – at least in any conventional sense. It not only has no plotters, it effectively has no plot. Significantly, it is the only play by Shakespeare for which there is no written source (all the others avail themselves to some extent of documentary origins). He made it all up – partly, one feels, as he went along. No plotters, only players – literally, people at play. For what, in sum, happens? A king and three lords take a vow to devote themselves to three years of study and chastity. *Immediately*, a princess and three ladies arrive on a diplomatic mission, and have to be received. *Immediately*, the men 'fall in love' with the women, and, sophistically arguing themselves out of their oaths, commence a series of wooing games, involving members of the lower orders in one of their court entertainments. It is all 'pass-time', pastimes. The games are interrupted by a messenger bringing news of the death of the Princess's father, and the play ends in abrupt dispersal, separation, and deferral – instead of the conventional comic resolution of union, consummation, and gathering-in. In fact, it has turned out not be a 'play', as Berowne recognizes in his last words. And yet of course it is – even if we have to see it as a play *about* play.

Shakespeare has moved from ancient Greece and Renaissance Italy to contemporary Reformist France. There was a Henry of Navarre with whom the Elizabethans had some links after the Massacre of St Bartholomew (severed when he re-converted to Catholicism in 1593). He was a patron of learning, and in 1583 an ambassador wrote to Walsingham that Navarre 'has furnished his Court with principal gentlemen of the Religion, and reformed his house'. The play contains echoes of a contemporary pamphlet war between Gabriel Harvey and Thomas Nashe, and the phrase 'school of night' (IV, iii, 254) has led to speculation about a political background involving the two factions of Essex and Southampton, and Ralegh and Northumberland. I think that all we need to bear in mind (and even this is not necessary for an enjoyment of the play), is the balanced summing-up of the Arden editor, R. W. David – 'all the evidence goes to show that *Love's Labor's Lost* was a battle in a private war between court factions' (and thus almost certainly first written for private performance in court circles). Shakespeare also draws on figures from the *Commedia dell'Arte* – for instance the Spanish fantastic Armado (and the name would, of course, have contemporary resonance) is closely related to the stock Braggart, always called Capitano Spavento del Vall'Inferno; and Holofernes, Nathaniel, and Costard have comparable relations. Though, of course, Shakespeare makes the figures all his own. They enable him to extend the range of the play from the initial court setting, out into the middle-class world of schoolmasters and curates, and down to the simpler world of constables, swains, and country wenches. Each social level is at play in its own way; at the same time, we feel they are a community. Though somewhat scattered at the end.

But, first and foremost, the action is in the language. Armado is said to speak in 'high-born words' of Spanish knights 'lost in the world's debate' (I, i, 171–2). Here, 'debate' carries the meaning of literal warfare (it derives from the same root as 'battle' – *battuere*, to beat); but, of course, it also sounds the meaning it has for us (philosophical debating societies based on the example of Plato were founded in Italy during the Renaissance, and spread to other parts of Europe). The meanings are nicely elided when the Princess refers to 'this civil war of wits' (II, i, 226) – for 'debating' can, indeed, amount to civil (also 'polite') war carried on by other means. Here, the characters 'tilt', joust, spar, fence, and otherwise compete – with words. And this of course, and pre-eminently, includes sexual 'tilting' as well. 'Well bandied both! a set of wit well played' (V, ii, 29), cries the Princess appreciatively. And here is Armado, delighted as ever by another pert sally from the quicksilver Moth: 'Now, by the salt wave of the Mediterranean, a sweet touch, a quick venew of wit! Snip, snap, quick and home! It rejoiceth my intellect. True wit!' (V, i, 59–61). We might stay with that word 'wit' for a moment. It occurs more often in this play than in any other by Shakespeare – and that by some considerable margin (forty-two times). It was a capacious word in the Renaissance, and could refer specifically to poetry, or more generally to felicities of eloquence. It bespeaks a particular zest in words, and points to that wonderful exhilaration experienced when language seems almost autonomously to release ever new potentialities, to take over and start to make happy discoveries off its own bat. In Barber's nice formulation – wit 'gives us something for nothing ... When wit flows happily, it is as though the resistance of the objective world had suddenly given way.' Wit is the champagne of language – for language can be champagne, as well as small beer. In good champagne, the bubbles keep on rising and rising, as if from nothing, to break at the surface. That is 'true wit'. And *Love's Labor's Lost* is mainly champagne. Which can, of course, become too 'heady', and people have sometimes found, perhaps justifiably, that there is here a superfluity of 'wit', a something too compulsive in the tireless straining after it. What is undeniable is that the play also shows how wit can be abused – that it has a strong anti-social potential, and may have a corrosive rather than generative effect on developing relationships.

I will return to that, but let us stay with the very real pleasures afforded by word-play – language on the loose – in the play. Armado is a representative figure. He is a man of 'fire-new words, fashion's own knight' (I, i, 177) who:

> hath a mint of phrases in his brain;
> One who the music of his own vain tongue
> Doth ravish like enchanting harmony
>
> (I, i, 164–6)

– in this, though, he is only the lords writ large, or hilariously caricatured. When his letter arrives at court in the first scene, Berowne says: 'be it as the style shall give us cause to climb in the merriness' (I, i, 198–9), while near the end we gather the King has told Armado that he is 'good at' – perhaps he meant 'good *for*' – 'eruptions and sudden breaking out of mirth' (V, i, 115). This very exactly describes the play, and its effect on the audience. Personal anecdotes are invariably rather pointless in this matter – but I did once see a perfect performance of this play, and I have never been so conscious of growing communal pleasure. The audience 'climbed in the merriness', and went on climbing and climbing. And, in large part, it was indeed 'the style' that 'gave us cause' – Granville Barker fastened on that word as characterizing the work's very essence, and it is, in every sense, the most 'stylish' of plays.

And not only are the spectators having a merry time, the characters are enjoying themselves, too, relishing every sally, each sparkling bubble. 'Pretty and apt,' says Armado to Moth appreciatively, 'A most fine figure ... sweet invocation of a child' (I, ii, 18, 55, 96). Costard listens with growing enjoyment to the bantering between the ladies and their attendant lord, Boyet. 'By my troth, most pleasant: how both did fit it.' The sexual *double entendres* grow increasingly broad (and wit is intimately involved with our sexual drives and interests), until Maria cries enough – 'Come, come, you talk greasily; your lips grow foul' (IV, i, 138). Costard loves it; and, wittingly or not, chooses just the right word: 'O' my troth, most sweet jests ... When it comes so smoothly off, so obscenely as it were, so fit!' (IV, i, 143–4). Holofernes intends generosity in his comment on one of Costard's rural efforts – 'a good luster of conceit in a turf of earth, fire enough for a flint, pearl enough for a swine. 'Tis pretty; it is well' (IV, ii, 88–90). But he shows the respectful admiration of the connoisseur when Armado refers to 'the posteriors of this day, which the rude multitude call the afternoon'.

The posterior of the day, most generous sir, is liable, congruent, and measurable for the afternoon. The word is well culled, chose, sweet and apt, I do assure you, sir, I do assure.

(V, i, 91–4)

So far from mocking the man's provincial pedantry, the audience is by this time usually helpless with laughter – and grateful.

*

The play starts solemnly enough, with the King announcing his intention to make his court into a 'little academe' to which he and his fellow lords will retire for a period of ascetic, celibate contemplation and study: turning their backs on the body, as it were, and making 'war' against 'the huge army of the world's desires' (I, i, 10). The first lines of the play give his reasons:

> Let fame, that all hunt after in their lives,
> Live regist'red upon our brazen tombs
> And then grace us in the disgrace of death

He is seeking honour and eternal 'fame' through this renunciation of the flesh. This way of pursuing 'fame' turns out to be drastically (comically) misdirected (not graceful, and not the way to gain 'grace'). The play makes two basic points about this aspiration. During the hunting scene, the Princess makes a generalization which is, retrospectively, very telling:

> Glory grows guilty of detested crimes,
> When, for fame's sake, for praise, an outward part,
> We bend to that the working of the heart
>
> (IV, i, 31–3)

She is not talking about the King (at least, not directly), but he *has* tried to 'bend ... the working of the heart' (what he called 'our affections') 'for fame's sake'. He is not exactly guilty of 'detested crimes', but in ordering that 'no woman shall come within a mile of my court ... on pain of losing her tongue' (I, i, 119–21), he is revealing a streak of patriarchal cruelty (only men talk here), as well as trying to 'bend' himself against the ways of nature. And when, at indeed 'the latest minute of the hour', he asks the Princess for her 'love', she demurs – his turn-around has been all too quick, 'A time, methinks, too short/To make a world-without-end bargain in' (V, ii, 789–90). 'World-without-end' (Amen) has, of course, a religious resonance; here suggesting, certainly, the till-death-do-us-part 'bargain' of marriage; and, perhaps, the 'bargain' we hope we have struck with God for eternal life. Either way, love and marriage point to the true lastingness, not any empty 'fame' won by perverse renunciations.

The King's plan is, of course, doomed to failure. When the imminent arrival of the Princess is announced (who, of course, must be afforded hospitality), Berowne, who goes along with the plan while commenting ironically on its impossibility, immediately points out:

> Necessity will make us all forsworn
> Three thousand times within this three years' space:
> For every man with his affects is born,
> Not by might mast'red, but by special grace.

(I, i, 148–51)

Later, he advances the same opinion:

> Young blood doth not obey an old decree.
> We cannot cross the cause why we were born

(IV, iii, 216–17)

This conviction seems to be quite central to the comedies. It is expressed most succinctly in *All's Well That Ends Well*: 'Our blood to us, this to our blood is born' (I, iii, 133) – 'this' being simply sexual desire. It is both risky and wrong – not to say hubristic – for a healthy young man to think he can 'bend' himself *completely* against 'this'. The King, if he could but hear it, receives an even prompter admonition when, immediately after he and his lords have sworn their oaths and taken their vows, Dull comes in with Costard, asking for the King, saying specifically: 'I would see his own person in flesh and blood' (I, i, 184) – which the King has that very minute been resolutely denying. Costard has been 'taken' with Jaquenetta, but, living in a more grounded and realistic world than the court, has no shame in admitting the forbidden deed. 'Such is the simplicity of man to hearken after the flesh', he says with a sort of rural resignation, adding 'Sir, I confess the wench' (I, i, 216, 278). The King and lords will shortly 'hearken after the flesh' themselves, and duly have to confess their wenches. Though of course, it will all be a much more elaborate, elaborated affair than anything offered by the forthright and literal-minded Costard. The simplest confrontation of all occurs between Armado and Jaquenetta, when he (of all people), embarrassed by his emotion, is reduced to the monosyllabic greeting – 'Maid!' To which she replies – 'Man?' (I, ii, 131–2). This is the basic exchange underlying all other exchanges between the sexes. All the rest is elaboration of one kind or another. Of course, it is those elaborations which provide occasions for grace and civility, not to mention fun and delight, and nobody would wish a two-word play. But that is where all love's labours start, and in a wondrous variety of ways is always being said. 'Maid!' 'Man?'

To read Berowne's seventy-five line paean in Act IV is to realize just what amazing elaborations 'love' can inspire, or permit. The occasion is the climax of the scene of multiple eavesdropping, when Berowne steps forward to 'whip hypocrisy', in the shape of the King, Longaville, and Dumaine, who have, in turn, caught and denounced each other for having love-letters and sonnets for the visiting ladies. Berowne triumphs in his 'over-view' – 'O what a scene of fool'ry I have seen' (IV, iii, 162) – and enjoys scorning 'men like you, men of inconstancy' (IV, iii, 179). At the peak of his derision, Jaquenetta comes in, bringing what turns out to be Berowne's love-letter to Rosaline to be read. Berowne collapses and confesses – 'you three fools lacked me fool to make up the mess' (IV, iii, 206). ('Mess' is one of those interesting words which seems to look both ways. Coming from a serving of food, or mixed food for an animal, it came to refer to any confused or shapeless mass – as now. But, in the Elizabethan period, it was also used to mean a small group or party of precisely four people – for meals, dances, games, whatever. Confusion *and* order; shapeless *and* exact. Strange.) Now that they are all discovered to have broken their vows, and fallen for women, they need to find 'some flattery for this evil ... Some tricks, some quillets [subtleties], how to cheat the devil' (IV, iii, 285–7) – in other words, some casuistry to somehow justify their perjury. Berowne is just the man for the task. Their real 'folly', he declares, is not their present state of being 'forsworn', but their original belief that they could and should 'forswear' women. Using a Christian argument with which we are now familiar in the comedies, he argues:

> Let us once lose our oaths to find ourselves,
> Or else we lose ourselves to keep our oaths.
>
> (IV, iii, 361–3)

There is a lot of sophistry, or 'glozing' (superficial word-play used to 'gloss', palliate, extenuate, etc.) in his speech; but, as Holofernes would say, 'the Gentles are at their game'. Berowne finally demonstrates to their group satisfaction that 'It is religion to be thus forsworn' (IV, iii, 362), and, happily bundling up his Christianity with his paganism, the relieved King cries out 'Saint Cupid then! And soldiers to the field!' (IV, iii, 365 – an invocation, incidentally, which echoes one by Armado at the end of Act I. In the matter of susceptibility to a woman, there is not much to tell between them).

Berowne is the most surprised at his susceptibility, as the long soliloquy starting – 'O, and I, forsooth, in love!' – which ends Act III, reveals (III, i, 175–207). He, too, reluctantly acknowledges the power of 'This wimpled, whining, purblind, wayward boy', but, initially at least, he has small thanks for 'this senior-junior, giant-dwarf, Dan Cupid' (III, i, 181–2). This love, or sudden infatuation, he feels is:

> a plague
> That Cupid will impose for my neglect
> Of his almighty dreadful little might.
>
> (III, i, 203–5)

That 'plague' metaphor is by no means all a joke. He returns to it at the end to describe the condition of his companions:

> Write 'Lord have mercy on us' on those three.
> They are infected, in their hearts it lies;
> They have the plague, and caught it of your eyes.
> These lords are visited ...
>
> (V, ii, 420–23)

A sign reading 'Lord have mercy on us' was hung on the door of a house which had been infected by the plague, which was also known as a 'visitation'. This play was written very close to, if not in, the year of 1592–3, which was one of the worst 'visitations'. This probably tells us something about how tough-minded the Elizabethans could be in their humour; but it reminds us that they also thought that love could be a sort of sickness, sometimes mortal. In a sudden dark moment (which anticipates the ending), while the ladies are joking about Cupid, there is this exchange:

Katharine. Ay, and a shrowd unhappy gallows too.
Rosaline. You'll ne'er be friends with him: a' killed your sister.
Katharine. He made her melancholy, sad, and heavy;
   And so she died. Had she been light, like you,
   Of such a merry, nimble, stirring spirit,
   She might ha' been a grandam ere she died.
   And so may you, for a light heart lives long.

(V, ii, 12–18)

'Gallows' here means someone fit for the gallows (in *Much Ado* Cupid is called a 'hangman', III, ii, 11). This play is almost exclusively for, by, and about 'merry, nimble, stirring spirits' playing with, and at, love. But here is a sudden chill reminder. Like the plague, Cupid can kill.

But in his long paean, it is the positive aspects of love which Berowne wants (has) to emphasize. He evokes its Orphic power – 'as sweet and musical/As bright Apollo's lute' (IV, iii, 341–2), and stresses its superior educative potency. His argument – or nimble sophistry, if you will – is, roughly, that we will learn much more from looking at our women, than from hanging over the books in our rotten old academy.

> For where is any author in the world
> Teaches such beauty as a woman's eye?
> . . .
> From women's eyes this doctrine I derive.
> They sparkle still the right Promethean fire;
> They are the books, the arts, the academes,
> That show, contain, and nourish all the world

(IV, iii, 311–12, 349–52)

'Eye(s)' occurs over fifty times in this play – more times than in any other by Shakespeare except *A Midsummer Night's Dream*, and most of the relationships and exchanges between the lords and ladies take place between sparkling, dancing, 'dazzling' eyes. We still speak of falling in love 'at first sight' (what the morose Puritan Richardson deprecated as 'the tindery fit' – no 'right Promethean fire' for him), and whatever it is the lords fall into, it is almost exclusively concerned with the eyes. Berowne's central contention is that 'love, first learned in a lady's eye', then

xcix

adds a precious seeing to the eye:
A lover's eyes will gaze an eagle blind

(IV, iii, 332–3)

It would be pointless to go through and examine occasions – eyes are looking and flashing everywhere. But there is one extraordinary description of that moment when an eye lights up at the sight of a beautiful person (someone who, as we say, catches the eye), which is like nothing else in the whole of Shakespeare. Boyet is describing to the Princess how he infers that the King has been 'infected' (again) by seeing her. He is going on what he nicely calls 'the heart's still rhetoric disclosed with eyes':

>   all his behaviors did make their retire
> To the court of his eye, peeping thorough desire.
> His heart, like an agate with your print impressed,
> Proud with his form, in his eye pride expressed.
> His tongue, all impatient to speak and not see,
> Did stumble with haste in his eyesight to be;
> All senses to that sense did make their repair,
> To feel only looking on fairest of fair.
> Methought all his senses were locked in his eye,
> As jewels in crystal for some prince to buy;
> Who, tend'ring their own worth from where they were glassed,
> Did point you to buy them, along as you passed.
> His face's own margent did quote such amazes
> That all eyes saw his eyes enchanted with gazes.

(II, i, 234–48)

The mysterious moment of sudden attraction has surely never been more amazingly elaborated than in these 'conceited' couplets. The tongue tripping up in its haste to join the other courtiers already crowded into the eye, peeping through desire ... (I note in passing that the imperturbably poised, endlessly amused, teasingly gallant, provocatively suggestive Boyet, is called by Berowne – he means to be rude – 'Monsieur the Nice' and 'honey-tongued Boyet', V, ii, 326, 335. One of the earliest, contemporary pieces of praise for Shakespeare – by Meres – contains the phrase 'mellifluous and honey-tongued Shakespeare'. Shakespeare could have been aware of this, and we may well have here an amiable, self-referential joke.

Certainly, only Shakespeare could have pulled off Boyet's amazing 'eye' conceit.)

But, is this *love*? One cannot help but feel that these young men most enjoy talking about it; trying to find clever ways of expressing how *they* feel, competing in hyperbolic praises of their adored ones. They seem to be caught up in – enjoyable – post-Petrarchan posturings. That the mere sight of the ladies has put paid to their absurd monkish resolves, is certain enough. They have been 'struck' – or indeed, 'infected'. But they don't seem to have moved beyond that to any consideration of the ladies as other individuals, nor given much thought to love as a *relationship* between two people (and none at all to the prospect of sexual consummation – possibly a chivalric touch). Barber rightly pointed out that Berowne's speeches on love tend to become 'autonomous rhapsodies' that 'almost forget the beloved'. When they discover that the ladies deceived them by wearing masks and changing favours – while they thought they were 'disguised' as Muscovites! – Berowne is the first to see the trick:

> The ladies did change favors, and then we,
> Following the signs, wooed but the sign of she.
>
> (V, ii, 469–70)

He speaks more truly than he knows; for they have, indeed, been wooing 'the sign of she' – i.e. not individuals, but the conventionalized, generic idea of the female. They never, we might say in today's parlance, moved beyond the sign to what, truly, it signified. Even when Berowne thinks he is trying to break out of artificiality, he shows himself to be still inextricably involved in it:

> *Berowne.* My love to thee is sound, sans crack or flaw.
> *Rosaline.* Sans 'sans', I pray you.
>
> (V, ii, 416–7)

Sincerity is an elusive thing – hard to detect in others, hard to be sure of even in oneself. Berowne, certainly, has not yet got the knack of it. Rosaline's wry response is definitive, and says it all.

None of what I have said about the young lords as would-be

'lovers' extends to the ladies. They are much more associated with 'grace'; not so much Christian redemptive grace, as the grace of genuinely good, humane, manners. To some extent, they have joined in the game – and with some pleasure, for they are, themselves, attracted to the men. But always in a controlled, realistic, non-deceptive (and non-deceiving) way. The Princess sums up how they took the lords' 'love-making':

> At courtship, pleasant jest, and courtesy,
> As bombast and as lining to the time.
> But more devout than this in our respects
> Have we not been, and therefore met your loves
> In their own fashion, like a merriment.

> (V, ii, 781–5)

And, we feel, they did absolutely right. *How* right has just been graphically demonstrated at the play, or entertainment (or show, or pageant, or antic, or . . .) put on for the court by the non-aristocratic locals. At the start, when the ladies were discussing the lords, they singled out a characteristic or attribute they all shared – a dangerously compulsive wit which could be 'ravishing', but also sharp to the point of cruelty – they are 'merry *mocking*' lords. Longaville's 'soil' is:

> a sharp wit matched with too blunt a will,
> Whose edge hath power to cut, whose will still wills
> It should none spare that come within his power.

> (II, i, 49–51)

Dumaine 'hath wit to make an ill shape good' (59), and Berowne turns everything 'to a mirth-moving jest' (71). When the locals put on their performance of the Nine Worthies – a performance as endearing as it is amusing – the King is worried that 'they will shame us' (V, ii, 510). In the event, the shame is all the lords'. The Princess is gracious and, as we have seen in the hunting scene, compassionate: 'Great thanks, great Pompey' – 'Alas! poor Maccabaeus, how he hath been baited!' (V, ii, 555, 632). (In rehearsal, Moth had spoken of 'the way to make an offense gracious, though few have the grace to do it', V, i, 141. The Princess has that 'grace'; the lords emphatically lack it.) The players are patient, well-mannered, deferential: 'Sweet Lord Longaville, rein thy tongue' (V, ii, 658). But the lords display the higher yobbery throughout, boorishly baiting and mocking the poor players without pause. There really *is* nothing like the bad manners of good society! We may learn from the Arden editor that it was customary for the courtiers to engage in what he rightly calls 'brutal' mockery at such entertainments. But, here again, I invoke my conviction that if we react to something as cruel, so did Shakespeare. As the crude, rude, mockery continues, we feel that if *this* is so-called wit, then it is wit at its most despicable, turned to bad ends. When poor, gentle Holofernes is catcalled completely 'out of countenance' and is jeered off the stage by Berowne as a Jude-ass, he is moved to make the reproach which should shame them all – 'This is not generous, not gentle, not humble' (V, ii, 630). This, too, is definitive. Berowne claimed that 'love' would teach them all they needed to know. These clever, selfish, self-regarding young aristocrats have learned nothing. The ladies are something more than justified in refusing to commit themselves to them in their unreconstructed state.

So – no weddings. As Berowne ruefully points out:

> Our wooing doth not end like an old play;
> Jack hath not Jill. These ladies' courtesy
> Might well have made our sport a comedy.
>
> (V, ii, 875–7)

This is the whole point. It is a 'sport' and *not* a 'comedy'. If it had been a comedy, Jack *would* have had Jill; if it had been a history, Jack would have been crowned; if it had been a tragedy, Jack and Jill would probably have both been dead. Here, Jack and Jill just go their separate ways. A play, in the sense of a drama, was, as Shakespeare constructed it, a representation, in some mode and form, of an arc of a significantly completed action – inasmuch as life knows of any completions. It might end, for example, in a marriage, a coronation, a funeral. If we are to regard *Love's Labor's Lost* as a drama, then we should see it as dramatizing how a 'sport' *fails* to become a 'comedy'. It is 'interrupted', or 'dashed', as real life will always interrupt mere 'pastime'; just as 'holiday' cannot go on forever, yet does not have any significant completion. It simply has to, at some time or another, give way to the exigencies of 'workday'. This 'interruption' has been adumbrated and prepared for. When the lords come dressed as Russians, Rosaline is about to start the dance, then stops it.

> Play, music, then. Nay, you must do it soon.
> Not yet! No dance! Thus change I like the moon.
>
> (V, ii, 211–12)

The episode ends with the 'frozen Muscovites' quite routed, and hopelessly 'out of count'nance' (V, ii, 273). Berowne can see what has happened:

> I see the trick on 't. Here was a consent,
> Knowing aforehand of our merriment,
> To dash it like a Christmas comedy.
>
> (V, ii, 461–3)

He is alluding to that custom of disrupting with mockery a seasonal entertainment put on by the local other-classes, which I mentioned. And, of course, the lords proceed to do exactly the same thing (only more cruelly) to the performance offered by the poor Worthies, 'dashing' it indeed, and putting the inexperienced players, exactly, quite 'out of countenance' (V, ii, 621). (These men, it should be noted, are all like Nathaniel, who is a 'marvellous good neighbour' but, in Costard's memorable formulation, 'a little o'erparted', 581–2. The lords trying to play at lovers are 'a little o'erparted', too.)

It is worth examining the point at which Shakespeare 'dashes' his own 'merriment'. The entertainment of the Worthies has collapsed, and threatens to end in a fight between Costard and Armado over Jaquenetta. They are supposed to strip to their shirts for combat, but Armado refuses:

> The naked truth of it is, I have no shirt. (V, ii, 710)

A man without a shirt is a speech without a metaphor. Immediately, the messenger Marcade enters with the naked, unadorned news of the death of the Princess's father. The 'merriment' is not only 'interrupted' (718) – it is definitively dashed. The Princess and her ladies retire to a 'mourning house' (809). The King is dispatched to 'some forlorn and *naked* hermitage' (796 – my italics). Berowne is sent to a hospital to try to 'move wild laughter in the throat of death', in the hope that that will 'choke a gibing spirit' (856, 859). Jaquenetta is two months' pregnant, and Armado promises to give up playing and take up 'ploughing' for her sake. The 'sport' is over, and it is back to the naked, unadorned realities of birth, work, sickness, and death. After Carnival, Lent. The play ends with pageant seasonal songs of Spring, *followed* by Winter. The festive interlude is over, and for the moment, it is more a matter of endings than renewals. The songs sing of the year-round, seasonal pleasures and labours of simple, communal rural life. The last line leaves us with the most homely and humble of pictures – 'While greasy Joan doth keel the pot'. Suddenly, we are a long way from princesses and court games. The very last sentence of the play is in larger type in the Quarto and may represent a non-Shakespearian addition. But it may be still Shakespeare – and the somewhat cryptic, enigmatic words are both ominous and fitting. The line is given to Armado; but ideally, I think, it should seem to come from nowhere, or some mysterious source, like the pronouncement of an oracle.

The words of Mercury are harsh after the songs of Apollo.

'Marcade', messenger of death, is a form of 'Mercury', messenger of the gods. Berowne invoked 'bright Apollo's lute', and tried to emulate his music. But Death always has the last word.

Thus Shakespeare soberly and sombrely ends his lightest, most 'play-ful' play. It is a bracing conclusion to a sufficiency of 'sport'. But I think we most remember the mounting pleasure which preceded it. I am reminded of a statement by Emerson concerning what it is we go to great artists for. 'We came this time for condiments, not for corn. We want the great genius only for joy . . .' Perhaps not *only* for joy, but I feel that the emphasis is right – that art should be, not primarily utilitarian and serviceable, but an addition, an excess, something over and above; not our daily bread, but an added spice, zest, relish. And this, surely, is true of *Love's Labor's Lost*. It gives great joy. I could say, simply, that it makes me laugh a lot. But, on this occasion, I prefer to put it that the heaving of my lungs provokes me to ridiculous smiling. It rejoiceth my intellect.

Come for the condiments.

*

ROMEO AND JULIET

> All things that we ordainèd festival
> Turn from their office to black funeral
>
> (IV, v, 84–5)
>
> Now art thou sociable, now art thou Romeo; now art thou what thou art, by art as well as by nature.
>
> (II, iv, 93–5)

Romeo and Juliet fails of being a 'comedy' by something under a minute (Juliet wakes up from her pseudo-death twenty-seven lines after Romeo has committed suicide). As a reason for including the play in a volume of Shakespeare's Comedies, this may seem, at best, a rather perverse piece of special pleading. The first good Quarto announced it clearly enough as 'THE MOST EXCELLENT AND LAMENTABLE TRAGEDY OF ROMEO AND JULIET', and by the end the five main protagonists are dead. Of course it is a tragedy. But it contains within it all the lineaments of a Classical comedy. Consider. Two young lovers set about circumventing the obstructiveness of intransigent parents, with the help of servants. When the Chorus announces at the beginning of Act II:

> Now old desire doth in his deathbed lie,
> And young affection gapes to be his heir

it is offering a precise definition of one of the most basic situations of all comedy. In addition, we have a standard Malcontent (or kill-joy, or spoil-sport) in Tybalt, who is a Malvolio at the feast, and, despite familial exhortations, will *not* be festive. Mercutio, full of bawdy jests, provocative, punning, playful, always buzzing in Romeo's ear, is a superb Clown. And we have a comic, garrulous Nurse, whose main interest is helping to get the young into bed together. There is a splendid dance and banquet (from which the churlish Tybalt is banished, and where the young lovers meet); and there is, indeed, a marriage whereby Romeo and Juliet are made 'incorporate two in one' (II, vi, 37) – which, as I have indicated elsewhere, is the ideal conclusion to a Shakespearian comedy. Only here, it happens at the end of Act II. Thereafter, 'ordained festival' does, indeed, turn to 'black funeral'. What (let us ask speculatively) was Shakespeare doing?

There has never been a way of deciding in which order Shakespeare wrote *Romeo and Juliet* and *A Midsummer Night's Dream*, and it seems at least likely that he was writing both plays *at the same time*. Both plays explore similar themes and subjects in, of course, a very different manner. Famously, the play of 'Pyramus and Thisby' put on by Bottom and the 'mechanicals' is a farcical redaction of the whole drama of *Romeo and Juliet* (Mercutio calls Romeo's loved one a 'Thisby' – if we needed a clue); and when Hippolyta pronounces it 'the silliest stuff that ever I heard' (V, i, 211), we can only guess at the fine, ironic pleasure Shakespeare must have had in writing the line. Mercutio's long, almost delirious, invocation of Queen Mab (I, iv, 53–94) seems to point directly to *A Midsummer Night's Dream* (some commentators think it really belongs there); while the cruelly prohibiting Egeus (trying to block and deflect his daughter, Hermia's, true love) is just such a father as the violent, tyrannical old Capulet becomes, when he threatens to turn Juliet out of house and home if she will not obey his orders. And so on – I won't pursue the similarities and echoes. In the one play, Shakespeare explores how 'comedy' can suddenly change, and veer precipitately into tragedy. He shows how everything can go terribly wrong. In the other play he demonstrates how things can all go, magically, right. The two plays were clearly conceived together; and, while I can hardly maintain that separating them is as risky as separating Siamese twins, from the point of view of a literary appreciation of what Shakespeare was doing, I think it is something of that order.

Let me give one example of the inter-involvement, the strange mutual reflectingness, of the two plays. Lysander, confronting the (usual) paternal blockage of his love for Hermia, complains, at length, that 'the course of true love never did run smooth' (a line which has become a truism because it is the simplest possible expression of a simple truth). He takes a perverse pleasure in elaborating on the number of ways in which true love can be variously impeded, frustrated, and otherwise derailed. Including this:

> Or, if there were a sympathy in choice,
> War, death, or sickness did lay siege to it,
> Making it momentary as a sound,
> Swift as a shadow, short as any dream,
> Brief as the lightning in the collied night,
> That, in a spleen, unfolds both heaven and earth,
> And, ere a man hath power to say 'Behold!'
> The jaws of darkness do devour it up:
> So quick bright things come to confusion.
>
> (*MSND*, I, i, 141–9)

That last line is one of the most haunting in the whole of Shakespeare – it is hard to imagine poetry doing more than this in seven simple words, six darting monosyllables brought to a halt in the relative tangle of a trisyllable. But let us just linger, with appropriate brevity, on 'lightning'. When Romeo is trying to swear his love to Juliet in the so-called balcony scene (II, ii), she holds, briefly, back:

> Well, do not swear. Although I joy in thee,
> I have no joy of this contract tonight.
> It is too rash, too unadvised, too sudden;
> Too like the lightning, which doth cease to be
> Ere one can say it lightens.
>
> (II, ii, 116–20)

Benvolio, describing the crucial 'bloody fray' to the Prince, tells how Romeo came looking for Tybalt, to revenge Mercutio, 'and to't they go like lightning' (III, i, 174) – anger can work like love: violent and (for whatever reasons), often short-lived, expiring in the performance. In his last speech, Romeo, imaginatively transforming Juliet's tomb into a festive chamber, says:

> How oft when men are at the point of death

Have they been merry! Which their keepers call
A lightning before death. O, how may I
Call this a lightning?

(V, iii, 88–91)

Shakespeare shows how – but I will return to that. Here, I just
want to suggest that both plays are concerned, imaginatively,
with the 'lightning' of young love. And its possible ramifications. So quick bright things come to confusion – in this play,
the confusion leads, tragically, to death; in the other, the
confusion is, comically, resolved.

*

The basic story of Romeo and Juliet can be traced back to
folklore, but it was first developed into a popular narrative by
a number of Italian *novelle* in the fifteenth and sixteenth
centuries. Shakespeare's primary source was unquestionably a
translation of the story into English by Arthur Brooke, in a
long poem entitled *The Tragicall History of Romeus and Juliet*
(published in 1562). Brooke was a Protestant moralist, and he
gave as the intention and justification of his poem – 'to
describe unto thee a couple of unfortunate lovers, thralling
themselves to unhonest desire, neglecting the authoritie and
advise of parents and frendes, conferring their principall
counsels with dronken gossypes, and superstitious friers,
attempting all adventures of peryll, for thattaynyng of their
wished lust ... abusing the honorable name of lawefull marriage, to cloke the shame of stolne contractes, finallye, by all
means of unhonest lyfe, hastyng to most unhappye deathe'. A
cautionary tale, indeed! To be fair, his actual poem is a good
deal more sympathetic to the young lovers than this stiff-
necked sententiousness suggests will be the case. But Shakespeare clearly had something very different in mind than a
demonstration of the folly of aroused youth ignoring parental
advice.

Shakespeare took a lot of matter from Brooke's poem (the
lyric brilliance of his transformation of Brooke's rather turgid,
lugubrious verse is a marvel in itself); but, as always, it is
particularly instructive to notice what he changed. He drasti-

cally foreshortens the time-scale of the action (as he will do in the one other tragedy he based on an Italian story of love and intrigue – *Othello*). Where Brooke has weeks between the ball and the lovers' meeting by moonlight, and months between their marriage and the death of Tybalt, Shakespeare makes these events occur on the same night and the same day, respectively. In Brooke, Juliet wakes up an hour after Romeo's suicide; in Shakespeare, it is less than a minute. In all, he collapses about seven months into, at most, four days. In Brooke, Romeo kills Tybalt in self-defence and Mercutio is not involved. In Shakespeare, Mercutio is first killed, mainly as a result of Romeo's attempt at pacifying interference (good intentions can have bad outcomes), and Romeo is obliged to adhere to the revenge code. Juliet is, in some versions, an eighteen-year-old; Brooke makes her sixteen; Shakespeare brings her down to just *fourteen*. Brooke leaves the entirely honourable Paris alive at the end; Shakespeare kills him off. Brooke describes the night after the wedding, when the young lovers legitimately consummate their love; Shakespeare shows only the dawn parting. I will, in due course, suggest reasons for all these changes. (One little change intrigues me, though I have no theories about it. Every other version of the story, including Brooke's, stresses that Mercutio has very cold hands – quite a nice touch, given his hot, lecherous banter. But Shakespeare deletes the manual chill!) Brooke – the Protestant moralist – stresses the malignancy of Fortune and Fate, on at least fifteen occasions. This was his gloomy addition to the Italian tale. In the words of H. B. Charlton, 'Brooke drenched the story in fatality.' Charlton thinks that Shakespeare took over this sense of Fate, and fatality, from Brooke, which is partly why, in his opinion, as a tragedy the play is a 'failure'. Thus: 'though *Romeo and Juliet* is set in a modern Christian country, with church and priest and full ecclesiastical institution, the whole universe of God's justice, vengeance, and providence is discarded and rejected from the directing forces of the play's dramatic movement. In its place, there is a theatrical resuscitation of the half-barbarian, half-Roman deities of Fate and Fortune.' And: 'Fate was no longer a deity strong enough to carry the responsibility of a tragic universe

... It fails to provide the indispensable inevitability.' One can see the point, but unhappily for Charlton's case, the word 'fortune' appears here less often than in any other play ('Fortune' is apostrophized twice); while 'fate', with a single appearance, is also a rarer visitor than is the case everywhere else. If anything, Shakespeare *drained* the story of 'fatality'.

I think Charlton is perhaps addressing the difficulty of locating the blame for what happens, of identifying the cause which makes the tragedy 'inevitable'. The point is an important one. In comedy, things are, precisely, 'evitable' (Susan Snyder has developed this point). If this doesn't work, we'll try that; let's hide in the forest, let's dress up as men; so-and-so will help us; we can get round this old man; I know a trick whereby ... Iron laws can be made to melt; irrevocable prohibitions are rescinded; obstacles are made to be removed or circumvented – it *will* be, somehow, all right in the end. *Romeo and Juliet* starts with something of that atmosphere – come on, let's gatecrash the Capulet ball, we can get away with it. The Friar and the Nurse continue to believe in 'evitability', the possible other way (try this drug, why not marry the other man?), but they become increasingly irrelevant figures. Somehow, the tragic imperatives close in and take over. Things do turn '*in*-evitable'. Only just; but, nevertheless, unmistakably. Why? Whence? How? This, of course, is *the* tragic question; and, at the end of the worst and longest day, we might do well to recall Cordelia's piercingly gentle words – 'No cause, no cause'.

Who or what is to 'blame' for what happens in *Romeo and Juliet*? There is the futile feud, but no explanation or origin of that is given – it is just one of those irrational things that *are*. (Charlton thought that feuds belong to the 'border country of civilization', and that it is impossible, or anachronistic, for Shakespeare to locate something so tribal and clan-based as a feud in such a civilized city as Verona. Civilized it certainly is, and was, but my sense of the matter is that 'feuding', in one form or another, can hardly be said to go out of date. And wasn't there something about the Guelphs and the Ghibellines, not to mention Yorkists and Lancastrians? The feud in Verona is a 'hurt' to the community, and, as such, it is like

Mercutio's fatal wound – "'tis not so deep as a well, nor so wide as a church door, but 'tis enough, 'twill serve', III, i, 97–8. As continued by the feeble old men, who need crutches more than swords, it has become ridiculous; but, as perpetuated by Tybalt, it is lethal enough.) It is the plague which is responsible for the temporary incarceration of the monk, who is thus prevented from delivering the Friar's all-explaining letter to Romeo – and the plague is another irrational thing which simply *is*. 'Prince of cats' Tybalt's violence certainly sets a train of events in motion. But, threatening and unpleasant as he is, Tybalt is hardly a proper villain. He appears, rather, as an obsessive psychopath who is only interested in killing Montagues. He is not a 'plotter', not a Richard III; not, certainly, a Iago (though explain why Iago is Iago if you can). An 'earthquake' is mentioned; and, in the case of this dangerously eruptive play, you might say that whatever it is that is really responsible for what happens, may be compared to whatever it is that causes earthquakes. But Fate and Fortune are not serious players – or not serious *as* players. Shakespeare's opening choric sonnet announces that the lovers are 'star-crossed' and their love 'death-marked'; but, although the play is full of premonitions and a growing sense of menace, we never experience it as a demonstration of astrological determinism. It is a very starlit play, even while the 'mark' of death is clearly on it: it is bright to the point of brilliance – and as dark as oblivion itself. The play itself is somewhat like a flash of lightning in the night. In a way, the young lovers *are* crossed with stars, are themselves crossing stars – but I will come to that.

Fate and Fortune figure minimally, and 'Providence' not once (it is, in any case, a rare word in Shakespeare's plays – six occurences have been counted. The Friar finally acknowledges 'A greater power than we can contradict /Hath thwarted our intents', V, iii, 153–4 – this is pious, but vague to the point of pointlessness. 'A greater power' – God? An earthquake? Who knows?). The Prince refers to 'heaven' (V, iii, 293) – but this is the habitation of the blind stars, as well as the residence of whatever gods there might be. But, the word 'haste' occurs *more* frequently than in any other Shakespeare play – except

Hamlet. In the case of *Hamlet*, this is something of a contributory irony, since it is at once the longest and the slowest of Shakespeare's tragedies. But in *Romeo and Juliet*, speed is, indeed, of the essence. It is among the fastest of the plays; as fast, perhaps, even as *Macbeth*, that black arrow of a play. But Macbeth wants to outrun his own mind, and he can never, *could* never, run fast enough. Whereas Romeo is always just too quick, too sudden, too soon. Finally, only by seconds – but it is enough to ensure catastrophe. Coleridge thought this play was particularly marked by 'precipitation', both in language and action, and that is just the right word. The falling in love, the marrying, the brawling, the killing, the plotting, the judgments and decrees, the suicides – all, all too precipitate. Paris says that Juliet is weeping for her cousin's death 'immoderately' (IV, i, 6). In his decent ignorance, he cannot realize that she is weeping for everything, including Juliet – but the word is tellingly apposite. Immoderation rules. Precipitate immoderation.

In this connection, Juliet's invocation to Phoebus *and Phaeton*, as she waits for Romeo on her bridal night, is understandable, apt – and ominous.

> Gallop apace, you fiery-footed steeds,
> Towards Phoebus' lodging! Such a wagoner
> As Phaeton would whip you to the west
> And bring in cloudy night immediately.
> Spread thy close curtain, love-performing night,
> That runaways' eyes may wink, and Romeo
> Leap to these arms untalked of and unseen.

(III, ii, 1–7)

She wants the sun to sink and night to fall as quickly as possible – of course she does. And, as we have seen Romeo 'leap' the orchard wall, we may be confident that he will manage this longed-for leap as well. But 'such a wagoner/ As Phaeton' (son of Phoebus) was too reckless and inexperienced; when he took over the horses of the sun, he could not control them – they ran unstoppably wild, and he fell, fatally, to earth. (It amuses me slightly that 'runaway's' – wherever the apostrophe belongs – remains a 'famous crux'. This is runaway speech in a runaway play full of runaways – it is a perfect word.) As Jonathan Bate, tracing the Ovidian reference, says – 'to put Phaeton in charge is to precipitate catastrophe'. The Phaeton–Romeo connection (or echo) is clinched when, at the end, the Prince, announcing the 'glooming peace' which follows the death of the too-dazzling lovers, predicts that, on this day – 'The sun for sorrow will not show his head' (V, iii, 306). This is a direct allusion to Golding's translation of Ovid, in which, after the fall of Phaeton, 'A day did pass without the Sunne.' Phaeton was another quick bright thing that came to confusion. The play is marked by sudden-ness – explosive outbursts of eruptive energies. Violent fighting in the street; urgent passion in the orchard. When Romeo doesn't need a sword, he needs a ladder, or a crowbar. It's all difficult – but, with sufficient determined energy, do-able. Penetrating an enemy, a new wife, a tomb – Romeo's youthful vigour is up to it all.

Shakespeare's play starts with lead and ends in gold: in between it is mainly silver, silvery, and iron (daggers are 'iron', while there are 'silver sounds', silver among the musicians, silver-tipped trees at night, and a prevalent silver moonlight). I have no doubt that Shakespeare was alluding to the classical idea of the four Ages of Mankind – as outlined in the first book of Ovid's *Metamorphoses*, for example – with the brass age here elided. But, this being Shakespeare, the Ages are here reversed – so that we are presented with, not the downward declensions of history, but the soaring ascensions of poetry. Romeo is all lead to start with, pure inertia. No dancing for him:

> I have a soul of lead
> So stakes me to the ground I cannot move.
> . . .
> I cannot bound a pitch above dull woe.
> Under love's heavy burden do I sink.
>
> (I, iv, 15–16, 21–2)

We will see him 'bounding' soon enough ('He ran this way and leapt this orchard wall', II, i, 5), but he has as yet to be sparked into lightness and leaping, soaring motion. In this,

unawakened youth is like age. Juliet, thinking the Nurse much
too slow, complains:

> But old folks, many feign as they were dead –
> Unwieldy, slow, heavy and pale as lead.
>
> (II, v, 16–17)

It is, of course, primarily Juliet herself who will 'feign as she
were dead' – the play is a tissue of unconscious and conscious
premonitions, but here, her 'warm youthful blood ... would
be as swift in motion as a ball' (II, v, 13–14).

Romeo, aroused, is now the reverse of leaden. 'O, let us
hence! I stand on sudden haste', he says impatiently to the
Friar; who replies, with a sagacity which no longer has any
purchase – 'Wisely and slow. They stumble that run fast' (II,
iii, 93–4). Nothing now can stop Romeo in his running – and
his stumbling. Contemplating the moment of his imminent
marriage, Romeo declares:

> But come what sorrow can,
> It cannot countervail the exchange of joy
> That one short minute gives me in her sight.
>
> (II, vi, 3–5)

Another omen – the joy *will* be 'countervailed' by exactly 'one
short minute' in the tomb. Here, it is the Friar who gives voice
to apprehensions:

> These violent delights have violent ends
> And in their triumph die, like fire and powder,
> Which, as they kiss, consume. The sweetest honey
> Is loathsome in his own deliciousness
> And in the taste confounds the appetite.
> Therefore love moderately: long love doth so;
> Too swift arrives as tardy as too slow.
>
> (II, vi, 9–15)

In many ways, these lines sum up the play. Apart from the
honey turning loathsome in its own deliciousness – that
belongs squarely in *Troilus and Cressida*, another of the only
three plays entitled by a couple's names (the third is *Antony and
Cleopatra* – of which, more in due course). Romeo and Juliet's
love is too quick and short to have time to curdle. It *is* violent

and explosive, and they kiss and 'consume' – and are consumed – at the same moment. In their 'triumph' – i.e. the flash-point of an explosion – they do, indeed, die. But also – they die in triumph, in the wider sense of the word; or, their death *is* their triumph. A triumph was probably originally a *thriambos*, a hymn to Bacchus; and, as Juliet and then Romeo toast each other in festal poison prior to death, that will do nicely for the occasion. 'Moderation' is, of course, out of the question; and 'long love' never on the cards. And they *are* too swift in their tardiness (or too tardy in their swiftness), arriving, and acting, somehow both too late and too soon. (When old Capulet says 'it is so very late/ That we may call it early by and by', III, iv, 34–5, he is in the spirit of the play – it is, invariably, both very late, and yet too early.) The precipitately planned marriage of Paris to Juliet 'should be slowed', as the Friar well knows (IV, i, 16). But some things won't be 'slowed' when they should be, just as other things refuse to be accelerated when they need to be. Explaining his failure to deliver the crucial letter to Romeo, Friar John describes how he was forcibly detained in a house of 'infectious pestilence ... So that my speed to Mantua there was stayed' (V, ii, 10, 12). Things are too fast, or, more rarely, too slow. Nothing seems to go at the right speed. The 'speed' of the young lovers is only 'stayed' in, and by, death. Thereafter, they are transformed into 'pure gold' statues. Permanently slowed – definitively stayed. Art forever.

They are, in a sense, simply too young – love hits them prematurely, as we may say (hence, I think the deliberate juvenalization of Juliet to fourteen; an age at which, even in those days and among high-born families, it was, apparently, very rare for a girl to marry). As John Lawlor puts it – 'in both we meet youth on the hither side of experience'. But, if it finds them pre- or im-mature, they are something very different by the end. In a sense (which we will have to explore), they have moved beyond considerations of maturity – as it feels, out of time altogether. But, in the world of the play, in hot, feasting, feuding, fighting, joking, courting, drudging, playing, Verona – where people are 'soon moody to be moved' (III, i, 14) – time is, as it were, everywhere. Characters think back over the years – wasn't that wedding twenty-five years ago, come Pentecost? The Nurse can tell Juliet's age 'to the hour'. In this play, you are never far from a clock, or a time check. Romeo's first words are 'Is the day so young?' 'But new struck nine', answers Benvolio (I, i, 163). Thereafter, Shakespeare 'sustains the emphasis on the continuous counterpoint between extended periods and an exactly stipulated day, hour, moment' in Brian Gibbons' felicitous formulation.

There is recurrent emphasis on the time of dawn – Romeo is described as walking in a sycamore grove at dawn, before we see him: he leaves the Capulet orchard at dawn: he leaves Juliet at dawn after their wedding night: Juliet's supposedly 'dead' body is found at dawn by the Nurse: and it is dawn when the Prince surveys the dead bodies and predicts that the sun will not rise that day. Dawn is, or should be, usually accompanied by a sense of new beginnings, a refreshing and renewing light dispelling the last of the darkness. But in this play, it is more characteristically associated with separation, departure and death. But, for Romeo and Juliet, might death not *be* a new kind of dawn? I think we should feel something like that. Certainly, everyday time is everywhere against them, down to that last single minute when Romeo, ever precipitate, kills himself far too quickly, just too soon. In the inner universe of love they have created for themselves, it is as if they, somehow, recede from the world's time into a private, ecstatic, timelessness. But these worlds collide, and clock time, calendar time, will not let them be. In other plays, time, 'ripe time', is often a restorative, regenerative force, helping to expose evil, bring justice, effect reconciliation. But not in this play. The ever-resourceful, benevolently plotting Friar, still thinks, or hopes, that he is living in a 'comic' world in which everything is still possible. So, after the sentence of exile has been passed, he packs Romeo off to Mantua:

> Where thou shalt live till we can find a time
> To blaze your marriage, reconcile your friends,
> Beg pardon of the Prince, and call thee back
> With twenty hundred thousand times more joy
> Than thou went'st forth in lamentation.
>
> (III, iii, 150–54)

In a comedy, this is just what would happen, one way or another. But it is too late, or too early – or too *something* – for that here. The Friar is always optimistic that he will 'find a time' – time for this, for that, for the other. But, here, there is no time to be found; and, as we say, no time to be lost, either. For Romeo and Juliet, there is just no time.

The Friar uses 'blaze' to mean 'make public'; but he could hardly have fastened on a more appropriate verb (it comes from older words meaning both 'blow' *and* 'shine'). The hot afternoon sun blazes down on the square in Verona, heating 'mad blood' to fighting point. In the great houses at night, the torches and fires are blazing as the feasting and dancing go forward. 'More torches here ... More light, more light!' is the host's cry. Romeo is a torch-bearer first and last – self-effacingly at the ball; brave and determined at the tomb. If his marriage to Juliet is as short as a flash of lightning, it is, for its duration, an incandescent blaze. Fires go out, or are quenched, as surely as lightning disappears. 'Come, we burn daylight ... We waste our lights in vain, like lights by day' (I, iv, 43–5), says Mercutio, impatient to get to the ball. There *is* something strange about, say, a candle flame in bright sun-shine, and 'burning daylight' is a graphic way of evoking that rather curious light-devouring-light phenomenon. The question becomes – is the 'blaze' ignited by Romeo and Juliet's love a wasted light? Or something else? 'What light through yonder window breaks?' (II, ii, 1) becomes, by the end, an almost metaphysical question.

But there is another source of light in the play, which is the reverse of transient – the stars. Before his feast, Capulet in a gracious invitation, declares:

> At my poor house look to behold this night
> Earth-treading stars that make dark heaven light.
>
> (I, ii, 24–5)

There are a number of references to 'earth'. Juliet is, for her father, 'the hopeful lady of my earth' (I, ii, 15), while Romeo addresses himself as 'dull earth' before he leaps the orchard wall, and starts to 'soar'. Beautiful young ladies are 'earth-treading stars' – so much is gallantry, a courteous conceit. But, in a much more powerful and dramatic way, Romeo and Juliet begin to emerge as 'earth-treading stars' in earnest, and it is the earth that they would be glad to leave behind, below. This is adumbrated by Romeo's reaction to his first sight of Juliet:

> O, she doth teach the torches to burn bright!
> It seems she hangs upon the cheek of night
> As a rich jewel in an Ethiop's ear –
> Beauty too rich for use, for earth too dear!
>
> (I, v, 46–9)

Not, finally, too expensive for the earth to purchase, since the tomb claims her at the end. But, as M. Mahood suggests, she *will* prove 'too rare a creature for mortal life'. Romeo, who at the start is a young posing, Petrarchan 'lover' who could have walked out of *Love's Labor's Lost*, is still indulging himself in self-congratulatory conceits – hence the 'Ethiop's ear' business. But, once inflamed, he soon 'blazes' into authentic, coruscating poetry. Juliet at the window, not only serves to 'kill the envious moon' (the planet of periodicity and cyclical time), but outshines the stars as well:

> Two of the fairest stars in all the heaven,
> Having some business, do entreat her eyes
> To twinkle in their spheres till they return.
> What if her eyes were there, they in her head?
> The brightness of her cheek would shame those stars
> As daylight doth a lamp [that phenomenon again!];
>   her eyes in heaven
> Would through the airy region stream so bright
> That birds would sing and think it were not night.
>
> (II, ii, 15–22)

Reciprocally, Juliet on her wedding night, addresses the darkness:

> Come, gentle night; come, loving, black-browed night;
> Give me my Romeo; and, when I shall die,
> Take him and cut him out in little stars,
> And he will make the face of heaven so fine

That all the world will be in love with night
And pay no worship to the garish sun.

(III, ii, 20–25)

As Professor Mahood very accurately puts it, Romeo and Juliet 'stellify each other'. And the reminder of how recently Juliet must have been cutting out stars in some child's nursery game, is not only exquisite. It reminds us that she has been, precipitately, launched into the seas of adult passion, with only a little girl's experience to draw on.

When he enters the tomb where Juliet is lying, sleeping-thought-dead, Romeo transforms this 'bed of death' into a version of a strange celebration. He denies that he is in a 'triumphant grave':

A grave? O, no, a lanthorn [lantern], slaught'red youth,
For here lies Juliet, and her beauty makes
This vault a feasting presence full of light.
Death, lie thou there, by a dead man interred.

(V, iii, 84–7)

He is laying down the corpse of the unfortunate Paris whom he has killed, and makes it into a burying of Death itself, turning the 'vault' into a 'feasting presence full of light'. This is the 'lightning' – light*e*ning – 'before death'. In this strange festal mood, he raises the poison and toasts his Juliet – 'Here's to my love!' (V, iii, 119), just as Juliet raised her drugged glass to him – 'Romeo, Romeo, Romeo, I drink to thee' (IV, iii, 58). They make their deaths into their own, private banquet. In the outside, public world, all things that were 'ordained festival' have been turned to 'black funeral'. The would-be 'comic' world is truly dead – that, I think, is why Shakespeare kills off the blameless Paris. It means that *all* the young protagonists are dead by the end. There is no 'young affection' gaping to be the heir to 'old desire' – a whole generation has been wiped out, and generational renewal is, here, out of the question. At the end, the scene is peopled entirely by old (or not young) people, standing reconciled but hopeless in the gloom of a sunless dawn. But, in his private world of poetry, Romeo has turned everything that was 'black funeral' into his own form of 'ordained festival', 'celebrating' on, and in, his own terms. The 'comedy', albeit in a rare form, is consummated in the dazzling Juliet-light inside the tomb.

As he dies, Romeo cries out 'O true apothecary!/Thy drugs are quick' (V, iii, 119-20). 'Quick' is 'fast', but it is also 'life' – as in the biblical 'the quick and the dead'. So in one of the many puns in this play (M. Mahood pointed out that they are more prevalent here than in any other play), Romeo is saying, at once, that the drug works very quickly, and that it is life-giving. Similarly Juliet, kissing his dead but still warm lips, hopes to imbibe some 'poison' there 'to make me die with a restorative' (V, iii, 166). The poison that can also be a medicine is a very ancient paradox, and it is very apt for the purposes of the young lovers. In this play, we have the Friar, who is an expert on herbal potions, and an apothecary who specializes in poisons. Shakespeare has extended his treatment of these aspects of the story (and, unlike Brooke, he does *not* have the apothecary hanged at the end), and we might have a word about the role of drugs etc. in this play. In his long disquisition on the properties of herbs, the Friar foregrounds their doubleness, or root ambiguity if you will – 'Within the infant rind of this weak flower/Poison hath residence and medicine power' (II, iii, 23–4). He tends to stress the bene-ficent side of nature:

> O, mickle is the powerful grace that lies
> In plants, herbs, stones, and their true qualities
>
> (II, iii, 15–16)

and he extrapolates from the opposite powers of different herbs, to the divided nature of man himself:

> Two such opposèd kings encamp them still
> In man as well as herbs – grace and rude will
>
> (II, iii, 27–8)

But things are not so separate, separable. The Friar is a healthy, benevolent man, and he tries to use his herbs for their 'powerful grace'; but, in the event, indirectly they help to destroy Juliet. By contrast, the Apothecary in his shop (the shop is Shakespeare's invention), looks like Death in a charnel house:

> Meager were his looks,
> Sharp misery had worn him to the bones;
> And in his needy shop a tortoise hung,
> An alligator stuffed, and other skins
> Of ill-shaped fishes; and about his shelves
> A beggarly account of empty boxes,
> Green earthen pots, bladders, and musty seeds,
> Remnants of packthread, and old cakes of roses
> Were thinly scatterèd, to make up a show.
>
> (V, i, 40–48)

– a wasteland, all sterility, used-up-ness, and desolation. But this is all 'a show'. He has, hidden, something supremely valuable, as far as Romeo is concerned – a pricelesss concoction which will cure all. Romeo pays for it in 'gold' – which, as money, is a 'worse poison to men's souls' (as monument, it will have another value entirely) – and goes away happy with the Apothecary's secret mixture which is now 'not poison' but 'cordial' (V, i, 80, 85) – or 'restorative', as Juliet will shortly call it. Nature's 'grace' comes in strange forms, and from strange places. And works in unpredictable ways – as these herbalist-artists show.

Dr Johnson said of Addison's prose that 'it never blazes into unexpected splendour'. Addison's prose is, in this context, neither here nor there. But we will hardly find a happier phrase than 'blazing into splendour' for what happens to Romeo and Juliet's love – and their poetry. In this, the play is closest in spirit and concluding feeling, to *Antony and Cleopatra* (the other couple-titled play that *is* relevant). There are interesting structural similarities. The feuding Montagues and Capulets may be matched, on a cosmic scale, by the oppugnant Rome and Egypt. In both cases, the putative death of the woman (Juliet by drugs, Cleopatra by false report), leads to the suicide of the man, followed by the real suicides of the women. The lovers in the first play are, at the outset, innocent children; while the later lovers are relatively old, and sexually experienced – we are confronted with spring-time, and then autumnal, love. All the lovers die, but in both cases we are made to feel that, in some way, the power of love has 'triumphed' over death. By the end, it is as 'paltry' to be a

Montague or a Capulet as it is to be Caesar. In both cases, the poetry of the lovers achieves an *incandescent* quality (= glowing with both heat and brightness), unequalled, I feel, elsewhere in Shakespeare. And the poetry of both plays is marked by the same two crucial qualities. Here is Juliet, expressing her love:

> My bounty is as boundless as the sea,
> My love as deep: the more I give to thee,
> The more I have, for both are infinite.

(II, ii, 133–5)

'Bounty' is the special mark of Antony, and 'boundlessness' is what distinguishes Antony and Cleopatra's love from severely bounded, banded, bonded, Rome. Cleopatra is known for her 'infinite variety': indeed, all four lovers have their eyes on the 'infinite'. And – as a result – their poetry really does 'blaze into unexpected splendour'.

Other forms of 'love' are intimated early in the play – empty Petrarchan idolatry, and coarse, bawdy cynicism, are first on the scene. Some of the sexual joking is very broad, particularly that coming from Mercutio. One of his lines might have a claim to be the bawdiest in Shakespeare. He says to Romeo that he wishes that Rosaline – Romeo's earlier Petrarchan 'love' object – was 'an open *et cetera*, thou a pop'rin pear' (II, i, 38). That '*et cetera*' was a subsequent delicacy, and the original line was almost certainly 'an open-arse and thou a poperin pear' – the replaced term being a dialect term for a medlar, a fruit often used to refer to female genitalia. In this form, the line could hardly be less unambiguous. But all this encircling vulgarity has an important dramatic role. Just as Romeo will quickly free himself from his residual Petrarchanism, so he must soar above this encroaching obscenity. He will have to find another language altogether. And he does.

The Friar tells Romeo that 'Thy love did read by rote, that could not spell' (II, iii, 88). And when he first kisses Juliet, she says 'You kiss by th' book' (I, v, 112). (The entirely conventional Paris is actually described as a book by Juliet's mother – at length: see I, iii, 80–94). The implication is clear: Romeo's love with Juliet will move beyond all the prescribed, prescripted forms. It will be something new. In one of his first speeches, concerning love and hate, Romeo indulges in some rather book-ish, modish, oxymorons:

> O heavy lightness, serious vanity,
> Misshapen chaos of well-seeming forms,
> Feather of lead, bright smoke, cold fire, sick health
>
> (I, i, 181–3)

and so on – clever young man! But, in his love, he will discover and live through, live out, *die* out, such seemingly impossible merged opposites. He will meet his end drinking poison as a cordial. And loving will become indistinguishable from, identical with, dying.

Their love is, indeed, from the start 'death-marked' – marked by, and marked (heading) *for* (towards) death. After their first anonymous encounter at the ball, Juliet asks the Nurse who the young man was.

> Go ask his name. – If he is marrièd,
> My grave is like to be my wedding bed.
>
> (I, v, 136–7)

And indeed, the one will follow so quickly upon the other as almost to merge with it (because, precisely, of his *name*). There is a lot of play with the idea of Death as bridegroom. When she hears that Romeo has been banished, Juliet says to the Nurse – 'I'll to my wedding bed;/And death, not Romeo, take my maidenhead!' (III, ii, 136–7). When told she must marry Paris, Juliet asks her mother, instead, to 'make the bridal bed/ In that dim monument where Tybalt lies' (III, v, 202–3) – that, too, shall come to pass. (Later, while Capulet is preparing the guest-list for the wedding of his daughter and Paris, and the cooks are busy with preparations in the kitchens, Juliet is upstairs fantasizing the nightmare of waking up in the tomb 'Where bloody Tybalt, yet but green in earth,/Lies fest'ring in his shroud', IV, iv, 42–3 – another lived-out oxymoron.) With desperate ambiguity, Juliet, on hearing of Tybalt's death, vows to her mother:

> Indeed I never shall be satisfied
> With Romeo till I behold him – dead –

which seems clear enough; but she continues

> Is my poor heart ...   (III, v, 94-6)

which is another kind of statement altogether. (Impossibly enough, though, *both* lovers will have the experience of beholding the loved one 'dead'. Juliet's vow will be kept for her.) On hearing of Juliet's 'death', her father explicitly says to Paris:

> O son, the night before thy wedding day
> Hath Death lain with thy wife. There she lies,
> Flower as she was, deflowerèd by him.
>
> (IV, v, 35–8)

Not true yet. But all in due course – and very soon. 'Beholding' Juliet's 'corpse', Romeo exclaims:

> Why art thou yet so fair? Shall I believe
> That unsubstantial Death is amorous,
> And that the lean abhorrèd monster keeps
> Thee here in dark to be his paramour?
>
> (V, iii, 102–5)

Death as 'amorous paramour', as *Romeo*, is almost literally enacted within a few minutes, when Juliet, beholding Romeo's corpse, says:

> ... I'll be brief. O happy dagger! [*Snatches Romeo's dagger.*]
> This is thy sheath; there rust, and let me die.
> [*She stabs herself and falls.*]
>
> (V, iii, 169–70)

Since 'die' was also used for sexual orgasm, the conflation could hardly be more complete. This is not to suggest that the young lovers have a 'death wish'. This is absolutely not Wagner. The feeling, rather, is that such a 'blaze' *can* only lead quickly to confusion, to extinction. 'Lightning' is indeed the word.

For the Montagues and Capulets, and people like them, marriage is a family business. According to their family, suitors are suitable, or unsuitable, for their children. Here, of course, the family name is everything. Everybody is born into a family name; it is *ineluctable* (literally – cannot be struggled out from). And, of course, for entirely irrational but entirely inescapable reasons, Montagues are *not* 'suitable' for Capulets. This is the point of Juliet's famous lament; uttered, notice, when Romeo, standing below in darkness, is both there and not there, invisible though within earshot, an absent presence. As Juliet asks, when he speaks – 'What *man* art thou ... thus bescreened in night ... ?' (my italics). In the penumbra of the moment, he is simply a generic 'man' without a social identity. Would that he could stay in that ontological pre-baptismal limbo! I want to examine Juliet's crucial speech, and before doing so I just want to point out the two 'o's in the name. This is Shakespeare's nomination – in Brooke, he is Rome*us*. He will do the same with *O*thell*o*, and I have speculated elsewhere on the significance of this – 'O' being, at once, a wordless sigh or cry of despair; the circle of perfection; the nought of nothingness. All this is very relevant to Othello, and I think it applies in the case of Romeo, too. So to Juliet's speech, which starts with a line containing nine 'o's!

> O Romeo, Romeo! Wherefore art thou Romeo?
> Deny thy father and refuse thy name;
> Or, if thou wilt not, be but sworn my love,
> And I'll no longer be a Capulet.
> ...
> 'Tis but thy name that is my enemy.
> Thou art thyself, though not a Montague.
> What's Montague? It is nor hand, nor foot,
> Nor arm, nor face. O, be some other name
> Belonging to a man.
> What's in a name? That which we call a rose
> By any other word would smell as sweet.
> So Romeo would, were he not Romeo called,
> Retain that dear perfection which he owes
> Without that title. Romeo, doff thy name;
> And for thy name, which is no part of thee,
> Take all myself.
>
> (II, ii, 33–6, 38–48)

(Strictly speaking, it is the name 'Montague' which is the 'enemy' – Romeo is a Christian name, not the family name. But I see no point in pursuing this. He is Romeo-the-known-Montague, and it is precisely the individual-inextricable-from-the-family that is being focused on.) Juliet goes to the very heart of the matter. Deny, refuse, doff – father, name, title. But it cannot be done.

Of course the *name* is *not* the *man*, nor is it like a physical *part* of the man. But it is an inseparable, constitutive part of what Henry James calls 'the impress which constitutes an identity'. Once born, a man cannot elude what Jacques Derrida calls 'the law of the name'.[1] Romeo simply cannot *be* Romeo without the name 'Romeo'. It is *not* the same for a rose. 'Rose', as Juliet correctly differentiates (even if the proverbial version does not) is a 'word' and *not* a 'name' ; and, yes, you could call it – what? a weed? – and it *would* smell as sweet. But the analogy does not hold when it comes to the human, familial, social realm. Wherefore is he Romeo? By virtue of having been born of whom, when, and where, he was. Truly speaking, a man's 'name' never can be denied or refused; it is not a hat to be doffed, nor, indeed, a hand to be cut off (this, whatever superficial substitutes are allowed, or 'aliases' had recourse to). Romeo would like to do it, of course:

> I take thee at thy word.
> Call me but love, and I'll be new baptized;
> Henceforth I never will be Romeo.

> (II, ii, 49–51)

There sometimes *are* 'new baptisms' in comedies of renewal and regeneration; but here, it is not an available option. Romeo would even like to get violent with his own name. What 'man' is he?

> By a name
> I know not how to tell thee who I am.
> My name, dear saint, is hateful to myself
> Because it is an enemy to thee.
> Had I it written, I would tear the word.

> (II, ii, 54–7)

1. I know that too much Derrida is the sort of thing that makes the British think twice about taking their holidays in France, but he has a remarkable meditation on the balcony scene, translated as 'Aphorism Countertime', which may be found in *Acts of Literature* (1992).

Not possible, either. Names are not detachable and eradic-
able; but, rather, somehow deeply implanted, at once everywhere and nowhere within us. When, later, Romeo hears how
Juliet has fallen down, weeping and calling his name, he
would like to be even more violent:

> As if that name,
> Shot from the deadly level of a gun,
> Did murder her; as that name's cursèd hand
> Murdered her kinsman. O, tell me, friar, tell me,
> In what vile part of this anatomy
> Doth my name lodge? Tell me, that I may sack
> The hateful mansion.

(III, iii, 102–8)

and he actually tries to stab himself. But, of course, something
as non-corporeal, im-material, as a name is quite beyond any
amputation. You can't kill *that* 'lodger' without killing the
mansion. On the other hand, in the social arena, a name can
be as lethal as a gun. And that is the point. The young lovers
would somehow like to get out (back? up? beyond?), to a non-
social realm where names no longer (or don't yet) matter, or
even obtain. But, as they quickly discover, the only way there
is by killing the mansion. Which, shortly, they do. Among
other things, this play may be seen as exploring the tragedy
latent in the naming process itself.

When Romeo snaps out of his callow 'driveling love' for
Rosaline, Mercutio congratulates him.

Now art thou sociable, now art thou Romeo; now art thou what thou
art, by art as well as by nature.

(II, iv, 93–5)

He means, simply enough, that Romeo is now 'sociable'
because, in addition to groaning away on the reproductive
side of his being, as nature prompts, he is also, now, composed,
clever, and witty, as culture promotes. As it happens, Romeo
would dearly like to be de-socialized altogether, as we have
seen. But Mercutio's words have a greater pregnancy for the
play – for Shakespeare – as a whole. Art, art, art, art, *by art*, 'as
well as by nature' – in the last great comic-romances, Shakespeare will show art and nature working together so that

characters can more truly become what they really are, or
'art'. Here, we may say that Romeo is rendered most truly and
fully *Romeo* by, in, and through Shakespeare's transforming
and perpetuating art, in addition to whatever, by nature, he
'sociably' was in Verona. Of course, from the point of view of
the inhabitants of Verona, left stunned and bereft in the
gloomy after-vacancy which follows the deaths of the young
lovers, it is all unmitigated tragedy. Earth-bound critics may
duly, dutifully join them there. But Verona is just exactly
where Romeo and Juliet no longer wanted to be, and they
have made a 'triumphant' and lightning/enlightening escape.
From the stellar perspective, it *is* a form of 'comedy'.

*

A MIDSUMMER NIGHT'S DREAM

> Through the house give *glimmering* light,
> By the dead and drowsy fire
>
> (V, i, 393-4)
>
> These things seem small and *undistinguishable*,
> Like far-off mountains turnèd into clouds.
>
> (IV, i, 190-91)

The two words which I have italicized occur more than once
in *A Midsummer Night's Dream* – and *in no other play by
Shakespeare*. I want them to, as it were, hover over the following
discussion.

*

When Romeo mentions to Mercutio 'I dreamt a dream
tonight', his sceptical, down-to-earth friend is dismissive –
'dreamers often lie'. Romeo prefers to keep a more open mind
about the possible veracity of dreams – 'In bed asleep, while
[= sometimes] they do dream things true.' This sets Mercutio
careering off on what is certainly the most surprising speech of
the play.

> O, then I see Queen Mab hath been with you.
> She is the fairies' midwife, and she comes
> In shape no bigger than an agate stone

> On the forefinger of an alderman,
> Drawn with a team of little atomies
> Over men's noses as they lie asleep;
> Her wagon spokes made of long spinners' legs,
> The cover, of the wings of grasshoppers;
> Her traces, of the smallest spider web;
> Her collars, of the moonshine's wat'ry beams;
> Her whip, of cricket's bone; the lash of film;
> Her wagoner, a small gray-coated gnat,
> ...
> Her chariot is an empty hazelnut,
> Made by the joiner squirrel or old grub,
> Time out o' mind the fairies' coachmakers.
> And in this state she gallops night by night
> Through lovers' brains, and then they dream of love ...
>
> *(Romeo and Juliet, I, iv, 49–71)*

and so on for another twenty-plus lines, all on the magical, and often mischievous, effects of Queen Mab and her entourage on human sleepers. Romeo cannot make head or tail of what he is saying – 'Thou talk'st of nothing'; and Mercutio, dismissive once more, agrees – 'True, I talk of dreams', as though he has made his point (I, v, 95–6). Romeo's bewilderment is entirely understandable. 'Mab' is Cymric (or Welsh) for 'small child', and Mercutio's 'little atomies', in their insect tiny-ness, their filminess, their domiciliation in the gossamer of spider webs and the 'watery beams' of moonshine, are undoubtedly British, primarily Celtic, fairies. They certainly have no place in Renaissance Verona. But what, then, are they – what is an English wood – doing, in *A Midsummer Night's Dream*, just outside ancient Athens?

The simplest, most general answer would be to suggest that Shakespeare wants to effect an accommodation, an assimilation of the ancient world of pagan, classical legend into the local, domestic world of folklore and popular, vernacular superstition (combining an extensive literary heritage with age-old English customs) – thus, perhaps, forging a new mythology, at least for the occasion (which was probably a noble wedding in a great house). Certainly, the occasion – the wedding(s) towards the consummation of which ('Lovers, to bed') the play moves – is more important than the plot, which is rudimentary, or, we might more appropriately say, as light as gossamer, as transparent as film, as solid as moonbeam. C. L. Barber is at his festive best on this play, and he shows how Shakespeare 'in developing a May game at length to express the will in nature that is consummated in marriage, brings out underlying magical meanings of the ritual'. The May game – the bringing in of summer – traditionally involved the whole community, and moved from the town, out to the woods or grove, and back again (as this play moves from palace to forest and back to palace). During these May games, the young men and maids 'ran gadding over night to the woods ... where they spend the whole night in pleasant pastimes', said Puritan Stubbes (as happens in the play, even if the pastimes are not unequivocally 'pleasant'). They might be presided over by a May king (Satan, as far as Stubbes was concerned), and there was also a Summer Lady, celebrating the most fertile time of the year. These popular games could be worked up into more sophisticated pageants to be presented at aristocratic entertainments. Midsummer Night itself was thought to be a magic time when spirits might be abroad, and young minds could be touched with madness ('midsummer madness', as Olivia expressly calls it in *Twelfth Night*). Maying and Midsummer could be easily conflated since, as Barber shows, people went Maying at various times. 'This Maying can be thought of as happening on a midsummer night, even on Midsummer Eve itself, so that its accidents are complicated by the delusions of a magic time ... The Maying is completed when Oberon and Titania with their trains come into the great chamber to bring the blessings of fertility. They are at once common and special, a May king and queen making their good luck visit to the manor house, and a pair of country gods, half-English and half-Ovid, come to bring their powers in tribute to great lords and ladies.'

Ovid. Jonathan Bate calls this play 'Shakespeare's most luminous *imitatio* of Ovid ... a displaced dramatization of Ovid'. Ovid, and the world of *Metamorphoses*, are everywhere in this play: in the gods, the characters, the animals; in the flowers and the woods; in the light and the water; in the turmoils of love, the experience of transformation, the unavoidability of change; in the language, the allusions, the symbols; in the very air they all breathe – *everywhere*. But it is Ovid refracted through Shakespeare, and so made new, made different, redirected or 'turned' (I'll come back to this important word). The most engagingly obvious signal of alteration is given by Helena, as, in a most unmaidenly way, she desperately pursues Demetrius:

> Run when you will, the story shall be changed:
> Apollo flies, and Daphne holds the chase
>
> (II, i, 230–31)

The most obvious substantial incorporation of Ovid is, of course, the play put on by Bottom and the 'mechanicals' – 'Pyramus and Thisby'. As performed by these worthy lads, it is Ovid with a difference indeed. A possible reason for this reversion of Ovid in Shakespeare's play, may become clear later. But here, I want to say something about the setting of the story in Ovid's own work. It is one of the stories told by Minyas' daughters while they are spinning. But this is not wholly innocent spinning. A feast day for the god Bacchus has been decreed, and all the Theban women have been ordered to leave their usual housework to celebrate rites in his honour. But Alcithoe, a daughter of Minyas, denies the divinity of Bacchus – 'rash girl' – and she and her sisters blaspheme against the god: they 'remain indoors and mar the festival/By their untimely spinning . . . ' Since a crucial figure in Shakespeare's play is a weaver, this is important: perhaps his 'weaving' will be more timely.

The girls tell three stories – including 'Pyramus and Thisbe' – to pass away the time while spinning, but their blasphemy is duly punished. This is what happens, in 'The Daughters of Minyas Transformed' (Book IV, 398–418), as translated by A. D. Melville:

> The tale was done, but still the girls worked on,
> Scorning the god, dishonouring his feast,
> When suddenly the crash of unseen drums
> Clamoured, and fifes and jingling brass
> Resounded, and the air was sweet with scents
> Of myrrh and saffron, and – beyond belief! –

The weaving all turned green, the hanging cloth
Grew leaves of ivy, part became a vine,
What had been threads formed tendrils, from the warp
Broad leaves unfurled, bunches of grapes were seen,
Matching the purple with their coloured sheen.
  And now the day was spent, the hour stole on
When one would doubt if it were light or dark,
Some lingering light at night's vague borderlands.
Suddenly the whole house began to shake,
The lamps flared up, and all the rooms were bright
With flashing crimson fires, and phantom forms
Of savage beasts of prey howled all around.

In Shakespeare's play, Theseus says to his Amazon bride-to-be:

Hippolyta, I wooed thee with my sword,
And won thy love, doing thee injuries;
But I will wed thee in another key,
With pomp, with triumph, and with reveling.

(I, i, 16–19)

The passage from Ovid is one of his great transformation scenes, and, like all his metamorphoses, it is injurious and marked by violence (like Theseus' early wooing). Shakespeare will give us this quintessential Ovid, but *in another key*. The clamouring drums and jingling brass will be quietened into lullabies and soft, sweet music; the purple grapes will be exchanged for a love-flower; the flaring lamps will be dimmed to 'glimmering'; and the savage beasts will be miniaturized into harmlessness (hedgehogs, spiders, beetles, worms, snails). The time of day will, however, remain the same – 'at night's vague borderlands' ('*dubiae confinia noctis*'), when things are 'undistinguishable'. As usual, where Ovid's transformations are invariably downward and lethal, Shakespeare's are, ultimately, upward and benign. His play concludes with blessings and purifications, while Ovid's tale ends in squeakings and hauntings. Minyas' daughters were transformed into *bats*; and it is perhaps worth noting that, while there are any number of small nocturnal animals in Shakespeare's wood, 'haunting … squeaking' bats (Ovid's words) have been banished, or 'turned forth'. As when Theseus gives the order:

Awake the pert and nimble spirit of mirth,
Turn melancholy forth to funerals

(I, i, 13–14)

That is the first 'turn' of the play. The first of many – as it turns out.

(It is perhaps interesting to note that, in Ovid, 'The Daughters of Minyas' follows immediately on from the concluding story of Book III, which is 'Pentheus and Bacchus'. Pentheus was another who defied the god, and he is punished by being torn to pieces by the Theban women – including his mother – thus being violently transformed into scattered scraps, or nothing at all. This story also contains one of the other great transformation scenes in Ovid, when the sailors who are supposed to be taking the child Bacchus to Naxos, change course, thinking they can sell the pretty child into slavery. The ship is becalmed, and is slowly thronged with ivy and vines, and panthers and savage beasts – just like the house of Minyas. Golding's translation of this scene inspired Ezra Pound to one of his greatest passages of poetry, in Canto II – 'void air taking pelt ... lynx-purr amid sea', marvellous line after marvellous line. What both stories address, and dramatize, is the potentially terrifying – as well as the savagely beautiful – power there is in the Dionysiac forces, and how foolish and dangerous it is to think they can be ignored, defied, or denied. How, in the broadest sense, we deal with Dionysus, the Dionysiac in all its guises, seems to me to be a generative concern close to the centre of all art. Be that as it may, I am sure that Shakespeare is very much aware of these Dionysiac monitory fables hovering just outside the edges of his own play, and I think that the implicit answer of his play is that the wisest way to recognize and accommodate Dionysus–Bacchus, is through, by, in – marriage.)

The main 'spinner' in Ovid's work is another god- or goddess-defying girl – Arachne. Challenging Pallas to a tapestry-weaving competition, she is duly transformed into a spider – an *animal* weaver – as punishment for her presumption. The different tapestries the two women weave in the competition are instructive. Pallas depicts the 'twelve great gods', imposing punishing metamorphoses on hapless humans.

INTRODUCTION

By way of response, Arachne depicts what Melville calls 'a hectic anthology of divine delinquency at the expense of deluded women' (some twenty of them) – gods *using* metamorphosis to abuse mortals. Angry Pallas tears up the tapestry (showing those 'crimes of heaven'), and turns Arachne into a spider; yet, at the end, Arachne 'as a spider, still/Weaving her web, pursues her former skill'. In her reduced form, she still keeps her web-spinning skills alive; in this, she is a key image or embodiment of the human spider-artist. And, in case you are wondering about the possible relevance of all this, I shall be suggesting that we think of Bottom the weaver as a version of Arachne the spinner – *in another key*. I quote now from Leonard Barkan's indispensable book, *The Gods Made Flesh*. 'It requires no great leap of the imagination to see in Arachne's tapestry all the elements of Ovid's own poetic form in the *Metamorphoses*, which is, after all, a poem that eschews a clear narrative structure and rather creates a finely woven fabric of stories related via transformation.' This, as it happens, is just what Shakespeare does in *A Midsummer Night's Dream* (and, as Arachne to Ovid, so Bottom to Shakespeare – but more of that later).

A Midsummer Night's Dream is like *Love's Labor's Lost* in having no one particular primary source – it makes them unique among Shakespeare's plays. But whereas *Love's Labor's Lost* has virtually no sources at all – a hint here, an echo there – *A Midsummer Night's Dream* draws *quite clearly* on perhaps as many as a dozen different works from the far and near of previous literature. It is Shakespeare's contribution – his genius – to select, arrange, combine, fuse, sew seamlessly together; these elements, fragments, patches, strains, skeins; extracted, snipped, cut, siphoned, and unwound from other works. As the admirable Arden editor, Harold Brooks, says, 'Shakespeare *weaves* together material from a whole series of sources' (my italics). He is not alone among editors in using that metaphor, and I confess I find it striking that they seem not provoked to pursue the possibly extra-pertinent implications it might have in connection with a play in which one of the main players – take him however you will – *is* a weaver.

A proper study of these multifarious sources would take half a book. Bullough, as usual, lays them out impeccably – I must briefly summarize (must – because an important part of the play is in the weaving). From Chaucer's *Knightes Tale* Shakespeare takes Theseus, the triumphant conqueror, happily married to Hippolyta (he also takes a pair of unhappy young lovers fighting in a wood). From Pluto's *Life of Theseus* he takes Theseus the law-giver and bringer of social order; but he deleted (almost entirely, though not quite) Theseus the notorious rapist and ravisher, and substituted for this a monogamous Theseus based on the parallel *Life of Romulus*. The fairies come, in part, from Lyly's *Endimion*, where they both pinch and kiss; and in part, of course, from the rural air he had breathed (and, possibly, Welsh lore he knew about). Puck looks back to a Cornish earth demon, 'pukka' or 'pixy'; and is identified by Shakespeare with Robin Goodfellow, who was something between a house-fairy and 'the national practical joker'. 'Titania' comes straight from bathing in a pool in Ovid, where it is another name for Diana ('Titania' does not appear in Golding's translation, a fact frequently adduced to show that Shakespeare read Ovid in the original). Oberon comes from a romance entitled *Huon of Bordeaux*, translated by Lord Berners before 1533. He is, as in Shakespeare, an Eastern fairy from the farthest steep of India. He is king of a wood and has 'marvelous' power over nature, though in the end 'all is but fantasie and enchauntments'. Oberon and Titania together owe something to the figures of Pluto and Proserpina in Chaucer's *Merchant's Tale*, where they sit in a garden and discuss the wayward sexual behaviour of the mortals they are watching. Shakespeare removes their divine detachment, and makes them pretty wayward themselves, but they are still fairy gods.

In this fairy-connection, a book by Reginald Scot entitled *The Discoverie of Witchcraft* (1584) should be mentioned. Scot ferociously attacks all belief in fairies, witches, and magic transformations in general. 'Whosoever beleeveth, that anie creature can be made or changed into better or woorsse, or transformed into anie other shape, or into anie other similitude, by anie other than by God hiself the creator of all things, without all doubt is an infidell, and woorsse than a pagan …

heretofore Robin Goodfellow, and Hob gobblin were as terrible, and also as credible to the people, as hags and witches be now: and inn time to come, a witch will be as much derided and contemned, and as plainlie perceived, as the illusion and knaverie of Robin goodfellow.' But, as is often the case with would-be castigators and casters-out, he provides a great deal of fascinating information, with vivid examples, of just what he is seeking to deride and discredit – in this case, fairies, elves, imps, changelings, dwarfs, spirits, witches, and magical (demonic) transformations. The less censorious, and rurally derived, Shakespeare must have loved it. Curiously, Scot gives details of a trick for setting 'an asses head upon a mans shoulders'; but the 'translation' of Bottom certainly owes more to *The Golden Ass* of Apuleius, which had been translated by Aldington in 1566. His amorous adventures – while an ass – with a princess, prefigure Bottom's amazing experience with Titania (I think there is also an echo of Pasiphae and her beloved bull). Elsewhere, Brooks finds traces of Spenser's *Shepheardes Calender*, and an overlooked debt to Seneca, particularly his *Hippolytus* (the hunting scene; Phaedra's self-abasement in love – like Helena's; and the nurse's invocation to three-formed Hecate – who also presides in Shakespeare's play). And the 'entertainment' which concludes the play, when all the various strands have been deftly woven together, is Ovid's 'Pyramus and Thisbe' – in, of course, another key. We are, inevitably, back with Ovid.

One of the alternative entertainments offered by Philostrate to Theseus is 'The battle with the Centaurs, to be sung/By an Athenian eunuch to the harp' (V, i, 44-5). 'We'll none of that' says Theseus quickly – and very understandably. Theseus took part in that battle which broke out at the marriage of Pirithous and Hippodame (Ovid, Book XII), and it must be the most disastrous and violent wedding on record, as some three hundred particularly bloody lines describe. Theseus acquitted himself honourably, as befits a hero; but it would hardly be an auspicious event to rehearse on *this* wedding day, just while they are waiting to consummate their marriages. (The figure of a eunuch would be no more auspicious on such an occasion!) But we noticed that there was the sign of the

Centaur displayed at the first inn in Shakespeare's works, and, here again, the figure of the half-animal, half-man (as opposed to the eunuch who is half-man, half nothing at all) has a general, if oblique, relevance to this play as well. Specifically, it refers us back to Bottom who, but recently, was half-ass, half-man. But it might remind us of another 'monstrous hybrid beast' in Ovid – the Minotaur (Book VIII). Minotaur, at the centre of his labyrinth or maze, was finally killed by Theseus, with the aid of Ariadne (whom he then abandoned, but whom Bacchus subsequently comforted and 'stellified'!). Bottom, also referred to as a 'monster', is somewhere at the centre of *this* play, which is also a 'maze', full of 'amazed' people. The difference is that, here, Theseus does no slaying; and Bottom, unmonstered, ends, in his own way, triumphant. Ovid in another key.

In Ovid's account of the story of Pyramus and Thisbe, the lovers agree to meet beneath a tree 'laden with snow-white fruit, a mulberry'. When Pyramus, thinking Thisbe has been devoured by a lion, fatally stabs himself, this is what happens:

> And as he lay outstretched his blood leaped high,
> As when a pipe bursts where the lead is flawed
> And water through the narrow hissing hole
> Shoots forth long leaping jets that cut the air.
> The berries of the tree, spattered with blood,
> Assumed a sable hue; the blood-soaked roots
> Tinged with purple dye the hanging fruits.

And, as a result, 'the mulberry retains its purple hue'. Quince and company, perhaps knowing their limitations, wisely do not attempt to re-enact this part of the story. But Shakespeare has a use for it, suitably changed, in *his* play. When Titania refuses to part with the changeling child, Oberon plans his revenge, and summons Puck for an errand. He recalls a magic moment involving mermaids, dolphins, civil seas, mad stars, and a maid's music:

> That very time I saw, but thou couldst not,
> Flying between the cold moon and the earth,
> Cupid all armed. [Puck couldn't see him, perhaps because he

was Cupid – certainly Puck is as much Cupid as he is Robin
Goodfellow.] A certain aim he took
At a fair vestal thronèd by the west,
And loosed his love shaft smartly from his bow,
As it should pierce a hundred thousand hearts.
But I might see young Cupid's fiery shaft
Quenched in the chaste beams of the wat'ry moon,
And the imperial vot'ress passèd on,
In maiden meditation, fancy-free.
Yet marked I where the bolt of Cupid fell.
It fell upon a little western flower,
Before milk-white, now purple with love's wound,
And maidens call it love-in-idleness.
Fetch me that flow'r; the herb I showed thee once:
The juice of it on sleeping eyelids laid
Will make or man or woman madly dote
Upon the next live creature that it sees.

(II, i, 155–72)

This play is much concerned with 'doting' (more or less mad
as the case may be – 'dote' occurs more often than in any other
play), to be seen against the background of the sane and
steady love of the mature figures, Theseus and Hippolyta. The
play ends with the marriages about to be consummated,
when, presumably, the bed sheets which were 'before milk-
white', like the flower, will soon also be 'purple with love's
wound'. And the laying on sleeping eyes of this love juice, is
seen to play a crucial, instrumental role in all the doting
madness (interestingly, Shakespeare uses a variety of different
verbs for the application of the juice to the eyes – from the
religious 'anoint' and the artistic 'streak', to the more downright 'sink' and 'crush'). Puck is guilty of putting the love juice
in the wrong eyes, but that is appropriate too, since Cupid is
blind, and love (sudden overwhelming attraction) strikes
randomly. That is the point to Shakespeare's 'metamorphosed' etiology. The white mulberry empurpled by the blood
of Pyramus in Ovid, has become the white pansy hit by 'young
Cupid's fiery shaft' which missed its intended virginal target.
William Carroll makes the very nice point that the pansy thus
becomes 'a deflowered flower'. He points to the wonderful
aptness of the malapropism uttered by Bottom–Pyramus

when, lamenting what he takes to be the death of Thisby, he says – 'lion vile hath here deflow'red my dear' (V, i, 293 – presumably he intends 'devoured'); for, as Carroll says, given the impending marriages, defloration is necessarily one of the play's main subjects, however understated or obliquely approached. Another lyric justification for having the love juice come from 'Cupid's *flower*'. It is worth noting that there is a flower which has the power to counter Cupid's, restoring the blind besotted to clear-eyed chastity. It is called 'Dian's bud' and this, too, is to hand for Oberon, king of the wood. As when he administers a curing restorative to Titania:

> Be as thou wast wont to be;
> See as thou wast wont to see.
> Dian's bud o'er Cupid's flower
> Hath such force and blessèd power.

> (IV, i, 74–7)

(We might recall the importance of good and bad herbs – medicine, poison, ambiguous 'restoratives' – in *Romeo and Juliet*.) These magically propertied flowers represent – figure forth – the uncomprehended force and untraceable power which causes love (we had perhaps better talk of desire and infatuation) to suddenly 'flare' up, and as suddenly to 'melt' away. When Demetrius is trying to explain the abrupt shifts and swerves in his passional attractions, he casts around:

> But, my good lord, I wot not by what power –
> But by some power it is . . .

> (IV, i, 168–9)

– that is actually, by way of explanation, about as far as he – perhaps as any of us – will ever get.

The juice is applied to the eyes because that is where all the 'dotings' start; this kind of sudden infatuation appearing as caused by (or intimately related to) an impairment, a dis- order, indeed a disease, of the eye. The involvement of the 'eye' in young love was prominent enough in *Love's Labor's Lost*, where the word occurred fifty-two times. But in this play it occurs fifty-six times (top score in Shakespeare's plays), and everything seems to come down to how we look, and how we see. Among the young courtly lovers, it is the men whose eyes malfunction as their affections go awry (as usual in Shakespeare, the young women hold firm); while among the fairies, it is Queen Titania whose seeing is so sorely and humiliatingly afflicted. (We are to infer that Theseus and Hippolyta are beyond such ocular madness and have achieved the Arnoldian vision, seeing life steadily and seeing it whole.) Helena effectively announces a major theme of the play in the first scene:

> Things base and vile, holding no quantity,
> Love can transpose to form and dignity.
> Love looks not with the eyes, but with the mind,
> And therefore is winged Cupid painted blind.
> Nor hath Love's mind of any judgment taste;
> Wings, and no eyes, figure unheedy haste:
> And therefore is Love said to be a child,
> Because in choice he is so oft beguiled.
>
> (I, i, 232–9)

It is the 'transposing' power of Cupidian love, along with its 'unheedy haste', which will be demonstrated in this play. We should note the number of verbs in the play carrying the prefix 'trans-': transpose, translate, transform, transfigure, and (perhaps most important), transport. For '**trans-**', the OED gives 'across, beyond, on or to the other side, into a different state or place' – which will do for now. When Oberon goes around near the end, setting things and people in their proper states and places, he applies his 'liquor' whose 'virtuous property' can make 'eyeballs roll with wonted sight' (III, ii, 369) – presumably, before the Cupidian glaze and slant came over them. Of Titania he says 'I will undo/This hateful imperfection of her eyes' (IV, i, 65–6), and promises:

> And then I will her charmèd eye release
> From monster's view, and all things shall be peace.
>
> (III, ii, 376–7)

As Puck says over the sleeping lovers, when their eyes have been duly corrected:

> And the country proverb known,
> That every man should take his own,

In your waking will be shown.
    Jack shall have Jill;
    Nought shall go ill;
That man shall have his mare again, and all shall be well.

                                                    (III, ii, 457–63)

That is the conclusion towards which the play moves. Bemused eyes are 'released' from all deformities and 'monstrosities' of vision (or vision of 'monsters'); all shall go well, and all things shall be at peace; and, unlike the stalled inconclusiveness which ends the 'dashed' wooing games of *Love's Labor's Lost*, here there is the certainty that Jack *shall* have his Jill. In this sense, at least, *A Midsummer Night's Dream* does 'end like an old play'.

But not before we have witnessed the confusions and 'transpositions' precipitated by doting infatuations touched with midsummer madness. The effect on the discrete but converging worlds of the courtiers, the fairies, and the mechanicals, is rather as Theseus describes 'a tangled chain' – there is 'nothing impaired, but all disordered' (V, i, 126). The 'disordering' is not exclusively due to the operations of the love juice. The blocking, or deflecting power of the paternal prohibition (familiar in comedy since comedy began – it is the negative which provokes the play, driving young love to stratagems of circumvention), comes into operation immediately, and effectively sends all the young lovers away from the palace and into the fairy-haunted wood. Egeus, father of Hermia, bursts into the first scene 'full of vexation'. He has promised Hermia to Demetrius, and accuses Lysander of having 'bewitched' her and 'stol'n the impression of her fantasy' (I, i, 32). It is an arresting charge, implying that he has, with all sorts of tricks and magics, corrupted (dis-figured, trans-figured?) her 'fantasy'; and, as Frank Kermode noted, one way and another, 'the disorders of fantasy (imagination) are the main topic of the play'. Egeus continues:

    With cunning hast thou filched my daughter's heart,
    Turned her obedience, which is due to me,
    To stubborn harshness.

                                                    (I, i, 36–8)

He then proceeds to set a fair example of 'stubborn harshness' himself, by begging 'the ancient privilege of Athens' by which he can 'dispose' of his daughter as he wishes – which here means, her obedience, or her death 'according to our law'. Theseus, the responsible ruler, reluctantly backs him up, telling Hermia that she must obey her father:

> Or else the law of Athens yields you up –
> Which by no means we may extenuate –
> To death, or to a vow of single life.
>
> (I, i, 119–21)

Near the end, when Egeus again cries 'I beg the law, the law', Theseus simply brushes him (and 'the law') aside – 'Egeus, I will overbear your will' (IV, i, 182). As usual, the 'unextenuatable' inflexibilities of 'the law' in Act I have, by some other 'law' of comedy, mysteriously melted away by the end of play. We are, somehow, in a different place. Trans-ported.

Egeus maintains that Lysander has worked on Hermia, and 'turned her obedience'. 'Turn' – comes from ancient words implying 'rotation' or 'deviation from a course'. If you just think of some of the compounds – turncoat, turnover (kind of tart, amount of business), turnstile, turn-up (on a garment, for the books, what a bad penny always does) – you can begin to get a sense of what an indispensable word it is concerning human doings and dealings and makings; and how wide-ranging are its ramifications and applications. And, of course, it is a simple word for 'metamorphosis' – when someone turns into someone, or something, else. It is such an unobtrusive, familiar word, that it can easily slip past unnoticed. And yet, this play 'turns' on it. There are, as I see it, three major deployments of the word, but when you start to look, you find that the play is full of turns and turnings. Hermia complains that love 'hath turned a heaven unto a hell' (I, i, 207), so she and Lysander resolve to 'from Athens turn away our eyes' (I, i, 218). Puck promises to pursue the frightened mechanicals through the woods, 'Like horse, hound, hog, bear, fire, at every turn' (III, i, 112). Dear, imperturbable, self-sufficient Bottom invariably has 'enough to serve mine own turn' (III, i, 152). To the drugged eyes of Demetrius, 'snow ... turns to a crow' set next to the whiteness of Helena's hand (III, ii, 142); while poor Helena simply thinks they are all laughing at her 'when I turn my back' (III, ii, 238). Oberon (whose name may be related to that of Auberon, god of the red light of dawn, in old French) sometimes makes 'sport' with 'Morning's love' as the first beam of the sun plays on Neptune's domain, and 'Turns into yellow gold his salt green streams' (III, ii, 392 – part of the everywhere ongoing alchemy of nature). When it comes to judgments – say, as between players – 'A mote will turn the balance, which Pyramus, which Thisby, is the better' (V, i, 320). And, if things can turn, so they can re-turn – as when the sobered and clarified Demetrius says of his heart 'to Helen is it home returned' (III, ii, 172).

More notably, when Oberon realizes that Puck has put the love juice in the wrong eyes, he says:

> Of thy misprision must perforce ensue
> Some true love turned, and not a false turned true.
>
> (III, ii, 91–2)

The 'misprisions' of love itself, when true, turns inexplicably to false, and false turns magically to true, are a central and animating concern of the play. When the young lovers wake up out of their night's madness, and find themselves, like Oberon and Titania, 'new in amity' (IV, i, 90), they cannot, looking back, quite believe that it was all real. Even now, they don't know if they are truly awake, or still asleep. One imagines them rubbing their eyes.

> *Demetrius.* These things seem small and undistinguishable,
>   Like far-off mountains turnèd into clouds.
> *Helena.* Methinks I see these things with parted eye,
>   When everything seems double.
>
> (IV, i, 190–93)

Mountains and clouds are both equally *real* – we can see them in the same landscape. But, where mountains are the very image of the solid, the immovable, the adamantine, clouds are definitively non-substantial; of ever drifting, shifting outline; self-dissipatingly vaporous – they seem like brief compressions of air, as opposed to the great compactions of the earth. What can 'turn' mountains into clouds? Distance? A trick of the eye? A poet's metaphor? Any of these can effect the metamorphosis. You can see mountains; and then you can see them as clouds. The human eye is like that – it can be 'parted' and 'see double'. Mountains–clouds: so, likewise, humans–animals, humans–fairies, humans–legends, humans–gods. There is a state of vision – it may only be brief – in which all these become 'undistinguishable'; in which the world, even at its heaviest, becomes nebulous, diaphanous, swimmingly dream-like. In this play – which takes place in silvery, watery moonlight, and glimmering starlight which turns dew to 'liquid pearl', and in which things can merge and melt, dissolve and change – Shakespeare brings about this state of vision in the spectators, who are kept, at once, rapt and awake.

One last turn – apt enough phrase for a performing art. In a famous speech at the start of the last Act, Theseus expresses his scepticism concerning the young lovers' 'strange' experiences during the midsummer night in the forest. In the process, he generalizes his reservations about the activities of the human imagination.

> I never may believe
> These antique fables, nor these fairy toys.
> Lovers and madmen have such seething brains,
> Such shaping fantasies, that apprehend
> More than cool reason ever comprehends.
> The lunatic, the lover and the poet
> Are of imagination all compact.
> One sees more devils than vast hell can hold,
> That is the madman. The lover, all as frantic,
> Sees Helen's beauty in a brow of Egypt.
> The poet's eye, in a fine frenzy rolling,
> Doth glance from heaven to earth, from earth to heaven;
> And as imagination bodies forth
> The forms of things unknown, the poet's pen
> *Turns them to shapes*, and gives to airy nothing
> A local habitation and a name.

> (V, i, 2–17, my italics)

Commentators have noted that the speech begins with Theseus saying, effectively – to start with, I don't believe in *me*; since of course *he* is pre-eminently a figure of 'antique fable', and a creation of that human imagination he goes on to deprecate and dismiss. Shakespeare is certainly having his fun here. But there is a serious issue. Shakespeare knew very well that the world of 'antique fable', or classical myth, was the Elizabethans' indispensable heritage – as it is ours. Christianity had, of course, intervened, and there were plenty of Christian apologists who were ready to dismiss all those 'antique fables' as childish nonsense or pagan iniquity – and a good deal more vehemently than Theseus. Shakespeare knew, of course, that when it came to products of the human imagination, questions of 'belief' were a good deal more complex and subtle than mere orthodoxy could comprehend. The poet may have the same sort of high-temperature imagination as the lunatic and the lover, but they simply 'see' (devils and beauties), whereas the poet intuits 'the forms of things unknown' and *then* 'turns them to shapes'. So *we* can see them, and share the vision. There is a hint here of the workman at his lathe; and, if we make *that* a metaphor, we can say that art is, indeed, just such a 'turning'. Another artist who clearly saw that art was a sort of 'turning' was Henry James. *The Turn of the Screw* – one of his most enigmatic works – is narrated, mainly, by a governess who is herself a (frustrated) lover, something of an (uncertified) lunatic, and (perhaps more than she knows) a poet, or creative artist. The word 'turn' features constantly in her narration, in all sorts of contexts; and, transcribing the moment when, to her mind, she first saw one of the figures haunting the house, she writes – 'What arrested me on the spot ... was the sense that my imagination had, in a flash, turned real.' She proceeds to turn the 'things unknown' to written shapes, which have driven critics to distraction ever since. But, the imagination 'turned real' is what all great art gives us, and, as Shakespeare clearly saw, we can 'believe' in these 'turnings' in a way quite differently from what is demanded by religion or science. For certainly, there are more things in heaven and earth than the 'cool reason' invoked by Theseus can ever fully 'comprehend'. And, in her response to Theseus, Hippolyta has the better of it.

INTRODUCTION

> But all the story of the night told over,
> And all their minds transfigured so together,
> More witnesseth than fancy's images,
> And grows to something of great constancy;
> But, howsoever, strange and admirable.
>
> (V, i, 23–7)

'Constancy' is an important notion for Shakespeare (and the Elizabethans), and the question of whether there was, or could somehow be inculcated, any 'persistive constancy in men' (*Troilus and Cressida*), was one which, one way and another, he addressed throughout his plays (and, looking at the hapless oscillations of Lysander and Demetrius, not to mention sundry other males in Shakespeare, and the invariable 'constancy' of the women, the emphasis does have to be on *men*). Spenser's 'Mutabilitie Cantos' (at the end of *The Faerie Queene*, and certainly written in the same decade as Shakespeare's play, even though they did not appear until 1609), are written 'UNDER THE LEGEND OF CONSTANCIE', and they tell how the goddess Mutability (and *Change*) tries to lay claim to the whole realm of Nature, since every thing and every creature in it is 'tost, and *turned*, with continuall change' (my italics). *Nature* acknowledges the power of the claim, but has an answer:

> I well consider all that ye have sayd,
> And find that all things stedfastness doe hate
> And changed be: yet being rightly wayd
> They are not changed from their first estate;
> But by their change their being doe dilate:
> And *turning* to themselves at length againe,
> Doe worke their owne perfection so by fate:
> Then over them Change doth not rule and raigne;
> But they raigne over change, and doe their states maintaine.
>
> (Canto VII, 58, my italics)

That, we might say, is the hope or dream of the mutability-obsessed Elizabethans; that there would be a

> time when no more *Change* shall be,
> But stedfast rest of all things firmely stayd
> Upon the pillours of Eternity
>
> (Canto VIII – 'unperfite'!)

cxlvii

I am not suggesting that Hippolyta had anything so meta-physical in mind; indeed, it is not very clear what she *does* mean by the 'something of great constancy' which might grow from all the 'transfigurations' which have made up 'the story of the night' (pregnant phrase). Perhaps a 'strange and admirable' exemplary narrative of young love righted, which may have perennial relevance (and Shakespeare's play has proved to be 'something of great constancy'). Or perhaps she is referring to the 'great constancy' which is both symbolized and enacted in the marriages they have all just entered into after all the confused wooing; (solemnized marriage vows are perhaps the only earthly way of overcoming mutability and change in Shakespeare). Whatever, she sees more value in the 'story' than the anti-imaginative Theseus.

The spectacle of an order (a 'constancy'?) coming out of a confusion, is part of the larger frame and setting of the play. Since Oberon and Titania are, in some sort, gods of the elements, it is not surprising that their quarrel is reflected in larger natural turbulences and disasters – contagious fogs, overflowing rivers, drowned fields, rotting corn, starved flocks. Titania evokes at length a veritable wasteland of nature gone wrong:

> The nine men's morris is filled up with mud;
> And the quaint *mazes* in the wanton green,
> For lack of tread, are *undistinguishable*.
> . . .
> The seasons alter: hoary-headed frosts
> Fall in the fresh lap of the crimson rose,
> And on old Hiems' thin and icy crown
> An odorous chaplet of sweet summer buds
> Is, as in mockery, set. The spring, the summer,
> The childing autumn, angry winter, change
> Their wonted liveries; and the *mazed* world,
> By their increase, now knows not which is which.
> And this same progeny of evil comes
> From our debate, from our dissension;
> We are their parents and original.
>
> (II, i, 98–117, my italics)

It is the only time in the play when the word 'evil' is used.

None of the active *agents* – gods, heroes, mortals, fairies – is
'evil' (though Egeus is, necessarily, a bit of a stick). Traditional fairies could be malign; but, as Oberon expressly says,
'we are spirits of another sort'.

But Titania reminds us of the possibility of 'evil' in nature
itself. She graphically depicts a vision of chaos, inversion, and
confusion, in which things have become 'undistinguishable'
(this is *bad* undistinguishability), and there is no traceable way
out of the 'maze', or labyrinth (remembering the presence of
Theseus, and ass-headed Bottom in the depths of the forest). It
is, indeed, a 'mazed world'. But, with the help of the magic in
the story of the night, the lovers find their way out, and
'dissension' gives way to 'amity' – dawn brings intimations of
new harmonies. These are announced, or evoked, by Theseus
and Hippolyta, leading a hunting party into the forest.
Theseus first remarks on 'the music of my hounds' ('matched
in mouth like bells' – a beautiful image), and says to
Hippolyta:

> We will, fair Queen, up to the mountain's top,
> And mark the musical confusion
> Of hounds and echo in conjunction.
>
> (IV, i, 112–14)

This reminds Hippolyta of a time she went hunting with
Hercules and Cadmus, and the famous 'hounds of Sparta':

> Never did I hear
> Such gallant chiding; for, besides the groves,
> The skies, the fountains, every region near
> Seemed all one mutual cry. I never heard
> So musical a discord, such sweet thunder.
>
> (IV, i, 117–21)

This signifies the achievement of a *concordia discors* on all levels.
When discord starts to sound like music, and thunder yields a
sweetness, (and salt sea turns to fresh) – when the dogs start
barking as sweetly as bells; you may be sure that what Walt
Whitman called 'the primal sanities of earth' have begun to
reassert themselves, and nature has mysteriously started putting itself to rights. It is a perfectly appropriate end to a

comedy. But there is one more act, in which Quince and his men will put on *their* play.

*

Before that, Bottom has had *his* dream. Bottom is the only person in Shakespeare to undergo a 'literal' metamorphosis; not that he seems to notice any difference, apart from feeling 'marvellous hairy about the face'. He is also the only human in the play who 'literally' sees the fairies; though he talks to Peaseblossom, Cobweb, and Mustardseed as they 'do him courtesies', as easily as he does to Quince, Snug, and Francis Flute – even if he does find himself asking for 'a bottle of hay'. And, when it comes to acting, Bottom reveals himself to be an extreme 'literalist', albeit willing and eager to play every part. When the distractedly doting Titania swears how much she loves him, he seems not to be greatly surprised, though it can hardly be said to go to his head – human or asinine.

Methinks, mistress, you should have little reason for that. And yet, to say the truth, reason and love keep little company together nowadays; the more the pity, that some honest neighbors will not make them friends.

(III, i, 143–7)

You will hardly find more wisdom in the wood than that.

His encounter with the inexplicably doting Titania must, perforce, be an amazing one, for all his imperturbability. Though, of course, we can hardly follow them when Titania gives the order to her fairies – 'Tie up my lover's tongue, bring him silently' (III, i, 201) – and disappears with Bottom into the impenetrable silence of the darkened forest. In this connection, it is both instructive and amusing to see how critics have responded to the temptation to speculate on what happened next. Representing the 'no sex please' British school, Brooks, with honourable *pudeur*, was sure that nothing happened at all – dammit, a fellow wouldn't *deliberately* plan for his wife to go off and have sexual intercourse with someone else. Speaking from the 'a man's a man' American point of view, Carroll has no doubts: 'Titania is tired of Bottom's voice and wants him to perform'. In, boy. Looking with his darkened East European eye, Jan Kott can only imagine bestiality and nightmare – 'the monstrous ass is being raped by the poetic Titania, while she still keeps chattering about flowers ... ' I suppose it depends where you are born. But this, more and less, prurient speculation seems to me most extraordinarily to miss the point. What 'happened' belongs, crucially and precisely, in the realm of what Henry James called 'the unspecified' (by implication, the unspecifiable). It is a gap, a silence, an unrecuperable missingness – a mystery. It is a vital blank which we never can fill in – and nor should we try. If anything, the preliminary intimations are more Platonic than sexual:

> And I will purge thy mortal grossness so,
> That thou shalt like an airy spirit go.
>
> (III, i, 161–2)

But, as to what *happened* – why, even Bottom cannot tell us that. As he makes clear in his quite amazing (and amazed) speech upon waking:

I have had a most rare vision. I have had a dream, past the wit of man to say what dream it was. Man is but an ass, if he go about to expound this dream. Methought I was – there is no man can tell what. Methought I was – and methought I had – but man is but a patched fool if he will offer to say what methought I had. The eye of man hath not heard, the ear of man hath not seen, man's hand is not able to taste, his tongue to conceive, nor his heart to report, what my dream was. I will get Peter Quince to write a ballet of this dream. It shall be called 'Bottom's Dream,' because it hath no bottom; and I will sing it in the latter end of a play, before the Duke. Peradventure to make it the more gracious, I shall sing it at her death.

(IV, i, 207–22)

He has been, of a truth, 'transported'. Long before Rimbaud, Bottom has clearly experienced a '*déréglement du sens*'. Though, as many commentators have noted, the relevant voice behind this comes from I Corinthians:

But we speak the wisdom of God in a mystery, even the hidden wisdom, which God ordained before the world unto our glory:
Which none of the princes of this world knew. ...
But as it is written, Eye hath not seen, nor ear heard, neither have

entered into the heart of man, the things which God hath prepared
for them that love him.

(2:7–9)

If Shakespeare can mutate Ovid, Bottom can scramble St
Paul. But this is not simply more fun and parody. Bottom has
had a *vision*. In *The Golden Ass*, Apuleius is finally reprieved
from his ass's shape by Isis; he has a vision of the goddess, and
is initiated into her mysteries – which entails never speaking
about them. St Paul also had a visionary initiation into the
mysteries of the very religion he had persecuted. Both these
men were transformed after being vouchsafed an experience of
divine love; and we may assume that Bottom's vision is
something comparable. It is certainly no ordinary dream;
such as, we may say, the young lovers feel they have been
through. It is, rather, in Frank Kermode's words, '*oneiros* or
somnium; ambiguous, enigmatic, of high import'. Bottom is
very distinctly *not* a 'prince of the world'; that designation
more properly fits Theseus who, as we have seen, believes only
in reason, and speaks disparagingly of all mysteries. Bottom is
more like a holy fool – perhaps only the lowest (a man–ass) and
the most literal, can see the highest and most sublime ('a most
rare vision'). His ecstatic garbling of St Paul merely intimates
that such a vision is beyond speaking of; he speaks, only to say
he can't tell. ('Masters, I am to discourse wonders: but ask me
not what; for if I tell you, I am not true Athenian', IV, ii,
29–30 – 'true Athenian' may be a quiet smile to Plato, who
also recognized and respected the ineffable.) This is one
occasion for which the over-used aphorism which concludes
Wittgenstein's *Tractatus Logico-Philosophicus* is absolutely pertinent: 'What we cannot speak about we must pass over in
silence.' Or we might like to recall that marvellous moment in
Dostoevsky's *The Brothers Karamazov*, when Dmitri wakes up in
prison and says – 'Gentlemen, I have had a good dream ... '

*

Bottom is a weaver, *and* an actor (= a 'patched fool') who feels
sure he can play every role (male, female, animal); just as
Arachne would represent all the Ovidian stories in her

tapestry. In this, he is surely like Shakespeare himself. Peter Quince is the carpenter/stage manager who tries to hammer and nail the play into a structured shape; Snug, the joiner, does what he can to join rather incompatible identities together; but it is Bottom who weaves it all into a seamless fabric. (The Elizabethan theatre was closer to the workshop than to the court.) Bottom is, indeed, a literalist; but, in being so, he makes basic discoveries about the art, or 'devices', of theatrical representation. At the first rehearsal, Bottom runs over what he believes to be the problems of audience reaction. Pyramus commits suicide, and you can't have *that* on stage. But Bottom has a saving 'device': he will 'tell them that I Pyramus am not Pyramus, but Bottom the weaver' (III, i, 20–21). Just so: an actor both is and is not himself. Playing the lion is even trickier, since 'to bring in ... a lion among ladies, is a most dreadful thing'. Bottom sees the way:

Nay, you must name his name, and half his face must be seen through the lion's neck, and he himself must speak through, saying thus, or to the same defect – 'Ladies' – or, 'Fair ladies – I would wish you' – or, 'I would request you' – or, 'I would entreat you – not to fear, not to tremble: my life for yours. If you think I come hither as a lion, it were pity of my life. No, I am no such thing. I am a man as other men are.' And there indeed let him name his name, and tell them plainly, he is Snug the joiner.

(III, i, 36–46)

Barkan makes the nice observation that this image of Snug showing himself as half-man and half-lion, is reminiscent of familiar book illustrations to the *Metamorphoses* of characters 'in the midst of Ovidian transformation'. Certainly, Bottom is here 'laying bare', in the simplest terms, a basic truth about the curious relation between an *actor* and his role, and a *character* and his metamorphosis. The others see comparable problems in the matter of the requisite moonlight, and the dividing wall. 'Two hard things', they say – 'to bring the moonlight into a chamber', and 'you can never bring in a wall'. (Joking allusions, here, to the orchard wall leapt by Romeo in the almost entirely moonlit other play – Shakespeare can, of course, accomplish these 'effects' effortlessly.) Quince and Bottom realize that they must use someone 'to disfigure, or to present, the person of Moonshine ... [and] to signify Wall' (III, i, 61, 70). First steps in symbolism – something or someone can stand for, present, signify, *dis*-figure (that happens, too) something or someone else; Shakespeare shows Theatre itself beginning to learn its own essential 'devices'. Of course, honest, literal Bottom–Bottom, feeling his way, is ensuring that any chance of achieving convincing 'illusion' in their performance is hilariously destroyed. But that is all right, since Bottom–Shakespeare can effortlessly contain it all within the larger illusion with which he is holding us entranced. 'Pyramus and Thisby' in *A Midsummer Night's Dream* is a play-within-a-play with a difference. *Romeo and Juliet* – in another key!

But why *this* play for a wedding night entertainment? Here we need to think of 'exorcism', as first suggested, I think, by Barber. The play is announced in (unintentional) Romeo-ish oxymorons which prompt Theseus to comment:

> Merry and tragical? Tedious and brief?
> That is, hot ice and wondrous strange snow.
> How shall we find the concord of this discord?
>
> (V, i, 58–60)

The 'discord' of the performance only serves to emphasize and enhance the 'concord' achieved in the main play. And a self-destroyingly bad play about self-destructive young lovers may be no bad thing to enact on a wedding night – one 'botch' laughingly driving out another, as it were. And, just in case anyone present is lingeringly disturbed even by this minimally convincing (indeed, maximally *un*convincing) representation of the ill-fated young lovers, Bottom ('dead' Pyramus) leaps up and, in a last, triumphant, speech, announces that no one is dead – 'No, I assure you; the wall is down that parted their fathers' (V, i, 353–4). This is the final 'turn' that Shakespeare gives to his re-vision, re-version, of *Romeo and Juliet*.

The main image in this bridal-night play is not of death, but, fittingly, of fertility. Titania gives us one of the loveliest descriptions of pregnancy in Shakespeare (indeed, I cannot think of another). It concerns the 'little changeling boy' Oberon is demanding:

His mother was a vot'ress of my order,
And, in the spicèd Indian air, by night,
Full often hath she gossiped by my side,
And sat with me on Neptune's yellow sands,
Marking th' embarkèd traders on the flood;
When we have laughed to see the sails conceive
And grow big-bellied with the wanton wind;
Which she, with pretty and with swimming gait
Following – her womb then rich with my young squire –
Would imitate, and sail upon the land,
To fetch me trifles, and return again,
As from a voyage, rich with merchandise.
But she, being mortal, of that boy did die;
And for her sake do I rear up her boy,
And for her sake I will not part with him.

(II, i, 123–37)

The smudge of mortality again; even this play has to carry it. But, notwithstanding, this is a glorious celebration of joyous, female fecundity. The 'changeling boy', who is the unwitting cause of the most seriously disruptive contentions, is a strange, enigmatic figure. He is the obscure, small, absent object of desire, at the heart of the play. And not really a 'changeling', since that was the name given to a (usually deformed) fairy child, substituted, so superstition had it, for a sound human baby. But this child *is* human ('she, being mortal ... '). My guess – it can only be that – is that, in a play so concerned with turns and transformations of all kinds, Shakespeare wanted that word ringing mysteriously somewhere in the woody depths of the play – change, changing, changeling. Changelings all, perhaps. But, 'to a great constancy' too.

At the end, the forest fairies enter the palace (as, earlier, the palace had entered the forest). Puck comes on with a broom, to sweep away all possible present and future ills: Robin–Cupid as good house-fairy (in due course, he will be transformed into Ariel – but that is another play).

> Not a mouse
> Shall disturb this hallowed house

(V, i, 389–90)

Titania bestows blessings and 'fairy grace' upon the whole

place. Oberon performs a lustration 'with this field-dew consecrate' ('dew' is another word which occurs more often in this play than elsewhere), and wards off all possible defects from the children to come:

> And the blots of Nature's hand
> Shall not in their issue stand.
> Never mole, harelip, nor scar,
> Nor mark prodigious, such as are
> Despisèd in nativity,
> Shall upon their children be.

(V, i, 411–16)

Some commentators have seen the whole play as operating as an exorcism of the anxieties and fears associated with leaving the virginal security of childhood, and entering the unknown territory of active sexuality (hence the assorted, though temporary and harmless, terrors and 'monsters' in the woods – the 'spotted snakes' near the sleeping Titania; Hermia's dream of a serpent eating her heart; the threatened 'vile thing' which turns out, however, to be Bottom). Certainly, by the end, all fears and worries have been purged, blessed, washed, wished away. And the sleeping palace is bathed in the distinctive light of the play:

> Through the house give glimmering light,
> By the dead and drowsy fire

(V, i, 393–4)

Glow, gleam, glint, glisten, glitter, glim, glimpse, glimmer (d*im* g*le*am), *glimmering* – all from old Saxon and German 'gl-' words describing a light, a something, which shines brightly, shines faintly, shines briefly. This is the almost indescribable light in which we see the play. 'If we shadows have offended' says Puck, coming forward at the end – well, just tell yourselves you fell asleep and had a silly dream. But supposing they haven't 'offended', but, rather, ravished us – what kind of experience shall we say we had then? Everyone will find their own words – but certainly, there is no experience quite like it. Critics often say that *A Midsummer Night's Dream* is Shakespeare's most lyrical play; and that is no less than the truth.

INTRODUCTION

Indeed, I cannot see that a more magical play has ever been written.

King's College, Cambridge, 1994   Tony Tanner

SELECT BIBLIOGRAPHY

_____

BIOGRAPHY
The standard biography is now Samuel Schoenbaum, *William Shakespeare: A Documentary Life*, Oxford University Press, Oxford, 1975. A shortened version of this excellent volume was published in 1977. For those interested in Shakespearian mythology, Schoenbaum has also produced *Shakespeare's Lives*, Clarendon Press, Oxford, 1970, a witty dissection of the myriad theories concerning the playwright's identity and the authorship of the plays. Rather in the same vein is Anthony Burgess, *Shakespeare*, Penguin, London, 1972, a lively introduction to the presumed facts of the poet's life, enhanced by novelistic licence.

BIBLIOGRAPHY
Among the vast quantity of Shakespeare criticism it is probably only useful to list texts which are both outstanding and easily available. This I do below. For further information the serious student may consult the bibliographies of works listed. There are also three major journals which record the flow of critical work: the *Shakespeare Quarterly*; and the *Shakespeare Survey* and *Shakespeare Studies* which are published annually.

CRITICISM
The two indispensable Shakespearian critics are Johnson and Coleridge. Their dispersed comments are collected in *Samuel Johnson on Shakespeare*, ed., H. R. Woodhuysen, Penguin, London, 1989, and S. T. Coleridge, *Shakespearian Criticism*, two vols., Everyman's Library, London, 1960.

THE COMEDIES: GENERAL
BARBER, C. L., *Shakespeare's Festive Comedy*, 1959.
BARKAN, L., *The Gods Made Flesh*, 1986.
BATE, J., *Shakespeare and Ovid*, 1993.
BERRY, R., *Shakespeare's Comedies*, 1972.
BRADBROOK, M. C., *The Growth and Structure of Elizabethan Comedy*, 1955.
BROWN, J. R., (ed.), *Early Shakespeare* (Stratford-upon-Avon Studies), 1961.
—*Shakespearian Comedy* (Stratford-upon-Avon Studies), 1972.
CALDERWOOD, J. C., *Shakespeare's Metadrama*, 1971.
CARROLL, W. C., *The Metamorphoses of Shakespearian Comedy*, 1985.
CHAMPION, L., *The Evolution of Shakespeare's Comedies*, 1973.

CHARLTON, H. B., *Shakespearian Comedy*, 1938.
EDWARDS, P., *Shakespeare and the Confines of Art*, 1968.
EVANS, B., *Shakespeare's Comedies*, 1960.
FRYE, N., *A Natural Perspective*, 1965.
HERRICK, M. T., *Comic Theory in the Sixteenth Century*, 1950.
HUSTON, J. D., *Shakespeare's Comedies of Play*, 1981.
KAHN, C., *Man's Estate: Masculine Identity in Shakespeare*, 1981.
LAROQUE, F., *Shakespeare's Festive World*, 1991.
LEGGATT, A., *Shakespeare's Comedy of Love*, 1974.
LEVIN, H., *Playboys and Killjoys*, 1987.
MCFARLAND, T., *Shakespeare's Pastoral Comedy*, 1972.
MUIR, K., (ed.), *Shakespeare: The Comedies*, 1968.
NEVO, R., *Comic Transformations in Shakespeare*, 1980.
PARROTT, T. M., *Shakespearian Comedy*, 1949.
PETTET, E. C., *Shakespeare and the Romance Tradition*, 1949.
PHIALAS, P. G., *Shakespeare's Romantic Comedies*, 1966.
SALINGAR, L., *Shakespeare and the Traditions of Comedy*, 1976.
SCRAGG, L., *Shakespeare's Mouldy Tales*, 1992.
SORELIUS, G., *Shakespeare's Early Comedies*, 1993.
WELSFORD, E., *The Fool*, 1935.
WILSON, J. D., *Shakespeare's Happy Comedies*, 1962.
YOUNG, D., *The Heart's Forest: A Study of Shakespeare's Pastoral Plays*, 1972.

Many of the above books contain chapters on the individual plays collected in this volume. What follows may be regarded as suggested supplementary reading.

THE COMEDY OF ERRORS

BALDWIN, T. W., *Shakespeare's Five Act Structure*, 1947.
CHARNEY, M., (ed.), *Shakespearean Comedy*, 1980.
ELLIOT, G. R., 'Weirdness in *The Comedy of Errors*', University of Toronto Quarterly LX (1939).
FERGUSSON, FRANCIS, 'Two Comedies' in *The Human Image in Dramatic Literature*, 1957.
FOAKES, R. A., (ed.), Introduction to the Arden edition, 1962.
LEA, K. M., *Italian Popular Comedy*, 1934.
SALGADO, G., ' "Time's Deformed Hand": Sequence, Consequence, and Inconsequence in *The Comedy of Errors*', Shakespeare Survey 25, 1972.
TETZELI VON ROSADOR, K., 'Plotting the Early Comedies', Shakespeare Survey 37, 1984.
THOMSON, J. A. K., *Shakespeare and the Classics*, 1952.

COMEDIES

THE TAMING OF THE SHREW

BARTON, A., *Shakespeare and the Idea of the Play*, 1962.

BRADBROOK, M. C., 'Dramatic Role as Social Image: A Study of *The Taming of the Shrew*', Shakespeare Jahrbuch, 1958.

BRUNVAND, J. H., 'The Folktale Origin of *The Taming of the Shrew*', Shakespeare Quarterly, 1966.

GARBER, M. B., *Dream in Shakespeare*, 1974.

GODDARD, H. C., *The Meaning of Shakespeare*, 1951.

GREER, G., *The Female Eunuch*, 1971.

JONES, E., *Scenic Form in Shakespeare*, 1971.

MORRIS, B., (ed.), Introduction to the Arden edition, 1981.

SEAGER, H. W., *Natural History in Shakespeare's Time*, 1896.

SERONSY, C. C., '"Supposes" as the Unifying Theme in *The Taming of the Shrew*', Shakespeare Quarterly, 1964.

TILLYARD, E. M. W., *Shakespeare's Early Comedies*, 1965.

WEBSTER, M., *Shakespeare Without Tears*, 1942.

WEST, M., 'The Folk Background of Petruchio's Wooing Dance: Male Supremacy in *The Taming of the Shrew*', Shakespeare Studies, 1974.

THE TWO GENTLEMEN OF VERONA

BERGGREN, P. S., '"More Grace than Boy": Male Disguise in *The Two Gentlemen of Verona*', Signet Classic edition, 1988.

BROOKS, H. F., 'Two Clowns in a Comedy (to say nothing of the Dog): Speed, Launce (and Crab) in *The Two Gentlemen of Verona*', Essays and Studies, 1963.

HOLMBERG, A., '*The Two Gentlemen of Verona*: Shakespearean Comedy as a Rite of Passage', Queen's Quarterly 90, 1983.

JARDINE, L., *Still Harping on Daughters*, 1983.

KEIFER, F., 'Love Letters in *The Two Gentlemen of Verona*', Shakespeare Studies 18, 1986.

LEECH, C., (ed.), Introduction to the Arden edition.

MACCARY, T., *Friends and Lovers: The Phenomenology of Desire in Shakespearean Comedy*, 1985.

ROSSKY, W., '*The Two Gentlemen of Verona* as Burlesque', English Literary Renaissance 12, 1982.

SLIGHTS, C. W., '*The Two Gentlemen of Verona* and the Courtesy Book Tradition', Shakespeare Studies 16, 1983.

WEIMANN, R., 'Laughing with the Audience: *The Two Gentlemen of Verona* and the Popular Tradition of Comedy', Shakespeare Survey 22, 1969.

WELLER, B., 'Identity and Representation in Shakespeare', English Literary History 49, 1982.

SELECT BIBLIOGRAPHY

WELLS, S., 'The Failure of *The Two Gentlemen of Verona*', Shakespeare Jahrbuch, 1963.

LOVE'S LABOR'S LOST

BRADBROOK, M. C., *The School of Night*, 1936.

CARROLL, W. C., *The Great Feast of Language in* Love's Labour's Lost, 1976.

HAWKINS, S., 'The Two Worlds of Shakespearean Comedy', Shakespeare Studies III, 1967.

HENNINGER, S. K., 'The Pattern of *Love's Labour's Lost*', Shakespeare Studies VII, 1974.

HUNTER, R. G., 'The Function of the Songs at the end of *Love's Labour's Lost*', Shakespeare Studies VII, 1974.

JOSEPH, M., *Shakespeare's Use of the Arts of Language*, 1947.

KERRIGAN, J., 'Shakespeare at Work: the Katharine Rosaline Tangle in *Love's Labour's Lost*', Review of English Studies 33, 1982.

LAMB, M. L., 'The Nature of Topicality in *Love's Labour's Lost*', Shakespeare Survey 38, 1985.

MONTROSE, L. A., *'Curious-Knotted Garden': The Forms, Themes, and Contexts of Shakespeare's* Love's Labour's Lost, 1977.

ROESEN, B., 'Love's Labour's Lost', Shakespeare Quarterly 4, 1953.

TRAVERSI, D., *The Early Comedies*, 1960.

VYVYAN, J., *Shakespeare and the Rose of Love*, 1960.

WESTLUND, J., 'Fancy and Achievement in *Love's Labour's Lost*', Shakespeare Quarterly 18, 1967.

YATES, F. A., *A Study of* Love's Labour's Lost, 1936.

ROMEO AND JULIET

BEVINGTON, D., *Action is Eloquence: Shakespeare's Language of Gesture*, 1984.

BONNARD, G. A., *'Romeo and Juliet*: a possible significance?', Review of English Studies, 1951.

DRAPER, J. W., 'Shakespeare's "Star-crossed Lovers"', Review of English Studies, 1939.

FERGUSSON, F., *Trope and Allegory: Themes Common to Shakespeare and Dante*, 1977.

GARBER, M., *Coming of Age in Shakespeare*, 1981.

GESNER, C., *Shakespeare and the Greek Romance*, 1981.

GIBBONS, B., (ed.), Introduction to the Arden edition.

GOLDMAN, M., *Shakespeare and the Energies of Drama*, 1972.

HOPPE, H. R., *The Bad Quarto of* Romeo and Juliet. *A Bibliographical and Textual Study*, 1948.

COMEDIES

LAW, R. A., 'On Shakespeare's changes of his source material in *Romeo and Juliet*', Studies in English 9, 1929.

MAHOOD, M. M., *Shakespeare's Wordplay*, 1957.

MOORE, O. H., *The Legend of Romeo and Juliet*, 1950.

MYERS, H. A., *Tragedy: A View of Life*, 1956.

RABKIN, N., *Shakespeare and the Common Understanding*, 1967.

RIBNER, I., *Patterns in Shakespearian Tragedy*, 1960.

SNYDER, S., *The Comic Matrix of Shakespeare's Tragedies*, 1979.

STAUFFER, D., *Shakespeare's World of Images*, 1949.

WILSON, H. S., *On the Design of Shakespearian Tragedy*, 1957.

A MIDSUMMER NIGHT'S DREAM

BRIGGS, K. M., *Fairies in Tradition and Literature*, 1967.

—*The Anatomy of Puck*, 1959.

BROOKE, S. A., *On Ten Plays of Shakespeare*, 1930.

BROOKS, H. F., (ed.), Introduction to the Arden edition.

CALDERWOOD, J. L., '*A Midsummer Night's Dream*: The Illusion of Drama', Modern Language Quarterly, 1965.

CHAMBERS, E. K., *Shakespearean Gleanings*, 1946.

CRAIK, T. W., *The Tudor Interlude*, 1967.

CRANE, M., *Shakespeare's Prose*, 1951.

DENT, R. W., 'Imagination in *A Midsummer Night's Dream*', Shakespeare Quarterly, 1964.

DONALDSON, E. T., *The Swan at the Well: Shakespeare Reading Chaucer*, 1985.

DORAN, M., *Shakespeare's Dramatic Language*, 1976.

FENDER, S., *Shakespeare: A Midsummer Night's Dream*, 1968.

GARBER, M., *Dream in Shakespeare: From Metaphor to Metamorphosis*, 1974.

HEMINGWAY, S. B., 'The Relation of *A Midsummer Night's Dream* to *Romeo and Juliet*', Modern Language Notes, 1911.

HUSTON, J. D., 'Bottom Waking: Shakespeare's "Most Rare Vision"', Studies in English Literature 13, 1973.

LAMB, M. E., '*A Midsummer Night's Dream*: The Myth of Theseus and the Minotaur', Texas Studies in Language and Literature 21, 1979.

LATHAM, M. W., *The Elizabethan Fairies*, 1930.

LONG, J. H., *Shakespeare's Use of Music: The Comedies*, 1955.

MILLER, R. F., '*A Midsummer Night's Dream*: The Faeries, Bottom, and the Mystery of Things', Shakespeare Quarterly 26, 1975.

NEMEROV, H., 'The Marriage of Theseus and Hippolyta', Kenyon Review, 1956.

OLSON, P. A., '*A Midsummer Night's Dream* and the Meaning of Court Marriage', English Literary History, 1957.

SELECT BIBLIOGRAPHY

ORMEROD, D., '*A Midsummer Night's Dream*: The Monster in the Labyrinth', Shakespeare Studies 11, 1978.

ROBINSON, J. W., 'Palpable Hot Ice: Dramatic Burlesque in *A Midsummer Night's Dream*', Studies in Philology, 1964.

SCHANZER, E., 'The Moon and the Fairies in *A Midsummer Night's Dream*', University of Toronto Quarterly, 1955.

SIEGEL, P. N., '*A Midsummer Night's Dream* and the Wedding Guests', Shakespeare Quarterly, 1953.

SPURGEON, C., *Shakespeare's Imagery*, 1935.

STROUP, T. B., 'Bottom's Name and His Epiphany', Shakespeare Quarterly 29, 1978.

WEINER, A. D., '"Multiformitie Uniforme": *A Midsummer Night's Dream*', English Literary History 38, 1971.

WELSFORD, E., *The Court Masque*, 1927.

WILSON KNIGHT, G., *The Shakespearean Tempest*, 1932.

WYRICK, D. B., 'The Ass Motif in *The Comedy of Errors* and *A Midsummer Night's Dream*', Shakespeare Quarterly 33, 1982.

YOUNG, D. P., *Something of Great Constancy, The Art of A Midsummer Night's Dream*', 1966.

DATE	AUTHOR'S LIFE	LITERARY CONTEXT
1564	Born in Stratford, Warwickshire, the eldest surviving son of John Shakespeare, glover and occasional dealer in wool, and Mary Arden, daughter of a prosperous farmer.	Birth of Christopher Marlowe.
1565	John Shakespeare elected Alderman of Stratford.	Clinthio: *Hecatommithi*. Edwards: *Damon and Pythias*.
1566	Birth of Shakespeare's brother Gilbert.	Gascoigne: *Supposes*.
1567		Udall: *Roister Doister*. Golding: *The Stories of Venus and Adonis and of Hermaphroditus and Salamcis*.
1568	His father is elected bailiff.	Gascoigne: *Jocasta*. Wilmot: *Tancred and Gismunda*. Second Edition of Vasari's *Lives of the Artists*.
1569	Probably starts attending the petty school attached to the King's New School in Stratford. Birth of his sister Joan.	
1570	His father involved in money-lending.	
1571	John Shakespeare is elected Chief Alderman and deputy to the new bailiff.	
1572		Whitgift's *Answer* to the 'Admonition' receives Cartwright's *Reply*, beginning the first literary debate between Anglicans and Puritans.
1573		Tasso: *Aminta*.
1574	Probably enters the Upper School (where studies include rhetoric, logic, the Latin poets, and a little Greek). Birth of his brother Richard.	

Death of Michelangelo. Birth of Galileo.

Rebellion against Spain in the Netherlands. Birth of the actor Edward Alleyn.
Birth of the actor Richard Burbage.

Mary Stuart flees to England from Scotland.

Northern Rebellion.

Excommunication of Elizabeth. *Baïf's* Academy founded in Paris to promote poetry, music and dance.
Ridolfi Plot. Puritan 'Admonition' to Parliament.

Dutch rebels conquer Holland and Zeeland. Massacre of St Bartholomew's Day in Paris.

Accession of Henry III and new outbreak of civil war in France. First Catholic missionaries arrive in England from Douai. Earl of Leicester's Men obtain licence to perform within the City of London.

DATE	AUTHOR'S LIFE	LITERARY CONTEXT
1575		*Gammer Gurton's Needle* is printed.
1576		Castiglione's *The Book of the Courtier* banned by the Spanish Inquisition.
		George Gascoigne: *The Steel Glass*.
1577		John Northbrooke's attack in *Treatise wherein Dicing, Dancing, Vain Plays etc are reproved*.
1578	Shakespeare family fortunes are in decline, and John is having to sell off property to pay off his increasing debts.	Sidney writes *The Lady of May* and begins the 'Old' *Arcadia*.
		George Whetstone: *Promos and Cassandra*.
		John Lyly: *Euphues, the Anatomy of Wit*.
		Pierre de Ronsard, leader of the Pléiade, publishes his *Sonnets pour Hélène*. He is said to have exercised a considerable influence on the English sonnet-writers of the sixteenth century.
1579		Spenser: *The Shepherd's Calendar*.
		North: translation of Plutarch.
		Gossen: *The School of Abuse, and Pleasant Invective against Poets, Pipers, Players etc*.
1580	Birth of Shakespeare's brother Edmund.	Sidney: *Apologie for Poetrie*.
		Lodge: *Defense of Plays*.
1581		John Newton's translation of Seneca's *Ten Tragedies*.
		Barnaby Rich: *Apolonius and Silla*.
1582	Shakespeare marries Anne Hathaway, a local farmer's daughter, 7 or 8 years his senior, who is already pregnant with their first child.	Tasso: *Gerusalemme Liberata*.
		Watson: *Hekatompathia* (First sonnet sequence published in England).
		Whetstone: *Heptameron of Civil Discourses*.
		Sidney begins *Astrophel and Stella* and the 'New' *Arcadia*.
		Lope de Vega writing for the Corrals in Madrid.

CHRONOLOGY

Kenilworth Revels.

Restricted by the City of London's order that no plays be performed within the City boundaries, James Burbage of The Earl of Leicester's Men builds The Theatre only just outside the boundaries in Shoreditch. The Blackfriars Theatre is built. End of civil war in France. Observatory of Uraniborg built for the Danish astronomer, Tycho Brahe. Death of Titian.
Drake's circumnavigation of the world. The Curtain Theatre built. Birth of Rubens.

First visit to England of the duc d'Alençon as a suitor to Elizabeth, provoking much opposition to a French match. The Corral de la Cruz built in Madrid.

Spanish conquest of Portugal. Jesuit mission arrives in England from Rome led by Edmund Campion and Parsons.
Stricter enforcement of treason laws and increased penalties on recusants. Campion captured and executed. Northern provinces of the Netherlands renounce their allegiance to Phillip II, and invite the duc d'Alençon to be their sovereign.
Sir Walter Ralegh established in the Queen's favour. The Corral del Principe built in Madrid.

COMEDIES

DATE	AUTHOR'S LIFE	LITERARY CONTEXT
1583	Birth of their daughter Susanna.	
1583–4	The players' companies of the Earls of Essex, Oxford and Leicester perform in Stratford.	Giordarno Bruno visits England.
1584		Bruno publishes *La cena de le Ceneri* and *Spaccio della bestia trionfante*. Reginald Scott: *The Discovery of Witchcraft*.
1585	Birth of Shakespeare's twins Hamnet and Judith. The following years until 1592 are the 'Lost Years' for which no documentary records of his life survive, only legends such as the one of deer-stealing and flight from prosecution, and conjectures such as ones that he became a schoolmaster, travelled in Europe, or went to London to be an actor as early as the mid 1580s.	Death of Pierre de Ronsard. Bruno: *De gli eroici furori*, dedicated to Sidney.
1586		Timothy Bright: *A Treatise of Melancholy*.
1586–7	Five players' companies visit Stratford, including the Queen's, Essex's, Leicester's and Stafford's.	
1587		Holinshed: *Chronicles of England, Scotland and Ireland*. Marlowe: First part of *Tamburlaine the Great* acted. New edition of *The Mirror for Magistrates*.
1588		Marlowe: Second part of *Tamburlaine*. Thomas Kyd: *The Spanish Tragedy*. Lope de Vega, serving with the Armada, writes some of *The Beauty of Angelica*.

CHRONOLOGY

COMEDIES

DATE	AUTHOR'S LIFE	LITERARY CONTEXT
1589	The earliest likely date at which Shakespeare began composition of his first play (1 *Henry VI*) when he would have been working as an actor at The Theatre, with Burbage's company.	Marlowe: *The Jew of Malta*. Thomas Nashe: *The Anatomy of Absurdity*. Richard Hakluyt: *Principal Navigations, Voyages and Discoveries of the English nation*.
1590	2 *Henry VI*, 3 *Henry VI*.	Spenser: first 3 books of *The Faerie Queen*. Publication of Sidney's 'New' *Arcadia*. Nashe: *An Almond for a Parrot*, one of the Marprelate Tracts. Greene: *Menaphon*. Guarina: *The Faithful Shepherd*.
1590–92	Performances of *Henry VI*, parts 2 and 3, *Titus* and *The Shrew* by the Earl of Pembroke's Men.	
1591	*Richard III* and *The Comedy of Errors* written.	Spenser's *Complaints* which includes his translation of fifteen of Joachim du Bellay's sonnets – du Bellay was a member of the Pléiade and responsible for its manifesto. Sir John Harington's translation of *Orlando Furioso*. Publication of Sidney's *Astrophel and Stella*.
1592	First recorded reference to Shakespeare as an actor and playwright in Greene's attack in *The Groatsworth of Wit* describing him as 'an upstart crow'.	Samuel Daniel: *Delia*. Marlowe's *Edward II* and *Doctor Faustus* performed. *Arden of Feversham* printed. Nashe: *Strange News*.
1592–4	*Titus Andronicus* written.	
1593	Publication of *Venus and Adonis*, dedicated to the Earl of Southampton. The *Sonnets* probably begun.	Marlowe: *Massacre of Paris*. *The Phoenix Nest*, miscellany of poems including ones by Ralegh, Lodge and Breton. Barnabe Barnes: *Parthenophil and Parthenope*. George Peele: *The Honour of the Garter*. Lodge: *Phillis*. Nashe: *Christ's Tears over Jerusalem*.
1593–4	*The Taming of the Shrew*; *The Two Gentlemen of Verona*.	

CHRONOLOGY

HISTORICAL EVENTS

Failure of the Portugal expedition. Henry III of France assassinated. English military aid sent to Henry of Navarre. Marlowe's tutor, Francis Ket, burned at the stake for atheism.

English government discovers and suppresses the Puritan printing press.

Earl of Essex given command of the English army in France. The last fight of the *Revenge* under Spanish attack.

Capture of Madre de Dios. Split in the main players' company. Shakespeare and Burbage's group remain at The Theatre, Alleyn's move to the Rose on Bankside. Plague in London: the theatres closed.

Marlowe arrested on blasphemy charges and murdered two weeks later. Kyd arrested for libel. Henry of Navarre converts to Catholicism in order to unite France.

COMEDIES

DATE	AUTHOR'S LIFE	LITERARY CONTEXT
1593–6		John Donne writing his early poems, the Satires and Elegies.
1594	*The Rape of Lucrece* dedicated to his patron Southampton. *The Comedy of Errors* and *Titus Andronicus* performed at the Rose. Shakespeare established as one of the shareholders in his company, The Chamberlain's Men, which performs before the Queen during the Christmas festivities.	Daniel: *Cleopatra*. Spenser: *Amoretti* and *Epithalamion*. Drayton: *Idea's Mirror*. Nashe: *The Terrors of the Night*, *The Unfortunate Traveller*. Greene: *Friar Bacon and Friar Bungay*.
1594–5	*Love's Labor's Lost* and *Romeo and Juliet* written.	
1595	*Richard II*.	Daniel: *The First Four Books of the Civil Wars between the two houses of Lancaster and York*. Sidney: *Defence of Poesy* published. Ralegh: *The Discovery of the Empire of Guiana*.
1595–6	*A Midsummer Night's Dream*.	
1596	Death of his son, Hamnet. *The Merchant of Venice*. Shakespeare living in Bishopsgate ward. His father, John, is granted a coat of arms. *King John* written.	Lodge: *Wits Miserle*. First complete edition of Spenser's *Faerie Queen*.
1597	*Henry IV* Part 1. First performance of *The Merry Wives of Windsor*. Shakespeare's company now under the patronage of the new Lord Chamberlain, Hunsdon. In Stratford, Shakespeare buys New Place, the second largest house in the town, with its own orchards and vines.	John Donne writes 'The Storme' and 'The Calme'. Francis Bacon: first edition of *Essays*. Jonson and Nashe imprisoned for writing *The Isle of Dogs*.
1597–8	*Henry IV* Part 2.	
1598	Shakespeare one of the 'principal comedians' with Richard Burbage, Heminge and Cordell in Jonson's *Every Man in his Humour*. For the second year, Shakespeare is listed as having failed to pay tax levied on all householders.	Publication of Sidney's *Works* and of Marlowe's *Hero and Leander* (together with Chapman's continuation). *Seven Books of the Iliads* (first of Chapman's Homeric translations). Meres: *Palladia Tamia*. New edition of Lodge's *Rosalynde*.

CHRONOLOGY

Henry of Navarre accepted as King in Paris. Rebellion in Ireland. The London theatres re-open. The Swan Theatre is built. Ralegh accused of blasphemy.

France declares war on Spain. Failure of the Indies voyage and death of Hawkins. Ralegh's expedition to Guiana.

England joins France in the war against Spain. Death of Drake. Raid on Cadiz led by Essex. In long-standing power struggle with Essex, Robert Cecil is appointed Secretary of State.

Islands Voyage led by Essex and Ralegh. The government suppresses the *Isle of Dogs* at the Swan and closes the theatres. Despite the continued hostility of the City of London, they soon re-open. James Burbage builds the second Blackfriars Theatre. Death of James Burbage.

Peace between France and Spain. Death of Philip II. Tyrone defeats the English at Armagh. Essex appointed Lord Deputy of Ireland.

DATE	AUTHOR'S LIFE	LITERARY CONTEXT
1598 *cont.*		Lope de Vega: *La Arcadia*. James VI of Scotland: *The True Law of Free Monarchies*.
1598–1600	*Much Ado About Nothing*.	
1599	*As You Like It, Henry V, Julius Caesar*. Shakespeare one of the shareholders in the Globe Theatre. He moves lodgings to Bankside. Publication of *The Passionate Pilgrim*, a miscellany of 20 poems, at least 5 by Shakespeare.	Jonson: *Every Man out of his Humour*. Dekker: *The Shoemaker's Holiday*. Sir John Hayward: *The First Part of the Life and Reign of King Henry IV*. Greene's translation of *Orlando Furioso*.
1599–1600	*Twelfth Night*.	
1600		'England's Helicon'.
1600–1	*Hamlet* (performed with Burbage as the Prince and Shakespeare as the Ghost).	
1601	*The Phoenix and the Turtle*. The Lord Chamberlain's Men paid by one of Essex's followers to perform *Richard II* on the day before the rebellion. Death of John Shakespeare.	
1601–2	*Troilus and Cressida*.	
1602	Shakespeare buys more property in Stratford.	
1602–4	*Alls Well That Ends Well*.	
1603	Shakespeare's company now under the patronage of King James. Shakespeare is one of the principal tragedians in Jonson's *Sejanus*.	Montaigne's *Essays* translated into English. Thomas Heywood: *A Woman Killed with Kindness*.
1604	Shakespeare known to be lodging in Silver Street with a Huguenot family called Mountjoy. *Othello*; first performance of *Measure for Measure*.	Chapman: *Bussy d'Ambois*. Marston: *The Malcontent*.
1604–5	Ten of his plays performed at court by the King's Men.	

CHRONOLOGY

The Burbage brothers, Richard and Cuthbert, pull down The Theatre and, with its timbers, build the Globe on Bankside. Essex's campaign fails in Ireland, and after returning without permission to court he is arrested. The government suppresses satirical writings, and burns pamphlets by Nashe and Harvey.

Essex released but still in disgrace. The Fortune Theatre built by Alleyn and Henslowe. Bruno executed for heresy by the Inquisition in Rome.

Essex's Rebellion. Essex and Southampton arrested, and the former executed. Spanish invasion of Ireland. Monopolies debates in Parliament.

Spanish troops defeated in Ireland.

Death of Elizabeth, and accession of James I. Ralegh imprisoned in the Tower. Plague in London. Sir Thomas Bodley re-founds the library of Oxford University.

Peace with Spain. Hampton Court Conference.

DATE	AUTHOR'S LIFE	LITERARY CONTEXT
1605	First performance of *King Lear* at the Globe, with Burbage as the King, and Robert Armin as the Fool. Shakespeare makes further investments in Stratford, buying a half interest in a lease of tithes.	Cervantes: *Don Quixote* (part one). Bacon: *The Proficience and Advancement of Learning*. Jonson and Inigo Jones: *The Masque of Blackness*. Jonson and co-authors imprisoned for libellous references to the court in *Eastward Ho*.
1605–6		Jonson: *Volpone*.
1606	First performance of *Macbeth*.	John Ford's masque *Honour Triumphant*.
1607	*Antony and Cleopatra*. Susanna marries John Hall, a physician. Death of Shakespeare's brother Edmund, an actor.	Tourneur's *The Revenger's Tragedy* printed. Barnes: *The Devil's Charter*.
1607–8	*Timon of Athens, Coriolanus, Pericles*.	
1608	Shakespeare one of the shareholders in the Blackfriars Theatre. Death of his mother.	Lope de Vega: *Peribanez*. Beaumont and Fletcher: *Philaster*. Jonson and Jones: *The Masque of Beauty*. Donne writes *La Corona*. Twelve books of Homer's *Iliad* (Chapman's translation).
1609	Publication, probably unauthorized, of the quarto edition of the *Sonnets* and *A Lover's Complaint*.	Jonson and Jones: *The Masque of Queens*. Donne's 'The Expiration' printed; 'Liturgie' and 'On the Annunciation' written. Bacon: *De Sapientia Veterum*. Lope de Vega: *New Art of Writing Plays for the Theatre*.
1609–10	*Cymbeline*.	
1610		Donne: *Pseudo-Martyr* printed and *The First Anniversarie* written. Jonson: *The Alchemist*. Beaumont and Fletcher: *The Maid's Tragedy*.
1610–11	*The Winter's Tale*.	
1611	*The Tempest* performed in the Banqueting House, Whitehall. Simon Forman records seeing performances of *Macbeth, The Winter's Tale* and *Cymbeline*.	Beaumont and Fletcher: *A King and No King, The Knight of the Burning Pestle*. Tourneur: *The Atheist's Tragedy*.

CHRONOLOGY

COMEDIES

DATE	AUTHOR'S LIFE	LITERARY CONTEXT
1611 *cont.*		Jonson and Jones: *Masque of Oberon*. Authorized Version of the Bible. Sir John Davies: *The Scourge of Folly*. Donne writes the *The Second Anniversarie* and a 'A Valediction: forbidding mourning'.
1612	Shakespeare appears as a witness in a Court of Requests case involving a dispute over a dowry owed by his former landlord, Mountjoy, to his son-in-law, Belott. Death of his brother Gilbert.	Webster: *The White Devil* printed. Tourneur: *The Nobleman*. Lope de Vega: *Fuente Ovejuna*.
1613	At a performance of his last play, *Henry VIII*, the Globe Theatre catches fire and is destroyed. As part of the court celebrations for the marriage of Princess Elizabeth, The King's Men perform 14 plays, including *Much Ado*, *Othello*, *The Winter's Tale* and *The Tempest*. Death of his brother Richard.	Sir Thomas Overbury: *The Wife*. Donne: 'Good Friday' and 'Epithalamion' on Princess Elizabeth's marriage. Cervantes: *Novelas ejemplares* – a collection of short stories.
1614	In Stratford, Shakespeare protects his property interests during a controversy over a threat to enclose the common fields.	Jonson: *Bartholomew Fair*. Webster: *The Duchess of Malfi*. Ralegh: *The History of the World*.
1615	The Warwick Assizes issue an order to prevent enclosures, which ends the dispute in Stratford.	Cervantes publishes 8 plays and *Don Quixote* (part two).
1616	Marriage of his daughter Judith to Thomas Quincy, a vintner, who a month later is tried for fornication with another woman whom he had made pregnant. Death of Shakespeare (23 April).	Jonson: *The Devil is an Ass*. Jonson publishes his *Works*.
1623	The players Heminge and Condell publish the plays of the First Folio.	

CHRONOLOGY

Death of Henry, Prince of Wales.

Marriage of Princess Elizabeth to Frederick, Elector Palatine. Bacon appointed Attorney-General.

The second Globe and the Hope Theatre built.

Inquiry into the murder of Sir Thomas Overbury in the Tower implicates the wife of the King's favourite, Somerset.

Ralegh released from the Tower to lead an expedition to Guiana; on his return he is executed.

WILLIAM SHAKESPEARE

THE COMEDY OF ERRORS

Edited by Harry Levin

[Dramatis Personae

SOLINUS, Duke of Ephesus
EGEON, a merchant of Syracuse
ANTIPHOLUS OF EPHESUS } twin brothers, and sons of Egeon
ANTIPHOLUS OF SYRACUSE } and Emilia
DROMIO OF EPHESUS } twin brothers, and bondmen to the
DROMIO OF SYRACUSE } two Antipholuses
BALTHASAR
ANGELO, a goldsmith
A MERCHANT, friend to Antipholus of Syracuse
ANOTHER MERCHANT, to whom Angelo is in debt
DOCTOR PINCH, a schoolmaster
EMILIA, an abbess at Ephesus, wife of Egeon
ADRIANA, wife of Antipholus of Ephesus
LUCIANA, her sister
LUCE, or NELL, kitchen maid to Adriana
COURTESAN
JAILER, HEADSMAN, OFFICERS, and OTHER ATTENDANTS

Scene: Ephesus]

THE COMEDY OF ERRORS

ACT I

Scene I. [*A public place.*]

Enter the Duke of Ephesus, with [Egeon] the Merchant of Syracusa, Jailer, and other Attendants.

EGEON Proceed, Solinus, to procure my fall,
And by the doom of death end woes and all.

DUKE Merchant of Syracusa, plead no more;
I am not partial to infringe our laws.
The enmity and discord which of late   5
Sprung from the rancorous outrage of your Duke
To merchants, our well-dealing countrymen,
Who, wanting guilders to redeem their lives,
Have sealed his rigorous statutes with their bloods,
Excludes all pity from our threat'ning looks.   10
For, since the mortal and intestine jars
'Twixt thy seditious countrymen and us,
It hath in solemn synods been decreed,
Both by the Syracusians and ourselves,

Text references are printed in **boldface** type; the annotation follows in roman type.
I.i.s.d. **Syracusa** Syracuse, ancient capital of Sicily   2 **doom** sentence   4 **partial** predisposed   8 **guilders** Dutch coins worth about forty cents   11 **intestine jars** internal conflicts

15   To admit no traffic to our adverse towns.
      Nay more; if any born at Ephesus
      Be seen at Syracusian marts and fairs;
      Again, if any Syracusian born
      Come to the bay of Ephesus, he dies,
20   His goods confiscate to the Duke's dispose,
      Unless a thousand marks be levièd
      To quit the penalty and to ransom him.
      Thy substance, valued at the highest rate,
      Cannot amount unto a hundred marks;
25   Therefore by law thou art condemned to die.

EGEON Yet this my comfort: when your words are
          done,
      My woes end likewise with the evening sun.

DUKE Well, Syracusian, say, in brief, the cause
      Why thou departed'st from thy native home,
30   And for what cause thou cam'st to Ephesus.

EGEON A heavier task could not have been imposed
      Than I to speak my griefs unspeakable;
      Yet, that the world may witness that my end
      Was wrought by nature, not by vile offense,
35   I'll utter what my sorrow gives me leave.
      In Syracusa was I born, and wed
      Unto a woman happy but for me,
      And by me, had not our hap been bad.
      With her I lived in joy, our wealth increased
40   By prosperous voyages I often made
      To Epidamnum, till my factor's death
      And the great care of goods at random left
      Drew me from kind embracements of my spouse;
      From whom my absence was not six months old,
45   Before herself—almost at fainting under
      The pleasing punishment that women bear—
      Had made provision for her following me,

---

15 **adverse** hostile   16 **Ephesus** (rich city on the coast of Asia Minor)   20 **dispose**
disposal   21 **marks** (valued at somewhat more than three dollars)   22 **quit** acquit
41 **Epidamnum** (Adriatic seaport)   41 **factor's** agent's

And soon and safe arrivèd where I was.
There had she not been long, but she became
A joyful mother of two goodly sons;   50
And, which was strange, the one so like the other,
As could not be distinguished but by names.
That very hour, and in the self-same inn,
A mean woman was deliverèd
Of such a burden male, twins both alike.   55
Those, for their parents were exceeding poor,
I bought, and brought up to attend my sons.
My wife, not meanly proud of two such boys,
Made daily motions for our home return.
Unwilling I agreed; alas, too soon   60
We came aboard.
A league from Epidamnum had we sailed
Before the always wind-obeying deep
Gave any tragic instance of our harm.
But longer did we not retain much hope;   65
For what obscurèd light the heavens did grant
Did but convey unto our fearful minds
A doubtful warrant of immediate death,
Which, though myself would gladly have embraced,
Yet the incessant weepings of my wife,   70
Weeping before for what she saw must come,
And piteous plainings of the pretty babes,
That mourned for fashion, ignorant what to fear,
Forced me to seek delays for them and me.
And this it was—for other means was none: 75
The sailors sought for safety by our boat,
And left the ship, then sinking-ripe, to us.
My wife, more careful for the latter-born,
Had fast'ned him unto a small spare mast,
Such as seafaring men provide for storms;   80
To him one of the other twins was bound,
Whilst I had been like heedful of the other.

54 **mean** poor   56 **for** because   58 **not meanly** more than a little   59 **motions**
proposals   64 **instance** token   68 **doubtful warrant** ominous sign   72 **plainings** wails   73 **fashion** custom   77 **sinking-ripe** ready to sink   78 **latter-born**
(but see line 124)

5

The children thus disposed, my wife and I,
Fixing our eyes on whom our care was fixed,
85   Fast'ned ourselves at either end the mast;
And floating straight, obedient to the stream,
Was carried towards Corinth, as we thought.
At length the sun, gazing upon the earth,
Dispersed those vapors that offended us,
90   And, by the benefit of his wishèd light,
The seas waxed calm, and we discoverèd
Two ships from far, making amain to us:
Of Corinth that, of Epidaurus this.
But ere they came—O, let me say no more!
95   Gather the sequel by that went before.

DUKE   Nay, forward, old man; do not break off so,
For we may pity, though not pardon thee.

EGEON   O, had the gods done so, I had not now
Worthily termed them merciless to us.
100   For, ere the ships could meet by twice five leagues,
We were encount'red by a mighty rock,
Which being violently borne upon,
Our helpful ship was splitted in the midst;
So that, in this unjust divorce of us,
105   Fortune had left to both of us alike
What to delight in, what to sorrow for.
Her part, poor soul, seeming as burdenèd
With lesser weight, but not with lesser woe,
Was carried with more speed before the wind;
110   And in our sight they three were taken up
By fishermen of Corinth, as we thought.
At length another ship had seized on us,
And, knowing whom it was their hap to save,
Gave healthful welcome to their shipwracked guests,
115   And would have reft the fishers of their prey,
Had not their bark been very slow of sail;
And therefore homeward did they bend their course.

---

87 **Corinth** (major Greek seaport)   90 **his wishèd** its wished-for   92 **amain** with full speed   93 **Epidaurus** (ancient name for both a Greek and an Adriatic town)   99 **Worthily** deservedly   103 **ship** i.e., the mast   115 **reft** robbed

Thus have you heard me severed from my bliss,
That by misfortunes was my life prolonged
To tell sad stories of my own mishaps.   120

DUKE And, for the sake of them thou sorrowest for,
Do me the favor to dilate at full
What have befall'n of them and thee till now.

EGEON My youngest boy, and yet my eldest care,
At eighteen years became inquisitive   125
After his brother, and importuned me
That his attendant—so his case was like,
Reft of his brother, but retained his name—
Might bear him company in the quest of him;
Whom whilst I labored of a love to see,   130
I hazarded the loss of whom I loved.
Five summers have I spent in farthest Greece,
Roaming clean through the bounds of Asia,
And coasting homeward, came to Ephesus,
Hopeless to find, yet loath to leave unsought   135
Or that or any place that harbors men.
But here must end the story of my life;
And happy were I in my timely death,
Could all my travels warrant me they live.

DUKE Hapless Egeon, whom the fates have marked   140
To bear the extremity of dire mishap!
Now trust me, were it not against our laws,
Against my crown, my oath, my dignity,
Which princes, would they, may not disannul,
My soul should sue as advocate for thee.   145
But though thou art adjudgèd to the death,
And passèd sentence may not be recalled
But to our honor's great disparagement,
Yet will I favor thee in what I can;
Therefore, merchant, I'll limit thee this day   150
To seek thy health by beneficial help.

122 dilate relate 130 of a love out of love 135 Hopeless to find without hope
of finding 136 Or either 139 travels (with the further implication of "tra-
vails") 143 dignity office 144 disannul cancel 146 adjudgèd sentenced
148 disparagement injury

Try all the friends thou hast in Ephesus—
Beg thou, or borrow, to make up the sum,
And live; if no, then thou art doomed to die.
155 Jailer, take him to thy custody.

JAILER I will, my lord.

EGEON Hopeless and helpless doth Egeon wend,
But to procrastinate his lifeless end.   *Exeunt.*

[Scene II. *The Mart.*]

Enter Antipholus [of Syracuse], a Merchant, and
Dromio [of Syracuse].

MERCHANT Therefore, give out you are of Epidamnum,
Lest that your goods too soon be confiscate.
This very day a Syracusian merchant
Is apprehended for arrival here,
5 And not being able to buy out his life,
According to the statute of the town,
Dies ere the weary sun set in the west.
There is your money that I had to keep.

S. ANTIPHOLUS Go bear it to the Centaur, where we
host,
10 And stay there, Dromio, till I come to thee;
Within this hour it will be dinnertime;
Till that, I'll view the manners of the town,
Peruse the traders, gaze upon the buildings,
And then return and sleep within mine inn;
15 For with long travel I am stiff and weary.
Get thee away.

S. DROMIO Many a man would take you at your word,
And go indeed, having so good a mean.
                                              Exit Dromio.

158 procrastinate postpone I.ii.s.d. Mart marketplace 5 buy out redeem
9 Centaur (name and sign of an inn) 9 host lodge 18 mean means

8

S. ANTIPHOLUS A trusty villain, sir, that very oft,
   When I am dull with care and melancholy,   20
   Lightens my humor with his merry jests.
   What, will you walk with me about the town,
   And then go to my inn and dine with me?

MERCHANT I am invited, sir, to certain merchants,
   Of whom I hope to make much benefit.   25
   I crave your pardon; soon at five o'clock,
   Please you, I'll meet with you upon the Mart,
   And afterward consort you till bedtime.
   My present business calls me from you now.

S. ANTIPHOLUS Farewell till then. I will go lose myself,   30
   And wander up and down to view the city.

MERCHANT Sir, I commend you to your own content.

Exit.

S. ANTIPHOLUS He that commends me to mine own
   content
   Commends me to the thing I cannot get.
   I to the world am like a drop of water   35
   That in the ocean seeks another drop,
   Who, falling there to find his fellow forth,
   Unseen, inquisitive, confounds himself.
   So I, to find a mother and a brother,
   In quest of them, unhappy, lose myself.   40

Enter Dromio of Ephesus.

Here comes the almanac of my true date.
What now? How chance thou art returned so soon?

E. DROMIO Returned so soon! Rather approached
   too late.
   The capon burns, the pig falls from the spit;
   The clock hath strucken twelve upon the bell;   45
   My mistress made it one upon my cheek.

---

19 **villain** (in the original sense of "bondman")   21 **humor** mood   28 **consort**
accompany   37 **find his fellow forth** seek his fellow out   38 **confounds** loses
40 **unhappy** unlucky   41 **almanac** (Dromio reminds Antipholus of his own
age)   45 **twelve** (dinnertime or later)

She is so hot because the meat is cold;
The meat is cold because you come not home;
You come not home because you have no stomach;
50   You have no stomach, having broke your fast.
But we, that know what 'tis to fast and pray,
Are penitent for your default today.

S. ANTIPHOLUS Stop in your wind, sir; tell me this,
    I pray:
Where have you left the money that I gave you?

55   E. DROMIO O, sixpence, that I had o' Wednesday last,
To pay the saddler for my mistress' crupper?
The saddler had it, sir, I kept it not.

S. ANTIPHOLUS I am not in a sportive humor now.
Tell me, and dally not, where is the money?
60   We being strangers here, how dar'st thou trust
So great a charge from thine own custody?

E. DROMIO I pray you, jest, sir, as you sit at dinner.
I from my mistress come to you in post;
If I return, I shall be post indeed,
65   For she will score your fault upon my pate.
Methinks your maw, like mine, should be your
    clock,
And strike you home without a messenger.

S. ANTIPHOLUS Come, Dromio, come, these jests are
    out of season;
Reserve them till a merrier hour than this.
70   Where is the gold I gave in charge to thee?

E. DROMIO To me, sir? Why, you gave no gold to me.

S. ANTIPHOLUS Come on, sir knave, have done your
    foolishness,
And tell me how thou hast disposed thy charge.

---

49 **stomach** appetite   52 **default** (1) sin (2) failure to appear   53 **wind** breath
56 **crupper** strap from saddle to horse's tail   63 **post** haste   64 **post** posted (to
pay account, with pun meaning "beaten")   65 **score** (with pun on "scour," beat)
66 **maw** stomach (ordinarily used of animals)

E. DROMIO My charge was but to fetch you from the
 Mart
 Home to your house, the Phoenix, sir, to dinner. 75
 My mistress and her sister stays for you.

S. ANTIPHOLUS Now, as I am a Christian, answer me,
 In what safe place you have bestowed my money;
 Or I shall break that merry sconce of yours
 That stands on tricks when I am undisposed. 80
 Where is the thousand marks thou hadst of me?

E. DROMIO I have some marks of yours upon my pate,
 Some of my mistress' marks upon my shoulders,
 But not a thousand marks between you both.
 If I should pay your worship those again, 85
 Perchance you will not bear them patiently.

S. ANTIPHOLUS Thy mistress' marks? What mistress,
 slave, hast thou?

E. DROMIO Your worship's wife, my mistress at the
 Phoenix;
 She that doth fast till you come home to dinner,
 And prays that you will hie you home to dinner. 90

S. ANTIPHOLUS What, wilt thou flout me thus unto my
 face,
 Being forbid? There, take you that, sir knave.
             [Beats him.]

E. DROMIO What mean you, sir? For God's sake, hold
 your hands!
 Nay, and you will not, sir, I'll take my heels.
            Exit Dromio E.

S. ANTIPHOLUS Upon my life, by some device or other, 95
 The villain is o'er-raught of all my money.
 They say this town is full of cozenage:
 As nimble jugglers that deceive the eye,

75 **Phoenix** i.e., house of Antipholus, denoted by the sign of his shop 78 **bestowed**
deposited 79 **sconce** head 80 **stands on** insists upon 85 **pay** (also meaning
"beat") 94 **and** if 96 **o'er-raught** overreached 97 **cozenage** cheating 98 **As**
such as

Dark-working sorcerers that change the mind,
100   Soul-killing witches that deform the body,
Disguisèd cheaters, prating mountebanks,
And many suchlike liberties of sin.
If it prove so, I will be gone the sooner.
I'll to the Centaur, to go seek this slave.
105   I greatly fear my money is not safe.   *Exit.*

101 **mountebanks** quacks   102 **liberties** uninhibited acts

ACT II

[Scene I. *The Phoenix*.]

*Enter Adriana, wife to Antipholus [of Ephesus], with
Luciana, her sister.*

ADRIANA Neither my husband nor the slave returned,
That in such haste I sent to seek his master.
Sure, Luciana, it is two o'clock.

LUCIANA Perhaps some merchant hath invited him,
And from the Mart he's somewhere gone to dinner.   5
Good sister, let us dine, and never fret;
A man is master of his liberty.
Time is their master, and when they see time,
They'll go or come; if so, be patient, sister.

ADRIANA Why should their liberty than ours be more?   10

LUCIANA Because their business still lies out o' door.

ADRIANA Look when I serve him so, he takes it ill.

LUCIANA O, know he is the bridle of your will.

ADRIANA There's none but asses will be bridled so.

LUCIANA Why, headstrong liberty is lashed with woe.   15
There's nothing situate under heaven's eye
But hath his bound, in earth, in sea, in sky.
The beasts, the fishes, and the wingèd fowls
Are their males' subjects, and at their controls;

II.i.11 **still** always 12 **Look when** whenever 15 **lashed** whipped 19 **controls** commands

13

20   Man, more divine, the master of all these,
     Lord of the wide world and wild wat'ry seas,
     Indued with intellectual sense and souls,
     Of more preeminence than fish and fowls,
     Are masters to their females, and their lords;
25   Then let your will attend on their accords.

ADRIANA This servitude makes you to keep unwed.

LUCIANA Not this, but troubles of the marriage bed.

ADRIANA But, were you wedded, you would bear some
     sway.

LUCIANA Ere I learn love, I'll practice to obey.

ADRIANA How if your husband start some other
30   where?

LUCIANA Till he come home again, I would forbear.

ADRIANA Patience unmoved! no marvel though she
         pause;
     They can be meek that have no other cause.
     A wretched soul, bruised with adversity,
35   We bid be quiet when we hear it cry;
     But were we burd'ned with like weight of pain,
     As much or more we should ourselves complain:
     So thou, that hast no unkind mate to grieve thee,
     With urging helpless patience would relieve me;
40   But, if thou live to see like right bereft,
     This fool-begged patience in thee will be left.

LUCIANA Well, I will marry one day, but to try.
     Here comes your man, now is your husband nigh.

          Enter Dromio of Ephesus.

ADRIANA Say, is your tardy master now at hand?

---

22 intellectual sense reason   28 sway authority   30 start some other where
pursue another woman   32 pause delay in getting married   33 cause motive
39 helpless unavailing   40 like right bereft your own rights denied
41 fool-begged i.e., assumed as one would assume responsibility for a fool

E. DROMIO Nay, he's at two hands with me, and that   45
  my two ears can witness.

ADRIANA Say, didst thou speak with him? Know'st thou
  his mind?

E. DROMIO Ay, ay, he told his mind upon mine ear.
  Beshrew his hand, I scarce could understand it.

LUCIANA Spake he so doubtfully, thou couldst not   50
  feel his meaning?

E. DROMIO Nay, he struck so plainly, I could too well
  feel his blows; and withal so doubtfully, that I could
  scarce understand them.

ADRIANA But say, I prithee, is he coming home?   55
  It seems he hath great care to please his wife.

E. DROMIO Why, mistress, sure my master is horn-mad.

ADRIANA Horn-mad, thou villain!

E. DROMIO   I mean not cuckold-mad,
  But sure he is stark mad.
  When I desired him to come home to dinner,   60
  He asked me for a thousand marks in gold.
  "'Tis dinnertime," quoth I. "My gold!" quoth he.
  "Your meat doth burn," quoth I. "My gold!" quoth
    he.
  "Will you come?" quoth I. "My gold!" quoth he.
  "Where is the thousand marks I gave thee, villain?"   65
  "The pig," quoth I, "is burned." "My gold!" quoth
    he.
  "My mistress, sir—" quoth I. "Hang up thy
    mistress!
  I know not thy mistress, out on thy mistress!"

LUCIANA Quoth who?

E. DROMIO Quoth my master.   70
  "I know," quoth he, "no house, no wife, no mistress."

48 **told** (with a pun on "tolled")   50 **doubtfully** uncertainty   54 **understand**
(pun on "stand under")   58 **Horn-mad** (1) like a mad bull (2) a cuckold
67 **Hang up** be hanged   68 **out on** (angry interjection)

So that my errand due unto my tongue,
I thank him, I bare home upon my shoulders;
For, in conclusion, he did beat me there.

ADRIANA Go back again, thou slave, and fetch him
75   home.

E. DROMIO Go back again, and be new beaten home?
For God's sake, send some other messenger.

ADRIANA Back, slave, or I will break thy pate across.

E. DROMIO And he will bless that cross with other
        beating;
80   Between you, I shall have a holy head.

ADRIANA Hence, prating peasant! Fetch thy master
        home.

E. DROMIO Am I so round with you, as you with me,
That like a football you do spurn me thus?
You spurn me hence, and he will spurn me hither;
85   If I last in this service, you must case me in leather.
                                              [Exit.]

LUCIANA Fie, how impatience lowereth in your face!

ADRIANA His company must do his minions grace,
Whilst I at home starve for a merry look:
Hath homely age th' alluring beauty took
90   From my poor cheek? Then he hath wasted it.
Are my discourses dull? Barren my wit?
If voluble and sharp discourse be marred,
Unkindness blunts it more than marble hard.
Do their gay vestments his affections bait?
95   That's not my fault; he's master of my state.
What ruins are in me that can be found,
By him not ruined? Then is he the ground
Of my defeatures. My decayèd fair

72 **due unto** appropriate to   73 **bare** bore   78 **across** (taken by Dromio as "a cross")   80 **holy** (quibbling on "full of holes")   82 **round** (1) plain-spoken (2) spherical   86 **lowereth** frowns   87 **minions** paramours   88 **starve** pine away   91 **discourses** conversations   94 **bait** entice   98 **defeatures** disfigurements   98 **decayèd fair** impaired beauty

A sunny look of his would soon repair.
But, too unruly deer, he breaks the pale,   100
And feeds from home; poor I am but his stale.

LUCIANA Self-harming jealousy! fie, beat it hence.

ADRIANA Unfeeling fools can with such wrongs
     dispense.
I know his eye doth homage otherwhere,
Or else what lets it but he would he here?   105
Sister, you know he promised me a chain.
Would that alone, alone he would detain,
So he would keep fair quarter with his bed!
I see the jewel best enamelèd
Will lose his beauty; yet the gold bides still   110
That others touch, and often touching will
Wear gold, and no man that hath a name
But falsehood and corruption doth it shame.
Since that my beauty cannot please his eye,
I'll weep what's left away, and weeping die.   115

LUCIANA How many fond fools serve mad jealousy!
                              Exit [with Adriana].

[Scene II. *The Mart.*]

Enter Antipholus [of Syracuse].

S. ANTIPHOLUS The gold I gave to Dromio is laid up
Safe at the Centaur, and the heedful slave
Is wand'red forth, in care to seek me out,
By computation and mine host's report.

---

100 **deer** (pun on "dear") 100 **pale** enclosure 101 **from** away from
101 **stale** dupe 103 **dispense** offer a dispensation 104 **otherwhere** elsewhere
105 **lets** prevents 107 **detain** keep back 108 **keep fair quarter** keep the peace
110 **his** its 109–113 **I see ... it shame** (through these ambiguous metaphors
Adriana seems to imply that she still values her husband, though he is made less
attractive by promiscuity) 116 **fond** foolish II.ii.4 **computation** calculation

5   I could not speak with Dromio since at first
           I sent him from the Mart! See, here he comes.

                    Enter Dromio of Syracuse.

           How now, sir, is your merry humor altered?
           As you love strokes, so jest with me again.
           You know no Centaur? You received no gold?
10   Your mistress sent to have me home to dinner?
           My house was at the Phoenix? Wast thou mad,
           That thus so madly thou didst answer me?

      S. DROMIO What answer, sir? When spake I such a
           word?

      S. ANTIPHOLUS Even now, even here, not half an hour
           since.

15   S. DROMIO I did not see you since you sent me hence,
           Home to the Centaur, with the gold you gave me.

      S. ANTIPHOLUS Villain, thou didst deny the gold's
           receipt,
           And told'st me of a mistress, and a dinner;
           For which, I hope, thou felt'st I was displeased.

20   S. DROMIO I am glad to see you in this merry vein.
           What means this jest? I pray you, master, tell me.

      S. ANTIPHOLUS Yea, dost thou jeer, and flout me in the
           teeth?
           Think'st thou, I jest? Hold, take thou that! And that!
                                         Beats Dromio.

      S. DROMIO Hold, sir, for God's sake! Now your jest is
           earnest.
25   Upon what bargain do you give it me?

      S. ANTIPHOLUS Because that I familiarly sometimes
           Do use you for my fool and chat with you,
           Your sauciness will jest upon my love,
           And make a common of my serious hours.
30   When the sun shines, let foolish gnats make sport;

22 **in the teeth** to my face   24 **earnest** (1) serious (2) a deposit   29 **common**
public property

18

But creep in crannies, when he hides his beams.
If you will jest with me, know my aspect,
And fashion your demeanor to my looks,
Or I will beat this method in your sconce.

S. DROMIO Sconce, call you it? So you would leave   35
battering, I had rather have it a head. And you use
these blows long, I must get a sconce for my head,
and ensconce it too, or else I shall seek my wit in
my shoulders. But, I pray, sir, why am I beaten?

S. ANTIPHOLUS Dost thou not know?   40

S. DROMIO Nothing, sir, but that I am beaten.

S. ANTIPHOLUS Shall I tell you why?

S. DROMIO Ay, sir, and wherefore; for they say every
why hath a wherefore.

S. ANTIPHOLUS Why, first for flouting me, and then
wherefore,   45
For urging it the second time to me.

S. DROMIO Was there ever any man thus beaten out of
season,
When in the why and the wherefore is neither rhyme
nor reason?
Well, sir, I thank you.

S. ANTIPHOLUS   Thank me, sir, for what?

S. DROMIO Marry, sir, for this something that you   50
gave me for nothing.

S. ANTIPHOLUS I'll make you amends next, to give you
nothing for something. But say, sir, is it dinnertime?

S. DROMIO No, sir. I think the meat wants that I
have.   55

S. ANTIPHOLUS In good time, sir. What's that?

---

32 **aspect** attitude (astrological term for planetary influence)   34 **sconce** (1) head
(2) fortification   38 **ensconce** screen   38 **wit** brains   50 **Marry** (mild exclamation, originally an oath by the Virgin Mary)   54 **wants that** lacks what   56 **In
good time** indeed

S. DROMIO Basting.

S. ANTIPHOLUS Well, sir, then 'twill be dry.

S. DROMIO If it be, sir, I pray you eat none of it.

60 S. ANTIPHOLUS Your reason?

S. DROMIO Lest it make you choleric and purchase me
another dry basting.

S. ANTIPHOLUS Well, sir, learn to jest in good time;
there's a time for all things.

65 S. DROMIO I durst have denied that, before you were
so choleric.

S. ANTIPHOLUS By what rule, sir?

S. DROMIO Marry, sir, by a rule as plain as the plain
bald pate of Father Time himself.

70 S. ANTIPHOLUS Let's hear it.

S. DROMIO There's no time for a man to recover his
hair that grows bald by nature.

S. ANTIPHOLUS May he not do it by fine and recovery?

75 S. DROMIO Yes, to pay a fine for a periwig and recover the lost hair of another man.

S. ANTIPHOLUS Why is Time such a niggard of hair,
being, as it is, so plentiful an excrement?

S. DROMIO Because it is a blessing that he bestows on
80   beasts: and what he hath scanted men in hair, he
hath given them in wit.

S. ANTIPHOLUS Why, but there's many a man hath
more hair than wit.

---

57 **Basting** (1) moistening meat (2) thrashing   61 **choleric** irascible (from a
surplus of choler, the humor of dryness)   62 **dry** bloodless   73–74 **fine and
recovery** (legal form of conveyance, with a pun on "foin," the fur of a polecat)
78 **excrement** outgrowth

S. DROMIO Not a man of those but he hath the wit to lose his hair.   85

S. ANTIPHOLUS Why, thou didst conclude hairy men plain dealers without wit.

S. DROMIO The plainer dealer, the sooner lost; yet he loseth it in a kind of jollity.

S. ANTIPHOLUS For what reason?   90

S. DROMIO For two; and sound ones too.

S. ANTIPHOLUS Nay, not sound, I pray you.

S. DROMIO Sure ones, then.

S. ANTIPHOLUS Nay, not sure, in a thing falsing.

S. DROMIO Certain ones, then.   95

S. ANTIPHOLUS Name them.

S. DROMIO The one, to save the money that he spends in tiring; the other, that at dinner they should not drop in his porridge.

S. ANTIPHOLUS You would all this time have proved there is no time for all things.   100

S. DROMIO Marry, and did, sir: namely, e'en no time to recover hair lost by nature.

S. ANTIPHOLUS But your reason was not substantial why there is no time to recover.   105

S. DROMIO Thus I mend it: Time himself is bald, and therefore, to the world's end, will have bald followers.

S. ANTIPHOLUS I knew 'twould be a bald conclusion.

Enter Adriana and Luciana.

But soft, who wafts us yonder?   110

89 **loseth it in a kind of jollity** (as a consequence of venereal disease)
91 **sound** (1) cogent (2) healthy   94 **falsing** deceptive   98 **tiring** hairdressing
109 **bald** (with a quibble on "trivial")   110 **wafts** beckons

21

ADRIANA Ay, ay, Antipholus, look strange and
  frown;
  Some other mistress hath thy sweet aspects.
  I am not Adriana, nor thy wife.
  The time was once when thou unurged wouldst vow
115 That never words were music to thine ear,
  That never object pleasing in thine eye,
  That never touch well welcome to thy hand,
  That never meat sweet-savored in thy taste,
  Unless I spake or looked or touched or carved to
   thee.
120 How comes it now, my husband, O how comes it,
  That thou art then estrangèd from thyself?
  Thyself I call it, being strange to me,
  That, undividable, incorporate,
  Am better than thy dear self's better part.
125 Ah, do not tear away thyself from me;
  For know, my love, as easy mayst thou fall
  A drop of water in the breaking gulf,
  And take unmingled thence that drop again
  Without addition or diminishing
130 As take from me thyself, and not me too.
  How dearly would it touch thee to the quick,
  Shouldst thou but hear I were licentious,
  And that this body, consecrate to thee,
  By ruffian lust should be contaminate!
135 Wouldst thou not spit at me, and spurn at me,
  And hurl the name of husband in my face,
  And tear the stained skin off my harlot brow,
  And from my false hand cut the wedding ring,
  And break it with a deep-divorcing vow?
140 I know thou canst, and therefore see thou do it.
  I am possessed with an adulterate blot.
  My blood is mingled with the crime of lust;
  For, if we two be one, and thou play false,
  I do digest the poison of thy flesh,
145 Being strumpeted by thy contagion.

111 **strange** distant 119 **carved** (a way of flirting at the dinner table)
124 **better part** soul 126 **fall** let fall 131 **dearly** grievously 142 **crime** sin

Keep then fair league and truce with thy true bed,
I live distained, thou undishonorèd.

S. ANTIPHOLUS Plead you to me, fair dame? I know
   you not.
In Ephesus I am but two hours old,
As strange unto your town as to your talk;   150
Who, every word by all my wit being scanned,
Wants wit in all one word to understand.

LUCIANA Fie, brother, how the world is changed with
   you.
When were you wont to use my sister thus?
She sent for you by Dromio home to dinner.   155

S. ANTIPHOLUS By Dromio?

S. DROMIO By me?

ADRIANA By thee, and this thou didst return from
   him:
That he did buffet thee, and in his blows
Denied my house for his, me for his wife.   160

S. ANTIPHOLUS Did you converse, sir, with this gentlewoman?
What is the course and drift of your compact?

S. DROMIO I, sir? I never saw her till this time.

S. ANTIPHOLUS Villain, thou liest; for even her very
   words
Didst thou deliver to me on the Mart.   165

S. DROMIO I never spake with her in all my life.

S. ANTIPHOLUS How can she thus then call us by our
   names,
Unless it be by inspiration?

ADRIANA How ill agrees it with your gravity
To counterfeit thus grossly with your slave,   170

146 **Keep then ... true bed** i.e., if you are faithful to your marriage
147 **distained** unstained   151 **Who** (refers to "I")   162 **course and drift**
general meaning   162 **compact** confederacy   170 **grossly** obviously

23

Abetting him to thwart me in my mood!
Be it my wrong you are from me exempt,
But wrong not that wrong with a more contempt.
Come, I will fasten on this sleeve of thine:
175   Thou art an elm, my husband, I a vine,
Whose weakness, married to thy stronger state,
Makes me with thy strength to communicate.
If aught possess thee from me, it is dross,
Usurping ivy, briar, or idle moss,
180   Who, all for want of pruning, with intrusion
Infect thy sap and live on thy confusion.

S. ANTIPHOLUS [*Aside*] To me she speaks, she moves
        me for her theme;
What, was I married to her in my dream?
Or sleep I now, and think I hear all this?
185   What error drives our eyes and ears amiss?
Until I know this sure uncertainty,
I'll entertain the offered fallacy.

LUCIANA Dromio, go bid the servants spread for
        dinner.

S. DROMIO O, for my beads! I cross me for a sinner.
190   This is the fairy land. O spite of spites!
We talk with goblins, owls, and sprites;
If we obey them not, this will ensue:
They'll suck our breath, or pinch us black and blue.

LUCIANA Why prat'st thou to thyself and answer'st
        not?
Dromio, thou drone, thou snail, thou slug, thou
195   sot.

S. DROMIO I am transformèd, master, am not I?

S. ANTIPHOLUS I think thou art in mind, and so am I.

---

172 **exempt** cut off   173 **But wrong … more contempt** i.e., do not compound
it by adding insult to injury   174 **fasten on** cling to   177 **communicate** share
178 **possess thee** take you away   179 **idle** worthless   181 **confusion** ruin
182 **moves me for her theme** appeals to me as her subject   187 **fallacy** delusion
189 **beads** rosary   195 **sot** dolt

S. DROMIO Nay, master, both in mind and in my
    shape.

S. ANTIPHOLUS Thou hast thine own form.

S. DROMIO   No, I am an ape.

LUCIANA If thou art changed to aught, 'tis to an ass.   200

S. DROMIO 'Tis true, she rides me and I long for
    grass.
  'Tis so, I am an ass; else it could never be
  But I should know her as well as she knows me.

ADRIANA Come, come, no longer will I be a fool,
  To put the finger in the eye and weep,   205
  Whilst man and master laughs my woes to scorn.
  Come, sir, to dinner. Dromio, keep the gate.
  Husband, I'll dine above with you today,
  And shrive you of a thousand idle pranks.
  Sirrah, if any ask you for your master,   210
  Say he dines forth, and let no creature enter.
  Come, sister. Dromio, play the porter well.

S. ANTIPHOLUS [*Aside*] Am I in earth, in heaven, or in
    hell?
  Sleeping or waking, mad or well-advised?
  Known unto these, and to myself disguised?   215
  I'll say as they say, and persever so,
  And in this mist at all adventures go.

S. DROMIO Master, shall I be porter at the gate?

ADRIANA Ay, and let none enter, lest I break your
    pate.

LUCIANA Come, come, Antipholus, we dine too late.   220
                                  [*Exeunt.*]

199 **ape** imitation (or fool)   201 **rides** teases   208 **above** upstairs (represented
by the upper stage)   209 **shrive** hear confession and absolve   210 **Sirrah** (term
used in addressing inferiors)   211 **forth** out   214 **well-advised** of sound mind
217 **adventures** hazards

ACT III

Scene I. [*Before the Phoenix*.]

*Enter Antipholus of Ephesus, his man Dromio,
Angelo the Goldsmith, and Balthasar the Merchant.*

E. ANTIPHOLUS Good Signor Angelo, you must ex-
    cuse us all;
    My wife is shrewish when I keep not hours.
    Say that I lingered with you at your shop
    To see the making of her carcanet,
5   And that tomorrow you will bring it home.
    But here's a villain that would face me down
    He met me on the Mart, and that I beat him,
    And charged him with a thousand marks in gold,
    And that I did deny my wife and house.
10   Thou drunkard, thou, what didst thou mean by this?

E. DROMIO Say what you will, sir, but I know what
    I know—
    That you beat me at the Mart, I have your hand to
    show;
    If the skin were parchment and the blows you gave
    were ink,
    Your own handwriting would tell you what I think.

E. ANTIPHOLUS I think thou art an ass.

III.i.1 **Signor** (the Italian title of respect is applied rather broadly by Shakespeare)
4 **carcanet** jeweled necklace 6 **face me down** contradict me by declaring
9 **deny** disown 12 **hand** (1) handwriting (2) blows

E. DROMIO   Marry, so it doth appear   15
  By the wrongs I suffer and the blows I bear.
  I should kick, being kicked, and being at that pass,
  You would keep from my heels and beware of an
    ass.

E. ANTIPHOLUS You're sad, Signor Balthasar; pray
    God, our cheer
  May answer my good will and your good welcome
    here.   20

BALTHASAR I hold your dainties cheap, sir, and your
    welcome dear.

E. ANTIPHOLUS O, Signor Balthasar, either at flesh or
    fish,
  A tableful of welcome makes scarce one dainty dish.

BALTHASAR Good meat, sir, is common; that every
    churl affords.

E. ANTIPHOLUS And welcome more common, for that's
    nothing but words.   25

BALTHASAR Small cheer and great welcome makes a
    merry feast.

E. ANTIPHOLUS Ay, to a niggardly host and more
    sparing guest.
  But though my cates be mean, take them in good
    part;
  Better cheer may you have, but not with better
    heart.
  But soft, my door is locked; go, bid them let us in. 30

E. DROMIO Maud, Bridget, Marian, Cicely, Gillian,
    Ginn!

S. DROMIO [*Within*] Mome, malt-horse, capon, cox-
    comb, idiot, patch!

17 **at that pass** in that predicament   19 **sad** serious   19 **cheer** entertainment
20 **answer** accord with   24 **churl** peasant   28 **cates** dainties   32 **Mome** ...
patch blockhead, drudge, cuckold, fool, idiot, jester

Either get thee from the door or sit down at the
    hatch.
Dost thou conjure for wenches, that thou call'st for
    such store,
When one is one too many? Go, get thee from the
35   door.

E. DROMIO What patch is made our porter? My
    master stays in the street.

S. DROMIO Let him walk from whence he came, lest
    he catch cold on's feet.

E. ANTIPHOLUS Who talks within there? Ho, open the
    door!

S. DROMIO Right sir, I'll tell you when, and you'll tell
    me wherefore.

E. ANTIPHOLUS Wherefore? For my dinner; I have not
40   dined today.

S. DROMIO Nor today here you must not; come again
    when you may.

E. ANTIPHOLUS What art thou that keep'st me out
    from the house I owe?

S. DROMIO The porter for this time, sir, and my name
    is Dromio.

E. DROMIO O villain, thou hast stol'n both mine office
    and my name.
The one ne'er got me credit, the other mickle
45   blame.
If thou hadst been Dromio today in my place,
Thou wouldst have changed thy face for a name,
    or thy name for an ass.

Enter Luce [above].

---

33 **hatch** lower part of a divided door 34 **store** abundance 37 **on's** in his
42 **owe** own 45 **mickle** much 47 **Thou wouldst ... an ass** you would have
been confused with someone else, or been made a fool of (?)

LUCE What a coil is there, Dromio? Who are those
    at the gate?

E. DROMIO Let my master in, Luce.

LUCE   Faith, no, he comes too late.
    And so tell your master.

E. DROMIO   O Lord, I must laugh!   50
    Have at you with a proverb: "Shall I set in my
    staff?"

LUCE Have at you with another: that's "When? Can
    you tell?"

S. DROMIO If thy name be called Luce—Luce, thou
    hast answered him well.

E. ANTIPHOLUS Do you hear, you minion? You'll let
    us in, I trow?

LUCE I thought to have asked you.

S. DROMIO   And you said no.   55

E. DROMIO So, come help! Well struck! There was
    blow for blow.

E. ANTIPHOLUS Thou baggage, let me in.

LUCE   Can you tell for whose sake?

E. DROMIO Master, knock the door hard.

LUCE   Let him knock till it ache.

E. ANTIPHOLUS You'll cry for this, minion, if I beat the
    door down.

LUCE What needs all that, and a pair of stocks in
    the town?   60

Enter Adriana [above].

---

48 **coil** turmoil   51 **proverb** (they bandy proverbial phrases)   51 **set in my staff** move in   52 **When? Can you tell?** (a contemptuous retort)   54 **minion** hussy   60 **stocks** device for the public confinement of offenders

ADRIANA Who is that at the door that keeps all this
noise?

S. DROMIO By my troth, your town is troubled with
unruly boys.

E. ANTIPHOLUS Are you there, wife? You might have
come before.

ADRIANA Your wife, sir knave! Go, get you from the
door.   [*Exit with Luce.*]

E. DROMIO If you went in pain, master, this knave
65   would go sore.

ANGELO Here is neither cheer, sir, nor welcome; we
would fain have either.

BALTHASAR In debating which was best, we shall part
with neither.

E. DROMIO They stand at the door, master. Bid
them welcome hither.

E. ANTIPHOLUS There is something in the wind, that
we cannot get in.

E. DROMIO You would say so, master, if your gar-
70   ments were thin.
Your cake here is warm within; you stand here in
the cold.
It would make a man mad as a buck to be so
bought and sold.

E. ANTIPHOLUS Go, fetch me something. I'll break ope
the gate.

S. DROMIO Break any breaking here, and I'll break
your knave's pate.

E. DROMIO A man may break a word with you, sir,
75   and words are but wind;

---

62 **boys** fellows   67 **part** depart   72 **buck** male deer (with an implication of
"horn-mad")   72 **bought and sold** cheated   75 **break** exchange   75 **words are
but wind** (a proverb, which Dromio vulgarly quibbles upon)

Ay, and break it in your face, so he break it not
    behind.

S. DROMIO It seems thou want'st breaking. Out upon
    thee, hind!

E. DROMIO Here's too much "out upon thee." I pray
    thee, let me in.

S. DROMIO Ay, when fowls have no feathers, and fish
    have no fin.

E. ANTIPHOLUS Well, I'll break in. Go borrow me a
    crow.   80

E. DROMIO A crow without feather? Master, mean
    you so?
    For a fish without a fin, there's a fowl without a
    feather.
    If a crow help us in, sirrah, we'll pluck a crow
    together.

E. ANTIPHOLUS Go, get thee gone, fetch me an iron
    crow.

BALTHASAR Have patience, sir, O, let it not be so!   85
    Herein you war against your reputation,
    And draw within the compass of suspect
    Th' unviolated honor of your wife.
    Once this—your long experience of her wisdom,
    Her sober virtue, years, and modesty,   90
    Plead on her part some cause to you unknown;
    And doubt not, sir, but she will well excuse
    Why at this time the doors are made against you.
    Be ruled by me, depart in patience,
    And let us to the Tiger all to dinner.   95
    And, about evening, come yourself alone,
    To know the reason of this strange restraint.
    If by strong hand you offer to break in,

77 **breaking** beating   77 **Out upon thee** (a mild curse)   77 **hind** menial
80 **crow** crowbar   83 **pluck a crow** pick a bone   87 **suspect** suspicion
89 **Once this** in summary   92 **excuse** explain   93 **made** shut   95 **Tiger** (name
and sign of an inn)   98 **offer** attempt

31

Now in the stirring passage of the day,
100   A vulgar comment will be made of it;
And that supposèd by the common rout
Against your yet ungallèd estimation,
That may with foul intrusion enter in
And dwell upon your grave when you are dead;
105   For slander lives upon succession,
For ever housed where it gets possession.

E. ANTIPHOLUS You have prevailed. I will depart in
        quiet,
And, in despite of mirth, mean to be merry.
I know a wench of excellent discourse,
110   Pretty and witty; wild and yet, too, gentle;
There will we dine: this woman that I mean,
My wife—but, I protest, without desert—
Hath oftentimes upbraided me withal.
To her will we to dinner. [*To Angelo*] Get you
        home,
115   And fetch the chain; by this, I know, 'tis made;
Bring it, I pray you, to the Porpentine,
For there's the house. That chain will I bestow—
Be it for nothing but to spite my wife—
Upon mine hostess there. Good sir, make haste.
120   Since mine own doors refuse to entertain me,
I'll knock elsewhere, to see if they'll disdain me.

ANGELO I'll meet you at that place some hour hence.

E. ANTIPHOLUS Do so. This jest shall cost me some
        expense.   *Exeunt*.

---

99 **stirring passage** busy traffic   100 **vulgar** public   101 **rout** multitude
102 **ungallèd estimation** unblemished repute   105 **succession** its consequences
108 **in despite of mirth** though disinclined to merriment   115 **by this** by this
time   116 **Porpentine** porcupine (name of the Courtesan's house)

[Scene II. *Above.*]

Enter Luciana, with Antipholus of Syracuse.

LUCIANA And may it be that you have quite forgot
   A husband's office? Shall, Antipholus, hate
   Even in the spring of love thy love-springs rot?
   Shall love, in building, grow so ruinate?
   If you did wed my sister for her wealth,   5
   Then for her wealth's sake use her with more
      kindness;
   Or, if you like elsewhere, do it by stealth,
   Muffle your false love with some show of blindness.
   Let not my sister read it in your eye;
   Be not thy tongue thy own shame's orator;   10
   Look sweet, speak fair, become disloyalty;
   Apparel vice like virtue's harbinger.
   Bear a fair presence, though your heart be tainted,
   Teach sin the carriage of a holy saint,
   Be secret-false: what need she be acquainted?   15
   What simple thief brags of his own attaint?
   'Tis double wrong to truant with your bed
   And let her read it in thy looks at board.
   Shame hath a bastard fame, well managèd;
   Ill deeds is doubled with an evil word.   20
   Alas, poor women! Make us but believe,
   Being compact of credit, that you love us;
   Though others have the arm, show us the sleeve:
   We in your motion turn, and you may move us.
   Then, gentle brother, get you in again;   25

III.ii.3 **love-springs** young plants of love 4 **ruinate** ruinous 7 **like elsewhere**
have some other love 11 **become disloyalty** make infidelity seem becoming
14 **carriage** bearing 16 **attaint** disgrace 17 **truant** play truant 18 **board** table
19 **bastard fame** illegitimate honor 22 **compact of credit** disposed to trust
24 **in your motion** by your moves

        Comfort my sister, cheer her, call her wife;
        'Tis holy sport, to be a little vain,
        When the sweet breath of flattery conquers strife.

S. ANTIPHOLUS Sweet mistress, what your name is else,
        I know not;
30   Nor by what wonder you do hit of mine;
        Less in your knowledge and your grace you show
           not
        Than our earth's wonder, more than earth divine.
        Teach me, dear creature, how to think and speak:
        Lay open to my earthy-gross conceit,
35   Smoth'red in errors, feeble, shallow, weak,
        The folded meaning of your words' deceit.
        Against my soul's pure truth why labor you
        To make it wander in an unknown field?
        Are you a god? Would you create me new?
40   Transform me, then, and to your pow'r I'll yield.
        But if that I am I, then well I know
        Your weeping sister is no wife of mine,
        Nor to her bed no homage do I owe;
        Far more, far more, to you do I decline.
45   O, train me not, sweet mermaid, with thy note,
        To drown me in thy sister's flood of tears.
        Sing, siren, for thyself, and I will dote;
        Spread o'er the silver waves thy golden hairs;
        And as a bed I'll take them, and there lie,
50   And, in that glorious supposition, think
        He gains by death that hath such means to die.
        Let Love, being light, be drownèd if she sink!

LUCIANA What, are you mad, that you do reason so?

S. ANTIPHOLUS Not mad, but mated—how, I do not
        know.

55 LUCIANA It is a fault that springeth from your eye.

---

27 **be a little vain** use a little flattery   30 **hit of** hit on   31 **show** appear
32 **earth's wonder** (these lines are sometimes taken as a compliment to Queen
Elizabeth)   34 **conceit** apprehension   36 **folded** hidden   44 **decline** incline
45 **train** lure   51 **die** (with an implication of sexual fulfillment)   52 **light** (1) not
heavy (2) wanton   54 **mated** (1) confounded (2) wedded

S. ANTIPHOLUS For gazing on your beams, fair sun,
    being by.

LUCIANA Gaze where you should, and that will clear
    your sight.

S. ANTIPHOLUS As good to wink, sweet love, as look
    on night.

LUCIANA Why call you me love? Call my sister so.

S. ANTIPHOLUS Thy sister's sister.

LUCIANA   That's my sister.

S. ANTIPHOLUS   No,   60
    It is thyself, mine own self's better part,
    Mine eye's clear eye, my dear heart's dearer heart;
    My food, my fortune, and my sweet hope's aim;
    My sole earth's heaven, and my heaven's claim.

LUCIANA All this my sister is, or else should be.   65

S. ANTIPHOLUS Call thyself sister, sweet, for I am thee;
    Thee will I love, and with thee lead my life;
    Thou hast no husband yet, nor I no wife.
    Give me thy hand.

LUCIANA   O, soft, sir, hold you still
    I'll fetch my sister, to get her good will.   *Exit*.   70

Enter Dromio of Syracuse.

S. ANTIPHOLUS Why, how now, Dromio! Where run'st
    thou so fast?

S. DROMIO Do you know me, sir? Am I Dromio? Am
    I your man? Am I myself?

S. ANTIPHOLUS Thou art Dromio, thou art my man,   75
    thou art thyself.

S. DROMIO I am an ass; I am a woman's man, and
    besides myself.

58 **wink** shut one's eyes   64 **heaven's claim** claim on heaven

S. ANTIPHOLUS What woman's man? And how besides
80   thyself?

S. DROMIO Marry, sir, besides myself, I am due to
a woman: one that claims me, one that haunts me,
one that will have me.

S. ANTIPHOLUS What claim lays she to thee?

85   S. DROMIO Marry, sir, such claim as you would lay
to your horse; and she would have me as a beast—
not that, I being a beast, she would have me, but
that she, being a very beastly creature, lays claim
to me.

90   S. ANTIPHOLUS What is she?

S. DROMIO A very reverend body; ay, such a one as
a man may not speak of without he say "sir-reverence." I have but lean luck in the match, and
yet is she a wondrous fat marriage.

95   S. ANTIPHOLUS How dost thou mean a fat marriage?

S. DROMIO Marry, sir, she's the kitchen-wench, and
all grease; and I know not what use to put her to,
but to make a lamp of her, and run from her by
her own light. I warrant her rags and the tallow in
100   them will burn a Poland winter. If she lives till
doomsday, she'll burn a week longer than the
whole world.

S. ANTIPHOLUS What complexion is she of?

S. DROMIO Swart, like my shoe, but her face noth-
105   ing like so clean kept; for why? She sweats; a man
may go over-shoes in the grime of it.

S. ANTIPHOLUS That's a fault that water will mend.

---

81 **besides myself** (1) out of my mind (2) in addition to me   81 **due** belonging
86 **a beast** (Elizabethan pronunciation made possible a pun on "abased")
92–93 **sir-reverence** save your reverence (meaning "pardon the expression")
97 **grease** (with a pun on "grace")   101 **week** (with a pun on "wick")   104 **Swart**
swarthy   106 **over-shoes** shoe-deep

s. DROMIO No, sir, 'tis in grain; Noah's flood could not do it.

s. ANTIPHOLUS What's her name?   110

s. DROMIO Nell, sir; but her name and three quarters—that's an ell and three quarters—will not measure her from hip to hip.

s. ANTIPHOLUS Then she bears some breadth?

s. DROMIO No longer from head to foot than from   115
hip to hip. She is spherical, like a globe. I could find out countries in her.

s. ANTIPHOLUS In what part of her body stands Ireland?

s. DROMIO Marry, sir, in her buttocks; I found it out   120
by the bogs.

s. ANTIPHOLUS Where Scotland?

s. DROMIO I found it by the barrenness, hard in the palm of the hand.

s. ANTIPHOLUS Where France?   125

s. DROMIO In her forehead, armed and reverted, making war against her heir.

s. ANTIPHOLUS Where England?

s. DROMIO I looked for the chalky cliffs, but I could find no whiteness in them. But I guess, it stood in   130
her chin, by the salt rheum that ran between France and it.

s. ANTIPHOLUS Where Spain?

s. DROMIO Faith, I saw it not; but I felt it hot in her breath.   135

s. ANTIPHOLUS Where America, the Indies?

108 **in grain** inherent   111 **Nell** (called Luce, III.i.49)   112 **ell** forty-five inches
126 **reverted** revolted   127 **heir** (interpreted as a contemporary allusion to the
struggle of the Catholic League against Henry of Navarre, who succeeded to the
throne of France in 1593)   129 **chalky cliffs** teeth   131 **rheum** moisture from
the nose

S. DROMIO O, sir, upon her nose, all o'er embellished
with rubies, carbuncles, sapphires, declining their
rich aspect to the hot breath of Spain, who sent
140   whole armadoes of carracks to be balleast at her
nose.

S. ANTIPHOLUS Where stood Belgia, the Netherlands?

S. DROMIO O, sir, I did not look so low. To conclude, this drudge, or diviner, laid claim to me,
145   called me Dromio, swore I was assured to her,
told me what privy marks I had about me, as the
mark of my shoulder, the mole in my neck, the
great wart on my left arm, that I, amazed, ran from
her as a witch.
And, I think, if my breast had not been made of
150   faith, and my heart of steel,
She had transformed me to a curtal dog, and made
me turn i' th' wheel.

S. ANTIPHOLUS Go, hie thee presently, post to the road,
And if the wind blow any way from shore,
I will not harbor in this town tonight.
155   If any bark put forth, come to the Mart,
Where I will walk till thou return to me.
If everyone knows us, and we know none,
'Tis time, I think, to trudge, pack, and begone.

S. DROMIO As from a bear a man would run for life,
160   So fly I from her that would be my wife.   *Exit*.

S. ANTIPHOLUS There's none but witches do inhabit
here,
And therefore 'tis high time that I were hence.
She that doth call me husband, even my soul
Doth for a wife abhor. But her fair sister,
165   Possessed with such a gentle sovereign grace,

138 **declining** inclining 140 **armadoes of carracks** fleets of galleons (with
possible reference to the Spanish Armada of 1588) 140 **ballast** loaded
142 **Belgia, the Netherlands** the Low Countries 144 **diviner** witch
145 **assured** betrothed 151 **curtal dog** dog with docked tail 151 **wheel** spit
152 **presently** immediately 152 **road** harbor 153 **And if** if 154 **harbor** lodge
158 **trudge, pack, and begone** (synonyms)

Of such enchanting presence and discourse,
Hath almost made me traitor to myself.
But, lest myself be guilty to self-wrong,
I'll stop mine ears against the mermaid's song.

Enter Angelo with the chain.

ANGELO Master Antipholus—

S. ANTIPHOLUS   Ay, that's my name.   170

ANGELO I know it well, sir. Lo, here is the chain.
I thought to have ta'en you at the Porpentine.
The chain unfinished made me stay thus long.

S. ANTIPHOLUS What is your will that I shall do with
    this?

ANGELO What please yourself, sir; I have made it for
    you.   175

S. ANTIPHOLUS Made it for me, sir? I bespoke it not.

ANGELO Not once, nor twice, but twenty times you
    have.
Go home with it and please your wife withal,
And soon at suppertime I'll visit you,
And then receive my money for the chain.   180

S. ANTIPHOLUS I pray you, sir, receive the money now,
For fear you ne'er see chain nor money more.

ANGELO You are a merry man, sir. Fare you well.
                                        Exit.

S. ANTIPHOLUS What I should think of this, I cannot
    tell:
But this I think, there's no man is so vain   185
That would refuse so fair an offered chain.
I see a man here needs not live by shifts,
When in the streets he meets such golden gifts.
I'll to the Mart, and there for Dromio stay;
If any ship put out, then straight away.   *Exit.*   190

---

168 **to** of   176 **bespoke** ordered   185 **vain** silly   187 **shifts** tricks   190 **straight**
without delay

39

ACT IV

Scene I. [*The Mart*.]

Enter a Merchant, [Angelo the] Goldsmith,
and an Officer.

MERCHANT You know since Pentecost the sum is due,
And since I have not much importuned you,
Nor now I had not, but that I am bound
To Persia, and want guilders for my voyage;
5   Therefore make present satisfaction,
Or I'll attach you by this officer.

ANGELO Even just the sum that I do owe to you
Is growing to me by Antipholus,
And in the instant that I met with you
10   He had of me a chain. At five o'clock
I shall receive the money for the same.
Pleaseth you, walk with me down to his house;
I will discharge my bond, and thank you too.

Enter Antipholus of Ephesus, [and] Dromio
[of Ephesus] from the Courtesan's.

OFFICER That labor may you save. See where he
comes.

E. ANTIPHOLUS While I go to the goldsmith's house,
15   go thou

IV.i.1 **Pentecost** the fiftieth day after Easter   5 **present** immediate   6 **attach**
arrest   8 **growing** accruing   12 **Pleaseth** may it please

And buy a rope's end; that will I bestow
Among my wife and her confederates,
For locking me out of my doors by day.
But soft, I see the goldsmith; get thee gone,
Buy thou a rope, and bring it home to me.   20

E. DROMIO I buy a thousand pound a year! I buy a
     rope!   *Exit Dromio.*

E. ANTIPHOLUS A man is well holp up that trusts to
     you!
I promisèd your presence and the chain,
But neither chain nor goldsmith came to me.
Belike you thought our love would last too long,   25
If it were chained together, and therefore came not.

ANGELO Saving your merry humor, here's the note
How much your chain weighs to the utmost carat,
The fineness of the gold and chargeful fashion—
Which doth amount to three odd ducats more   30
Than I stand debted to this gentleman.
I pray you, see him presently discharged,
For he is bound to sea, and stays but for it.

E. ANTIPHOLUS I am not furnished with the present
     money.
Besides, I have some business in the town.   35
Good signor, take the stranger to my house,
And with you take the chain, and bid my wife
Disburse the sum on the receipt thereof.
Perchance I will be there as soon as you.

ANGELO Then you will bring the chain to her your-
     self?   40

E. ANTIPHOLUS No, bear it with you, lest I come not
     time enough.

16 rope's end (for flogging) 21 I buy ... a rope! (Dromio's obscure irony seems
motivated by his awareness that the rope's end could be used on him) 22 holp
helped 29 chargeful costly 30 ducats gold coins of varying origin and value
32 presently instantly 41 time enough in time

ANGELO Well, sir, I will. Have you the chain about
    you?

E. ANTIPHOLUS And if I have not, sir, I hope you
    have,
Or else you may return without your money.

45 ANGELO Nay, come, I pray you, sir, give me the chain:
Both wind and tide stays for this gentleman,
And I, to blame, have held him here too long.

E. ANTIPHOLUS Good Lord, you use this dalliance
    to excuse
Your breach of promise to the Porpentine.
50 I should have chid you for not bringing it,
But, like a shrew, you first begin to brawl.

MERCHANT The hour steals on; I pray you, sir, dis-
    patch.

ANGELO You hear how he importunes me—the chain!

E. ANTIPHOLUS Why, give it to my wife, and fetch
    your money.

ANGELO Come, come, you know, I gave it you even
55 now;
Either send the chain or send me by some token.

E. ANTIPHOLUS Fie, now you run this humor out of
    breath.
Come, where's the chain? I pray you, let me see it.

MERCHANT My business cannot brook this dalliance.
60 Good sir, say whe'er you'll answer me or no:
If not, I'll leave him to the officer.

E. ANTIPHOLUS I answer you! What should I answer
    you?

ANGELO The money that you owe me for the chain.

E. ANTIPHOLUS I owe you none till I receive the chain.

65 ANGELO You know I gave it you half an hour since.

---

47 **to blame** blameworthy 48 **dalliance** tarrying 51 **shrew** scold (male or
female) 60 **whe'er** whether 60 **answer** pay

E. ANTIPHOLUS You gave me none; you wrong me
   much to say so.

ANGELO You wrong me more, sir, in denying it.
   Consider how it stands upon my credit.

MERCHANT Well, officer, arrest him at my suit.

OFFICER I do,   70
   And charge you in the Duke's name to obey me.

ANGELO This touches me in reputation.
   Either consent to pay this sum for me,
   Or I attach you by this officer.

E. ANTIPHOLUS Consent to pay thee that I never had!   75
   Arrest me, foolish fellow, if thou dar'st.

ANGELO Here is thy fee; arrest him, officer.
   I would not spare my brother in this case,
   If he should scorn me so apparently.

OFFICER I do arrest you, sir; you hear the suit.   80

E. ANTIPHOLUS I do obey thee, till I give thee bail.
   But, sirrah, you shall buy this sport as dear
   As all the metal in your shop will answer.

ANGELO Sir, sir, I shall have law in Ephesus,
   To your notorious shame, I doubt it not.   85

     Enter Dromio of Syracuse from the Bay.

S. DROMIO Master, there's a bark of Epidamnum,
   That stays but till her owner comes aboard,
   And then she bears away. Our fraughtage, sir,
   I have conveyed aboard, and I have bought
   The oil, the balsamum, and aqua-vitae.   90
   The ship is in her trim, the merry wind
   Blows fair from land; they stay for nought at all
   But for their owner, master, and yourself.

---

68 **stands upon** concerns 79 **apparently** openly 88 **fraughtage** cargo
90 **balsamum** balm 90 **aqua-vitae** brandy 91 **in her trim** ready to sail
93 **master** captain (?)

E. ANTIPHOLUS How now! a madman? Why, thou
    peevish sheep,
95   What ship of Epidamnum stays for me?

S. DROMIO A ship you sent me to, to hire waftage.

E. ANTIPHOLUS Thou drunken slave, I sent thee for a
    rope,
    And told thee to what purpose and what end.

S. DROMIO You sent me for a rope's end as soon.
100   You sent me to the bay, sir, for a bark.

E. ANTIPHOLUS I will debate this matter at more
    leisure,
    And teach your ears to list me with more heed.
    To Adriana, villain, hie thee straight;
    Give her this key, and tell her, in the desk
105   That's covered o'er with Turkish tapestry
    There is a purse of ducats; let her send it.
    Tell her I am arrested in the street,
    And that shall bail me. Hie thee, slave, begone.
    On, officer, to prison till it come.

                      Exeunt [all but Dromio].

110 S. DROMIO To Adriana—that is where we dined,
    Where Dowsabel did claim me for her husband.
    She is too big, I hope, for me to compass.
    Thither I must, although against my will;
    For servants must their masters' minds fulfill.

                            Exit.

---

94 **peevish** silly   94 **sheep** (with a pun on "ship")   96 **waftage** passage by sea
99 **rope's end** (in the sense of "halter" here)   102 **list** listen to   111 **Dowsabel**
(from *douce et belle*, sweet and pretty, an elaborate name for a heroine, ironically
applied to Nell)   112 **compass** (1) obtain (2) embrace

[Scene II. *Before the Phoenix.*]

Enter Adriana and Luciana.

ADRIANA Ah, Luciana, did he tempt thee so?
  Mightst thou perceive austerely in his eye,
  That he did plead in earnest, yea or no?
  Looked he or red or pale, or sad or merrily?
  What observation mad'st thou in this case   5
  Of his heart's meteors tilting in his face?

LUCIANA First, he denied you had in him no right.

ADRIANA He meant he did me none; the more my
    spite.

LUCIANA Then swore he that he was a stranger here.

ADRIANA And true he swore, though yet forsworn he
    were.   10

LUCIANA Then pleaded I for you.

ADRIANA   And what said he?

LUCIANA That love I begged for you he begged of me.

ADRIANA With what persuasion did he tempt thy love?

LUCIANA With words that in an honest suit might
    move.
  First he did praise my beauty, then my speech.   15

ADRIANA Didst speak him fair?

LUCIANA   Have patience, I beseech.

IV.ii.2 **austerely** by the austerity   6 **heart's meteors tilting** emotions tossing
7 **denied ... no right** (double negative)   8 **spite** vexation   14 **honest** honorable
16 **speak him fair** speak to him kindly

ADRIANA I cannot, nor I will not, hold me still.
 My tongue, though not my heart, shall have his will.
 He is deformèd, crookèd, old and sere,
20 Ill-faced, worse bodied, shapeless everywhere:
 Vicious, ungentle, foolish, blunt, unkind,
 Stigmatical in making, worse in mind.

LUCIANA Who would be jealous then of such a one?
 No evil lost is wailed when it is gone.

25 ADRIANA Ah, but I think him better than I say;
 And yet would herein others' eyes were worse.
 Far from her nest the lapwing cries away;
 My heart prays for him, though my tongue do curse.

Enter Dromio of Syracuse.

S. DROMIO Here, go—the desk, the purse! Sweet, now, make haste.

LUCIANA How hast thou lost thy breath?

30 S. DROMIO   By running fast.

ADRIANA Where is thy master, Dromio? Is he well?

S. DROMIO No, he's in Tartar limbo, worse than hell:
 A devil in an everlasting garment hath him;
 One whose hard heart is buttoned up with steel:
35 A fiend, a fairy, pitiless and rough:
 A wolf, nay worse, a fellow all in buff:
 A back-friend, a shoulder-clapper, one that countermands
 The passages of alleys, creeks, and narrow lands;

---

18 **his** its 20 **shapeless** unshapely 22 **Stigmatical in making** deformed in appearance 27 **lapwing** peewit (who draws intruders away from its nest in the manner described) 32 **Tartar limbo** prison, as well as the outskirts of hell (the pagan Tartarus) 33 **everlasting garment** leather coat, the police uniform 35 **fairy** malignant spirit 36 **buff** ox-hide 37 **back-friend** false friend (with a quibble on the mode of arrest) 37 **shoulder-clapper** bailiff 37 **countermands** prohibits 38 **creeks** winding alleys

A hound that runs counter, and yet draws dry-
    foot well;
One that, before the judgment, carries poor souls
    to hell.   40

ADRIANA Why, man, what is the matter?

S. DROMIO I do not know the matter, he is 'rested
    on the case.

ADRIANA What, is he arrested? Tell me, at whose suit.

S. DROMIO I know not at whose suit he is arrested
    well;
But is in a suit of buff which 'rested him, that can
    I tell.   45
Will you send him, Mistress Redemption, the
    money in his desk?

ADRIANA Go fetch it, sister. This I wonder at,
                             Exit Luciana.
Thus he, unknown to me, should be in debt.
Tell me, was he arrested on a band?

S. DROMIO Not on a band, but on a stronger thing: 50
A chain, a chain! Do you not hear it ring?

ADRIANA What, the chain?

S. DROMIO   No, no, the bell; 'tis time
    that I were gone.
It was two ere I left him, and now the clock strikes
    one.

ADRIANA The hours come back! That did I never hear.

S. DROMIO O yes. If any hour meet a sergeant, 'a
    turns back for very fear.   55

---

39 **counter** (1) contrary (2) Counter, a debtors' prison   39 **draws dry-foot** hunts
by scent   42 **'rested** arrested   42 **case** (1) special case at law (2) suit of clothes
49 **band** bond   53 **one** (with a pun on "on")   55 **hour** (pun on "whore")
55 **'a** (colloquial form of "he," "she," or "it")

ADRIANA As if time were in debt! How fondly dost
         thou reason!

S. DROMIO Time is a very bankrupt, and owes more
         than he's worth to season.
      Nay, he's a thief too: have you not heard men say,
      That time comes stealing on by night and day?
60   If 'a be in debt and theft, and a sergeant in the way,
      Hath he not reason to turn back an hour in a day?

                    Enter Luciana.

ADRIANA Go, Dromio. There's the money, bear it
         straight,
      And bring thy master home immediately.
      Come, sister. I am pressed down with conceit:
65   Conceit, my comfort and my injury.
                         Exit [with Luciana and Dromio].

              [Scene III. *The Mart.*]

            Enter Antipholus of Syracuse.

S. ANTIPHOLUS There's not a man I meet but doth
         salute me
      As if I were their well-acquainted friend;
      And everyone doth call me by my name.
      Some tender money to me, some invite me;
5   Some other give me thanks for kindnesses;
      Some offer me commodities to buy.
      Even now a tailor called me in his shop
      And showed me silks that he had bought for me,
      And therewithal took measure of my body.
10   Sure, these are but imaginary wiles,
      And Lapland sorcerers inhabit here.

56 fondly foolishly   57 **season** occasion (?), ripen (?)   64 **conceit** imagination
IV.iii.5 **other** others   10 **imaginary wiles** tricks of the imagination   11 **Lap-
land** (notorious for sorcery)

Enter Dromio of Syracuse.

S. DROMIO Master, here's the gold you sent me for. What, have you got the picture of old Adam new-appareled?

S. ANTIPHOLUS What gold is this? What Adam dost thou   15
mean?

S. DROMIO Not that Adam that kept the paradise, but that Adam that keeps the prison; he that goes in the calf's skin that was killed for the Prodigal; he that came behind you, sir, like an evil angel, and bid   20
you forsake your liberty.

S. ANTIPHOLUS I understand thee not.

S. DROMIO No? Why, 'tis a plain case: he that went, like a bass-viol, in a case of leather; the man, sir, that, when gentlemen are tired gives them a sob   25
and 'rests them; he, sir, that takes pity on decayed men, and gives them suits of durance; he that sets up his rest to do more exploits with his mace than a morris-pike.

S. ANTIPHOLUS What, thou mean'st an officer?   30

S. DROMIO Ay, sir, the sergeant of the band: he that brings any man to answer it that breaks his band; one that thinks a man always going to bed, and says, "God give you good rest!"

S. ANTIPHOLUS Well, sir, there rest in your foolery.   35
Is there any ships puts forth tonight? May we be gone?

S. DROMIO Why, sir, I brought you word an hour

---

13 **old Adam** the sergeant in his buff coat (?)   18-19 **goes in the calf's skin** wears the leather garb (with a quibble on the fatted calf in the parable)   23 **case** (1) situation (2) box (3) suit   25 **sob** rest given a horse to recover its wind (with quibbles)   27 **suits of durance** durable clothing (with puns on "lawsuits" and "imprisonment")   27-28 **sets up his rest** stakes all   28 **mace** staff of authority   29 **morris-pike** Moorish lance   32 **band** (with pun on "bond")   34 **rest** (with the usual pun)

40   since that the bark *Expedition* put forth tonight,
          and then were you hind'red by the sergeant to tarry
          for the hoy *Delay*. Here are the angels that you
          sent for to deliver you.

S. ANTIPHOLUS The fellow is distract, and so am I,
          And here we wander in illusions.
45   Some blessèd power deliver us from hence!

Enter a Courtesan.

COURTESAN Well met, well met, Master Antipholus.
          I see, sir, you have found the goldsmith now.
          Is that the chain you promised me today?

S. ANTIPHOLUS Satan, avoid! I charge thee, tempt me
          not!

50   S. DROMIO Master, is this Mistress Satan?

S. ANTIPHOLUS It is the devil.

S. DROMIO Nay, she is worse, she is the devil's dam;
          and here she comes in the habit of a light wench,
          and thereof comes that the wenches say, "God
55   damn me." That's as much to say, "God make me
          a light wench." It is written, they appear to men
          like angels of light. Light is an effect of fire, and
          fire will burn: ergo, light wenches will burn.
          Come not near her.

COURTESAN Your man and you are marvelous merry,
60   sir.
          Will you go with me? We'll mend our dinner here.

S. DROMIO Master, if you do, expect spoon-meat, or
          bespeak a long spoon.

S. ANTIPHOLUS Why, Dromio?

___

39 **bark** ship (allegorically named by Dromio)   41 **hoy** coasting vessel   41 **angels** coins worth ten shillings (with pun)   49 **avoid** begone (Matthew 4:10)   52 **dam** mother   53 **habit** dress   53 **light** (with implication of loose morals)   58 **ergo** it follows logically   58 **burn** infect with disease   61 **mend** complete   62 **spoon-meat** soft food (introducing an allusion to the proverb about the devil)

S. DROMIO Marry, he must have a long spoon that   65
  must eat with the devil.

S. ANTIPHOLUS Avoid, then, fiend! What tell'st thou
    me of supping?
  Thou art, as you are all, a sorceress.
  I conjure thee to leave me and be gone.

COURTESAN Give me the ring of mine you had at
    dinner,   70
  Or, for my diamond, the chain you promised,
  And I'll be gone, sir, and not trouble you.

S. DROMIO Some devils ask but the parings of one's
    nail,
  A rush, a hair, a drop of blood, a pin,
  A nut, a cherry-stone;   75
  But she, more covetous, would have a chain.
  Master, be wise; and if you give it her,
  The devil will shake her chain, and fright us with it.

COURTESAN I pray you, sir, my ring, or else the chain.
  I hope you do not mean to cheat me so!   80

S. ANTIPHOLUS Avaunt, thou witch! Come, Dromio,
    let us go.

S. DROMIO Fly pride, says the peacock. Mistress,
    that you know.   *Exit [with Antipholus].*

COURTESAN Now, out of doubt, Antipholus is mad,
  Else would he never so demean himself.
  A ring he hath of mine worth forty ducats,   85
  And for the same he promised me a chain;
  Both one and other he denies me now.
  The reason that I gather he is mad,
  Besides this present instance of his rage,
  Is a mad tale he told today at dinner,   90
  Of his own doors being shut against his entrance.

69 **conjure** solemnly call on   73 **parings** (witchcraft requires such appurtenances
in order to cast a spell)   79 **chain** (cf. Revelation, 20:1-2)   81 **Avaunt** away
82 **peacock** (emblem of pride, which was also personified by a harlot)
84 **demean** behave   89 **rage** madness

Belike his wife, acquainted with his fits,
On purpose shut the doors against his way.
My way is now to hie home to his house,
95   And tell his wife that, being lunatic,
He rushed into my house and took perforce
My ring away. This course I fittest choose,
For forty ducats is too much to lose.   [*Exit.*]

[Scene IV. *The same.*]

Enter Antipholus of Ephesus with a Jailer.

E. ANTIPHOLUS Fear me not, man, I will not break
       away.
I'll give thee, ere I leave thee, so much money,
To warrant thee, as I am 'rested for.
My wife is in a wayward mood today,
5   And will not lightly trust the messenger
That I should be attached in Ephesus;
I tell you, 'twill sound harshly in her ears.

Enter Dromio of Ephesus, with a rope's end.

Here comes my man, I think he brings the money.
How now, sir! Have you that I sent you for?

E. DROMIO Here's that, I warrant you, will pay them
10   all.

E. ANTIPHOLUS But where's the money?

E. DROMIO Why, sir, I gave the money for the rope.

E. ANTIPHOLUS Five hundred ducats, villain, for a
       rope?

E. DROMIO I'll serve you, sir, five hundred at the
       rate.

96 **perforce** by force   IV.iv.3 **warrant** secure   6 **attached** arrested   10 **pay**
(with a beating)   14 **serve you** supply you with

E. ANTIPHOLUS To what end did I bid thee hie thee
    home?   15

E. DROMIO To a rope's end, sir, and to that end am
    I returned.

E. ANTIPHOLUS And to that end, sir, I will welcome
    you.   [*Beats Dromio.*]

OFFICER Good sir, be patient.

E. DROMIO Nay, 'tis for me to be patient; I am in
    adversity.   20

OFFICER Good now, hold thy tongue.

E. DROMIO Nay, rather persuade him to hold his
    hands.

E. ANTIPHOLUS Thou whoreson, senseless villain!

E. DROMIO I would I were senseless, sir, that I might   25
    not feel your blows.

E. ANTIPHOLUS Thou art sensible in nothing but
    blows, and so is an ass.

E. DROMIO I am an ass, indeed; you may prove it by
    my long ears. I have served him from the hour of   30
    my nativity to this instant, and have nothing at his
    hands for my service but blows. When I am cold,
    he heats me with beating; when I am warm, he
    cools me with beating. I am waked with it when
    I sleep, raised with it when I sit, driven out of   35
    doors with it when I go from home, welcomed
    home with it when I return; nay, I bear it on my
    shoulders, as a beggar wont her brat; and, I think,
    when he hath lamed me, I shall beg with it from
    door to door.   40

Enter Adriana, Luciana, Courtesan, and a
Schoolmaster called Pinch.

15 **end** purpose (on which Dromio quibbles)   21 **Good** (used vocatively)
24 **whoreson** bastard   27 **sensible** (1) reasonable (2) sensitive   30 **ears** (pun on
"years")   38 **wont** habitually does

53

E. ANTIPHOLUS Come, go along; my wife is coming
 yonder.

E. DROMIO Mistress, *"respice finem,"* respect your
 end; or rather, the prophecy like the parrot, "beware the rope's end."

45 E. ANTIPHOLUS Wilt thou still talk?   *Beats Dromio.*

COURTESAN How say you now? Is not your husband
 mad?

ADRIANA His incivility confirms no less.
 Good Doctor Pinch, you are a conjurer;
 Establish him in his true sense again,
50 And I will please you what you will demand.

LUCIANA Alas, how fiery and how sharp he looks!

COURTESAN Mark how he trembles in his ecstasy!

PINCH Give me your hand, and let me feel your pulse.
         [Antipholus strikes him.]

E. ANTIPHOLUS There is my hand, and let it feel
 your ear!

55 PINCH I charge thee, Satan, housed within this man,
 To yield possession to my holy prayers,
 And to thy state of darkness hie thee straight;
 I conjure thee by all the saints in heaven.

E. ANTIPHOLUS Peace, doting wizard, peace; I am not
 mad.

60 ADRIANA O, that thou wert not, poor distressèd soul!

E. ANTIPHOLUS You minion, you, are these your
 customers?
 Did this companion with the saffron face
 Revel and feast it at my house today,

42 **respice finem** (this proverbial phrase, which Dromio translates, was sometimes punningly altered to *"respice funem,"* remember the rope) 43 **parrot**
(parrots were taught to cry "rope") 48 **conjurer** (who can exorcise evil spirits,
also called "Doctor" because of his learning) 50 **please** satisfy 52 **ecstasy**
frenzy 61 **minion** harlot 62 **companion** low fellow 62 **saffron** yellow

Whilst upon me the guilty doors were shut,
And I denied to enter in my house?   65

ADRIANA O, husband, God doth know you dined at
home,
Where would you had remained until this time,
Free from these slanders and this open shame!

E. ANTIPHOLUS Dined at home! Thou villain, what
sayest thou?

E. DROMIO Sir, sooth to say, you did not dine at
home.   70

E. ANTIPHOLUS Were not my doors locked up, and I
shut out?

E. DROMIO Perdie, your doors were locked, and you
shut out.

E. ANTIPHOLUS And did not she herself revile me
there?

E. DROMIO *Sans fable*, she herself reviled you there.

E. ANTIPHOLUS Did not her kitchen maid rail, taunt,
and scorn me?   75

E. DROMIO Certes, she did; the kitchen vestal
scorned you.

E. ANTIPHOLUS And did not I in rage depart from
thence?

E. DROMIO In verity, you did; my bones bears witness,
That since have felt the vigor of his rage.

ADRIANA Is't good to soothe him in these contraries?   80

PINCH It is no shame; the fellow finds his vein,
And yielding to him humors well his frenzy.

---

65 **denied** not allowed   72 **Perdie** by God ("*par Dieu*")   74 **Sans fable** without
lying (French)   76 **Certes** certainly   76 **kitchen vestal** (so called, as Dr.
Johnson pointed out, because she kept the fire burning, like the vestal virgins of
Rome)   80 **soothe** humor

E. ANTIPHOLUS Thou hast suborned the goldsmith to
    arrest me.

ADRIANA Alas, I sent you money to redeem you,
85   By Dromio here, who came in haste for it.

E. DROMIO Money by me? Heart and goodwill you
    might,
    But, surely, master, not a rag of money.

E. ANTIPHOLUS Went'st not thou to her for a purse
    of ducats?

ADRIANA He came to me, and I delivered it.

90 LUCIANA And I am witness with her that she did.

E. DROMIO God and the rope-maker bear me witness
    That I was sent for nothing but a rope.

PINCH Mistress, both man and master is possessed;
    I know it by their pale and deadly looks.
95   They must be bound, and laid in some dark room.

E. ANTIPHOLUS Say, wherefore didst thou lock me
    forth today,
    And why dost thou deny the bag of gold?

ADRIANA I did not, gentle husband, lock thee forth.

E. DROMIO And, gentle master, I received no gold;
100   But I confess, sir, that we were locked out.

ADRIANA Dissembling villain, thou speak'st false in
    both.

E. ANTIPHOLUS Dissembling harlot, thou art false in
    all,
    And art confederate with a damnèd pack
    To make a loathsome abject scorn of me;
105   But with these nails I'll pluck out these false eyes
    That would behold in me this shameful sport.

Enter three or four, and offer to bind him.
He strives.

83 **suborned** colluded with 87 **rag** (slang for farthing) 96 **forth** out
103 **confederate** in conspiracy 103 **pack** gang of rogues

ADRIANA O, bind him, bind him, let him not come
   near me!

PINCH More company! The fiend is strong within him.

LUCIANA Ay me, poor man, how pale and wan he
   looks.

E. ANTIPHOLUS What, will you murder me? Thou
   jailer, thou,   110
  I am thy prisoner; wilt thou suffer them
  To make a rescue?

OFFICER   Masters, let him go.
  He is my prisoner, and you shall not have him.

PINCH Go, bind this man, for he is frantic too.

ADRIANA What wilt thou do, thou peevish officer?   115
  Hast thou delight to see a wretched man
  Do outrage and displeasure to himself?

OFFICER He is my prisoner; if I let him go,
  The debt he owes will be required of me.

ADRIANA I will discharge thee ere I go from thee.   120
  Bear me forthwith unto his creditor,
  And, knowing how the debt grows, I will pay it.
  Good master doctor, see him safe conveyed
  Home to my house. O most unhappy day!

E. ANTIPHOLUS O most unhappy strumpet!   125

E. DROMIO Master, I am here ent'red in bond for you.

E. ANTIPHOLUS Out on thee, villain! Wherefore dost
   thou mad me?

E. DROMIO Will you be bound for nothing? Be mad,
   good master;
  Cry, "The devil!"

LUCIANA God help, poor souls, how idly do they
   talk!   130

109 Ay me (expression of sympathy) 112 rescue deliverance by force
115 peevish stupid 117 displeasure offense 120 discharge pay
124 unhappy unfortunate 127 mad madden 130 idly foolishly

ADRIANA Go bear him hence. Sister, go you with me.

*Exeunt [Pinch and others with Antipholus of
Ephesus and Dromio of Ephesus]. Manet Officer,
Adriana, Luciana, Courtesan.*

Say now, whose suit is he arrested at?

OFFICER One Angelo, a goldsmith, do you know him?

ADRIANA I know the man. What is the sum he owes?

OFFICER Two hundred ducats.

135 ADRIANA   Say, how grows it due?

OFFICER Due for a chain your husband had of him.

ADRIANA He did bespeak a chain for me, but had it
    not.

COURTESAN Whenas your husband, all in rage, today
    Came to my house, and took away my ring—
140 The ring I saw upon his finger now—
    Straight after did I meet him with a chain.

ADRIANA It may be so, but I did never see it.
    Come, jailer, bring me where the goldsmith is;
    I long to know the truth hereof at large.

*Enter Antipholus of Syracuse, with his rapier
drawn, and Dromio of Syracuse.*

145 LUCIANA God for thy mercy, they are loose again.

ADRIANA And come with naked swords. Let's call
    more help
To have them bound again.

OFFICER   Away, they'll kill us!

*Run all out. Exeunt omnes as fast as may be,
frighted.*

S. ANTIPHOLUS I see these witches are afraid of swords.

131s.d. **Manet** remains (Latin; third person singular, but common with a plural
subject) 135 **grows** comes 146 **naked** drawn

S. DROMIO She that would be your wife now ran from
    you.

S. ANTIPHOLUS Come to the Centaur; fetch our stuff
    from thence.   150
    I long that we were safe and sound aboard.

S. DROMIO Faith, stay here this night; they will surely
    do us no harm. You saw they speak us fair, give
    us gold. Methinks they are such a gentle nation
    that, but for the mountain of mad flesh that claims   155
    marriage of me, I could find in my heart to stay here
    still, and turn witch.

S. ANTIPHOLUS I will not stay tonight for all the town;
    Therefore away, to get our stuff aboard.   *Exeunt.*

150 stuff baggage   157 still always

ACT V

Scene I. [*Before the Phoenix.*]

Enter [Another] Merchant and [Angelo] the
Goldsmith.

ANGELO I am sorry, sir, that I have hind'red you;
But I protest he had the chain of me.
Though most dishonestly he doth deny it.

MERCHANT How is the man esteemed here in the city?

5 ANGELO Of very reverend reputation, sir,
Of credit infinite, highly beloved,
Second to none that lives here in the city.
His word might bear my wealth at any time.

MERCHANT Speak softly; yonder, as I think, he walks.

Enter Antipholus and Dromio of Syracuse again.

10 ANGELO 'Tis so; and that self chain about his neck,
Which he forswore most monstrously to have.
Good sir, draw near to me; I'll speak to him.
Signor Antipholus, I wonder much
That you would put me to this shame and trouble,
15 And not without some scandal to yourself,
With circumstance and oaths so to deny
This chain which now you wear so openly.

V.i.8 **bear** command the support of   10 **self** same   11 **forswore** denied on oath
16 **circumstance** detailed argument

Besides the charge, the shame, imprisonment,
You have done wrong to this my honest friend,
Who, but for staying on our controversy,   20
Had hoisted sail and put to sea today.
This chain you had of me, can you deny it?

S. ANTIPHOLUS I think I had; I never did deny it.

MERCHANT Yes, that you did, sir, and forswore it too.

S. ANTIPHOLUS Who heard me to deny it or forswear
    it?   25

MERCHANT These ears of mine, thou know'st, did hear
    thee.
Fie on thee, wretch! 'Tis pity that thou liv'st
To walk where any honest men resort.

S. ANTIPHOLUS Thou art a villain to impeach me thus.
I'll prove mine honor and mine honesty   30
Against thee presently, if thou dar'st stand.

MERCHANT I dare, and do defy thee for a villain!

They draw. Enter Adriana, Luciana, Courtesan,
and others.

ADRIANA Hold, hurt him not, for God's sake! He is
    mad.
Some get within him, take his sword away.
Bind Dromio too, and bear them to my house.   35

S. DROMIO Run, master, run; for God's sake, take a
    house!
This is some priory. In, or we are spoiled.
                                        Exeunt to the Priory.

Enter Lady Abbess.

ABBESS Be quiet, people. Wherefore throng you
    hither?

ADRIANA To fetch my poor distracted husband hence.

18 **charge** expense   29 **impeach** accuse   31 **presently** at once   31 **stand**
prepare to fight   34 **within him** inside his guard   36 **take a house** get inside

40   Let us come in, that we may bind him fast,
        And bear him home for his recovery.

ANGELO I knew he was not in his perfect wits.

MERCHANT I am sorry now that I did draw on him.

ABBESS How long hath this possession held the man?

45   ADRIANA This week he hath been heavy, sour, sad,
        And much different from the man he was;
        But till this afternoon his passion
        Ne'er brake into extremity of rage.

        ABBESS Hath he not lost much wealth by wrack of sea?
50   Buried some dear friend? Hath not else his eye
        Strayed his affection in unlawful love—
        A sin prevailing much in youthful men,
        Who give their eyes the liberty of gazing?
        Which of these sorrows is he subject to?

55   ADRIANA To none of these, except it be the last,
        Namely, some love that drew him oft from home.

        ABBESS You should for that have reprehended him.

        ADRIANA Why, so I did.

        ABBESS   Ay, but not rough enough.

        ADRIANA As roughly as my modesty would let me.

        ABBESS Haply, in private.

60   ADRIANA   And in assemblies too.

        ABBESS Ay, but not enough.

        ADRIANA It was the copy of our conference.
        In bed he slept not for my urging it;
        At board he fed not for my urging it;
65   Alone, it was the subject of my theme:
        In company I often glancèd it;
        Still did I tell him it was vile and bad.

---

44 **possession** (by evil spirits)   49 **wrack of sea** shipwreck   51 **Strayed** led astray
62 **copy** topic   63 **for** because of   66 **glancèd** touched on   67 **Still** continually

ABBESS And thereof came it that the man was mad.
　The venom clamors of a jealous woman
　Poisons more deadly than a mad dog's tooth.   70
　It seems his sleeps were hind'red by thy railing,
　And thereof comes it that his head is light.
　Thou say'st his meat was sauced with thy
　　upbraidings;
　Unquiet meals make ill digestions;
　Thereof the raging fire of fever bred—   75
　And what's a fever but a fit of madness?
　Thou sayest his sports were hind'red by thy brawls;
　Sweet recreation barred, what doth ensue
　But moody and dull melancholy,
　Kinsman to grim and comfortless despair,   80
　And at her heels a huge infectious troop
　Of pale distemperatures and foes to life?
　In food, in sport, and life-preserving rest
　To be disturbed, would mad or man or beast.
　The consequence is, then, thy jealous fits   85
　Hath scared thy husband from the use of wits.

LUCIANA She never reprehended him but mildly,
　When he demeaned himself rough, rude, and
　　wildly.
　Why bear you these rebukes and answer not?

ADRIANA She did betray me to my own reproof.   90
　Good people, enter and lay hold on him.

ABBESS No, not a creature enters in my house.

ADRIANA Then, let your servants bring my husband
　forth.

ABBESS Neither. He took this place for sanctuary,
　And it shall privilege him from your hands   95
　Till I have brought him to his wits again,
　Or lose my labor in assaying it.

69 venom venomous 82 distemperatures disorders 84 mad madden
88 demeaned conducted 90 my own reproof self-accusation 94 sanctuary
right of asylum 95 privilege him grant him immunity 97 assaying attempting

63

ADRIANA I will attend my husband, be his nurse,
Diet his sickness, for it is my office,
100 And will have no attorney but myself;
And therefore let me have him home with me.

ABBESS Be patient, for I will not let him stir
Till I have used the approvèd means I have,
With wholesome syrups, drugs, and holy prayers,
105 To make of him a formal man again.
It is a branch and parcel of mine oath,
A charitable duty of my order;
Therefore depart, and leave him here with me.

ADRIANA I will not hence, and leave my husband here;
110 And ill it doth beseem your holiness
To separate the husband and the wife.

ABBESS Be quiet and depart, thou shalt not have him.
                                        [Exit.]

LUCIANA Complain unto the Duke of this indignity.

ADRIANA Come, go. I will fall prostrate at his feet,
115 And never rise until my tears and prayers
Have won his Grace to come in person hither,
And take perforce my husband from the Abbess.

MERCHANT By this, I think, the dial points at five:
Anon, I'm sure, the Duke himself in person
120 Comes this way to the melancholy vale,
The place of death and sorry execution,
Behind the ditches of the abbey here.

ANGELO Upon what cause?

MERCHANT To see a reverend Syracusian merchant,
125 Who put unluckily into this bay
Against the laws and statutes of this town,
Beheaded publicly for his offense.

ANGELO See, where they come. We will behold his
death.

100 **attorney** agent   103 **approvèd** tested   105 **formal** normal   106 **branch
and parcel** part and parcel   121 **sorry** sorrowful

LUCIANA Kneel to the Duke before he pass the abbey.

Enter the Duke of Ephesus and [Egeon] the
Merchant of Syracuse, barehead, with the Heads-
man and other Officers.

DUKE Yet once again proclaim it publicly,   130
   If any friend will pay the sum for him,
   He shall not die; so much we tender him.

ADRIANA Justice, most sacred Duke, against the
   Abbess!

DUKE She is a virtuous and a reverend lady.
   It cannot be that she hath done thee wrong.   135

ADRIANA May it please your Grace, Antipholus, my
   husband,
   Who I made lord of me and all I had
   At your important letters, this ill day
   A most outrageous fit of madness took him:
   That desp'rately he hurried through the street,   140
   With him his bondman all as mad as he,
   Doing displeasure to the citizens
   By rushing in their houses, bearing thence
   Rings, jewels, anything his rage did like.
   Once did I get him bound, and sent him home,   145
   Whilst to take order for the wrongs I went,
   That here and there his fury had committed.
   Anon, I wot not by what strong escape,
   He broke from those that had the guard of him,
   And with his mad attendant and himself,   150
   Each one with ireful passion, with drawn swords,
   Met us again and, madly bent on us,
   Chased us away, till, raising of more aid,
   We came again to bind them. Then they fled
   Into this abbey, whither we pursued them;   155
   And here the Abbess shuts the gates on us,
   And will not suffer us to fetch him out,
   Nor send him forth that we may bear him hence.

132 **tender** regard   138 **important** pressing   140 **That** so that   141 **bondman**
slave   142 **displeasure** harm   146 **take order** settle   148 **wot** know
148 **strong** violent

160

Therefore, most gracious Duke, with thy command,
Let him be brought forth and borne hence for help.

DUKE Long since thy husband served me in my wars;
And I to thee engaged a prince's word,
When thou didst make him master of thy bed,
To do him all the grace and good I could.

165

Go, some of you, knock at the abbey gate,
And bid the Lady Abbess come to me.
I will determine this before I stir.

Enter a Messenger.

MESSENGER O mistress, mistress, shift and save
   yourself.
My master and his man are both broke loose,

170

Beaten the maids a-row, and bound the doctor,
Whose beard they have singed off with brands of
   fire,
And ever as it blazed, they threw on him
Great pails of puddled mire to quench the hair.
My master preaches patience to him, and the while

175

His man with scissors nicks him like a fool;
And, sure, unless you send some present help,
Between them they will kill the conjurer.

ADRIANA Peace, fool, thy master and his man are here,
And that is false thou dost report to us.

180

MESSENGER Mistress, upon my life, I tell you true;
I have not breathed almost since I did see it.
He cries for you and vows, if he can take you,
To scorch your face and to disfigure you.

Cry within.

Hark, hark! I hear him, mistress. Fly, begone.

DUKE Come, stand by me; fear nothing. Guard with

185

   halberds!

170 **a-row** one after another   173 **puddled** muddied   175 **fool** (Elizabethan
fools had their hair cut off)   181 **not breathed almost** hardly breathed
185 **halberds** (poles with heads like battle-axes)

ADRIANA Ay me, it is my husband! Witness you,
That he is borne about invisible.
Even now we housed him in the abbey here,
And now he's there, past thought of human
reason.

Enter Antipholus and Dromio of Ephesus.

E. ANTIPHOLUS Justice, most gracious Duke! O, grant
me justice,   190
Even for the service that long since I did thee,
When I bestrid thee in the wars, and took
Deep scars to save thy life; even for the blood
That then I lost for thee, now grant me justice.

EGEON Unless the fear of death doth make me dote,   195
I see my son Antipholus and Dromio.

E. ANTIPHOLUS Justice, sweet Prince, against that
woman there!
She whom thou gav'st to me to be my wife;
That hath abusèd and dishonored me,
Even in the strength and height of injury: 200
Beyond imagination is the wrong
That she this day hath shameless thrown on me.

DUKE Discover how, and thou shalt find me just.

E. ANTIPHOLUS This day, great Duke, she shut the
doors upon me,
While she with harlots feasted in my house.   205

DUKE A grievous fault. Say, woman, didst thou so?

ADRIANA No, my good lord. Myself, he, and my sister
Today did dine together; so befall my soul
As this is false he burdens me withal.

LUCIANA Ne'er may I look on day, nor sleep on night,   210
But she tells to your Highness simple truth.

188 **housed him** pursued him to shelter 192 **bestrid** defended by standing
over 200 **in the strength and height** to the strongest degree 203 **Discover**
reveal 205 **harlots** rascals 208-09 **so befall ... me withal** i.e., I stake my soul
that what he charges me with is false 210 **on night** at night

ANGELO O perjured woman! They are both forsworn.
In this the madman justly chargeth them.

E. ANTIPHOLUS My liege, I am advisèd what I say,
215   Neither disturbed with the effect of wine,
Nor heady-rash, provoked with raging ire,
Albeit my wrongs might make one wiser mad.
This woman locked me out this day from dinner.
That goldsmith there, were he not packed with
      her,
220   Could witness it; for he was with me then,
Who parted with me to go fetch a chain,
Promising to bring it to the Porpentine,
Where Balthasar and I did dine together.
Our dinner done, and he not coming thither,
225   I went to seek him. In the street I met him,
And in his company that gentleman.
There did this perjured goldsmith swear me down
That I this day of him received the chain,
Which, God he knows, I saw not; for the which,
230   He did arrest me with an officer.
I did obey, and sent my peasant home
For certain ducats; he with none returned.
Then fairly I bespoke the officer
To go in person with me to my house.
235   By th' way we met
My wife, her sister, and a rabble more
Of vile confederates. Along with them
They brought one Pinch, a hungry lean-faced
      villain;
A mere anatomy, a mountebank,
240   A threadbare juggler and a fortune-teller,
A needy-hollow-eyed-sharp-looking wretch;
A living dead man. This pernicious slave,
Forsooth, took on him as a conjurer;
And, gazing in mine eyes, feeling my pulse,

214 **advisèd** well aware of   219 **packed** conspiring   231 **peasant** bondman
233 **fairly I bespoke** politely I addressed   239 **mere anatomy** sheer skeleton
240 **juggler** sorcerer   243 **took on him as** assumed the part of

And with no face, as 'twere, out-facing me,   245
Cries out, I was possessed. Then all together
They fell upon me, bound me, bore me thence,
And in a dark and dankish vault at home
There left me and my man, both bound together,
Till gnawing with my teeth my bonds in sunder,   250
I gained my freedom; and immediately
Ran hither to your Grace, whom I beseech
To give me ample satisfaction
For these deep shames and great indignities.

ANGELO My lord, in truth, thus far I witness with him: 255
That he dined not at home, but was locked out.

DUKE But had he such a chain of thee, or no?

ANGELO He had, my lord, and when he ran in here
These people saw the chain about his neck.

MERCHANT Besides, I will be sworn these ears of mine   260
Heard you confess you had the chain of him,
After you first forswore it on the Mart;
And, thereupon, I drew my sword on you;
And then you fled into this abbey here,
From whence, I think, you are come by miracle.   265

E. ANTIPHOLUS I never came within these abbey walls,
Nor ever didst thou draw thy sword on me.
I never saw the chain, so help me Heaven!
And this is false you burden me withal.

DUKE Why, what an intricate impeach is this!   270
I think you all have drunk of Circe's cup.
If here you housed him, here he would have been;
If he were mad, he would not plead so coldly.
You say he dined at home, the goldsmith here
Denies that saying. Sirrah, what say you?   275

E. DROMIO Sir, he dined with her there at the
      Porpentine.

250 in sunder asunder 270 impeach accusation 271 Circe's cup (potion
which, in Greek mythology, turns men into beasts) 273 coldly rationally

COURTESAN He did, and from my finger snatched that
     ring.

E. ANTIPHOLUS 'Tis true, my liege, this ring I had of
     her.

DUKE Saw'st thou him enter at the abbey here?

280 COURTESAN As sure, my liege, as I do see your Grace.

DUKE Why, this is strange. Go call the Abbess hither.
     I think you are all mated, or stark mad.
                              Exit One to the Abbey.

EGEON Most mighty Duke, vouchsafe me speak a
     word.
     Haply I see a friend will save my life,
285   And pay the sum that may deliver me.

DUKE Speak freely, Syracusian, what thou wilt.

EGEON Is not your name, sir, called Antipholus?
     And is not that your bondman Dromio?

E. DROMIO Within this hour I was his bondman, sir,
290   But he, I thank him, gnawed in two my cords.
     Now am I Dromio, and his man, unbound.

EGEON I am sure you both of you remember me.

E. DROMIO Ourselves we do remember, sir, by you;
     For lately we were bound, as you are now.
295   You are not Pinch's patient, are you, sir?

EGEON Why look you strange on me? You know me
     well.

E. ANTIPHOLUS I never saw you in my life till now.

EGEON O, grief hath changed me since you saw me
     last,
     And careful hours with time's deformèd hand
300   Have written strange defeatures in my face.

282 **mated** confounded   283 **vouchsafe me** allow me to   284 **Haply** perchance
294 **bound** (pun on being a bondservant and being literally bound as a madman)
299 **careful** full of care   300 **defeatures** disfigurements

But tell me yet, dost thou not know my voice?

E. ANTIPHOLUS Neither.

EGEON Dromio, nor thou?

E. DROMIO   No, trust me, sir, nor I.

EGEON I am sure thou dost!

E. DROMIO Ay, sir, but I am sure I do not; and what-   305
    soever a man denies, you are now bound to believe
    him.

EGEON Not know my voice! O, time's extremity,
    Hast thou so cracked and splitted my poor tongue
    In seven short years, that here my only son   310
    Knows not my feeble key of untuned cares?
    Though now this grainèd face of mine be hid
    In sap-consuming winter's drizzled snow,
    And all the conduits of my blood froze up,
    Yet hath my night of life some memory;   315
    My wasting lamps some fading glimmer left;
    My dull deaf ears a little use to hear.
    All these old witnesses—I cannot err—
    Tell me thou art my son Antipholus.

E. ANTIPHOLUS I never saw my father in my life.   320

EGEON But seven years since, in Syracusa, boy,
    Thou know'st we parted; but perhaps, my son,
    Thou sham'st to acknowledge me in misery.

E. ANTIPHOLUS The Duke and all that know me in
    the city
    Can witness with me that it is not so.   325
    I ne'er saw Syracusa in my life.

DUKE I tell thee, Syracusian, twenty years
    Have I been patron to Antipholus,
    During which time he ne'er saw Syracusa.   330
    I see thy age and dangers make thee dote.

306 **bound** (a further quibble)   311 **feeble key of untuned cares** voice enfeebled
by discordant cares   312 **grainèd** furrowed   316 **wasting lamps** dimming eyes

*Enter the Abbess with Antipholus of Syracuse
and Dromio of Syracuse.*

ABBESS Most mighty Duke, behold a man much
    wronged. *All gather to see them.*

ADRIANA I see two husbands, or mine eyes deceive me.

DUKE One of these men is genius to the other;
    And so of these, which is the natural man,
335   And which the spirit? Who deciphers them?

S. DROMIO I, sir, am Dromio; command him away.

E. DROMIO I, sir, am Dromio; pray let me stay.

S. ANTIPHOLUS Egeon art thou not, or else his ghost?

S. DROMIO O, my old master! Who hath bound him
    here?

340 ABBESS Whoever bound him, I will loose his bonds,
    And gain a husband by his liberty.
    Speak, old Egeon, if thou beest the man
    That hadst a wife once called Emilia,
    That bore thee at a burden two fair sons!
345   O, if thou beest the same Egeon, speak;
    And speak unto the same Emilia.

DUKE [*Aside*] Why, here begins his morning story right:
    These two Antipholus', these two so like,
    And these two Dromios, one in semblance,
350   Besides her urging of her wrack at sea;
    These are the parents to these children,
    Which accidentally are met together.

EGEON If I dream not, thou art Emilia.
    If thou art she, tell me where is that son
355   That floated with thee on the fatal raft?

ABBESS By men of Epidamnum, he and I
    And the twin Dromio, all were taken up;

333 **genius** attendant spirit   344 **burden** birth   349 **semblance** appearance
350 **urging** account

But by and by rude fishermen of Corinth
By force took Dromio and my son from them,
And me they left with those of Epidamnum.   360
What then became of them, I cannot tell;
I to this fortune that you see me in.

DUKE Antipholus, thou cam'st from Corinth first.

S. ANTIPHOLUS No, sir, not I; I came from Syracuse.

DUKE Stay, stand apart; I know not which is which.   365

E. ANTIPHOLUS I came from Corinth, my most
    gracious lord.

E. DROMIO And I with him.

E. ANTIPHOLUS Brought to this town by that most
    famous warrior,
    Duke Menaphon, your most renownèd uncle.

ADRIANA Which of you two did dine with me today?   370

S. ANTIPHOLUS I, gentle mistress.

ADRIANA   And are not you my husband?

E. ANTIPHOLUS No, I say nay to that.

S. ANTIPHOLUS And so do I, yet did she call me so;
    And this fair gentlewoman, her sister here,
    Did call me brother. What I told you then   375
    I hope I shall have leisure to make good,
    If this be not a dream I see and hear.

ANGELO That is the chain, sir, which you had of me.

S. ANTIPHOLUS I think it be, sir; I deny it not.

E. ANTIPHOLUS And you, sir, for this chain arrested   380
    me.

ANGELO I think I did, sir. I deny it not.

ADRIANA I sent you money, sir, to be your bail,
    By Dromio; but I think he brought it not.

E. DROMIO No, none by me.

362 I to] I came to

73

S. ANTIPHOLUS This purse of ducats I received from
385   you,
And Dromio, my man, did bring them me.
I see we still did meet each other's man,
And I was ta'en for him, and he for me,
And thereupon these errors are arose.

E. ANTIPHOLUS These ducats pawn I for my father
390   here.

DUKE It shall not need; thy father hath his life.

COURTESAN Sir, I must have that diamond from you.

E. ANTIPHOLUS There, take it, and much thanks for
my good cheer.

ABBESS Renownèd Duke, vouchsafe to take the pains
395   To go with us into the abbey here,
And hear at large discoursèd all our fortunes;
And all that are assembled in this place,
That by this sympathizèd one day's error
Have suffered wrong, go, keep us company,
400   And we shall make full satisfaction.
Thirty-three years have I but gone in travail
Of you, my sons, and till this present hour
My heavy burden ne'er delivered.
The Duke, my husband, and my children both,
405   And you the calendars of their nativity,
Go to a gossips' feast, and joy with me
After so long grief such nativity.

DUKE With all my heart I'll gossip at this feast.
                    *Exeunt [all except] the two Dromios
                              and two Brothers.*

S. DROMIO Master, shall I fetch your stuff from ship-
board?

387 **still** repeatedly   398 **sympathizèd** shared   401 **travail** childbirth (with a
pun on "travel")   405 **calendars** (the Dromios mark the age of the Antipholuses)
406 **gossips** godparents   407 **nativity** a christening party (suggested emendations are "festivity" and "felicity")   408 **gossip** make merry

E. ANTIPHOLUS Dromio, what stuff of mine hast thou
    embarked?   410

S. DROMIO Your goods that lay at host, sir, in the
    Centaur.

S. ANTIPHOLUS He speaks to me. I am your master,
    Dromio.
Come, go with us; we'll look to that anon.
Embrace thy brother there; rejoice with him.
              Exit [*with Antipholus of Ephesus*].

S. DROMIO There is a fat friend at your master's
    house,   415
That kitchened me for you today at dinner;
She now shall be my sister, not my wife.

E. DROMIO Methinks you are my glass, and not my
    brother;
I see by you I am a sweet-faced youth.
Will you walk in to see their gossiping?   420

S. DROMIO Not I, sir, you are my elder.

E. DROMIO That's a question; how shall we try it?

S. DROMIO We'll draw cuts for the senior; till then,
    lead thou first.

E. DROMIO Nay, then, thus: 425
We came into the world like brother and brother:
And now let's go hand in hand, not one before
    another.   *Exeunt*.

FINIS

411 at host in the care of the host   416 kitchened entertained in the kitchen
419 sweet-faced good-looking

Textual Note

The Comedy of Errors was first published in the Folio of 1623, which provides the only authoritative text. It is possible that the copy for the Folio was Shakespeare's manuscript; the ambiguity of some names in stage directions and in speech prefixes would have been confusing in a promptbook. For example, Egeon is *Mer(chant)* in I.i., but other merchants appear in other scenes without distinctive titles. More important, *E. Dro(mio)* is, as might be expected, *Dromio of Ephesus*; but *E. Ant.* is Antipholus of Syracuse, an abbreviation of his earlier designation, *Ant. Errotis*—which is perhaps an approximation of *erraticus*, wandering. A promptbook doubtless would have clarified the nomenclature.

The Folio's text is a good one, presenting the editor with relatively few problems. In the present edition the speech prefixes and names in stage directions have been regularized, spelling and punctuation have been modernized, and obvious typographical errors have been corrected. A few passages that the Folio prints as prose are given in verse, and the positions of a few stage directions have been slightly altered. Act division (translated from the Latin) is that of the Folio; scene division is that of the Globe text. Other departures from the Folio are listed below, with the adopted reading first, in bold, and the original reading next, in roman.

I.i.17 **at** at any   42 **the** he   102 **upon** vp   116 **bark** backe   123 **thee** they   151 **health** helpe

I.ii.s.d. **Antipholus of Syracuse** Antipholis Erotes   4 **arrival** a riuall   30 **lose** loose   32s.d. **Exit** Exeunt   40 **unhappy** vnhappie a   65 **score** scoure   66 **clock** cooke   93 **God's** God   94s.d. **Exit** Exeunt

II.i.s.d. **Antipholus of Ephesus** Antipholis Sereptus   11 **o' door** adore   12 **ill** thus   45 **two** too   61 **thousand** hundred   72 **errand** arrant   107 **alone, alone** alone, a loue   112 **Wear** Where   113 **But** By

II.ii.s.d. **Antipholus of Syracuse** Antipholis Errotis   12 **didst** did didst   80 **men** them   98 **tiring** trying   102 **e'en** in   176 **stronger** stranger   187 **offered** free'd   195 **drone** Dromio   196 **am not I** am I not

III.i.54 **trow** hope   75 **you** your   89 **her** your   91 **her** your

76

III.ii.s.d. **Luciana** Iuliana   1 **Luciana** Iulia   2 **Antipholus, hate** Antipholus
4 **building** buildings   16 **attaint** attaine   21 **but** not   26 **wife** wise   46 **sister's**
sister   49 **bed** bud   49 **them** thee   57 **where** when   111 **and** is   129 **chalky**
chalkle   171 **here is** here's

IV.i.17 **her** their   28 **carat** charect   47 **to blame** too blame   88 **then she** then sir
she

IV.ii.6 **Of** Oh   60 **'a** I

IV.iii.1. **S. Antipholus** [F omits]   62 **if you do** if do

V.i.s.d. **Another Merchant** the Merchant   33 **God's** God   121 **death** depth
168 **Messenger** [F omits]   246 **all together** altogether   282s.d. **Abbey** Abbesse
403 **ne'er** are   406 **joy with** go with   408s.d. **Exeunt** Exeunt omnes. Manet
423 **senior** Signior

WILLIAM SHAKESPEARE

THE TAMING OF THE SHREW

Edited by Robert B. Heilman

Induction (and ending of Act I, Scene i)
  CHRISTOPHER SLY, a tinker
  HOSTESS OF AN ALEHOUSE
  A LORD
  HUNTSMEN and SERVANTS OF THE LORD
  PLAYERS IN A TRAVELING COMPANY
  BARTHOLOMEW, a page
Acts I-V
  BAPTISTA MINOLA, of Padua, father of Kate and Bianca
  KATE, the shrew
  BIANCA
  PETRUCHIO, of Verona, suitor of Kate
  LUCENTIO (Cambio) ⎫
  GREMIO, a pantaloon ⎬ suitors of Bianca
  HORTENSIO (Litio) ⎭
  VINCENTIO, of Pisa, father of Lucentio
  A PEDANT (impersonating Vincentio)
  TRANIO (later impersonating ⎫
    Lucentio) ⎬ servants of Lucentio
  BIONDELLO ⎭
  GRUMIO ⎫
  CURTIS ⎪
  NATHANIEL, NICHOLAS ⎬ servants of Petruchio
  JOSEPH, PHILIP, PETER ⎭
  A TAILOR
  A HABERDASHER
  A WIDOW
  SERVANTS OF BAPTISTA and LUCENTIO

Scene: Warwick (Induction);
Padua; the country near Verona]

THE TAMING OF
THE SHREW

[INDUCTION]

Scene I. [*Outside rural alehouse.*]

Enter Hostess and Beggar, Christophero Sly.

SLY I'll pheeze you, in faith.

HOSTESS A pair of stocks, you rogue!

SLY Y'are a baggage, the Slys are no rogues. Look in
the chronicles: we came in with Richard Conqueror. Therefore, *paucas pallabris*; let the world   5
slide. Sessa!

HOSTESS You will not pay for the glasses you have
burst?

SLY No, not a denier. Go, by St. Jeronimy, go to
thy cold bed and warm thee.   10

HOSTESS I know my remedy: I must go fetch the
thirdborough.   [*Exit.*]

SLY Third or fourth or fifth borough, I'll answer him
by law. I'll not budge an inch, boy; let him come
and kindly.   *Falls asleep.* 15

Text references are printed in **boldface**; the annotation follows in roman type.
Ind.i.1 **pheeze** do for (cf. *faze*)   2 **stocks** (threatened punishment)   4 **Richard**
(he means William)   5 **paucas pallabris** few words (Spanish *pocas palabras*)
6 **slide** go by (proverb; cf. Ind.ii.143)   6 **Sessa** scram (?) shut up (?)   9 **denier**
very small coin (cf. "a copper")   9 **Jeronimy** (Sly's oath inaccurately reflects a
line in Kyd's *Spanish Tragedy*)   12 **thirdborough** constable   14 **boy** wretch
15 **kindly** by all means

81

Wind horns. Enter a Lord from hunting,
with his train.

LORD Huntsman, I charge thee, tender well my
    hounds.
    Broach Merriman—the poor cur is embossed—
    And couple Clowder with the deep-mouthed brach.
    Saw'st thou not, boy, how Silver made it good
20   At the hedge-corner in the coldest fault?
    I would not lose the dog for twenty pound.

FIRST HUNTSMAN Why, Bellman is as good as he, my
    lord;
    He cried upon it at the merest loss
    And twice today picked out the dullest scent.
25   Trust me, I take him for the better dog.

LORD Thou art a fool. If Echo were as fleet,
    I would esteem him worth a dozen such.
    But sup them well and look unto them all.
    Tomorrow I intend to hunt again.

30 FIRST HUNTSMAN I will, my lord.

LORD What's here? One dead or drunk? See, doth
    he breathe?

SECOND HUNTSMAN He breathes, my lord. Were he not
    warmed with ale,
    This were a bed but cold to sleep so soundly.

LORD O monstrous beast, how like a swine he lies!
35   Grim death, how foul and loathsome is thine image!
    Sirs, I will practice on this drunken man.
    What think you, if he were conveyed to bed,
    Wrapped in sweet clothes, rings put upon his
    fingers,
    A most delicious banquet by his bed,

15s.d. **Wind blow**   16 **tender** look after   17 **Broach** bleed, i.e., medicate (some
editors emend to *Breathe*)   17 **embossed** foaming at the mouth   18 **brach**
hunting bitch   20 **fault** lost ("cold") scent   23 **cried ... loss** gave cry despite
complete loss (of scent)   36 **practice on** play a trick on

And brave attendants near him when he wakes—   40
Would not the beggar then forget himself?

FIRST HUNTSMAN Believe me, lord, I think he cannot
   choose.

SECOND HUNTSMAN It would seem strange unto him
   when he waked.

LORD Even as a flatt'ring dream or worthless fancy.
Then take him up and manage well the jest.   45
Carry him gently to my fairest chamber
And hang it round with all my wanton pictures;
Balm his foul head in warm distillèd waters
And burn sweet wood to make the lodging sweet.
Procure me music ready when he wakes   50
To make a dulcet and a heavenly sound;
And if he chance to speak, be ready straight
And with a low submissive reverence
Say, "What is it your honor will command?"
Let one attend him with a silver basin   55
Full of rose water and bestrewed with flowers;
Another bear the ewer, the third a diaper,
And say, "Will't please your lordship cool your
   hands?"
Some one be ready with a costly suit
And ask him what apparel he will wear,   60
Another tell him of his hounds and horse
And that his lady mourns at his disease.
Persuade him that he hath been lunatic,
And when he says he is, say that he dreams,
For he is nothing but a mighty lord.   65
This do, and do it kindly, gentle sirs.
It will be pastime passing excellent
If it be husbanded with modesty.

FIRST HUNTSMAN My lord, I warrant you we will play
   our part

40 **brave** well dressed   47 **wanton** gay   48 **Balm** bathe   51 **dulcet** sweet
52 **straight** without delay   57 **diaper** towel   64 **is** i.e., is "lunatic" now
66 **kindly** naturally   68 **husbanded with modesty** carried out with moderation

83

70   As he shall think by our true diligence
       He is no less than what we say he is.

   LORD Take him up gently and to bed with him,
       And each one to his office when he wakes.
                             [*Sly is carried out.*] *Sound trumpets.*
       Sirrah, go see what trumpet 'tis that sounds.
                                        [*Exit Servingman.*]
75   Belike some noble gentleman that means,
       Traveling some journey, to repose him here.

                     Enter Servingman.

       How now? Who is it?

   SERVINGMAN   An't please your honor, players
       That offer service to your lordship.

                       Enter Players.

   LORD Bid them come near.
                        Now, fellows, you are welcome.

80 PLAYERS We thank your honor.

   LORD Do you intend to stay with me tonight?

   A PLAYER So please your lordship to accept our duty.

   LORD With all my heart. This fellow I remember
       Since once he played a farmer's eldest son;
85   'Twas where you wooed the gentlewoman so well.
       I have forgot your name, but sure that part
       Was aptly fitted and naturally performed.

   SECOND PLAYER I think 'twas Soto that your honor
       means.

   LORD 'Tis very true; thou didst it excellent.
90   Well, you are come to me in happy time,
       The rather for I have some sport in hand

70 **As** so that   73 **office** assignment   74 **Sirrah** (term of address used to inferiors)
75 **Belike** likely   77 **An't** if it   82 **duty** respectful greeting   87 **aptly fitted**
well suited (to you)   88 **Soto** (in John Fletcher's *Women Pleased*, 1620; reference
possibly inserted here later)   90 **in happy** at the right   91 **The rather for**
especially because

84

Wherein your cunning can assist me much.
There is a lord will hear you play tonight.
But I am doubtful of your modesties,
Lest over-eyeing of his odd behavior—   95
For yet his honor never heard a play—
You break into some merry passion
And so offend him, for I tell you, sirs,
If you should smile he grows impatient.

A PLAYER Fear not, my lord, we can contain ourselves   100
Were he the veriest antic in the world.

LORD Go, sirrah, take them to the buttery
And give them friendly welcome every one.
Let them want nothing that my house affords.
                              Exit one with the Players.
Sirrah, go you to Barthol'mew my page   105
And see him dressed in all suits like a lady.
That done, conduct him to the drunkard's chamber
And call him "madam"; do him obeisance.
Tell him from me—as he will win my love—
He bear himself with honorable action   110
Such as he hath observed in noble ladies
Unto their lords, by them accomplishèd.
Such duty to the drunkard let him do
With soft low tongue and lowly courtesy,
And say, "What is't your honor will command   115
Wherein your lady and your humble wife
May show her duty and make known her love?"
And then, with kind embracements, tempting kisses,
And with declining head into his bosom,
Bid him shed tears, as being overjoyed   120
To see her noble lord restored to health
Who for this seven years hath esteemèd him
No better than a poor and loathsome beggar.
And if the boy have not a woman's gift

92 **cunning** talent 94 **modesties** self-restraint 95 **over-eyeing** seeing
97 **merry passion** fit of merriment 101 **antic** odd person 102 **buttery** liquor
pantry, bar 104 **want** lack 106 **suits** respects (with pun) 109 **as he will** if he
wishes to 112 **by them accomplishèd** i.e., as carried out by the ladies

125   To rain a shower of commanded tears,
         An onion will do well for such a shift,
         Which in a napkin being close conveyed
         Shall in despite enforce a watery eye.
         See this dispatched with all the haste thou canst;
130   Anon I'll give thee more instructions.

                                     Exit a Servingman.

         I know the boy will well usurp the grace,
         Voice, gait, and action of a gentlewoman.
         I long to hear him call the drunkard husband,
         And how my men will stay themselves from laughter
135   When they do homage to this simple peasant.
         I'll in to counsel them; haply my presence
         May well abate the over-merry spleen
         Which otherwise would grow into extremes.

                                         [Exeunt.]

[Scene II. *Bedroom in the Lord's house.*]

*Enter aloft the Drunkard [Sly] with Attendants—some
with apparel, basin and ewer, and other appurtenances—
and Lord.*

SLY   For God's sake, a pot of small ale!

FIRST SERVINGMAN   Will't please your lordship drink a
    cup of sack?

SECOND SERVINGMAN   Will't please your honor taste of
    these conserves?

THIRD SERVINGMAN   What raiment will your honor
    wear today?

126 **shift** purpose   127 **napkin** handkerchief   127 **close conveyed** secretly
carried   128 **Shall in despite** can't fail to   130 **Anon** then   131 **usurp** take
on   136 **haply** perhaps   137 **spleen** spirit Ind.ii.s.d. **aloft** (on balcony above
stage at back)   1 **small** thin, diluted (inexpensive)   2 **sack** imported sherry
(costly)   3 **conserves** i.e., of fruit

SLY I am Christophero Sly; call not me "honor" nor   5
"lordship." I ne'er drank sack in my life, and if you
give me any conserves, give me conserves of beef.
Ne'er ask me what raiment I'll wear, for I have no
more doublets than backs, no more stockings than
legs nor no more shoes than feet—nay, sometime   10
more feet than shoes or such shoes as my toes look
through the overleather.

LORD Heaven cease this idle humor in your honor!
O that a mighty man of such descent,
Of such possessions and so high esteem,   15
Should be infusèd with so foul a spirit!

SLY What, would you make me mad? Am not I Christopher Sly, old Sly's son of Burton-heath, by birth
a peddler, by education a cardmaker, by transmu-
tation a bearherd, and now by present profession   20
a tinker? Ask Marian Hacket, the fat ale-wife of
Wincot, if she know me not. If she say I am not
fourteen pence on the score for sheer ale, score
me up for the lying'st knave in Christendom. What,
I am not bestraught! Here's—   25

THIRD SERVINGMAN O, this it is that makes your lady
        mourn.

SECOND SERVINGMAN O, this it is that makes your ser-
        vants droop.

LORD Hence comes it that your kindred shuns your
        house
As beaten hence by your strange lunacy.
O noble lord, bethink thee of thy birth,   30
Call home thy ancient thoughts from banishment

---

7 **conserves of beef** salt beef   9 **doublets** close-fitting jackets   13 **idle humor**
unreasonable fantasy   18 **Burton-heath** (probably Barton-on-the-Heath, south
of Stratford)   19 **cardmaker** maker of cards, or combs, for arranging wool fibers
before spinning   20 **bearherd** leader of a tame bear   22 **Wincot** village near
Stratford (some Hackets lived there)   23 **score** charge account   23 **sheer ale** ale
alone (?) undiluted ale (?)   25 **bestraught** distraught, crazy   31 **ancient thoughts**
original sanity

And banish hence these abject lowly dreams.
Look how thy servants do attend on thee,
Each in his office ready at thy beck.
35 Wilt thou have music? Hark, Apollo plays,   *Music.*
And twenty cagèd nightingales do sing.
Or wilt thou sleep? We'll have thee to a couch
Softer and sweeter than the lustful bed
On purpose trimmed up for Semiramis.
40 Say thou wilt walk, we will bestrow the ground.
Or wilt thou ride? Thy horses shall be trapped,
Their harness studded all with gold and pearl.
Dost thou love hawking? Thou hast hawks will soar
Above the morning lark. Or wilt thou hunt?
45 Thy hounds shall make the welkin answer them
And fetch shrill echoes from the hollow earth.

FIRST SERVINGMAN Say thou wilt course, thy grey-
    hounds are as swift
As breathèd stags, ay, fleeter than the roe.

SECOND SERVINGMAN Dost thou love pictures? We will
    fetch thee straight
50 Adonis painted by a running brook
And Cytherea all in sedges hid,
Which seem to move and wanton with her breath
Even as the waving sedges play with wind.

LORD We'll show thee Io as she was a maid
55 And how she was beguilèd and surprised,
As lively painted as the deed was done.

THIRD SERVINGMAN Or Daphne roaming through a
    thorny wood,

---

35 **Apollo** here, god of music   39 **Semiramis** mythical Assyrian queen, noted for
beauty and sexuality (cf. *Titus Andronicus*, II.i.22, II.iii.118)   40 **bestrow** cover
41 **trapped** decorated   45 **welkin** sky   47 **course** hunt hares   48 **breathèd**
having good wind   48 **roe** small deer   50 **Adonis** young hunter loved by Venus
(Cytherea) and killed by wild boar   51 **sedges** grasslike plant growing in marshy
places   52 **wanton** sway sinuously   54 **Io** mortal loved by Zeus and changed into
a heifer   56 **lively** lifelike   57 **Daphne** nymph loved by Apollo and changed into
laurel to evade him

Scratching her legs that one shall swear she bleeds,
And at that sight shall sad Apollo weep,
So workmanly the blood and tears are drawn.   60

LORD Thou art a lord and nothing but a lord.
Thou hast a lady far more beautiful
Than any woman in this waning age.

FIRST SERVINGMAN And till the tears that she hath shed
    for thee
Like envious floods o'errun her lovely face,   65
She was the fairest creature in the world,
And yet she is inferior to none.

SLY Am I a lord, and have I such a lady?
Or do I dream? Or have I dreamed till now?
I do not sleep: I see, I hear, I speak,   70
I smell sweet savors and I feel soft things.
Upon my life, I am a lord indeed
And not a tinker nor Christopher Sly.
Well, bring our lady hither to our sight,
And once again a pot o' th' smallest ale.   75

SECOND SERVINGMAN Will't please your mightiness to
    wash your hands?
O, how we joy to see your wit restored!
O, that once more you knew but what you are!
These fifteen years you have been in a dream,
Or when you waked so waked as if you slept.   80

SLY These fifteen years! By my fay, a goodly nap.
But did I never speak of all that time?

FIRST SERVINGMAN O yes, my lord, but very idle words,
For though you lay here in this goodly chamber,
Yet would you say ye were beaten out of door   85
And rail upon the hostess of the house
And say you would present her at the leet

---

63 **waning** decadent   67 **yet** now, still   75 **smallest** weakest   77 **wit** mind
81 **fay** faith   82 **of** in   86 **house** inn   87 **present her at the leet** accuse her at
the court under lord of a manor

Because she brought stone jugs and no sealed
quarts.
Sometimes you would call out for Cicely Hacket.

90 SLY Ay, the woman's maid of the house.

THIRD SERVINGMAN Why, sir, you know no house nor
no such maid
Nor no such men as you have reckoned up,
As Stephen Sly and old John Naps of Greece,
And Peter Turph and Henry Pimpernell,
95 And twenty more such names and men as these
Which never were nor no man ever saw.

SLY Now, Lord be thankèd for my good amends!

ALL Amen.

Enter [the Page, as a] Lady, with Attendants.

SLY I thank thee; thou shalt not lose by it.

100 PAGE How fares my noble lord?

SLY Marry, I fare well, for here is cheer enough.
Where is my wife?

PAGE Here, noble lord. What is thy will with her?

SLY Are you my wife and will not call me husband?
My men should call me "lord"; I am your good-
105 man.

PAGE My husband and my lord, my lord and husband,
I am your wife in all obedience.

SLY I know it well. What must I call her?

LORD Madam.

110 SLY Al'ce madam or Joan madam?

LORD Madam and nothing else. So lords call ladies.

---

88 **sealed** marked by a seal guaranteeing quantity 93 **Stephen Sly** Stratford
man (Naps, etc., may also be names of real persons) 93 **Greece** the Green (?)
Greet, hamlet not far from Stratford (?) 97 **amends** recovery 101 **Marry** in
truth (originally, [by St.] Mary) 105 **goodman** husband

SLY Madam wife, they say that I have dreamed
And slept above some fifteen year or more.

PAGE Ay, and the time seems thirty unto me,
Being all this time abandoned from your bed.   115

SLY 'Tis much. Servants, leave me and her alone.
Madam, undress you and come now to bed.

PAGE Thrice noble lord, let me entreat of you
To pardon me yet for a night or two
Or, if not so, until the sun be set.   120
For your physicians have expressly charged,
In peril to incur your former malady,
That I should yet absent me from your bed.
I hope this reason stands for my excuse.

SLY Ay, it stands so that I may hardly tarry so long,   125
but I would be loath to fall into my dreams again.
I will therefore tarry in despite of the flesh and the
blood.

Enter a Messenger.

MESSENGER Your Honor's players, hearing your
amendment,
Are come to play a pleasant comedy.   130
For so your doctors hold it very meet,
Seeing too much sadness hath congealed your blood,
And melancholy is the nurse of frenzy.
Therefore they thought it good you hear a play
And frame your mind to mirth and merriment,   135
Which bars a thousand harms and lengthens life.

SLY Marry, I will let them play it. Is not a comontie
a Christmas gambold or a tumbling trick?

PAGE No, my good lord, it is more pleasing stuff.

---

115 **abandoned** excluded   122 **In peril to incur** because of the danger of a
return of   125 **stands so** will do (with phallic pun, playing on "reason," which
was pronounced much like "raising")   133 **frenzy** mental illness   137 **comontie**
comedy (as pronounced by Sly)   138 **gambold** gambol (game, dance, frolic)

140 SLY What, household stuff?

PAGE It is a kind of history.

SLY Well, we'll see't. Come, madam wife, sit by my
side
And let the world slip. We shall ne'er be younger.

---

140 **stuff** (with sexual innuendo: see Eric Partridge, *Shakespeare's Bawdy*)
143 **slip** go by

[ACT I

Scene I. *Padua. A street.*]

Flourish. Enter Lucentio and his man Tranio.

LUCENTIO Tranio, since for the great desire I had
  To see fair Padua, nursery of arts,
  I am arrived for fruitful Lombardy,
  The pleasant garden of great Italy,
  And by my father's love and leave am armed   5
  With his good will and thy good company,
  My trusty servant well approved in all,
  Here let us breathe and haply institute
  A course of learning and ingenious studies.
  Pisa, renownèd for grave citizens,   10
  Gave me my being and my father first,
  A merchant of great traffic through the world,
  Vincentio, come of the Bentivolii.
  Vincentio's son, brought up in Florence,
  It shall become to serve all hopes conceived,   15
  To deck his fortune with his virtuous deeds;
  And therefore, Tranio, for the time I study,
  Virtue and that part of philosophy
  Will I apply that treats of happiness
  By virtue specially to be achieved.   20
  Tell me thy mind, for I have Pisa left
  And am to Padua come, as he that leaves

I.i.s.d. **Flourish** fanfare of trumpets   s.d. **man** servant   2 **Padua** (noted for its university)   7 **approved** proved, found reliable   9 **ingenious** mind-training   11 **first** i.e., before that   12 **traffic** business   15 **serve** work for   19 **apply** apply myself to

A shallow plash to plunge him in the deep
And with satiety seeks to quench his thirst.

25 TRANIO *Mi perdonato*, gentle master mine,
I am in all affected as yourself,
Glad that you thus continue your resolve
To suck the sweets of sweet philosophy.
Only, good master, while we do admire
30 This virtue and this moral discipline,
Let's be no stoics nor no stocks, I pray,
Or so devote to Aristotle's checks
As Ovid be an outcast quite abjured.
Balk logic with acquaintance that you have
35 And practice rhetoric in your common talk.
Music and poesy use to quicken you.
The mathematics and the metaphysics,
Fall to them as you find your stomach serves you.
No profit grows where is no pleasure ta'en.
40 In brief, sir, study what you most affect.

LUCENTIO Gramercies, Tranio, well dost thou advise.
If, Biondello, thou wert come ashore,
We could at once put us in readiness
And take a lodging fit to entertain
45 Such friends as time in Padua shall beget.
But stay awhile, what company is this?

TRANIO Master, some show to welcome us to town.

*Enter Baptista with his two daughters, Kate and Bianca;
Gremio, a pantaloon; [and] Hortensio, suitor to Bianca.
Lucentio [and] Tranio stand by.*

BAPTISTA Gentlemen, importune me no farther,
For how I firmly am resolved you know,
50 That is, not to bestow my youngest daughter

---

23 **plash** pool   25 **Mi perdonato** pardon me   26 **affected** inclined   31 **stocks**
sticks (with pun on Stoics)   32 **devote** devoted   32 **checks** restraints   33 **As** so
that   33 **Ovid** Roman love poet (cf. III.i.28-29, IV.ii.8)   34 **Balk logic** engage
in arguments   36 **quicken** make alive   38 **stomach** taste, preference   40 **affect**
like   41 **Gramercies** many thanks   47s.d. **pantaloon** laughable old man (a stock
character with baggy pants, in Italian Renaissance comedy)   47s.d. **by** nearby

Before I have a husband for the elder.
If either of you both love Katherina,
Because I know you well and love you well,
Leave shall you have to court her at your pleasure.

GREMIO To cart her rather. She's too rough for me.   55
There, there, Hortensio, will you any wife?

KATE I pray you, sir, is it your will
To make a stale of me amongst these mates?

HORTENSIO Mates, maid? How mean you that? No
        mates for you
Unless you were of gentler, milder mold.   60

KATE I' faith, sir, you shall never need to fear:
Iwis it is not halfway to her heart.
But if it were, doubt not her care should be
To comb your noddle with a three-legged stool
And paint your face and use you like a fool.   65

HORTENSIO From all such devils, good Lord deliver us!

GREMIO And me too, good Lord!

TRANIO [Aside] Husht, master, here's some good
        pastime toward.
That wench is stark mad or wonderful froward.

LUCENTIO [Aside] But in the other's silence do I see   70
Maid's mild behavior and sobriety.
Peace, Tranio.

TRANIO [Aside] Well said, master. Mum, and gaze
        your fill.

BAPTISTA Gentlemen, that I may soon make good
What I have said: Bianca, get you in,   75
And let it not displease thee, good Bianca,

---

55 **cart** drive around in an open cart (a punishment for prostitutes) 58 **stale**
(1) laughingstock (2) prostitute 58 **mates** low fellows (with pun on *stalemate* and
leading to pun on *mate* = husband) 62 **Iwis** certainly 62 **it** i.e., getting a
mate 62 **her** Kate's 65 **paint** i.e., red with blood 68 **toward** coming up
69 **froward** willful

For I will love thee ne'er the less, my girl.

KATE   A pretty peat! It is best
Put finger in the eye, and she knew why.

80 BIANCA Sister, content you in my discontent.
Sir, to your pleasure humbly I subscribe.
My books and instruments shall be my company,
On them to look and practice by myself.

LUCENTIO [*Aside*] Hark, Tranio, thou mayst hear
Minerva speak.

85 HORTENSIO Signior Baptista, will you be so strange?
Sorry am I that our good will effects
Bianca's grief.

GREMIO   Why will you mew her up,
Signior Baptista, for this fiend of hell
And make her bear the penance of her tongue?

90 BAPTISTA Gentlemen, content ye. I am resolved.
Go in, Bianca.   [*Exit Bianca.*]
And for I know she taketh most delight
In music, instruments, and poetry,
Schoolmasters will I keep within my house,
95 Fit to instruct her youth. If you, Hortensio,
Or Signior Gremio, you, know any such,
Prefer them hither; for to cunning men
I will be very kind, and liberal
To mine own children in good bringing up.
100 And so, farewell. Katherina, you may stay,
For I have more to commune with Bianca.   *Exit.*

KATE   Why, and I trust I may go too, may I not?
What, shall I be appointed hours, as though, belike,
I knew not what to take and what to leave? Ha!
                                        Exit.

---

78 **peat** pet (cf. "teacher's pet")   79 **Put finger in the eye** cry   79 **and** if
84 **Minerva** goddess of wisdom   85 **strange** rigid   87 **mew** cage (falconry term)
92 **for** because   97 **Prefer** recommend   97 **cunning** talented   101 **commune
with** communicate to   103 **belike** it seems likely

GREMIO You may go to the devil's dam; your gifts 105
are so good, here's none will hold you. Their love is
not so great, Hortensio, but we may blow our
nails together and fast it fairly out. Our cake's
dough on both sides. Farewell. Yet for the love I
bear my sweet Bianca, if I can by any means light 110
on a fit man to teach her that wherein she delights,
I will wish him to her father.

HORTENSIO So will I, Signior Gremio. But a word, I
pray. Though the nature of our quarrel yet never
brooked parle, know now, upon advice, it touch- 115
eth us both—that we may yet again have access
to our fair mistress and be happy rivals in Bianca's
love—to labor and effect one thing specially.

GREMIO What's that, I pray?

HORTENSIO Marry, sir, to get a husband for her sister. 120

GREMIO A husband! A devil.

HORTENSIO I say, a husband.

GREMIO I say, a devil. Think'st thou, Hortensio,
though her father be very rich, any man is so very
a fool to be married to hell? 125

HORTENSIO Tush, Gremio, though it pass your patience and mine to endure her loud alarums, why,
man, there be good fellows in the world, and a man
could light on them, would take her with all faults,
and money enough. 130

GREMIO I cannot tell, but I had as lief take her
dowry with this condition, to be whipped at the
high cross every morning.

---

105 **dam** mother (used of animals)   107 **great** important   107-08 **blow our
nails together** i.e., wait patiently   108-09 **Our cake's dough on both sides**
we've both failed (proverbial)   112 **wish** commend   115 **brooked parle** allowed
negotiation   115 **advice** consideration   115-16 **toucheth** concerns   124 **very**
thorough   125 **to** as to   127 **alarums** outcries   128 **and** if   131 **had as lief**
would as willingly   133 **high cross** market cross (prominent spot)

HORTENSIO Faith, as you say, there's small choice in
135   rotten apples. But come, since this bar in law
makes us friends, it shall be so far forth friendly
maintained, till by helping Baptista's eldest daughter to a husband, we set his youngest free for a
husband, and then have to't afresh. Sweet Bianca!
140   Happy man be his dole! He that runs fastest gets
the ring. How say you, Signior Gremio?

GREMIO I am agreed, and would I had given him the
best horse in Padua to begin his wooing, that
would thoroughly woo her, wed her, and bed her
145   and rid the house of her. Come on.

Exeunt ambo. Manet Tranio and Lucentio.

TRANIO I pray, sir, tell me, is it possible
That love should of a sudden take such hold?

LUCENTIO O Tranio, till I found it to be true
I never thought it possible or likely.
150   But see, while idly I stood looking on,
I found the effect of love-in-idleness
And now in plainness do confess to thee,
That art to me as secret and as dear
As Anna to the Queen of Carthage was,
155   Tranio, I burn, I pine, I perish, Tranio,
If I achieve not this young modest girl.
Counsel me, Tranio, for I know thou canst.
Assist me, Tranio, for I know thou wilt.

TRANIO Master, it is no time to chide you now.
160   Affection is not rated from the heart.

---

135 **bar in law** legal action of preventive sort 136 **so far forth** so long
139 **have to't** renew our competition 140 **Happy man be his dole** let being a
happy man be his (the winner's) destiny 143 **that** (antecedent is *his*)
145s.d. **ambo** both 145s.d. **Manet** remain (though the Latin plural is properly
manent, the singular with a plural subject is common in Elizabethan texts)
151 **love-in-idleness** popular name for pansy (believed to have mysterious power
in love; cf. *Midsummer Night's Dream*, II.i.165ff.) 153 **to me as secret** as much
in my confidence 154 **Anna** sister and confidante of Queen Dido 160 **rated**
scolded

If love have touched you, naught remains but so,
"*Redime te captum, quam queas minimo.*"

LUCENTIO Gramercies, lad, go forward. This contents.
The rest will comfort, for thy counsel's sound.

TRANIO Master, you looked so longly on the maid,   165
Perhaps you marked not what's the pith of all.

LUCENTIO O yes, I saw sweet beauty in her face,
Such as the daughter of Agenor had,
That made great Jove to humble him to her hand
When with his knees he kissed the Cretan strond.   170

TRANIO Saw you no more? Marked you not how her
sister
Began to scold and raise up such a storm
That mortal ears might hardly endure the din?

LUCENTIO Tranio, I saw her coral lips to move
And with her breath she did perfume the air.   175
Sacred and sweet was all I saw in her.

TRANIO Nay, then, 'tis time to stir him from his trance.
I pray, awake, sir. If you love the maid,
Bend thoughts and wits to achieve her. Thus it
stands:
Her elder sister is so curst and shrewd   180
That till the father rid his hands of her,
Master, your love must live a maid at home;
And therefore has he closely mewed her up,
Because she will not be annoyed with suitors.

LUCENTIO Ah, Tranio, what a cruel father's he!   185
But art thou not advised he took some care
To get her cunning schoolmasters to instruct her?

161 **so** to act thus   162 **Redime ... minimo** ransom yourself, a captive, at the smallest possible price (from Terence's play *The Eunuch*, as quoted inaccurately in Lilly's *Latin Grammar*)   163 **Gramercies** many thanks   165 **longly** (1) longingly (2) interminably   166 **pith of all** heart of the matter   168 **daughter of Agenor** Europa, loved by Jupiter, who, in the form of a bull, carried her to Crete   170 **strond** strand, shore   180 **curst and shrewd** sharp-tempered and shrewish   183 **mewed** caged   184 **Because** so that   186 **advised** informed   187 **cunning** knowing

TRANIO Ay, marry, am I, sir—and now 'tis plotted!

LUCENTIO I have it, Tranio!

TRANIO   Master, for my hand,
190   Both our inventions meet and jump in one.

LUCENTIO Tell me thine first.

TRANIO   You will be schoolmaster
    And undertake the teaching of the maid.
    That's your device.

LUCENTIO   It is. May it be done?

TRANIO Not possible, for who shall bear your part
195   And be in Padua here Vincentio's son?
    Keep house and ply his book, welcome his friends,
    Visit his countrymen and banquet them?

LUCENTIO *Basta*, content thee, for I have it full.
    We have not yet been seen in any house,
200   Nor can we be distinguished by our faces
    For man or master. Then it follows thus:
    Thou shalt be master, Tranio, in my stead,
    Keep house and port and servants as I should.
    I will some other be—some Florentine,
205   Some Neapolitan, or meaner man of Pisa.
    'Tis hatched and shall be so. Tranio, at once
    Uncase thee, take my colored hat and cloak.
    When Biondello comes he waits on thee,
    But I will charm him first to keep his tongue.

210   TRANIO So had you need.
    In brief, sir, sith it your pleasure is
    And I am tied to be obedient—
    For so your father charged me at our parting;

---

188 'tis plotted I've a scheme   189 for I bet   190 inventions schemes
190 jump in one are identical   194 bear act   198 Basta enough (Italian)
198 full fully (worked out)   203 port style   205 meaner of lower rank
207 Uncase undress   207 colored (masters dressed colorfully; servants wore
dark blue)   209 charm exercise power over (he tells him a fanciful tale, lines
225–34)   211 sith since   212 tied obligated

"Be serviceable to my son," quoth he,
Although I think 'twas in another sense—   215
I am content to be Lucentio
Because so well I love Lucentio.

LUCENTIO Tranio, be so, because Lucentio loves,
And let me be a slave, t'achieve that maid
Whose sudden sight hath thralled my wounded eye.   220

Enter Biondello.

Here comes the rogue. Sirrah, where have you been?

BIONDELLO Where have I been? Nay, how now, where
are you?
Master, has my fellow Tranio stol'n your clothes,
Or you stol'n his, or both? Pray, what's the news?

LUCENTIO Sirrah, come hither. 'Tis no time to jest,   225
And therefore frame your manners to the time.
Your fellow Tranio, here, to save my life,
Puts my apparel and my count'nance on,
And I for my escape have put on his,
For in a quarrel since I came ashore   230
I killed a man and fear I was descried.
Wait you on him, I charge you, as becomes,
While I make way from hence to save my life.
You understand me?

BIONDELLO   I, sir? Ne'er a whit.

LUCENTIO And not a jot of Tranio in your mouth.   235
Tranio is changed into Lucentio.

BIONDELLO The better for him. Would I were so too.

TRANIO So could I, faith, boy, to have the next wish
after,
That Lucentio indeed had Baptista's youngest
daughter.

___

220 **thralled** enslaved 226 **frame your manners to the time** adjust your
conduct to the situation 228 **count'nance** demeanor 231 **decried** seen,
recognized

But, sirrah, not for my sake but your master's,
240   I advise
You use your manners discreetly in all kind of
    companies.
When I am alone, why, then I am Tranio,
But in all places else your master, Lucentio.

LUCENTIO Tranio, let's go.
245   One thing more rests, that thyself execute—
To make one among these wooers. If thou ask me
    why,
Sufficeth my reasons are both good and weighty.

                                            Exeunt.

                The Presenters above speaks.

FIRST SERVINGMAN My lord, you nod; you do not mind
    the play.

SLY Yes, by Saint Anne, do I. A good matter, surely.
250   Comes there any more of it?

PAGE My lord, 'tis but begun.

SLY 'Tis a very excellent piece of work, madam lady.
    Would 'twere done!   *They sit and mark.*

        [Scene II. *Padua. The street in front of
                    Hortensio's house.*]

        Enter Petruchio and his man Grumio.

PETRUCHIO Verona, for a while I take my leave
    To see my friends in Padua, but of all
    My best belovèd and approvèd friend,

---

245 **rests** remains   245 **execute** are to perform   247s.d. **Presenters** commentators, actors thought of collectively, hence the singular verb   248 **mind** pay attention to   253s.d. **mark** observe   I.ii.s.d. **Petruchio** (correct form *Petrucio*, with *c* pronounced *tch*)

Hortensio, and I trow this is his house.
Here, sirrah Grumio, knock, I say.   5

GRUMIO Knock, sir? Whom should I knock? Is there
any man has rebused your worship?

PETRUCHIO Villain, I say, knock me here soundly.

GRUMIO Knock you here, sir? Why, sir, what am I,
sir, that I should knock you here, sir?   10

PETRUCHIO Villain, I say, knock me at this gate
And rap me well or I'll knock your knave's pate.

GRUMIO My master is grown quarrelsome. I should
knock you first,
And then I know after who comes by the worst.

PETRUCHIO Will it not be?   15
Faith, sirrah, and you'll not knock, I'll ring it;
I'll try how you can *sol, fa,* and sing it.
                                        He wrings him by the ears.

GRUMIO Help, masters, help! My master is mad.

PETRUCHIO Now, knock when I bid you, sirrah villain.

                          Enter Hortensio.

HORTENSIO How now, what's the matter? My old   20
friend Grumio, and my good friend Petruchio! How
do you all at Verona?

PETRUCHIO Signior Hortensio, come you to part the
fray?
Con tutto il cuore ben trovato, may I say.

HORTENSIO *Alla nostra casa ben venuto, molto hono-*   25
rato signior mio Petruchio.

---

4 **trow** think   7 **rebused** (Grumio means *abused*)   8 **knock me here** knock here
for me (Grumio plays game of misunderstanding, taking "me here" as "my ear")
11 **gate** door   12 **pate** head   16 **and** if   16 **ring** (pun on *wring*)   17 **sol, fa** go
up and down the scales (possibly with puns on meanings now lost)   24 **Con ...
trovato** with all [my] heart well found (i.e., welcome)   25–26 **Alla ... Petruchio**
welcome to our house, my much honored Signior Petruchio

Rise, Grumio, rise. We will compound this quarrel.

GRUMIO Nay, 'tis no matter, sir, what he 'leges in
Latin. If this be not a lawful cause for me to leave
30   his service—look you, sir, he bid me knock him and
rap him soundly, sir. Well, was it fit for a servant to
use his master so, being perhaps, for aught I see,
two-and-thirty, a peep out?
Whom would to God I had well knocked at first,
35   Then had not Grumio come by the worst.

PETRUCHIO A senseless villain! Good Hortensio,
I bade the rascal knock upon your gate
And could not get him for my heart to do it.

GRUMIO Knock at the gate? O heavens! Spake you
40   not these words plain, "Sirrah, knock me here, rap
me here, knock me well, and knock me soundly"?
And come you now with "knocking at the gate"?

PETRUCHIO Sirrah, be gone or talk not, I advise you.

HORTENSIO Petruchio, patience, I am Grumio's pledge.
45   Why, this's a heavy chance 'twixt him and you,
Your ancient, trusty, pleasant servant Grumio.
And tell me now, sweet friend, what happy gale
Blows you to Padua here from old Verona?

PETRUCHIO Such wind as scatters young men through
   the world
50   To seek their fortunes farther than at home,
Where small experience grows. But in a few,
Signior Hortensio, thus it stands with me:
Antonio my father is deceased,
And I have thrust myself into this maze,
55   Happily to wive and thrive as best I may.

---

27 **compound** settle   28 **'leges** alleges   29 **Latin** (as if he were English, Grumio does not recognize Italian)   33 **two-and-thirty, a peep out** (1) an implication that Petruchio is aged (2) a term from cards, slang for "drunk" (*peep* is an old form of *pip*, a marking on a card)   38 **heart** life   45 **heavy chance** sad happening   51 **few** i.e., words   54 **maze** traveling; uncertain course   55 **Happily** haply, perchance

Crowns in my purse I have and goods at home
And so am come abroad to see the world.

HORTENSIO Petruchio, shall I then come roundly to
 thee
And wish thee to a shrewd ill-favored wife?
Thou'ldst thank me but a little for my counsel—   60
And yet I'll promise thee she shall be rich,
And very rich—but thou'rt too much my friend,
And I'll not wish thee to her.

PETRUCHIO Signior Hortensio, 'twixt such friends as we
Few words suffice; and therefore if thou know   65
One rich enough to be Petruchio's wife—
As wealth is burthen of my wooing dance—
Be she as foul as was Florentius' love,
As old as Sibyl, and as curst and shrewd
As Socrates' Xanthippe or a worse,   70
She moves me not, or not removes, at least,
Affection's edge in me, were she as rough
As are the swelling Adriatic seas.
I come to wive it wealthily in Padua;
If wealthily, then happily in Padua.   75

GRUMIO Nay, look you, sir, he tells you flatly what
his mind is. Why, give him gold enough and marry
him to a puppet or an aglet-baby or an old trot
with ne'er a tooth in her head, though she have as
many diseases as two-and-fifty horses. Why, nothing   80
comes amiss so money comes withal.

HORTENSIO Petruchio, since we are stepped thus far in,
I will continue that I broached in jest.
I can, Petruchio, help thee to a wife
With wealth enough and young and beauteous,   85

---

58 **come roundly** talk frankly   59 **shrewd ill-favored** shrewish, poorly qualified
67 **burthen** burden (musical accompaniment)   68 **foul** homely   68 **Florentius**
knight in Gower's *Confessio Amantis* (cf. Chaucer's Wife of Bath's Tale; knight
marries hag who turns into beautiful girl)   69 **Sibyl** prophetess in Greek and
Roman myth   70 **Xanthippe** Socrates' wife, legendarily shrewish   78 **aglet-
baby** small female figure forming metal tip of cord or lace (French *aiguillette*, point)
78 **trot** hag   81 **withal** with it   83 **that** what

Brought up as best becomes a gentlewoman.
Her only fault—and that is faults enough—
Is that she is intolerable curst
And shrewd and froward, so beyond all measure
90 That were my state far worser than it is,
I would not wed her for a mine of gold.

PETRUCHIO Hortensio, peace. Thou know'st not gold's
    effect.
Tell me her father's name, and 'tis enough,
For I will board her though she chide as loud
95 As thunder when the clouds in autumn crack.

HORTENSIO Her father is Baptista Minola,
An affable and courteous gentleman.
Her name is Katherina Minola,
Renowned in Padua for her scolding tongue.

100 PETRUCHIO I know her father though I know not her,
And he knew my deceasèd father well.
I will not sleep, Hortensio, till I see her,
And therefore let me be thus bold with you,
To give you over at this first encounter
105 Unless you will accompany me thither.

GRUMIO I pray you, sir, let him go while the humor
lasts. A my word, and she knew him as well as I
do, she would think scolding would do little good
upon him. She may perhaps call him half a score
110 knaves or so—why, that's nothing. And he begin
once, he'll rail in his rope-tricks. I'll tell you what,
sir, and she stand him but a little, he will throw a
figure in her face and so disfigure her with it that
she shall have no more eyes to see withal than a
115 cat. You know him not, sir.

---

88 **intolerable curst** intolerably sharp-tempered   89 **froward** willful   90 **state** estate, revenue   94 **board** naval term, with double sense: (1) accost (2) go on board   95 **crack** make explosive roars   104 **give you over** leave you   106 **humor** mood   107 **A** on   107 **and** if (also at lines 110 and 112)   108 **do little good** have little effect   111 **rope-tricks** (1) Grumio's version of *rhetoric*, going with *figure* just below (2) rascally conduct, deserving hanging (3) possible sexual innuendo, as in following lines   112 **stand** withstand

HORTENSIO Tarry, Petruchio, I must go with thee,
 For in Baptista's keep my treasure is.
 He hath the jewel of my life in hold,
 His youngest daughter, beautiful Bianca,
 And her withholds from me and other more,   120
 Suitors to her and rivals in my love,
 Supposing it a thing impossible,
 For those defects I have before rehearsed,
 That ever Katherina will be wooed.
 Therefore this order hath Baptista ta'en,   125
 That none shall have access unto Bianca
 Till Katherine the curst have got a husband.

GRUMIO Katherine the curst!
 A title for a maid of all titles the worst.

HORTENSIO Now shall my friend Petruchio do me
  grace   130
 And offer me, disguised in sober robes,
 To old Baptista as a schoolmaster
 Well seen in music, to instruct Bianca,
 That so I may, by this device, at least
 Have leave and leisure to make love to her   135
 And unsuspected court her by herself.

   Enter Gremio, and Lucentio disguised
    [as a schoolmaster, Cambio].

GRUMIO Here's no knavery! See, to beguile the old
 folks, how the young folks lay their heads together!
 Master, master, look about you. Who goes there,
 ha?   140

HORTENSIO Peace, Grumio. It is the rival of my love.
 Petruchio, stand by awhile.   *[They eavesdrop.]*

GRUMIO A proper stripling, and an amorous!

GREMIO O, very well, I have perused the note.

117 **keep** heavily fortified inner tower of castle 118 **hold** stronghold 123 **For** because of 125 **order** step 130 **grace** a favor 131 **offer** present, introduce 133 **seen** trained 143 **proper stripling** handsome youth (sarcastic comment on Gremio) 144 **note** memorandum (reading list for Bianca)

145 Hark you, sir, I'll have them very fairly bound—
All books of love, see that at any hand,
And see you read no other lectures to her.
You understand me. Over and beside
Signior Baptista's liberality,
150 I'll mend it with a largess. Take your paper too
And let me have them very well perfumed,
For she is sweeter than perfume itself
To whom they go to. What will you read to her?

LUCENTIO Whate'er I read to her, I'll plead for you
155 As for my patron, stand you so assured,
As firmly as yourself were still in place—
Yea, and perhaps with more successful words
Than you unless you were a scholar, sir.

GREMIO O this learning, what a thing it is!

160 GRUMIO [*Aside*] O this woodcock, what an ass it is!

PETRUCHIO Peace, sirrah!

HORTENSIO Grumio, mum! [*Coming forward*] God save
you, Signior Gremio.

GREMIO And you are well met, Signior Hortensio.
Trow you whither I am going? To Baptista Minola.
165 I promised to inquire carefully
About a schoolmaster for the fair Bianca,
And, by good fortune, I have lighted well
On this young man—for learning and behavior
Fit for her turn, well read in poetry
170 And other books, good ones I warrant ye.

HORTENSIO 'Tis well. And I have met a gentleman
Hath promised me to help me to another,
A fine musician to instruct our mistress.

146 **at any hand** in any case   147 **read no other lectures** assign no other
readings   150 **mend it with a largess** add a gift of money to it   150 **paper** note
(line 144)   151 **them** i.e., the books   156 **as** as if you   156 **in place** present
160 **woodcock** bird easily trapped, so considered silly   164 **Trow** know   168 **for**
in   169 **turn** situation (with unconscious bawdy pun on the sense of "copulation")
172 **help me to** (1) find (2) become (Hortensio's jest)

So shall I no whit be behind in duty
To fair Bianca, so beloved of me.   175

GREMIO Beloved of me, and that my deeds shall
    prove.

GRUMIO [*Aside*] And that his bags shall prove.

HORTENSIO Gremio, 'tis now no time to vent our love.
    Listen to me, and if you speak me fair,
    I'll tell you news indifferent good for either.   180
    Here is a gentleman whom by chance I met,
    Upon agreement from us to his liking,
    Will undertake to woo curst Katherine,
    Yea, and to marry her if her dowry please.

GREMIO So said, so done, is well.   185
    Hortensio, have you told him all her faults?

PETRUCHIO I know she is an irksome, brawling scold;
    If that be all, masters, I hear no harm.

GREMIO No, say'st me so, friend? What countryman?

PETRUCHIO Born in Verona, old Antonio's son.   190
    My father dead, my fortune lives for me,
    And I do hope good days and long to see.

GREMIO O, sir, such a life with such a wife were
    strange.
    But if you have a stomach, to't a God's name;
    You shall have me assisting you in all.   195
    But will you woo this wildcat?

PETRUCHIO   Will I live?

GRUMIO [*Aside*] Will he woo her? Ay, or I'll hang her.

PETRUCHIO Why came I hither but to that intent?
    Think you a little din can daunt mine ears?
    Have I not in my time heard lions roar?   200
    Have I not heard the sea, puffed up with winds,
    Rage like an angry boar chafèd with sweat?

177 **bags** i.e., of money 178 **vent** express 180 **indifferent** equally
182 **Upon ... liking** if we agree to his terms (paying costs) 183 **undertake**
promise 194 **stomach** inclination 194 **a** in

Have I not heard great ordnance in the field
And heaven's artillery thunder in the skies?
205   Have I not in a pitchèd battle heard
Loud 'larums, neighing steeds, and trumpets'
    clang?
And do you tell me of a woman's tongue,
That gives not half so great a blow to hear
As will a chestnut in a farmer's fire?
Tush, tush, fear boys with bugs.

210 GRUMIO [*Aside*]   For he fears none.

GREMIO Hortensio, hark.
This gentleman is happily arrived,
My mind presumes, for his own good and ours.

HORTENSIO I promised we would be contributors
215   And bear his charge of wooing, whatsoe'er.

GREMIO And so we will, provided that he win her.

GRUMIO [*Aside*] I would I were as sure of a good
dinner.

Enter Tranio brave [as Lucentio] and Biondello.

TRANIO Gentlemen, God save you. If I may be bold,
Tell me, I beseech you, which is the readiest way
220   To the house of Signior Baptista Minola?

BIONDELLO He that has the two fair daughters? Is't
he you mean?

TRANIO Even he, Biondello.

GREMIO Hark you, sir. You mean not her to—

TRANIO Perhaps, him and her, sir. What have you
to do?

PETRUCHIO Not her that chides, sir, at any hand, I
225   pray.

---

203 **ordnance** cannon 206 **'larums** calls to arms, sudden attacks 210 **fear**
frighten 210 **bugs** bugbears 215 **his charge** of the cost of his 217s.d. **brave**
elegantly attired 224 **to do** i.e., to do with this 225 **at any hand** in any case

TRANIO I love no chiders, sir. Biondello, let's away.

LUCENTIO [*Aside*] Well begun, Tranio.

HORTENSIO   Sir, a word ere
  you go.
  Are you a suitor to the maid you talk of, yea or no?

TRANIO And if I be, sir, is it any offense?

GREMIO No, if without more words you will get you
  hence.   230

TRANIO Why, sir, I pray, are not the streets as free
  For me as for you?

GREMIO   But so is not she.

TRANIO For what reason, I beseech you?

GREMIO For this reason, if you'll know,
  That she's the choice love of Signior Gremio.   235

HORTENSIO That she's the chosen of Signior Hortensio.

TRANIO Softly, my masters! If you be gentlemen,
  Do me this right: hear me with patience.
  Baptista is a noble gentleman
  To whom my father is not all unknown,   240
  And were his daughter fairer than she is,
  She may more suitors have, and me for one.
  Fair Leda's daughter had a thousand wooers;
  Then well one more may fair Bianca have.
  And so she shall. Lucentio shall make one,   245
  Though Paris came in hope to speed alone.

GREMIO What, this gentleman will out-talk us all.

LUCENTIO Sir, give him head. I know he'll prove a
  jade.

PETRUCHIO Hortensio, to what end are all these words?

235 **choice** chosen   243 **Leda's daughter** Helen of Troy   246 **Paris** lover who
took Helen to Troy (legendary cause of Trojan War)   246 **came** should come
246 **speed** succeed   248 **prove a jade** soon tire (cf. "jaded")

250 HORTENSIO Sir, let me be so bold as ask you,
       Did you yet ever see Baptista's daughter?

    TRANIO No, sir, but hear I do that he hath two,
       The one as famous for a scolding tongue
       As is the other for beauteous modesty.

255 PETRUCHIO Sir, sir, the first's for me; let her go by.

    GREMIO Yea, leave that labor to great Hercules,
       And let it be more than Alcides' twelve.

    PETRUCHIO Sir, understand you this of me in sooth:
       The youngest daughter, whom you hearken for,
260   Her father keeps from all access of suitors
       And will not promise her to any man
       Until the elder sister first be wed.
       The younger then is free, and not before.

    TRANIO If it be so, sir, that you are the man
265   Must stead us all, and me amongst the rest,
       And if you break the ice and do this feat,
       Achieve the elder, set the younger free
       For our access, whose hap shall be to have her
       Will not so graceless be to be ingrate.

    HORTENSIO Sir, you say well, and well you do
270   conceive,
       And since you do profess to be a suitor,
       You must, as we do, gratify this gentleman
       To whom we all rest generally beholding.

    TRANIO Sir, I shall not be slack, in sign whereof,
275   Please ye we may contrive this afternoon
       And quaff carouses to our mistress' health
       And do as adversaries do in law,
       Strive mightily but eat and drink as friends.

---

257 **Alcides** Hercules (after Alcaeus, a family ancestor) 258 **sooth** truth
259 **hearken** long 265 **stead** aid 267 **Achieve** succeed with 268 **whose hap**
the man whose luck 269 **to be ingrate** as to be ungrateful 270 **conceive** put
the case 272 **gratify** compensate 273 **rest** remain 273 **beholding** indebted
275 **contrive** pass 276 **quaff carouses** empty our cups 277 **adversaries**
attorneys

GRUMIO, BIONDELLO O excellent motion! Fellows, let's
   be gone.

HORTENSIO The motion's good indeed, and be it so.   280
   Petruchio, I shall be your *ben venuto*.   *Exeunt*.

---

281 ben venuto welcome (i.e., host)

[ACT II

Scene I. *In Baptista's house.*]

Enter Kate and Bianca [with her hands tied].

BIANCA Good sister, wrong me not nor wrong
    yourself
    To make a bondmaid and a slave of me.
    That I disdain. But for these other gawds,
    Unbind my hands, I'll pull them off myself,
5   Yea, all my raiment, to my petticoat,
    Or what you will command me will I do,
    So well I know my duty to my elders.

KATE Of all thy suitors, here I charge thee, tell
    Whom thou lov'st best. See thou dissemble not.

10 BIANCA Believe me, sister, of all the men alive
    I never yet beheld that special face
    Which I could fancy more than any other.

KATE Minion, thou liest. Is't not Hortensio?

BIANCA If you affect him, sister, here I swear
15   I'll plead for you myself but you shall have him.

KATE O then, belike, you fancy riches more:
    You will have Gremio to keep you fair.

BIANCA Is it for him you do envy me so?
    Nay, then you jest, and now I well perceive
20   You have but jested with me all this while.
    I prithee, sister Kate, untie my hands.

II.i.3 **gawds** adornments 13 **Minion** impudent creature 14 **affect** like
16 **belike** probably 17 **fair** in fine clothes 18 **envy** hate

KATE If that be jest then all the rest was so.
                              Strikes her.
            Enter Baptista.

BAPTISTA Why, how now, dame, whence grows this
      insolence?
    Bianca, stand aside. Poor girl, she weeps.
    Go ply thy needle; meddle not with her.   25
    For shame, thou hilding of a devilish spirit,
    Why dost thou wrong her that did ne'er wrong
      thee?
    When did she cross thee with a bitter word?

KATE Her silence flouts me and I'll be revenged.
                          Flies after Bianca.

BAPTISTA What, in my sight? Bianca, get thee in.   30
                            Exit [Bianca].

KATE What, will you not suffer me? Nay, now I see
    She is your treasure, she must have a husband;
    I must dance barefoot on her wedding day,
    And, for your love to her, lead apes in hell.
    Talk not to me; I will go sit and weep   35
    Till I can find occasion of revenge.   *[Exit.]*

BAPTISTA Was ever gentleman thus grieved as I?
    But who comes here?

    *Enter Gremio, Lucentio in the habit of a mean man
    [Cambio], Petruchio, with [Hortensio as a music teacher,
    Litio, and] Tranio [as Lucentio], with his boy
              [Biondello] bearing a lute and books.*

GREMIO Good morrow, neighbor Baptista.

BAPTISTA Good morrow, neighbor Gremio. God save   40
    you, gentlemen.

PETRUCHIO And you, good sir. Pray, have you not a
      daughter

26 **hilding** base wretch   31 **suffer** permit (i.e., to deal with you)   33 **dance ...**
day (expected of older maiden sisters)   34 **lead apes in hell** (proverbial occupa-
tion of old maids; cf. *Much Ado About Nothing*, II.i.41)   38s.d. **mean** lower class

Called Katherina, fair and virtuous?

BAPTISTA I have a daughter, sir, called Katherina.

45 GREMIO [*Aside*] You are too blunt; go to it orderly.

PETRUCHIO [*Aside*] You wrong me, Signior Gremio,
    give me leave.
    [*To Baptista*] I am a gentleman of Verona, sir,
    That, hearing of her beauty and her wit,
    Her affability and bashful modesty,
50 Her wondrous qualities and mild behavior,
    Am bold to show myself a forward guest
    Within your house, to make mine eye the witness
    Of that report which I so oft have heard.
    And, for an entrance to my entertainment,
55 I do present you with a man of mine,
                        [*presenting Hortensio*]
    Cunning in music and the mathematics,
    To instruct her fully in those sciences,
    Whereof I know she is not ignorant.
    Accept of him, or else you do me wrong.
60 His name is Litio, born in Mantua.

BAPTISTA Y'are welcome, sir, and he for your good sake.
    But for my daughter Katherine, this I know,
    She is not for your turn, the more my grief.

PETRUCHIO I see you do not mean to part with her,
65 Or else you like not of my company.

BAPTISTA Mistake me not; I speak but as I find.
    Whence are you, sir? What may I call your name?

PETRUCHIO Petruchio is my name, Antonio's son,
    A man well known throughout all Italy.

BAPTISTA I know him well. You are welcome for his
70 sake.

GREMIO Saving your tale, Petruchio, I pray,

45 **orderly** gradually 51 **forward** eager 54 **entrance to** price of admission for
54 **entertainment** reception 63 **turn** purpose (again, with bawdy pun)
71 **Saving** with all respect for

Let us, that are poor petitioners, speak too.
Backare, you are marvelous forward.

PETRUCHIO O pardon me, Signior Gremio, I would
fain be doing.

GREMIO I doubt it not, sir, but you will curse your
wooing.   75
Neighbor, this is a gift very grateful, I am sure of
it. To express the like kindness myself, that have
been more kindly beholding to you than any, freely
give unto you this young scholar [*presenting Lucentio*] that hath been long studying at Rheims—as   80
cunning in Greek, Latin, and other languages, as
the other in music and mathematics. His name is
Cambio. Pray accept his service.

BAPTISTA A thousand thanks, Signior Gremio. Welcome, good Cambio. [*To Tranio*] But, gentle sir,   85
methinks you walk like a stranger. May I be so
bold to know the cause of your coming?

TRANIO Pardon me, sir, the boldness is mine own,
That, being a stranger in this city here,
Do make myself a suitor to your daughter,   90
Unto Bianca, fair and virtuous.
Nor is your firm resolve unknown to me
In the preferment of the eldest sister.
This liberty is all that I request,
That, upon knowledge of my parentage,   95
I may have welcome 'mongst the rest that woo
And free access and favor as the rest.
And, toward the education of your daughters
I here bestow a simple instrument,
And this small packet of Greek and Latin books.   100
If you accept them, then their worth is great.

---

73 **Backare** back (proverbial quasi-Latin)   73 **marvelous** very   74 **would fain**
am eager to   74 **doing** (with a sexual jest)   76 **grateful** worthy of gratitude
77 **myself, that** I myself, who   83 **Cambio** (Italian for "exchange")   86 **walk**
like have the bearing of   89 **That** who   93 **preferment of** giving priority to
97 **favor** countenance, acceptance   99 **instrument** i.e., the lute

BAPTISTA [*Looking at books*] Lucentio is your name.
    Of whence, I pray?

TRANIO Of Pisa, sir, son to Vincentio.

BAPTISTA A mighty man of Pisa; by report
105   I know him well. You are very welcome, sir.
    [*To Hortensio*] Take you the lute, [*to Lucentio*]
      and you the set of books;
    You shall go see your pupils presently.
    Holla, within!

Enter a Servant.

                Sirrah, lead these gentlemen
    To my daughters and tell them both
110   These are their tutors; bid them use them well.
                  [*Exit Servant, with Lucentio,*
                  Hortensio, and Biondello following.]
    We will go walk a little in the orchard
    And then to dinner. You are passing welcome,
    And so I pray you all to think yourselves.

PETRUCHIO Signior Baptista, my business asketh haste,
115   And every day I cannot come to woo.
    You knew my father well, and in him me,
    Left solely heir to all his lands and goods,
    Which I have bettered rather than decreased.
    Then tell me, if I get your daughter's love
120   What dowry shall I have with her to wife?

BAPTISTA After my death the one half of my lands,
    And in possession twenty thousand crowns.

PETRUCHIO And, for that dowry, I'll assure her of
    Her widowhood, be it that she survive me,
125   In all my lands and leases whatsoever.
    Let specialties be therefore drawn between us
    That covenants may be kept on either hand.

---

105 **him** his name   107 **presently** at once   111 **orchard** garden   112 **passing** very   122 **possession** i.e., at the time of marriage   124 **widowhood** estate settled on a widow (Johnson)   126 **specialties** special contracts

BAPTISTA Ay, when the special thing is well obtained,
　　That is, her love, for that is all in all.

PETRUCHIO Why, that is nothing, for I tell you, father,　130
　　I am as peremptory as she proud-minded.
　　And where two raging fires meet together
　　They do consume the thing that feeds their fury.
　　Though little fire grows great with little wind,
　　Yet extreme gusts will blow out fire and all.　135
　　So I to her, and so she yields to me,
　　For I am rough and woo not like a babe.

BAPTISTA Well mayst thou woo, and happy be thy
　　　　speed!
　　But be thou armed for some unhappy words.

PETRUCHIO Ay, to the proof, as mountains are for
　　　　winds　140
　　That shakes not, though they blow perpetually.

Enter Hortensio with his head broke.

BAPTISTA How now, my friend, why dost thou look
　　　　so pale?

HORTENSIO For fear, I promise you, if I look pale.

BAPTISTA What, will my daughter prove a good
　　　　musician?

HORTENSIO I think she'll sooner prove a soldier.　145
　　Iron may hold with her, but never lutes.

BAPTISTA Why, then thou canst not break her to
　　　　the lute?

HORTENSIO Why, no, for she hath broke the lute to me.
　　I did but tell her she mistook her frets
　　And bowed her hand to teach her fingering,　150
　　When, with a most impatient devilish spirit,
　　"Fret, call you these?" quoth she; "I'll fume with
　　　　them."

131 **peremptory** resolved 138 **speed** progress 140 **to the proof** in tested steel
armor 146 **hold with her** stand her treatment 147 **break** train 149 **frets**
ridges where strings are pressed 150 **bowed** bent

And with that word she stroke me on the head,
And through the instrument my pate made way.
155 And there I stood amazèd for a while
As on a pillory, looking through the lute,
While she did call me rascal, fiddler,
And twangling Jack, with twenty such vile terms
As had she studied to misuse me so.

160 PETRUCHIO Now, by the world, it is a lusty wench!
I love her ten times more than e'er I did.
O how I long to have some chat with her!

BAPTISTA [*To Hortensio*] Well, go with me, and be
not so discomfited.
Proceed in practice with my younger daughter;
165 She's apt to learn and thankful for good turns.
Signior Petruchio, will you go with us
Or shall I send my daughter Kate to you?
           Exit [Baptista, with Gremio, Tranio, and
                          Hortensio]. Manet Petruchio.

PETRUCHIO I pray you do. I'll attend her here
And woo her with some spirit when she comes.
170 Say that she rail, why then I'll tell her plain
She sings as sweetly as a nightingale.
Say that she frown, I'll say she looks as clear
As morning roses newly washed with dew.
Say she be mute and will not speak a word,
175 Then I'll commend her volubility
And say she uttereth piercing eloquence.
If she do bid me pack, I'll give her thanks
As though she bid me stay by her a week.
If she deny to wed, I'll crave the day
180 When I shall ask the banns and when be marrièd.
But here she comes, and now, Petruchio, speak.

---

153 **stroke** struck   156 **pillory** i.e., with a wooden collar (old structure for public punishment)   158 **Jack** (term of contempt)   159 **As** as if   159 **studied** prepared   160 **lusty** spirited   164 **practice** instruction   165 **apt** disposed   167s.d. (is in the F position, which need not be changed; Petruchio speaks to the departing Baptista)   168 **attend** wait for   170 **rail** scold, scoff   177 **pack** go away   179 **deny** refuse   180 **banns** public announcement in church of intent to marry

Good morrow, Kate, for that's your name, I hear.

KATE Well have you heard, but something hard of
    hearing.
They call me Katherine that do talk of me.

PETRUCHIO You lie, in faith, for you are called plain
    Kate,   185
And bonny Kate, and sometimes Kate the curst.
But, Kate, the prettiest Kate in Christendom,
Kate of Kate Hall, my super-dainty Kate,
For dainties are all Kates, and therefore, Kate,
Take this of me, Kate of my consolation.   190
Hearing thy mildness praised in every town,
Thy virtues spoke of, and thy beauty sounded—
Yet not so deeply as to thee belongs—
Myself am moved to woo thee for my wife.

KATE Moved! In good time, let him that moved you
    hither   195
Remove you hence. I knew you at the first
You were a movable.

PETRUCHIO   Why, what's a movable?

KATE A joint stool.

PETRUCHIO   Thou hast hit it; come sit on me.

KATE Asses are made to bear and so are you.

PETRUCHIO Women are made to bear and so are you.   200

KATE No such jade as you, if me you mean.

---

183 **heard** (pun: pronounced like *hard*)   186 **bonny** big, fine (perhaps with pun
on *bony*, the F spelling)   188 **Kate Hall** (possible topical reference; several places
have been proposed)   189 **dainties** delicacies   189 **Kates** i.e., *cates*, delicacies
192 **sounded** (1) measured (effect of *deeply*) (2) spoken of (pun)   195 **In good
time** indeed   197 **movable** article of furniture (with pun)   198 **joint stool** stool
made by a joiner (standard term of disparagement)   199 **bear** carry   200 **bear**
i.e., bear children (with second sexual meaning in Petruchio's "I will not burden
thee")   201 **jade** worn-out horse (Kate has now called him both "ass" and "sorry
horse")

PETRUCHIO Alas, good Kate, I will not burden thee,
For, knowing thee to be but young and light—

KATE Too light for such a swain as you to catch
205   And yet as heavy as my weight should be.

PETRUCHIO Should be! Should—buzz!

KATE   Well ta'en, and like a buzzard.

PETRUCHIO O slow-winged turtle, shall a buzzard
take thee?

KATE Ay, for a turtle, as he takes a buzzard.

PETRUCHIO Come, come, you wasp, i' faith you are
too angry.

210 KATE If I be waspish, best beware my sting.

PETRUCHIO My remedy is then to pluck it out.

KATE Ay, if the fool could find it where it lies.

PETRUCHIO Who knows not where a wasp does wear
his sting?
In his tail.

KATE   In his tongue.

PETRUCHIO   Whose tongue?

215 KATE Yours, if you talk of tales, and so farewell.

PETRUCHIO What, with my tongue in your tail? Nay,
come again.
Good Kate, I am a gentleman—

KATE   That I'll try.
                                        She strikes him.

PETRUCHIO I swear I'll cuff you if you strike again.

---

204 **swain** country boy   206 **be** (pun on *bee*; hence *buzz*, scandal, i.e., about "light" woman)   206 **buzzard** hawk unteachable in falconry (hence idiot) 207 **turtle** turtledove, noted for affectionateness   207 **take** capture (with pun, "mistake for," in next line)   208 **buzzard** buzzing insect (hence "wasp") 215 **of tales** idle tales (leading to bawdy pun on *tail* = pudend)

KATE So may you lose your arms:
   If you strike me you are no gentleman,   220
   And if no gentleman, why then no arms.

PETRUCHIO A herald, Kate? O, put me in thy books.

KATE What is your crest? A coxcomb?

PETRUCHIO A combless cock, so Kate will be my hen.

KATE No cock of mine; you crow too like a craven.   225

PETRUCHIO Nay, come, Kate, come, you must not look
   so sour.

KATE It is my fashion when I see a crab.

PETRUCHIO Why, here's no crab, and therefore look
   not sour.

KATE There is, there is.

PETRUCHIO Then show it me.

KATE   Had I a glass I would.   230

PETRUCHIO What, you mean my face?

KATE   Well aimed of
   such a young one.

PETRUCHIO Now, by Saint George, I am too young
   for you.

KATE Yet you are withered.

PETRUCHIO   'Tis with cares.

KATE   I care not.

PETRUCHIO Nay, hear you, Kate, in sooth you scape
   not so.

KATE I chafe you if I tarry. Let me go.   235

219 arms (pun on "coat of arms") 222 herald one skilled in heraldry
222 books registers of heraldry (with pun on "in your good books") 223 crest
heraldic device 223 coxcomb identifying feature of court Fool's cap; the cap
itself 224 combless i.e., unwarlike 224 so if 225 craven defeated cock
227 crab crab apple 230 glass mirror 231 well aimed of a good shot (in the
dark) 234 sooth truth 234 scape escape 235 chafe (1) annoy (2) warm up

PETRUCHIO No, not a whit. I find you passing gentle.
'Twas told me you were rough and coy and sullen,
And now I find report a very liar,
For thou art pleasant, gamesome, passing courteous,
240 But slow in speech, yet sweet as springtime flowers.
Thou canst not frown, thou canst not look askance,
Nor bite the lip as angry wenches will,
Nor hast thou pleasure to be cross in talk,
But thou with mildness entertain'st thy wooers,
245 With gentle conference, soft and affable.
Why does the world report that Kate doth limp?
O sland'rous world! Kate like the hazel-twig
Is straight and slender, and as brown in hue
As hazelnuts and sweeter than the kernels.
250 O, let me see thee walk. Thou dost not halt.

KATE Go, fool, and whom thou keep'st command.

PETRUCHIO Did ever Dian so become a grove
As Kate this chamber with her princely gait?
O, be thou Dian and let her be Kate,
255 And then let Kate be chaste and Dian sportful!

KATE Where did you study all this goodly speech?

PETRUCHIO It is extempore, from my mother-wit.

KATE A witty mother! Witless else her son.

PETRUCHIO Am I not wise?

KATE   Yes, keep you warm.

PETRUCHIO Marry, so I mean, sweet Katherine,
260   in thy bed.
And therefore, setting all this chat aside,
Thus in plain terms: your father hath consented
That you shall be my wife, your dowry 'greed on,
And will you, nill you, I will marry you.

---

237 **coy** offish   245 **conference** conversation   250 **halt** limp   251 **whom thou keep'st** i.e., your servants   252 **Dian** Diana, goddess of hunting and virginity   255 **sportful** (i.e., in the game of love)   257 **mother-wit** natural intelligence   258 **else** otherwise would be   259 **Yes** yes, just enough to (refers to a proverbial saying)   264 **nill** won't

Now, Kate, I am a husband for your turn,   265
For, by this light, whereby I see thy beauty—
Thy beauty that doth make me like thee well—
Thou must be married to no man but me.

Enter Baptista, Gremio, Tranio.

For I am he am born to tame you, Kate,
And bring you from a wild Kate to a Kate   270
Conformable as other household Kates.
Here comes your father. Never make denial;
I must and will have Katherine to my wife.

BAPTISTA Now, Signior Petruchio, how speed you
with my daughter?

PETRUCHIO How but well, sir? How but well?   275
It were impossible I should speed amiss.

BAPTISTA Why, how now, daughter Katherine, in your
dumps?

KATE Call you me daughter? Now, I promise you
You have showed a tender fatherly regard
To wish me wed to one half lunatic,   280
A madcap ruffian and a swearing Jack
That thinks with oaths to face the matter out.

PETRUCHIO Father, 'tis thus: yourself and all the world
That talked of her have talked amiss of her.
If she be curst it is for policy,   285
For she's not froward but modest as the dove.
She is not hot but temperate as the morn;
For patience she will prove a second Grissel
And Roman Lucrece for her chastity.
And to conclude, we have 'greed so well together   290
That upon Sunday is the wedding day.

KATE I'll see thee hanged on Sunday first.

265 turn advantage (with bawdy second meaning)   270 wild Kate (pun on
"wildcat")   271 Conformable submissive   274 speed get on   277 dumps low
spirits   278 promise tell   282 face brazen   285 policy tactics   287 hot
intemperate   288 Grissel Griselda (patient wife in Chaucer's Clerk's Tale)
289 Lucrece (killed herself after Tarquin raped her)

GREMIO Hark, Petruchio, she says she'll see thee
    hanged first.

TRANIO Is this your speeding? Nay, then good night
    our part!

PETRUCHIO Be patient, gentlemen, I choose her for
295   myself.
    If she and I be pleased, what's that to you?
    'Tis bargained 'twixt us twain, being alone,
    That she shall still be curst in company.
    I tell you, 'tis incredible to believe
300   How much she loves me. O, the kindest Kate,
    She hung about my neck, and kiss on kiss
    She vied so fast, protesting oath on oath,
    That in a twink she won me to her love.
    O, you are novices. 'Tis a world to see
305   How tame, when men and women are alone,
    A meacock wretch can make the curstest shrew.
    Give me thy hand, Kate. I will unto Venice
    To buy apparel 'gainst the wedding day.
    Provide the feast, father, and bid the guests;
310   I will be sure my Katherine shall be fine.

BAPTISTA I know not what to say, but give me your
    hands.
    God send you joy, Petruchio! 'Tis a match.

GREMIO, TRANIO Amen, say we. We will be witnesses.

PETRUCHIO Father, and wife, and gentlemen, adieu.
315   I will to Venice; Sunday comes apace.
    We will have rings and things and fine array,
    And, kiss me, Kate, "We will be married a Sun-
    day."

                     Exit Petruchio and Kate.

GREMIO Was ever match clapped up so suddenly?

---

294 **speeding** success   302 **vied** made higher bids (card-playing terms), i.e.,
kissed more frequently   303 **twink** twinkling   304 **world** wonder   306 **mea-
cock** timid   308 **'gainst** in preparation for   310 **fine** well dressed   317 **"We ...
Sunday"** (line from a ballad)   318 **clapped** fixed

BAPTISTA Faith, gentlemen, now I play a merchant's
    part
  And venture madly on a desperate mart.   320

TRANIO 'Twas a commodity lay fretting by you;
  'Twill bring you gain or perish on the seas.

BAPTISTA The gain I seek is quiet in the match.

GREMIO No doubt but he hath got a quiet catch.
  But now, Baptista, to your younger daughter;   325
  Now is the day we long have lookèd for.
  I am your neighbor and was suitor first.

TRANIO And I am one that love Bianca more
  Than words can witness or your thoughts can guess.

GREMIO Youngling, thou canst not love so dear as I.   330

TRANIO Graybeard, thy love doth freeze.

GREMIO   But thine doth fry.
  Skipper, stand back, 'tis age that nourisheth.

TRANIO But youth in ladies' eyes that flourisheth.

BAPTISTA Content you, gentlemen; I will compound
    this strife.
  'Tis deeds must win the prize, and he of both   335
  That can assure my daughter greatest dower
  Shall have my Bianca's love.
  Say, Signior Gremio, what can you assure her?

GREMIO First, as you know, my house within the city
  Is richly furnishèd with plate and gold,   340
  Basins and ewers to lave her dainty hands;
  My hangings all of Tyrian tapestry;
  In ivory coffers I have stuffed my crowns,
  In cypress chests my arras counterpoints,

---

320 mart "deal" 321 commodity (here a coarse term for women; see Partridge, *Shakespeare's Bawdy*) 321 fretting decaying in storage (with pun) 332 Skipper skipping (irresponsible) fellow 334 compound settle 335 he of both the one of you two 336 dower man's gift to bride 341 lave wash 342 Tyrian purple 344 arras counterpoints counterpanes woven in Arras

345   Costly apparel, tents, and canopies,
       Fine linen, Turkey cushions bossed with pearl,
       Valance of Venice gold in needlework,
       Pewter and brass, and all things that belongs
       To house or housekeeping. Then, at my farm
350   I have a hundred milch-kine to the pail,
       Six score fat oxen standing in my stalls
       And all things answerable to this portion.
       Myself am struck in years, I must confess,
       And if I die tomorrow, this is hers,
355   If whilst I live she will be only mine.

       TRANIO That "only" came well in. Sir, list to me.
       I am my father's heir and only son.
       If I may have your daughter to my wife,
       I'll leave her houses three or four as good,
360   Within rich Pisa wall, as any one
       Old Signior Gremio has in Padua,
       Besides two thousand ducats by the year
       Of fruitful land, all which shall be her jointure.
       What, have I pinched you, Signior Gremio?

       GREMIO [Aside] Two thousand ducats by the year of
365   land!
       My land amounts not to so much in all.
       [To others] That she shall have besides an argosy
       That now is lying in Marcellus' road.
       What, have I choked you with an argosy?

370   TRANIO Gremio, 'tis known my father hath no less
       Than three great argosies, besides two galliasses
       And twelve tight galleys. These I will assure her
       And twice as much, whate'er thou off'rest next.

---

345 **tents** bed tester (hanging cover)   346 **bossed** embroidered   347 **Valance**
bed fringes and drapes   350 **milch-kine to the pail** cows producing milk for
human use   352 **answerable to this portion** corresponding to this settlement (?)   353 **struck** advanced   362 **ducats** Venetian gold coins   363 **Of** from
363 **jointure** settlement   364 **pinched** put the screws on   367 **argosy** largest
type of merchant ship   368 **Marcellus' road** Marseilles' harbor   371 **galliasses**
large galleys   372 **tight** watertight

GREMIO Nay, I have off'red all. I have no more,
And she can have no more than all I have.   375
If you like me, she shall have me and mine.

TRANIO Why, then the maid is mine from all the world
By your firm promise. Gremio is outvied.

BAPTISTA I must confess your offer is the best,
And let your father make her the assurance,   380
She is your own; else you must pardon me.
If you should die before him, where's her dower?

TRANIO That's but a cavil. He is old, I young.

GREMIO And may not young men die as well as old?

BAPTISTA Well, gentlemen,   385
I am thus resolved. On Sunday next, you know,
My daughter Katherine is to be married.
Now on the Sunday following shall Bianca
Be pride to you if you make this assurance;
If not, to Signior Gremio.   390
And so I take my leave and thank you both.   *Exit.*

GREMIO Adieu, good neighbor. Now I fear thee not.
Sirrah young gamester, your father were a fool
To give thee all and in his waning age
Set foot under thy table. Tut, a toy!   395
An old Italian fox is not so kind, my boy.   *Exit.*

TRANIO A vengeance on your crafty withered hide!
Yet I have faced it with a card of ten.
'Tis in my head to do my master good.
I see no reason but supposed Lucentio   400
Must get a father, called "supposed Vincentio,"
And that's a wonder. Fathers commonly
Do get their children, but in this case of wooing
A child shall get a sire if I fail not of my cunning.
                                              Exit.

378 **outvied** outbid 380 **assurance** guarantee 383 **cavil** small point
393 **Sirrah** (used contemptuously) 393 **gamester** gambler 393 **were** would
be 395 **Set foot under thy table** be dependent on you 395 **a toy** a joke
398 **faced it with a card of ten** bluffed with a ten-spot 401 **get** beget

ACT III

[Scene I. *Padua. In Baptista's house.*]

*Enter Lucentio [as Cambio], Hortensio [as Litio],
and Bianca.*

LUCENTIO Fiddler, forbear. You grow too forward, sir.
Have you so soon forgot the entertainment
Her sister Katherine welcomed you withal?

HORTENSIO But, wrangling pedant, this is
5   The patroness of heavenly harmony.
Then give me leave to have prerogative,
And when in music we have spent an hour,
Your lecture shall have leisure for as much.

LUCENTIO Preposterous ass, that never read so far
10   To know the cause why music was ordained!
Was it not to refresh the mind of man
After his studies or his usual pain?
Then give me leave to read philosophy,
And while I pause, serve in your harmony.

HORTENSIO Sirrah, I will not bear these braves of
15   thine.

BIANCA Why, gentlemen, you do me double wrong
To strive for that which resteth in my choice.

III.i.2 **entertainment** i.e., "pillorying" him with the lute   6 **prerogative** priority
8 **lecture** instruction   9 **Preposterous** putting later things (*post-*) first (*pre-*)
12 **pain** labor   13 **read** give a lesson in   15 **braves** defiances

I am no breeching scholar in the schools.
I'll not be tied to hours nor 'pointed times,
But learn my lessons as I please myself.   20
And, to cut off all strife, here sit we down.
[*To Hortensio*] Take you your instrument, play you
    the whiles;
His lecture will be done ere you have tuned.

HORTENSIO You'll leave his lecture when I am in tune?

LUCENTIO That will be never. Tune your instrument.   25

BIANCA Where left we last?

LUCENTIO Here, madam:
    Hic ibat Simois, hic est Sigeia tellus,
        Hic steterat Priami regia celsa senis.

BIANCA Conster them.   30

LUCENTIO *Hic ibat*, as I told you before, *Simois*, I am
    Lucentio, *hic est*, son unto Vincentio of Pisa, *Sigeia
    tellus*, disguised thus to get your love, *Hic steterat*,
    and that Lucentio that comes a wooing, *Priami*, is
    my man Tranio, *regia*, bearing my port, *celsa senis*,   35
    that we might beguile the old pantaloon.

HORTENSIO [*Breaks in*] Madam, my instrument's in
    tune.

BIANCA Let's hear. O fie, the treble jars.

LUCENTIO Spit in the hole, man, and tune again.

BIANCA Now let me see if I can conster it. *Hic ibat*   40
    Simois, I know you not, *hic est Sigeia tellus*, I trust
    you not, *Hic steterat Priami*, take heed he hear us
    not, *regia*, presume not, *celsa senis*, despair not.

HORTENSIO [*Breaks in again*] Madam, 'tis now in tune.

---

18 breeching (1) in breeches (young) (2) whippable 18 **scholar** schoolboy
22 the whiles meanwhile 28-29 Hic ... senis here flowed the Simois, here is
the Sigeian (Trojan) land, here had stood old Priam's high palace (Ovid)
30 Conster construe 35 **bearing my port** taking on my style 36 **pantaloon**
Gremio (see I.i.47s.d. note) 38 **treble jars** highest tone is off

LUCENTIO   All but the bass.

HORTENSIO The bass is right; 'tis the base knave that
45   jars.
        [*Aside*] How fiery and forward our pedant is!
        Now, for my life, the knave doth court my love.
        Pedascule, I'll watch you better yet.

BIANCA In time I may believe, yet I mistrust.

50 LUCENTIO Mistrust it not, for sure Aeacides
        Was Ajax, called so from his grandfather.

BIANCA I must believe my master; else, I promise you,
        I should be arguing still upon that doubt.
        But let it rest. Now, Litio, to you.
55   Good master, take it not unkindly, pray,
        That I have been thus pleasant with you both.

HORTENSIO [*To Lucentio*] You may go walk and give
        me leave a while.
        My lessons make no music in three parts.

LUCENTIO Are you so formal, sir? [*Aside*] Well, I
        must wait
60   And watch withal, for but I be deceived,
        Our fine musician groweth amorous.

HORTENSIO Madam, before you touch the instrument,
        To learn the order of my fingering,
        I must begin with rudiments of art
65   To teach you gamut in a briefer sort,
        More pleasant, pithy, and effectual,
        Than hath been taught by any of my trade;
        And there it is in writing, fairly drawn.

BIANCA Why, I am past my gamut long ago.

70 HORTENSIO Yet read the gamut of Hortensio.

---

48 **Pedascule** little pedant (disparaging quasi-Latin)   50–51 **Aeacides/Was Ajax**
Ajax, Greek warrior at Troy, was grandson of Aeacus (Lucentio comments on next
passage in Ovid)   56 **pleasant** merry   57 **give me leave** leave me alone   58 **in
three parts** for three voices   60 **withal** besides   60 **but** unless   65 **gamut** the
scale

BIANCA [*Reads*]
　Gamut I am, the ground of all accord.
　　A re, to plead Hortensio's passion:
　B mi, Bianca, take him for thy lord,
　　C fa ut, that loves with all affection;
　D sol re, one clef, two notes have I: 75
　　E la mi, show pity or I die.

　Call you this gamut? Tut, I like it not.
　Old fashions please me best; I am not so nice
　To change true rules for odd inventions.

　　　　　　　Enter a Messenger.

MESSENGER Mistress, your father prays you leave your
　　　books   80
　And help to dress your sister's chamber up.
　You know tomorrow is the wedding day.

BIANCA Farewell, sweet masters both, I must be gone.
　　　　　　[Exeunt Bianca and Messenger.]

LUCENTIO Faith, mistress, then I have no cause to stay.
　　　　　　　　　　　　　　　　　　　　　[Exit.]

HORTENSIO But I have cause to pry into this pedant.   85
　Methinks he looks as though he were in love.
　Yet if thy thoughts, Bianca, be so humble
　To cast thy wand'ring eyes on every stale,
　Seize thee that list. If once I find thee ranging,
　Hortensio will be quit with thee by changing.   *Exit.*   90

71 **ground** beginning, first note   71 **accord** harmony   78 **nice** whimsical
88 **stale** lure (as in hunting)   89 **Seize thee that list** let him who likes capture
you   89 **ranging** going astray   90 **changing** i.e., sweethearts

[Scene II. *Padua. The street in front of Baptista's house.*]

Enter Baptista, Gremio, Tranio [as Lucentio], Kate, Bianca, [Lucentio as Cambio] and others, Attendants.

BAPTISTA [*To Tranio*] Signior Lucentio, this is the
        'pointed day
    That Katherine and Petruchio should be marrièd,
    And yet we hear not of our son-in-law.
    What will be said? What mockery will it be
5   To want the bridegroom when the priest attends
    To speak the ceremonial rites of marriage!
    What says Lucentio to this shame of ours?

KATE No shame but mine. I must, forsooth, be forced
    To give my hand opposed against my heart
10   Unto a mad-brain rudesby, full of spleen,
    Who wooed in haste and means to wed at leisure.
    I told you, I, he was a frantic fool,
    Hiding his bitter jests in blunt behavior.
    And to be noted for a merry man,
15   He'll woo a thousand, 'point the day of marriage,
    Make friends, invite, and proclaim the banns,
    Yet never means to wed where he hath wooed.
    Now must the world point at poor Katherine
    And say, "Lo, there is mad Petruchio's wife,
20   If it would please him come and marry her."

TRANIO Patience, good Katherine, and Baptista too.
    Upon my life, Petruchio means but well,
    Whatever fortune stays him from his word.

III.ii.5 **want** be without   10 **rudesby** uncouth fellow   10 **spleen** caprice
14 **noted for** reputed   16 **Make friends, invite** (some editors emend to "Make
feast, invite friends")   23 **stays** keeps

Though he be blunt, I know him passing wise;
Though he be merry, yet withal he's honest.   25

KATE Would Katherine had never seen him though!
Exit weeping [followed by Bianca and others].

BAPTISTA Go, girl, I cannot blame thee now to weep.
For such an injury would vex a very saint,
Much more a shrew of thy impatient humor.

Enter Biondello.

BIONDELLO Master, master, news! And such old news   30
as you never heard of!

BAPTISTA Is it new and old too? How may that be?

BIONDELLO Why, is it not news to hear of Petruchio's
coming?

BAPTISTA Is he come?   35

BIONDELLO Why, no, sir.

BAPTISTA What then?

BIONDELLO He is coming.

BAPTISTA When will he be here?

BIONDELLO When he stands where I am and sees you   40
there.

TRANIO But, say, what to thine old news?

BIONDELLO Why, Petruchio is coming in a new hat and
an old jerkin; a pair of old breeches thrice turned;
a pair of boots that have been candle-cases, one   45
buckled, another laced; an old rusty sword ta'en
out of the town armory, with a broken hilt and
chapeless; with two broken points; his horse
hipped (with an old mothy saddle and stirrups of

24 **passing** very   29 **humor** temper   30 **old** strange   44 **jerkin** short outer coat
44 **turned** i.e., inside out (to conceal wear and tear)   45 **candle-cases** worn-out
boots used to keep candle ends in   48 **chapeless** lacking the metal mounting at
end of scabbard   48 **points** laces to fasten hose to garment above   49 **hipped**
with dislocated hip

50   no kindred), besides, possessed with the glanders
      and like to mose in the chine; troubled with the
      lampass, infected with the fashions, full of wind-
      galls, sped with spavins, rayed with the yellows,
      past cure of the fives, stark spoiled with the stag-
55   gers, begnawn with the bots, swayed in the
      back, and shoulder-shotten; near-legged before,
      and with a half-cheeked bit and a head-stall of
      sheep's leather, which, being restrained to keep
      him from stumbling, hath been often burst and
60   now repaired with knots; one girth six times
      pieced, and a woman's crupper of velure, which
      hath two letters for her name fairly set down in
      studs, and here and there pierced with packthread.

BAPTISTA Who comes with him?

65   BIONDELLO O sir, his lackey, for all the world capari-
      soned like the horse: with a linen stock on one
      leg and a kersey boot-hose on the other, gart'red
      with a red and blue list; an old hat, and the humor
      of forty fancies pricked in't for a feather—a mon-
70   ster, a very monster in apparel, and not like a Chris-
      tian footboy or a gentleman's lackey.

49–50 **of no kindred** not matching   50 **glanders** bacterial disease affecting
mouth and nose   51 **mose in the chine** (1) glanders (2) nasal discharge
52 **lampass** swollen mouth   52 **fashions** tumors (related to glanders)
52–53 **windgalls** swellings on lower leg   53 **spavins** swellings on upper hind
leg   53 **rayed** soiled   53 **yellows** jaundice   54 **fives** vives: swelling of submax-
illary glands   54–55 **staggers** nervous disorder causing loss of balance
55 **begnawn with the bots** gnawed by parasitic worms (larvae of the botfly)
55 **swayed** sagging   56 **shoulder-shotten** with dislocated shoulder   56 **near-
legged before** with forefeet knocking together   57 **half-cheeked** wrongly
adjusted to bridle and affording less control   57 **head-stall** part of bridle which
surrounds head   58 **sheep's leather** (weaker than pigskin)   58 **restrained**
pulled back   60 **girth** saddle strap under belly   61 **pieced** patched   61 **crupper**
leather loop under horse's tail to help steady saddle   61 **velure** velvet   63 **studs**
large-headed nails of brass or silver   63 **pieced with packthread** tied together
with coarse thread   65–66 **caparisoned** outfitted   66 **stock** stocking   67 **kersey
boot-hose** coarse stocking worn with riding boot   68 **list** strip of discarded
border-cloth   68–69 **humor of forty fancies** fanciful decoration (in place of
feather)   69 **pricked** pinned   71 **footboy** page in livery

TRANIO 'Tis some odd humor pricks him to this
      fashion,
   Yet oftentimes he goes but mean-appareled.

BAPTISTA I am glad he's come, howsoe'er he comes.

BIONDELLO Why, sir, he comes not.   75

BAPTISTA Didst thou not say he comes?

BIONDELLO Who? That Petruchio came?

BAPTISTA Ay, that Petruchio came.

BIONDELLO No, sir, I say his horse comes, with him
   on his back.   80

BAPTISTA Why, that's all one.

BIONDELLO [Sings]   Nay, by Saint Jamy,
                    I hold you a penny,
                    A horse and a man
                    Is more than one   85
                    And yet not many.

                  Enter Petruchio and Grumio.

PETRUCHIO Come, where be these gallants? Who's at
      home?

BAPTISTA You are welcome, sir.

PETRUCHIO   And yet I come not well.

BAPTISTA And yet you halt not.

TRANIO   Not so well appareled
   As I wish you were.   90

PETRUCHIO Were it better, I should rush in thus.
   But where is Kate? Where is my lovely bride?
   How does my father? Gentles, methinks you frown.

---

72 **humor** mood, fancy   72 **pricks** incites   81 **all one** the same thing   83 **hold**
bet   87 **gallants** men of fashion   89 **halt** limp (pun on *come* meaning "walk")
91 **Were it better** even if I were better   93 **Gentles** sirs

And wherefore gaze this goodly company
95 As if they saw some wondrous monument,
Some comet or unusual prodigy?

BAPTISTA Why, sir, you know this is your wedding day.
First were we sad, fearing you would not come,
Now sadder that you come so unprovided.
100 Fie, doff this habit, shame to your estate,
An eyesore to our solemn festival.

TRANIO And tell us what occasion of import
Hath all so long detained you from your wife
And sent you hither so unlike yourself.

105 PETRUCHIO Tedious it were to tell and harsh to hear.
Sufficeth, I am come to keep my word
Though in some part enforcèd to digress,
Which, at more leisure, I will so excuse
As you shall well be satisfied with all.
110 But where is Kate? I stay too long from her.
The morning wears, 'tis time we were at church.

TRANIO See not your bride in these unreverent robes.
Go to my chamber; put on clothes of mine.

PETRUCHIO Not I, believe me; thus I'll visit her.

115 BAPTISTA But thus, I trust, you will not marry her.

PETRUCHIO Good sooth, even thus; therefore ha' done
with words.
To me she's married, not unto my clothes.
Could I repair what she will wear in me
As I can change these poor accoutrements,
120 'Twere well for Kate and better for myself.
But what a fool am I to chat with you
When I should bid good morrow to my bride
And seal the title with a lovely kiss.

Exit [with Grumio].

95 **monument** warning sign   96 **prodigy** marvel   99 **unprovided** ill-outfitted
100 **habit** costume   100 **estate** status   102 **of import** important   107 **enforcèd
to digress** forced to depart (perhaps from his plan to "buy apparel 'gainst the
wedding day," II.i.308)   116 **Good sooth** yes indeed   118 **wear** wear out
123 **title** i.e., as of ownership   123 **lovely** loving

TRANIO He hath some meaning in his mad attire.
We will persuade him, be it possible,   125
To put on better ere he go to church.

BAPTISTA I'll after him and see the event of this.
                    Exit [with Gremio and Attendants].

TRANIO But to her love concerneth us to add
Her father's liking, which to bring to pass,
As I before imparted to your worship,   130
I am to get a man—whate'er he be
It skills not much, we'll fit him to our turn—
And he shall be Vincentio of Pisa,
And make assurance here in Padua
Of greater sums than I have promisèd.   135
So shall you quietly enjoy your hope
And marry sweet Bianca with consent.

LUCENTIO Were it not that my fellow schoolmaster
Doth watch Bianca's steps so narrowly,
'Twere good, methinks, to seal our marriage,   140
Which once performed, let all the world say no,
I'll keep mine own despite of all the world.

TRANIO That by degrees we mean to look into
And watch our vantage in this business.
We'll overreach the graybeard, Gremio,   145
The narrow-prying father, Minola,
The quaint musician, amorous Litio—
All for my master's sake, Lucentio.

                    Enter Gremio.

Signior Gremio, came you from the church?

GREMIO As willingly as e'er I came from school.   150

TRANIO And is the bride and bridegroom coming
home?

GREMIO A bridegroom say you? 'Tis a groom indeed,

127 event upshot, outcome   132 skills matters   132 turn purpose   134 assurance guarantee   140 steal our marriage elope   144 vantage advantage
145 overreach get the better of   147 quaint artful   152 groom menial (i.e.,
coarse fellow)

A grumbling groom, and that the girl shall find.

TRANIO Curster than she? Why, 'tis impossible.

155 GREMIO Why, he's a devil, a devil, a very fiend.

TRANIO Why, she's a devil, a devil, the devil's dam.

GREMIO Tut, she's a lamb, a dove, a fool to him.
I'll tell you, Sir Lucentio, when the priest
Should ask, if Katherine should be his wife,
"Ay, by goggs woones!" quoth he and swore so
160   loud
That, all amazed, the priest let fall the book,
And as he stooped again to take it up,
This mad-brained bridegroom took him such a cuff
That down fell priest and book and book and priest.
165 "Now, take them up," quoth he, "if any list."

TRANIO What said the wench when he rose again?

GREMIO Trembled and shook, for why he stamped
       and swore
As if the vicar meant to cozen him.
But after many ceremonies done
170 He calls for wine. "A health!" quoth he as if
He had been aboard, carousing to his mates
After a storm; quaffed off the muscadel
And threw the sops all in the sexton's face,
Having no other reason
175 But that his beard grew thin and hungerly,
And seemed to ask him sops as he was drinking.
This done, he took the bride about the neck
And kissed her lips with such a clamorous smack
That at the parting all the church did echo,
180 And I, seeing this, came thence for very shame.

---

156 **dam** mother 157 **fool to** harmless person compared with 160 **goggs woones** by God's wounds (a common oath) 163 **took** gave 165 **list** pleases to 167 **for why** because 168 **cozen** cheat 171 **carousing** calling "Bottoms up" 172 **muscadel** sweet wine, conventionally drunk after marriage service 173 **sop** pieces of cake soaked in wine; dregs 175 **hungerly** as if poorly nourished

And after me, I know, the rout is coming.
Such a mad marriage never was before.
Hark, hark, I hear the minstrels play.   *Music plays.*

*Enter Petruchio, Kate, Bianca, Hortensio [as Litio],
Baptista [with Grumio and others].*

PETRUCHIO Gentlemen and friends, I thank you for
    your pains.
I know you think to dine with me today   185
And have prepared great store of wedding cheer,
But so it is, my haste doth call me hence
And therefore here I mean to take my leave.

BAPTISTA Is't possible you will away tonight?

PETRUCHIO I must away today, before night come.   190
    Make it no wonder; if you knew my business,
    You would entreat me rather go than stay.
    And, honest company, I thank you all
    That have beheld me give away myself
    To this most patient, sweet, and virtuous wife.   195
    Dine with my father, drink a health to me,
    For I must hence, and farewell to you all.

TRANIO Let us entreat you stay till after dinner.

PETRUCHIO It may not be.

GREMIO   Let me entreat you.

PETRUCHIO It cannot be.

KATE   Let me entreat you.   200

PETRUCHIO I am content.

KATE   Are you content to stay?

PETRUCHIO I am content you shall entreat me stay,
    But yet not stay, entreat me how you can.

KATE Now if you love me, stay.

PETRUCHIO   Grumio, my horse!

181 **rout** crowd   186 **cheer** food and drink   191 **Make it no wonder** don't be
surprised   204 **horse** horses

205   GRUMIO Ay, sir, they be ready; the oats have eaten
         the horses.

       KATE Nay then,
         Do what thou canst, I will not go today,
         No, nor tomorrow, not till I please myself.
210   The door is open, sir, there lies your way.
         You may be jogging whiles your boots are green;
         For me, I'll not be gone till I please myself.
         'Tis like you'll prove a jolly surly groom,
         That take it on you at the first so roundly.

       PETRUCHIO O Kate, content thee; prithee, be not
215   angry.

       KATE I will be angry. What hast thou to do?
         Father, be quiet; he shall stay my leisure.

       GREMIO Ay, marry, sir, now it begins to work.

       KATE Gentlemen, forward to the bridal dinner.
220   I see a woman may be made a fool
         If she had not a spirit to resist.

       PETRUCHIO They shall go forward, Kate, at thy
         command.
         Obey the bride, you that attend on her.
         Go to the feast, revel and domineer,
225   Carouse full measure to her maidenhead,
         Be mad and merry, or go hang yourselves.
         But for my bonny Kate, she must with me.
         Nay, look not big, nor stamp, nor stare, nor fret;
         I will be master of what is mine own.
230   She is my goods, my chattels; she is my house,
         My household stuff, my field, my barn,
         My horse, my ox, my ass, my anything,

205-06 oats have eaten the horses (1) a slip of the tongue or (2) an ironic jest
211 You ... green (proverbial way of suggesting departure to a guest, *green* =
new, cleaned) 213 jolly domineering 214 take it on you do as you please
214 roundly roughly 215 prithee I pray thee 216 What hast thou to do
what do you have to do with it 217 stay my leisure await my willingness
224 domineer cut up in a lordly fashion 228 bid challenging 228 stare
swagger 232 My horse ... anything (echoing Tenth Commandment)

And here she stands. Touch her whoever dare,
I'll bring mine action on the proudest he
That stops my way in Padua. Grumio,   235
Draw forth thy weapon, we are beset with thieves.
Rescue thy mistress, if thou be a man.
Fear not, sweet wench; they shall not touch thee,
   Kate.
I'll buckler thee against a million.
                    Exeunt Petruchio, Kate [and Grumio].

BAPTISTA Nay, let them go, a couple of quiet ones.   240

GREMIO Went they not quickly, I should die with
   laughing.

TRANIO Of all mad matches never was the like.

LUCENTIO Mistress, what's your opinion of your sister?

BIANCA That being mad herself, she's madly mated.

GREMIO I warrant him, Petruchio is Kated.   245

BAPTISTA Neighbors and friends, though bride and
   bridegroom wants
For to supply the places at the table,
You know there wants no junkets at the feast.
[*To Tranio*] Lucentio, you shall supply the bride-
   groom's place,
And let Bianca take her sister's room.   250

TRANIO Shall sweet Bianca practice how to bride it?

BAPTISTA She shall, Lucentio. Come, gentlemen, let's
   go.   *Exeunt.*

---

234 action   239 buckler shield   246 wants are lacking   248 junkets sweetmeats, confections

[ACT IV

Scene I. *Petruchio's country house.*]

Enter Grumio.

GRUMIO Fie, fie, on all tired jades, on all mad masters, and all foul ways! Was ever man so beaten?
Was ever man so rayed? Was ever man so weary?
I am sent before to make a fire, and they are coming
5   after to warm them. Now were not I a little pot and
soon hot, my very lips might freeze to my teeth,
my tongue to the roof of my mouth, my heart in my
belly, ere I should come by a fire to thaw me. But I
with blowing the fire shall warm myself, for con-
10 sidering the weather, a taller man than I will take
cold. Holla, ho, Curtis!

Enter Curtis [a Servant].

CURTIS Who is that calls so coldly?

GRUMIO A piece of ice. If thou doubt it, thou mayst
slide from my shoulder to my heel with no greater
15 a run but my head and my neck. A fire, good
Curtis.

CURTIS Is my master and his wife coming, Grumio?

IV.i.1 **jades** worthless horses   2 **foul ways** bad roads   3 **rayed** befouled
5-6 **little pot and soon hot** (proverbial for small person of short temper)
10 **taller** sturdier (with allusion to "little pot")   15 **run** running start

GRUMIO O ay, Curtis, ay, and therefore fire, fire; cast on no water.

CURTIS Is she so hot a shrew as she's reported?   20

GRUMIO She was, good Curtis, before this frost, but thou know'st winter tames man, woman, and beast; for it hath tamed my old master, and my new mistress, and myself, fellow Curtis.

CURTIS Away, you three-inch fool! I am no beast.   25

GRUMIO Am I but three inches? Why, thy horn is a foot, and so long am I at the least. But wilt thou make a fire, or shall I complain on thee to our mistress, whose hand—she being now at hand—thou shalt soon feel, to thy cold comfort, for being slow   30 in thy hot office?

CURTIS I prithee, good Grumio, tell me, how goes the world?

GRUMIO A cold world, Curtis, in every office but thine, and therefore, fire. Do thy duty and have thy   35 duty, for my master and mistress are almost frozen to death.

CURTIS There's fire ready, and therefore, good Grumio, the news.

GRUMIO Why, "Jack boy, ho boy!" and as much   40 news as wilt thou.

CURTIS Come, you are so full of cony-catching.

GRUMIO Why therefore fire, for I have caught extreme cold. Where's the cook? Is supper ready, the house trimmed, rushes strewed, cobwebs swept, the   45

---

19 **cast on no water** (alters "Cast on more water" in a well-known round)
25 **three-inch** (1) another allusion to Grumio's small stature (2) a phallic jest, the first of several   26 **horn** (symbol of cuckold)   31 **hot office** job of making a fire
35-36 **thy duty** what is due thee   40 **"Jack boy, ho boy!"** (from another round or catch)   42 **cony-catching** rabbit-catching (i.e., tricking simpletons; with pun on *catch*, the song)   45 **strewed** i.e., on floor (for special occasion)

servingmen in their new fustian, the white stockings, and every officer his wedding garment on? Be the jacks fair within, the jills fair without, the carpets laid and everything in order?

50 CURTIS All ready, and therefore, I pray thee, news.

GRUMIO First, know my horse is tired, my master and mistress fall'n out.

CURTIS How?

GRUMIO Out of their saddles into the dirt—and
55 thereby hangs a tale.

CURTIS Let's ha't, good Grumio.

GRUMIO Lend thine ear.

CURTIS Here.

GRUMIO There.   [Strikes him.]

60 CURTIS This 'tis to feel a tale, not to hear a tale.

GRUMIO And therefore 'tis called a sensible tale, and this cuff was but to knock at your ear and beseech list'ning. Now I begin. *Imprimis*, we came down a foul hill, my master riding behind my mistress—

65 CURTIS Both of one horse?

GRUMIO What's that to thee?

CURTIS Why, a horse.

GRUMIO Tell thou the tale. But hadst thou not crossed me thou shouldst have heard how her
70 horse fell and she under her horse. Thou shouldst have heard in how miry a place, how she was bemoiled, how he left her with the horse upon her, how he beat me because her horse stumbled, how

46 **fustian** coarse cloth (cotton and flax) 47 **officer** servant 48 **jacks** (1) menservants (2) half-pint leather drinking cups 48 **jills** (1) maids (2) gill-size metal drinking cups 48-49 **carpets** table covers 61 **sensible** (1) rational (2) "feel"-able 63 **Imprimis** first 64 **foul** muddy 65 **of** on 69 **crossed** interrupted 72 **bemoiled** muddied

she waded through the dirt to pluck him off me;
how he swore, how she prayed that never prayed   75
before; how I cried, how the horses ran away, how
her bridle was burst, how I lost my crupper, with
many things of worthy memory which now shall
die in oblivion, and thou return unexperienced to
thy grave.   80

CURTIS By this reck'ning he is more shrew than she.

GRUMIO Ay, and that thou and the proudest of you
all shall find when he comes home. But what talk
I of this? Call forth Nathaniel, Joseph, Nicholas,
Philip, Walter, Sugarsop, and the rest. Let their   85
heads be slickly combed, their blue coats brushed,
and their garters of an indifferent knit. Let them
curtsy with their left legs and not presume to touch
a hair of my master's horsetail till they kiss their
hands. Are they all ready?   90

CURTIS They are.

GRUMIO Call them forth.

CURTIS Do you hear, ho? You must meet my master
to countenance my mistress.

GRUMIO Why, she hath a face of her own.   95

CURTIS Who knows not that?

GRUMIO Thou, it seems, that calls for company to
countenance her.

CURTIS I call them forth to credit her.

GRUMIO Why, she comes to borrow nothing of them.   100

Enter four or five Servingmen.

NATHANIEL Welcome home, Grumio!

---

79 **unexperienced** uninformed 81 **reck'ning** account 83 **what** why
86 **slickly** smoothly 86 **blue** (usual color of servants' clothing) 87 **indifferent**
matching (?) appropriate (?) 94 **countenance** show respect to (with puns
following) 99 **credit** honor

PHILIP How now, Grumio?

JOSEPH What, Grumio!

NICHOLAS Fellow Grumio!

105 NATHANIEL How now, old lad!

GRUMIO Welcome, you; how now, you; what, you; fellow, you; and thus much for greeting. Now, my spruce companions, is all ready and all things neat?

NATHANIEL All things is ready. How near is our
110 master?

GRUMIO E'en at hand, alighted by this, and therefore be not—Cock's passion, silence! I hear my master.

Enter Petruchio and Kate.

PETRUCHIO Where be these knaves? What, no man at door
115 To hold my stirrup nor to take my horse?
Where is Nathaniel, Gregory, Philip?

ALL SERVINGMEN Here, here, sir, here, sir.

PETRUCHIO Here, sir, here, sir, here, sir, here, sir!
You loggerheaded and unpolished grooms!
120 What, no attendance? No regard? No duty?
Where is the foolish knave I sent before?

GRUMIO Here, sir, as foolish as I was before.

PETRUCHIO You peasant swain! You whoreson malt-horse drudge!
Did I not bid thee meet me in the park
125 And bring along these rascal knaves with thee?

GRUMIO Nathaniel's coat, sir, was not fully made
And Gabrel's pumps were all unpinked i' th' heel.

111 **this** now   112 **Cock's** God's (i.e., Christ's)   119 **loggerheaded** blockheaded
123 **swain** bumpkin   123 **whoreson** bastardly   123 **malt-horse drudge** slow
horse on brewery treadmill   124 **park** country-house grounds   127 **unpinked**
lacking embellishment made by pinking (making small holes in leather)

There was no link to color Peter's hat,
And Walter's dagger was not come from sheathing.
There were none fine but Adam, Rafe, and Gregory;   130
The rest were ragged, old, and beggarly.
Yet, as they are, here are they come to meet you.

PETRUCHIO Go, rascals, go, and fetch my supper in.
                                        Exeunt Servants.

[*Sings*] "Where is the life that late I led?"

Where are those—Sit down, Kate, and welcome.   135
    Soud, soud, soud, soud!

                Enter Servants with supper.

Why, when, I say?—Nay, good sweet Kate, be
    merry.—
Off with my boots, you rogues, you villains! When?
    [*Sings*] "It was the friar of orders gray,
    As he forth walkèd on his way"—   140
Out, you rogue, you pluck my foot awry!
Take that, and mend the plucking of the other.
                                        [*Strikes him.*]
Be merry, Kate. Some water here! What ho!

                Enter one with water.

Where's my spaniel Troilus? Sirrah, get you hence
And bid my cousin Ferdinand come hither—   145
                                        [*Exit Servant.*]
One, Kate, that you must kiss and be acquainted with.
Where are my slippers? Shall I have some water?
Come, Kate, and wash, and welcome heartily.
You whoreson villain, will you let it fall?
                                        [*Strikes him.*]

KATE Patience, I pray you. 'Twas a fault unwilling.   150

PETRUCHIO A whoreson, beetle-headed, flap-eared
    knave!

128 **link** torch, providing blacking 129 **sheathing** repairing scabbard
134 **"Where ... led?"** (from an old ballad) 135 **those** servants 136 **Soud**
(exclamation variously explained; some editors emend to *Food*) 137 **when** (exclamation of annoyance, as in next line) 139-40 **"It was ... his way"** (from
another old song) 142 **mend** improve 151 **beetle-headed** mallet-headed

Come, Kate, sit down; I know you have a stomach.
Will you give thanks, sweet Kate, or else shall I?
What's this? Mutton?

FIRST SERVINGMAN   Ay.

PETRUCHIO   Who brought it?

PETER   I.

155 PETRUCHIO 'Tis burnt, and so is all the meat.
What dogs are these! Where is the rascal cook?
How durst you, villains, bring it from the dresser,
And serve it thus to me that love it not?
There, take it to you, trenchers, cups, and all,
                        [*Throws food and dishes at them.*]
160 You heedless joltheads and unmannered slaves!
What, do you grumble? I'll be with you straight.

KATE   I pray you, husband, be not so disquiet.
The meat was well if you were so contented.

PETRUCHIO   I tell thee, Kate, 'twas burnt and dried away,
165 And I expressly am forbid to touch it,
For it engenders choler, planteth anger,
And better 'twere that both of us did fast—
Since of ourselves, ourselves are choleric—
Than feed it with such overroasted flesh.
170 Be patient. Tomorrow't shall be mended,
And for this night we'll fast for company.
Come, I will bring thee to thy bridal chamber.
                                    Exeunt.

Enter Servants severally.

NATHANIEL   Peter, didst ever see the like?

PETER   He kills her in her own humor.

152 **stomach** (1) hunger (2) irascibility   153 **give thanks** say grace
157 **dresser** sideboard   159 **trenchers** wooden platters   160 **joltheads** bone-
heads (*jolt* is related to *jaw* or *jowl*)   161 **with** even with   161 **straight** directly
163 **so contented** willing to see it as it was   166 **choler** bile, the "humor" (fluid)
supposed to produce anger   168 **choleric** bilious, i.e., hot-tempered   169 **it** i.e.,
their choler   170 **'t shall be mended** things will be better   171 **for company**
together   174 **kills her in her own humor** conquers her by using her own
disposition

Enter Curtis, a Servant.

GRUMIO Where is he?   175

CURTIS In her chamber, making a sermon of continency
   to her,
   And rails and swears and rates, that she, poor soul,
   Knows not which way to stand, to look, to speak,
   And sits as one new-risen from a dream.   180
   Away, away, for he is coming hither.   [*Exeunt.*]

Enter Petruchio.

PETRUCHIO Thus have I politicly begun my reign,
   And 'tis my hope to end successfully.
   My falcon now is sharp and passing empty,
   And till she stoop she must not be full gorged,   185
   For then she never looks upon her lure.
   Another way I have to man my haggard,
   To make her come and know her keeper's call,
   That is, to watch her as we watch these kites
   That bate and beat and will not be obedient.   190
   She eat no meat today, nor none shall eat.
   Last night she slept not, nor tonight she shall not.
   As with the meat, some undeservèd fault
   I'll find about the making of the bed,
   And here I'll fling the pillow, there the bolster,   195
   This way the coverlet, another way the sheets.
   Ay, and amid this hurly I intend
   That all is done in reverent care of her,
   And in conclusion she shall watch all night.
   And if she chance to nod I'll rail and brawl   200
   And with the clamor keep her still awake.

---

178 **rates** scolds   182 **politicly** with a calculated plan   184 **falcon** hawk trained
for hunting (falconry figures continue for seven lines)   184 **sharp** pinched with
hunger   185 **stoop** (1) obey (2) swoop to the lure   185 **full gorged** fully fed
186 **lure** device used in training a hawk to return from flight   187 **man** (1) tame
(2) be a man to   187 **haggard** hawk captured after reaching maturity   189 **watch**
keep from sleep   189 **kites** type of small hawk   190 **bate and beat** flap and
flutter (i.e., in jittery resistance to training)   191 **eat** ate (pronounced *et*, as still in
Britain)   195 **bolster** cushion extending width of bed as under-support for pillows
197 **hurly** disturbance   197 **intend** profess   199 **watch** stay awake

This is a way to kill a wife with kindness,
And thus I'll curb her mad and headstrong humor.
He that knows better how to tame a shrew,
205   Now let him speak—'tis charity to show.   *Exit.*

[Scene II. *Padua. The street in front of*
Baptista's house.]

Enter Tranio [as Lucentio] and Hortensio [as Litio].

TRANIO Is't possible, friend Litio, that Mistress Bianca
Doth fancy any other but Lucentio?
I tell you, sir, she bears me fair in hand.

HORTENSIO Sir, to satisfy you in what I have said,
5   Stand by and mark the manner of his teaching.
                                        [*They eavesdrop.*]

Enter Bianca [and Lucentio as Cambio].

LUCENTIO Now mistress, profit you in what you read?

BIANCA What, master, read you? First resolve me that.

LUCENTIO I read that I profess, the Art to Love.

BIANCA And may you prove, sir, master of your art.

LUCENTIO While you, sweet dear, prove mistress of my
10   heart.   [*They court.*]

HORTENSIO Quick proceeders, marry! Now, tell me,
        I pray,
You that durst swear that your mistress Bianca
Loved none in the world so well as Lucentio.

---

202 **kill a wife with kindness** (ironic allusion to proverb on ruining a wife by pampering)   204 **shrew** (rhymes with "show")   IV.ii.2 **fancy** like   3 **bears me fair in hand** leads me on   7 **resolve** answer   8 **that** what   8 **profess** avow, practice   8 **Art to Love** (i.e., Ovid's *Ars Amandi*)   11 **proceeders** (pun on idiom "proceed Master of Arts"; cf. line 9)   11 **marry** by Mary (mild exclamation)

TRANIO O despiteful love! Unconstant womankind!
  I tell thee, Litio, this is wonderful.   15

HORTENSIO Mistake no more. I am not Litio,
  Nor a musician, as I seem to be,
  But one that scorn to live in this disguise,
  For such a one as leaves a gentleman
  And makes a god of such a cullion.   20
  Know, sir, that I am called Hortensio.

TRANIO Signior Hortensio, I have often heard
  Of your entire affection to Bianca,
  And since mine eyes are witness of her lightness,
  I will with you, if you be so contented,   25
  Forswear Bianca and her love forever.

HORTENSIO See, how they kiss and court! Signior
    Lucentio,
  Here is my hand and here I firmly vow
  Never to woo her more, but do forswear her,
  As one unworthy all the former favors   30
  That I have fondly flattered her withal.

TRANIO And here I take the like unfeignèd oath,
  Never to marry with her though she would entreat.
  Fie on her! See how beastly she doth court him.

HORTENSIO Would all the world but he had quite
    forsworn.   35
  For me, that I may surely keep mine oath,
  I will be married to a wealthy widow
  Ere three days pass, which hath as long loved me
  As I have loved this proud disdainful haggard.
  And so farewell, Signior Lucentio.   40
  Kindness in women, not their beauteous looks,
  Shall win my love, and so I take my leave
  In resolution as I swore before.   [Exit.]

---

14 despiteful spiteful 15 wonderful causing wonder 20 cullion low fellow
(literally, testicle) 24 lightness (cf. "light woman") 26 Forswear "swear off"
30 favors marks of esteem 31 fondly foolishly 34 beastly unashamedly
35 Would ... forsworn i.e., would she had only one lover 38 which who
39 haggard (cf. IV.i.187)

TRANIO Mistress Bianca, bless you with such grace
45   As 'longeth to a lover's blessèd case.
        Nay, I have ta'en you napping, gentle love,
        And have forsworn you with Hortensio.

BIANCA Tranio, you jest. But have you both forsworn
        me?

TRANIO Mistress, we have.

LUCENTIO   Then we are rid of Litio.

50 TRANIO I' faith, he'll have a lusty widow now,
        That shall be wooed and wedded in a day.

BIANCA God give him joy!

TRANIO Ay, and he'll tame her.

BIANCA   He says so, Tranio.

TRANIO Faith, he is gone unto the taming school.

BIANCA The taming school! What, is there such a
55   place?

TRANIO Ay, mistress, and Petruchio is the master,
        That teacheth tricks eleven and twenty long
        To tame a shrew and charm her chattering tongue.

Enter Biondello.

BIONDELLO O master, master, I have watched so long
60   That I am dog-weary, but at last I spied
        An ancient angel coming down the hill
        Will serve the turn.

TRANIO   What is he, Biondello?

BIONDELLO Master, a mercatante or a pedant,
        I know not what, but formal in apparel,

---

46 **ta'en you napping** seen you "kiss and court" (line 27)   50 **lusty** lively
57 **tricks eleven and twenty long** (1) many tricks (2) possibly an allusion to card
game "thirty-one" (cf. I.ii.33)   61 **ancient angel** man of good old stamp (*angel* =
coin; cf. "gentleman of the old school")   62 **Will serve the turn** who will do for
our purposes   62 **What** what kind of man   63 **mercatante** merchant   63 **pedant**
schoolmaster

In gait and countenance surely like a father.   65

LUCENTIO And what of him, Tranio?

TRANIO If he be credulous and trust my tale,
I'll make him glad to seem Vincentio,
And give assurance to Baptista Minola
As if he were the right Vincentio.   70
Take in your love and then let me alone.
                      [*Exeunt Lucentio and Bianca.*]

                  Enter a Pedant.

PEDANT God save you, sir.

TRANIO   And you, sir. You are welcome.
Travel you far on, or are you at the farthest?

PEDANT Sir, at the farthest for a week or two,
But then up farther and as far as Rome,   75
And so to Tripoli if God lend me life.

TRANIO What countryman, I pray?

PEDANT   Of Mantua.

TRANIO Of Mantua, sir? Marry, God forbid!
And come to Padua, careless of your life?

PEDANT My life, sir? How, I pray? For that goes
hard.   80

TRANIO 'Tis death for anyone in Mantua
To come to Padua. Know you not the cause?
Your ships are stayed at Venice and the Duke,
For private quarrel 'twixt your duke and him,
Hath published and proclaimed it openly.   85
'Tis marvel, but that you are but newly come,
You might have heard it else proclaimed about.

PEDANT Alas, sir, it is worse for me than so,
For I have bills for money by exchange
From Florence and must here deliver them.   90

65 **gait and countenance** bearing and style   77 **What countryman** a man of
what country   80 **goes hard** (cf. "is rough")   83 **stayed** held   88 **than so** than
it appears so far

TRANIO Well, sir, to do you courtesy,
This will I do and this I will advise you.
First tell me, have you ever been at Pisa?

PEDANT Ay, sir, in Pisa have I often been—
95   Pisa, renownèd for grave citizens.

TRANIO Among them, know you one Vincentio?

PEDANT I know him not but I have heard of him—
A merchant of incomparable wealth.

TRANIO He is my father, sir, and, sooth to say,
100   In count'nance somewhat doth resemble you.

BIONDELLO [*Aside*] As much as an apple doth an
oyster, and all one.

TRANIO To save your life in this extremity,
This favor will I do you for his sake,
105   And think it not the worst of all your fortunes
That you are like to Sir Vincentio.
His name and credit shall you undertake,
And in my house you shall be friendly lodged.
Look that you take upon you as you should.
110   You understand me, sir? So shall you stay
Till you have done your business in the city.
If this be court'sy, sir, accept of it.

PEDANT O sir, I do, and will repute you ever
The patron of my life and liberty.

115 TRANIO Then go with me to make the matter good.
This, by the way, I let you understand:
My father is here looked for every day
To pass assurance of a dower in marriage
'Twixt me and one Baptista's daughter here.
120   In all these circumstances I'll instruct you.
Go with me to clothe you as becomes you.   *Exeunt.*

---

92 **advise** explain to 102 **all one** no difference 107 **credit** standing
107 **undertake** adopt 109 **take upon you** assume your role 113 **repute** esteem
116 **by the way** as we walk along 118 **pass assurance** give a guarantee

[Scene III. *In Petruchio's house.*]

Enter Kate and Grumio.

GRUMIO No, no, forsooth, I dare not for my life.

KATE The more my wrong, the more his spite
    appears.
  What, did he marry me to famish me?
  Beggars that come unto my father's door,
  Upon entreaty have a present alms;   5
  If not, elsewhere they meet with charity.
  But I, who never knew how to entreat
  Nor never needed that I should entreat,
  Am starved for meat, giddy for lack of sleep,
  With oaths kept waking and with brawling fed.   10
  And that which spites me more than all these wants,
  He does it under name of perfect love,
  As who should say, if I should sleep or eat
  'Twere deadly sickness or else present death.
  I prithee go and get me some repast,   15
  I care not what, so it be wholesome food.

GRUMIO What say you to a neat's foot?

KATE 'Tis passing good; I prithee let me have it.

GRUMIO I fear it is too choleric a meat.
  How say you to a fat tripe finely broiled?   20

KATE I like it well. Good Grumio, fetch it me.

GRUMIO I cannot tell, I fear 'tis choleric.
  What say you to a piece of beef and mustard?

IV.iii.2 **The more my wrong the greater the wrong done me   5 present** prompt
9 **meat** food   13 **As who should say** as if to say   16 **so** as long as   17 **neat's**
ox's or calf's   19 **choleric** temper-producing

KATE A dish that I do love to feed upon.

25 GRUMIO Ay, but the mustard is too hot a little.

KATE Why then, the beef, and let the mustard rest.

GRUMIO Nay then, I will not. You shall have the
mustard
Or else you get no beef of Grumio.

KATE Then both or one, or anything thou wilt.

30 GRUMIO Why then, the mustard without the beef.

KATE Go, get thee gone, thou false deluding slave,

Beats him.

That feed'st me with the very name of meat.
Sorrow on thee and all the pack of you
That triumph thus upon my misery.
35 Go, get thee gone, I say.

Enter Petruchio and Hortensio with meat.

PETRUCHIO How fares my Kate? What, sweeting, all
amort?

HORTENSIO Mistress, what cheer?

KATE   Faith, as cold as can be.

PETRUCHIO Pluck up thy spirits; look cheerfully upon
me.
Here, love, thou seest how diligent I am
40 To dress thy meat myself and bring it thee.
I am sure, sweet Kate, this kindness merits thanks.
What, not a word? Nay then, thou lov'st it not,
And all my pains is sorted to no proof.
Here, take away this dish.

KATE   I pray you, let it stand.

45 PETRUCHIO The poorest service is repaid with thanks,
And so shall mine before you touch the meat.

32 **very name** name only   36 **all amort** depressed, lifeless (cf. "mortified")
37 **what cheer** how are things   37 **cold** (cf. "not so hot"; "cold comfort,"
IV.i.30)   40 **To dress thy meat** in fixing your food   43 **sorted to no proof**
have come to nothing

KATE I thank you, sir.

HORTENSIO Signior Petruchio, fie, you are to blame.
Come, Mistress Kate, I'll bear you company.

PETRUCHIO [*Aside*] Eat it up all, Hortensio, if thou
  lovest me;   50
Much good do it unto thy gentle heart.
Kate, eat apace. And now, my honey love,
Will we return unto thy father's house
And revel it as bravely as the best,
With silken coats and caps and golden rings,   55
With ruffs and cuffs and fardingales and things,
With scarfs and fans and double change of brav'ry,
With amber bracelets, beads, and all this knav'ry.
What, hast thou dined? The tailor stays thy leisure
To deck thy body with his ruffling treasure.   60

Enter Tailor.

Come, tailor, let us see these ornaments.

Enter Haberdasher.

Lay forth the gown. What news with you, sir?

HABERDASHER Here is the cap your Worship did
  bespeak.

PETRUCHIO Why, this was molded on a porringer—
A velvet dish. Fie, fie, 'tis lewd and filthy.   65
Why, 'tis a cockle or a walnut shell,
A knack, a toy, a trick, a baby's cap.
Away with it! Come, let me have a bigger.

KATE I'll have no bigger. This doth fit the time,
And gentlewomen wear such caps as these.   70

---

54 **bravely** handsomely dressed   56 **ruffs** stiffly starched, wheel-shaped collars
56 **fardingales** farthingales, hooped skirts of petticoats   57 **brav'ry** handsome
clothes   58 **knav'ry** girlish things   59 **stays thy leisure** awaits your permission
60 **ruffling** gaily ruffled   63 **bespeak** order   64 **porringer** soup bowl   65 **lewd**
vile   66 **cockle** shell of a mollusk   67 **knack** knickknack   67 **trick** plaything
69 **doth fit the time** is in fashion

PETRUCHIO When you are gentle you shall have
         one too,
      And not till then.

HORTENSIO [*Aside*] That will not be in haste.

KATE Why, sir, I trust I may have leave to speak,
      And speak I will. I am no child, no babe.
75   Your betters have endured me say my mind,
      And if you cannot, best you stop your ears.
      My tongue will tell the anger of my heart,
      Or else my heart, concealing it, will break,
      And rather than it shall I will be free
80   Even to the uttermost, as I please, in words.

PETRUCHIO Why, thou sayst true. It is a paltry cap,
      A custard-coffin, a bauble, a silken pie.
      I love thee well in that thou lik'st it not.

KATE Love me or love me not, I like the cap,
85   And it I will have or I will have none.
                              [*Exit Haberdasher.*]

PETRUCHIO Thy gown? Why, ay. Come, tailor,
         let us see't.
      O mercy, God! What masquing stuff is here?
      What's this? A sleeve? 'Tis like a demi-cannon.
      What, up and down, carved like an apple tart?
90   Here's snip and nip and cut and slish and slash,
      Like to a censer in a barber's shop.
      Why, what, a devil's name, tailor, call'st thou this?

HORTENSIO [*Aside*] I see she's like to have neither cap
         nor gown.

TAILOR You bid me make it orderly and well,
95   According to the fashion and the time.

PETRUCHIO Marry, and did, but if you be rememb'red,

---

82 **custard-coffin** custard crust   82 **pie** meat pie   87 **masquing** for masquer-
ades or actors' costumes   88 **demi-cannon** big cannon   89 **up and down** entirely
91 **censer** incense burner with perforated top   92 **a** in the

I did not bid you mar it to the time.
Go, hop me over every kennel home,
For you shall hop without my custom, sir.
I'll none of it. Hence, make your best of it.   100

KATE I never saw a better-fashioned gown,
More quaint, more pleasing, nor more commend-
able.
Belike you mean to make a puppet of me.

PETRUCHIO Why, true, he means to make a puppet of
thee.

TAILOR She says your worship means to make a
puppet of her.   105

PETRUCHIO O monstrous arrogance!
Thou liest, thou thread, thou thimble,
Thou yard, three-quarters, half-yard, quarter, nail!
Thou flea, thou nit, thou winter cricket thou!
Braved in mine own house with a skein of thread!   110
Away, thou rag, thou quantity, thou remnant,
Or I shall so bemete thee with thy yard
As thou shalt think on prating whilst thou liv'st.
I tell thee, I, that thou hast marred her gown.

TAILOR Your worship is deceived. The gown is made   115
Just as my master had direction.
Grumio gave order how it should be done.

GRUMIO I gave him no order; I gave him the stuff.

TAILOR But how did you desire it should be made?

GRUMIO Marry, sir, with needle and thread.   120

TAILOR But did you not request to have it cut?

GRUMIO Thou hast faced many things.

97 **to the time** for all time (cf. line 95, in which "the time" is "the contemporary style") 98 **kennel** gutter (canal) 102 **quaint** skillfully made 103 **Belike** no doubt 108 **nail** 1/16 of a yard 109 **nit** louse's egg 110 **Braved** defied 110 **with** by 111 **quantity** fragment 112 **bemete** (1) measure (2) beat 113 **think on prating** remember your silly talk 116 **had direction** received orders 122 **faced** trimmed

TAILOR I have.

125 GRUMIO Face not me. Thou hast braved many men; brave not me. I will neither be faced nor braved. I say unto thee, I bid thy master cut out the gown, but I did not bid him cut it to pieces. *Ergo*, thou liest.

TAILOR Why, here is the note of the fashion to testify.

130 PETRUCHIO Read it.

GRUMIO The note lies in's throat if he say I said so.

TAILOR "*Imprimis*, a loose-bodied gown."

GRUMIO Master, if ever I said loose-bodied gown, sew me in the skirts of it and beat me to death with a
135 bottom of brown thread. I said, a gown.

PETRUCHIO Proceed.

TAILOR "With a small compassed cape."

GRUMIO I confess the cape.

TAILOR "With a trunk sleeve."

140 GRUMIO I confess two sleeves.

TAILOR "The sleeves curiously cut."

PETRUCHIO Ay, there's the villainy.

GRUMIO Error i' th' bill, sir, error i' th' bill. I commanded the sleeves should be cut out and sewed
145 up again, and that I'll prove upon thee, though thy little finger be armed in a thimble.

TAILOR This is true that I say. And I had thee in place where, thou shouldst know it.

---

124 **Face** challenge 124 **braved** equipped with finery 125 **brave** defy
127 **Ergo** therefore 129 **note** written notation 131 **in's throat** from the heart,
with premeditation 131 **he** it 132 **Imprimis** first 132 **loose-bodied gown**
(worn by prostitutes, with *loose* in pun) 135 **bottom** spool 137 **compassed**
with circular edge 139 **trunk** full (cf. line 88) 141 **curiously** painstakingly
143 **bill** i.e., the "note" 145 **prove upon** test by dueling with 147 **And** if
148 **place where** the right place

GRUMIO I am for thee straight. Take thou the bill,
    give me thy mete-yard, and spare not me.   150

HORTENSIO God-a-mercy, Grumio, then he shall have
    no odds.

PETRUCHIO Well, sir, in brief, the gown is not for me.

GRUMIO You are i' th' right, sir, 'tis for my mistress.

PETRUCHIO Go, take it up unto thy master's use.   155

GRUMIO Villain, not for thy life! Take up my mistress'
    gown for thy master's use!

PETRUCHIO Why sir, what's your conceit in that?

GRUMIO O sir, the conceit is deeper than you think
    for.
    Take up my mistress' gown to his master's use!   160
    O, fie, fie, fie!

PETRUCHIO [*Aside*] Hortensio, say thou wilt see the
    tailor paid.
    [*To Tailor*] Go take it hence; be gone and say no
    more.

HORTENSIO Tailor, I'll pay thee for thy gown
    tomorrow;
    Take no unkindness of his hasty words.   165
    Away, I say, commend me to thy master.
                       Exit Tailor.

PETRUCHIO Well, come, my Kate, we will unto your
    father's,
    Even in these honest mean habiliments.
    Our purses shall be proud, our garments poor,
    For 'tis the mind that makes the body rich,   170
    And as the sun breaks through the darkest clouds
    So honor peereth in the meanest habit.

149 for ready for 149 straight right now 149 bill (1) written order (2) long-handled weapon 150 mete-yard yardstick 155 up unto away for 15 use i.e., in whatever way he can; Grumio uses these words for a sex joke 158 conceit idea 168 habiliments clothes 172 peereth is recognized 172 habit clothes

What, is the jay more precious than the lark
Because his feathers are more beautiful?
175   Or is the adder better than the eel
Because his painted skin contents the eye?
O no, good Kate, neither art thou the worse
For this poor furniture and mean array.
If thou account'st it shame, lay it on me,
180   And therefore frolic. We will hence forthwith
To feast and sport us at thy father's house.
[*To Grumio*] Go call my men, and let us straight
    to him;
And bring our horses unto Long-lane end.
There will we mount, and thither walk on foot.
185   Let's see, I think 'tis now some seven o'clock,
And well we may come there by dinnertime.

KATE   I dare assure you, sir, 'tis almost two,
And 'twill be suppertime ere you come there.

PETRUCHIO   It shall be seven ere I go to horse.
190   Look what I speak or do or think to do,
You are still crossing it. Sirs, let't alone:
I will not go today, and ere I do,
It shall be what o'clock I say it is.

HORTENSIO [*Aside*] Why, so this gallant will command
    the sun.   [*Exeunt.*]

178 **furniture** outfit   179 **lay** blame   186 **dinnertime** midday   190 **Look what**
whatever   191 **crossing** obstructing, going counter to

164

[Scene IV. *Padua. The street in front
of Baptista's house.*]

*Enter Tranio [as Lucentio] and the Pedant
dressed like Vincentio.*

TRANIO Sir, this is the house. Please it you that I call?

PEDANT Ay, what else? And but I be deceived,
Signior Baptista may remember me
Near twenty years ago in Genoa,
Where we were lodgers at the Pegasus.   5

TRANIO 'Tis well, and hold your own in any case
With such austerity as 'longeth to a father.

PEDANT I warrant you. But sir, here comes your boy;
'Twere good he were schooled.

Enter Biondello.

TRANIO Fear you not him. Sirrah Biondello,   10
Now do your duty throughly, I advise you.
Imagine 'twere the right Vincentio.

BIONDELLO Tut, fear not me.

TRANIO But hast thou done thy errand to Baptista?

BIONDELLO I told him that your father was at Venice   15
And that you looked for him this day in Padua.

TRANIO Th' art a tall fellow. Hold thee that to drink.
Here comes Baptista. Set your countenance, sir.

IV.iv.2 **but** unless   3-5 **Signior Baptista ... Pegasus** (the Pedant is practicing as
Vincentio)   5 **Pegasus** common English inn name (after mythical winged horse
symbolizing poetic inspiration)   6 **hold your own** act your role   8 **warrant**
guarantee   9 **schooled** informed (about his role)   11 **throughly** thoroughly
17 **tall** excellent   17 **Hold thee that** i.e, take this tip

Enter Baptista and Lucentio [as Cambio].
Pedant booted and bareheaded.

Signior Baptista, you are happily met.
[*To the Pedant*] Sir, this is the gentleman I told
20   you of.
I pray you, stand good father to me now,
Give me Bianca for my patrimony.

PEDANT Soft, son.
Sir, by your leave. Having come to Padua
25   To gather in some debts, my son Lucentio
Made me acquainted with a weighty cause
Of love between your daughter and himself.
And—for the good report I hear of you,
And for the love he beareth to your daughter,
30   And she to him—to stay him not too long,
I am content, in a good father's care,
To have him matched. And if you please to like
No worse than I, upon some agreement
Me shall you find ready and willing
35   With one consent to have her so bestowed,
For curious I cannot be with you,
Signior Baptista, of whom I hear so well.

BAPTISTA Sir, pardon me in what I have to say.
Your plainness and your shortness please me well.
40   Right true it is, your son Lucentio here
Doth love my daughter and she loveth him—
Or both dissemble deeply their affections—
And therefore, if you say no more than this,
That like a father you will deal with him
45   And pass my daughter a sufficient dower,
The match is made, and all is done.
Your son shall have my daughter with consent.

18s.d. **booted and bareheaded** i.e., arriving from a journey and courteously
greeting Baptista   23 **soft** take it easy   26 **weighty cause** important matter
30 **stay** delay   32 **like** i.e., the match   36 **curious** overinsistent on fine points
39 **shortness** conciseness   45 **pass** legally settle upon

TRANIO I thank you, sir. Where, then, do you know
    best
    We be affied and such assurance ta'en
    As shall with either part's agreement stand?   50

BAPTISTA Not in my house, Lucentio, for you know
    Pitchers have ears, and I have many servants.
    Besides, old Gremio is heark'ning still,
    And happily we might be interrupted.

TRANIO Then at my lodging and it like you.   55
    There doth my father lie, and there this night
    We'll pass the business privately and well.
    Send for your daughter by your servant here;
    My boy shall fetch the scrivener presently.
    The worst is this, that at so slender warning   60
    You are like to have a thin and slender pittance.

BAPTISTA It likes me well. Cambio, hie you home
    And bid Bianca make her ready straight,
    And, if you will, tell what hath happenèd:
    Lucentio's father is arrived in Padua,   65
    And how she's like to be Lucentio's wife.
                                            [*Exit Lucentio.*]

BIONDELLO I pray the gods she may with all my heart!
                                            Exit.

TRANIO Dally not with the gods, but get thee gone.
    Signior Baptista, shall I lead the way?
    Welcome, one mess is like to be your cheer.   70
    Come, sir, we will better it in Pisa.

BAPTISTA I follow you.   *Exeunt.*

        Enter Lucentio [as Cambio] and Biondello.

BIONDELLO Cambio!

LUCENTIO What sayst thou, Biondello?

48 **know** think   49 **affied** formally engaged   50 **part's** party's   53 **heark'ning still** listening constantly   54 **happily** perchance   55 **and it like** if it please   56 **lie** stay   57 **pass** settle   59 **scrivener** notary   60 **slender warning** short notice   61 **pittance** meal   62 **likes** pleases   70 **mess** dish   70 **cheer** entertainment

75   BIONDELLO You saw my master wink and laugh upon
         you?

      LUCENTIO Biondello, what of that?

      BIONDELLO Faith, nothing, but has left me here be-
         hind to expound the meaning or moral of his signs
80   and tokens.

      LUCENTIO I pray thee, moralize them.

      BIONDELLO Then thus. Baptista is safe, talking with
         the deceiving father of a deceitful son.

      LUCENTIO And what of him?

85   BIONDELLO His daughter is to be brought by you to
         the supper.

      LUCENTIO And then?

      BIONDELLO The old priest at Saint Luke's church is at
         your command at all hours.

90   LUCENTIO And what of all this?

      BIONDELLO I cannot tell, except they are busied about
         a counterfeit assurance. Take you assurance of
         her, "*cum previlegio ad impremendum solem.*" To
         th' church! Take the priest, clerk, and some suffi-
95   cient honest witnesses.
         If this be not that you look for, I have no more to say,
         But bid Bianca farewell forever and a day.

      LUCENTIO Hear'st thou, Biondello?

      BIONDELLO I cannot tarry. I knew a wench married
100   in an afternoon as she went to the garden for pars-
         ley to stuff a rabbit. And so may you, sir. And so
         adieu, sir. My master hath appointed me to go to

      75 my master i.e., Tranio; cf. line 59   78 has he has   81 moralize "expound"
      92 assurance betrothal document   92 Take you assurance make sure   93 cum
      ... solem (Biondello's version of *cum previlegio ad imprimendum solum*, "with right
      of sole printing," a licensing phrase, with sexual pun in *imprimendum*, literally
      "pressing upon")

Saint Luke's, to bid the priest be ready to come
against you come with your appendix.   *Exit.*

LUCENTIO I may, and will, if she be so contented.   105
She will be pleased; then wherefore should I doubt?
Hap what hap may, I'll roundly go about her.
It shall go hard if Cambio go without her.   *Exit.*

[Scene V. *The road to Padua.*]

*Enter Petruchio, Kate, Hortensio
[with Servants.]*

PETRUCHIO Come on, a God's name, once more to-
          ward our father's.
Good lord, how bright and goodly shines the moon.

KATE The moon? The sun. It is not moonlight now.

PETRUCHIO I say it is the moon that shines so bright.

KATE I know it is the sun that shines so bright.   5

PETRUCHIO Now, by my mother's son, and that's
          myself,
It shall be moon or star or what I list,
Or ere I journey to your father's house.
[*To Servants*] Go on and fetch our horses back
          again.
Evermore crossed and crossed, nothing but crossed!   10

HORTENSIO [*To Kate*] Say as he says or we shall never
          go.

KATE Forward, I pray, since we have come so far,
And be it moon or sun or what you please.

---

104 **against you come** in preparing for your coming   104 **appendix** (1) servant
(2) wife (another metaphor from printing)   107 **roundly** directly   107 **about** after
IV.v.1 **a** in   7 **list** please   8 **Or ere** before   10 **crossed** opposed, challenged

And if you please to call it a rush-candle,
15   Henceforth I vow it shall be so for me.

PETRUCHIO I say it is the moon.

KATE   I know it is the moon.

PETRUCHIO Nay, then you lie. It is the blessèd sun.

KATE Then God be blessed, it is the blessèd sun.
But sun it is not when you say it is not,
20   And the moon changes even as your mind.
What you will have it named, even that it is,
And so it shall be so for Katherine.

HORTENSIO [*Aside*] Petruchio, go thy ways. The field
is won.

PETRUCHIO Well, forward, forward! Thus the bowl
should run
25   And not unluckily against the bias.
But soft, company is coming here.

Enter Vincentio.

[*To Vincentio*] Good morrow, gentle mistress;
where away?
Tell me, sweet Kate, and tell me truly too,
Hast thou beheld a fresher gentlewoman?
30   Such war of white and red within her cheeks!
What stars do spangle heaven with such beauty
As those two eyes become that heavenly face?
Fair lovely maid, once more good day to thee.
Sweet Kate, embrace her for her beauty's sake.

35   HORTENSIO [*Aside*] 'A will make the man mad, to
make a woman of him.

KATE Young budding virgin, fair and fresh and sweet,
Whither away, or where is thy abode?

14 **rush-candle** rush dipped in grease and used as candle   24 **bowl** bowling ball
25 **against the bias** not in the planned curving route, made possible by a lead
insertion (bias) weighting one side of the ball   26 **soft** hush   26 **company**
someone   29 **fresher** more radiant   35 **'A** he

Happy the parents of so fair a child!
Happier the man whom favorable stars   40
Allots thee for his lovely bedfellow!

PETRUCHIO Why, how now, Kate, I hope thou are not
  mad.
This is a man, old, wrinkled, faded, withered,
And not a maiden, as thou sayst he is.

KATE Pardon, old father, my mistaking eyes   45
That have been so bedazzled with the sun
That everything I look on seemeth green.
Now I perceive thou art a reverend father;
Pardon, I pray thee, for my mad mistaking.

PETRUCHIO Do, good old grandsire, and withal make
  known   50
Which way thou travelest. If along with us,
We shall be joyful of thy company.

VINCENTIO Fair sir, and you my merry mistress,
That with your strange encounter much amazed me,
My name is called Vincentio, my dwelling Pisa,   55
And bound I am to Padua, there to visit
A son of mine which long I have not seen.

PETRUCHIO What is his name?

VINCENTIO   Lucentio, gentle sir.

PETRUCHIO Happily met, the happier for thy son.
And now by law as well as reverend age,   60
I may entitle thee my loving father.
The sister to my wife, this gentlewoman,
Thy son by this hath married. Wonder not
Nor be not grieved. She is of good esteem,
Her dowry wealthy, and of worthy birth;   65
Beside, so qualified as may beseem
The spouse of any noble gentleman.
Let me embrace with old Vincentio

47 green young   54 encounter mode of address   63 this now   66 so qualified
having qualities   66 beseem befit

And wander we to see thy honest son,
70   Who will of thy arrival be full joyous.

VINCENTIO But is this true, or is it else your pleasure,
Like pleasant travelers, to break a jest
Upon the company you overtake?

HORTENSIO I do assure thee, father, so it is.

75   PETRUCHIO Come, go along, and see the truth hereof,
For our first merriment hath made thee jealous.

Exeunt [all but Hortensio].

HORTENSIO Well, Petruchio, this has put me in heart.
Have to my widow, and if she be froward,
Then hast thou taught Hortensio to be untoward.

Exit.

---

72 **pleasant** addicted to pleasantries   76 **jealous** suspicious   78 **Have to** on to
78 **froward** fractious   79 **untoward** difficult

[ACT V

Scene I. *Padua. The street in front
of Lucentio's house.*]

*Enter Biondello, Lucentio [as Cambio],
and Bianca; Gremio is out before.*

BIONDELLO Softly and swiftly, sir, for the priest is
ready.

LUCENTIO I fly, Biondello. But they may chance to
need thee at home; therefore leave us.
Exit [with Bianca].

BIONDELLO Nay, faith, I'll see the church a your back,   5
and then come back to my master's as soon as I
can.   *[Exit.]*

GREMIO I marvel Cambio comes not all this while.

*Enter Petruchio, Kate, Vincentio, [and] Grumio,
with Attendants.*

PETRUCHIO Sir, here's the door, this is Lucentio's
house.
My father's bears more toward the marketplace;   10
Thither must I, and here I leave you, sir.

VINCENTIO You shall not choose but drink before you
go.
I think I shall command your welcome here,
And by all likelihood some cheer is toward.   *Knock.*

V.i.s.d. **out before** precedes, and does not see, the others   5 **a your back** on your
back (see you enter the church? or, married?)   10 **bears** lies   14 **toward** at hand

173

15   GREMIO They're busy within. You were best knock
     louder.

> *Pedant [as Vincentio] looks out of*
> *the window [above].*

PEDANT What's he that knocks as he would beat
     down the gate?

VINCENTIO Is Signior Lucentio within, sir?

20   PEDANT He's within, sir, but not to be spoken withal.

VINCENTIO What if a man bring him a hundred pound
     or two, to make merry withal?

PEDANT Keep your hundred pounds to yourself; he
     shall need none so long as I live.

25   PETRUCHIO Nay, I told you your son was well beloved
     in Padua. Do you hear, sir? To leave frivolous cir-
     cumstances, I pray you tell Signior Lucentio that
     his father is come from Pisa and is here at the door
     to speak with him.

30   PEDANT Thou liest. His father is come from Padua
     and here looking out at the window.

VINCENTIO Art thou his father?

PEDANT Ay sir, so his mother says, if I may believe
     her.

35   PETRUCHIO [*To Vincentio*] Why how now, gentleman?
     Why this is flat knavery, to take upon you another
     man's name.

PEDANT Lay hands on the villain. I believe 'a means
     to cozen somebody in this city under my counte-
40   nance.

Enter Biondello.

17 **What's** who is   20 **withal** with   26–27 **frivolous circumstances** trivial
matters   30 **Padua** (perhaps Shakespeare's slip of the pen for *Pisa*, home of the
real Vincentio, or *Mantua*, where the Pedant comes from; cf. IV.ii.77)   36 **flat**
unvarnished   38 **'a** he   39 **cozen** defraud   39–40 **countenance** identity

BIONDELLO I have seen them in the church together;
God send 'em good shipping! But who is here?
Mine old master, Vincentio! Now we are undone
and brought to nothing.

VINCENTIO Come hither, crack-hemp.   45

BIONDELLO I hope I may choose, sir.

VINCENTIO Come hither, you rogue. What, have you
forgot me?

BIONDELLO Forgot you? No, sir. I could not forget you,
for I never saw you before in all my life.   50

VINCENTIO What, you notorious villain, didst thou
never see thy master's father, Vincentio?

BIONDELLO What, my old worshipful old master? Yes,
marry, sir, see where he looks out of the window.

VINCENTIO Is't so, indeed?   *He beats Biondello.*   55

BIONDELLO Help, help, help! Here's a madman will
murder me.   [*Exit.*]

PEDANT Help, son! Help, Signior Baptista!
                                    [*Exit from above.*]

PETRUCHIO Prithee, Kate, let's stand aside and see the
end of this controversy.   60
                                    [*They stand aside.*]

*Enter Pedant [below] with Servants, Baptista,
[and] Tranio [as Lucentio].*

TRANIO Sir, what are you that offer to beat my
servant?

VINCENTIO What am I, sir? Nay, what are you, sir?
O immortal gods! O fine villain! A silken doublet,

42 **shipping** journey 43 **undone** defeated 44 **brought to nothing**
(cf. "annihilated") 45 **crack-hemp** rope-stretcher (i.e., subject for hanging)
46 **choose** have some choice (in the matter) 51 **notorious** extraordinary
61 **offer** attempt 64 **fine** well dressed

65   a velvet hose, a scarlet cloak, and a copatain hat!
O, I am undone, I am undone! While I play the
good husband at home, my son and my servant
spend all at the university.

TRANIO How now, what's the matter?

70 BAPTISTA What, is the man lunatic?

TRANIO Sir, you seem a sober ancient gentleman by
your habit, but your words show you a madman.
Why sir, what 'cerns it you if I wear pearl and
gold? I thank my good father, I am able to main-
75   tain it.

VINCENTIO Thy father! O villain, he is a sailmaker in
Bergamo.

BAPTISTA You mistake, sir, you mistake, sir. Pray,
what do you think is his name?

80 VINCENTIO His name! As if I knew not his name! I
have brought him up ever since he was three years
old, and his name is Tranio.

PEDANT Away, away, mad ass! His name is Lucentio,
and he is mine only son and heir to the lands of me,
85   Signior Vincentio.

VINCENTIO Lucentio! O he hath murd'red his master.
Lay hold on him, I charge you in the Duke's name.
O my son, my son! Tell me, thou villain, where is
my son Lucentio?

90 TRANIO Call forth an officer.

[*Enter an Officer.*]

Carry this mad knave to the jail. Father Baptista,
I charge you see that he be forthcoming.

VINCENTIO Carry me to the jail!

---

65 **copatain** high conical   67 **husband** manager   72 **habit** manner   73 **'cerns**
concerns   92 **forthcoming** available (for trial)

GREMIO Stay, officer. He shall not go to prison.

BAPTISTA Talk not, Signior Gremio. I say he shall go   95
to prison.

GREMIO Take heed, Signior Baptista, lest you be cony-
catched in this business. I dare swear this is the
right Vincentio.

PEDANT Swear, if thou dar'st.   100

GREMIO Nay, I dare not swear it.

TRANIO Then thou wert best say that I am not
Lucentio.

GREMIO Yes, I know thee to be Signior Lucentio.

BAPTISTA Away with the dotard, to the jail with him!   105

VINCENTIO Thus strangers may be haled and abused.
O monstrous villain!

Enter Biondello, Lucentio, and Bianca.

BIONDELLO O we are spoiled—and yonder he is. Deny
him, forswear him, or else we are all undone.
Exit Biondello, Tranio, and Pedant as fast as may be.

LUCENTIO Pardon, sweet father.   *Kneel.*

VINCENTIO   Lives my sweet son?   110

BIANCA Pardon, dear father.

BAPTISTA   How hast thou offended?
Where is Lucentio?

LUCENTIO   Here's Lucentio,
Right son to the right Vincentio,
That have by marriage made thy daughter mine
While counterfeit supposes bleared thine eyne.   115

97-98 **cony-catched** fooled 102 **thou wert best** maybe you'll dare
105 **dotard** old fool 106 **haled** pulled about 108 **spoiled** ruined 115 **supposes** pretendings (evidently an allusion to Gascoigne's play *Supposes*, one of
Shakespeare's sources) 115 **eyne** eyes

GREMIO Here's packing, with a witness, to deceive
us all!

VINCENTIO Where is that damnèd villain Tranio
That faced and braved me in this matter so?

120 BAPTISTA Why, tell me, is not this my Cambio?

BIANCA Cambio is changed into Lucentio.

LUCENTIO Love wrought these miracles. Bianca's love
Made me exchange my state with Tranio
While he did bear my countenance in the town,
125 And happily I have arrived at the last
Unto the wishèd haven of my bliss.
What Tranio did, myself enforced him to.
Then pardon him, sweet father, for my sake.

VINCENTIO I'll slit the villain's nose that would have
130 sent me to the jail.

BAPTISTA [*To Lucentio*] But do you hear, sir? Have
you married my daughter without asking my good
will?

VINCENTIO Fear not, Baptista; we will content you, go
135 to. But I will in, to be revenged for this villainy.
Exit.

BAPTISTA And I, to sound the depth of this knavery.
Exit.

LUCENTIO Look not pale, Bianca. Thy father will not
frown.   *Exeunt* [*Lucentio and Bianca*].

GREMIO My cake is dough, but I'll in among the rest
140 Out of hope of all but my share of the feast. [*Exit*.]

KATE Husband, let's follow, to see the end of this ado.

PETRUCHIO First kiss me, Kate, and we will.

116 **packing** plotting 116 **with a witness** outright, unabashed 119 **faced and braved** impudently challenged and defied 124 **bear my countenance** take on my identity 134-35 **go to** (mild remonstrance; cf. "go on," "come, come," "don't worry") 136 **sound the depth** get to the bottom of 139 **cake is dough** project hasn't worked out (proverbial; cf. I.i.108-09)

KATE What, in the midst of the street?

PETRUCHIO What, art thou ashamed of me?

KATE No sir, God forbid, but ashamed to kiss.   145

PETRUCHIO Why, then let's home again.   [*To Grumio*]
    Come sirrah, let's away.

KATE Nay, I will give thee a kiss. Now pray thee, love,
    stay.

PETRUCHIO Is not this well? Come, my sweet Kate.
    Better once than never, for never too late.   *Exeunt.*

[Scene II. *Padua. In Lucentio's house.*]

*Enter Baptista, Vincentio, Gremio, the Pedant, Lucentio,
and Bianca, [Petruchio, Kate, Hortensio,] Tranio,
Biondello, Grumio, and Widow; the Servingmen with
Tranio bringing in a banquet.*

LUCENTIO At last, though long, our jarring notes agree,
    And time it is, when raging war is done,
    To smile at 'scapes and perils overblown.
    My fair Bianca, bid my father welcome
    While I with self-same kindness welcome thine.   5
    Brother Petruchio, sister Katherina,
    And thou, Hortensio, with thy loving widow,
    Feast with the best and welcome to my house.
    My banquet is to close our stomachs up
    After our great good cheer. Pray you, sit down,   10
    For now we sit to chat as well as eat.

PETRUCHIO Nothing but sit and sit, and eat and eat.

---

149 **once** at some time 149 **Better … late** better late than never
V.ii.s.d. **banquet** dessert 1 **At last, though long** at long last 3 **over-blown**
that have blown over 9 **stomachs** (with pun on "irascibility"; cf. IV.i.152)
10 **cheer** (reception at Baptista's)

BAPTISTA Padua affords this kindness, son Petruchio.

PETRUCHIO Padua affords nothing but what is kind.

HORTENSIO For both our sakes I would that word were
15   true.

PETRUCHIO Now, for my life, Hortensio fears his
      widow.

WIDOW Then never trust me if I be afeard.

PETRUCHIO You are very sensible and yet you miss my
      sense:
   I mean Hortensio is afeard of you.

20 WIDOW He that is giddy thinks the world turns round.

PETRUCHIO Roundly replied.

KATE   Mistress, how mean you that?

WIDOW Thus I conceive by him.

PETRUCHIO Conceives by me! How likes Hortensio
      that?

HORTENSIO My widow says, thus she conceives her
      tale.

PETRUCHIO Very well mended. Kiss him for that, good
25   widow.

KATE "He that is giddy thinks the world turns round."
   I pray you, tell me what you meant by that.

WIDOW Your husband, being troubled with a shrew,
   Measures my husband's sorrow by his woe,
30   And now you know my meaning.

KATE A very mean meaning.

---

16 **fears** is afraid of (the Widow puns on the meaning "frightens")   17 **afeard**
(1) frightened (2) suspected   21 **Roundly** outspokenly   22 **conceive by**
understand   23 **Conceives by** is made pregnant by   24 **conceives her tale**
understands her statement (with another pun)   29 **Measures** estimates   29 **his**
his own   31 **mean** paltry

WIDOW   Right, I mean you.

KATE And I am mean indeed, respecting you.

PETRUCHIO To her, Kate!

HORTENSIO To her, widow!

PETRUCHIO A hundred marks, my Kate does put her
    down.   35

HORTENSIO That's my office.

PETRUCHIO Spoke like an officer. Ha' to thee, lad.
                              Drinks to Hortensio.

BAPTISTA How likes Gremio these quick-witted folks?

GREMIO Believe me, sir, they butt together well.

BIANCA Head and butt! An hasty-witted body   40
    Would say your head and butt were head and horn.

VINCENTIO Ay, mistress bride, hath that awakened
    you?

BIANCA Ay, but not frighted me; therefore I'll sleep
    again.

PETRUCHIO Nay, that you shall not. Since you have
    begun,
    Have at you for a bitter jest or two.   45

BIANCA Am I your bird? I mean to shift my bush,
    And then pursue me as you draw your bow.
    You are welcome all.
                  Exit Bianca [with Kate and Widow].

PETRUCHIO She hath prevented me. Here, Signior
    Tranio,

---

32 **am mean** (1) am moderate (2) have a low opinion   35 **put her down** defeat
her (with sexual pun by Hortensio)   36 **office** job   37 **Ha'** here's, hail   39 **butt**
(perhaps also "but," i.e., argue or differ)   40 **butt** (with pun on "bottom")
41 **horn** (1) butting instrument (2) symbol of cuckoldry (3) phallus   45 **Have at
you** let's have   45 **bitter** biting (but good-natured)   46 **bird** prey   49 **prevented me** beaten me to it

50   This bird you aimed at, though you hit her not;
      Therefore a health to all that shot and missed.

TRANIO O sir, Lucentio slipped me, like his grey-
      hound,
      Which runs himself and catches for his master.

PETRUCHIO A good swift simile but something currish.

55   TRANIO 'Tis well, sir, that you hunted for yourself;
      'Tis thought your deer does hold you at a bay.

BAPTISTA O, O, Petruchio, Tranio hits you now.

LUCENTIO I thank thee for that gird, good Tranio.

HORTENSIO Confess, confess, hath he not hit you here?

60   PETRUCHIO 'A has a little galled me, I confess,
      And as the jest did glance away from me,
      'Tis ten to one it maimed you two outright.

BAPTISTA Now, in good sadness, son Petruchio,
      I think thou hast the veriest shrew of all.

PETRUCHIO Well, I say no. And therefore, for
65   assurance,
      Let's each one send unto his wife,
      And he whose wife is most obedient
      To come at first when he doth send for her
      Shall win the wager which we will propose.

HORTENSIO Content. What's the wager?

70   LUCENTIO   Twenty crowns.

PETRUCHIO Twenty crowns!
      I'll venture so much of my hawk or hound,
      But twenty times so much upon my wife.

LUCENTIO A hundred then.

HORTENSIO   Content.

52 **slipped** unleashed   54 **swift** quick-witted   56 **deer** (1) doe (2) dear   56 **at a
bay** at bay (i.e., backed up at a safe distance)   58 **gird** gibe   60 **galled** chafed
63 **sadness** seriousness   64 **veriest** most genuine   65 **assurance** proof   72 **of**
on   74 **Content** agreed

PETRUCHIO   A match, 'tis done.

HORTENSIO Who shall begin?

LUCENTIO   That will I.   75
  Go Biondello, bid your mistress come to me.

BIONDELLO I go.   *Exit.*

BAPTISTA Son, I'll be your half, Bianca comes.

LUCENTIO I'll have no halves; I'll bear it all myself.

                    Enter Biondello.

  How now, what news?

BIONDELLO   Sir, my mistress sends you
      word   80
  That she is busy and she cannot come.

PETRUCHIO How? She's busy and she cannot come?
  Is that an answer?

GREMIO   Ay, and a kind one too.
  Pray God, sir, your wife send you not a worse.

PETRUCHIO I hope, better.   85

HORTENSIO Sirrah Biondello, go and entreat my wife
  To come to me forthwith.   *Exit Biondello.*

PETRUCHIO   O ho, entreat her!
  Nay, then she must needs come.

HORTENSIO   I am afraid, sir,
  Do what you can, yours will not be entreated.

                    Enter Biondello.

  Now where's my wife?   90

BIONDELLO She says you have some goodly jest in hand.
  She will not come. She bids you come to her.

---

74 **A match** (it's) a bet   78 **be your half** assume half your bet   80 **How now** (mild exclamation; cf. "well")   82 **How** what   87 **forthwith** right away

PETRUCHIO Worse and worse. She will not come.
    O vile,
Intolerable, not to be endured!
95   Sirrah Grumio, go to your mistress; say
I command her come to me.   *Exit* [*Grumio*].

HORTENSIO I know her answer.

PETRUCHIO   What?

HORTENSIO   She will not.

PETRUCHIO The fouler fortune mine, and there an end.

Enter Kate.

BAPTISTA Now, by my holidame, here comes Katherina.

100 KATE What is your will, sir, that you send for me?

PETRUCHIO Where is your sister and Hortensio's wife?

KATE They sit conferring by the parlor fire.

PETRUCHIO Go fetch them hither. If they deny to
    come,
Swinge me them soundly forth unto their
    husbands.
105 Away, I say, and bring them hither straight.
                        [*Exit Kate.*]

LUCENTIO Here is a wonder, if you talk of a wonder.

HORTENSIO And so it is. I wonder what it bodes.

PETRUCHIO Marry, peace it bodes, and love, and quiet
    life,
An awful rule and right supremacy;
110 And, to be short, what not that's sweet and happy.

BAPTISTA Now fair befall thee, good Petruchio.

---

99 **holidame** holy dame (some editors emend to *halidom*, sacred place or relic)
102 **conferring** conversing 103 **deny** refuse 104 **Swinge** thrash
104 **soundly** thoroughly (cf. "sound beating") 109 **awful** inspiring respect
110 **what not** i.e., everything 111 **fair befall** good luck to

The wager thou hast won, and I will add
Unto their losses twenty thousand crowns,
Another dowry to another daughter,
For she is changed as she had never been.   115

PETRUCHIO Nay, I will win my wager better yet
And show more sign of her obedience,
Her new-built virtue and obedience.

Enter Kate, Bianca, and Widow.

See where she comes and brings your froward
     wives
As prisoners to her womanly persuasion.   120
Katherine, that cap of yours becomes you not.
Off with that bauble, throw it under foot.

                                        [*She throws it.*]

WIDOW Lord, let me never have a cause to sigh
Till I be brought to such a silly pass.

BIANCA Fie, what a foolish—duty call you this?   125

LUCENTIO I would your duty were as foolish too.
The wisdom of your duty, fair Bianca,
Hath cost me five hundred crowns since supper-
     time.

BIANCA The more fool you for laying on my duty.

PETRUCHIO Katherine, I charge thee, tell these head-
     strong women   130
What duty they do owe their lords and husbands.

WIDOW Come, come, you're mocking. We will have
     no telling.

PETRUCHIO Come on, I say, and first begin with her.

WIDOW She shall not.

---

119 **froward** uncooperative   124 **pass** situation   128 **five hundred** (1) Lucentio
makes it look worse than it is, or (2) he made several bets, or (3) the text errs (some
editors emend to "a hundred," assuming that the manuscript's "a" was misread as
the Roman numeral v)   129 **laying** betting

135 PETRUCHIO I say she shall—and first begin with her.

    KATE Fie, fie, unknit that threatening unkind brow
    And dart not scornful glances from those eyes
    To wound thy lord, thy king, thy governor.
    It blots thy beauty as frosts do bite the meads,
    Confounds thy fame as whirlwinds shake fair
140   buds,
    And in no sense is meet or amiable.
    A woman moved is like a fountain troubled,
    Muddy, ill-seeming, thick, bereft of beauty,
    And while it is so, none so dry or thirsty
145   Will deign to sip or touch one drop of it.
    Thy husband is thy lord, thy life, thy keeper,
    Thy head, thy sovereign—one that cares for thee,
    And for thy maintenance commits his body
    To painful labor both by sea and land,
150   To watch the night in storms, the day in cold,
    Whilst thou li'st warm at home, secure and safe;
    And craves no other tribute at thy hands
    But love, fair looks, and true obedience:
    Too little payment for so great a debt.
155   Such duty as the subject owes the prince,
    Even such a woman oweth to her husband,
    And when she is froward, peevish, sullen, sour,
    And not obedient to his honest will,
    What is she but a foul contending rebel
160   And graceless traitor to her loving lord?
    I am ashamed that women are so simple
    To offer war where they should kneel for peace,
    Or seek for rule, supremacy, and sway,
    When they are bound to serve, love, and obey.
165   Why are our bodies soft and weak and smooth,
    Unapt to toil and trouble in the world,
    But that our soft conditions and our hearts
    Should well agree with our external parts?

135 **unkind** hostile 140 **Confounds thy fame** spoils people's opinion of you
140 **shake** shake off 142 **moved** i.e., by ill temper 150 **watch** stay awake, be
alert during 158 **honest** honorable 161 **simple** silly 166 **Unapt to** unfitted
for 167 **conditions** qualities

Come, come, you froward and unable worms,
My mind hath been as big as one of yours,   170
My heart as great, my reason haply more,
To bandy word for word and frown for frown.
But now I see our lances are but straws,
Our strength as weak, our weakness past compare,
That seeming to be most which we indeed least are.   175
Then vail your stomachs, for it is no boot,
And place your hands below your husband's foot,
In token of which duty, if he please,
My hand is ready, may it do him ease.

PETRUCHIO Why, there's a wench! Come on and kiss
    me, Kate.   180

LUCENTIO Well, go thy ways, old lad, for thou shalt
    ha't.

VINCENTIO 'Tis a good hearing when children are
    toward.

LUCENTIO But a harsh hearing when women are
    froward.

PETRUCHIO Come, Kate, we'll to bed.
    We three are married, but you two are sped.   185
    'Twas I won the wager, [to Lucentio] though you
        hit the white,
    And, being a winner, God give you good night.
                                    Exit Petruchio [with Kate].

HORTENSIO Now, go thy ways; thou hast tamed a curst
    shrow.

LUCENTIO 'Tis a wonder, by your leave, she will be
    tamèd so.   [Exeunt.]

FINIS

169 **unable worms** weak, lowly creatures   170 **big** inflated (cf. "think big")
176 **vail your stomachs** fell your pride   176 **no boot** useless, profitless
179 **may it** (1) I hope it may (2) if it may   182 **hearing** thing to hear; report
182 **toward** tractable   185 **sped** done   for   186 **white** (1) bull's eye
(2) *Bianca* means white

Textual Note

The authority for the present text is the Folio of 1623 (F). Based on it were the Quarto of 1631 and three later folios. These introduce a number of errors of their own but also make some corrections and some changes accepted by most subsequent editors. The present text adheres as closely as possible to F, accepting standard emendations only when F seems clearly erroneous. These emendations come mainly from such early editors as Rowe, Theobald, and Capell.

F's incomplete division into acts is almost universally altered by modern editors, and present text conforms to standard practice. F has "*Actus primus. Scoena [sic] Prima*" at the beginning, whereas in modern practice approximately the first 275 lines are placed in an "Induction" with two scenes. F lacks a designation for Act II. F's "*Actus Tertia [sic]*," beginning with Lucentio's "Fiddler, forbear, etc.," is universally accepted. F's "*Actus Quartus. Scena Prima*" generally becomes modern IV.iii, and F's "*Actus Quintus*," modern V.ii.

F makes a number of erroneous or unclear speech assignments (at one time naming an actor, Sincklo, instead of the character). These are at Ind.i.88; III.i.46ff.; IV.ii.4ff. They are specifically listed below. Names of speakers, nearly always abbreviated in F, are regularly spelled out in the present edition. Speakers in F designated *Beggar*, *Lady*, and *Man* are given as *Sly*, *Page*, and *Servingman*, respectively.

F is not consistent in the spelling of some proper names. In the stage directions, the shrew, for instance, appears as *Katerina*, *Katherina*, *Katherine* (sometimes with *a* in the second syllable), and *Kate*; she is spoken to and of as *Katherine* and *Kate*; her speeches are headed *Ka*, *Kat*, and *Kate*. Since *Kate* is the most frequent form, this edition uses it throughout and does not include the change in the following list. In F, the name adopted by Hortensio when he pretends to be a music teacher appears three times as *Litio*, which we use here, and four times as *Lisio*. Many editors follow F2 and Rowe in emending to *Licio*.

Editors vary in the treatment of F's short lines, sometimes letting a short line stand independently, and sometimes joining several short lines into a quasi-pentameter. The latter practice is generally followed in the present edition. Modern editors are quite consistent in identifying as verse a few passages set as prose in F, and vice versa.

Errors in foreign languages in F are allowed to stand if they are conceivably errors made by the speaker, e.g., errors in Latin and Spanish. Spellings of English words are corrected and modernized. The punctuation is modern. Obvious typographical errors, of which there are a great many, are corrected silently. The following materials, lacking in F, are given in square brackets in this edition: cast of characters, missing act and scene designations, indications of place of action, certain stage directions (F has an unusually copious supply of stage directions, some of which make interesting references to properties).

The following list includes all significant variations from F. The reading in the present text is in bold, followed by the F reading in roman.

Ind.i.s.d. **Hostess and Beggar** Begger and Hostes 12 **thirdborough** Head-borough 17 **Broach** Brach 82 **A Player** 2. Player 88 **2. Player** Sincklo

Ind.ii.2 **lordship** Lord 18 **Sly's** Sies 137 **play it. Is** play, it is

I.i.13 **Vincentio** Vincentio's 25 **Mi perdonato** Me Pardonato 47s.d. **suitor** sister 73 **Master** Mr 162 **captum** captam 207 **colored** Conlord 243 **your** you

I.ii.13 **master** Mr 17s.d. **wrings** rings 18 **masters** mistris 24 **Con ... trovato** Contutti le core bene trobatto 25 **ben** bene 25 **molto** multo 45 **this's** this 69, 89 **shrewd** shrow'd 70 **Xanthippe** Zentippe 72 **she** she is 120 **me and other** me. Other 172 **help me** helpe one 190 **Antonio's** Butonios 213 **ours** yours 266 **feat** seeke

II.i.3 **gawds** goods 8 **charge thee** charge 73 **Backare** Bacare 75–76 **wooing. Neighbor,** wooing neighbors: 79 **unto you this** vnto this 104 **Pisa; by report** Pisa by report 158 **vile** vilde 186 **bonny** bony 241 **askance a sconce** 323 **in me**

189

TEXTUAL NOTE

III.i.28 **Sigeia** Sigeria (also in 32, 41)   46 [*Aside*] Luc.   49 **Bianca** [F omits]
50 **Lucentio** Bian.   52 **Bianca** Hort.   73 **B mi** Beeme   79 **change** charge
79 **odd** old   80 **Messenger** Nicke

III.ii.29 **of thy** of   30 **such old** such   33 **hear** heard   55 **swayed** Waid
57 **half-cheeked** halfe-chekt   128 **to her love sir,** Loue   130 **As I** As

IV.i.25 **Curtis** Grumio   100s.d. **Enter ... Servingmen** [F places after 99]
174s.d. [in F, after 175]   198 **reverent** reuerend

IV.ii.4 **Hortensio** Luc.   6 **Lucentio** Hor.   8 **Lucentio** Hor.   13 **none** me
31 **her** them   63 **mercatante** Marcantant   71 **Take in** Par. Take me.

IV.iii.63 **Haberdasher** Fel.   81 **is a** is   88 **like a** like   179 **account'st**
accountedst

IV.iv.1 **Sir** Sirs   5 [in F, Tranio's speech begins here]   9s.d. [F places after 7]
19 **Signior** Tra. Signior   68 [F adds s.d., Enter Peter]   91 **except** expect

IV.v.18 **is in** 36 **make a** make the   38 **Whither** Whether   38 **where** whether
41 **Allots** A lots   48 **reverend** reuerent (also in 60)   78 **she be** she

V.i.6 **master's** mistris   52 **master's** Mistris   107s.d. [F places after 105]
145 **No** Mo

V.ii.2 **done** come   37 **thee, lad** the lad   45 **bitter** better   65 **for** sir

WILLIAM SHAKESPEARE

THE TWO GENTLEMEN OF VERONA

Edited by Bertrand Evans

The Names of All the Actors

DUKE [OF MILAN], father to Silvia

VALENTINE ⎱ the two gentlemen
PROTEUS ⎰

ANTONIO, father to Proteus

THURIO, a foolish rival to Valentine

EGLAMOUR, agent for Silvia in her escape

HOST, where Julia lodges

OUTLAWS, with Valentine

SPEED, a clownish servant to Valentine

LAUNCE, the like to Proteus

PANTHINO, servant to Antonio

JULIA, beloved of Proteus

SILVIA, beloved of Valentine

LUCETTA, waiting woman to Julia

[SERVANTS, MUSICIANS

Scene: Verona; Milan; a forest]

THE TWO GENTLEMEN
OF VERONA

ACT I

Scene I. [*Verona. An open place.*]

[Enter] Valentine [and] Proteus.

VALENTINE Cease to persuade, my loving Proteus:
　　Home-keeping youth have ever homely wits.
　　Were't not affection chains thy tender days
　　To the sweet glances of thy honored love,
　　I rather would entreat thy company　　　　　　　5
　　To see the wonders of the world abroad,
　　Than, living dully sluggardized at home,
　　Wear out thy youth with shapeless idleness.
　　But since thou lov'st, love still, and thrive therein,
　　Even as I would, when I to love begin.　　　　　10

PROTEUS Wilt thou be gone? Sweet Valentine, adieu!
　　Think on thy Proteus when thou haply seest
　　Some rare noteworthy object in thy travel:
　　Wish me partaker in thy happiness
　　When thou dost meet good hap; and in thy danger,　15

Text references are printed in **boldface** type; the annotation follows in roman type.
I.i.12 **haply** by chance　15 **hap** luck

If ever danger do environ thee,
Commend thy grievance to my holy prayers,
For I will be thy beadsman, Valentine.

VALENTINE And on a love-book pray for my success?

20 PROTEUS Upon some book I love I'll pray for thee.

VALENTINE That's on some shallow story of deep love:
How young Leander crossed the Hellespont.

PROTEUS That's a deep story of a deeper love,
For he was more than over shoes in love.

25 VALENTINE 'Tis true, for you are over boots in love,
And yet you never swum the Hellespont.

PROTEUS Over the boots? Nay, give me not the boots.

VALENTINE No, I will not, for it boots thee not.

PROTEUS   What?

VALENTINE To be in love—where scorn is bought with
groans,
Coy looks with heartsore sighs, one fading
30 moment's mirth
With twenty watchful, weary, tedious nights;
If haply won, perhaps a hapless gain;
If lost, why then a grievous labor won;
However, but a folly bought with wit,
35 Or else a wit by folly vanquishèd.

PROTEUS So, by your circumstance, you call me fool.

VALENTINE So, by your circumstance, I fear you'll
prove.

PROTEUS 'Tis love you cavil at. I am not Love.

VALENTINE Love is your master, for he masters you;

18 **beadsman** one who contracts to pray in behalf of another   19 **love-book** i.e.,
instead of a prayer book   22 **Leander** (legendary Greek youth who nightly swam
the Hellespont to visit his beloved Hero and, one night, was drowned)   27 **give
me not the boots** i.e., don't jest with me   28 **boots** benefits (with pun on
preceding line)   32 **hapless** luckless   34 **However** in either case   36 **by your
circumstance** i.e., by your argument (in the next line the same phrase means "in
your condition [of love]")

And he that is so yokèd by a fool, 40
Methinks, should not be chronicled for wise.

PROTEUS Yet writers say, as in the sweetest bud
The eating canker dwells, so eating love
Inhabits in the finest wits of all.

VALENTINE And writers say, as the most forward bud 45
Is eaten by the canker ere it blow,
Even so by love the young and tender wit
Is turned to folly, blasting in the bud,
Losing his verdure even in the prime,
And all the fair effects of future hopes. 50
But wherefore waste I time to counsel thee,
That art a votary to fond desire?
Once more adieu! My father at the road
Expects my coming, there to see me shipped.

PROTEUS And thither will I bring thee, Valentine. 55

VALENTINE Sweet Proteus, no; now let us take our
leave.
To Milan let me hear from thee by letters
Of thy success in love, and what news else
Betideth here in absence of thy friend,
And I likewise will visit thee with mine. 60

PROTEUS All happiness bechance to thee in Milan!

VALENTINE As much to you at home! And so, farewell.
Exit.

PROTEUS He after honor hunts, I after love.
He leaves his friends to dignify them more,
I leave myself, my friends, and all, for love. 65
Thou, Julia, thou hast metamorphized me,
Made me neglect my studies, lose my time,
War with good counsel, set the world at nought,
Made wit with musing weak, heart sick with
thought.

41 **chronicled** written down   43 **canker** cankerworm   45 **most forward** earliest
46 **blow** bloom   48 **blasting** withering   49 **prime** spring   53 **road** harbor
55 **bring** accompany   58 **success** fortune (good or bad)

[*Enter Speed.*]

70   SPEED Sir Proteus, save you! Saw you my master?

PROTEUS But now he parted hence, to embark for
         Milan.

SPEED Twenty to one, then, he is shipped already,
       And I have played the sheep in losing him.

PROTEUS Indeed, a sheep doth very often stray,
75   And if the shepherd be awhile away.

SPEED You conclude that my master is a shepherd,
       then, and I a sheep?

PROTEUS I do.

SPEED Why then, my horns are his horns, whether I
80   wake or sleep.

PROTEUS A silly answer, and fitting well a sheep.

SPEED This proves me still a sheep.

PROTEUS True, and thy master a shepherd.

SPEED Nay, that I can deny by a circumstance.

85   PROTEUS It shall go hard but I'll prove it by another.

SPEED The shepherd seeks the sheep, and not the
       sheep the shepherd; but I seek my master, and my
       master seeks not me. Therefore I am no sheep.

PROTEUS The sheep for fodder follow the shepherd;
90   the shepherd for food follows not the sheep; thou
         for wages followest thy master, thy master for
         wages follows not thee. Therefore thou art a sheep.

SPEED Such another proof will make me cry "baa."

PROTEUS But, dost thou hear? Gav'st thou my letter to
95   Julia?

---

70 **save you** (a greeting)   73 **sheep** (pun on "ship")   75 **And if** if   79 **my horns are his horns** i.e., my (sheep's) horns belong to him (making him a cuckold)   84 **circumstance** logical proof

SPEED Ay, sir: I, a lost mutton, gave your letter to her, a laced mutton, and she, a laced mutton, gave me, a lost mutton, nothing for my labor.

PROTEUS Here's too small a pasture for such store of muttons.   100

SPEED If the ground be overcharged, you were best stick her.

PROTEUS Nay, in that you are astray; 'twere best pound you.

SPEED Nay, sir, less than a pound shall serve me for   105
carrying your letter.

PROTEUS You mistake. I mean the pound—a pinfold.

SPEED From a pound to a pin? Fold it over and over, 'Tis threefold too little for carrying a letter to your lover.

PROTEUS But what said she?   110

SPEED [Nodding] Ay.

PROTEUS Nod—ay. Why, that's noddy.

SPEED You mistook, sir. I say she did nod; and you ask me if she did nod, and I say, "Ay."

PROTEUS And that set together is noddy.   115

SPEED Now you have taken the pains to set it together, take it for your pains.

PROTEUS No, no. You shall have it for bearing the letter.

SPEED Well, I perceive I must be fain to bear with you.   120

PROTEUS Why, sir, how do you bear with me?

96–97 **lost mutton ... laced mutton** i.e., lost sheep and laced courtesan (probably "lost" and "laced" were similarly pronounced) 101 **overcharged** overgrazed 102 **stick** stab (slaughter) 104 **pound** impound (with pun) 112 **noddy** fool

SPEED Marry, sir, the letter, very orderly; having nothing but the word "noddy" for my pains.

125 PROTEUS Beshrew me, but you have a quick wit.

SPEED And yet it cannot overtake your slow purse.

PROTEUS Come, come, open the matter in brief. What said she?

SPEED Open your purse, that the money and the mat-
130 ter may be both at once delivered.

PROTEUS Well, sir, here is for your pains. What said she?

SPEED Truly, sir, I think you'll hardly win her.

PROTEUS Why, couldst thou perceive so much from
135 her?

SPEED Sir, I could perceive nothing at all from her; no, not so much as a ducat for delivering your letter. And being so hard to me that brought your mind, I fear she'll prove as hard to you in telling your
140 mind. Give her no token but stones; for she's as hard as steel.

PROTEUS What said she? Nothing?

SPEED No, not so much as "Take this for thy pains." To testify your bounty, I thank you, you have tes-
145 terned me; in requital whereof, henceforth carry your letters yourself. And so, sir, I'll commend you to my master.

PROTEUS Go, go, be gone, to save your ship from wrack, Which cannot perish, having thee aboard,
150 Being destined to a drier death on shore.
                                              [*Exit Speed.*]

---

123 **Marry** by the Virgin Mary (a casual oath)   125 **Beshrew** curse (used casually)   140 **stones** (in addition to punning on its meanings of "jewels" and "worthless gifts," Speed may be punning on another meaning, "testicles")
144-45 **testerned me** i.e., given me a testern (sixpence)   150 **Being destined ... shore** i.e., being destined to hang

I must go send some better messenger;
I fear my Julia would not deign my lines,
Receiving them from such a worthless post.   *Exit.*

Scene II. [*Verona. Julia's house.*]

Enter Julia and Lucetta.

JULIA But say, Lucetta, now we are alone,
　　Wouldst thou, then, counsel me to fall in love?

LUCETTA Ay, madam; so you stumble not unheedfully.

JULIA Of all the fair resort of gentlemen
　　That every day with parle encounter me,　　　　　5
　　In thy opinion which is worthiest love?

LUCETTA Please you repeat their names, I'll show my
　　　　mind
　　According to my shallow simple skill.

JULIA What think'st thou of the fair Sir Eglamour?

LUCETTA As of a knight well-spoken, neat, and fine;　　10
　　But, were I you, he never should be mine.

JULIA What think'st thou of the rich Mercatio?

LUCETTA Well of his wealth; but of himself, so so.

JULIA What think'st thou of the gentle Proteus?

LUCETTA Lord, Lord! To see what folly reigns in us!　　15

JULIA How now! What means this passion at his
　　　　name?

LUCETTA Pardon, dear madam; 'tis a passing shame
　　That I, unworthy body as I am,
　　Should censure thus on lovely gentlemen.

153 **post** messenger   I.ii.4 **resort of gentlemen** crowd of suitors   5 **parle** parley
16 **passion** emotion   17 **passing** surpassing   19 **censure** pass judgment

20 JULIA Why not on Proteus, as of all the rest?

LUCETTA Then thus: of many good I think him best.

JULIA Your reason?

LUCETTA I have no other but a woman's reason:
I think him so because I think him so.

25 JULIA And wouldst thou have me cast my love on him?

LUCETTA Ay, if you thought your love not cast away.

JULIA Why, he, of all the rest, hath never moved me.

LUCETTA Yet he, of all the rest, I think, best loves ye.

JULIA His little speaking shows his love but small.

30 LUCETTA Fire that's closest kept burns most of all.

JULIA They do not love that do not show their love.

LUCETTA O, they love least that let men know their love.

JULIA I would I knew his mind.

LUCETTA Peruse this paper, madam.

35 JULIA "To Julia."—Say, from whom?

LUCETTA That the contents will show.

JULIA Say, say, who gave it thee?

LUCETTA Sir Valentine's page; and sent, I think, from
Proteus.
He would have given it you; but I, being in the way,
40 Did in your name receive it. Pardon the fault, I pray.

JULIA Now, by my modesty, a goodly broker!
Dare you presume to harbor wanton lines?
To whisper and conspire against my youth?
Now, trust me, 'tis an office of great worth,
45 And you an officer fit for the place.
There, take the paper; see it be returned,
Or else return no more into my sight.

27 moved i.e., proposed to   41 broker go-between

LUCETTA To plead for love deserves more fee than hate.

JULIA Will ye be gone?

LUCETTA   That you may ruminate.   *Exit*.

JULIA And yet I would I had o'erlooked the letter.   50
It were a shame to call her back again,
And pray her to a fault for which I chid her.
What fool is she, that knows I am a maid,
And would not force the letter to my view!
Since maids, in modesty, say "no" to that   55
Which they would have the profferer construe "ay."
Fie, fie, how wayward is this foolish love,
That, like a testy babe, will scratch the nurse,
And presently, all humbled, kiss the rod!
How churlishly I chid Lucetta hence,   60
When willingly I would have had her here!
How angerly I taught my brow to frown,
When inward joy enforced my heart to smile!
My penance is to call Lucetta back
And ask remission for my folly past.   65
What, ho! Lucetta!

[Enter Lucetta.]

LUCETTA   What would your ladyship?

JULIA Is't near dinnertime?

LUCETTA   I would it were;
That you might kill your stomach on your meat,
And not upon your maid.

JULIA What is't that you took up so gingerly?   70

LUCETTA Nothing.

JULIA Why didst thou stoop, then?

LUCETTA To take a paper up that I let fall.

---

50 o'erlooked perused   52 pray her to apologize to her for   58 testy irritable
59 **presently** immediately   68 **kill your stomach** (1) allay your vexation
(2) appease your hunger   68-69 **meat . . . maid** (pun on "mate")

JULIA And is that paper nothing?

75 LUCETTA Nothing concerning me.

JULIA Then let it lie for those that it concerns.

LUCETTA Madam, it will not lie where it concerns,
Unless it have a false interpreter.

JULIA Some love of yours hath writ to you in rhyme.

80 LUCETTA That I might sing it, madam, to a tune.
Give me a note: your ladyship can set.

JULIA As little by such toys as may be possible.
Best sing it to the tune of "Light o' love."

LUCETTA It is too heavy for so light a tune.

85 JULIA Heavy! Belike it hath some burden, then?

LUCETTA Ay, and melodious were it, would you sing it.

JULIA And why not you?

LUCETTA   I cannot reach so high.

JULIA Let's see your song. [*Takes the letter.*] How now,
minion!

LUCETTA Keep tune there still, so you will sing it out:
90 And yet methinks I do not like this tune.

JULIA You do not?

LUCETTA   No, madam; 'tis too sharp.

JULIA You, minion, are too saucy.

LUCETTA Nay, now you are too flat,
And mar the concord with too harsh a descant.
95 There wanteth but a mean to fill your song.

JULIA The mean is drowned with your unruly bass.

---

77 **lie where it concerns** i.e., express its content falsely (with quibble on preceding line) 81 **set** set to music 82 **toys** trifles 83 **Light o' love** a contemporary popular ditty 85 **burden** bass refrain (with pun) 94 **descant** improvised harmony 95 **wanteth but a mean** lacks a tenor part (Proteus?)

LUCETTA Indeed, I bid the base for Proteus.

JULIA This babble shall not henceforth trouble me.
   Here is a coil with protestation!   [*Tears the letter.*]
   Go get you gone, and let the papers lie;   100
   You would be fing'ring them, to anger me.

LUCETTA She makes it strange; but she would be best
    pleased
   To be so ang'red with another letter.   [*Exit.*]

JULIA Nay, would I were so ang'red with the same!
   O hateful hands, to tear such loving words!   105
   Injurious wasps, to feed on such sweet honey,
   And kill the bees, that yield it, with your stings!
   I'll kiss each several paper for amends.
   Look, here is writ "kind Julia." Unkind Julia!
   As in revenge of thy ingratitude,   110
   I throw thy name against the bruising stones,
   Trampling contemptuously on thy disdain.
   And here is writ "love-wounded Proteus."
   Poor wounded name! My bosom, as a bed,
   Shall lodge thee, till thy wound be throughly
    healed;   115
   And thus I search it with a sovereign kiss.
   But twice or thrice was "Proteus" written down.
   Be calm, good wind, blow not a word away
   Till I have found each letter in the letter,
   Except mine own name: that some whirlwind bear   120
   Unto a ragged, fearful-hanging rock,
   And throw it thence into the raging sea!
   Lo, here in one line is his name twice writ,
   "Poor forlorn Proteus, passionate Proteus,
   To the sweet Julia." That I'll tear away.—   125
   And yet I will not, sith so prettily
   He couples it to his complaining names.

97 bid the base (in the game of Prisoner's Base, a challenge to a test of speed
[with pun]) 99 coil with protestation much ado made up of lover's protestations
102 makes it strange i.e., pretends that it is nothing to her 108 several separate
115 throughly thoroughly 116 search probe (as in cleaning a wound)
126 sith since

Thus will I fold them one upon another.
Now kiss, embrace, contend, do what you will.

[*Enter Lucetta.*]

130 LUCETTA Madam,
Dinner is ready, and your father stays.

JULIA Well, let us go.

LUCETTA What, shall these papers lie like telltales here?

JULIA If you respect them, best to take them up.

135 LUCETTA Nay, I was taken up for laying them down;
Yet here they shall not lie, for catching cold.

JULIA I see you have a month's mind to them.

LUCETTA Ay, madam, you may say what sights you see;
I see things too, although you judge I wink.

140 JULIA Come, come; will't please you go?   *Exeunt.*

Scene III. [*Verona. Antonio's house.*]

Enter Antonio and Panthino.

ANTONIO Tell me, Panthino, what sad talk was that
Wherewith my brother held you in the cloister?

PANTHINO 'Twas of his nephew Proteus, your son.

ANTONIO Why, what of him?

PANTHINO   He wond'red that your lordship
5   Would suffer him to spend his youth at home,
While other men, of slender reputation,
Put forth their sons to seek preferment out:

137 **month's mind** i.e., lasting desire   139 **wink** have my eyes shut, see nothing
I.iii.1 **sad** serious   6 **slender reputation** unimportant place

Some to the wars, to try their fortune there,
Some to discover islands far away,
Some to the studious universities.   10
For any, or for all these exercises,
He said that Proteus your son was meet,
And did request me to importune you
To let him spend his time no more at home,
Which would be great impeachment to his age,   15
In having known no travel in his youth.

ANTONIO Nor need'st thou much importune me to that
Whereon this month I have been hammering.
I have considered well his loss of time,
And how he cannot be a perfect man,   20
Not being tried and tutored in the world.
Experience is by industry achieved,
And perfected by the swift course of time.
Then, tell me, whither were I best to send him?

PANTHINO I think your lordship is not ignorant   25
How his companion, youthful Valentine,
Attends the Emperor in his royal court.

ANTONIO I know it well.

PANTHINO 'Twere good, I think, your lordship sent him
    thither.
There shall he practice tilts and tournaments,   30
Hear sweet discourse, converse with noblemen,
And be in eye of every exercise
Worthy his youth and nobleness of birth.

ANTONIO I like thy counsel; well hast thou advised.
And that thou mayst perceive how well I like it,   35
The execution of it shall make known.
Even with the speediest expedition
I will dispatch him to the Emperor's court.

PANTHINO Tomorrow, may it please you,
    Don Alphonso,

12 meet fitted 15 impeachment detriment 18 hammering i.e., pondering
23 perfected (accented on first syllable) 27 Emperor i.e., Duke (of Milan)
32 be in eye of have sight of 37 expedition haste

40   With other gentlemen of good esteem,
      Are journeying to salute the Emperor,
      And to commend their service to his will.

ANTONIO Good company; with them shall Proteus go.
      And—in good time! Now will we break with him.

[*Enter Proteus.*]

45 PROTEUS Sweet love! Sweet lines! Sweet life!
      Here is her hand, the agent of her heart.
      Here is her oath for love, her honor's pawn.
      O, that our fathers would applaud our loves,
      To seal our happiness with their consents!
50   O heavenly Julia!

ANTONIO How now! What letter are you reading there?

PROTEUS May't please your lordship, 'tis a word or two
      Of commendations sent from Valentine,
      Delivered by a friend that came from him.

55 ANTONIO Lend me the letter; let me see what news.

PROTEUS There is no news, my lord, but that he writes
      How happily he lives, how well beloved
      And daily gracèd by the Emperor,
      Wishing me with him, partner of his fortune.

60 ANTONIO And how stand you affected to his wish?

PROTEUS As one relying on your lordship's will,
      And not depending on his friendly wish.

ANTONIO My will is something sorted with his wish.
      Muse not that I thus suddenly proceed,
65   For what I will, I will, and there an end.
      I am resolved that thou shalt spend some time
      With Valentinus in the Emperor's court.
      What maintenance he from his friends receives,
      Like exhibition thou shalt have from me.
70   Tomorrow be in readiness to go.

44 **break with** break the news to   47 **pawn** pledge   53 **commendations** greetings
63 **something sorted** somewhat in accord   69 **exhibition** allowance

Excuse it not, for I am peremptory.

PROTEUS My lord, I cannot be so soon provided.
Please you, deliberate a day or two.

ANTONIO Look what thou want'st shall be sent after
thee.
No more of stay! Tomorrow thou must go.   75
Come on, Panthino; you shall be employed
To hasten on his expedition.
                    [*Exeunt Antonio and Panthino.*]

PROTEUS Thus have I shunned the fire for fear of
burning,
And drenched me in the sea, where I am drowned.
I feared to show my father Julia's letter,   80
Lest he should take exceptions to my love;
And with the vantage of mine own excuse
Hath he expected most against my love.
O, how this spring of love resembleth
The uncertain glory of an April day,   85
Which now shows all the beauty of the sun,
And by and by a cloud takes all away!

                [*Enter Panthino.*]

PANTHINO Sir Proteus, your father calls for you.
He is in haste; therefore, I pray you, go.

PROTEUS Why, this it is: my heart accords thereto,   90
And yet a thousand times it answers "no."   *Exeunt.*

---

71 **Excuse it not** offer no excuses   71 **peremptory** determined   74 **Look what**
whatever   82-83 **with the vantage ... my love** i.e., he took advantage of my
own device (the pretended letter from Valentine) to strike the heaviest blow to my
affair of love (with Julia)

ACT II

Scene I. [*Milan. The Duke's palace.*]

Enter Valentine [and] Speed.

SPEED Sir, your glove.

VALENTINE Not mine; my gloves are on.

SPEED Why, then, this may be yours, for this is but
one.

VALENTINE Ha, let me see. Ay, give it me, it's mine.
Sweet ornament that decks a thing divine!
5 Ah, Silvia, Silvia!

SPEED Madam Silvia! Madam Silvia!

VALENTINE How now, sirrah?

SPEED She is not within hearing, sir.

VALENTINE Why, sir, who bade you call her?

10 SPEED Your worship, sir, or else I mistook.

VALENTINE Well, you'll still be too forward.

SPEED And yet I was last chidden for being too slow.

VALENTINE Go to, sir. Tell me, do you know Madam
Silvia?

II.i.1–2 **on ... one** (a pun in Elizabethan speech) 7 **sirrah** (common form of
address to inferiors) 11 **still** always

SPEED She that your worship loves?   15

VALENTINE Why, how know you that I am in love?

SPEED Marry, by these special marks: first, you have
learned, like Sir Proteus, to wreathe your arms, like
a malcontent; to relish a love song, like a robin red-
breast; to walk alone, like one that had the pesti-   20
lence; to sigh, like a schoolboy that had lost his
ABC; to weep, like a young wench that had buried
her grandam; to fast, like one that takes diet; to
watch, like one that fears robbing; to speak puling,
like a beggar at Hallowmas. You were wont, when   25
you laughed, to crow like a cock; when you walked,
to walk like one of the lions; when you fasted, it
was presently after dinner; when you looked sadly,
it was for want of money. And now you are metamorphized with a mistress, that, when I look on   30
you, I can hardly think you my master.

VALENTINE Are all these things perceived in me?

SPEED They are all perceived without ye.

VALENTINE Without me? They cannot.

SPEED Without you? Nay, that's certain, for, without   35
you were so simple, none else would. But you are
so without these follies, that these follies are within
you, and shine through you like the water in an
urinal, that not an eye that sees you but is a physi-
cian to comment on your malady.   40

VALENTINE But tell me, dost thou know my lady Silvia?

SPEED She that you gaze on so as she sits at supper?

VALENTINE Hast thou observed that? Even she, I mean.

SPEED Why, sir, I know her not.

---

24 **watch** lie awake   24 **puling** whiningly   25 **at Hallowmas** on All Saints' Day
(when beggars vied for special treats)   30 **that** so that   33 **without ye** i.e., by
external signs (here begins a series of quibbles)   35 **without** unless

45   VALENTINE Dost thou know her by my gazing on her,
     and yet know'st her not?

     SPEED Is she not hard-favored, sir?

     VALENTINE Not so fair, boy, as well-favored.

     SPEED Sir, I know that well enough.

50   VALENTINE What dost thou know?

     SPEED That she is not so fair as, of you, well favored.

     VALENTINE I mean that her beauty is exquisite, but her
     favor infinite.

     SPEED That's because the one is painted, and the other
55   out of all count.

     VALENTINE How painted? And how out of count?

     SPEED Marry, sir, so painted, to make her fair, that
     no man counts of her beauty.

     VALENTINE How esteem'st thou me? I account of her
60   beauty.

     SPEED You never saw her since she was deformed.

     VALENTINE How long hath she been deformed?

     SPEED Ever since you loved her.

     VALENTINE I have loved her ever since I saw her; and
65   still I see her beautiful.

     SPEED If you love her, you cannot see her.

     VALENTINE Why?

     SPEED Because Love is blind. O, that you had mine
     eyes; or your own eyes had the lights they were wont
70   to have when you chid at Sir Proteus for going
     ungartered!

---

47 **hard-favored** homely   53 **favor** charm, graciousness   55 **out of all count**
beyond counting   58 **counts of** takes account of   61 **deformed** i.e., distorted by
your lover's view   70–71 **going ungartered** (a sure sign that one is in love; see *As
You Like It*, III.ii.371)

VALENTINE What should I see then?

SPEED Your own present folly, and her passing de-
  formity. For he, being in love, could not see to
  garter his hose; and you, being in love, cannot see   75
  to put on your hose.

VALENTINE Belike, boy, then, you are in love; for last
  morning you could not see to wipe my shoes.

SPEED True, sir; I was in love with my bed. I thank
  you, you swinged me for my love, which makes   80
  me the bolder to chide you for yours.

VALENTINE In conclusion, I stand affected to her.

SPEED I would you were set, so your affection would
  cease.

VALENTINE Last night she enjoined me to write some   85
  lines to one she loves.

SPEED And have you?

VALENTINE I have.

SPEED Are they not lamely writ?

VALENTINE No, boy, but as well as I can do them.   90
  Peace! Here she comes.

SPEED [*Aside*] O excellent motion! O exceeding puppet! Now will he interpret to her.

[*Enter Silvia.*]

VALENTINE Madam and mistress, a thousand good
  morrows.   95

SPEED [*Aside*] O, give ye good ev'n! Here's a million
  of manners.

SILVIA Sir Valentine and servant, to you two thousand.

73 **passing** surpassing, extreme   80 **swinged** beat   83 **set** seated (quibble on
"stand")   92–93 **motion . . . puppet . . . interpret** (the puppeteer's voice "inter-
prets" for the figures in the puppet play, or "motion")   98 **servant** gallant lover
(i.e., alludes not to Speed but to Valentine)

SPEED [*Aside*] He should give her interest, and she
100 gives it him.

VALENTINE As you enjoined me, I have writ your letter
Unto the secret nameless friend of yours,
Which I was much unwilling to proceed in,
But for my duty to your ladyship.

SILVIA I thank you, gentle servant; 'tis very clerkly
105 done.

VALENTINE Now trust me, madam, it came hardly off;
For, being ignorant to whom it goes,
I writ at random, very doubtfully.

SILVIA Perchance you think too much of so much
pains?

110 VALENTINE No, madam; so it stead you, I will write,
Please you command, a thousand times as much.
And yet—

SILVIA A pretty period! Well, I guess the sequel;
And yet I will not name it; and yet I care not;
115 And yet take this again; and yet I thank you,
Meaning henceforth to trouble you no more.

SPEED [*Aside*] And yet you will; and yet another "yet."

VALENTINE What means your ladyship? Do you not
like it?

SILVIA Yes, yes: the lines are very quaintly writ;
120 But since unwillingly, take them again.
Nay, take them.

VALENTINE Madam, they are for you.

SILVIA Ay, ay. You writ them, sir, at my request;
But I will none of them; they are for you;
125 I would have had them writ more movingly.

VALENTINE Please you, I'll write your ladyship another.

SILVIA And when it's writ, for my sake read it over,

105 **clerkly** scholarly   110 **stead** be useful to   113 **period** full stop
119 **quaintly** ingeniously

And if it please you, so; if not, why, so.

VALENTINE If it please me, madam, what then?

SILVIA Why, if it please you, take it for your labor;   130
And so, good morrow, servant.   *Exit Silvia.*

SPEED O jest unseen, inscrutable, invisible,
As a nose on a man's face, or a weathercock on a
steeple!
My master sues to her, and she hath taught her
suitor,
He being her pupil, to become her tutor.   135
O excellent device! Was there ever heard a better,
That my master, being scribe, to himself should
write the letter?

VALENTINE How now, sir? What are you reasoning with
yourself?

SPEED Nay, I was rhyming; 'tis you that have the   140
reason.

VALENTINE To do what?

SPEED To be spokesman from Madam Silvia.

VALENTINE To whom?

SPEED To yourself. Why, she woos you by a figure.   145

VALENTINE What figure?

SPEED By a letter, I should say.

VALENTINE Why, she hath not writ to me?

SPEED What need she, when she hath made you write
to yourself? Why, do you not perceive the jest?   150

VALENTINE No, believe me.

SPEED No believing you, indeed, sir. But did you
perceive her earnest?

VALENTINE She gave me none, except an angry word.

145 **by a figure** by indirect means   153 **earnest** (1) seriousness (2) token
payment

155 SPEED Why, she hath given you a letter.

VALENTINE That's the letter I writ to her friend.

SPEED And that letter hath she delivered, and there
an end.

VALENTINE I would it were no worse.

160 SPEED I'll warrant you, 'tis as well;
For often have you writ to her, and she, in modesty,
Or else for want of idle time, could not again reply;
Or fearing else some messenger that might her mind
discover,
Herself have taught her love himself to write unto
her lover.
165 All this I speak in print, for in print I found it.
Why muse you, sir? 'Tis dinnertime.

VALENTINE I have dined.

SPEED Ay, but hearken, sir; though the chameleon
Love can feed on the air, I am one that am nour-
170 ished by my victuals, and would fain have meat. O,
be not like your mistress; be moved, be moved.

Exeunt.

Scene II. [*Verona. Julia's house.*]

Enter Proteus [and] Julia.

PROTEUS Have patience, gentle Julia.

JULIA I must, where is no remedy.

PROTEUS When possibly I can, I will return.

---

163 **discover** reveal   165 **speak in print** i.e., quote   168–69 **chameleon ... the
air** (the chameleon was thought to eat nothing but air; see also II.iv.24–26 and
Hamlet III.ii.95)

JULIA If you turn not, you will return the sooner.
  Keep this remembrance for thy Julia's sake.   5
                                     [Giving a ring.]

PROTEUS Why, then, we'll make exchange; here, take
  you this.

JULIA And seal the bargain with a holy kiss.

PROTEUS Here is my hand for my true constancy;
  And when that hour o'erslips me in the day
  Wherein I sigh not, Julia, for thy sake,   10
  The next ensuing hour some foul mischance
  Torment me for my love's forgetfulness!
  My father stays my coming; answer not;
  The tide is now:—nay, not thy tide of tears;
  That tide will stay me longer than I should.   15
  Julia, farewell!   *[Exit Julia.]*
          What, gone without a word?
  Ay, so true love should do: it cannot speak;
  For truth hath better deeds than words to grace it.

                [Enter Panthino.]

PANTHINO Sir Proteus, you are stayed for.

PROTEUS Go; I come, I come.   20
  Alas! This parting strikes poor lovers dumb. *Exeunt.*

            Scene III. [*Verona. A street.*]

          Enter Launce, [leading a dog].

LAUNCE Nay, 'twill be this hour ere I have done weeping; all the kind of the Launces have this very fault.
  I have received my proportion, like the prodigious

II.ii.4 **turn** i.e., change your affection (perhaps with the additional meaning of
"engage in sexual acts")   13 **stays** waits for   III.iii.3 **proportion** (Launce's
blunder for "portion")   3 **prodigious** (blunder for "prodigal")

5   son, and am going with Sir Proteus to the Imperial's
court. I think Crab my dog be the sourest-natured
dog that lives. My mother weeping, my father wailing, my sister crying, our maid howling, our cat
wringing her hands, and all our house in a great
perplexity, yet did not this cruel-hearted cur shed
10   one tear. He is a stone, a very pebble stone, and
has no more pity in him than a dog. A Jew would
have wept to have seen our parting. Why, my
grandam, having no eyes, look you, wept herself
blind at my parting. Nay, I'll show you the manner
15   of it. This shoe is my father; no, this left shoe is
my father. No, no, this left shoe is my mother; nay,
that cannot be so neither. Yes, it is so, it is so, it
hath the worser sole. This shoe, with the hole in it,
is my mother, and this my father; a vengeance on't!
20   There 'tis. Now, sir, this staff is my sister, for, look
you, she is as white as a lily, and as small as a
wand. This hat is Nan, our maid. I am the dog. No,
the dog is himself, and I am the dog. Oh! The dog
is me, and I am myself; ay, so, so. Now come I to
25   my father: Father, your blessing. Now should not
the shoe speak a word for weeping: now should I
kiss my father: well, he weeps on. Now come I to
my mother. Oh, that she could speak now like a
wood woman! Well, I kiss her; why, there 'tis.
30   Here's my mother's breath up and down. Now
come I to my sister; mark the moan she makes.
Now the dog all this while sheds not a tear, nor
speaks a word; but see how I lay the dust with my
tears.

[Enter Panthino.]

35   PANTHINO Launce, away, away, aboard! Thy master is
shipped, and thou art to post after with oars. What's
the matter? Why weep'st thou, man? Away, ass!
You'll lose the tide, if you tarry any longer.

28-29 **Oh, that ... wood woman** (Launce laments that his [wooden] shoe is not
really his mother, madly distressed [wood] as she was at parting)   30 **up and
down** identically

LAUNCE It is no matter if the tied were lost; for it is
the unkindest tied that ever any man tied.   40

PANTHINO What's the unkindest tide?

LAUNCE Why, he that's tied here, Crab, my dog.

PANTHINO Tut, man, I mean thou'lt lose the flood,
and, in losing the flood, lose thy voyage, and, in
losing thy voyage, lose thy master, and, in losing   45
thy master, lose thy service, and, in losing thy service— Why dost thou stop my mouth?

LAUNCE For fear thou shouldst lose thy tongue.

PANTHINO Where should I lose my tongue?

LAUNCE In thy tale.   50

PANTHINO In thy tail!

LAUNCE Lose the tide, and the voyage, and the master,
and the service, and the tied! Why, man, if the river
were dry, I am able to fill it with my tears; if the
wind were down, I could drive the boat with my   55
sighs.

PANTHINO Come, come away, man; I was sent to call
thee.

LAUNCE Sir, call me what thou dar'st.

PANTHINO Wilt thou go?   60

LAUNCE Well, I will go.   *Exeunt.*

Scene IV. [*Milan. The Duke's palace.*]

Enter Valentine, Silvia, Thurio, [and] Speed.

SILVIA Servant!

VALENTINE Mistress?

43 **flood** full tide

SPEED Master, Sir Thurio frowns on you.

VALENTINE Ay, boy, it's for love.

5 SPEED Not of you.

VALENTINE Of my mistress, then.

SPEED 'Twere good you knocked him.   [*Exit.*]

SILVIA Servant, you are sad.

VALENTINE Indeed, madam, I seem so.

10 THURIO Seem you that you are not?

VALENTINE Haply I do.

THURIO So do counterfeits.

VALENTINE So do you.

THURIO What seem I that I am not?

15 VALENTINE Wise.

THURIO What instance of the contrary?

VALENTINE Your folly.

THURIO And how quote you my folly?

VALENTINE I quote it in your jerkin.

20 THURIO My jerkin is a doublet.

VALENTINE Well, then, I'll double your folly.

THURIO How?

SILVIA What, angry, Sir Thurio! Do you change color?

VALENTINE Give him leave, madam; he is a kind of
25   chameleon.

THURIO That hath more mind to feed on your blood
    than live in your air.

VALENTINE You have said, sir.

II.iv.18 **quote** observe (pronounced "coat")   20 **doublet** close-fitting jacket

THURIO Ay, sir, and done too, for this time.

VALENTINE I know it well, sir; you always end ere you   30
  begin.

SILVIA A fine volley of words, gentlemen, and quickly
  shot off.

VALENTINE 'Tis indeed, madam; we thank the giver.

SILVIA Who is that, servant?   35

VALENTINE Yourself, sweet lady; for you gave the fire.
  Sir Thurio borrows his wit from your ladyship's
  looks, and spends what he borrows kindly in your
  company.

THURIO Sir, if you spend word for word with me, I   40
  shall make your wit bankrupt.

VALENTINE I know it well, sir. You have an exchequer
  of words, and, I think, no other treasure to give
  your followers, for it appears by their bare liveries
  that they live by your bare words.   45

SILVIA No more, gentlemen, no more—here comes my
  father.

[*Enter Duke.*]

DUKE Now, daughter Silvia, you are hard beset.
  Sir Valentine, your father's in good health.
  What say you to a letter from your friends   50
  Of much good news?

VALENTINE   My lord, I will be thankful
  To any happy messenger from thence.

DUKE Know ye Don Antonio, your countryman?

VALENTINE Ay, my good lord, I know the gentleman
  To be of worth, and worthy estimation,   55
  And not without desert so well reputed.

DUKE Hath he not a son?

44 bare threadbare   52 happy messenger i.e., bringer of good news

VALENTINE Ay, my good lord, a son that well deserves
The honor and regard of such a father.

60 DUKE You know him well?

VALENTINE I knew him as myself; for from our infancy
We have conversed and spent our hours together;
And though myself have been an idle truant,
Omitting the sweet benefit of time
65   To clothe mine age with angel-like perfection,
Yet hath Sir Proteus, for that's his name,
Made use and fair advantage of his days;
His years but young, but his experience old;
His head unmellowed, but his judgment ripe.
70   And, in a word, for far behind his worth
Comes all the praises that I now bestow,
He is complete in feature and in mind
With all good grace to grace a gentleman.

DUKE Beshrew me, sir, but if he make this good,
75   He is as worthy for an empress' love
As meet to be an emperor's counselor.
Well, sir, this gentleman is come to me
With commendation from great potentates,
And here he means to spend his time awhile.
80 I think 'tis no unwelcome news to you.

VALENTINE Should I have wished a thing, it had been he.

DUKE Welcome him, then, according to his worth.
Silvia, I speak to you, and you, Sir Thurio;
For Valentine, I need not cite him to it.
85 I will send him hither to you presently.   [*Exit.*]

VALENTINE This is the gentleman I told your ladyship
Had come along with me, but that his mistress
Did hold his eyes locked in her crystal looks.

SILVIA Belike that now she hath enfranchised them,
90   Upon some other pawn for fealty.

---

76 **meet** fitted   84 **cite** incite, urge   90 **pawn for fealty** pledge for loyalty

VALENTINE Nay, sure, I think she holds them prisoners
    still.

SILVIA Nay, then, he should be blind; and, being blind,
    How could he see his way to seek out you?

VALENTINE Why, lady, Love hath twenty pair of eyes.

THURIO They say that Love hath not an eye at all.   95

VALENTINE To see such lovers, Thurio, as yourself.
    Upon a homely object Love can wink. [*Exit Thurio.*]

SILVIA Have done, have done; here comes the gentle-
    man.

[*Enter Proteus.*]

VALENTINE Welcome, dear Proteus! Mistress, I beseech
    you,
    Confirm his welcome with some special favor.   100

SILVIA His worth is warrant for his welcome hither,
    If this be he you oft have wished to hear from.

VALENTINE Mistress, it is. Sweet lady, entertain him
    To be my fellow servant to your ladyship.

SILVIA Too low a mistress for so high a servant.   105

PROTEUS Not so, sweet lady, but too mean a servant
    To have a look of such a worthy mistress.

VALENTINE Leave off discourse of disability.
    Sweet lady, entertain him for your servant.

PROTEUS My duty will I boast of, nothing else.   110

SILVIA And duty never yet did want his meed.
    Servant, you are welcome to a worthless mistress.

PROTEUS I'll die on him that says so but yourself.

SILVIA That you are welcome?

103 entertain welcome   106 mean low, humble   108 Leave ... disability i.e.,
cease this modest talk   111 want his meed lack its reward   113 die on fight to
the death

PROTEUS   That you are worthless.

[*Enter Thurio.*]

SERVANT Madam, my lord your father would speak
115   with you.

SILVIA I wait upon his pleasure. [*Exit Servant.*] Come,
    Sir Thurio,
    Go with me. Once more, new servant, welcome.
    I'll leave you to confer of home affairs.
    When you have done, we look to hear from you.

120 PROTEUS We'll both attend upon your ladyship.
                          [*Exeunt Silvia and Thurio.*]

VALENTINE Now, tell me, how do all from whence you
    came?

PROTEUS Your friends are well, and have them much
    commended.

VALENTINE And how do yours?

PROTEUS   I left them all in health.

VALENTINE How does your lady? And how thrives your
    love?

125 PROTEUS My tales of love were wont to weary you;
    I know you joy not in a love discourse.

VALENTINE Ay, Proteus, but that life is altered now.
    I have done penance for contemning Love,
    Whose high imperious thoughts have punished me
130   With bitter fasts, with penitential groans,
    With nightly tears, and daily heartsore sighs;
    For, in revenge of my contempt of love,
    Love hath chased sleep from my enthrallèd eyes,
    And made them watchers of mine own heart's
    sorrow.
135   O gentle Proteus, Love's a mighty lord,
    And hath so humbled me, as I confess

122 have them much commended i.e., themselves to you   136 as that

There is no woe to his correction,
Nor to his service no such joy on earth.
Now no discourse, except it be of love;
Now can I break my fast, dine, sup, and sleep   140
Upon the very naked name of love.

PROTEUS Enough; I read your fortune in your eye.
Was this the idol that you worship so?

VALENTINE Even she; and is she not a heavenly saint?

PROTEUS No; but she is an earthly paragon.   145

VALENTINE Call her divine.

PROTEUS   I will not flatter her.

VALENTINE O, flatter me, for love delights in praises.

PROTEUS When I was sick, you gave me bitter pills,
And I must minister the like to you.

VALENTINE Then speak the truth by her; if not divine,   150
Yet let her be a principality,
Sovereign to all the creatures on the earth.

PROTEUS Except my mistress.

VALENTINE   Sweet, except not any,
Except thou wilt except against my love.

PROTEUS Have I not reason to prefer mine own?   155

VALENTINE And I will help thee to prefer her too.
She shall be dignified with this high honor—
To bear my lady's train, lest the base earth
Should from her vesture chance to steal a kiss,
And, of so great a favor growing proud,   160
Disdain to root the summer-swelling flow'r,
And make rough winter everlastingly.

PROTEUS Why, Valentine, what braggardism is this?

VALENTINE Pardon me, Proteus. All I can is nothing

137 to like unto   154 Except thou wilt except against unless you will take
exception to   156 prefer advance

165   To her, whose worth makes other worthies nothing;
        She is alone.

PROTEUS   Then let her alone.

VALENTINE Not for the world. Why, man, she is mine
            own,
        And I as rich in having such a jewel
        As twenty seas, if all their sand were pearl,
170   The water nectar, and the rocks pure gold.
        Forgive me that I do not dream on thee,
        Because thou see'st me dote upon my love.
        My foolish rival, that her father likes
        Only for his possessions are so huge,
175   Is gone with her along; and I must after,
        For love, thou know'st, is full of jealousy.

PROTEUS But she loves you?

VALENTINE Ay, and we are betrothed; nay, more, our
            marriage hour,
        With all the cunning manner of our flight,
180   Determined of: how I must climb her window,
        The ladder made of cords, and all the means
        Plotted and 'greed on for my happiness.
        Good Proteus, go with me to my chamber,
        In these affairs to aid me with thy counsel.

185 PROTEUS Go on before; I shall inquire you forth.
        I must unto the road, to disembark
        Some necessaries that I needs must use,
        And then I'll presently attend you.

VALENTINE Will you make haste?

190 PROTEUS I will.   *Exit* [*Valentine*].
        Even as one heat another heat expels,
        Or as one nail by strength drives out another,
        So the remembrance of my former love
        Is by a newer object quite forgotten.
195   Is it mine eye, or Valentine's praise,
        Her true perfection, or my false transgression,

171 on of

That makes me reasonless to reason thus?
She is fair; and so is Julia, that I love—
That I did love, for now my love is thawed,
Which, like a waxen image 'gainst a fire,   200
Bears no impression of the thing it was.
Methinks my zeal to Valentine is cold,
And that I love him not as I was wont.
O, but I love his lady too too much!
And that's the reason I love him so little.   205
How shall I dote on her with more advice,
That thus without advice begin to love her!
'Tis but her picture I have yet beheld,
And that hath dazzled my reason's light;
But when I look on her perfections,   210
There is no reason but I shall be blind.
If I can check my erring love, I will;
If not, to compass her I'll use my skill.   *Exit.*

Scene V. [*Milan. A street.*]

Enter Speed and Launce [meeting].

SPEED Launce! By mine honesty, welcome to Padua!

LAUNCE Forswear not thyself, sweet youth; for I am
not welcome. I reckon this always—that a man is
never undone till he be hanged, nor never welcome
to a place till some certain shot be paid, and the   5
hostess say "Welcome!"

SPEED Come on, you madcap, I'll to the alehouse with
you presently, where, for one shot of five pence,
thou shalt have five thousand welcomes. But, sirrah,
how did thy master part with Madam Julia?   10

197 **reasonless** without justification 206 **advice** careful thought 208 **picture**
i.e, her visible being, outward appearance 211 **reason** question 213 **compass**
get, achieve II.v.1 **padua** (apparently Shakespeare forgot that his characters are
in Milan) 2 **Forswear** perjure 5 **shot** alehouse bill

LAUNCE Marry, after they closed in earnest, they parted very fairly in jest.

SPEED But shall she marry him?

LAUNCE No.

15 SPEED How, then? Shall he marry her?

LAUNCE No, neither.

SPEED What, are they broken?

LAUNCE No, they are both as whole as a fish.

SPEED Why, then, how stands the matter with them?

20 LAUNCE Marry, thus: when it stands well with him, it stands well with her.

SPEED What an ass art thou! I understand thee not.

LAUNCE What a block art thou, that thou canst not! My staff understands me.

25 SPEED What thou sayest?

LAUNCE Ay, and what I do too. Look thee, I'll but lean, and my staff understands me.

SPEED It stands under thee, indeed.

LAUNCE Why, stand-under and under-stand is all one.

30 SPEED But tell me true, will't be a match?

LAUNCE Ask my dog. If he say ay, it will; if he say, no, it will; if he shake his tail and say nothing, it will.

SPEED The conclusion is, then, that it will.

35 LAUNCE Thou shalt never get such a secret from me but by a parable.

SPEED 'Tis well that I get it so. But, Launce, how

---

11 **closed in earnest** (1) formally agreed (2) embraced   36 **by a parable** i.e., by indirect affirmation

sayest thou, that my master is become a notable lover?

LAUNCE I never knew him otherwise.   40

SPEED Than how?

LAUNCE A notable lubber, as thou reportest him to be.

SPEED Why, thou whoreson ass, thou mistak'st me.

LAUNCE Why fool, I meant not thee; I meant thy master.   45

SPEED I tell thee, my master is become a hot lover.

LAUNCE Why, I tell thee, I care not though he burn himself in love. If thou wilt, go with me to the ale-house; if not, thou art an Hebrew, a Jew, and not worth the name of a Christian.   50

SPEED Why?

LAUNCE Because thou hast not so much charity in thee as to go to the ale with a Christian. Wilt thou go?

SPEED At thy service.   *Exeunt.*

Scene VI. [*Milan. The Duke's palace.*]

Enter Proteus solus.

PROTEUS To leave my Julia shall I be forsworn;
 To love fair Silvia shall I be forsworn;
 To wrong my friend, I shall be much forsworn;
 And ev'n that pow'r which gave me first my oath
 Provokes me to this threefold perjury: 5
 Love bade me swear, and Love bids me forswear.
 O sweet-suggesting Love, if thou hast sinned,

37-38 **how sayest thou** what do you think about this   53 **go to the ale with a Christian** i.e., attend a church-benefit festivity   II.vi.s.d. **solus** alone (Latin)

Teach me, thy tempted subject, to excuse it!
At first I did adore a twinkling star,
10 But now I worship a celestial sun.
Unheedful vows may heedfully be broken;
And he wants wit that wants resolvèd will
To learn his wit t' exchange the bad for better.
Fie, fie, unreverend tongue! To call her bad,
15 Whose sovereignty so oft thou hast preferred
With twenty thousand soul-confirming oaths.
I cannot leave to love, and yet I do;
But there I leave to love where I should love.
Julia I lose, and Valentine I lose.
20 If I keep them, I needs must lose myself;
If I lose them, thus find I by their loss
For Valentine, myself, for Julia, Silvia.
I to myself am dearer than a friend,
For love is still most precious in itself;
25 And Silvia—witness Heaven, that made her fair!—
Shows Julia but a swarthy Ethiope.
I will forget that Julia is alive,
Rememb'ring that my love to her is dead;
And Valentine I'll hold an enemy,
30 Aiming at Silvia as a sweeter friend.
I cannot now prove constant to myself,
Without some treachery used to Valentine.
This night he meaneth with a corded ladder
To climb celestial Silvia's chamber window,
35 Myself in counsel, his competitor.
Now presently I'll give her father notice
Of their disguising and pretended flight;
Who, all enraged, will banish Valentine;
For Thurio, he intends, shall wed his daughter.
40 But, Valentine being gone, I'll quickly cross
By some sly trick blunt Thurio's dull proceeding.
Love, lend me wings to make my purpose swift,
As thou hast lent me wit to plot this drift!   *Exit.*

12 **wants** lacks   13 **learn** teach   35 **competitor** accomplice   37 **pretended** intended   43 **drift** device

Scene VII. [*Verona. Julia's house.*]

Enter Julia and Lucetta.

JULIA Counsel, Lucetta; gentle girl, assist me;
And, ev'n in kind love, I do conjure thee,
Who art the table wherein all my thoughts
Are visibly charactered and engraved,
To lesson me, and tell me some good mean,   5
How, with my honor, I may undertake
A journey to my loving Proteus.

LUCETTA Alas, the way is wearisome and long!

JULIA A true-devoted pilgrim is not weary
To measure kingdoms with his feeble steps;   10
Much less shall she that hath Love's wings to fly—
And when the flight is made to one so dear,
Of such divine perfection, as Sir Proteus.

LUCETTA Better forbear till Proteus make return.

JULIA O, know'st thou not his looks are my soul's
    food?   15
Pity the dearth that I have pinèd in
By longing for that food so long a time.
Didst thou but know the inly touch of love,
Thou wouldst as soon go kindle fire with snow
As seek to quench the fire of love with words.   20

LUCETTA I do not seek to quench your love's hot fire,
But qualify the fire's extreme rage,
Lest it should burn above the bounds of reason.

JULIA The more thou damm'st it up, the more it burns.
The current that with gentle murmur glides,   25
Thou know'st, being stopped, impatiently doth rage;
But when his fair course is not hinderèd,
He makes sweet music with th' enameled stones,

II.vii.3 **table** tablet   6 **with my honor** preserving my honor   18 **inly** inward
22 **qualify** mitigate   28 **enameled** shiny

229

Giving a gentle kiss to every sedge
30   He overtaketh in his pilgrimage;
And so by many winding nooks he strays,
With willing sport, to the wild ocean.
Then let me go, and hinder not my course.
I'll be as patient as a gentle stream,
35   And make a pastime of each weary step,
Till the last step have brought me to my love;
And there I'll rest, as after much turmoil
A blessèd soul doth in Elysium.

LUCETTA But in what habit will you go along?

40 JULIA Not like a woman, for I would prevent
The loose encounters of lascivious men.
Gentle Lucetta, fit me with such weeds
As may beseem some well-reputed page.

LUCETTA Why, then, your ladyship must cut your hair.

45 JULIA No, girl; I'll knit it up in silken strings
With twenty odd-conceited truelove knots.
To be fantastic may become a youth
Of greater time than I shall show to be.

LUCETTA What fashion, madam, shall I make your
breeches?

50 JULIA That fits as well as, "Tell me, good my lord,
What compass will you wear your farthingale?"
Why, ev'n what fashion thou best likes, Lucetta.

LUCETTA You must needs have them with a codpiece,
madam.

JULIA Out, out, Lucetta! That will be ill-favored.

55 LUCETTA A round hose, madam, now'st not worth a pin,
Unless you have a codpiece to stick pins on.

JULIA Lucetta, as thou lov'st me, let me have

39 **habit** costume   42 **weeds** garments   46 **odd-conceited** ingeniously devised
48 **Of greater time** i.e., older   51 **compass** circumference   51 **farthingale**
hooped petticoat   53 **codpiece** pocket or bag at front of men's breeches (**round
hose**, line 55), often fashionably exaggerated   54 **Out, out** fie, fie

What thou think'st meet, and is most mannerly.
But tell me, wench, how will the world repute me
For undertaking so unstaid a journey?   60
I fear me, it will make me scandalized.

LUCETTA If you think so, then stay at home, and go not.

JULIA Nay, that I will not.

LUCETTA Then never dream on infamy, but go.
If Proteus like your journey when you come,   65
No matter who's displeased when you are gone:
I fear me, he will scarce be pleased withal.

JULIA That is the least, Lucetta, of my fear.
A thousand oaths, an ocean of his tears,
And instances of infinite of love   70
Warrant me welcome to my Proteus.

LUCETTA All these are servants to deceitful men.

JULIA Base men, that use them to so base effect!
But truer stars did govern Proteus' birth.
His words are bonds, his oaths are oracles;   75
His love sincere, his thoughts immaculate;
His tears pure messengers sent from his heart:
His heart as far from fraud as heaven from earth.

LUCETTA Pray heav'n he prove so, when you come to
   him!

JULIA Now, as thou lov'st me, do him not that wrong,   80
To bear a hard opinion of his truth.
Only deserve my love by loving him,
And presently go with me to my chamber
To take a note of what I stand in need of
To furnish me upon my longing journey.   85
All that is mine I leave at thy dispose,
My goods, my lands, my reputation;
Only, in lieu thereof, dispatch me hence.
Come, answer not, but to it presently!
I am impatient of my tarriance.   *Exeunt.*   90

60 **unstaid** unbecoming   67 **withal** with it   70 **infinite** infinity   85 **longing**
i.e., occasioned by my longing

ACT III

Scene I. [*Milan. The Duke's palace.*]

Enter Duke, Thurio, [and] Proteus.

DUKE Sir Thurio, give us leave, I pray, awhile;
We have some secrets to confer about.

[*Exit Thurio.*]
Now, tell me, Proteus, what's your will with me?

PROTEUS My gracious lord, that which I would
discover
5   The law of friendship bids me to conceal;
But when I call to mind your gracious favors
Done to me, undeserving as I am,
My duty pricks me on to utter that
Which else no worldly good should draw from me.
10   Know, worthy prince, Sir Valentine, my friend,
This night intends to steal away your daughter.
Myself am one made privy to the plot.
I know you have determined to bestow her
On Thurio, whom your gentle daughter hates,
15   And should she thus be stol'n away from you,
It would be much vexation to your age.
Thus, for my duty's sake, I rather chose

III.i.4 **discover** disclose

To cross my friend in his intended drift
Than, by concealing it, heap on your head
A pack of sorrows which would press you down,   20
Being unprevented, to your timeless grave.

DUKE Proteus, I thank thee for thine honest care,
Which to requite, command me while I live.
This love of theirs myself have often seen,
Haply when they have judged me fast asleep;   25
And oftentimes have purposed to forbid
Sir Valentine her company and my court.
But, fearing lest my jealous aim might err,
And so, unworthily disgrace the man,
A rashness that I ever yet have shunned,   30
I gave him gentle looks; thereby to find
That which thyself hast now disclosed to me.
And, that thou mayst perceive my fear of this,
Knowing that tender youth is soon suggested,
I nightly lodge her in an upper tow'r,   35
The key whereof myself have ever kept;
And thence she cannot be conveyed away.

PROTEUS Know, noble lord, they have devised a mean
How he her chamber window will ascend,
And with a corded ladder fetch her down;   40
For which the youthful lover now is gone,
And this way comes he with it presently,
Where, if it please you, you may intercept him.
But, good my lord, do it so cunningly
That my discovery be not aimèd at;   45
For love of you, not hate unto my friend,
Hath made me publisher of this pretense.

DUKE Upon mine honor, he shall never know
That I had any light from thee of this.

PROTEUS Adieu, my lord; Sir Valentine is coming.   50
                                                    [*Exit.*]

---

21 **timeless** untimely   28 **jealous** suspicious   34 **suggested** tempted, prompted
45 **aimèd at** guessed   47 **pretense** intention

[*Enter Valentine.*]

DUKE Sir Valentine, whither away so fast?

VALENTINE Please it your Grace, there is a messenger
  That stays to hear my letters to my friends,
  And I am going to deliver them.

55 DUKE Be they of much import?

VALENTINE The tenor of them doth but signify
  My health and happy being at your court.

DUKE Nay then, no matter; stay with me awhile.
  I am to break with thee of some affairs
60 That touch me near, wherein thou must be secret.
  'Tis not unknown to thee that I have sought
  To match my friend Sir Thurio to my daughter.

VALENTINE I know it well, my lord; and, sure, the
    match
  Were rich and honorable; besides, the gentleman
65 Is full of virtue, bounty, worth, and qualities
  Beseeming such a wife as your fair daughter.
  Cannot your Grace win her to fancy him?

DUKE No, trust me; she is peevish, sullen, froward,
  Proud, disobedient, stubborn, lacking duty,
70 Neither regarding that she is my child
  Nor fearing me as if I were her father.
  And, may I say to thee, this pride of hers,
  Upon advice, hath drawn my love from her;
  And, where I thought the remnant of mine age
75 Should have been cherished by her childlike duty,
  I now am full resolved to take a wife,
  And turn her out to who will take her in.
  Then let her beauty be her wedding dow'r,
  For me and my possessions she esteems not.

VALENTINE What would your Grace have me to do in
80   this?

68 **peevish ... froward** obstinate ... willful 73 **advice** consideration
73 **drawn** withdrawn

DUKE There is a lady in Verona here
    Whom I affect; but she is nice and coy,
    And nought esteems my agèd eloquence.
    Now, therefore, would I have thee to my tutor—
    For long agone I have forgot to court;   85
    Besides, the fashion of the time is changed—
    How and which way I may bestow myself,
    To be regarded in her sun-bright eye.

VALENTINE Win her with gifts, if she respect not words.
    Dumb jewels often in their silent kind   90
    More than quick words do move a woman's mind.

DUKE But she did scorn a present that I sent her.

VALENTINE A woman sometime scorns what best
    contents her.
    Send her another; never give her o'er;
    For scorn at first makes after-love the more.   95
    If she do frown, 'tis not in hate of you,
    But rather to beget more love in you.
    If she do chide, 'tis not to have you gone;
    For why, the fools are mad, if left alone.
    Take no repulse, whatever she doth say;   100
    For "get you gone," she doth not mean "away!"
    Flatter and praise, commend, extol their graces;
    Though ne'er so black, say they have angels' faces.
    That man that hath a tongue, I say, is no man,
    If with his tongue he cannot win a woman.   105

DUKE But she I mean is promised by her friends
    Unto a youthful gentleman of worth,
    And kept severely from resort of men,
    That no man hath access by day to her.

VALENTINE Why, then, I would resort to her by night.   110

DUKE Ay, but the doors be locked, and keys kept safe,
    That no man hath recourse to her by night.

81 in Verona here (some editors emend in to "of," but probably Shakespeare
forgot his characters are now in Milan) 82 nice fastidious 87 bestow conduct
90 kind nature

VALENTINE What lets but one may enter at her
    window?

DUKE Her chamber is aloft, far from the ground,
115   And built so shelving that one cannot climb it
    Without apparent hazard of his life.

VALENTINE Why, then, a ladder, quaintly made of
    cords,
    To cast up, with a pair of anchoring hooks,
    Would serve to scale another Hero's tow'r,
120   So bold Leander would adventure it.

DUKE Now, as thou art a gentleman of blood,
    Advise me where I may have such a ladder.

VALENTINE When would you use it? Pray, sir, tell me
    that.

DUKE This very night; for Love is like a child,
125   That longs for everything that he can come by.

VALENTINE By seven o'clock I'll get you such a ladder.

DUKE But, hark thee; I will go to her alone.
    How shall I best convey the ladder thither?

VALENTINE It will be light, my lord, that you may
    bear it
130   Under a cloak that is of any length.

DUKE A cloak as long as thine will serve the turn?

VALENTINE Ay, my good lord.

DUKE   Then let me see thy cloak.
    I'll get me one of such another length.

VALENTINE Why, any cloak will serve the turn, my lord.

135 DUKE How shall I fashion me to wear a cloak?
    I pray thee, let me feel thy cloak upon me.
                      [*Opens Valentine's cloak.*]
    What letter is this same? What's here?
    "To Silvia"—

113 **lets** prevents   115 **shelving** steeply sloping   121 **of blood** i.e., of noble
blood

And here an engine fit for my proceeding.
I'll be so bold to break the seal for once.   [*Reads.*]
"My thoughts do harbor with my Silvia nightly;   140
  And slaves they are to me, that send them flying.
O, could their master come and go as lightly,
  Himself would lodge where senseless they are
    lying!
My herald thoughts in thy pure bosom rest them,
  While I, their king, that thither them importune,   145
Do curse the grace that with such grace hath blessed
  them,
  Because myself do want my servants' fortune.
I curse myself, for they are sent by me,
That they should harbor where their lord should be."
What's here?   150
"Silvia, this night I will enfranchise thee."
'Tis so; and here's the ladder for the purpose.
Why, Phaethon—for thou art Merops' son—
Wilt thou aspire to guide the heavenly car,
And with thy daring folly burn the world?   155
Wilt thou reach stars, because they shine on thee?
Go, base intruder! Overweening slave!
Bestow thy fawning smiles on equal mates,
And think my patience, more than thy desert,
Is privilege for thy departure hence.   160
Thank me for this more than for all the favors
Which all too much I have bestowed on thee.
But if thou linger in my territories
Longer than swiftest expedition
Will give thee time to leave our royal court,   165
By heaven, my wrath shall far exceed the love
I ever bore my daughter or thyself.
Be gone! I will not hear thy vain excuse;
But, as thou lov'st thy life, make speed from hence.
                      [*Exit.*]

---

138 **engine** contrivance (here, the ladder)   153-55 **Phaethon ... the world**
(Phaethon's father, Phoebus—not Merops, who was his mother's husband—let the
youth drive the horses of the sun across the sky, with dire results)   164 **expedition**
speed

VALENTINE And why not death rather than living
170   torment?
        To die is to be banished from myself;
        And Silvia is myself. Banished from her
        Is self from self: a deadly banishment!
        What light is light, if Silvia be not seen?
175   What joy is joy, if Silvia be not by?—
        Unless it be to think that she is by,
        And feed upon the shadow of perfection.
        Except I be by Silvia in the night,
        There is no music in the nightingale;
180   Unless I look on Silvia in the day,
        There is no day for me to look upon.
        She is my essence, and I leave to be,
        If I be not by her fair influence
        Fostered, illumined, cherished, kept alive.
185   I fly not death, to fly his deadly doom:
        Tarry I here, I but attend on death;
        But, fly I hence, I fly away from life.

[Enter Proteus and Launce.]

PROTEUS Run, boy, run, run, and seek him out.

LAUNCE Soho, soho!

190 PROTEUS What seest thou?

LAUNCE Him we go to find. There's not a hair on's
        head but 'tis a Valentine.

PROTEUS Valentine?

VALENTINE No.

195 PROTEUS Who then? His spirit?

VALENTINE Neither.

PROTEUS What then?

---

177 **shadow** mere image 182 **leave** cease 183 **influence** i.e., like that of the
stars (see especially Sonnet 15) 191 **hair** (with pun on "hare," prepared by
preceding **Soho**, a hunting cry) 192 **Valentine** (with pun, as in lines 210–14
below)

VALENTINE Nothing.

LAUNCE Can nothing speak? Master, shall I strike?

PROTEUS Who wouldst thou strike?   200

LAUNCE Nothing.

PROTEUS Villain, forbear.

LAUNCE Why, sir, I'll strike nothing. I pray you—

PROTEUS Sirrah, I say, forbear. Friend Valentine, a
   word.

VALENTINE My ears are stopped, and cannot hear good
      news,   205
   So much of bad already hath possessed them.

PROTEUS Then in dumb silence will I bury mine,
   For they are harsh, untunable, and bad.

VALENTINE Is Silvia dead?

PROTEUS No, Valentine.   210

VALENTINE No Valentine, indeed, for sacred Silvia.
   Hath she forsworn me?

PROTEUS No, Valentine.

VALENTINE No Valentine, if Silvia have forsworn me.
   What is your news?   215

LAUNCE Sir, there is a proclamation that you are vanished.

PROTEUS That thou art banishèd—O, that's the
      news—
   From hence, from Silvia, and from me thy friend.

VALENTINE O, I have fed upon this woe already,   220
   And now excess of it will make me surfeit.
   Doth Silvia know that I am banishèd?

PROTEUS Ay, ay, and she hath offered to the doom—
   Which, unreversed, stands in effectual force—
   A sea of melting pearl, which some call tears: 225
   Those at her father's churlish feet she tendered;

With them, upon her knees, her humble self;
Wringing her hands, whose whiteness so became
    them
As if but now they waxèd pale for woe.
230 But neither bended knees, pure hands held up,
Sad sighs, deep groans, nor silver-shedding tears,
Could penetrate her uncompassionate sire;
But Valentine, if he be ta'en, must die.
Besides, her intercession chafed him so,
235 When she for thy repeal was suppliant,
That to close prison he commanded her,
With many bitter threats of biding there.

VALENTINE No more; unless the next word that thou
    speak'st
Have some malignant power upon my life.
240 If so, I pray thee, breathe it in mine ear,
As ending anthem of my endless dolor.

PROTEUS Cease to lament for that thou canst not help,
And study help for that which thou lament'st.
Time is the nurse and breeder of all good.
245 Here if thou stay, thou canst not see thy love;
Besides, thy staying will abridge thy life.
Hope is a lover's staff; walk hence with that,
And manage it against despairing thoughts.
Thy letters may be here, though thou art hence;
250 Which, being writ to me, shall be delivered
Even in the milk-white bosom of thy love.
The time now serves not to expostulate.
Come, I'll convey thee through the city gate,
And, ere I part with thee, confer at large
255 Of all that may concern thy love affairs.
As thou lov'st Silvia, though not for thyself,
Regard thy danger, and along with me!

VALENTINE I pray thee, Launce, and if thou seest my
    boy,
Bid him make haste, and meet me at the Northgate.

237 **biding** i.e., permanent incarceration   241 **ending anthem** funeral hymn
258 **and if** if

PROTEUS Go, sirrah, find him out. Come, Valentine.   260

VALENTINE O my dear Silvia! Hapless Valentine!
                    [*Exeunt Valentine and Proteus.*]

LAUNCE I am but a fool, look you, and yet I have the
wit to think my master is a kind of a knave. But
that's all one, if he be but one knave. He lives not
now that knows me to be in love, yet I am in love;   265
but a team of horse shall not pluck that from me,
nor who 'tis I love, and yet 'tis a woman; but what
woman, I will not tell myself, and yet 'tis a milk-
maid; yet 'tis not a maid, for she hath had gossips;
yet 'tis a maid, for she is her master's maid, and   270
serves for wages. She hath more qualities than a
water spaniel—which is much in a bare Christian.
[*Pulling out a paper*] Here is the cate-log of her
condition. "Imprimis: She can fetch and carry."
Why, a horse can do no more: nay, a horse cannot   275
fetch, but only carry; therefore is she better than a
jade. "Item: She can milk"; look you, a sweet virtue in a maid with clean hands.

                    [*Enter Speed.*]

SPEED How now, Signior Launce! What news with
your mastership?   280

LAUNCE With my master's ship? Why, it is at sea.

SPEED Well, your old vice still; mistake the word.
What news, then, in your paper?

LAUNCE The black'st news that ever thou heard'st.

SPEED Why, man, how black?   285

LAUNCE Why, as black as ink.

SPEED Let me read them.

LAUNCE Fie on thee, jolthead! Thou canst not read.

269 gossips godparents (for her own child)   274 Imprimis in the first place
277 jade nag   288 jolthead blockhead

SPEED Thou liest; I can.

290 LAUNCE I will try thee. Tell me this: who begot thee?

SPEED Marry, the son of my grandfather.

LAUNCE O illiterate loiterer! It was the son of thy grandmother. This proves that thou canst not read.

SPEED Come, fool, come; try me in thy paper.

295 LAUNCE There; and Saint Nicholas be thy speed!

SPEED [*Reads*] "Imprimis: She can milk."

LAUNCE Ay, that she can.

SPEED "Item: She brews good ale."

LAUNCE And thereof comes the proverb: "Blessing of
300 your heart, you brew good ale."

SPEED "Item: She can sew."

LAUNCE That's as much as to say, Can she so?

SPEED "Item: She can knit."

LAUNCE What need a man care for a stock with a
305 wench when she can knit him a stock?

SPEED "Item: She can wash and scour."

LAUNCE A special virtue; for then she need not be washed and scoured.

SPEED "Item: She can spin."

310 LAUNCE Then may I set the world on wheels, when she can spin for her living.

SPEED "Item: She hath many nameless virtues."

LAUNCE That's as much as to say, bastard virtues—that, indeed, know not their fathers, and therefore
315 have no names.

295 **Saint Nicholas** patron saint of scholars (among others)   295 **speed** aid
304 **stock** dowry (pun follows)   310 **set the world on wheels** take life easy

SPEED "Here follow her vices."

LAUNCE Close at the heels of her virtues.

SPEED "Item: She is not to be kissed fasting, in respect of her breath."

LAUNCE Well, that fault may be mended with a break-   320
fast. Read on.

SPEED "Item: She hath a sweet mouth."

LAUNCE That makes amends for her sour breath.

SPEED "Item: She doth talk in her sleep."

LAUNCE It's no matter for that, so she sleep not in her   325
talk.

SPEED "Item: She is slow in words."

LAUNCE O villain, that set this down among her vices!
To be slow in words is a woman's only virtue. I
pray thee, out with't, and place it for her chief   330
virtue.

SPEED "Item: She is proud."

LAUNCE Out with that too; it was Eve's legacy, and
cannot be ta'en from her.

SPEED "Item: she hath no teeth."   335

LAUNCE I care not for that neither, because I love
crusts.

SPEED "Item: She is curst."

LAUNCE Well, the best is, she hath no teeth to bite.

SPEED "Item: She will often praise her liquor."   340

LAUNCE If her liquor be good, she shall; if she will not,
I will, for good things should be praised.

SPEED "Item: She is too liberal."

LAUNCE Of her tongue she cannot, for that's writ down

322 hath a sweet mouth i.e., likes sweets   338 curst shrewish

345 she is slow of; of her purse she shall not, for that
I'll keep shut. Now, of another thing she may, and
that cannot I help. Well, proceed.

SPEED "Item: She hath more hair than wit, and more
faults than hairs and more wealth than faults."

350 LAUNCE Stop there; I'll have her. She was mine, and
not mine, twice or thrice in that last article. Rehearse that once more.

SPEED "Item: She hath more hair than wit"—

LAUNCE More hair than wit? It may be; I'll prove it.
355 The cover of the salt hides the salt, and therefore
it is more than the salt; the hair that covers the wit is
more than the wit, for the greater hides the less.
What's next?

SPEED "And more faults than hairs"—

360 LAUNCE That's monstrous. O, that that were out!

SPEED "And more wealth than faults."

LAUNCE Why, that word makes the faults gracious.
Well, I'll have her; and if it be a match, as nothing
is impossible—

365 SPEED What then?

LAUNCE Why, then will I tell thee—that thy master
stays for thee at the Northgate?

SPEED For me?

LAUNCE For thee! Ay, who art thou? He hath stayed
370 for a better man than thee.

SPEED And must I go to him?

LAUNCE Thou must run to him, for thou hast stayed
so long that going will scarce serve the turn.

SPEED Why didst not tell me sooner? Pox of your love
375 letters!   [Exit.]

355 **salt** saltcellar   373 **going** i.e., merely walking   374 **Pox of** plague (literally, syphilis) on

244

LAUNCE Now will he be swinged for reading my letter
—an unmannerly slave, that will thrust himself into
secrets! I'll after, to rejoice in the boy's correction.
[*Exit.*]

Scene II. [*Milan. The Duke's palace.*]

Enter Duke [*and*] *Thurio.*

DUKE Sir Thurio, fear not but that she will love you,
Now Valentine is banished from her sight.

THURIO Since his exile she hath despised me most,
Forsworn my company, and railed at me,
That I am desperate of obtaining her.   5

DUKE This weak impress of love is as a figure
Trenchèd in ice, which with an hour's heat
Dissolves to water, and doth lose his form.
A little time will melt her frozen thoughts,
And worthless Valentine shall be forgot.   10

[*Enter Proteus.*]

How now, Sir Proteus! Is your countryman,
According to our proclamation, gone?

PROTEUS Gone, my good lord.

DUKE My daughter takes his going grievously.

PROTEUS A little time, my lord, will kill that grief.   15

DUKE So I believe, but Thurio thinks not so.
Proteus, the good conceit I hold of thee—
For thou hast shown some sign of good desert—
Makes me the better to confer with thee.

III.ii.6 **impress** impression (dent, groove)   17 **conceit** opinion

245

20   PROTEUS Longer than I prove loyal to your Grace,
          Let me not live to look upon your Grace.

      DUKE Thou know'st how willingly I would effect
          The match between Sir Thurio and my daughter.

      PROTEUS I do, my lord.

25   DUKE And also, I think, thou art not ignorant
          How she opposes her against my will.

      PROTEUS She did, my lord, when Valentine was here.

      DUKE Ay, and perversely she persevers so.
          What might we do to make the girl forget
30   The love of Valentine, and love Sir Thurio?

      PROTEUS The best way is to slander Valentine
          With falsehood, cowardice, and poor descent,
          Three things that women highly hold in hate.

      DUKE Ay, but she'll think that it is spoke in hate.

35   PROTEUS Ay, if his enemy deliver it;
          Therefore it must with circumstance be spoken
          By one whom she esteemeth as his friend.

      DUKE Then you must undertake to slander him.

      PROTEUS And that, my lord, I shall be loath to do.
40   'Tis an ill office for a gentleman,
          Especially against his very friend.

      DUKE Where your good word cannot advantage him,
          Your slander never can endamage him;
          Therefore the office is indifferent,
45   Being entreated to it by your friend.

      PROTEUS You have prevailed, my lord. If I can do it
          By aught that I can speak in his dispraise,
          She shall not long continue love to him.
          But say this weed her love from Valentine,
50   It follows not that she will love Sir Thurio.

      THURIO Therefore, as you unwind her love from him,

36 **circumstance** circumstantial detail   44 **indifferent** neutral in effect

246

Lest it should ravel and be good to none,
You must provide to bottom it on me;
Which must be done by praising me as much
As you in worth dispraise Sir Valentine.   55

DUKE And, Proteus, we dare trust you in this kind,
Because we know, on Valentine's report,
You are already Love's firm votary
And cannot soon revolt and change your mind.
Upon this warrant shall you have access   60
Where you with Silvia may confer at large;
For she is lumpish, heavy, melancholy,
And, for your friend's sake, will be glad of you;
Where you may temper her by your persuasion
To hate young Valentine and love my friend.   65

PROTEUS As much as I can do, I will effect.
But you, Sir Thurio, are not sharp enough;
You must lay lime to tangle her desires
By wailful sonnets, whose composèd rhymes
Should be full-fraught with serviceable vows.   70

DUKE Ay,
Much is the force of heaven-bred poesy.

PROTEUS Say that upon the altar of her beauty
You sacrifice your tears, your sighs, your heart.
Write till your ink be dry, and with your tears   75
Moist it again, and frame some feeling line
That may discover such integrity.
For Orpheus' lute was strung with poets' sinews,
Whose golden touch could soften steel and stones,
Make tigers tame, and huge leviathans   80
Forsake unsounded deeps to dance on sands.
After your dire-lamenting elegies,
Visit by night your lady's chamber window

53 **bottom** anchor, tie (as a weaver's thread)   56 **kind** i.e., an affair of this
nature   64 **temper** make pliant, shape   68 **lime to tangle** birdlime to ensnare
(birdlime is a sticky substance spread on branches to catch birds)   70 **full-fraught
with serviceable vows** loaded with vows to serve faithfully   77 **discover such
integrity** exhibit such devotion   78–81 **Orpheus' lute ... sands** (cf. *Merchant of
Venice*, V.i for a simpler tribute to the musician of Thrace)

With some sweet consort; to their instruments
85   Tune a deploring dump. The night's dead silence
Will well become such sweet-complaining
          grievance.
This, or else nothing, will inherit her.

DUKE   This discipline shows thou hast been in love.

THURIO   And thy advice this night I'll put in practice.
90   Therefore, sweet Proteus, my direction-giver,
Let us into the city presently
To sort some gentlemen well skilled in music.
I have a sonnet that will serve the turn
To give the onset to thy good advice.

95   DUKE   About it, gentlemen!

PROTEUS   We'll wait upon your Grace till after supper,
And afterward determine our proceedings.

DUKE   Even now about it! I will pardon you.   *Exeunt*.

---

84 **sweet consort** i.e., company of musicians   85 **deploring dump** doleful ditty
87 **inherit** obtain   88 **discipline** instruction   92 **sort** sort out, select
94 **give the onset** make a beginning

ACT IV

Scene I. [*A forest*.]

Enter certain Outlaws.

FIRST OUTLAW Fellows, stand fast; I see a passenger.

SECOND OUTLAW If there be ten, shrink not, but down
with 'em.

[*Enter Valentine and Speed*.]

THIRD OUTLAW Stand, sir, and throw us that you have
about ye.
If not, we'll make you sit, and rifle you.

SPEED Sir, we are undone; these are the villains   5
That all the travelers do fear so much.

VALENTINE My friends—

FIRST OUTLAW That's not so, sir; we are your enemies.

SECOND OUTLAW Peace! We'll hear him.

THIRD OUTLAW Ay, by my beard, will we, for he's a
proper man.   10

VALENTINE Then know that I have little wealth to lose.
A man I am crossed with adversity.
My riches are these poor habiliments,

___

IV.i.1 **passenger** pedestrian   3 **that** that which   10 **proper** handsome

249

Of which if you should here disfurnish me,
You take the sum and substance that I have.

SECOND OUTLAW Whither travel you?

VALENTINE To Verona.

FIRST OUTLAW Whence came you?

VALENTINE From Milan.

THIRD OUTLAW Have you long sojourned there?

VALENTINE Some sixteen months, and longer might
    have stayed
  If crooked fortune had not thwarted me.

FIRST OUTLAW What, were you banished thence?

VALENTINE I was.

SECOND OUTLAW For what offense?

VALENTINE For that which now torments me to re-
    hearse:
  I killed a man, whose death I much repent;
  But yet I slew him manfully in fight,
  Without false vantage or base treachery.

FIRST OUTLAW Why, ne'er repent it, if it were done so.
  But were you banished for so small a fault?

VALENTINE I was, and held me glad of such a doom.

SECOND OUTLAW Have you the tongues?

VALENTINE My youthful travel therein made me happy,
  Or else I often had been miserable.

THIRD OUTLAW By the bare scalp of Robin Hood's fat
    friar,
  This fellow were a king for our wild faction!

FIRST OUTLAW We'll have him. Sirs, a word.

---

14 **disfurnish** deprive 29 **false vantage** i.e., such advantage as is gained by deceit 32 **doom** sentence 33 **Have you the tongues** do you know foreign languages 34 **happy** fortunate

SPEED Master, be one of them; it's an honorable kind
   of thievery.   40

VALENTINE Peace, villain!

SECOND OUTLAW Tell us this: have you anything to
   take to?

VALENTINE Nothing but my fortune.

THIRD OUTLAW Know, then, that some of us are
   gentlemen,
   Such as the fury of ungoverned youth   45
   Thrust from the company of awful men:
   Myself was from Verona banishèd
   For practicing to steal away a lady,
   An heir, and near allied unto the Duke.

SECOND OUTLAW And I from Mantua, for a gentleman   50
   Who, in my mood, I stabbed unto the heart.

FIRST OUTLAW And I for suchlike petty crimes as these.
   But to the purpose—for we cite our faults,
   That they may hold excused our lawless lives;
   And partly, seeing you are beautified   55
   With goodly shape, and by your own report
   A linguist, and a man of such perfection
   As we do in our quality much want—

SECOND OUTLAW Indeed, because you are a banished
   man,
   Therefore, above the rest, we parley to you.   60
   Are you content to be our general,
   To make a virtue of necessity,
   And live, as we do, in this wilderness?

THIRD OUTLAW What say'st thou? Wilt thou be of our
   consort?
   Say ay, and be the captain of us all.   65

---

42 **anything to take to** any trade to take up 46 **awful** deeply respectful (but
possibly a printer's slip for "lawful") 48 **practicing** plotting 58 **in our
quality much want** much lack in our profession

We'll do thee homage and be ruled by thee,
Love thee as our commander and our king.

FIRST OUTLAW But if thou scorn our courtesy, thou
   diest.

SECOND OUTLAW Thou shalt not live to brag what we
   have offered.

70 VALENTINE I take your offer, and will live with you,
   Provided that you do no outrages
   On silly women or poor passengers.

THIRD OUTLAW No, we detest such vile base practices.
   Come, go with us; we'll bring thee to our crews
75 And show thee all the treasure we have got,
   Which, with ourselves, all rest at thy dispose.

                                        Exeunt.

Scene II. [*Milan. Beneath Silvia's window.*]

Enter Proteus.

PROTEUS Already have I been false to Valentine,
   And now I must be as unjust to Thurio.
   Under the color of commending him,
   I have access my own love to prefer.
5 But Silvia is too fair, too true, too holy
   To be corrupted with my worthless gifts.
   When I protest true loyalty to her,
   She twits me with my falsehood to my friend;
   When to her beauty I commend my vows,
10 She bids me think how I have been forsworn
   In breaking faith with Julia whom I loved.
   And notwithstanding all her sudden quips,
   The least whereof would quell a lover's hope,
   Yet, spaniel-like, the more she spurns my love,

---

72 **silly** defenseless   IV.ii.3 **color** pretense   4 **prefer** advance

The more it grows, and fawneth on her still.   15
But here comes Thurio; now must we to her window
And give some evening music to her ear.

[*Enter Thurio and Musicians.*]

THURIO How now, Sir Proteus, are you crept before
    us?

PROTEUS Ay, gentle Thurio, for you know that love
    Will creep in service where it cannot go.   20

THURIO Ay, but I hope, sir, that you love not here.

PROTEUS Sir, but I do; or else I would be hence.

THURIO Who? Silvia?

PROTEUS   Ay, Silvia, for your sake.

THURIO I thank you for your own. Now, gentlemen,
    Let's tune, and to it lustily awhile.   25

[*Enter, at a distance, Host, and Julia in boy's
clothes.*]

HOST Now, my young guest, methinks you're ally-
    cholly. I pray you, why is it?

JULIA Marry, mine host, because I cannot be merry.

HOST Come, we'll have you merry. I'll bring you where
    you shall hear music, and see the gentleman that   30
    you asked for.

JULIA But shall I hear him speak?

HOST Ay, that you shall.

JULIA That will be music.   [*Music plays.*]

HOST Hark, hark!   35

JULIA Is he among these?

HOST Ay, but, peace! Let's hear 'em.

20 go walk upright   26-27 allycholly i.e., melancholy

Song.

Who is Silvia, what is she,
　That all our swains commend her?
40 Holy, fair, and wise is she;
　The heaven such grace did lend her,
That she might admirèd be.

Is she kind as she is fair?
　For beauty lives with kindness.
45 Love doth to her eyes repair,
　To help him of his blindness,
And, being helped, inhabits there.

Then to Silvia let us sing,
　That Silvia is excelling;
50 She excels each mortal thing
　Upon the dull earth dwelling.
To her let us garlands bring.

HOST How now! Are you sadder than you were before?
　How do you, man? The music likes you not.

55 JULIA You mistake; the musician likes me not.

HOST Why, my pretty youth?

JULIA He plays false, father.

HOST How? Out of tune on the strings?

JULIA Not so; but yet so false that he grieves my very
60 　heartstrings.

HOST You have a quick ear.

JULIA Ay, I would I were deaf; it makes me have a
　slow heart.

HOST I perceive you delight not in music.

65 JULIA Not a whit, when it jars so.

54 **likes** pleases   63 **slow** i.e., heavy

254

HOST Hark, what fine change is in the music!

JULIA Ay, that change is the spite.

HOST You would have them always play but one thing?

JULIA I would always have one play but one thing.
But, host, doth this Sir Proteus that we talk on   70
Often resort unto this gentlewoman?

HOST I tell you what Launce, his man, told me—he
loved her out of all nick.

JULIA Where is Launce?

HOST Gone to seek his dog, which tomorrow, by his   75
master's command, he must carry for a present to
his lady.

JULIA Peace! Stand aside. The company parts.

PROTEUS Sir Thurio, fear not you. I will so plead
That you shall say my cunning drift excels.   80

THURIO Where meet we?

PROTEUS   At Saint Gregory's well.

THURIO   Farewell.
[*Exeunt Thurio and Musicians.*]

[*Enter Silvia above.*]

PROTEUS Madam, good even to your ladyship.

SILVIA I thank you for your music, gentlemen.
Who is that that spake?

PROTEUS One, lady, if you knew his pure heart's truth,   85
You would quickly learn to know him by his voice.

SILVIA Sir Proteus, as I take it.

PROTEUS Sir Proteus, gentle lady, and your servant.

---

66 **change** modulation (in the next line Julia puns, alluding to the change in Proteus' affections)   73 **out of all nick** beyond measure

SILVIA What's your will?

PROTEUS   That I may compass yours.

90 SILVIA You have your wish; my will is even this:
That presently you hie you home to bed.
Thou subtle, perjured, false, disloyal man!
Think'st thou I am so shallow, so conceitless,
To be seducèd by thy flattery,
95 That hast deceived so many with thy vows?
Return, return, and make thy love amends.
For me, by this pale queen of night I swear,
I am so far from granting thy request
That I despise thee for thy wrongful suit,
100 And by and by intend to chide myself
Even for this time I spend in talking to thee.

PROTEUS I grant, sweet love, that I did love a lady;
But she is dead.

JULIA [Aside] 'Twere false, if I should speak it,
105 For I am sure she is not burièd.

SILVIA Say that she be; yet Valentine thy friend
Survives, to whom, thyself art witness,
I am betrothed. And art thou not ashamed
To wrong him with thy importunacy?

110 PROTEUS I likewise hear that Valentine is dead.

SILVIA And so suppose am I, for in his grave
Assure thyself my love is burièd.

PROTEUS Sweet lady, let me rake it from the earth.

SILVIA Go to thy lady's grave, and call hers thence;
115 Or, at the least, in hers sepulcher thine.

JULIA [Aside] He heard not that.

PROTEUS Madam, if your heart be so obdurate,
Vouchsafe me yet your picture for my love,
The picture that is hanging in your chamber.
120 To that I'll speak, to that I'll sigh and weep;
For since the substance of your perfect self

93 conceitless witless   118 Vouchsafe grant

Is else devoted, I am but a shadow,
And to your shadow will I make true love.

JULIA [*Aside*] If 'twere a substance, you would, sure,
    deceive it,
And make it but a shadow, as I am.   125

SILVIA I am very loath to be your idol, sir;
But since your falsehood shall become you well
To worship shadows and adore false shapes,
Send to me in the morning, and I'll send it.
And so, good rest.

PROTEUS   As wretches have o'ernight   130
That wait for execution in the morn.
                [*Exeunt Proteus and Silvia severally.*]

JULIA Host, will you go?

HOST By my halidom, I was fast asleep.

JULIA Pray you, where lies Sir Proteus?

HOST Marry, at my house. Trust me, I think 'tis almost   135
day.

JULIA Not so; but it hath been the longest night
That e'er I watched, and the most heaviest.
                                          [*Exeunt.*]

Scene III. [*Milan. Beneath Silvia's window.*]

Enter Eglamour.

EGLAMOUR This is the hour that Madam Silvia
Entreated me to call and know her mind.
There's some great matter she'd employ me in.
Madam, madam!

---

122 **else devoted** vowed to someone else   123 **shadow** portrait   133 **halidom**
sacred relic (a mild oath)   134 **lies** lodges

[*Enter Silvia above.*]

SILVIA Who calls?

5   EGLAMOUR   Your servant and your friend,
    One that attends your ladyship's command.

SILVIA Sir Eglamour, a thousand times good morrow.

EGLAMOUR As many, worthy lady, to yourself.
    According to your ladyship's impose,
10   I am thus early come to know what service
    It is your pleasure to command me in.

SILVIA O Eglamour, thou art a gentleman—
    Think not I flatter, for I swear I do not—
    Valiant, wise, remorseful, well accomplished.
15   Thou art not ignorant what dear good will
    I bear unto the banished Valentine,
    Nor how my father would enforce me marry
    Vain Thurio, whom my very soul abhors.
    Thyself hast loved, and I have heard thee say
20   No grief did ever come so near thy heart
    As when thy lady and thy true love died,
    Upon whose grave thou vow'dst pure chastity.
    Sir Eglamour, I would to Valentine,
    To Mantua, where I hear he makes abode;
25   And, for the ways are dangerous to pass,
    I do desire thy worthy company,
    Upon whose faith and honor I repose.
    Urge not my father's anger, Eglamour,
    But think upon my grief, a lady's grief,
30   And on the justice of my flying hence
    To keep me from a most unholy match,
    Which heaven and fortune still rewards with plagues.
    I do desire thee, even from a heart
    As full of sorrows as the sea of sands,
35   To bear me company, and go with me:
    If not, to hide what I have said to thee,
    That I may venture to depart alone.

IV.iii.9 **impose** command   14 **remorseful** compassionate

EGLAMOUR Madam, I pity much your grievances,
    Which since I know they virtuously are placed,
    I give consent to go along with you,   40
    Recking as little what betideth me
    As much I wish all good befortune you.
    When will you go?

SILVIA   This evening coming.

EGLAMOUR Where shall I meet you?

SILVIA   At Friar Patrick's cell,
    Where I intend holy confession.   45

EGLAMOUR I will not fail your ladyship. Good morrow,
    gentle lady.

SILVIA Good morrow, kind Sir Eglamour.
                                        Exeunt [severally].

Scene IV. [*Milan. Beneath Silvia's window.*]

Enter Launce, [with his dog].

LAUNCE When a man's servant shall play the cur with
    him, look you, it goes hard: one that I brought up
    of a puppy; one that I saved from drowning, when
    three or four of his blind brothers and sisters went
    to it! I have taught him, even as one would say pre-   5
    cisely, "thus I would teach a dog." I was sent to
    deliver him as a present to Mistress Silvia from my
    master, and I came no sooner into the dining cham-
    ber, but he steps me to her trencher and steals her
    capon's leg. O, 'tis a foul thing when a cur cannot   10
    keep himself in all companies! I would have, as
    one should say, one that takes upon him to be a
    dog indeed, to be as it were, a dog at all things. If
    I had not had more wit than he, to take a fault upon
    me that he did, I think verily he had been hanged   15

IV.iv.3 of from   9 trencher wooden plate   11 keep control

for't; sure as I live, he had suffered for't. You shall
judge. He thrusts me himself into the company of
three or four gentlemanlike dogs under the Duke's
table; he had not been there—bless the mark!—a
20 pissing while, but all the chamber smelt him. "Out
with the dog!" says one. "What cur is that?" says
another. "Whip him out," says the third. "Hang him
up," says the Duke. I, having been acquainted with
the smell before, knew it was Crab, and goes me to
25 the fellow that whips the dogs. "Friend," quoth I,
"you mean to whip the dog?" "Ay, marry, do I,"
quoth he. "You do him the more wrong," quoth I;
"'twas I did the thing you wot of." He makes me
no more ado, but whips me out of the chamber.
30 How many masters would do this for his servant?
Nay, I'll be sworn, I have sat in the stocks for puddings he hath stol'n; otherwise he had been executed. I have stood on the pillory for geese he hath
killed; otherwise he had suffered for't. Thou think'st
35 not of this now. Nay, I remember the trick you
served me when I took my leave of Madam Silvia.
Did not I bid thee still mark me, and do as I do?
When didst thou see me heave up my leg, and make
water against a gentlewoman's farthingale? Didst
40 thou ever see me do such a trick?

[*Enter Proteus and Julia.*]

PROTEUS Sebastian is thy name? I like thee well.
And will employ thee in some service presently.

JULIA In what you please. I'll do what I can.

PROTEUS I hope thou wilt. [*To Launce.*] How now, you
whoreson peasant!
45 Where have you been these two days loitering?

LAUNCE Marry, sir, I carried Mistress Silvia the dog
you bade me.

PROTEUS And what says she to my little jewel?

28 **wot** know   31-32 **puddings** sausages

LAUNCE Marry, she says your dog was a cur, and tells
   you currish thanks is good enough for such a present.   50

PROTEUS But she received my dog?

LAUNCE No, indeed, did she not. Here have I brought
   him back again.

PROTEUS What, didst thou offer her this from me?

LAUNCE Ay, sir. The other squirrel was stol'n from   55
   me by the hangman's boys in the market place, and
   then I offered her mine own, who is a dog as big
   as ten of yours, and therefore the gift the greater.

PROTEUS Go get thee hence and find my dog again,
   Or ne'er return again into my sight.   60
   Away, I say! Stayest thou to vex me here?
                              [*Exit Launce.*]
   A slave, that still an end turns me to shame!
   Sebastian, I have entertainèd thee
   Partly that I have need of such a youth
   That can with some discretion do my business,   65
   For 'tis no trusting to yond foolish lout;
   But chiefly for thy face and thy behavior,
   Which, if my augury deceive me not,
   Witness good bringing up, fortune, and truth.
   Therefore, know thou, for this I entertain thee.   70
   Go presently, and take this ring with thee;
   Deliver it to Madam Silvia.
   She loved me well delivered it to me.

JULIA It seems you loved not her, to leave her token.
   She is dead, belike?

PROTEUS   Not so; I think she lives.   75

JULIA Alas!

PROTEUS Why dost thou cry "Alas"?

---

55 **squirrel** i.e., little dog   56 **hangman's boys** i.e., boys who will surely belong
to the hangman (hang) at last   62 **still an end** forevermore   63 **entertainèd**
retained   64 **Partly that** in part because

JULIA   I cannot choose
But pity her.

PROTEUS   Wherefore shouldst thou pity her?

JULIA Because methinks that she loved you as well
80   As you do love your lady Silvia.
She dreams on him that has forgot her love;
You dote on her that cares not for your love.
'Tis pity love should be so contrary;
And thinking on it makes me cry "Alas!"

85   PROTEUS Well, give her that ring, and therewithal
This letter. That's her chamber. Tell my lady
I claim the promise for her heavenly picture.
Your message done, hie home unto my chamber,
Where thou shalt find me, sad and solitary.   [Exit.]

90   JULIA How many women would do such a message?
Alas, poor Proteus! Thou hast entertained
A fox to be the shepherd of thy lambs.
Alas, poor fool! Why do I pity him
That with his very heart despiseth me?
95   Because he loves her, he despiseth me;
Because I love him, I must pity him.
This ring I gave him when he parted from me,
To bind him to remember my good will;
And now am I, unhappy messenger,
100   To plead for that which I would not obtain,
To carry that which I would have refused,
To praise his faith which I would have dispraised.
I am my master's true-confirmèd love,
But cannot be true servant to my master
105   Unless I prove false traitor to myself.
Yet will I woo for him, but yet so coldly
As, heaven it knows, I would not have him speed.

[Enter Silvia, attended.]

Gentlewoman, good day! I pray you, be my mean
To bring me where to speak with Madam Silvia.

107 **speed** prosper, succeed

SILVIA What would you with her, if that I be she?   110

JULIA If you be she, I do entreat your patience
To hear me speak the message I am sent on.

SILVIA From whom?

JULIA From my master, Sir Proteus, madam.

SILVIA O, he sends you for a picture.   115

JULIA Ay, madam.

SILVIA Ursula, bring my picture there.
Go give your master this. Tell him, from me,
One Julia, that his changing thoughts forget,
Would better fit his chamber than this shadow.   120

JULIA Madam, please you peruse this letter—
Pardon me, madam; I have unadvised
Delivered you a paper that I should not.
This is the letter to your ladyship.

SILVIA I pray thee, let me look on that again.   125

JULIA It may not be; good madam, pardon me.

SILVIA There, hold!
I will not look upon your master's lines.
I know they are stuffed with protestations,
And full of new-found oaths which he will break   130
As easily as I do tear his paper.

JULIA Madam, he sends your ladyship this ring.

SILVIA The more shame for him that he sends it me,
For I have heard him say a thousand times
His Julia gave it him at his departure.   135
Though his false finger have profaned the ring,
Mine shall not do his Julia so much wrong.

JULIA She thanks you.

SILVIA What say'st thou?

122 **unadvised** unintentionally

140   JULIA I thank you, madam, that you tender her.
          Poor gentlewoman! My master wrongs her much.

      SILVIA Dost thou know her?

      JULIA Almost as well as I do know myself.
          To think upon her woes, I do protest
145   That I have wept a hundred several times.

      SILVIA Belike she thinks that Proteus hath forsook her.

      JULIA I think she doth; and that's her cause of sorrow.

      SILVIA Is she not passing fair?

      JULIA She hath been fairer, madam, than she is.
150   When she did think my master loved her well,
          She, in my judgment, was as fair as you.
          But since she did neglect her looking glass,
          And threw her sun-expelling mask away,
          The air hath starved the roses in her cheeks
155   And pinched the lily-tincture of her face,
          That now she is become as black as I.

      SILVIA How tall was she?

      JULIA About my stature: for, at Pentecost,
          When all our pageants of delight were played,
160   Our youth got me to play the woman's part,
          And I was trimmed in Madam Julia's gown,
          Which servèd me as fit, by all men's judgments,
          As if the garment had been made for me.
          Therefore I know she is about my height.
165   And at that time I made her weep agood,
          For I did play a lamentable part.
          Madam, 'twas Ariadne passioning
          For Theseus' perjury and unjust flight,
          Which I so lively acted with my tears
170   That my poor mistress, movèd therewithal,

140 **tender her** i.e., have a care for her interest   145 **several** separate
148 **passing** surpassingly   156 **black** i.e., from the sun   158 **Pentecost** (Whit-
sunday [seventh Sunday after Easter], an occasion for morris dances, "pageants of
delight," and such outdoor festivities)   165 **agood** aplenty   167 **Ariadne**
(daughter of King Minos, who aided Theseus' flight from the Cretan labyrinth,
only to be abandoned on the isle of Naxos)

Wept bitterly; and would I might be dead
If I in thought felt not her very sorrow!

SILVIA She is beholding to thee, gentle youth.
Alas, poor lady, desolate and left!
I weep myself to think upon thy words.   175
Here, youth, there is my purse. I give thee this
For thy sweet mistress' sake, because thou lov'st her.
Farewell.   [*Exit Silvia, with attendants.*]

JULIA And she shall thank you for't, if e'er you know her.
A virtuous gentlewoman, mild and beautiful!   180
I hope my master's suit will be but cold,
Since she respects my mistress' love so much.
Alas, how love can trifle with itself!
Here is her picture: let me see; I think,
If I had such a tire, this face of mine   185
Were full as lovely as is this of hers.
And yet the painter flattered her a little,
Unless I flatter with myself too much.
Her hair is auburn, mine is perfect yellow:
If that be all the difference in his love,   190
I'll get me such a colored periwig.
Her eyes are gray as glass, and so are mine:
Ay, but her forehead's low, and mine's as high.
What should it be that he respects in her,
But I can make respective in myself,   195
If this fond Love were not a blinded god?
Come, shadow, come, and take this shadow up,
For 'tis thy rival. O thou senseless form,
Thou shalt be worshipped, kissed, loved, and adored!
And, were there sense in his idolatry,   200
My substance should be statue in thy stead.
I'll use thee kindly for thy mistress' sake,
That used me so; or else, by Jove I vow,
I should have scratched out your unseeing eyes,
To make my master out of love with thee!   *Exit.* 205

173 **beholding** indebted   185 **tire** headdress   195 **respective** worthy of respect
196 **fond Love** i.e., foolish Cupid   197 **Come ... shadow up** come, shadow (of
my former self), and "take on" this other shadow (Silvia's portrait)

ACT V

Scene I. [*Milan. An abbey.*]

Enter Eglamour.

EGLAMOUR The sun begins to gild the western sky,
    And now it is about the very hour
    That Silvia, at Friar Patrick's cell, should meet me.
    She will not fail, for lovers break not hours,
5   Unless it be to come before their time,
    So much they spur their expedition.
    See where she comes.

[Enter Silvia.]

               Lady, a happy evening!

SILVIA Amen, amen! Go on, good Eglamour,
    Out at the postern by the abbey wall.
10   I fear I am attended by some spies.

EGLAMOUR Fear not; the forest is not three leagues off.
    If we recover that, we are sure enough.   *Exeunt.*

V.i.9 **postern** small door at side or rear   10 **attended** followed   12 **recover** reach

Scene II. [*Milan. The Duke's palace.*]

Enter Thurio, Proteus, [and] Julia.

THURIO Sir Proteus, what says Silvia to my suit?

PROTEUS O, sir, I find her milder than she was;
And yet she takes exceptions at your person.

THURIO What, that my leg is too long?

PROTEUS No; that it is too little.   5

THURIO I'll wear a boot, to make it somewhat rounder.

JULIA [*Aside*] But love will not be spurred to what
it loathes.

THURIO What says she to my face?

PROTEUS She says it is a fair one.

THURIO Nay then, the wanton lies; my face is black.   10

PROTEUS But pearls are fair; and the old saying is,
Black men are pearls in beauteous ladies' eyes.

JULIA [*Aside*] 'Tis true, such pearls as put out ladies'
eyes;
For I had rather wink than look on them.

THURIO How likes she my discourse?   15

PROTEUS Ill, when you talk of war.

THURIO But well, when I discourse of love and peace?

JULIA [*Aside*] But better, indeed, when you hold your
peace.

V.ii.7 **spurred** (with reference to preceding "boot")   15 **discourse** conversational ability

THURIO What says she to my valor?

20 PROTEUS O, sir, she makes no doubt of that.

JULIA [*Aside*] She needs not, when she knows it cow-
        ardice.

THURIO What says she to my birth?

PROTEUS That you are well derived.

JULIA [*Aside*] True, from a gentleman to a fool.

25 THURIO Considers she my possessions?

PROTEUS O, ay, and pities them.

THURIO Wherefore?

JULIA [*Aside*] That such an ass should owe them.

PROTEUS That they are out by lease.

30 JULIA Here comes the Duke.

[*Enter Duke.*]

DUKE How now, Sir Proteus! Now now, Thurio!
      Which of you saw Sir Eglamour of late?

THURIO Not I.

PROTEUS   Nor I.

DUKE   Saw you my daughter?

PROTEUS   Neither.

DUKE Why then,
35   She's fled unto that peasant Valentine,
        And Eglamour is in her company.
        'Tis true; for Friar Laurence met them both
        As he in penance wandered through the forest.
        Him he knew well, and guessed that it was she,
40   But, being masked, he was not sure of it;
        Besides, she did intend confession

---

28 **owe** own   29 **out by lease** i.e., because Thurio is such a fool, he will surely
hold onto his possessions only temporarily

At Patrick's cell this even, and there she was not.
These likelihoods confirm her flight from hence.
Therefore, I pray you, stand not to discourse,
But mount you presently, and meet with me   45
Upon the rising of the mountain foot
That leads toward Mantua, whither they are fled.
Dispatch, sweet gentlemen, and follow me.   [*Exit.*]

THURIO Why, this it is to be a peevish girl
  That flies her fortune when it follows her.   50
  I'll after, more to be revenged on Eglamour
  Than for the love of reckless Silvia.   [*Exit.*]

PROTEUS And I will follow, more for Silvia's love
  Than hate of Eglamour, that goes with her.   [*Exit.*]

JULIA And I will follow, more to cross that love   55
  Than hate for Silvia, that is gone for love.   [*Exit.*]

Scene III. [*A forest.*]

[*Enter*] Silvia [*and*] Outlaws.

FIRST OUTLAW Come, come,
  Be patient; we must bring you to our captain.

SILVIA A thousand more mischances than this one
  Have learned me how to brook this patiently.

SECOND OUTLAW Come, bring her away.   5

FIRST OUTLAW Where is the gentleman that was with her?

THIRD OUTLAW Being nimble footed, he hath outrun us,
  But Moyses and Valerius follow him.
  Go thou with her to the west end of the wood;
  There is our captain. We'll follow him that's fled;   10
  The thicket is beset; he cannot 'scape.

46 rising of the mountain foot i.e., foothill   V.iii.4 learned me how to brook
taught me how to endure   11 beset surrounded

FIRST OUTLAW Come, I must bring you to our captain's
    cave.
    Fear not; he bears an honorable mind,
    And will not use a woman lawlessly.

15   SILVIA O Valentine, this I endure for thee!   *Exeunt.*

Scene IV. [*Another part of the forest.*]

Enter Valentine.

VALENTINE How use doth breed a habit in a man!
    This shadowy desert, unfrequented woods,
    I better brook than flourishing peopled towns.
    Here can I sit alone, unseen of any,
5   And to the nightingale's complaining notes
    Tune my distresses and record my woes.
    O thou that dost inhabit in my breast,
    Leave not the mansion so long tenantless,
    Lest, growing ruinous, the building fall,
10   And leave no memory of what it was!
    Repair me with thy presence, Silvia;
    Thou gentle nymph, cherish thy forlorn swain!
                        [*Noise within.*]
    What halloing and what stir is this today?
    These are my mates, that make their wills their law,
15   Have some unhappy passenger in chase.
    They love me well; yet I have much to do
    To keep them from uncivil outrages.
    Withdraw thee, Valentine. Who's this comes here?
                           [*Retires.*]

[*Enter Proteus, Silvia, and Julia.*]

PROTEUS Madam, this service I have done for you—
20   Though you respect not aught your servant doth—

V.iv.1 **use** custom   2 **shadowy desert** wild place inhabited only with shadows (of
trees)   15 **Have** who have

To hazard life, and rescue you from him
That would have forced your honor and your love.
Vouchsafe me, for my meed, but one fair look;
A smaller boon than this I cannot beg,
And less than this, I am sure, you cannot give.   25

VALENTINE [*Aside*] How like a dream is this I see and
     hear!
Love, lend me patience to forbear awhile.

SILVIA O miserable, unhappy that I am!

PROTEUS Unhappy were you, madam, ere I came;
But by my coming I have made you happy.   30

SILVIA By thy approach thou mak'st me most unhappy.

JULIA [*Aside*] And me, when he approacheth to your
     presence.

SILVIA Had I been seizèd by a hungry lion,
I would have been a breakfast to the beast
Rather than have false Proteus rescue me.   35
O, heaven be judge how I love Valentine
Whose life's as tender to me as my soul!
And full as much, for more there cannot be,
I do detest false perjured Proteus.
Therefore be gone; solicit me no more.   40

PROTEUS What dangerous action, stood it next to death,
Would I not undergo for one calm look!
O 'tis the curse in love, and still approved,
When women cannot love where they're beloved!

SILVIA When Proteus cannot love where he's beloved!   45
Read over Julia's heart, thy first, best love,
For whose dear sake thou didst then rend thy faith
Into a thousand oaths; and all those oaths
Descended into perjury, to love me.
Thou hast no faith left now, unless thou'dst two,   50
And that's far worse than none; better have none
Than plural faith, which is too much by one.
Thou counterfeit to thy true friend!

37 tender precious   43 still approved perennially proved true

PROTEUS   In love,
Who respects friend?

SILVIA   All men but Proteus.

55 PROTEUS Nay, if the gentle spirit of moving words
        Can no way change you to a milder form,
        I'll woo you like a soldier, at arms' end,
        And love you 'gainst the nature of love—force ye.

SILVIA O heaven!

PROTEUS   I'll force thee yield to my desire.

VALENTINE [*Advancing*] Ruffian, let go that rude uncivil
60   touch,
        Thou friend of an ill fashion!

PROTEUS   Valentine!

VALENTINE Thou common friend, that's without faith
        or love—
        For such is a friend now; treacherous man!
        Thou hast beguiled my hopes; nought but mine eye
65   Could have persuaded me. Now I dare not say
        I have one friend alive; thou wouldst disprove me.
        Who should be trusted, when one's right hand
        Is perjured to the bosom? Proteus,
        I am sorry I must never trust thee more,
70   But count the world a stranger for thy sake.
        The private wound is deepest. O time most accurst,
        'Mongst all foes that a friend should be the worst!

PROTEUS My shame and guilt confounds me.
        Forgive me, Valentine. If hearty sorrow
75   Be a sufficient ransom for offense,
        I tender't here; I do as truly suffer
        As e'er I did commit.

VALENTINE   Then I am paid;

61 **friend of an ill fashion** i.e., false friend   62 **common** i.e., no better than the
ordinary   71 **private** intimate (here, given by a friend)   73 **confounds** destroys
76–77 **I do ... did commit** i.e., I do indeed suffer, as truly as I did commit the
fault   77 **paid** satisfied

And once again I do receive thee honest.
Who by repentance is not satisfied
Is nor of heaven nor earth, for these are pleased.   80
By penitence th' Eternal's wrath's appeased;
And, that my love may appear plain and free,
All that was mine in Silvia I give thee.

JULIA O me unhappy!   [*Swoons.*]

PROTEUS Look to the boy.   85

VALENTINE Why, boy! Why, wag! How now! What's
   the matter? Look up; speak.

JULIA O good sir, my master charged me to deliver a
   ring to Madam Silvia, which, out of my neglect, was
   never done.   90

PROTEUS Where is that ring, boy?

JULIA   Here 'tis; this is it.

PROTEUS How! Let me see.
   Why, this is the ring I gave to Julia.

JULIA O, cry you mercy, sir, I have mistook.
   This is the ring you sent to Silvia.   95

PROTEUS But how cam'st thou by this ring? At my
   depart I gave this unto Julia.

JULIA And Julia herself did give it me;
   And Julia herself hath brought it hither.

PROTEUS How! Julia!   100

JULIA Behold her that gave aim to all thy oaths,
   And entertained 'em deeply in her heart.
   How oft hast thou with perjury cleft the root!
   O Proteus, let this habit make thee blush!
   Be thou ashamed that I have took upon me   105
   Such an immodest raiment, if shame live
   In a disguise of love.

---

78 **receive thee honest** accept you as being honorable 94 **cry you mercy** I beg
your pardon 101 **gave aim to** was the object (target) of 104 **habit** i.e., her
boy's garb 106–07 **if shame ... of love** if it can be shameful to disguise oneself
for the sake of love

It is the lesser blot, modesty finds,
Women to change their shapes than men their
    minds.

PROTEUS Than men their minds! 'Tis true. O heaven,
110   were man
But constant, he were perfect! That one error
Fills him with faults, makes him run through all th'
    sins:
Inconstancy falls off ere it begins.
What is in Silvia's face, but I may spy
115   More fresh in Julia's with a constant eye?

VALENTINE Come, come, a hand from either.
Let me be blest to make this happy close;
'Twere pity two such friends should be long foes.

PROTEUS Bear witness, Heaven, I have my wish forever.

120 JULIA And I mine.

[*Enter Outlaws, with Duke and Thurio.*]

OUTLAWS A prize, a prize, a prize!

VALENTINE Forbear, forbear, I say! It is my lord the
    Duke.
Your Grace is welcome to a man disgraced,
Banished Valentine.

DUKE   Sir Valentine!

125 THURIO Yonder is Silvia, and Silvia's mine.

VALENTINE Thurio, give back, or else embrace thy
    death.
Come not within the measure of my wrath.
Do not name Silvia thine; if once again,
Verona shall not hold thee. Here she stands.
130   Take but possession of her with a touch:
I dare thee but to breathe upon my love.

---

113 **Inconstancy ... begins** i.e., the inconstant man proves false even before
he begins to love 117 **close** joining of hands 126 **give back** back off
127 **measure** range, reach 129 **Verona** i.e., Milan; see III.i.81,n.)

THURIO Sir Valentine, I care not for her, I.
  I hold him but a fool that will endanger
  His body for a girl that loves him not.
  I claim her not, and therefore she is thine.   135

DUKE The more degenerate and base art thou,
  To make such means for her as thou hast done,
  And leave her on such slight conditions.
  Now, by the honor of my ancestry,
  I do applaud thy spirit, Valentine,   140
  And think thee worthy of an empress' love.
  Know, then, I here forget all former griefs,
  Cancel all grudge, repeal thee home again,
  Plead a new state in thy unrivaled merit,
  To which I thus subscribe: Sir Valentine,   145
  Thou art a gentleman, and well derived;
  Take thou thy Silvia, for thou hast deserved her.

VALENTINE I thank your Grace; the gift hath made me
      happy.
  I now beseech you, for your daughter's sake,
  To grant one boon that I shall ask of you.   150

DUKE I grant it, for thine own, whate'er it be.

VALENTINE These banished men that I have kept withal
  Are men endued with worthy qualities.
  Forgive them what they have committed here,
  And let them be recalled from their exile: 155
  They are reformèd, civil, full of good,
  And fit for great employment, worthy lord.

DUKE Thou hast prevailed; I pardon them and thee.
  Dispose of them as thou know'st their deserts.
  Come, let us go. We will include all jars   160
  With triumphs, mirth, and rare solemnity.

---

137 **means for** efforts to win   143 **repeal** recall (from banishment)   144 **plead ... merit** (the general sense appears to be one of the following: (1) plead to be restored to your good graces, having formerly misjudged them (2) proclaim that you are elevated to a new place in my favor, earned by your unrivaled merit) 152 **kept withal** lived with   153 **endued** endowed   160 **include all jars** conclude all discords   161 **triumphs ... solemnity** celebrations ... festivity

VALENTINE And, as we walk along, I dare be bold
With our discourse to make your Grace to smile.
What think you of this page, my lord?

165 DUKE I think the boy hath grace in him; he blushes.

VALENTINE I warrant you, my lord, more grace than
boy.

DUKE What mean you by that saying?

VALENTINE Please you, I'll tell you as we pass along,
That you will wonder what hath fortunèd.
170 Come, Proteus; 'tis your penance but to hear
The story of your loves discoverèd.
That done, our day of marriage shall be yours;
One feast, one house, one mutual happiness.

Exeunt.

FINIS

169 **fortunèd** chanced   170 **'tis your penance but** your only penance is
171 **discoverèd** revealed

Textual Note

The Two Gentlemen of Verona was first printed in the First Folio of 1623, which is the authority for the present text. In the Folio it is the second play, standing between *The Tempest* and *The Merry Wives of Windsor*, the title of the latter play mistakenly appearing at the top of the final two pages. Names of characters who participate in each scene are grouped at the head of the scene, without notice made of the point of their entrance. The present edition deletes these names, and provides them, in square brackets, at the appropriate places later in the scenes. The Folio gives "Protheus" for "Proteus" and places the dramatis personae at the end of the text. Certain irregularities occur in place names, as though Shakespeare had changed his mind or become confused about principal locations; thus in II.v Padua rather than Milan is identified as the place of action by Speed, and in III.i the Duke of Milan speaks of a lady "in Verona here." In the present edition, speech prefixes have been regularized, spelling and punctuation have been modernized, and obvious typographical errors have been corrected. Added material (stage directions, etc.) is set in brackets. Act and scene divisions are those of the Folio, translated from Latin into English. The relatively few emendations of the Folio text are indicated below: the present reading is given in bold, followed by the Folio reading in roman.

I.i.65 **leave loue** loue   77 **a sheep** Sheepe   144-45 **testerned** cestern'd

I.ii.88 **your** you

I.iii.91 **Exeunt** Exeunt. Finis

II.iii.29 **wood** would

II.iv.49 **father's in** father is in   107 **mistress a** Mistresse   165 **makes** make   195 **Is it mine eye** It is mine   213 **Exit** Exeunt

II.v.38 **that my** that that my

III.i.281 **master's ship** Mastership   318 **kissed fasting** fasting   378s.d. **Exit** Exeunt

277

TEXTUAL NOTE

IV.i.10 **he's** he is   35 **miserable** often miserable   49 **An** And   49 **near** Neece

IV.ii.111 **his** her

IV.iii.18 **abhors** abhor'd

IV.iv.70 **thou** thee   74 **to leave** not leaue   205 **Exit** Exeunt

V.ii.18 **your peace** you peace   32 **Sir Eglamour** Eglamoure   56 **Exit** Exeunt

WILLIAM SHAKESPEARE

LOVE'S LABOR'S LOST

Edited by John Arthos

[*Dramatis Personae*

FERDINAND, King of Navarre
BEROWNE
LONGAVILLE } young lords attending on the King
DUMAINE
BOYET, an elderly lord attending on the Princess of France
MARCADE, a messenger
DON ADRIANO DE ARMADO, a fantastical Spaniard
SIR NATHANIEL, a curate
DULL, a constable
HOLOFERNES, a schoolmaster
COSTARD, a clown
MOTH, page to Don Armado
A FORESTER
THE PRINCESS OF FRANCE
ROSALINE
MARIA } ladies attending on the Princess
KATHARINE
JAQUENETTA, a country wench
OFFICERS AND OTHERS ATTENDANT ON THE KING AND
 PRINCESS

Scene: Navarre]

LOVE'S LABOR'S LOST

[ACT I

Scene I. *The park of the King of Navarre.*]

Enter Ferdinand King of Navarre, Berowne,
Longaville, and Dumaine.

KING Let fame, that all hunt after in their lives,
Live regist'red upon our brazen tombs
And then grace us in the disgrace of death,
When, spite of cormorant devouring time,
Th' endeavor of this present breath may buy   5
That honor which shall bate his scythe's keen edge
And make us heirs of all eternity.
Therefore, brave conquerors—for so you are
That war against your own affections
And the huge army of the world's desires—   10
Our late edict shall strongly stand in force:
Navarre shall be the wonder of the world;
Our court shall be a little academe,
Still and contemplative in living art.

Text references are printed in **boldface** type; the annotation follows in roman
type.
I.i.3 **disgrace** degradation 4 **cormorant** ravenous 6 **bate** make dull
13 **academe** academy 14 **Still ... art** continually studying the art of living

281

15   You three, Berowne, Dumaine, and Longaville,
        Have sworn for three years' term to live with me,
        My fellow scholars, and to keep those statutes
        That are recorded in this schedule here.
        Your oaths are passed; and now subscribe your
            names,
20   That his own hand may strike his honor down
        That violates the smallest branch herein.
        If you are armed to do as sworn to do,
        Subscribe to your deep oaths, and keep it too.

    LONGAVILLE I am resolved. 'Tis but a three years' fast.
25   The mind shall banquet though the body pine.
        Fat paunches have lean pates, and dainty bits
        Make rich the ribs, but bankrout quite the wits.

    DUMAINE My loving lord, Dumaine is mortified.
        The grosser manner of these world's delights
30   He throws upon the gross world's baser slaves.
        To love, to wealth, to pomp, I pine and die,
        With all these living in philosophy.

    BEROWNE I can but say their protestation over—
        So much, dear liege, I have already sworn,
35   That is, to live and study here three years.
        But there are other strict observances:
        As not to see a woman in that term—
        Which I hope well is not enrollèd there;
        And one day in a week to touch no food,
40   And but one meal on every day beside—
        The which I hope is not enrollèd there;
        And then to sleep but three hours in the night,
        And not be seen to wink of all the day
        (When I was wont to think no harm all night
45   And make a dark night too of half the day)—
        Which I hope well is not enrollèd there.
        O, these are barren tasks, too hard to keep,
        Not to see ladies, study, fast, not sleep!

22 **armed** resolved   27 **bankrout** bankrupt   28 **mortified** dead to worldly
pleasures   33 **say their protestation over** repeat their solemn declarations
43 **wink of** close the eyes during

KING Your oath is passed, to pass away from these.

BEROWNE Let me say no, my liege, and if you please.   50
   I only swore to study with your Grace
   And stay here in your court for three years' space.

LONGAVILLE You swore to that, Berowne, and to the
   rest.

BEROWNE By yea and nay, sir, then I swore in jest.
   What is the end of study, let me know?   55

KING Why, that to know which else we should not
   know.

BEROWNE Things hid and barred, you mean, from
   common sense?

KING Ay, that is study's godlike recompense.

BEROWNE Come on then, I will swear to study so,
   To know the thing I am forbid to know: 60
   As thus—to study where I well may dine
   When I to feast expressly am forbid;
   Or study where to meet some mistress fine
   When mistresses from common sense are hid;
   Or having sworn too hard-a-keeping oath,   65
   Study to break it and not break my troth.
   If study's gain be thus, and this be so,
   Study knows that which yet it doth not know.
   Swear me to this, and I will ne'er say no.

KING These be the stops that hinder study quite   70
   And train our intellects to vain delight.

BEROWNE Why, all delights are vain, but that most
   vain
   Which, with pain purchased, doth inherit pain:
   As, painfully to pore upon a book,
   To seek the light of truth, while truth the while   75
   Doth falsely blind the eyesight of his look.

---

50 and if if   54 By yea and nay in all earnestness   66 troth faith   70 stops
obstructions   71 train entice   76 falsely treacherously

Light seeking light doth light of light beguile;
So, ere you find where light in darkness lies,
Your light grows dark by losing of your eyes.
80 Study me how to please the eye indeed
By fixing it upon a fairer eye,
Who dazzling so, that eye shall be his heed
And give him light that it was blinded by.
Study is like the heaven's glorious sun,
85 That will not be deep-searched with saucy looks.
Small have continual plodders ever won
Save base authority from others' books.
These earthly godfathers of heaven's lights,
That give a name to every fixèd star
90 Have no more profit of their shining nights
Than those that walk and wot not what they are.
Too much to know is to know nought but fame;
And every godfather can give a name.

KING How well he's read to reason against reading!

95 DUMAINE Proceeded well, to stop all good proceeding!

LONGAVILLE He weeds the corn, and still lets grow the
    weeding.

BEROWNE The spring is near, when green geese are
    a-breeding.

DUMAINE How follows that?

BEROWNE   Fit in his place and time.

DUMAINE In reason nothing.

BEROWNE   Something then in rhyme.

100 KING Berowne is like an envious sneaping frost
    That bites the first-born infants of the spring.

---

77 **Light ... beguile** i.e., eyes in seeking truth lose their sight in too much
seeking 82 **heed** protector 88 **earthly godfathers** i.e., astronomers 91 **wot**
know 92 **fame** report 95 **Proceeded** took a degree at the university 96 **corn**
wheat 96 **weeding** weeds 97 **green geese** geese born the previous autumn
100 **sneaping** nipping (Berowne's "rhyme" is taken as "rime" or frost)

BEROWNE Well, say I am! Why should proud summer boast
  Before the birds have any cause to sing?
  Why should I joy in an abortive birth?
  At Christmas I no more desire a rose   105
  Than wish a snow in May's new-fangled shows,
  But like of each thing that in season grows.
  So you—to study now it is too late—
  Climb o'er the house to unlock the little gate.

KING Well, sit you out. Go home, Berowne. Adieu.   110

BEROWNE No, my good lord, I have sworn to stay with you;
  And though I have for barbarism spoke more
  Than for that angel knowledge you can say,
  Yet confident I'll keep what I have swore,
  And bide the penance of each three years' day.   115
  Give me the paper, let me read the same,
  And to the strictest decrees I'll write my name.

KING How well this yielding rescues thee from shame!

BEROWNE [*Reads*] "Item. That no woman shall come within a mile of my court—" Hath this been pro-   120
claimed?

LONGAVILLE Four days ago.

BEROWNE Let's see the penalty. [*Reads*] "—on pain of losing her tongue." Who devised this penalty?

LONGAVILLE Marry, that did I.

BEROWNE   Sweet lord, and why?   125

LONGAVILLE To fright them hence with that dread penalty.

BEROWNE A dangerous law against gentility!
  [*Reads*] "Item. If any man be seen to talk with a woman within the term of three years, he shall

112 **barbarism** philistinism   115 **each three years' day** each day of the three years   125 **Marry** By Mary (mild oath)   127 **gentility** good manners

130   endure such public shame as the rest of the court
       can possibly devise."
       This article, my liege, yourself must break;
       For well you know here comes in embassy
       The French king's daughter with yourself to speak,
135   A maid of grace and complete majesty,
       About surrender up of Aquitaine
       To her decrepit, sick, and bed-rid father.
       Therefore this article is made in vain,
       Or vainly comes th' admirèd princess hither.

140 KING What say you, lords? Why, this was quite forgot.

    BEROWNE So study evermore is overshot.
       While it doth study to have what it would,
       It doth forget to do the thing it should;
       And when it hath the thing it hunteth most,
145   'Tis won as towns with fire—so won, so lost.

    KING We must of force dispense with this decree.
       She must lie here on mere necessity.

    BEROWNE Necessity will make us all forsworn
       Three thousand times within this three years' space:
150   For every man with his affects is born,
       Not by might mast'red, but by special grace.
       If I break faith, this word shall speak for me,
       I am forsworn "on mere necessity."
       So to the laws at large I write my name;
                                          [*Subscribes.*]
155   And he that breaks them in the least degree
       Stands in attainder of eternal shame.
       Suggestions are to other as to me,
       But I believe, although I seem so loath,
       I am the last that will last keep his oath.
160   But is there no quick recreation granted?

    KING Ay, that there is. Our court, you know, is
              haunted

141 **overshot** wide of the mark   145 **won as towns with fire** destroyed in being
won   146 **of force** of necessity   147 **lie** lodge   147 **mere** simple   150 **affects**
passions   156 **in attainder of** to be condemned to   157 **Suggestions** temptations
158 **loath** reluctant

With a refinèd traveler of Spain,
A man in all the world's new fashion planted,
That hath a mint of phrases in his brain;
One who the music of his own vain tongue   165
Doth ravish like enchanting harmony;
A man of complements, whom right and wrong
Have chose as umpire of their mutiny.
This child of fancy, that Armado hight,
For interim to our studies shall relate   170
In high-born words the worth of many a knight
From tawny Spain, lost in the world's debate.
How you delight, my lords, I know not, I,
But, I protest, I love to hear him lie,
And I will use him for my minstrelsy.   175

BEROWNE Armado is a most illustrious wight,
A man of fire-new words, fashion's own knight.

LONGAVILLE Costard the swain and he shall be our
    sport;
And so to study three years is but short.

    Enter [Dull,] a Constable, with Costard, [a Clown,]
                    with a letter.

DULL Which is the duke's own person?   180

BEROWNE This, fellow. What wouldst?

DULL I myself reprehend his own person, for I am
his Grace's farborough. But I would see his own
person in flesh and blood.

BEROWNE This is he.   185

DULL Signior Arm—Arm—commends you. There's
villainy abroad. This letter will tell you more.

COSTARD Sir, the contempts thereof are as touching
me.

167 **complements** formal manners 169 **hight** is named 170 **interim** interruption 175 **minstrelsy** court entertainer 177 **fire-new** fresh from the mint 178 **swain** countryman 182 **reprehend** (Dull means to say, "represent") 183 **farborough** petty constable 188 **contempts** (Costard means the "contents" of the letter)

190   KING A letter from the magnificent Armado.

BEROWNE How long soever the matter, I hope in God for high words.

LONGAVILLE A high hope for a low heaven. God grant us patience!

195   BEROWNE To hear, or forbear hearing?

LONGAVILLE To hear meekly, sir, and to laugh moderately, or to forbear both.

BEROWNE Well, sir, be it as the style shall give us cause to climb in the merriness.

200   COSTARD The matter is to me, sir, as concerning Jaquenetta. The manner of it is, I was taken with the manner.

BEROWNE In what manner?

COSTARD In manner and form following, sir—all those
205   three: I was seen with her in the manor-house, sitting with her upon the form, and taken following her into the park; which, put together, is, in manner and form, following. Now, sir, for the manner—it is the manner of a man to speak to a woman.
210   For the form—in some form.

BEROWNE For the following, sir?

COSTARD As it shall follow in my correction, and God defend the right!

KING Will you hear this letter with attention?

215   BEROWNE As we would hear an oracle.

COSTARD Such is the simplicity of man to hearken after the flesh.

KING [*Reads*] "Great deputy, the welkin's vicegerent, and sole dominator of Navarre, my soul's earth's
220   God, and body's fost'ring patron—"

201-02 **with the manner** in the act   206 **form** bench   212 **correction** punishment   218 **welkin's vicegerent** deputy-ruler of heaven

288

COSTARD Not a word of Costard yet.

KING "So it is—"

COSTARD It may be so; but if he say it is so, he is, in telling true, but so.

KING Peace!   225

COSTARD Be to me and every man that dares not fight.

KING No words!

COSTARD Of other men's secrets, I beseech you.

KING [Reads] "So it is, besieged with sable-colored melancholy, I did commend the black-oppressing   230 humor to the most wholesome physic of thy health-giving air; and, as I am a gentleman, betook myself to walk. The time When? About the sixth hour; when beasts most graze, birds best peck, and men sit down to that nourishment which is   235 called supper. So much for the time When. Now for the ground Which? Which, I mean, I walked upon. It is ycleped thy park. Then for the place Where? Where, I mean, I did encounter that obscene and most preposterous event, that draweth   240 from my snow-white pen the ebon-colored ink, which here thou viewest, beholdest, surveyest, or seest. But to the place Where? It standeth northnorth-east and by east from the west corner of thy curious-knotted garden. There did I see that low-   245 spirited swain, that base minnow of thy mirth—"

COSTARD Me?

KING "that unlettered small-knowing soul—"

COSTARD Me?

KING "that shallow vassal—"   250

224 but so not worth much   230-31 black-oppressing humor fluid in the body that causes melancholy   231 physic treatment   238 ycleped called   241 snow-white pen goose-quill   245 curious-knotted flower beds and paths in intricate patterns   248 unlettered illiterate   250 vassal underling

COSTARD Still me!

KING "which, as I remember, hight Costard—"

COSTARD O me!

255 KING "snorted and consorted, contrary to thy established proclaimed edict and continent canon, which with—O, with—but with this I passion to say wherewith—"

COSTARD With a wench.

260 KING "with a child of our grandmother Eve, a female; or, for thy more sweet understanding, a woman. Him I (as my ever-esteemed duty pricks me on) have sent to thee, to receive the meed of punishment, by thy sweet Grace's officer, Anthony Dull, a man of good repute, carriage, bearing, and esti-
265 mation."

DULL Me, an 't shall please you: I am Anthony Dull.

KING "For Jaquenetta (so is the weaker vessel called), which I apprehended with the aforesaid swain, I keep her as a vessel of thy law's fury, and
270 shall, at the least of thy sweet notice, bring her to trial. Thine in all compliments of devoted and heart-burning heat of duty,

                          Don Adriano de Armado."

BEROWNE This is not so well as I looked for, but the
275 best that ever I heard.

KING Ay, the best for the worst. But, sirrah, what say you to this?

COSTARD Sir, I confess the wench.

KING Did you hear the proclamation?

---

252 **hight** called   255 **continent canon** the decree restraining the members of the Academy   261 **pricks** spurs   262 **meed** reward   267 **weaker vessel** (general phrase for "womankind")   270 **at the least ... notice** at the slightest indication of thy concern   276 **sirrah** (term of address used to an inferior)

COSTARD I do confess much of the hearing it, but little 280
of the marking of it.

KING It was proclaimed a year's imprisonment to be
taken with a wench.

COSTARD I was taken with none, sir; I was taken with
a damsel. 285

KING Well, it was proclaimed "damsel."

COSTARD This was no damsel neither, sir, she was a
virgin.

KING It is so varied too, for it was proclaimed
"virgin." 290

COSTARD If it were, I deny her virginity. I was taken
with a maid.

KING This maid will not serve your turn, sir.

COSTARD This maid will serve my turn, sir.

KING Sir, I will pronounce your sentence: you shall 295
fast a week with bran and water.

COSTARD I had rather pray a month with mutton and
porridge.

KING And Don Armado shall be your keeper.
My Lord Berowne, see him delivered o'er. 300
And go we, lords, to put in practice that
Which each to other hath so strongly sworn.
        [*Exeunt King, Longaville, and Dumaine.*]

BEROWNE I'll lay my head to any good man's hat,
These oaths and laws will prove an idle scorn.
Sirrah, come on. 305

COSTARD I suffer for the truth, sir, for true it is I was
taken with Jaquenetta, and Jaquenetta is a true
girl. And therefore welcome the sour cup of prosperity! Affliction may one day smile again, and till
then sit thee down, sorrow!   *Exeunt.* 310

289 **varied** distinguished 294 **turn** (Costard uses the word in a bawdy sense)
303 **lay** bet   307 **true** honest

[Scene II. *The park*.]

Enter Armado and Moth, his Page.

ARMADO Boy, what sign is it when a man of great
spirit grows melancholy?

MOTH A great sign, sir, that he will look sad.

ARMADO Why, sadness is one and the selfsame thing,
5　dear imp.

MOTH No, no, O Lord, sir, no!

ARMADO How canst thou part sadness and melancholy, my tender juvenal?

MOTH By a familiar demonstration of the working,
10　my tough signor.

ARMADO Why tough signor? Why tough signor?

MOTH Why tender juvenal? Why tender juvenal?

ARMADO I spoke it, tender juvenal, as a congruent
epitheton appertaining to thy young days, which
15　we may nominate tender.

MOTH And I, tough signor, as an appertinent title to
your old time, which we may name tough.

ARMADO Pretty and apt.

MOTH How mean you, sir? I pretty, and my saying
20　apt? Or I apt and my saying pretty?

I.ii.s.d. **Moth** (probably pronounced, and with the meaning of, "mote," i.e., speck)
7 **part** distinguish between　8 **juvenal** youth (it may also signify *Juvenal*, the
Roman satirist, and allude to the nickname of Thomas Nashe, Elizabethan writer)
10 **signor** (with a pun on "senior")　13-14 **congruent epitheton** appropriate
adjective

ARMADO Thou pretty, because little.

MOTH Little pretty, because little. Wherefore apt?

ARMADO And therefore apt because quick.

MOTH Speak you this in my praise, master?

ARMADO In thy condign praise.   25

MOTH I will praise an eel with the same praise.

ARMADO What, that an eel is ingenious?

MOTH That an eel is quick.

ARMADO I do say thou art quick in answers. Thou
heat'st my blood.   30

MOTH I am answered, sir.

ARMADO I love not to be crossed.

MOTH [*Aside*] He speaks the mere contrary—crosses
love not him.

ARMADO I have promised to study three years with the   35
duke.

MOTH You may do it in an hour, sir.

ARMADO Impossible.

MOTH How many is one thrice told?

ARMADO I am ill at reck'ning—it fitteth the spirit of a   40
tapster.

MOTH You are a gentleman and a gamester, sir.

ARMADO I confess both. They are both the varnish of a
complete man.

MOTH Then I am sure you know how much the gross   45
sum of deuce–ace amounts to.

ARMADO It doth amount to one more than two.

25 **condign** well-deserved   33 **crosses** coins (so named for the crosses engraved
on them)   41 **tapster** bartender   43 **varnish** outward gloss

293

MOTH Which the base vulgar do call three.

ARMADO True.

50 MOTH Why, sir, is this such a piece of study? Now
here is three studied ere ye'll thrice wink; and how
easy it is to put "years" to the word "three," and
study three years in two words, the dancing horse
will tell you.

55 ARMADO A most fine figure.

MOTH [*Aside*] To prove you a cipher.

ARMADO I will hereupon confess I am in love, and
as it is base for a soldier to love, so am I in love
with a base wench. If drawing my sword against
60 the humor of affection would deliver me from the
reprobate thought of it, I would take Desire prisoner and ransom him to any French courtier for
a new devised cursy. I think scorn to sigh: methinks I should outswear Cupid. Comfort me, boy.
65 What great men have been in love?

MOTH Hercules, master.

ARMADO Most sweet Hercules! More authority, dear
boy, name more; and, sweet my child, let them
be men of good repute and carriage.

70 MOTH Samson, master—he was a man of good carriage, great carriage, for he carried the town-gates
on his back like a porter, and he was in love.

ARMADO O well-knit Samson, strong-jointed Samson!
I do excel thee in my rapier as much as thou didst
75 me in carrying gates. I am in love too. Who was
Samson's love, my dear Moth?

MOTH A woman, master.

---

53 **dancing horse** (a performing horse well-known for beating out numbers)
55 **figure** figure of speech   60 **humor** innate disposition   63 **new devised cursy**
novel mannerism   63 **think scorn** disdain   64 **outswear** forswear

ARMADO Of what complexion?

MOTH Of all the four, or the three, or the two, or
one of the four.   80

ARMADO Tell me precisely of what complexion.

MOTH Of the sea-water green, sir.

ARMADO Is that one of the four complexions?

MOTH As I have read, sir, and the best of them too.

ARMADO Green indeed is the color of lovers. But to   85
have a love of that color, methinks Samson had
small reason for it. He surely affected her for her
wit.

MOTH It was so, sir, for she had a green wit.

ARMADO My love is most immaculate white and red.   90

MOTH Most maculate thoughts, master, are masked
under such colors.

ARMADO Define, define, well-educated infant.

MOTH My father's wit, and my mother's tongue, assist
me!   95

ARMADO Sweet invocation of a child, most pretty and
pathetical.

MOTH If she be made of white and red,
        Her faults will ne'er be known,
    For blushing cheeks by faults are bred,   100
        And fears by pale white shown.
    Then if she fear or be to blame,
        By this you shall not know,
    For still her cheeks possess the same
        Which native she doth owe.   105
A dangerous rhyme, master, against the reason of
white and red.

78 complexion disposition 79 all the four (the four humors or fluids of the
body: blood, phlegm, bile, black bile) 85 Green (immature) 88 wit mind
91 maculate spotted 105 native by nature 105 owe possess

ARMADO Is there not a ballet, boy, of the King and
the Beggar?

110 MOTH The world was very guilty of such a ballet
some three ages since. But I think now 'tis not to
be found, or if it were, it would neither serve for
the writing nor the tune.

ARMADO I will have that subject newly writ o'er, that
115 I may example my digression by some mighty
precedent. Boy, I do love that country girl that I
took in the park with the rational hind, Costard.
She deserves well.

MOTH [*Aside*] To be whipped—and yet a better love
120 than my master.

ARMADO Sing, boy. My spirit grows heavy in love.

MOTH And that's great marvel, loving a light wench.

ARMADO I say, sing.

MOTH Forbear till this company be past.

*Enter [Costard, the] Clown, [Dull, the]
Constable, and [Jaquenetta, a] Wench.*

125 DULL Sir, the duke's pleasure is that you keep Costard
safe, and you must suffer him to take no delight
nor no penance, but 'a must fast three days a
week. For this damsel, I must keep her at the park
—she is allowed for the day-woman. Fare you
130 well.

ARMADO I do betray myself with blushing. Maid!

JAQUENETTA Man?

ARMADO I will visit thee at the lodge.

JAQUENETTA That's hereby.

---

108 **ballet** ballad   115 **digression** (Armado means to say, "transgression")
117 **rational hind** intelligent yokel   127 **penance** (perhaps Dull means to say
"pleasance," meaning pleasure)   127 **'a** he   129 **allowed for the day-woman**
admitted as the dairy maid

ARMADO I know where it is situate.   135

JAQUENETTA Lord, how wise you are!

ARMADO I will tell thee wonders.

JAQUENETTA With that face?

ARMADO I love thee.

JAQUENETTA So I heard you say.   140

ARMADO And so farewell.

JAQUENETTA Fair weather after you!

DULL Come, Jaquenetta, away!
                    Exeunt [Dull and Jaquenetta].

ARMADO Villain, thou shalt fast for thy offenses ere
    thou be pardoned.   145

COSTARD Well, sir, I hope when I do it I shall do it
    on a full stomach.

ARMADO Thou shalt be heavily punished.

COSTARD I am more bound to you than your fellows,
    for they are but lightly rewarded.   150

ARMADO Take away this villain. Shut him up.

MOTH Come, you transgressing slave, away!

COSTARD Let me not be pent up, sir. I will fast, being
    loose.

MOTH No, sir, that were fast and loose. Thou shalt   155
    to prison.

COSTARD Well, if ever I do see the merry days of
    desolation that I have seen, some shall see.

MOTH What shall some see?

---

147 **on a full stomach** bravely   149 **fellows** servants   155 **fast and loose** not
playing fairly

160 COSTARD Nay, nothing, Master Moth, but what they
     look upon. It is not for prisoners to be too silent
     in their words, and therefore I will say nothing. I
     thank God I have as little patience as another man,
     and therefore I can be quiet.   *Exit [with Moth].*

165 ARMADO I do affect the very ground (which is base)
     where her shoe (which is baser) guided by her foot
     (which is basest) doth tread. I shall be forsworn
     (which is a great argument of falsehood) if I love.
     And how can that be true love which is falsely at-
170 tempted? Love is a familiar; Love is a devil. There
     is no evil angel but Love. Yet was Samson so
     tempted, and he had an excellent strength; yet was
     Solomon so seduced, and he had a very good wit.
     Cupid's butt-shaft is too hard for Hercules' club,
175 and therefore too much odds for a Spaniard's
     rapier. The first and second cause will not serve
     my turn; the *passado* he respects not, the *duello*
     he regards not. His disgrace is to be called boy, but
     his glory is to subdue men. Adieu, valor; rust, ra-
180 pier; be still, drum; for your manager is in love;
     yea, he loveth. Assist me some extemporal god of
     rhyme, for I am sure I shall turn sonnet. Devise,
     wit; write, pen; for I am for whole volumes in folio.
                                                      Exit.

---

162 **words** (probably with pun on wards = cells)   165 **affect** love   170 **familiar**
attendant spirit   174 **butt-shaft** unbarbed arrow   176 **first and second cause**
(referring to rules governing the conduct of a duel)   177 **passado** forward thrust
177 **duello** correct way of dueling   181-82 **extemporal god of rhyme** god of
rhymes written on the spur of the moment   182 **turn sonnet** compose a sonnet

[ACT II

Scene I. *The park.*]

*Enter the Princess of France, with three attending Ladies
[Maria, Katharine, Rosaline] and three Lords, [one
named Boyet].*

BOYET Now, madam, summon up your dearest
 spirits.
Consider who the king your father sends,
To whom he sends, and what's his embassy:
Yourself, held precious in the world's esteem,
To parley with the sole inheritor   5
Of all perfections that a man may owe,
Matchless Navarre; the plea of no less weight
Than Aquitaine, a dowry for a queen.
Be now as prodigal of all dear grace
As Nature was in making graces dear   10
When she did starve the general world beside,
And prodigally gave them all to you.

PRINCESS Good Lord Boyet, my beauty, though but
 mean,
Needs not the painted flourish of your praise.
Beauty is bought by judgment of the eye,   15
Not utt'red by base sale of chapmen's tongues.

II.i.1 **dearest spirits** best intelligence 5 **inheritor** possessor 6 **owe** own
10 **graces dear** beauty scarce 14 **painted flourish** elaborate ornament
16 **utt'red ... tongues** put up for sale by hucksters

I am less proud to hear you tell my worth
Than you much willing to be counted wise
In spending your wit in the praise of mine.
20   But now to task the tasker: good Boyet,
You are not ignorant all-telling fame
Doth noise abroad Navarre hath made a vow,
Till painful study shall outwear three years,
No woman may approach his silent court.
25   Therefore to's seemeth it a needful course,
Before we enter his forbidden gates,
To know his pleasure; and in that behalf,
Bold of your worthiness, we single you
As our best-moving fair solicitor.
30   Tell him the daughter of the king of France,
On serious business, craving quick dispatch,
Importunes personal conference with his Grace.
Haste, signify so much while we attend
Like humble-visaged suitors his high will.

35   BOYET Proud of employment, willingly I go.

                                        Exit Boyet.

PRINCESS All pride is willing pride, and yours is so.
Who are the votaries, my loving lords,
That are vow-fellows with this virtuous duke?

LORD Longaville is one.

PRINCESS   Know you the man?

40   MARIA I know him, madam. At a marriage feast
Between Lord Perigort and the beauteous heir
Of Jacques Falconbridge solemnizèd
In Normandy saw I this Longaville.
A man of sovereign parts he is esteemed,
45   Well fitted in arts, glorious in arms.
Nothing becomes him ill that he would well.
The only soil of his fair virtue's gloss—

20 **task the tasker** set a task to the one who sets tasks 28 **Bold of your worthiness** confident of your worth 29 **best-moving** most persuasive 37 **votaries** those who have sworn a vow 44 **sovereign parts** lordly qualities 46 **Nothing . . . well** nothing that he values is unbecoming to him

If virtue's gloss will stain with any soil—
Is a sharp wit matched with too blunt a will,
Whose edge hath power to cut, whose will still wills   50
It should none spare that come within his power.

PRINCESS Some merry mocking lord, belike—is 't so?

MARIA They say so most that most his humors know.

PRINCESS Such short-lived wits do wither as they grow.
Who are the rest?   55

KATHARINE The young Dumaine, a well-accomplished
youth,
Of all that virtue love for virtue loved;
Most power to do most harm, least knowing ill,
For he hath wit to make an ill shape good,
And shape to win grace though he had no wit.   60
I saw him at the Duke Alençon's once;
And much too little of that good I saw
Is my report to his great worthiness.

ROSALINE Another of these students at that time
Was there with him, if I have heard a truth.   65
Berowne they call him; but a merrier man,
Within the limit of becoming mirth,
I never spent an hour's talk withal.
His eye begets occasion for his wit;
For every object that the one doth catch   70
The other turns to a mirth-moving jest,
Which his fair tongue (conceit's expositor)
Delivers in such apt and gracious words,
That agèd ears play truant at his tales,
And younger hearings are quite ravishèd,   75
So sweet and voluble is his discourse.

PRINCESS God bless my ladies! Are they all in love,
That every one her own hath garnishèd
With such bedecking ornaments of praise?

62 **much too little** far short   63 **to** compared to   68 **withal** with   69 **begets occasion** finds opportunity   72 **conceit's expositor** one who explains an ingenious notion

LORD   Here comes Boyet.

Enter Boyet.

80   PRINCESS   Now, what admittance, lord?

BOYET   Navarre had notice of your fair approach;
And he and his competitors in oath
Were all addressed to meet you, gentle lady,
Before I came. Marry, thus much I have learnt;
85   He rather means to lodge you in the field,
Like one that comes here to besiege his court,
Than seek a dispensation for his oath
To let you enter his unpeopled house.

[*The Ladies mask.*]

Enter Navarre, Longaville, Dumaine, and
Berowne, [with Attendants].

Here comes Navarre.

90   KING   Fair princess, welcome to the court of Navarre.

PRINCESS   "Fair" I give you back again; and "welcome" I have not yet. The roof of this court is too high to be yours, and welcome to the wide fields too base to be mine.

95   KING   You shall be welcome, madam, to my court.

PRINCESS   I will be welcome, then. Conduct me thither.

KING   Hear me, dear lady—I have sworn an oath.

PRINCESS   Our Lady help my lord! He'll be forsworn.

KING   Not for the world, fair madam, by my will.

PRINCESS   Why, will shall break it, will, and nothing
100   else.

KING   Your ladyship is ignorant what it is.

---

80 **admittance** permission to enter   82 **competitors** partners   83 **addressed** ready

PRINCESS Were my lord so, his ignorance were wise,
　　Where now his knowledge must prove ignorance.
　　I hear your Grace hath sworn out house-keeping.
　　'Tis deadly sin to keep that oath, my lord,　　　　105
　　And sin to break it.
　　But pardon me, I am too sudden-bold;
　　To teach a teacher ill beseemeth me.
　　Vouchsafe to read the purpose of my coming,
　　And suddenly resolve me in my suit.　　　　　　110
　　　　　　　　　　　　　[Gives a paper.]

KING Madam, I will, if suddenly I may.

PRINCESS You will the sooner that I were away,
　　For you'll prove perjured if you make me stay.

BEROWNE Did not I dance with you in Brabant once?

ROSALINE Did not I dance with you in Brabant once?　　115

BEROWNE I know you did.

ROSALINE　　　　　　　How needless was it then
　　To ask the question!

BEROWNE　　　　　　　You must not be so quick.

ROSALINE 'Tis long of you that spur me with such
　　questions.

BEROWNE Your wit's too hot, it speeds too fast, 'twill
　　tire.

ROSALINE Not till it leave the rider in the mire.　　120

BEROWNE What time o' day?

ROSALINE The hour that fools should ask.

BEROWNE Now fair befall your mask!

ROSALINE Fair fall the face it covers!

BEROWNE And send you many lovers!　　　　　　125

---

104 **sworn out house-keeping** sworn not to keep house or offer hospitality
110 **suddenly resolve me** quickly give me a decision 118 **long** because
123 **fair befall** good luck to

ROSALINE Amen, so you be none.

BEROWNE Nay, then will I be gone.

KING Madam, your father here doth intimate
The payment of a hundred thousand crowns,
130　Being but the one half of an entire sum
Disbursèd by my father in his wars.
But say that he, or we (as neither have),
Received that sum, yet there remains unpaid
A hundred thousand more, in surety of the which,
135　One part of Aquitaine is bound to us,
Although not valued to the money's worth.
If then the king your father will restore
But that one half which is unsatisfied,
We will give up our right in Aquitaine,
140　And hold fair friendship with his Majesty.
But that, it seems, he little purposeth,
For here he doth demand to have repaid
A hundred thousand crowns; and not demands,
On payment of a hundred thousand crowns,
145　To have his title live in Aquitaine;
Which we much rather had depart withal,
And have the money by our father lent,
Than Aquitaine, so gelded as it is.
Dear princess, were not his requests so far
150　From reason's yielding, your fair self should make
A yielding 'gainst some reason in my breast,
And go well satisfied to France again.

PRINCESS You do the king my father too much wrong,
And wrong the reputation of your name,
155　In so unseeming to confess receipt
Of that which hath so faithfully been paid.

KING I do protest I never heard of it;
And if you prove it, I'll repay it back
Or yield up Aquitaine.

---

128 **intimate** make known 146 **depart withal** give up 148 **gelded** cut up
155 **unseeming** not appearing

PRINCESS   We arrest your word.
  Boyet, you can produce acquittances   160
  For such a sum from special officers
  Of Charles his father.

KING   Satisfy me so.

BOYET So please your Grace, the packet is not come
  Where that and other specialties are bound.
  Tomorrow you shall have a sight of them.   165

KING It shall suffice me—at which interview
  All liberal reason I will yield unto.
  Meantime, receive such welcome at my hand
  As honor (without breach of honor) may
  Make tender of to thy true worthiness.   170
  You may not come, fair princess, within my gates;
  But here without you shall be so received
  As you shall deem yourself lodged in my heart,
  Though so denied fair harbor in my house.
  Your own good thoughts excuse me, and farewell.   175
  Tomorrow shall we visit you again.

PRINCESS Sweet health and fair desires consort your
    Grace.

KING Thy own wish wish I thee in every place.
                          Exit [King and his Train].

BEROWNE Lady, I will commend you to mine own
    heart.   180

ROSALINE Pray you, do my commendations, I would
    be glad to see it.

BEROWNE I would you heard it groan.

ROSALINE Is the fool sick?

BEROWNE Sick at the heart.   185

ROSALINE Alack, let it blood!

159 arrest your word take your word as security 160 acquittances receipts
163 packet package 164 specialties particular legal documents 170 Make
tender of offer 177 consort accompany 186 let it blood bleed him

BEROWNE Would that do it good?

ROSALINE My physic says ay.

BEROWNE Will you prick 't with your eye?

190 ROSALINE No point, with my knife.

BEROWNE Now, God save thy life!

ROSALINE And yours from long living!

BEROWNE I cannot stay thanksgiving.   *Exit.*

Enter Dumaine.

DUMAINE Sir, I pray you a word. What lady is that
same?

195 BOYET The heir of Alençon, Katharine her name.

DUMAINE A gallant lady. Monsieur, fare you well.

Exit.

[Enter Longaville.]

LONGAVILLE I beseech you a word. What is she in the
white?

BOYET A woman sometimes, and you saw her in the
light.

LONGAVILLE Perchance light in the light. I desire her
name.

BOYET She hath but one for herself. To desire that
200 were a shame.

LONGAVILLE Pray you, sir, whose daughter?

BOYET Her mother's, I have heard.

LONGAVILLE God's blessing on your beard!

---

190 **No point** not at all   193 **stay thanksgiving** stay long enough to give you
proper thanks (for your unkind remark) 198 **and** if 199 **light in the light**
wanton if rightly perceived

BOYET Good sir, be not offended.
  She is an heir of Falconbridge.   205

LONGAVILLE Nay, my choler is ended.
  She is a most sweet lady.

BOYET Not unlike, sir; that may be.

                                        Exit Longaville.

                    Enter Berowne.

BEROWNE What's her name in the cap?

BOYET Rosaline, by good hap.   210

BEROWNE Is she wedded or no?

BOYET To her will, sir, or so.

BEROWNE O, you are welcome, sir! Adieu.

BOYET Farewell to me, sir, and welcome to you.

                                        Exit Berowne.

MARIA That last is Berowne, the merry madcap lord.   215
  Not a word with him but a jest.

BOYET   And every jest but a word.

PRINCESS It was well done of you to take him at his
    word.

BOYET I was as willing to grapple as he was to board.

KATHARINE Two hot sheeps, marry!

BOYET   And wherefore not ships?
  No sheep, sweet lamb, unless we feed on your lips.   220

KATHARINE You sheep, and I pasture. Shall that finish
    the jest?

BOYET So you grant pasture for me.

                                        [*Offers to kiss her.*]

206 **choler** wrath   212 **or so** something like that

KATHARINE   Not so, gentle beast.
My lips are no common, though several they be.

BOYET Belonging to whom?

KATHARINE   To my fortunes and me.

PRINCESS Good wits will be jangling; but, gentles,
225   agree.
This civil war of wits were much better used
On Navarre and his book-men, for here 'tis abused.

BOYET If my observation (which very seldom lies)
By the heart's still rhetoric disclosèd with eyes
230   Deceive me not now, Navarre is infected.

PRINCESS With what?

BOYET With that which we lovers entitle "affected."

PRINCESS Your reason?

BOYET Why, all his behaviors did make their retire
235   To the court of his eye, peeping thorough desire.
His heart, like an agate with your print impressed,
Proud with his form, in his eye pride expressed.
His tongue, all impatient to speak and not see,
Did stumble with haste in his eyesight to be;
240   All senses to that sense did make their repair,
To feel only looking on fairest of fair.
Methought all his senses were locked in his eye,
As jewels in crystal for some prince to buy;
Who, tend'ring their own worth from where they
      were glassed,
245   Did point you to buy them, along as you passed.

---

223 **no common** i.e., not like pasture held in common   223 **several** two (the word also, in this context, signifies "private property")   232 **affected** impassioned 234 **behaviors** expression of his feelings   235 **court** watch-post   236 **agate** (stone used for the engraving of images)   236 **impressed** imprinted   238 **His tongue ... see** his tongue, vexed at having the power of speaking without having the power of seeing   241 **To feel ... fair** (sight is translated into feeling in regarding her)   244 **tend'ring** offering   244 **glassed** enclosed in glass 245 **point** urge

His face's own margent did quote such amazes
That all eyes saw his eyes enchanted with gazes.
I'll give you Aquitaine, and all that is his,
And you give him for my sake but one loving kiss.

PRINCESS Come to our pavilion. Boyet is disposed.   250

BOYET But to speak that in words which his eye hath
disclosed.
I only have made a mouth of his eye
By adding a tongue which I know will not lie.

ROSALINE Thou art an old love-monger, and speakest
skillfully.

MARIA He is Cupid's grandfather, and learns news of
him.   255

KATHARINE Then was Venus like her mother, for her
father is but grim.

BOYET Do you hear, my mad wenches?

ROSALINE   No.

BOYET   What then? Do you see?

ROSALINE Ay, our way to be gone.

BOYET   You are too hard for me.
                                        Exeunt omnes.

<hr>

246–47 **His face's ... gazes** i.e., the amazement in Navarre's face drew attention, like comments in a book's margin, to the love in his eyes 249 **And** if 258s.d. **omnes** all (Latin)

[ACT III

Scene I. *The park*.]

Enter [Armado, the] Braggart, and [Moth,] his Boy.

ARMADO Warble, child, make passionate my sense of
hearing.

MOTH [*Sings.*] Concolinel.

ARMADO Sweet air! Go, tenderness of years, take
5   this key, give enlargement to the swain, bring him
festinately hither. I must employ him in a letter
to my love.

MOTH Master, will you win your love with a French
brawl?

10   ARMADO How meanest thou? Brawling in French?

MOTH No, my complete master; but to jig off a tune
at the tongue's end, canary to it with your feet,
humor it with turning up your eyelids, sigh a note
and sing a note, sometime through the throat as if
15   you swallowed love with singing love, sometime
through the nose as if you snuffed up love by smelling love, with your hat penthouse-like o'er the shop

---

III.i.3 **Concolinel** (perhaps the name of a song) 4 **tenderness of years**
(affected talk for "young fellow") 5 **enlargement** freedom 6 **festinately**
quickly 8–9 **French brawl** French dance 12 **canary to it** dance in a lively way

of your eyes, with your arms crossed on your
thin-belly doublet like a rabbit on a spit, or your
hands in your pocket like a man after the old paint-   20
ing; and keep not too long in one tune, but a snip
and away. These are complements, these are humors, these betray nice wenches (that would be
betrayed without these), and make them men of
note—do you note me?—that most are affected   25
to these.

ARMADO How hast thou purchased this experience?

MOTH By my penny of observation.

ARMADO But O—but O—

MOTH "The hobby-horse is forgot."   30

ARMADO Call'st thou my love "hobby-horse"?

MOTH No, master. The hobby-horse is but a colt, and
your love perhaps a hackney. But have you forgot your love?

ARMADO Almost I had.   35

MOTH Negligent student, learn her by heart.

ARMADO By heart, and in heart, boy.

MOTH And out of heart, master. All those three I will
prove.

ARMADO What wilt thou prove?   40

MOTH A man, if I live; and this, by, in, and without,
upon the instant. By heart you love her, because
your heart cannot come by her; in heart you love
her, because your heart is in love with her; and
out of heart you love her, being out of heart that   45
you cannot enjoy her.

18 **arms crossed** (a sign of melancholy) 19 **thin-belly doublet** garment
unpadded in the lower part (across your thin belly) 21 **snip** snatch 22 **comple-**
ments accompaniments 25-26 **affected** to taken with 30 **"The hobby-horse**
is forgot" (perhaps a phrase from an old song) 32-33 **hobby-horse, colt,**
hackney (slang words for "whore")

ARMADO I am all these three.

MOTH [*Aside*] And three times as much more, and
yet nothing at all.

50   ARMADO Fetch hither the swain. He must carry me a
letter.

MOTH A message well sympathized—a horse to be
ambassador for an ass.

ARMADO Ha, ha, what sayest thou?

55   MOTH Marry, sir, you must send the ass upon the
horse, for he is very slow-gaited. But I go.

ARMADO The way is but short. Away!

MOTH As swift as lead, sir.

ARMADO The meaning, pretty ingenious?
60   Is not lead a metal heavy, dull, and slow?

MOTH *Minime*, honest master; or rather, master, no.

ARMADO I say, lead is slow.

MOTH   You are too swift, sir, to say so.
Is that lead slow which is fired from a gun?

ARMADO Sweet smoke of rhetoric!
65   He reputes me a cannon; and the bullet, that's he:
I shoot thee at the swain.

MOTH   Thump, then, and I flee.
[*Exit.*]

ARMADO A most acute juvenal, voluble and free of
grace!
By thy favor, sweet welkin, I must sigh in thy
face:
Most rude melancholy, valor gives thee place.
70   My herald is returned.

52 **well sympathized** in proper accord 61 **Minime** by no means (Latin)
67 **juvenal** (in two senses) young fellow, satirist 68 **welkin** heaven 69 **gives
thee place** gives place to you

Enter [Moth, the] Page and [Costard, the] Clown.

MOTH A wonder, master! Here's a costard broken in a
    shin.

ARMADO Some enigma, some riddle. Come, thy l'envoy
    —begin.

COSTARD No egma, no riddle, no l'envoy; no salve
    in the mail, sir. O, sir, plantain, a plain plantain.
    No l'envoy, no l'envoy, no salve, sir, but a plantain. 75

ARMADO By virtue, thou enforcest laughter; thy silly
    thought, my spleen; the heaving of my lungs pro-
    vokes me to ridiculous smiling. O, pardon me, my
    stars! Doth the inconsiderate take salve for
    l'envoy, and the word l'envoy for a salve? 80

MOTH Do the wise think them other? Is not l'envoy
    a salve?

ARMADO No, page; it is an epilogue, or discourse to
    make plain
    Some obscure precedence that hath tofore been
    sain.
    I will example it: 85
        The fox, the ape, and the humble-bee
        Were still at odds, being but three.
    There's the moral. Now the l'envoy.

MOTH I will add the l'envoy. Say the moral again.

ARMADO The fox, the ape, and the humble-bee 90
        Were still at odds, being but three.

MOTH   Until the goose came out of door,
        And stayed the odds by adding four.

---

71 **costard** apple, or head 72 **l'envoy** words ending a composition by way of
leave-taking 73 **salve** (with a pun on *salve*, the Latin word for salute) 74 **mail**
bag, container 74 **plantain** tree whose leaves were used for healing 77 **spleen**
mirth 79 **inconsiderate** unthinking 84 **precedence** preceding statement
84 **tofore been sain** been said before 93 **stayed . . . four** turned them into evens
by adding a fourth

Now will I begin your moral, and do you follow
95   with my l'envoy.
          The fox, the ape, and the humble-bee
          Were still at odds, being but three.

ARMADO Until the goose came out of door,
          Staying the odds by adding four.

100   MOTH A good l'envoy, ending in the goose. Would you
          desire more?

COSTARD The boy hath sold him a bargain, a goose
          —that's flat.
          Sir, your pennyworth is good, and your goose be fat.
          To sell a bargain well is as cunning as fast and loose.
105   Let me see: a fat l'envoy—ay, that's a fat goose.

ARMADO Come hither, come hither. How did this
          argument begin?

MOTH By saying that a costard was broken in a shin.
          Then called you for the l'envoy.

COSTARD True, and I for a plantain; thus came your
          argument in;
          Then the boy's fat l'envoy, the goose that you
110   bought,
          And he ended the market.

ARMADO But tell me, how was there a costard broken
          in a shin?

MOTH I will tell you sensibly.

115   COSTARD Thou hast no feeling of it, Moth. I will speak
          that l'envoy:
          I, Costard, running out, that was safely within,
          Fell over the threshold and broke my shin.

ARMADO We will talk no more of this matter.

120   COSTARD Till there be more matter in the shin.

---

102 **sold him a bargain** made a fool of him   103 **and** if   104 **fast and loose**
cheating   114 **sensibly** with feeling   120 **matter** pus

ARMADO Sirrah Costard, I will enfranchise thee.

COSTARD O, marry me to one Frances! I smell some
l'envoy, some goose, in this.

ARMADO By my sweet soul, I mean setting thee at
liberty, enfreedoming thy person. Thou wert im-   125
mured, restrained, captivated, bound.

COSTARD True, true, and now you will be my purga-
tion and let me loose.

ARMADO I give thee thy liberty, set thee from durance, and in lieu thereof, impose on thee nothing   130
but this. [*Gives a letter.*] Bear this significant to
the country maid Jaquenetta. [*Gives a coin.*] There
is remuneration; for the best ward of mine honor
is rewarding my dependents. Moth, follow.

MOTH Like the sequel, I. Signior Costard, adieu.   135
                              Exit [*Armado, followed by Moth*].

COSTARD My sweet ounce of man's flesh, my incony
Jew!—Now will I look to his remuneration. Re-
remuneration? O that's the Latin word for three farthings. Three farthings—remuneration. "What's the
price of this inkle?" "One penny." "No, I'll give   140
you a remuneration." Why, it carries it! Remuneration! Why, it is a fairer name than French
crown. I will never buy and sell out of this word.

                              Enter Berowne.

BEROWNE O my good knave Costard, exceedingly well
met.   145

COSTARD Pray you, sir, how much carnation ribbon
may a man buy for a remuneration?

BEROWNE O, what is a remuneration?

121 enfranchise set free 131 significant letter 133 ward protection
136 incony darling 140 inkle band of linen 142-43 French crown (in two
senses: a coin, and the baldness caused by syphilis, the so-called "French disease")
146 carnation flesh-colored

315

COSTARD Marry, sir, halfpenny farthing.

150 BEROWNE O, why then, three-farthing-worth of silk.

COSTARD I thank your worship. God be wi' you!

BEROWNE O stay, slave, I must employ thee.
As thou wilt win my favor, good my knave,
Do one thing for me that I shall entreat.

155 COSTARD When would you have it done, sir?

BEROWNE O, this afternoon.

COSTARD Well, I will do it, sir. Fare you well.

BEROWNE O, thou knowest not what it is.

COSTARD I shall know, sir, when I have done it.

160 BEROWNE Why, villain, thou must know first.

COSTARD I will come to your worship tomorrow morning.

BEROWNE It must be done this afternoon. Hark, slave,
it is but this:
165 The princess comes to hunt here in the park,
And in her train there is a gentle lady;
When tongues speak sweetly, then they name her
name,
And Rosaline they call her. Ask for her,
And to her white hand see thou do commend
This sealed-up counsel. [*Gives him a letter and a*
170 *shilling.*] There's thy guerdon. Go.

COSTARD Gardon, O sweet gardon! Better than remuneration—a 'leven-pence farthing better. Most
sweet gardon! I will do it, sir, in print. Gardon!
Remuneration!   *Exit.*

175 BEROWNE O, and I, forsooth, in love!
I, that have been love's whip,
A very beadle to a humorous sigh,

170 **guerdon** reward   173 **in print** most carefully   177 **beadle** parish constable

316

A critic, nay, a night-watch constable,
A domineering pedant o'er the boy,
Than whom no mortal so magnificent!   180
This wimpled, whining, purblind, wayward boy,
This senior-junior, giant-dwarf, Dan Cupid,
Regent of love-rhymes, lord of folded arms,
Th' anointed sovereign of sighs and groans,
Liege of all loiterers and malcontents,   185
Dread prince of plackets, king of codpieces,
Sole imperator and great general
Of trotting paritors—O my little heart!—
And I to be a corporal of his field,
And wear his colors like a tumbler's hoop!   190
What? I love? I sue? I seek a wife?
A woman that is like a German clock,
Still a-repairing, ever out of frame,
And never going aright, being a watch,
But being watched that it may still go right!   195
Nay, to be perjured, which is worst of all;
And, among three, to love the worst of all,
A whitely wanton with a velvet brow,
With two pitch balls stuck in her face for eyes.
Ay, and, by heaven, one that will do the deed,   200
Though Argus were her eunuch and her guard!
And I to sigh for her, to watch for her,
To pray for her! Go to, it is a plague
That Cupid will impose for my neglect
Of his almighty dreadful little might.   205
Well, I will love, write, sigh, pray, sue, groan.
Some men must love my lady, and some Joan.
                                          [*Exit.*]

---

181 **wimpled** covered with a muffler   181 **purblind** completely blind   182 **Dan** ("don," a derivation of *dominus*, lord)   185 **Liege** lord   186 **plackets** slits in petticoats (vulgar term for women)   186 **codpieces** cloth covering the opening in men's breeches   188 **paritors** (officers of the Ecclesiastical Court who serve summonses for certain, often sexual, offenses)   189 **corporal of his field** aide to a general   190 **tumbler's** acrobat's   193 **frame** order   198 **whitely** pale   200 **do the deed** perform the act of coition   201 **Argus** (ancient mythological being with a hundred eyes)

[ACT IV

Scene I. *The park*.]

*Enter the Princess, a Forester, her Ladies,
and her Lords.*

PRINCESS Was that the King, that spurred his horse so
    hard
    Against the steep uprising of the hill?

FORESTER I know not, but I think it was not he.

PRINCESS Whoe'er 'a was, 'a showed a mounting
    mind.
5   Well, lords, today we shall have our dispatch;
    On Saturday we will return to France.
    Then, forester, my friend, where is the bush
    That we must stand and play the murderer in?

FORESTER Hereby, upon the edge of yonder coppice,
10   A stand where you may make the fairest shoot.

PRINCESS I thank my beauty, I am fair that shoot,
    And thereupon thou speak'st the fairest shoot.

FORESTER Pardon me, madam, for I meant not so.

PRINCESS What, what? First praise me, and again say
    no?
15   O short-lived pride! Not fair? Alack for woe!

IV.i.4 **'a** he 4 **mounting mind** lofty spirit (with pun on "mountain")
9 **coppice** undergrowth of small trees

FORESTER Yes, madam, fair.

PRINCESS   Nay, never paint me now!
  Where fair is not, praise cannot mend the brow.
  Here, good my glass, take this for telling true—
                        [*giving him money*]
  Fair payment for foul words is more than due.

FORESTER Nothing but fair is that which you inherit.   20

PRINCESS See, see—my beauty will be saved by
    merit!
  O heresy in fair, fit for these days!
  A giving hand, though foul, shall have fair praise.
  But come, the bow! Now mercy goes to kill,
  And shooting well is then accounted ill.   25
  Thus will I save my credit in the shoot:
  Not wounding, pity would not let me do 't;
  If wounding, then it was to show my skill,
  That more for praise than purpose meant to kill.
  And out of question so it is sometimes,   30
  Glory grows guilty of detested crimes,
  When, for fame's sake, for praise, an outward part,
  We bend to that the working of the heart;
  As I for praise alone now seek to spill
  The poor deer's blood that my heart means no ill.   35

BOYET Do not curst wives hold that self-sovereignty
  Only for praise sake, when they strive to be
  Lords o'er their lords?

PRINCESS Only for praise, and praise we may afford
  To any lady that subdues a lord.   40

Enter [Costard, the] Clown.

BOYET Here comes a member of the commonwealth.

16 **paint** flatter   17 **mend the brow** make the brow more beautiful   18 **good my glass** my fine mirror   21 **saved by merit** saved by what I truly deserve   22 **heresy in fair** heresy with respect to beauty   24 **mercy goes to kill** (the merciful huntsman goes forth to kill—instead of leaving the prey wounded—but such killing is not well regarded)   31 **Glory** i.e., ambition for glory   36 **curst** peevish   41 **member of the commonwealth** i.e., one of our group

COSTARD God dig-you-den all! Pray you, which is
the head lady?

PRINCESS Thou shalt know her, fellow, by the rest
45   that have no heads.

COSTARD Which is the greatest lady, the highest?

PRINCESS The thickest and the tallest.

COSTARD The thickest and the tallest—it is so. Truth
is truth.
50   And your waist, mistress, were as slender as my wit,
One o' these maids' girdles for your waist should
   be fit.
Are not you the chief woman? You are the thickest
   here.

PRINCESS What's your will, sir? What's your will?

COSTARD I have a letter from Monsieur Berowne to
one Lady Rosaline.

PRINCESS O thy letter, thy letter! He's a good friend
55   of mine.
Stand aside, good bearer. Boyet, you can carve—
Break up this capon.

BOYET   I am bound to serve.
This letter is mistook; it importeth none here.
It is writ to Jaquenetta.

PRINCESS   We will read it, I swear.
60   Break the neck of the wax, and every one give ear.

BOYET (*Reads*) "By heaven, that thou art fair is
most infallible; true that thou art beauteous; truth
itself that thou art lovely. More fairer than fair,
beautiful than beauteous, truer than truth itself,

---

42 **God dig-you-den** God give you good evening   50 **And** if   56 **carve** (with
pun on the sense "flirt")   57 **Break up this capon** (1) carve this chicken (2) open
this love-letter   58 **importeth** concerns   60 **Break the neck** (still referring to
the capon)

have commiseration on thy heroical vassal. The   65
magnanimous and most illustrate king Cophetua
set eye upon the pernicious and indubitate beggar
Zenelophon, and he it was that might rightly say
veni, vidi, vici; which to annothanize in the vulgar
(O base and obscure vulgar!) *videlicet*, he came,   70
saw, and overcame. He came, one; saw, two;
overcame, three. Who came? The king. Why did
he come? To see. Why did he see? To overcome.
To whom came he? To the beggar. What saw he?
The beggar. Who overcame he? The beggar. The   75
conclusion is victory. On whose side? The king's.
The captive is enriched. On whose side? The beggar's. The catastrophe is a nuptial. On whose side?
The king's. No—on both in one, or one in both.
I am the king, for so stands the comparison, thou   80
the beggar, for so witnesseth thy lowliness. Shall
I command thy love? I may. Shall I enforce thy
love? I could. Shall I entreat thy love? I will. What
shalt thou exchange for rags? Robes. For tittles?
Titles. For thyself? Me. Thus, expecting thy reply,   85
I profane my lips on thy foot, my eyes on thy pic-
ture, and my heart on thy every part.
        Thine in the dearest design of industry,
                    Don Adriano de Armado.
Thus dost thou hear the Nemean lion roar   90
    'Gainst thee, thou lamb, that standest as his prey.
Submissive fall his princely feet before,
    And he from forage will incline to play.
But if thou strive, poor soul, what art thou then?
Food for his rage, repasture for his den."   95

PRINCESS What plume of feathers is he that indited
    this letter?

---

66 **illustrate** illustrious   67 **indubitate** undoubted   68 **Zenelophon** (character
in the ballad of King Cophetua and the Beggar)   69 **annothanize** anatomize (or a
mock-Latin word to mean "annotate")   70 **videlicet** namely (Latin)   84 **tittles**
small jottings in ink   88 **industry** faithful service   90 **Nemean lion** (lion killed
by Hercules)   93 **from forage** turning away from feeding   95 **repasture** food
96 **indited** wrote

What vane? What weathercock? Did you ever hear better?

BOYET I am much deceived but I remember the style.

PRINCESS Else your memory is bad, going o'er it erewhile.

BOYET This Armado is a Spaniard that keeps here in court;
100　　A phantasime, a Monarcho, and one that makes sport
To the prince and his book-mates.

PRINCESS 　　　　　　　　　　Thou fellow, a word.
Who gave thee this letter?

COSTARD 　　　　　　　　I told you—my lord.

PRINCESS To whom shouldst thou give it?

COSTARD 　　　　　　　　　　From my lord to my lady.

105　PRINCESS From which lord to which lady?

COSTARD From my lord Berowne, a good master of mine,
To a lady of France that he called Rosaline.

PRINCESS Thou hast mistaken his letter. Come, lords, away.
Here, sweet, put up this; 'twill be thine another day.
[*Exeunt Princess and Train. Boyet remains.*]

BOYET Who is the suitor? Who is the suitor?

110　ROSALINE 　　　　　　　Shall I teach you to know?

BOYET Ay, my continent of beauty.

ROSALINE 　　　　　　　Why, she that bears the bow.
Finely put off!

---

97 **vane** weather-vane 97 **weather-cock** ostentatious thing 101 **phantasime** person of wild imaginings 101 **Monarcho** (nickname of a crazy Italian at the court of Elizabeth) 108 **mistaken** taken to the wrong person 110 **suitor** (pronounced "shooter") 111 **continent** container 112 **put off** repulsed

BOYET My lady goes to kill horns, but, if thou marry,
Hang me by the neck if horns that year miscarry.
Finely put on!   115

ROSALINE Well then, I am the shooter.

BOYET   And who is your deer?

ROSALINE If we choose by the horns, yourself. Come
not near.
Finely put on indeed!

MARIA You still wrangle with her, Boyet, and she strikes
at the brow.

BOYET But she herself is hit lower. Have I hit her now?   120

ROSALINE Shall I come upon thee with an old saying
that was a man when King Pepin of France was a
little boy, as touching the hit it?

BOYET So I may answer thee with one as old, that was
a woman when Queen Guinever of Britain was a   125
little wench, as touching the hit it.

ROSALINE "Thou canst not hit it, hit it, hit it,
Thou canst not hit it, my good man.

BOYET   "And I cannot, cannot, cannot,
And I cannot, another can."   130
                              Exit [Rosaline with Katharine].

COSTARD By my troth, most pleasant, how both did
fit it!

MARIA A mark marvelous well shot, for they both did
hit it.

BOYET A mark! O, mark but that mark! A mark,
says my lady!

---

114 **if horns that year miscarry** i.e., if someone is not made a cuckold 115 **put on** lay on, as a blow 119 **strikes at the brow** takes careful aim (with an allusion to the cuckold's horns) 123 **hit it** name of a dance tune (leading to pun on the sense of *hit* = to copulate) 129 **And if** 133 **mark** (1) target (2) pudend

Let the mark have a prick in 't, to mete at if it
    may be.

MARIA Wide o' the bow hand! I' faith, your hand
135   is out.

COSTARD Indeed 'a must shoot nearer, or he'll ne'er
    hit the clout.

BOYET And if my hand be out, then belike your hand
    is in.

COSTARD Then will she get the upshoot by cleaving
    the pin.

MARIA Come, come, you talk greasily; your lips grow
    foul.

COSTARD She's too hard for you at pricks, sir.
140   Challenge her to bowl.

BOYET I fear too much rubbing. Good night, my
    good owl.

                      [Exeunt Boyet and Maria.]

COSTARD By my soul, a swain, a most simple clown!
    Lord, lord, how the ladies and I have put him down!
    O' my troth, most sweet jests, most incony
        vulgar wit.
    When it comes so smoothly off, so obscenely as it
145   were, so fit!
    Armado to th' one side—O, a most dainty man!
    To see him walk before a lady, and to bear her fan!
    To see him kiss his hand, and how most sweetly
        a' will swear!

---

134 **prick** mark within the target (with additional bawdy suggestion)   134 **mete** aim   135 **Wide o' the bow hand** far from the target on the bow-hand side   136 **clout** nail in the center of the target   138 **upshoot** best shot   138 **cleaving the pin** (1) striking the center of the target (2) causing emission in the male   139 **greasily** indecently   141 **rubbing** (bowling balls striking each other; with sexual innuendo)   142 **swain** herdsman   144 **O' my troth** by my faith   144 **incony** fine

And his page o' t' other side, that handful of wit,
Ah, heavens, it is a most pathetical nit!   150

Shout within.

Sola, sola!   [*Exit.*]

[Scene II. *The park.*]

Enter Dull, Holofernes the Pedant, and Nathaniel.

NATHANIEL Very reverend sport, truly, and done in
the testimony of a good conscience.

HOLOFERNES The deer was, as you know, *sanguis*, in
blood; ripe as the pomewater, who now hangeth
like a jewel in the ear of *coelo*, the sky, the welkin,   5
the heaven; and anon falleth like a crab on the
face of *terra*, the soil, the land, the earth.

NATHANIEL Truly, Master Holofernes, the epithets are
sweetly varied, like a scholar at the least. But sir,
I assure ye it was a buck of the first head.   10

HOLOFERNES Sir Nathaniel, *haud credo*.

DULL 'Twas not a *haud credo*, 'twas a pricket.

HOLOFERNES Most barbarous intimation! Yet a kind
of insinuation, as it were, *in via*, in way, of expli-
cation; *facere*, as it were, replication, or rather,   15
ostentare, to show, as it were, his inclination—after
his undressed, unpolished, uneducated, unpruned,
untrained, or, rather, unlettered, or, ratherest, un-

---

150 nit small thing (louse)   151 Sola (a hunting cry)   IV.ii.2 testimony approval
4 pomewater (variety of a sweet apple)   6 crab crab apple   10 buck of the
first head full-grown buck   11 haud credo I do not believe it (Latin; in the next
line, Dull apparently takes the words as *old gray doe*)   12 pricket two-year old red
deer   13 intimation (a pedantic substitute for "insinuation")   14-15 explica-
tion explanation   15 facere to make   15 replication unfolding, revelation

20   confirmed fashion—to insert again my *haud credo* for a deer.

DULL I said the deer was not a *haud credo*, 'twas a pricket.

HOLOFERNES Twice sod simplicity, *bis coctus!*
O thou monster Ignorance, how deformed dost thou look!

NATHANIEL Sir, he hath never fed of the dainties that
25   are bred in a book.
He hath not eat paper, as it were, he hath not drunk ink. His intellect is not replenished. He is only an animal, only sensible in the duller parts.
And such barren plants are set before us that we thankful should be,
Which we of taste and feeling are, for those parts
30   that do fructify in us more than he.
For as it would ill become me to be vain, indiscreet, or a fool,
So were there a patch set on learning, to see him in a school.
But, *omne bene*, say I, being of an old father's mind,
Many can brook the weather that love not the wind.

DULL You two are book-men. Can you tell me by
35   your wit
What was a month old at Cain's birth that's not five weeks old as yet?

HOLOFERNES Dictynna, goodman Dull. Dictynna, goodman Dull.

DULL What is Dictynna?

NATHANIEL A title to Phoebe, to Luna, to the moon.

---

23 **Twice sod** soaked twice (again and again) 23 **bis coctus** cooked twice
30 **fructify** bear fruit 32 **patch** fool 33 **omne bene** all is well 34 **brook** endure
37 **Dictynna** Diana, the moon

HOLOFERNES The moon was a month old when Adam
    was no more,   40
  And raught not to five weeks when he came to
    fivescore.
  Th' allusion holds in the exchange.

DULL 'Tis true indeed; the collusion holds in the exchange.

HOLOFERNES God comfort thy capacity! I say th' allu-   45
  sion holds in the exchange.

DULL And I say the pollution holds in the exchange,
  for the moon is never but a month old; and I say
  beside that 'twas a pricket that the princess killed.

HOLOFERNES Sir Nathaniel, will you hear an extempo-   50
  ral epitaph on the death of the deer? And, to
  humor the ignorant, I call the deer the princess
  killed, a pricket.

NATHANIEL *Perge*, good Master Holofernes, *perge*, so
  it shall please you to abrogate scurrility.   55

HOLOFERNES I will something affect the letter for it
  argues facility.
  The preyful princess pierced and pricked a pretty
    pleasing pricket;
  Some say a sore, but not a sore till now made sore
    with shooting.
  The dogs did yell. Put L to sore, then sorel jumps
    from thicket;
  Or pricket, sore, or else sorel. The people fall a
    hooting.   60
  If sore be sore, then L to sore makes fifty sores—
    o' sorel.

---

41 **raught** attained   42 **Th' allusion ... exchange** (the riddle serves for Adam as
well as for Cain)   43 **collusion** (a pedantic misunderstanding)   50–51 **extemporal** on the spur of the moment   54 **Perge** continue   55 **abrogate scurrility**
put aside foul talk   56 **affect the letter** alliterate   57 **preyful** killing much prey
58 **sore** four-year old buck   59 **L** (the Roman numeral fifty)   59 **sorel** young
buck

Of one sore I an hundred make by adding but one
   more L.

NATHANIEL A rare talent!

DULL If a talent be a claw, look how he claws him
65 with a talent.

HOLOFERNES This is a gift that I have, simple, simple;
a foolish extravagant spirit, full of forms, figures,
shapes, objects, ideas, apprehensions, motions, revolutions. These are begot in the ventricle of mem-
70 ory, nourished in the womb of *pia mater*, and
delivered upon the mellowing of occasion. But the
gift is good in those in whom it is acute, and I am
thankful for it.

NATHANIEL Sir, I praise the Lord for you, and so may
75 my parishioners, for their sons are well tutored by
you, and their daughters profit very greatly under
you. You are a good member of the commonwealth.

HOLOFERNES Mehercle, if their sons be ingenious, they
shall want no instruction; if their daughters be ca-
80 pable, I will put it to them. But *vir sapit qui pauca
loquitur*. A soul feminine saluteth us.

   Enter Jaquenetta and [Costard,] the Clown.

JAQUENETTA God give you good morrow, Master Parson.

HOLOFERNES Master Parson, *quasi* pierce-one? And if
85 one should be pierced, which is the one?

COSTARD Marry, Master Schoolmaster, he that is likest
to a hogshead.

HOLOFERNES Of piercing a hogshead! A good luster

---

63 **talent** talon   64 **claws** flatters   69 **ventricle** part of the brain containing the
memory   70 **pia mater** membrane enclosing the brain   71 **mellowing of
occasion** fit time   78 **Mehercle** By Hercules   80–81 **vir ... loquitur** "the man
is wise who speaks little"   84 **quasi** as if   87 **hogshead** fathead   88 **piercing a
hogshead** getting drunk

of conceit in a turf of earth, fire enough for a
flint, pearl enough for a swine. 'Tis pretty; it is well.   90

JAQUENETTA Good master Parson, be so good as read
me this letter. It was given me by Costard, and
sent me from Don Armado. I beseech you read it.

HOLOFERNES *Fauste, precor, gelida quando pecus omne*
sub umbra ruminat, and so forth. Ah, good old   95
Mantuan. I may speak of thee as the traveler doth
of Venice:
> *Venetia, Venetia,*
> *Chi non ti vede, non ti pretia.*

Old Mantuan, old Mantuan! Who understandeth   100
thee not, loves thee not. *Ut, re, sol, la, mi, fa.* Under pardon, sir, what are the contents? Or, rather,
as Horace says in his—What, my soul, verses?

NATHANIEL Ay, sir, and very learned.

HOLOFERNES Let me hear a staff, a stanze, a verse.   105
Lege, domine.

[*Nathaniel reads.*] "If love make me forsworn, how
> shall I swear to love?
Ah, never faith could hold if not to beauty
> vowed!
Though to myself forsworn, to thee I'll faithful
> prove;
Those thoughts to me were oaks, to thee like
> osiers bowed.   110
Study his bias leaves and makes his book thine
> eyes,
Where all those pleasures live that art would
> comprehend.
If knowledge be the mark, to know thee shall
> suffice:

88–89 hunter of conceit brilliant idea   89 turf clod   94–95 Fauste ... ruminat "I pray thee, Faustus, when all the cattle ruminate beneath the cool shade" (a
quotation from a Latin poem by Mantuan, an Italian Renaissance poet)
98–99 Venetia ... pretia "Venice, Venice, only those who do not see thee do not
value thee" (Italian)   105 staff stanza   106 Lege, domine read, master
111 Study his bias leaves (the student leaves his favorite studies)

> Well learnèd is that tongue that well can thee
>   commend,
115 All ignorant that soul that sees thee without wonder;
>   Which is to me some praise, that I thy parts
>   admire.
>   Thy eye Jove's lightning bears, thy voice his dread-
>   ful thunder,
>   Which, not to anger bent, is music and sweet fire.
>   Celestial as thou art, O pardon love this wrong,
>   That sings heaven's praise with such an earthly
120   tongue!"

HOLOFERNES You find not the apostrophus, and so
miss the accent. Let me supervise the canzonet.
Here are only numbers ratified; but, for the ele-
gancy, facility, and golden cadence of poesy, *caret*.
125 Ovidius Naso was the man; and why indeed
"Naso" but for smelling out the odoriferous flowers of fancy, the jerks of invention? *Imitari* is
nothing. So doth the hound his master, the ape his
keeper, the tired horse his rider. But, damosella
130 virgin, was this directed to you?

JAQUENETTA Ay, sir, from one Monsieur Berowne, one
of the strange queen's lords.

HOLOFERNES I will overglance the superscript. "To
the snow-white hand of the most beauteous Lady
135 Rosaline." I will look again on the intellect of the
letter for the nomination of the party writing to
the person written unto. "Your ladyship's, in all
desired employment, Berowne." Sir Nathaniel, this
Berowne is one of the votaries with the king; and
140 here he hath framed a letter to a sequent of the

---

121 **apostrophus** (mark of punctuation taking the place of a vowel)
122 **canzonet** song   123 **numbers ratified** rhythm regularized   124 **caret** it is
deficient 126 **Naso** nose   127 **jerks of invention** clever strokes of wit
127 **Imitari** to imitate 132 **strange** foreign 133 **superscript** address
135 **intellect** purport   136 **nomination** name   139 **votaries** persons who have
taken a vow   140 **framed** devised   140 **sequent** follower

stranger queen's, which accidentally, or by the way
of progression, hath miscarried. Trip and go, my
sweet, deliver this paper into the royal hand of the
king; it may concern much. Stay not thy compliment; I forgive thy duty. Adieu.   145

JAQUENETTA Good Costard, go with me. Sir, God save
your life.

COSTARD Have with thee, my girl.
                              Exit [with Jaquenetta].

NATHANIEL Sir, you have done this in the fear of God
very religiously; and as a certain father saith—   150

HOLOFERNES Sir, tell not me of the father, I do fear
colorable colors. But to return to the verses—did
they please you, Sir Nathaniel?

NATHANIEL Marvelous well for the pen.

HOLOFERNES I do dine today at the father's of a certain   155
pupil of mine, where, if before repast it shall please
you to gratify the table with a grace, I will, on my
privilege I have with the parents of the foresaid
child or pupil, undertake your *ben venuto*; where
I will prove those verses to be very unlearned,   160
neither savoring of poetry, wit, nor invention. I beseech your society.

NATHANIEL And thank you too, for society (saith the
text) is the happiness of life.

HOLOFERNES And, certes, the text most infallibly con-   165
cludes it. *[To Dull]* Sir, I do invite you too; you
shall not say me nay. *Pauca verba.* Away! The
gentles are at their game, and we will to our recreation.   *Exeunt.*

141–42 by the way of progression on its way   142 Trip and go (phrase used of
a morris dance)   144–45 Stay not thy compliment do not wait on ceremony
152 colorable colors plausible excuses   154 pen penmanship, or style of writing
159 ben venuto welcome (Italian)   165 certes certainly   167 Pauca verba few
words

[Scene III. *The park.*]

Enter Berowne with a paper in his hand, alone.

BEROWNE The king he is hunting the deer; I am coursing myself. They have pitched a toil; I am toiling
in a pitch—pitch that defiles. Defile—a foul word!
Well, set thee down, sorrow, for so they say the
5   fool said, and so say I, and I the fool. Well proved,
wit! By the Lord, this love is as mad as Ajax:
it kills sheep; it kills me—I a sheep. Well proved
again o' my side! I will not love; if I do, hang me!
I' faith, I will not. O but her eye! By this light, but
10 for her eye, I would not love her—yes, for her two
eyes. Well, I do nothing in the world but lie, and
lie in my throat. By heaven, I do love, and it hath
taught me to rhyme, and to be melancholy; and here
is part of my rhyme, and here my melancholy. Well,
15 she hath one o' my sonnets already. The clown
bore it, the fool sent it, and the lady hath it—
sweet clown, sweeter fool, sweetest lady! By the
world, I would not care a pin if the other three
were in. Here comes one with a paper. God give
20 him grace to groan!   *He stands aside.*

The King ent'reth [with a paper].

KING Ay me!

BEROWNE [*Aside*] Shot, by heaven! Proceed, sweet
Cupid. Thou hast thumped him with thy bird-bolt
under the left pap. In faith, secrets!

IV.iii.1–2 **coursing** chasing 2 **pitched a toil** set a snare 6 **Ajax** (ancient Greek
warrior who, going mad, killed sheep, believing them his enemies) 23 **bird-bolt**
arrow for shooting birds 24 **pap** breast

KING [*Reads*] "So sweet a kiss the golden sun gives   25
    not
    To those fresh morning drops upon the rose,
As thy eye-beams when their fresh rays have smote
    The night of dew that on my cheeks down flows.
Nor shines the silver moon one half so bright
    Through the transparent bosom of the deep   30
As doth thy face, through tears of mine, give light.
    Thou shin'st in every tear that I do weep;
No drop but as a coach doth carry thee.
    So ridest thou triumphing in my woe.
Do but behold the tears that swell in me,   35
    And they thy glory through my grief will show.
But do not love thyself—then thou will keep
My tears for glasses and still make me weep.
O queen of queens, how far dost thou excel
No thought can think, nor tongue of mortal tell!"   40
How shall she know my griefs? I'll drop the paper.
Sweet leaves, shade folly. Who is he comes here?

Enter Longaville [with a paper]. The King steps aside.

What, Longaville, and reading! Listen, ear.

BEROWNE Now, in thy likeness, one more fool appear!

LONGAVILLE Ay me, I am forsworn.   45

BEROWNE Why, he comes in like a perjure, wearing
papers.

KING In love, I hope—sweet fellowship in shame!

BEROWNE One drunkard loves another of the name.

LONGAVILLE Am I the first that have been perjured so?   50

BEROWNE I could put thee in comfort—not by two
    that I know.

---

38 **glasses** mirrors   46 **perjure** perjurer   46 **wearing papers** (a punishment for perjury, to wear a paper on the head as a public shame; presumably Longaville has a sonnet in his hatband)

Thou makest the triumviry, the corner-cap of
    society,
The shape of Love's Tyburn, that hangs up
    simplicity.

LONGAVILLE I fear these stubborn lines lack power to
    move.
55   O sweet Maria, empress of my love!
These numbers will I tear, and write in prose.

BEROWNE O, rhymes are guards on wanton Cupid's
    hose;
Disfigure not his shop.

LONGAVILLE   This same shall go.

He reads the sonnet.

"Did not the heavenly rhetoric of thine eye,
60   'Gainst whom the world cannot hold argument,
Persuade my heart to this false perjury?
    Vows for thee broke deserve not punishment.
A woman I forswore, but I will prove,
    Thou being a goddess, I forswore not thee.
65 My vow was earthly, thou a heavenly love;
    Thy grace, being gained, cures all disgrace in me.
Vows are but breath, and breath a vapor is;
    Then thou, fair sun, which on my earth dost
      shine,
Exhal'st this vapor-vow; in thee it is.
70   If broken then, it is no fault of mine;
If by me broke, what fool is not so wise
To lose an oath to win a paradise?"

BEROWNE This is the liver-vein, which makes flesh a
    deity,
A green goose a goddess. Pure, pure idolatry.

---

52 **triumviry** triumvirate 52 **corner-cap** cap with corners (worn by divines,
judges, and scholars) 53 **Tyburn** place of execution (the triangular-shaped
gallows bears a resemblance to a corner-cap) 57 **guards** ornaments 58 **shop**
organ of generation, or codpiece 73 **liver-vein** vein coming from the liver (the
place of the origin of love) 74 **green goose** goose born the previous autumn (and
so, a young girl)

God amend us, God amend! We are much out o'
  th' way.   75

      Enter Dumaine [with a paper].

LONGAVILLE By whom shall I send this?—Company?
  Stay.   [*Steps aside.*]

BEROWNE All hid, all hid—an old infant play.
  Like a demi-god here sit I in the sky,
  And wretched fools' secrets heedfully o'er-eye.
  More sacks to the mill—O heavens, I have my
    wish!   80
  Dumaine transformed! Four woodcocks in a dish!

DUMAINE O most divine Kate!

BEROWNE O most profane coxcomb!

DUMAINE By heaven, the wonder in a mortal eye!

BEROWNE By earth, she is not, Corporal. There you
  lie!   85

DUMAINE Her amber hairs for foul hath amber
  quoted.

BEROWNE An amber-colored raven was well noted.

DUMAINE As upright as the cedar.

BEROWNE   Stoop, I say—
  Her shoulder is with child.

DUMAINE   As fair as day.

BEROWNE Ay, as some days; but then no sun must
  shine.   90

DUMAINE O that I had my wish!

LONGAVILLE   And I had mine!

75 **out o' th' way** on the wrong track   77 **All hid** (formula from a child's game)
80 **More sacks to the mill** more yet to do   81 **woodcocks** silly birds
85 **Corporal** officer (with a pun on the word for bodily, human)   86 **Her amber
... quoted** her amber-colored hair made amber look ugly by contrast
88 **Stoop** stooped   89 **with child** i.e., rounded

KING And I mine too, good Lord!

BEROWNE Amen, so I had mine! Is not that a good
word?

DUMAINE I would forget her, but a fever she
95 Reigns in my blood, and will rememb'red be.

BEROWNE A fever in your blood? Why, then incision
Would let her out in saucers. Sweet misprision!

DUMAINE Once more I'll read the ode that I have writ.

BEROWNE Once more I'll mark how love can vary wit.

Dumaine reads his sonnet.

100 DUMAINE
"On a day—alack the day!—
Love, whose month is ever May,
Spied a blossom passing fair
Playing in the wanton air.
Through the velvet leaves the wind,
105 All unseen, can passage find;
That the lover, sick to death,
Wished himself the heaven's breath.
Air, quoth he, thy cheeks may blow;
Air, would I might triumph so!
100 But, alack, my hand is sworn
Ne'er to pluck thee from thy thorn.
Vow, alack, for youth unmeet,
Youth so apt to pluck a sweet!
Do not call it sin in me,
115 That I am forsworn for thee;
Thou for whom Jove would swear
Juno but an Ethiop were,
And deny himself for Jove,
Turning mortal for thy love."
120 This will I send, and something else more plain,
That shall express my true love's fasting pain.
O, would the king, Berowne, and Longaville

---

97 **misprision** mistake 117 **Ethiop** black person 121 **fasting pain** pain
caused by deprivation

Were lovers too! Ill, to example ill,
Would from my forehead wipe a perjured note,
For none offend where all alike do dote.   125

LONGAVILLE [*Advancing*] Dumaine, thy love is far from
        charity,
That in love's grief desir'st society.
You may look pale, but I should blush, I know,
To be o'erheard and taken napping so.

KING [*Advancing*] Come, sir, you blush! As his your
        case is such;   130
You chide at him, offending twice as much.
You do not love Maria! Longaville
Did never sonnet for her sake compile,
Nor never lay his wreathèd arms athwart
His loving bosom to keep down his heart.   135
I have been closely shrouded in this bush,
And marked you both, and for you both did blush.
I heard your guilty rhymes, observed your fashion,
Saw sighs reek from you, noted well your passion.
"Ay me!" says one; "O Jove!" the other cries.   140
One, her hairs were gold; crystal, the other's eyes.
[*To Longaville*] You would for paradise break faith
        and troth,
[*To Dumaine*] And Jove, for your love, would in-
        fringe an oath.
What will Berowne say when that he shall hear
Faith infringèd, which such zeal did swear?   145
How will he scorn, how will he spend his wit!
How will he triumph, leap and laugh at it!
For all the wealth that ever I did see,
I would not have him know so much by me.

BEROWNE [*Advancing*] Now step I forth to whip
        hypocrisy.   150
Ah, good my liege, I pray thee pardon me.
Good heart, what grace hast thou, thus to reprove

123–24 Ill ... note wickedness, not liking to make itself an example, would
remove from me the papers I bear as the punishment for perjury   139 reek exhale
149 by me concerning me

These worms for loving, that art most in love?
Your eyes do make no coaches; in your tears
155   There is no certain princess that appears.
You'll not be perjured, 'tis a hateful thing.
Tush, none but minstrels like of sonneting!
But are you not ashamed? Nay, are you not,
All three of you, to be thus much o'ershot?
160   You found his mote, the king your mote did see;
But I a beam do find in each of three.
O what a scene of fool'ry have I seen,
Of sighs, of groans, of sorrow, and of teen!
O me, with what strict patience have I sat,
165   To see a king transformèd to a gnat!
To see great Hercules whipping a gig,
And profound Solomon to tune a jig,
And Nestor play at push-pin with the boys,
And critic Timon laugh at idle toys!
170   Where lies thy grief? O, tell me, good Dumaine.
And, gentle Longaville, where lies thy pain?
And where my liege's? All about the breast.
A caudle, ho!

KING   Too bitter is thy jest.
Are we betrayed thus to thy over-view?

175   BEROWNE Not you by me, but I betrayed to you;
I that am honest, I that hold it sin
To break the vow I am engagèd in,
I am betrayed by keeping company
With men like you, men of inconstancy.
180   When shall you see me write a thing in rhyme?
Or groan for Joan? Or spend a minute's time
In pruning me? When shall you hear that I
Will praise a hand, a foot, a face, an eye,
A gait, a state, a brow, a breast, a waist,
A leg, a limb—

154 **coaches** (for love to ride in—as in line 33)   159 **o'ershot** wide of the mark
160-61 **mote ... beam** (the contrast is between small and large faults; see Matthew
7:3–5; Luke 6:41–42)   163 **teen** grief   166 **gig** top   168 **Nestor** ancient Greek
sage   168 **push-pin** child's game   169 **critic** Timon Greek misanthrope
173 **caudle** healing drink for an invalid   182 **pruning** preening

KING   Soft! Whither away so fast?   185
  A true man or a thief, that gallops so?

BEROWNE I post from love. Good lover, let me go.

          Enter Jaquenetta and [Costard, the] Clown.

JAQUENETTA God bless the king!

KING   What present hast thou there?

COSTARD Some certain treason.

KING   What makes treason here?

COSTARD Nay, it makes nothing, sir.

KING   If it mar nothing neither,   190
  The treason and you go in peace away together.

JAQUENETTA I beseech your Grace let this letter be read.
  Our parson misdoubts it; 'twas treason, he said.

KING Berowne, read it over.
                    He [Berowne] reads the letter.
  Where hadst thou it?

JAQUENETTA Of Costard.

KING Where hadst thou it?   195

COSTARD Of Dun Adramadio, Dun Adramadio.
                    [Berowne tears the letter.]

KING How now, what is in you? Why dost thou tear it?

BEROWNE A toy, my liege, a toy. Your Grace needs not
  fear it.   200

LONGAVILLE It did move him to passion, and therefore
  let's hear it.

DUMAINE *[Gathering up the pieces]* It is Berowne's writing,
  and here is his name.

---

185 **Soft** wait a minute (an exclamation) 186 **true** honest 187 **post** ride in haste
189 **makes** does 193 **misdoubts** mistrusts

BEROWNE [*To Costard*] Ah, you whoreson loggerhead,
  you were born to do me shame!
Guilty, my lord, guilty. I confess, I confess.

205 KING What?

BEROWNE That you three fools lacked me fool to make
  up the mess.
He, he, and you—and you, my liege, and I,
Are pick-purses in love, and we deserve to die.
O dismiss this audience, and I shall tell you more.

DUMAINE Now the number is even.

210 BEROWNE   True, true, we are four.
  Will these turtles be gone?

KING   Hence, sirs, away!

COSTARD Walk aside the true folk, and let the traitors
  stay.   [*Exeunt Costard and Jaquenetta.*]

BEROWNE Sweet lords, sweet lovers, O let us embrace!
  As true we are as flesh and blood can be.
215 The sea will ebb and flow, heaven show his face;
  Young blood doth not obey an old decree.
  We cannot cross the cause why we were born;
  Therefore of all hands must we be forsworn.

KING What, did these rent lines show some love of
  thine?

BEROWNE Did they? quoth you. Who sees the heavenly
220 Rosaline,
  That, like a rude and savage man of Inde
  At the first op'ning of the gorgeous East,
  Bows not his vassal head and, strooken blind,
  Kisses the base ground with obedient breast?
225 What peremptory eagle-sighted eye
  Dares look upon the heaven of her brow
  That is not blinded by her majesty?

203 **whoreson loggerhead** rascally blockhead   206 **mess** party of four at table
211 **turtles** turtledoves, lovers   217 **cross** thwart   219 **rent** damaged
225 **peremptory** resolute

KING What zeal, what fury, hath inspired thee now?
  My love, her mistress, is a gracious moon;
  She, an attending star, scarce seen a light.   230

BEROWNE My eyes are then no eyes, nor I Berowne.
  O, but for my love, day would turn to night!
  Of all complexions the culled sovereignty
  Do meet, as at a fair, in her fair cheek,
  Where several worthies make one dignity,   235
  Where nothing wants that want itself doth seek.
  Lend me the flourish of all gentle tongues—
  Fie, painted rhetoric! O, she needs it not!
  To things of sale a seller's praise belongs:
  She passes praise; then praise too short doth blot.   240
  A withered hermit, five-score winters worn,
  Might shake off fifty, looking in her eye.
  Beauty doth varnish age as if new-born,
  And gives the crutch the cradle's infancy.
  O, 'tis the sun that maketh all things shine.   245

KING By heaven, thy love is black as ebony!

BEROWNE Is ebony like her? O wood divine!
  A wife of such wood were felicity.
  O, who can give an oath? Where is a book?
  That I may swear beauty doth beauty lack   250
  If that she learn not of her eye to look.
  No face is fair that is not full so black.

KING O paradox! Black is the badge of hell,
  The hue of dungeons, and the school of night;
  And beauty's crest becomes the heavens well.   255

BEROWNE Devils soonest tempt, resembling spirits of
  light.

233 culled sovereignty chosen as the best   235 worthies good qualities
236 wants lacks   237 flourish adornment   238 painted rhetoric extravagant
speech   239 of sale for sale   243 varnish lend freshness   254 school of night
(some editors emend "school" to "suit" or to "shade," but perhaps the term
means a place for learning dark things)   255 beauty's ... well true beauty, which
is bright, is heavenly, but if blackness is taken as the sign of beauty, it would be
ironic to link beauty with heaven, which is the source of light

O, if in black my lady's brows be decked,
It mourns that painting and usurping hair
Should ravish doters with a false aspect;
260　　And therefore is she born to make black fair.
Her favor turns the fashion of the days,
For native blood is counted painting now;
And therefore red that would avoid dispraise
Paints itself black to imitate her brow.

DUMAINE　To look like her are chimney-sweepers
265　　black.

LONGAVILLE　And since her time are colliers counted
bright.

KING　And Ethiops of their sweet complexion crack.

DUMAINE　Dark needs no candles now, for dark is
light.

BEROWNE　Your mistresses dare never come in rain,
270　　For fear their colors should be washed away.

KING　'Twere good yours did; for, sir, to tell you plain,
I'll find a fairer face not washed today.

BEROWNE　I'll prove her fair or talk till doomsday here.

KING　No devil will fright thee then so much as she.

275　DUMAINE　I never knew man hold vile stuff so dear.

LONGAVILLE　Look, here's thy love; [*showing his shoe*]
my foot and her face see.

BEROWNE　O, if the streets were pavèd with thine eyes,
Her feet were much too dainty for such tread.

DUMAINE　O vile! Then, as she goes, what upward lies
280　　The street should see as she walked overhead.

KING　But what of this? Are we not all in love?

258 usurping false　259 aspect appearance　261 favor complexion　262 native
blood naturally red complexion　266 colliers coal-men　267 crack boast
276 my foot (he is wearing black shoes)

BEROWNE O, nothing so sure, and thereby all
   forsworn.

KING Then leave this chat, and, good Berowne, now
   prove
Our loving lawful and our faith not torn.

DUMAINE Ay marry, there, some flattery for this evil! 285

LONGAVILLE O, some authority how to proceed!
   Some tricks, some quillets, how to cheat the devil!

DUMAINE Some salve for perjury.

BEROWNE   O, 'tis more than need!
   Have at you, then, affection's men-at-arms!
Consider what you first did swear unto. 290
To fast, to study, and to see no woman—
Flat treason 'gainst the kingly state of youth.
Say, can you fast? Your stomachs are too young,
And abstinence engenders maladies.
[And where that you have vowed to study, lords, 295
In that each of you have forsworn his book,
Can you still dream and pore and thereon look?
For when would you, my lord, or you, or you,
Have found the ground of study's excellence
Without the beauty of a woman's face? 300
From women's eyes this doctrine I derive:
They are the ground, the books, the academes,
From whence doth spring the true Promethean
   fire.
Why, universal plodding poisons up
The nimble spirits in the arteries, 305
As motion and long-during action tires
The sinewy vigor of the traveler.
Now for not looking on a woman's face,

---

287 **quillets** subtleties 289 **affection's men-at-arms** love's warriors
295 **where that** whereas (after writing lines 295-316, here bracketed, Shakespeare
apparently decided he could do better, and rewrote the passage in the ensuing
lines, but the printer mistakenly printed both versions) 302 **academes** academies
303 **Promethean fire** fire stolen from heaven by Prometheus 304 **poisons**
(some editors emend to *prisons*) 306 **long-during** long-lasting

You have in that forsworn the use of eyes,
310   And study too, the causer of your vow;
For where is any author in the world
Teaches such beauty as a woman's eye?
Learning is but an adjunct to ourself,
And where we are our learning likewise is.
315   Then when ourselves we see in ladies' eyes,
Do we not likewise see our learning there?]
O, we have made a vow to study, lords,
And in that vow we have forsworn our books;
For when would you, my liege, or you, or you,
320   In leaden contemplation have found out
Such fiery numbers as the prompting eyes
Of beauty's tutors have enriched you with?
Other slow arts entirely keep the brain,
And therefore, finding barren practisers,
325   Scarce show a harvest of their heavy toil;
But love, first learnèd in a lady's eyes,
Lives not alone immurèd in the brain,
But with the motion of all elements,
Courses as swift as thought in every power,
330   And gives to every power a double power
Above their functions and their offices.
It adds a precious seeing to the eye:
A lover's eyes will gaze an eagle blind.
A lover's ear will hear the lowest sound,
335   When the suspicious head of theft is stopped.
Love's feeling is more soft and sensible
Than are the tender horns of cockled snails.
Love's tongue proves dainty Bacchus gross in taste.
For valor, is not Love a Hercules,
340   Still climbing trees in the Hesperides?
Subtle as Sphinx; as sweet and musical
As bright Apollo's lute, strung with his hair.
And when Love speaks, the voice of all the gods

---

321 **fiery numbers** passionate verses   328 **with the motion of all elements**
i.e., with the force of all the components of the universe   335 **the suspicious
head of theft** i.e., a thief's hearing, suspicious of every sound   337 **cockled** in
shells   340 **Hesperides** (garden where Hercules picked the golden apples)

Make heaven drowsy with the harmony.
Never durst poet touch a pen to write   345
Until his ink were temp'red with Love's sighs.
O, then his lines would ravish savage ears
And plant in tyrants mild humility.
From women's eyes this doctrine I derive.
They sparkle still the right Promethean fire;   350
They are the books, the arts, the academes,
That show, contain, and nourish all the world;
Else none at all in aught proves excellent.
Then fools you were these women to forswear,
Or, keeping what is sworn, you will prove fools.   355
For wisdom's sake, a word that all men love,
Or for love's sake, a word that loves all men,
Or for men's sake, the authors of these women,
Or women's sake, by whom we men are men—
Let us once lose our oaths to find ourselves,   360
Or else we lose ourselves to keep our oaths.
It is religion to be thus forsworn,
For charity itself fulfils the law,
And who can sever love from charity?

KING Saint Cupid then! And, soldiers, to the field!   365

BEROWNE Advance your standards, and upon them,
    lords!
Pell-mell, down with them! But be first advised,
In conflict that you get the sun of them.

LONGAVILLE Now to plain-dealing. Lay these glozes
    by.
Shall we resolve to woo these girls of France?   370

KING And win them too! Therefore let us devise
Some entertainment for them in their tents.

BEROWNE First from the park let us conduct them
    thither;
Then homeward every man attach the hand

363 charity ... law (Romans 13:8: "he that loveth another hath fulfilled the law") 368 get the sun of them approach when the sun is in their eyes 369 glozes trivial comments

375　Of his fair mistress. In the afternoon
　　We will with some strange pastime solace them,
　　Such as the shortness of the time can shape;
　　For revels, dances, masks, and merry hours
　　Forerun fair Love, strewing her way with flowers.

380　KING　Away, away! No time shall be omitted
　　That will be time, and may by us be fitted.

BEROWNE　*Allons! Allons!* Sowed cockle reaped no
　　corn,
　　And justice always whirls in equal measure.
　　Light wenches may prove plagues to men forsworn;
385　If so, our copper buys no better treasure.　[*Exeunt.*]

381 **be time** come to pass　382 **Allons** let's go (French)　382 **Sowed ... corn** if weeds are sown, wheat is not reaped

[ACT V

Scene I. *The park.*]

Enter [Holofernes,] the Pedant, [Nathaniel,] the Curate, and Dull, [the Constable].

HOLOFERNES *Satis quid sufficit.*

NATHANIEL I praise God for you, sir. Your reasons
at dinner have been sharp and sententious, pleasant without scurrility, witty without affection,
audacious without impudency, learned without   5
opinion, and strange without heresy. I did converse this *quondam* day with a companion of the
king's, who is intituled, nominated, or called, Don
Adriano de Armado.

HOLOFERNES *Novi hominem tanquam te.* His humor   10
is lofty, his discourse peremptory, his tongue
filed, his eye ambitious, his gait majestical, and his
general behavior vain, ridiculous, and thrasonical.
He is too picked, too spruce, too affected,
too odd, as it were, too peregrinate, as I may   15
call it.

V.i.1 Satis quid sufficit enough is as good as a feast 2 reasons discourses
3 sententious full of meaning 4 affection affectation 6 opinion dogmatism
7 quondam former 10 Novi hominem tanquam te I know the man as well as
I know you 11 peremptory decisive 12 filed polished 13-14 thrasonical
boastful 14 picked refined 15 peregrinate foreign in manner

NATHANIEL A most singular and choice epithet.

Draw out his table-book.

HOLOFERNES He draweth out the thread of his ver-
bosity finer than the staple of his argument. I
20 abhor such fanatical phantasimes, such insociable
and point-devise companions; such rackers of
orthography as to speak "dout" fine when he
should say "doubt," "det" when he should pronounce "debt"—d, e, b, t, not d, e, t. He clepeth
25 a calf "cauf," half "hauf," neighbor *vocatur*
"nebor," neigh abbreviated "ne." This is abhomina-
ble, which he would call "abominable." It insinuateth me of insanie. *Ne intelligis, domine?* To
make frantic, lunatic.

30 NATHANIEL *Laus Deo bone intelligo.*

HOLOFERNES *Bone? Bone* for *bene!* Priscian a little
scratched; 'twill serve.

*Enter [Armado, the] Braggart, [Moth, the] Boy,
[and Costard, the Clown].*

NATHANIEL *Videsne quis venit?*

HOLOFERNES *Video, et gaudeo.*

35 ARMADO *[To Moth]* Chirrah!

HOLOFERNES *Quare* "chirrah," not "sirrah"?

ARMADO Men of peace, well encount'red.

17s.d. **table-book** tablet (stage directions are often, as here, in the imperative)
19 **staple** fiber 20 **phantasimes** wild imaginers 20 **insociable** impossible to
associate with 21 **point-devise** perfectly correct 21 **rackers** torturers
24 **clepeth** calls 25 **vocatur** is called 27–28 **insinuateth me of insanie**
suggests insanity to me 28 **Ne intelligis, domine** do you not understand,
sir? 30 **Laus Deo bone intelligo** praise be to God, I well understand 31 **Bone**
(probably a mixture of Latin *bene* and French *bon*) 31 **Priscian** Latin grammarian of sixth century A.D. 32 **scratched** damaged 33 **Videsne quis venit?**
do you see who is coming? 34 **Video, et gaudeo** I see, and I rejoice
35 **Chirrah** (dialect form for "sirrah") 36 **Quare** why?

HOLOFERNES Most military sir, salutation.

MOTH [*Aside to Costard*] They have been at a great
feast of languages and stol'n the scraps.   40

COSTARD O, they have lived long on the alms-basket
of words. I marvel thy master hath not eaten thee
for a word; for thou art not so long by the head
as *honorificabilitudinitatibus*. Thou art easier swallowed than a flapdragon.   45

MOTH Peace! The peal begins.

ARMADO Monsieur, are you not lett'red?

MOTH Yes, yes! He teaches boys the hornbook.
What is a, b, spelled backward with the horn on
his head?   50

HOLOFERNES Ba, *pueritia*, with a horn added.

MOTH Ba, most silly sheep with a horn. You hear his
learning.

HOLOFERNES *Quis, quis*, thou consonant?

MOTH The last of the five vowels, if you repeat them;   55
or the fifth, if I.

HOLOFERNES I will repeat them: a, e, i—

MOTH The sheep. The other two concludes it—o, u.

ARMADO Now, by the salt wave of the Mediterranean,
a sweet touch, a quick venew of wit! Snip, snap,   60
quick and home! It rejoiceth my intellect. True wit!

MOTH Offered by a child to an old man—which is
wit-old.

41 alms-basket (basket used at feasts to collect scraps from the table for the
poor) 44 honorificabilitudinitatibus (Latin tongue-twister, thought to be the
longest word known) 45 flapdragon (burning raisin or plum floating in liquor,
and so drunk) 46 peal (of bells) 47 lett'red man of letters 48 hornbook
(parchment with alphabet and numbers, covered with transparent horn, for
teaching spelling and counting) 51 pueritia childishness 54 Quis what?
60 venew thrust 63 wit-old i.e., mentally feeble (with pun on *wittol* = cuckold)

HOLOFERNES What is the figure? What is the figure?

65 MOTH Horns.

HOLOFERNES Thou disputes like an infant. Go whip thy gig.

MOTH Lend me your horn to make one, and I will whip about your infamy *manu cita*. A gig of a
70 cuckold's horn.

COSTARD And I had but one penny in the world, thou shouldst have it to buy gingerbread. Hold, there is the very remuneration I had of thy master, thou halfpenny purse of wit, thou pigeon-egg of
75 discretion. O, and the heavens were so pleased that thou wert but my bastard, what a joyful father wouldest thou make me! Go to, thou hast it *ad* dunghill, at the fingers' ends, as they say.

HOLOFERNES O, I smell false Latin! "Dunghill" for
80 *unguem*.

ARMADO Arts-man, preambulate. We will be singled from the barbarous. Do you not educate youth at the charge-house on the top of the mountain?

HOLOFERNES Or *mons*, the hill.

85 ARMADO At your sweet pleasure, for the mountain.

HOLOFERNES I do, *sans question*.

ARMADO Sir, it is the king's most sweet pleasure and affection to congratulate the princess at her pavilion in the posteriors of this day, which the rude mul-
90 titude call the afternoon.

HOLOFERNES The posterior of the day, most generous

---

64 **figure** figure of speech   67 **gig** top   69 **manu cita** with a swift hand   71 **And if**   77–78 **ad dunghill** (perhaps a schoolboy's corruption of the proverb "ad unguem," to the fingernail, meaning "precisely")   81 **Arts-man** learned man 81 **preambulate** walk forth   83 **charge-house** school (perhaps an allusion to a specific school on a hill, mentioned by Erasmus)   89 **posteriors** hind parts

sir, is liable, congruent, and measurable for the
afternoon. The word is well culled, chose, sweet
and apt, I do assure you, sir, I do assure.

ARMADO Sir, the king is a noble gentleman, and my   95
familiar, I do assure ye, very good friend. For
what is inward between us, let it pass. I do beseech thee, remember thy courtesy. I beseech thee
apparel thy head. And among other importunate
and most serious designs, and of great import in-   100
deed, too—but let that pass; for I must tell thee,
it will please his Grace, by the world, sometime to
lean upon my poor shoulder, and with his royal
finger thus dally with my excrement, with my
mustachio—but, sweet heart, let that pass. By the   105
world, I recount no fable! Some certain special
honors it pleaseth his greatness to impart to Armado, a soldier, a man of travel, that hath seen
the world—but let that pass. The very all of all
is (but, sweet heart, I do implore secrecy) that the   110
king would have me present the princess (sweet
chuck) with some delightful ostentation, or show,
or pageant, or antic, or fire-work. Now, understanding that the curate and your sweet self are
good at such eruptions and sudden breaking out   115
of mirth, as it were, I have acquainted you withal,
to the end to crave your assistance.

HOLOFERNES Sir, you shall present before her the Nine
Worthies. Sir Nathaniel, as concerning some entertainment of time, some show in the posterior of   120
this day, to be rend'red by our assistance, the king's
command, and this most gallant, illustrate, and

---

92 **liable, congruent, measurable** (all synonyms for "suitable")   96 **familiar**
close friend   97 **inward** private   98 **remember thy courtesy** (possibly: remove
your hat when the king's name is mentioned)   104 **excrement** that which grows
out (such as hair, nails, feathers)   113 **antic** fanciful pageant   118–19 **Nine
Worthies** (traditionally, Hector, Caesar, Joshua, David, Judas Maccabaeus, Alexander, King Arthur, Charlemagne, Godfrey of Boulogne; here Hercules and
Pompey are included)

learned gentleman, before the princess—I say, none so fit as to present the Nine Worthies.

125 NATHANIEL Where will you find men worthy enough to present them?

HOLOFERNES Joshua, yourself; myself; and this gallant gentleman, Judas Maccabaeus; this swain, because of his great limb or joint, shall pass Pompey the
130 Great; the page, Hercules—

ARMADO Pardon, sir—error! He is not quantity enough for that Worthy's thumb; he is not so big as the end of his club.

HOLOFERNES Shall I have audience? He shall present
135 Hercules in minority. His enter and exit shall be strangling a snake; and I will have an apology for that purpose.

MOTH An excellent device! So if any of the audience hiss, you may cry, "Well done, Hercules! Now
140 thou crushest the snake!" That is the way to make an offense gracious, though few have the grace to do it.

ARMADO For the rest of the Worthies?

HOLOFERNES I will play three myself.

145 MOTH Thrice-worthy gentleman!

ARMADO Shall I tell you a thing?

HOLOFERNES We attend.

ARMADO We will have, if this fadge not, an antic. I beseech you, follow.

150 HOLOFERNES *Via*, goodman Dull! Thou hast spoken no word all this while.

DULL Nor understood none neither, sir.

---

129 **pass** represent   134 **have audience** be heard   135 **minority** early youth
136 **apology** justification   148 **fadge** succeed   150 **Via** come on (Italian)

HOLOFERNES *Allons*, we will employ thee.

DULL I'll make one in a dance, or so; or I will play
on the tabor to the Worthies, and let them dance   155
the hay.

HOLOFERNES Most dull, honest Dull! To our sport,
away!   *Exeunt.*

[Scene II. *The park.*]

*Enter the Ladies [the Princess, Katharine,
Rosaline, and Maria].*

PRINCESS Sweet hearts, we shall be rich ere we depart
If fairings come thus plentifully in.
A lady walled about with diamonds!
Look you what I have from the loving king.

ROSALINE Madam, came nothing else along with that?   5

PRINCESS Nothing but this? Yes, as much love in
rhyme
As would be crammed up in a sheet of paper,
Writ o' both sides the leaf, margent and all,
That he was fain to seal on Cupid's name.

ROSALINE That was the way to make his godhead
wax,   10
For he hath been five thousand year a boy.

KATHARINE Ay, and a shrowd unhappy gallows too.

ROSALINE You'll ne'er be friends with him: 'a killed
your sister.

155 **tabor** small drum 156 **hay** country dance V.ii.2 **fairings** presents
8 **margent** margin 9 **fain** eager 10 **wax** grow (and with a pun on sealing-wax)
12 **shrowd** accursed 12 **gallows** one fit to be hanged

353

KATHARINE He made her melancholy, sad, and heavy;
15   And so she died. Had she been light, like you,
          Of such a merry, nimble, stirring spirit,
          She might ha' been a grandam ere she died.
          And so may you, for a light heart lives long.

ROSALINE What's your dark meaning, mouse, of this
          light word?

20   KATHARINE A light condition in a beauty dark.

ROSALINE We need more light to find your meaning
          out.

KATHARINE You'll mar the light by taking it in snuff,
          Therefore, I'll darkly end the argument.

ROSALINE Look what you do, you do it still i' th' dark.

25   KATHARINE So do not you, for you are a light wench.

ROSALINE Indeed I weigh not you, and therefore
          light.

KATHARINE You weigh me not? O, that's you care not
          for me!

ROSALINE Great reason, for past care is still past cure.

PRINCESS Well bandied both! A set of wit well
          played.
30   But Rosaline, you have a favor too—
          Who sent it? And what is it?

ROSALINE   I would you knew.
          And if my face were but as fair as yours,
          My favor were as great. Be witness this.
          Nay, I have verses too, I thank Berowne;
35   The numbers true, and, were the numb'ring too,
          I were the fairest goddess on the ground.

---

22 **taking it in snuff** being annoyed   24 **Look what** whatever   26 **weigh** value
at a certain rate   29 **bandied** hit back and forth (figure from tennis)   35 **numbers**
meter   35 **numb'ring** estimate

I am compared to twenty thousand fairs.
O, he hath drawn my picture in his letter!

PRINCESS Anything like?

ROSALINE Much in the letters, nothing in the praise.   40

PRINCESS Beauteous as ink—a good conclusion.

KATHARINE Fair as a text B in a copy-book.

ROSALINE 'Ware pencils, ho! Let me not die your
     debtor,
My red dominical, my golden letter.
O, that your face were not so full of O's!   45

PRINCESS A pox of that jest, and I beshrow all
     shrows!
But Katharine, what was sent to you from fair
     Dumaine?

KATHARINE Madam, this glove.

PRINCESS   Did he not send you twain?

KATHARINE Yes, madam; and moreover,
Some thousand verses of a faithful lover.   50
A huge translation of hypocrisy,
Vilely compiled, profound simplicity.

MARIA This, and these pearls, to me sent Longaville.
The letter is too long by half a mile.

PRINCESS I think no less. Dost thou not wish in heart   55
The chain were longer and the letter short?

MARIA Ay, or I would these hands might never part.

PRINCESS We are wise girls to mock our lovers so.

ROSALINE They are worse fools to purchase mocking so.

---

37 fairs beautiful women   43 'Ware beware   44 red dominical red S (for Sunday,
the Lord's Day)   45 O's smallpox scars   46 A pox of may a plague strike
46 beshrow all shrows curse all shrews   52 simplicity simple-mindedness

60   That same Berowne I'll torture ere I go.
        O that I knew he were but in by th' week!
        How I would make him fawn, and beg, and seek,
        And wait the season, and observe the times,
        And spend his prodigal wits in bootless rhymes,
65   And shape his service wholly to my hests,
        And make him proud to make me proud that jests!
        So pertaunt-like would I o'ersway his state
        That he should be my fool, and I his fate.

    PRINCESS None are so surely caught, when they are
            catched,
70   As wit turned fool. Folly, in wisdom hatched,
        Hath wisdom's warrant and the help of school
        And wit's own grace to grace a learnèd fool.

    ROSALINE The blood of youth burns not with such
            excess
        As gravity's revolt to wantonness.

75 MARIA Folly in fools bears not so strong a note
        As fool'ry in the wise when wit doth dote;
        Since all the power thereof it doth apply
        To prove, by wit, worth in simplicity.

                    Enter Boyet.

    PRINCESS Here comes Boyet, and mirth is in his face.

    BOYET O, I am stabbed with laughter! Where's her
80   Grace?

    PRINCESS Thy news, Boyet?

    BOYET   Prepare, madam, prepare!
        Arm, wenches, arm! Encounters mounted are
        Against your peace. Love doth approach disguised,
        Armèd in arguments; you'll be surprised.
85   Muster your wits; stand in your own defense,
        Or hide your heads like cowards and fly hence.

61 in by th' week trapped   65 hests commands   67 pertaunt-like (like a winning
hand [*Pair-taunt*] in a certain card game)   67 o'ersway his state overrule
his power

PRINCESS Saint Denis to Saint Cupid! What are they
    That charge their breath against us? Say, scout, say.

BOYET Under the cool shade of a sycamore
    I thought to close mine eyes some half an hour,   90
    When, lo, to interrupt my purposed rest,
    Toward that shade I might behold addrest
    The king and his companions! Warily
    I stole into a neighbor thicket by,
    And overheard what you shall overhear—   95
    That, by and by, disguised they will be here.
    Their herald is a pretty knavish page
    That well by heart hath conned his embassage.
    Action and accent did they teach him there:
    "Thus must thou speak, and thus thy body bear."   100
    And ever and anon they made a doubt
    Presence majestical would put him out;
    "For," quoth the king, "an angel shalt thou see,
    Yet fear not thou, but speak audaciously."
    The boy replied, "An angel is not evil;   105
    I should have feared her had she been a devil."
    With that all laughed and clapped him on the
        shoulder,
    Making the bold wag by their praises bolder.
    One rubbed his elbow thus, and fleered, and swore
    A better speech was never spoke before.   110
    Another, with his finger and his thumb,
    Cried "Via, we will do 't, come what will come!"
    The third he capered and cried, "All goes well!"
    The fourth turned on the toe, and down he fell.
    With that they all did tumble on the ground   115
    With such a zealous laughter, so profound,
    That in this spleen ridiculous appears,
    To check their folly, passion's solemn tears.

PRINCESS But what, but what? Come they to visit us?

BOYET They do, they do, and are apparelled thus—   120

87 **Saint Denis** patron saint of France 92 **addresst** approaching 98 **conned
his embassage** learned his commission 101 **made a doubt** expressed a fear
109 **fleered** grinned 114 **turned on the toe** turned quickly to leave 117 **spleen**
excess of mirth

Like Muscovites or Russians, as I guess.
Their purpose is to parley, court and dance,
And every one his love-feat will advance
Unto his several mistress, which they'll know
125   By favors several which they did bestow.

PRINCESS And will they so? The gallants shall be
          tasked;
        For, ladies, we will every one be masked,
        And not a man of them shall have the grace,
        Despite of suit, to see a lady's face.
130   Hold, Rosaline, this favor thou shalt wear,
        And then the king will court thee for his dear.
        Hold, take thou this, my sweet, and give me thine;
        So shall Berowne take me for Rosaline.
        And change you favors too; so shall your loves
135   Woo contrary, deceived by these removes.

ROSALINE Come on, then; wear the favors most in
          sight.

KATHARINE But in this changing what is your intent?

PRINCESS The effect of my intent is to cross theirs.
        They do it but in mockery merriment,
140   And mock for mock is only my intent.
        Their several counsels they unbosom shall
        To loves mistook and so be mocked withal
        Upon the next occasion that we meet,
        With visages displayed, to talk and greet.

145 ROSALINE But shall we dance if they desire us to 't?

PRINCESS No, to the death we will not move a foot,
        Nor to their penned speech render we no grace,
        But while 'tis spoke each turn away her face.

BOYET Why, that contempt will kill the speaker's
        heart,
150   And quite divorce his memory from his part.

122 **parley** hold a conference 123 **love-feat** exploit prompted by love
126 **tasked** tested 129 **Despite of suit** in spite of his pleading 135 **removes**
changes 136 **most in sight** conspicuously 138 **cross** thwart 141 **unbosom**
confide 146 **to the death** as long as we live

PRINCESS Therefore I do it, and I make no doubt
The rest will e'er come in if he be out.
There's no such sport as sport by sport o'erthrown,
To make theirs ours, and ours none but our own.
So shall we stay, mocking intended game,   155
And they, well mocked, depart away with shame.
                                        Sound trumpet.

BOYET The trumpet sounds. Be masked—the maskers
come.
                                [*The Ladies mask.*]

*Enter Blackamoors with music; [Moth,] the Boy, with a
speech, and [the King, Berowne, and] the rest of the
Lords [in Russian dress and] disguised.*

MOTH "All hail, the richest beauties on the earth!"

BOYET Beauties no richer than rich taffeta.

MOTH "A holy parcel of the fairest dames,   160
                The Ladies turn their backs to him.
That ever turned their backs to mortal views!"

BEROWNE "Their eyes," villain, "their eyes!"

MOTH "That ever turned their eyes to mortal views!
Out—"

BOYET True. "Out" indeed!   165

MOTH "Out of your favors, heavenly spirits, vouchsafe
Not to behold"—

BEROWNE "Once to behold," rogue!

MOTH "Once to behold with your sun-beamèd eyes,
—with your sun-beamèd eyes"—   170

BOYET They will not answer to that epithet.
You were best call it "daughter-beamèd eyes."

MOTH They do not mark me, and that brings me out.

155 game sport   173 brings puts

359

BEROWNE Is this your perfectness? Be gone, you rogue!
                                              [*Exit Moth.*]

ROSALINE What would these strangers? Know their
175   minds, Boyet.
           If they do speak our language, 'tis our will
           That some plain man recount their purposes.
           Know what they would.

BOYET What would you with the Princess?

180 BEROWNE Nothing but peace and gentle visitation.

ROSALINE What would they, say they?

BOYET Nothing but peace and gentle visitation.

ROSALINE Why, that they have, and bid them so be
           gone.

BOYET She says you have it and you may be gone.

185 KING Say to her, we have measured many miles,
           To tread a measure with her on this grass.

BOYET They say that they have measured many a mile,
           To tread a measure with you on this grass.

ROSALINE It is not so. Ask them how many inches
190   Is in one mile. If they have measured many,
           The measure then of one is eas'ly told.

BOYET If to come hither you have measured miles,
           And many miles, the princess bids you tell
           How many inches doth fill up one mile.

195 BEROWNE Tell her we measure them by weary steps.

BOYET She hears herself.

ROSALINE   How many weary steps,
           Of many weary miles you have o'ergone,
           Are numb'red in the travel of one mile?

BEROWNE We number nothing that we spend for you.
200   Our duty is so rich, so infinite,

188 **measure** stately dance

That we may do it still without accompt.
Vouchsafe to show the sunshine of your face,
That we like savages may worship it.

ROSALINE My face is but a moon, and clouded too.

KING Blessèd are clouds, to do as such clouds do.   205
Vouchsafe, bright moon, and these thy stars, to
      shine
(Those clouds removed) upon our watery eyne.

ROSALINE O vain petitioner, beg a greater matter!
Thou now requests but moonshine in the water.

KING Then in our measure do but vouchsafe one
      change.   210
Thou bid'st me beg; this begging is not strange.

ROSALINE Play, music then. Nay, you must do it soon.
                    [*The musicians play.*]
Not yet? No dance! Thus change I like the moon.

KING Will you not dance? How come you thus
      estrangèd?

ROSALINE You took the moon at full, but now she's
      changèd.   215

KING Yet still she is the moon, and I the man.
The music plays; vouchsafe some motion to it.

ROSALINE Our ears vouchsafe it.

KING   But your legs should do it.

ROSALINE Since you are strangers and come here by
      chance,
We'll not be nice. Take hands. We will not dance.   220

KING Why take we hands then?

ROSALINE   Only to part friends.
Curtsy, sweet hearts. And so the measure ends.

201 **accompt** reckoning 207 **eyne** eyes 209 **moonshine in the water** a mere
nothing 210 **change** round of dancing 211 **not strange** not unsuitably foreign
220 **nice** fastidious

KING   More measure of this measure! Be not nice.

ROSALINE   We can afford no more at such a price.

225   KING   Price you yourselves. What buys your company?

ROSALINE   Your absence only.

KING   That can never be.

ROSALINE   Then cannot we be bought; and so adieu—
Twice to your visor, and half once to you.

KING   If you deny to dance, let's hold more chat.

ROSALINE   In private then.

230   KING   I am best pleased with that.
                                [They converse apart.]

BEROWNE   White-handed mistress, one sweet word with
thee.

PRINCESS   Honey, and milk, and sugar—there is three.

BEROWNE   Nay then, two treys, an if you grow so
nice,
Metheglin, wort, and malmsey. Well run, dice!
There's half a dozen sweets.

235   PRINCESS   Seventh sweet, adieu.
Since you can cog, I'll play no more with you.

BEROWNE   One word in secret.

PRINCESS   Let it not be sweet.

BEROWNE   Thou grievest my gall.

PRINCESS   Gall! Bitter.

BEROWNE   Therefore meet.
                                [They converse apart.]

---

228 **visor** mask   233 **treys** threes (at dice)   233 **an if** if   234 **Metheglin** drink
mixed with honey   234 **wort** unfermented beer   234 **malmsey** a Mediterranean
wine   236 **cog** cheat   238 **gall** sore spot   238 **meet** fitting

DUMAINE Will you vouchsafe with me to change a
   word?

MARIA Name it.

DUMAINE   Fair lady—

MARIA   Say you so? Fair lord.   240
  Take that for your "fair lady."

DUMAINE   Please it you,
  As much in private, and I'll bid adieu.
                         [*They converse apart.*]

KATHARINE What, was your vizard made without a
   tongue?

LONGAVILLE I know the reason, lady, why you ask.

KATHARINE O for your reason! Quickly, sir, I long.   245

LONGAVILLE You have a double tongue within your
   mask
  And would afford my speechless vizard half.

KATHARINE "Veal," quoth the Dutchman. Is not
  "veal" a calf?

LONGAVILLE A calf, fair lady?

KATHARINE   No, a fair lord calf.

LONGAVILLE Let's part the word.

KATHARINE   No, I'll not be your half.   250
  Take all and wean it, it may prove an ox.

LONGAVILLE Look how you butt yourself in these sharp
   mocks.
  Will you give horns, chaste lady? Do not so.

KATHARINE Then die a calf before your horns do grow.

LONGAVILLE One word in private with you ere I die.   255

---

239 **change** exchange 243 **vizard** mask 246 **double tongue** (an inner projection or tongue held in the mouth to keep the mask in place) 248 **Veal** (Dutch or German pronunciation of "well") 253 **give horns** prove unfaithful

KATHARINE Bleat softly then. The butcher hears you
    cry.   [*They converse apart.*]

BOYET The tongues of mocking wenches are as keen
    As is the razor's edge invisible,
    Cutting a smaller hair than may be seen,
260   Above the sense of sense; so sensible
    Seemeth their conference, their conceits have wings
    Fleeter than arrows, bullets, wind, thought, swifter
    things.

ROSALINE Not one word more, my maids, break off,
    break off.

BEROWNE By heaven, all dry-beaten with pure scoff!

265 KING Farewell, mad wenches. You have simple wits.
              Exeunt [*King, Lords, and Blackamoors*].

PRINCESS Twenty adieus, my frozen Muscovits.
    Are these the breed of wits so wondered at?

BOYET Tapers they are, with your sweet breaths
    puffed out.

ROSALINE Well-liking wits they have; gross, gross;
    fat, fat.

270 PRINCESS O poverty in wit, kingly-poor flout!
    Will they not, think you, hang themselves tonight?
    Or ever but in vizards show their faces?
    This pert Berowne was out of count'nance quite.

ROSALINE They were all in lamentable cases.
275   The king was weeping-ripe for a good word.

PRINCESS Berowne did swear himself out of all suit.

MARIA Dumaine was at my service, and his sword.
    "No point," quoth I; my servant straight was mute.

---

260 **Above the sense** above the reach 261 **conference** conferring 261 **conceits**
witticisms 264 **dry-beaten** beaten with blood being drawn 269 **Well-liking**
plump, sleek 270 **kingly-poor flout** a poor jest for a king 274 **cases** (with pun
on the sense "masks" or "costumes") 275 **weeping-ripe** about to weep
276 **out of all suit** beyond all reasonableness 278 **No point** not at all

KATHARINE Lord Longaville said I came o'er his heart;
  And trow you what he called me?

PRINCESS   Qualm, perhaps.   280

KATHARINE Yes, in good faith.

PRINCESS   Go, sickness as thou art!

ROSALINE Well, better wits have worn plain statute-
    caps.
  But will you hear? The king is my love sworn.

PRINCESS And quick Berowne hath plighted faith to
  me.

KATHARINE And Longaville was for my service born.   285

MARIA Dumaine is mine as sure as bark on tree.

BOYET Madam, and pretty mistresses, give ear.
  Immediately they will again be here
  In their own shapes, for it can never be
  They will digest this harsh indignity.   290

PRINCESS Will they return?

BOYET   They will, they will, God knows,
  And leap for joy though they are lame with blows.
  Therefore change favors, and when they repair,
  Blow like sweet roses in this summer air.

PRINCESS How blow? How blow? Speak to be under-
    stood.   295

BOYET Fair ladies masked are roses in their bud;
  Dismasked, their damask sweet commixture shown,
  Are angels vailing clouds, or roses blown.

PRINCESS Avaunt, perplexity! What shall we do
  If they return in their own shapes to woo?   300

---

280 trow know 280 Qualm sudden sickness 282 statute-caps caps appren-
tices were required to wear 293 change exchange 293 repair come again
294 blow blossom 297 damask red and white (like the Damascus rose)
298 vailing letting fall 299 Avaunt, perplexity away, confusion

ROSALINE Good madam, if by me you'll be advised,
Let's mock them still, as well known as disguised.
Let us complain to them what fools were here,
Disguised like Muscovites in shapeless gear;
305 And wonder what they were, and to what end
Their shallow shows and prologue vilely penned,
And their rough carriage so ridiculous,
Should be presented at our tent to us.

BOYET Ladies, withdraw. The gallants are at hand.

310 PRINCESS Whip to our tents, as roes run o'er land.
                    Exeunt [Princess and Ladies].

*Enter the King and the rest: [Berowne, Longaville,
        and Dumaine, all in their proper habits].*

KING Fair sir, God save you. Where's the princess?

BOYET Gone to her tent. Please it your Majesty
Command me any service to her thither?

KING That she vouchsafe me audience for one word.

315 BOYET I will; and so will she, I know, my lord.   *Exit.*

BEROWNE This fellow pecks up wit, as pigeons peas,
And utters it again when God doth please.
He is wit's pedlar, and retails his wares
At wakes and wassails, meetings, markets, fairs;
320 And we that sell by gross, the Lord doth know,
Have not the grace to grace it with such show.
This gallant pins the wenches on his sleeve.
Had he been Adam, he had tempted Eve.
'A can carve too, and lisp. Why, this is he
325 That kissed his hand away in courtesy.
This is the ape of form, Monsieur the Nice,
That, when he plays at tables, chides the dice
In honorable terms. Nay, he can sing

---

304 **gear** outfit   319 **wakes** vigils and feastings   319 **wassails** revelry   322 **pins
the wenches** wears maidens' favors   324 **carve** make gestures of courtship
326 **form** etiquette   326 **Nice** exquisite   327 **at tables** backgammon

A mean most meanly; and in ushering
Mend him who can. The ladies call him sweet.   330
The stairs, as he treads on them, kiss his feet.
This is the flow'r that smiles on every one,
To show his teeth as white as whalës-bone;
And consciences that will not die in debt
Pay him the due of "honey-tongued Boyet."   335

KING A blister on his sweet tongue, with my heart,
That put Armado's page out of his part!

Enter [the Princess and] the Ladies [with Boyet].

BEROWNE See where it comes! Behavior, what wert
thou
Till this madman showed thee, and what art thou
now?

KING All hail, sweet madam, and fair time of day.   340

PRINCESS "Fair" in "all hail" is foul, as I conceive.

KING Construe my speeches better, if you may.

PRINCESS Then wish me better, I will give you leave.

KING We came to visit you, and purpose now
To lead you to our court. Vouchsafe it then.   345

PRINCESS This field shall hold me, and so hold your
vow.
Nor God nor I delights in perjured men.

KING Rebuke me not for that which you provoke.
The virtue of your eye must break my oath.

PRINCESS You nickname virtue. "Vice" you should
have spoke;   350
For virtue's office never breaks men's troth.
Now, by my maiden honor, yet as pure
As the unsullied lily, I protest,

329 mean intermediate part   330 Mend surpass   341 hail (with a pun on hail
meaning "sleet")   349 virtue power   350 nickname name by mistake

A world of torments though I should endure,
355   I would not yield to be your house's guest,
So much I hate a breaking cause to be
Of heavenly oaths, vowed with integrity.

KING O, you have lived in desolation here,
Unseen, unvisited, much to our shame.

360 PRINCESS Not so, my lord. It is not so, I swear.
We have had pastimes here and pleasant game.
A mess of Russians left us but of late.

KING How, madam? Russians?

PRINCESS   Ay, in truth, my lord;
Trim gallants, full of courtship and of state.

365 ROSALINE Madam, speak true. It is not so, my lord.
My lady, to the manner of the days,
In courtesy gives undeserving praise.
We four indeed confronted were with four
In Russian habit. Here they stayed an hour
370   And talked apace; and in that hour, my lord,
They did not bless us with one happy word.
I dare not call them fools, but this I think,
When they are thirsty, fools would fain have drink.

BEROWNE This jest is dry to me. Gentle sweet,
375   Your wit makes wise things foolish. When we greet
With eyes best seeing heaven's fiery eye,
By light we lose light. Your capacity
Is of that nature that to your huge store
Wise things seem foolish and rich things but poor.

ROSALINE This proves you wise and rich, for in my
380   eye—

BEROWNE I am a fool, and full of poverty.

ROSALINE But that you take what doth to you belong,
It were a fault to snatch words from my tongue.

356 **breaking cause** cause for breaking off   362 **mess** group of four   366 **to the manner of the days** according to the fashion of the time   369 **habit** dress
371 **happy** appropriate   376 **heaven's fiery eye** the sun

BEROWNE O, I am yours, and all that I possess.

ROSALINE All the fool mine?

BEROWNE   I cannot give you less.   385

ROSALINE Which of the vizards was it that you wore?

BEROWNE Where, when, what vizard? Why demand
   you this?

ROSALINE There, then, that vizard, that superfluous
   case
   That hid the worse, and showed the better face.

KING We were descried. They'll mock us now downright.   390

DUMAINE Let us confess, and turn it to a jest.

PRINCESS Amazed, my lord? Why looks your Highness sad?

ROSALINE Help! Hold his brows! He'll sound. Why
   look you pale?
   Seasick, I think, coming from Muscovy.

BEROWNE Thus pour the stars down plagues for
   perjury.   395
   Can any face of brass hold longer out?
   Here stand I, lady, dart thy skill at me.
   Bruise me with scorn, confound me with a flout,
   Thrust thy sharp wit quite through my ignorance,
   Cut me to pieces with thy keen conceit,   400
   And I will wish thee never more to dance,
   Nor never more in Russian habit wait.
   O, never will I trust to speeches penned,
   Nor to the motion of a schoolboy's tongue,
   Nor never come in vizard to my friend,   405
   Nor woo in rhyme, like a blind harper's song!
   Taffeta phrases, silken terms precise,
   Three-piled hyperboles, spruce affectation,

388 case covering 393 sound swoon 396 face of brass brazen manner
400 conceit imagination 407 Taffeta phrases fine speech 408 Three-piled
(the finest weight velvet)

Figures pedantical—these summer flies
410   Have blown me full of maggot ostentation.
I do forswear them; and I here protest
By this white glove (how white the hand, God
        knows!)
Henceforth my wooing mind shall be expressed
In russet yeas and honest kersey noes.
415   And to begin, wench—so God help me, law!—
My love to thee is sound, sans crack or flaw.

ROSALINE Sans "sans," I pray you.

BEROWNE   Yet I have a trick
Of the old rage. Bear with me, I am sick.
I'll leave it by degrees. Soft, let us see—
420   Write "Lord have mercy on us" on those three.
They are infected, in their hearts it lies;
They have the plague, and caught it of your eyes.
These lords are visited; you are not free,
For the Lord's tokens on you do I see.

425 PRINCESS No, they are free that gave these tokens to us.

BEROWNE Our states are forfeit. Seek not to undo us.

ROSALINE It is not so, for how can this be true,
That you stand forfeit, being those that sue?

BEROWNE Peace! for I will not have to do with you.

430 ROSALINE Nor shall not if I do as I intend.

BEROWNE Speak for yourselves. My wit is at an end.

KING Teach us, sweet madam, for our rude
        transgression
Some fair excuse.

PRINCESS   The fairest is confession.
Were not you here but even now disguised?

409 **Figures** figures of speech   410 **blown** filled   414 **russet** (characteristic red-
brown color of peasants' clothes)   414 **kersey** plain wool cloth   416 **sans** without
417 **trick** trace   420 **Lord have mercy on us** (inscription posted on the doors of
houses harboring the plague)   423 **visited** attacked by plague   423 **free** free of
infection   424 **the Lord's tokens** plague spots   426 **states** estates

KING Madam, I was.

PRINCESS   And were you well advised?   435

KING I was, fair madam.

PRINCESS   When you then were here,
    What did you whisper in your lady's ear?

KING That more than all the world I did respect her.

PRINCESS When she shall challenge this, you will
    reject her.

KING Upon mine honor, no.

PRINCESS   Peace, peace, forbear!   440
    Your oath once broke, you force not to forswear.

KING Despise me when I break this oath of mine.

PRINCESS I will, and therefore keep it. Rosaline,
    What did the Russian whisper in your ear?

ROSALINE Madame, he swore that he did hold me dear 445
    As precious eyesight, and did value me
    Above this world; adding thereto, moreover,
    That he would wed me or else die my lover.

PRINCESS God give thee joy of him. The noble lord
    Most honorably doth uphold his word.   450

KING What mean you, madam? By my life, my troth,
    I never swore this lady such an oath.

ROSALINE By heaven you did! And to confirm it plain,
    You gave me this, but take it, sir, again.

KING My faith and this the princess I did give.   455
    I knew her by this jewel on her sleeve.

PRINCESS Pardon me, sir, this jewel did she wear,
    And Lord Berowne, I thank him, is my dear.
    What! Will you have me, or your pearl again?

BEROWNE Neither of either, I remit both twain.   460
    I see the trick on 't. Here was a consent,

---

441 force not do not think it wrong

Knowing aforehand of our merriment,
To dash it like a Christmas comedy.
Some carry-tale, some please-man, some slight
    zany,
Some mumble-news, some trencher-knight, some
465   Dick
That smiles his cheek in years, and knows the trick
To make my lady laugh when she's disposed,
Told our intents before; which once disclosed,
The ladies did change favors, and then we,
470   Following the signs, wooed but the sign of she.
Now, to our perjury to add more terror,
We are again forsworn, in will and error.
Much upon this 'tis. [*To Boyet*] And might not you
Forestall our sport, to make us thus untrue?
475   Do not you know my lady's foot by th' squier,
And laugh upon the apple of her eye?
And stand between her back, sir, and the fire,
Holding a trencher, jesting merrily?
You put our page out. Go, you are allowed.
480   Die when you will, a smock shall be your shroud.
You leer upon me, do you? There's an eye
Wounds like a leaden sword.

BOYET   Full merrily
Hath this brave manage, this career, been run.

BEROWNE Lo, he is tilting straight. Peace! I have
    done.

Enter [Costard, the] Clown.

485   Welcome, pure wit! Thou part'st a fair fray.

---

463 **dash** ridicule   464 **please-man** toady   464 **zany** buffoon   465 **mumble-news** prattler   465 **trencher-knight** brave man at the table   465 **Dick** fellow   466 **smiles his cheek in years** laughs his face into wrinkles   473 **Much upon this 'tis** it is very much like this   475 **by th' squier** by the rule (that is, have her measure)   476 **laugh ... eye** laugh, looking closely into her eyes   478 **trencher** wooden plate   479 **put our page out** take him out of his part   479 **allowed** permitted (licensed, like a court fool)   480 **smock** woman's garment   483 **manage** display of horsemanship   483 **career** charge   484 **tilting straight** already jousting

COSTARD O Lord, sir, they would know
    Whether the three Worthies shall come in or no.

BEROWNE What, are there but three?

COSTARD   No, sir, but it is vara fine,
    For every one pursents three.

BEROWNE   And three times thrice is nine.

COSTARD Not so, sir, under correction, sir, I hope, it
    is not so.   490
    You cannot beg us, sir, I can assure you, sir; we
    know what we know.
    I hope, sir, three times thrice, sir—

BEROWNE   Is not nine?

COSTARD Under correction, sir, we know whereuntil it
    doth amount.

BEROWNE By Jove, I always took three threes for nine.   495

COSTARD O Lord, sir, it were pity you should get your
    living by reck'ning, sir.

BEROWNE How much is it?

COSTARD O Lord, sir, the parties themselves, the ac-
    tors, sir, will show whereuntil it doth amount. For   500
    mine own part, I am, as they say, but to parfect
    one man in one poor man—Pompion the Great,
    sir.

BEROWNE Art thou one of the Worthies?

COSTARD It pleased them to think me worthy of Pom-   505
    pey the Great. For mine own part, I know not the
    degree of the Worthy, but I am to stand for him.

BEROWNE Go, bid them prepare.

COSTARD We will turn it finely off, sir; we will take
    some care.   *Exit*.

---

488 **vara** (northern pronunciation of "very") 489 **pursents** represents
491 **beg us** prove us fools 501 **parfect** play the part of 502 **Pompion**
pumpkin (for Pompey) 507 **degree** rank

KING Berowne, they will shame us. Let them not
510   approach.

BEROWNE We are shame-proof, my lord; and 'tis some
    policy
    To have one show worse than the king's and his
    company.

KING I say they shall not come.

PRINCESS Nay, my good lord, let me o'errule you now.
515   That sport best pleases that doth least know how,
    Where zeal strives to content, and the contents
    Dies in the zeal of that which it presents.
    Their form confounded makes most form in mirth
    When great things laboring perish in their birth.

520 BEROWNE A right description of our sport, my lord.

        Enter [Armado, the] Braggart.

ARMADO Anointed, I implore so much expense of thy
    royal sweet breath as will utter a brace of words.
            [*Converses apart with the King, and delivers
                a paper to him.*]

PRINCESS Doth this man serve God?

BEROWNE Why ask you?

525 PRINCESS 'A speaks not like a man of God his making.

ARMADO That is all one, my fair, sweet, honey mon-
    arch; for, I protest, the schoolmaster is exceeding
    fantastical; too-too vain, too-too vain; but we will
    put it, as they say, to *fortuna de la guerra*. I wish
530   you the peace of mind, most royal couplement!
                                            Exit.

KING Here is like to be a good presence of Worthies.

---

511 **policy** crafty device   516-17 **contents ... presents** i.e., the substance is
destroyed by the excessive zeal in presenting it   518 **Their form ... mirth** i.e.,
art that is confused is most laughable entertainment   522 **brace** pair   529 **fortuna
de la guerra** fortune of war (Italian)   530 **couplement** pair

He presents Hector of Troy; the swain, Pompey the
Great; the parish curate, Alexander; Armado's page,
Hercules; the pedant, Judas Maccabaeus:
And if these four Worthies in their first show thrive,   535
These four will change habits and present the
     other five.

BEROWNE There is five in the first show.

KING You are deceivèd, 'tis not so.

BEROWNE The pedant, the braggart, the hedge-priest,
     the fool, and the boy—   540
Abate throw at novum, and the whole world again
Cannot pick out five such, take each one in his
     vein.

KING The ship is under sail, and here she comes
     amain.

Enter [Costard, for] Pompey.

COSTARD "I Pompey am—"

BEROWNE   You lie, you are not he!

COSTARD "I Pompey am—"

BOYET   With libbard's head on knee.   545

BEROWNE Well said, old mocker. I must needs be
     friends with thee.

COSTARD "I Pompey am, Pompey surnamed the Big—"

DUMAINE The "Great."

COSTARD It is "Great," sir—"Pompey surnamed the
     Great,
That oft in field, with targe and shield, did make
     my foe to sweat,   550
And traveling along this coast I here am come by
     chance,

536 habits costumes   539 hedge-priest unlearned priest   541 Abate throw at
novum except for the throw at nine (in a game of dice)   542 vein characteristic
way   543 amain swiftly   545 libbard's head heraldic painting of leopard
550 targe shield

And lay my arms before the legs of this sweet lass
of France."
If your ladyship would say, "Thanks, Pompey," I
had done.

555 PRINCESS Great thanks, great Pompey.

COSTARD 'Tis not so much worth, but I hope I was
perfect. I made a little fault in "Great."

BEROWNE My hat to a halfpenny, Pompey proves the
best Worthy.

Enter [Nathaniel, the] Curate, for Alexander.

NATHANIEL "When in the world I lived, I was the
560   world's commander;
By east, west, north, and south, I spread my
     conquering might;
My scutcheon plain declares that I am
     Alisander—"

BOYET Your nose says, no, you are not; for it stands
too right.

BEROWNE Your nose smells "no" in this, most tender-
smelling knight.

PRINCESS The conqueror is dismayed. Proceed, good
565   Alexander.

NATHANIEL "When in the world I lived, I was the
world's commander—"

BOYET Most true, 'tis right—you were so, Alisander.

BEROWNE Pompey the Great—

COSTARD Your servant, and Costard.

570 BEROWNE Take away the conqueror, take away Alisander.

COSTARD [*To Nathaniel*] O, sir, you have overthrown

562 **scutcheon** coat of arms   563 **right** straight (Alexander's neck was a little
awry)

Alisander the conqueror! You will be scraped out
of the painted cloth for this. Your lion that holds
his pole-ax sitting on a close-stool will be given   575
to Ajax. He will be the ninth Worthy. A conqueror, and afeard to speak? Run away for shame,
Alisander. [*Nathaniel stands aside.*] There, an 't
shall please you, a foolish mild man; an honest
man, look you, and soon dashed. He is a marvelous   580
good neighbor, faith, and very good bowler; but
for Alisander—alas! you see how 'tis—a little o'erparted. But there are Worthies a-coming will speak
their mind in some other sort.

PRINCESS Stand aside, good Pompey.   585

[Costard stands aside.]

*Enter [Holofernes, the] Pedant, for Judas, and
[Moth,] the Boy, for Hercules.*

HOLOFERNES "Great Hercules is presented by this imp,
Whose club killed Cerberus, that three-headed
    canus;
And when he was a babe, a child, a shrimp,
Thus did he strangle serpents in his *manus*.
Quoniam he seemeth in minority,   590
Ergo I come with this apology."
Keep some state in thy exit, and vanish.

Exit Boy [to one side].

"Judas I am—"

DUMAINE A Judas?

HOLOFERNES Not Iscariot, sir.   595
"Judas I am, ycleped Maccabaeus."

DUMAINE Judas Maccabaeus clipt is plain Judas.

---

574 **painted cloth** wall-hanging 575 **pole-ax** battle-ax (and penis) 575 **close-stool** commode 576 **Ajax** Greek warrior (with a pun on "jakes," privy) 578 **an 't** if it 582–83 **o'erparted** having too difficult a part 586 **imp** child 587 **canus** (from Latin *canis*) dog 589 **manus** hand 590 **Quoniam** since 590 **in minority** under age 591 **Ergo** therefore 592 **state** dignity 596 **ycleped** called 596 **Maccabaeus** Hebrew warrior 597 **clipt** (1) cut (2) embraced

377

BEROWNE A kissing traitor. How, art thou proved Judas?

600 HOLOFERNES "Judas I am—"

DUMAINE The more shame for you, Judas.

HOLOFERNES What mean you, sir?

BOYET To make Judas hang himself.

HOLOFERNES Begin, sir; you are my elder.

605 BEROWNE Well followed: Judas was hanged on an elder.

HOLOFERNES I will not be put out of countenance.

BEROWNE Because thou hast no face.

HOLOFERNES What is this?

610 BOYET A cittern-head.

DUMAINE The head of a bodkin.

BEROWNE A death's face in a ring.

LONGAVILLE The face of an old Roman coin, scarce seen.

615 BOYET The pommel of Caesar's falchion.

DUMAINE The carved-bone face on a flask.

BEROWNE Saint George's half-cheek in a brooch.

DUMAINE Ay, and in a brooch of lead.

BEROWNE Ay, and worn in the cap of a toothdrawer.
620 And now forward, for we have put thee in countenance.

HOLOFERNES You have put me out of countenance.

---

606 **elder** a kind of tree   610 **cittern-head** head of a stringed musical instrument
611 **bodkin** long hairpin   612 **death's face in a ring** finger ring with the carving
of a skull   615 **falchion** sword   617 **half-cheek** profile   618 **brooch of lead**
ornament worn in cap as badge of dentist's trade   622 **out of countenance**
disconcerted

378

BEROWNE False. We have given thee faces.

HOLOFERNES But you have outfaced them all.

BEROWNE And thou wert a lion, we would do so.   625

BOYET Therefore as he is an ass, let him go.
And so adieu, sweet Jude. Nay, why dost thou stay?

DUMAINE For the latter end of his name.

BEROWNE For the ass to the Jude? Give it him. Jud-as,
away!

HOLOFERNES This is not generous, not gentle, not
humble.   630

BOYET A light for Monsieur Judas! It grows dark, he
may stumble.   [Holofernes stands aside.]

PRINCESS Alas, poor Maccabaeus, how hath he been
baited!

Enter [Armado, the] Braggart, [for Hector].

BEROWNE Hide thy head, Achilles! Here comes Hector in arms.

DUMAINE Though my mocks come home by me, I   635
will now be merry.

KING Hector was but a Troyan in respect of this.

BOYET But is this Hector?

KING I think Hector was not so clean-timbered.

LONGAVILLE His leg is too big for Hector's.   640

DUMAINE More calf, certain.

BOYET No; he is best indued in the small.

BEROWNE This cannot be Hector.

DUMAINE He's a god or a painter; for he makes faces.

625 And if   632 baited tormented   633-34 Achilles ... Hector (the Greek and
Trojan champions)   639 clean-timbered clean-limbed   642 small lower part of
the leg

ARMADO "The armipotent Mars, of lances the al-
645   mighty,
     Gave Hector a gift—"

DUMAINE A gilt nutmeg.

BEROWNE A lemon.

LONGAVILLE Stuck with cloves.

650 DUMAINE No, cloven.

ARMADO Peace!
     "The armipotent Mars, of lances the almighty,
     Gave Hector a gift, the heir of Ilion;
     A man so breathed that certain he would fight, yea
655 From morn till night, out of his pavilion.
     I am that flower—"

DUMAINE   That mint.

LONGAVILLE   That columbine.

ARMADO Sweet Lord Longaville, rein thy tongue.

LONGAVILLE I must rather give it the rein, for it runs
     against Hector.

660 DUMAINE Ay, and Hector's a greyhound.

ARMADO The sweet war-man is dead and rotten.
     Sweet chucks, beat not the bones of the buried.
     When he breathed, he was a man. But I will for-
     ward with my device. [*To the Princess*] Sweet roy-
665 alty, bestow on me the sense of hearing.
                    Berowne steps forth [*to whisper to Costard*].

PRINCESS Speak, brave Hector; we are much delighted.

ARMADO I do adore thy sweet Grace's slipper.

BOYET [*Aside to Dumaine*] Loves her by the foot.

DUMAINE [*Aside to Boyet*] He may not by the yard.

645 **armipotent** powerful in arms 647 **gilt nutmeg** (with special icing)
654 **breathed** well-exercised 655 **pavilion** tent for a champion at a tournament
669 **yard** (slang word for male organ)

ARMADO "This Hector far surmounted Hannibal—"   670
    The party is gone.

COSTARD Fellow Hector, she is gone. She is two months
    on her way.

ARMADO What meanest thou?

COSTARD Faith, unless you play the honest Troyan,   675
    the poor wench is cast away. She's quick; the child
    brags in her belly already. 'Tis yours.

ARMADO Dost thou infamonize me among poten-
    tates? Thou shalt die.

COSTARD Then shall Hector be whipped for Jaquenetta   680
    that is quick by him, and hanged for Pompey that
    is dead by him.

DUMAINE Most rare Pompey!

BOYET Renowned Pompey!

BEROWNE Greater than great. Great, great, great Pom-   685
    pey! Pompey the Huge!

DUMAINE Hector trembles.

BEROWNE Pompey is moved. More Ates, more Ates!
    Stir them on, stir them on!

DUMAINE Hector will challenge him.   690

BEROWNE Ay, if 'a have no more man's blood in his
    belly than will sup a flea.

ARMADO By the North Pole, I do challenge thee.

COSTARD I will not fight with a pole, like a northern
    man. I'll slash; I'll do it by the sword. I bepray   695
    you, let me borrow my arms again.

DUMAINE Room for the incensed Worthies!

COSTARD I'll do it in my shirt.

671 **The party is gone** (referring to Hector)   672 **she is gone** she is pregnant
676 **quick** pregnant   678 **infamonize** defame   688 **Ates** goddess of mischief

DUMAINE Most resolute Pompey!

700 MOTH Master, let me take you a buttonhole lower.
Do you not see, Pompey is uncasing for the combat? What mean you? You will lose your reputation.

ARMADO Gentlemen and soldiers, pardon me. I will
705 not combat in my shirt.

DUMAINE You may not deny it. Pompey hath made
the challenge.

ARMADO Sweet bloods, I both may and will.

BEROWNE What reason have you for 't?

710 ARMADO The naked truth of it is, I have no shirt. I
go woolward for penance.

BOYET True, and it was enjoined him in Rome for
want of linen; since when, I'll be sworn he wore
none but a dishclout of Jaquenetta's, and that 'a
715 wears next his heart for a favor.

Enter a Messenger, Monsieur Marcade.

MARCADE God save you, madam.

PRINCESS Welcome, Marcade,
But that thou interrupt'st our merriment.

MARCADE I am sorry, madam, for the news I bring
720 Is heavy in my tongue. The king your father—

PRINCESS Dead, for my life!

MARCADE Even so. My tale is told.

BEROWNE Worthies, away! The scene begins to cloud.

ARMADO For mine own part, I breathe free breath.

---

700 **take you a buttonhole lower** take you down a peg   701 **uncasing** removing his coat   711 **go woolward** wearing wool next to the skin   712 **enjoined** commanded

I have seen the day of wrong through the little hole   725
of discretion, and I will right myself like a soldier.
                                    Exeunt Worthies.

KING How fares your Majesty?

PRINCESS Boyet, prepare. I will away tonight.

KING Madam, not so. I do beseech you, stay.

PRINCESS Prepare, I say. I thank you, gracious lords,   730
   For all your fair endeavors, and entreat
   Out of a new-sad soul that you vouchsafe
   In your rich wisdom to excuse, or hide
   The liberal opposition of our spirits,
   If over-boldly we have borne ourselves   735
   In the converse of breath. Your gentleness
   Was guilty of it. Farewell, worthy lord.
   A heavy heart bears not a humble tongue.
   Excuse me so, coming too short of thanks
   For my great suit so easily obtained.   740

KING The extreme parts of time extremely forms
   All causes to the purpose of his speed,
   And often at his very loose decides
   That which long process could not arbitrate.
   And though the mourning brow of progeny   745
   Forbid the smiling courtesy of love
   The holy suit which fain it would convince,
   Yet, since love's argument was first on foot,
   Let not the cloud of sorrow justle it
   From what it purposed; since to wail friends lost   750
   Is not by much so wholesome-profitable
   As to rejoice at friends but newly found.

PRINCESS I understand you not. My griefs are double.

BEROWNE Honest plain words best pierce the ear of grief;
   And by these badges understand the king.   755

736 **converse of breath** conversation   738 **humble** i.e., civil, tactful   741–42
The extreme . . . speed time, as it runs out, directs everything towards its conclusion
743 **at his very loose** in the act of letting go   745 **progeny** descendants
747 **convince** prove   755 **badges** tokens

For your fair sakes have we neglected time,
Played foul play with our oaths. Your beauty,
    ladies,
Hath much deformed us, fashioning our humors
Even to the opposèd end of our intents;
760   And what in us hath seemed ridiculous—
As love is full of unbefitting strains,
All wanton as a child, skipping and vain,
Formed by the eye and therefore, like the eye,
Full of straying shapes, of habits and of forms,
765   Varying in subjects as the eye doth roll
To every varied object in his glance;
Which parti-coated presence of loose love
Put on by us, if, in your heavenly eyes,
Have misbecomed our oaths and gravities,
770   Those heavenly eyes that look into these faults
Suggested us to make. Therefore, ladies,
Our love being yours, the error that love makes
Is likewise yours. We to ourselves prove false,
By being once false forever to be true
775   To those that make us both—fair ladies, you.
And even that falsehood, in itself a sin,
Thus purifies itself and turns to grace.

PRINCESS   We have received your letters, full of love;
Your favors, the ambassadors of love;
780   And in our maiden council rated them
At courtship, pleasant jest, and courtesy,
As bombast and as lining to the time.
But more devout than this in our respects
Have we not been, and therefore met your loves
785   In their own fashion, like a merriment.

DUMAINE   Our letters, madam, showed much more
    than jest.

LONGAVILLE   So did our looks.

ROSALINE   We did not quote them so.

767 **parti-coated** fool's motley   771 **Suggested** tempted   780 **rated** valued
782 **bombast** padding   787 **quote** regard

384

KING Now, at the latest minute of the hour
   Grant us your loves.

PRINCESS   A time, methinks, too short
   To make a world-without-end bargain in.   790
   No, no, my lord, your Grace is perjured much,
   Full of dear guiltiness; and therefore this—
   If for my love (as there is no such cause)
   You will do aught, this shall you do for me:
   Your oath I will not trust, but go with speed   795
   To some forlorn and naked hermitage,
   Remote from all the pleasures of the world;
   There stay until the twelve celestial signs
   Have brought about the annual reckoning.
   If this austere insociable life   800
   Change not your offer made in heat of blood—
   If frosts and fasts, hard lodging and thin weeds,
   Nip not the gaudy blossoms of your love,
   But that it bear this trial, and last love—
   Then, at the expiration of the year,   805
   Come challenge me, challenge me by these deserts,
   And, by this virgin palm now kissing thine,
   I will be thine; and till that instant, shut
   My woeful self up in a mourning house,
   Raining the tears of lamentation   810
   For the remembrance of my father's death.
   If this thou do deny, let our hands part,
   Neither entitled in the other's heart.

KING If this, or more than this, I would deny,
   To flatter up these powers of mine with rest,   815
   The sudden hand of death close up mine eye!
   Hence hermit then—my heart is in thy breast.

[BEROWNE And what to me, my love? and what to me?

ROSALINE You must be purgèd, too, your sins are
    rank,
   You are attaint with faults and perjury;   820

798 twelve celestial signs (of the Zodiac) 802 weeds garments 815 flatter
up pamper 820 attaint charged

Therefore, if you my favor mean to get,
A twelvemonth shall you spend, and never rest,
But seek the weary beds of people sick.]

DUMAINE But what to me, my love? But what to me?
825   A wife?

KATHARINE   A beard, fair health, and honesty;
With three-fold love I wish you all these three.

DUMAINE O, shall I say "I thank you, gentle wife"?

KATHARINE Not so, my lord. A twelvemonth and a day
I'll mark no words that smooth-faced wooers say.
830   Come when the king doth to my lady come;
Then, if I have much love, I'll give you some.

DUMAINE I'll serve thee true and faithfully till then.

KATHARINE Yet swear not, lest ye be forsworn again.

LONGAVILLE What says Maria?

MARIA   At the twelvemonth's end
835   I'll change my black gown for a faithful friend.

LONGAVILLE I'll stay with patience, but the time is long.

MARIA The liker you! Few taller are so young.

BEROWNE Studies my lady? Mistress, look on me.
Behold the window of my heart, mine eye,
840   What humble suit attends thy answer there.
Impose some service on me for thy love.

ROSALINE Oft have I heard of you, my Lord Berowne,
Before I saw you, and the world's large tongue
Proclaims you for a man replete with mocks,
845   Full of comparisons and wounding flouts,
Which you on all estates will execute
That lie within the mercy of your wit.

818-23 (lines 824-35) duplicate this passage in an expanded form; probably
Shakespeare failed to indicate clearly that these six lines had been superseded)
837 **liker** more like   845 **wounding flouts** painful jokes   846 **all estates** men of
all kinds

To weed this wormwood from your fructful brain,
And therewithal to win me, if you please,
Without the which I am not to be won,   850
You shall this twelvemonth term from day to day
Visit the speechless sick, and still converse
With groaning wretches; and your task shall be
With all the fierce endeavor of your wit
To enforce the painèd impotent to smile.   855

BEROWNE To move wild laughter in the throat of
    death?
    It cannot be; it is impossible;
    Mirth cannot move a soul in agony.

ROSALINE Why, that's the way to choke a gibing spirit,
    Whose influence is begot of that loose grace   860
    Which shallow laughing hearers give to fools.
    A jest's prosperity lies in the ear
    Of him that hears it, never in the tongue
    Of him that makes it. Then, if sickly ears,
    Deafed with the clamors of their own dear groans,   865
    Will hear your idle scorns, continue then,
    And I will have you and that fault withal;
    But if they will not, throw away that spirit,
    And I shall find you empty of that fault,
    Right joyful of your reformation.   870

BEROWNE A twelvemonth? Well, befall what will
    befall,
    I'll jest a twelvemonth in an hospital.

PRINCESS [To the King] Ay, sweet my lord, and so I
    take my leave.

KING No, madam, we will bring you on your way.

BEROWNE Our wooing doth not end like an old play;   875
    Jack hath not Jill. These ladies' courtesy
    Might well have made our sport a comedy.

---

848 **wormwood** bitterness   848 **fructful** fruitful   852 **still** always

KING Come, sir, it wants a twelvemonth and a day,
And then 'twill end.

BEROWNE   That's too long for a play.

Enter [Armado, the] Braggart.

880 ARMADO Sweet Majesty, vouchsafe me—

PRINCESS Was not that Hector?

DUMAINE The worthy knight of Troy.

ARMADO I will kiss thy royal finger, and take leave.
I am a votary; I have vowed to Jaquenetta to hold
885 the plough for her sweet love three year. But, most
esteemed greatness, will you hear the dialogue that
the two learned men have compiled in praise of the
owl and the cuckoo? It should have followed in
the end of our show.

890 KING Call them forth quickly; we will do so.

ARMADO Holla! Approach.

Enter all.

This side is *Hiems*, Winter; this *Ver*, the Spring;
the one maintained by the owl, th' other by the
cuckoo. *Ver*, begin.

The Song.

895 [*Spring.*] When daisies pied and violets blue
                 And lady-smocks all silver-white
              And cuckoo-buds of yellow hue
                 Do paint the meadows with delight,
              The cuckoo then, on every tree,
900   Mocks married men; for thus sings he,
                                      "Cuckoo!

---

884 **votary** sworn follower 895 **pied** parti-colored 896 **lady-smocks** water-
cresses, or cuckoo flowers 897 **cuckoo-buds** crowfoot, or buttercup

Cuckoo, cuckoo!" O word of fear,
Unpleasing to a married ear!
When shepherds pipe on oaten straws,
 And merry larks are ploughmen's clocks, 905
When turtles tread, and rooks, and daws,
 And maidens bleach their summer smocks,
The cuckoo then, on every tree,
Mocks married men; for thus sings he,
         "Cuckoo! 910

Cuckoo, cuckoo!" O word of fear,
Unpleasing to a married ear!

Winter. When icicles hang by the wall,
 And Dick the shepherd blows his nail,
And Tom bears logs into the hall, 915
 And milk comes frozen home in pail,
When blood is nipped, and ways be foul,
Then nightly sings the staring owl,
         "Tu-whit,
Tu-who!" a merry note, 920
While greasy Joan doth keel the pot.

When all aloud the wind doth blow,
 And coughing drowns the parson's saw,
And birds sit brooding in the snow,
 And Marian's nose looks red and raw, 925
When roasted crabs hiss in the bowl,
Then nightly sings the staring owl,
         "Tu-whit,
Tu-who!" a merry note,
While greasy Joan doth keel the pot. 930

[ARMADO] The words of Mercury are harsh after the
 songs of Apollo. [You that way, we this way.
             Exeunt omnes.]

FINIS

906 **turtles tread** turtledoves mate 914 **blows his nail** blows on his fingernails
to warm them (and so, waiting patiently) 921 **keel** cool, by stirring or skimming
923 **saw** wise saying 926 **crabs** crab apples 931-32 **The words ... Apollo**
i.e., let us end with the songs, because clever words of the god Mercury would
come harshly after the songs of Apollo, the god of poetry

Textual Note

This edition is based upon the quarto of 1598, which, it is generally agreed, was printed from a manuscript in Shakespeare's own hand. The title page reads: "A / Pleasant / Conceited Comedie / Called, / Loues labors lost. / As it was presented before her Highnes / this last Christmas. / Newly corrected and augmented / By W. Shakespere. / Imprinted at London by W. W. / for Cutbert Burby. / 1598."

Although here there may be a reference to a previous printing, there is no trace of an earlier edition. "Newly corrected and augmented" probably refers to revisions in the manuscript, some of which, as it happens, may be detected in examining the printed text. (See footnotes at IV.iii.295 and V.ii.818-23.)

The printing of the 1623 Folio is based upon the quarto. It corrects some errors of the quarto and adds a number of its own. It provides act divisions (mistakenly heading the fifth act "Actus Quartus"), but the scene divisions as well as the list of the names of the persons in the play are the contributions of later editors.

Apart from a considerable number of misreadings the most noteworthy confusions in the quarto are in the speech headings. It is not merely that occasionally *Nathaniel* stands for *Holofernes*, that the *King* is sometimes *Navarre* and sometimes *Ferdinand* in the early part of the second act, and that in the same part of the play Rosaline and Katharine are confused. In the next act the character previously identified as Armado becomes "Braggart," Moth, the Page, becomes "Boy," Holofernes becomes "Pedant," Costard becomes "Clown." Later Sir Nathaniel becomes "Curate" and "Constable" becomes "Dull." The use of the generic names to take the place of the individual ones may be evidence of Shakespeare's revisions. In the present edition the speech headings have been made consistent, but the later substitutions are made evident by the supplementary stage directions indicating the entrances of the various characters.

The revision of the manuscript has left a couple of other obvious confusions. Berowne's speech in Act IV, Scene iii contains lines that belong to an earlier version, and some of these should have been canceled. If lines 295-316 were omitted, the speech would continue connectedly and without obvious repetitions. It also seems that the exchange between Berowne and Rosaline in Act V, Scene ii, lines 818-23, was meant to be struck out. In the present edition these passages are retained, but enclosed in square brackets.

The text of this edition is based upon the Heber-Daniel copy of the quarto in the British Museum; the spelling and punctuation have been modernized, obvious misspellings and wrong speech headings corrected, and the quotations from foreign languages regularized. Other departures from the quarto text are listed below: the adopted reading is given first, in bold, followed immediately by the quarto reading in roman letters.

I.i.24 **three** thee   31 **pomp** pome   62 **feast** fast   104 **an** any   114 **swore** sworne 127-31 [Q gives to Longaville]   127 **gentility** gentletie   130 **public** publibue   131 **possibly** possible   218 **welkin's vicegerent** welkis Vizgerent 240 **preposterous** propostrous   276 **worst** wost   289 **King** Ber.   308-09 **prosperity** prosperie

I.ii.14 **epitheton** apethaton   100 **blushing** blush-in   143 **Dull** Clo.

II.i.32 **Importunes** Importuous   34 **visaged** visage   44 **parts** peerelsse 88 **unpeopled** vnpeeled   115-26 [the lines here given to Rosaline are in Q given to Katharine]   130 **half of an** halfe of, of an   140 **friendship** faiendship 142 **demand** pemaund   144 **On One**   179 **mine own** my none   195 **Katharine** Rosalin   210 **Rosaline** Katherin   221 [Q gives to La.]   222-23 [Q gives to Lad.]   224 [Q gives to La.]   236 **agate** Agot   246 **quote** coate   254 [Q gives to Lad.]   255 [Q gives to Lad. 2]   256 [Q gives to Lad. 3]   257 [Q gives to Lad.] 258 [Q gives to Lad.]

III.i.14 **throat as if** throate, if   16 **through the nose** through: nose   19 **thinbelly** thinbellies   25 **note me?—that** note men that   28 **penny** penne 67 **voluble** volable   74 **the mail** thee male   74 **plain** pline   136 **ounce** ouce 139 **remuneration** remuration   140 **One penny** i.d.   177 **beadle** Bedell 178 **critic** Crietick   182 **senior-junior** signior Iunios   186 **plackets** Placcats 188 **paritors** Parrators   192 **German clock** Iermane Cloake   198 **whitely** whitly   206 **sue** shue

IV.i.6 **On** Ore   33 **heart** hart   71 **saw...saw** See...see   72 **overcame** couercame 76 **king's** King   110 **suitor ... suitor** shooter ... shooter   122 **Pepin** Pippen

125 **Guinever** Guinouer 132 **hit it** hit 134 **mete** meate 136 **ne'er** neare 138 **pin is** in 140 **too** to 146 **to th'** one ath toothen 149 **o' t'** other atother 150 **a** most most 150s.d. *Shout* Shoot 151 **Exit** Exeunt

IV.ii.5 **coelo** Celo 8 **epithets** epythithes 30 **we of taste** we taste 31 **indiscreet** indistreell 37 **Dictynna ... Dictynna** Dictisima ... dictisima 38 **Dictynna** dictima 52 **ignorant, I call** ignorault cald 55 **scurrility** squirilitie 57 **preyful** prayfull 61 **sores o' sorel** sores o sorell 66–150 [all speech prefixes of Holofernes and Nathaniel are reversed in Q, except at 107] 70 **pia mater** primater 72 **those in whom** those whom 78 **ingenious** ingenous 80 **sapit** sapis 84 **pierce-one** Person 86 **likest** liklest 94–95 **Fauste ... ruminat** Facile precor gellida, quando pecas omnia sub vmbra ruminat 98–99 **Venetia ... pretia** vemchie, vencha, que non te vnde, que non te perreche 122 **canzonet** cangenet 136 **writing** written 138 **Sir Nathaniel** Ped. Sir Holofernes 159 **ben** bien

IV.iii.13,14 **melancholy** mallicholie 48 **King** Long 52 **triumviry** triumpherie 74 **idolatry** ydotarie 86 **quoted** coted 92 **And I mine** And mine 98 **ode** Odo 107 **Wished** Wish 111 **thorn** throne 129 **o'erheard** ore-hard 154 **coaches** couches 160 **mote ... mote** Moth ... Moth 179 **men like you, men** men like men 181 **Joan** Ione 247 **wood** word 258 **painting and usurping** painting vsurping 259 **doters** dooters 312 **woman's** womas 315–16 [between these lines Q has: With our selues] 322 **beauty's** beautis 358 **authors** authour 360 **Let us** Lets vs 382 **Allons!** Allons! **Alone** alone 384 **forsworn** forsorne

V.i.10 **hominem** hominum 28 **insanie** infamie 30 **bone** bene 31 **Bone? Bone for bene!** Priscian Bome boon for boon prescian 34 **gaudeo** gaudio 36 **Quare** Quari 51 **pueritia** puericia 52 **silly** seely 59 **wave** wane 59 **Mediterranean** meditaranium 60 **venew** vene we 69 **manu** vnũ 78 **dunghill** dungil 79 **Dunghill** dunghel 99 **importunate** importunt 110 **secrecy** secretie 119 **Nathaniel** Holofernes 121 **rend'red** rended 153 **Allons** Alone

V.ii.13 **ne'er** neare 17 **ha' been a grandam** a bin Grandam 43 **'Ware pencils, ho! Ware** pensalls, How? 53 **pearls** Pearle 65 **hests** deuice 74 **wantonness** wantons be 80 **stabbed** stable 89 **sycamore** Siccamone 93 **Warily** warely 95 **overheard** ouer hard 96 **they** thy 122 **parley, court** parlee, to court 134 **too** two 148 **her** his 152 **e'er** ere 159 [Q gives to Berowne] 163 **ever** euen 175 **strangers** stranges 217 [Q gives to Rosaline] 225 **Price** Prise 243–56 [Q gives "Maria" for "Katherine"] 298 **vailing** varling 300 **woo** woo woe 310 **run** runs 324 **too** to 329 **ushering** hushering 342 **Construe** Consture 353 **unsullied** vnsallied 375 **wit** wits 408 **affectation** affection 461 **on't** ant 464 **zany** saine 483 **manage** nuage 501 **they** thy 515 **least** best 529 **de la guerra** delaguar 564 **this** his 584 [Q has "Exit Curat"] 598 **proved** proud 647 **gilt** gift 689 **Stir them on, stir** stir them, or stir 751 **wholesome** holdsome 779 **the ambassadors** embassadours 783 **this in our** this our 787 **quote** cote 808 **instant** instance 813 **entitled** intiled 817 **hermit** herrite 819 **rank** rackt 825 **A wife?** [included in following speech in Q] 829 **smoothed-faced** smothfast 896–97 [these lines transposed in Q] 917 **foul** full 929–30 **The words ... Apollo** [printed in larger type in Q without any speech-heading; F adds **You that way: we this way**, and heading **Brag.**]

WILLIAM SHAKESPEARE

THE TRAGEDY OF ROMEO AND JULIET

Edited by J. A. Bryant, Jr.

[*Dramatis Personae*

CHORUS

ESCALUS, Prince of Verona

PARIS, a young count, kinsman to the Prince

MONTAGUE

CAPULET

AN OLD MAN, of the Capulet family

ROMEO, son to Montague

MERCUTIO, kinsman to the Prince and friend to Romeo

BENVOLIO, nephew to Montague and friend to Romeo

TYBALT, nephew to Lady Capulet

FRIAR LAWRENCE } Franciscans
FRIAR JOHN

BALTHASAR, servant to Romeo

SAMPSON } servants to Capulet
GREGORY

PETER, servant to Juliet's nurse

ABRAM, servant to Montague

AN APOTHECARY

THREE MUSICIANS

AN OFFICER

LADY MONTAGUE, wife to Montague

LADY CAPULET, wife to Capulet

JULIET, daughter to Capulet

NURSE TO JULIET

CITIZENS OF VERONA, GENTLEMEN AND GENTLEWOMEN OF BOTH
    HOUSES, MASKERS, TORCHBEARERS, PAGES, GUARDS, WATCH-
    MEN, SERVANTS, AND ATTENDANTS

Scene: Verona; Mantua]

THE TRAGEDY OF
ROMEO AND
JULIET

THE PROLOGUE

[Enter Chorus.]

CHORUS Two households, both alike in dignity,
    In fair Verona, where we lay our scene,
From ancient grudge break to new mutiny,
    Where civil blood makes civil hands unclean.
From forth the fatal loins of these two foes   5
    A pair of star-crossed lovers take their life;
Whose misadventured piteous overthrows
    Doth with their death bury their parents' strife.
The fearful passage of their death-marked love,
    And the continuance of their parents' rage,   10
Which, but their children's end, naught could
      remove,
    Is now the two hours' traffic of our stage;
The which if you with patient ears attend,
What here shall miss, our toil shall strive to mend.

                               [Exit.]

Text references are printed in **boldface** type; the annotation follows in roman type.
Prologue 1 **dignity** rank   3 **mutiny** violence   6 **star-crossed** fated to disaster
12 **two hours' traffic of our stage** i.e., the business of our play

[ACT I

Scene I. *Verona. A public place.*]

Enter Sampson and Gregory, with swords and
bucklers, of the house of Capulet.

SAMPSON Gregory, on my word, we'll not carry coals.

GREGORY No, for then we should be colliers.

SAMPSON I mean, and we be in choler, we'll draw.

GREGORY Ay, while you live, draw your neck out of
⁵   collar.

SAMPSON I strike quickly, being moved.

GREGORY But thou art not quickly moved to strike.

SAMPSON A dog of the house of Montague moves me.

GREGORY To move is to stir, and to be valiant is to
¹⁰   stand. Therefore, if thou art moved, thou run'st
        away.

SAMPSON A dog of that house shall move me to
        stand. I will take the wall of any man or maid of
        Montague's.

I.i.s.d. **bucklers** small shields   1 **carry coals** endure insults   2 **colliers** coal
venders (this leads to puns on "choler" = anger, and "collar" = hangman's
noose)   3 **and** if   3 **draw** draw swords   13 **take the wall** take the preferred
place on the walk

GREGORY That shows thee a weak slave; for the weak-   15
est goes to the wall.

SAMPSON 'Tis true; and therefore women, being the
weaker vessels, are ever thrust to the wall. Therefore I will push Montague's men from the wall and
thrust his maids to the wall.   20

GREGORY The quarrel is between our masters and us
their men.

SAMPSON 'Tis all one. I will show myself a tyrant.
When I have fought with the men, I will be civil
with the maids—I will cut off their heads.   25

GREGORY The heads of the maids?

SAMPSON Ay, the heads of the maids or their maiden-
heads. Take it in what sense thou wilt.

GREGORY They must take it in sense that feel it.

SAMPSON Me they shall feel while I am able to stand;   30
and 'tis known I am a pretty piece of flesh.

GREGORY 'Tis well thou art not fish; if thou hadst,
thou hadst been Poor John. Draw thy tool! Here
comes two of the house of Montagues.

Enter two other Servingmen [Abram and Balthasar].

SAMPSON My naked weapon is out. Quarrel! I will   35
back thee.

GREGORY How? Turn thy back and run?

SAMPSON Fear me not.

GREGORY No, marry. I fear thee!

15-16 **weakest goes to the wall** i.e., is pushed to the rear   18 **thrust to the wall**
assaulted against the wall   33 **Poor John** hake salted and dried (poor man's fare)
33 **tool** weapon (with bawdy innuendo)   39 **marry** (an interjection, from "By the
Virgin Mary")

40 SAMPSON Let us take the law of our sides; let them begin.

GREGORY I will frown as I pass by, and let them take it as they list.

SAMPSON Nay, as they dare. I will bite my thumb at
45 them, which is disgrace to them if they bear it.

ABRAM Do you bite your thumb at us, sir?

SAMPSON I do bite my thumb, sir.

ABRAM Do you bite your thumb at us, sir?

SAMPSON [*Aside to Gregory*] Is the law of our side if I
50 say ay?

GREGORY [*Aside to Sampson*] No.

SAMPSON No, sir, I do not bite my thumb at you, sir; but I bite my thumb, sir.

GREGORY Do you quarrel, sir?

55 ABRAM Quarrel, sir? No, sir.

SAMPSON But if you do, sir, I am for you. I serve as good a man as you.

ABRAM No better.

SAMPSON Well, sir.

Enter Benvolio.

60 GREGORY Say "better." Here comes one of my master's kinsmen.

SAMPSON Yes, better, sir.

ABRAM You lie.

SAMPSON Draw, if you be men. Gregory, remember
65 thy swashing blow.   *They fight.*

40 **take the law of our sides** keep ourselves in the right   44 **bite my thumb** i.e., make a gesture of contempt   65 **swashing** slashing

398

BENVOLIO Part, fools!
  Put up your swords. You know not what you do.

Enter Tybalt.

TYBALT What, art thou drawn among these heartless
    hinds?
  Turn thee, Benvolio; look upon thy death.

BENVOLIO I do but keep the peace. Put up thy sword,   70
  Or manage it to part these men with me.

TYBALT What, drawn, and talk of peace? I hate the
    word
  As I hate hell, all Montagues, and thee.
  Have at thee, coward!   *[They fight.]*

Enter [an Officer, and] three or four Citizens
with clubs or partisans.

OFFICER Clubs, bills, and partisans! Strike! Beat them   75
  down! Down with the Capulets! Down with the
  Montagues!

Enter old Capulet in his gown, and his Wife.

CAPULET What noise is this? Give me my long sword,
  ho!

LADY CAPULET A crutch, a crutch! Why call you for
  a sword?

CAPULET My sword, I say! Old Montague is come   80
  And flourishes his blade in spite of me.

Enter old Montague and his Wife.

MONTAGUE Thou villain Capulet!—Hold me not; let
  me go.

LADY MONTAGUE Thou shalt not stir one foot to seek
  a foe.

---

68 **heartless hinds** cowardly rustics   75 **bills, and partisans** varieties of
halberd, a combination spear and battle-ax   81 **spite** defiance

Enter Prince Escalus, with his Train.

PRINCE Rebellious subjects, enemies to peace,
85   Profaners of this neighbor-stainèd steel—
      Will they not hear? What, ho! You men, you beasts,
      That quench the fire of your pernicious rage
      With purple fountains issuing from your veins!
      On pain of torture, from those bloody hands
90   Throw your mistempered weapons to the ground
      And hear the sentence of your movèd prince.
      Three civil brawls, bred of an airy word
      By thee, old Capulet, and Montague,
      Have thrice disturbed the quiet of our streets
95   And made Verona's ancient citizens
      Cast by their grave beseeming ornaments
      To wield old partisans, in hands as old,
      Cank'red with peace, to part your cank'red hate.
      If ever you disturb our streets again,
100   Your lives shall pay the forfeit of the peace.
      For this time all the rest depart away.
      You, Capulet, shall go along with me;
      And, Montague, come you this afternoon,
      To know our farther pleasure in this case,
105   To old Freetown, our common judgment place.
      Once more, on pain of death, all men depart.
                          Exeunt [all but Montague, his Wife,
                                       and Benvolio].

MONTAGUE Who set this ancient quarrel new abroach?
      Speak, nephew, were you by when it began?

BENVOLIO Here were the servants of your adversary
110   And yours, close fighting ere I did approach.
      I drew to part them. In the instant came
      The fiery Tybalt, with his sword prepared;
      Which, as he breathed defiance to my ears,
      He swung about his head and cut the winds,

---

90 **mistempered** (1) ill-made (2) used with ill will   96 **grave beseeming**
dignified and appropriate   98 **can'kred ... cank'red** rusted ... malignant
107 **new abroach** newly open

Who, nothing hurt withal, hissed him in scorn. 115
While we were interchanging thrusts and blows,
Came more and more, and fought on part and
 part,
Till the Prince came, who parted either part.

LADY MONTAGUE O, where is Romeo? Saw you him
 today?
Right glad I am he was not at this fray. 120

BENVOLIO Madam, an hour before the worshiped sun
Peered forth the golden window of the East,
A troubled mind drave me to walk abroad;
Where, underneath the grove of sycamore
That westward rooteth from this city side, 125
So early walking did I see your son.
Towards him I made, but he was ware of me
And stole into the covert of the wood.
I, measuring his affections by my own,
Which then most sought where most might not be
 found, 130
Being one too many by my weary self,
Pursued my humor not pursuing his,
And gladly shunned who gladly fled from me.

MONTAGUE Many a morning hath he there been seen,
With tears augmenting the fresh morning's dew, 135
Adding to clouds more clouds with his deep sighs;
But all so soon as the all-cheering sun
Should in the farthest East begin to draw
The shady curtains from Aurora's bed,
Away from light steals home my heavy son 140
And private in his chamber pens himself,
Shuts up his windows, locks fair daylight out,
And makes himself an artificial night.

---

115 **withal** thereby   117 **on part and part** some on one side, some on another
127 **ware** aware   130 **most sought ... found** i.e., wanted most to be alone
132 **Pursued ... his** i.e., followed my own inclination by not inquiring into his
mood   139 **Aurora** goddess of the dawn   140 **heavy** melancholy, moody

    Black and portentous must this humor prove
145   Unless good counsel may the cause remove.

BENVOLIO My noble uncle, do you know the cause?

MONTAGUE I neither know it nor can learn of him.

BENVOLIO Have you importuned him by any means?

MONTAGUE Both by myself and many other friends;
150   But he, his own affections' counselor,
    Is to himself—I will not say how true—
    But to himself so secret and so close,
    So far from sounding and discovery,
    As is the bud bit with an envious worm
155   Ere he can spread his sweet leaves to the air
    Or dedicate his beauty to the sun.
    Could we but learn from whence his sorrows grow,
    We would as willingly give cure as know.

Enter Romeo.

BENVOLIO See, where he comes. So please you step
    aside;
160   I'll know his grievance, or be much denied.

MONTAGUE I would thou wert so happy by thy stay
    To hear true shrift. Come, madam, let's away.
                  Exeunt [Montague and Wife].

BENVOLIO Good morrow, cousin.

ROMEO   Is the day so young?

BENVOLIO But new struck nine.

ROMEO   Ay me! Sad hours seem long.
165   Was that my father that went hence so fast?

BENVOLIO It was. What sadness lengthens Romeo's
    hours?

---

144 **humor** mood   153 **So far from sounding** so far from measuring the depth
of his mood   154 **envious** malign   161 **happy** lucky   162 **true shrift** i.e.,
Romeo's confession of the truth   163 **morrow** morning

ROMEO Not having that which having makes them
    short.

BENVOLIO In love?

ROMEO Out—

BENVOLIO Of love?   170

ROMEO Out of her favor where I am in love.

BENVOLIO Alas that love, so gentle in his view,
    Should be so tyrannous and rough in proof!

ROMEO Alas that love, whose view is muffled still,
    Should without eyes see pathways to his will!   175
    Where shall we dine? O me! What fray was here?
    Yet tell me not, for I have heard it all.
    Here's much to do with hate, but more with love.
    Why then, O brawling love, O loving hate,
    O anything, of nothing first created!   180
    O heavy lightness, serious vanity,
    Misshapen chaos of well-seeming forms,
    Feather of lead, bright smoke, cold fire, sick health,
    Still-waking sleep, that is not what it is!
    This love feel I, that feel no love in this.   185
    Dost thou not laugh?

BENVOLIO   No, coz, I rather weep.

ROMEO Good heart, at what?

BENVOLIO   At thy good heart's oppression.

ROMEO Why, such is love's transgression.
    Griefs of mine own lie heavy in my breast,
    Which thou wilt propagate, to have it prest   190
    With more of thine. This love that thou hast shown

---

172 gentle in his view mild in appearance   174 muffled still always blindfolded
178 more with love i.e., the combatants enjoyed their fighting   180 O anything, of nothing first created (Romeo here relates his own succession of witty
paradoxes to the dogma that God created everything out of nothing)   186 coz
cousin (relative)   190 Which ... prest i.e., which griefs you will increase by
burdening my breast

Doth add more grief to too much of mine own.
Love is a smoke made with the fume of sighs;
Being purged, a fire sparkling in lovers' eyes;
195 Being vexed, a sea nourished with loving tears.
What is it else? A madness most discreet,
A choking gall, and a preserving sweet.
Farewell, my coz.

BENVOLIO   Soft! I will go along.
And if you leave me so, you do me wrong.

200 ROMEO Tut! I have lost myself; I am not here;
This is not Romeo, he's some other where.

BENVOLIO Tell me in sadness, who is that you love?

ROMEO What, shall I groan and tell thee?

BENVOLIO   Groan? Why, no;
But sadly tell me who.

205 ROMEO Bid a sick man in sadness make his will.
Ah, word ill urged to one that is so ill!
In sadness, cousin, I do love a woman.

BENVOLIO I aimed so near when I supposed you loved.

ROMEO A right good markman. And she's fair I love.

210 BENVOLIO A right fair mark, fair coz, is soonest hit.

ROMEO Well, in that hit you miss. She'll not be hit
With Cupid's arrow. She hath Dian's wit,
And, in strong proof of chastity well armed,
From Love's weak childish bow she lives un-
          charmed.
215 She will not stay the siege of loving terms,
Nor bide th' encounter of assailing eyes,

---

196 **discreet** discriminating   198 **Soft** hold on   199 **And if** if   202 **in sadness**
in all seriousness   204 **sadly** seriously   205 **in sadness** (1) in seriousness (2) in
unhappiness at the prospect of death   210 **fair mark** target easily seen   212 **Dian's
wit** the cunning of Diana, huntress and goddess of chastity   213 **proof** tested
power   215 **stay** submit to   216 **bide** abide (put up with)

Nor ope her lap to saint-seducing gold.
O, she is rich in beauty; only poor
That, when she dies, with beauty dies her store.

BENVOLIO Then she hath sworn that she will still live
    chaste?   220

ROMEO She hath, and in that sparing make huge
    waste;
For beauty, starved with her severity,
Cuts beauty off from all posterity.
She is too fair, too wise, wisely too fair,
To merit bliss by making me despair.   225
She hath forsworn to love, and in that vow
Do I live dead that live to tell it now.

BENVOLIO Be ruled by me; forget to think of her.

ROMEO O, teach me how I should forget to think!

BENVOLIO By giving liberty unto thine eyes.   230
Examine other beauties.

ROMEO   'Tis the way
To call hers, exquisite, in question more.
These happy masks that kiss fair ladies' brows,
Being black puts us in mind they hide the fair.
He that is strucken blind cannot forget   235
The precious treasure of his eyesight lost.
Show me a mistress that is passing fair:
What doth her beauty serve but as a note
Where I may read who passed that passing fair?
Farewell. Thou canst not teach me to forget.   240

BENVOLIO I'll pay that doctrine, or else die in debt.
                                                Exeunt.

---

219 **with beauty dies her store** i.e., she will leave no progeny to perpetuate her
beauty 220 **still** always 225 **merit bliss** win heavenly bliss 232 **To call hers**
... **in question** to keep bringing her beauty to mind 238 **note** written reminder
241 **I'll ... debt** I will teach you or else die trying

[Scene II. *A street.*]

Enter Capulet, County Paris, and the Clown,
[his Servant].

CAPULET But Montague is bound as well as I,
In penalty alike; and 'tis not hard, I think,
For men so old as we to keep the peace.

PARIS Of honorable reckoning are you both,
5   And pity 'tis you lived at odds so long.
But now, my lord, what say you to my suit?

CAPULET But saying o'er what I have said before:
My child is yet a stranger in the world,
She hath not seen the change of fourteen years;
10   Let two more summers wither in their pride
Ere we may think her ripe to be a bride.

PARIS Younger than she are happy mothers made.

CAPULET And too soon marred are those so early
        made.
Earth hath swallowèd all my hopes but she;
15   She is the hopeful lady of my earth.
But woo her, gentle Paris, get her heart;
My will to her consent is but a part.
And she agreed, within her scope of choice
Lies my consent and fair according voice.
20   This night I hold an old accustomed feast,
Whereto I have invited many a guest,
Such as I love; and you among the store,
One more, most welcome, makes my number more.

I.ii.1 **bound** under bond 4 **reckoning** reputation 14 **hopes** children 18 **And
she agreed** if she agrees 18 **within her scope of choice** among those she favors
19 **according** agreeing 20 **accustomed** established by custom

At my poor house look to behold this night
Earth-treading stars that make dark heaven light.   25
Such comfort as do lusty young men feel
When well-appareled April on the heel
Of limping Winter treads, even such delight
Among fresh fennel buds shall you this night
Inherit at my house. Hear all, all see,   30
And like her most whose merit most shall be;
Which, on more view of many, mine, being one,
May stand in number, though in reck'ning none.
Come, go with me. [*To Servant, giving him a paper*]
    Go, sirrah, trudge about
Through fair Verona; find those persons out   35
Whose names are written there, and to them say
My house and welcome on their pleasure stay.
                                                Exit [*with Paris*].

SERVANT Find them out whose names are written here?
It is written that the shoemaker should meddle with
his yard and the tailor with his last, the fisher with   40
his pencil and the painter with his nets; but I am
sent to find those persons whose names are here
writ, and can never find what names the writing
person hath here writ. I must to the learned. In
good time!   45

Enter Benvolio and Romeo.

BENVOLIO Tut, man, one fire burns out another's
        burning;
    One pain is less'ned by another's anguish;
    Turn giddy, and be holp by backward turning;

---

25 **Earth-treading stars** i.e., young girls   29 **fennel** flowering herb   30 **Inherit**
have   33 **stand in number** constitute one of the crowd   33 **in reck'ning none**
not worth special consideration   34 **sirrah** (a term of familiar address)   37 **stay**
wait   39–41 **shoemaker ... nets** i.e., one should stick to what one knows how to
do (but the servant, being illiterate, reverses the proverbial expressions)   43 **find**
understand   44–45 **In good time** i.e., here come some learned ones
47 **another's anguish** the pain of another   48 **be holp by backward turning** be
helped by turning in the opposite direction

One desperate grief cures with another's languish.
50 Take thou some new infection to thy eye,
And the rank poison of the old will die.

ROMEO Your plantain leaf is excellent for that.

BENVOLIO For what, I pray thee?

ROMEO   For your broken shin.

BENVOLIO Why, Romeo, art thou mad?

55 ROMEO Not mad, but bound more than a madman is;
Shut up in prison, kept without my food,
Whipped and tormented—and God-den, good
    fellow.

SERVANT God gi' go-den. I pray, sir, can you read?

ROMEO Ay, mine own fortune in my misery.

60 SERVANT Perhaps you have learned it without book.
But, I pray, can you read anything you see?

ROMEO Ay, if I know the letters and the language.

SERVANT Ye say honestly. Rest you merry.

ROMEO Stay, fellow; I can read.   *He reads the letter.*
65 "Signior Martino and his wife and daughters;
County Anselm and his beauteous sisters;
The lady widow of Vitruvio;
Signior Placentio and his lovely nieces;
Mercutio and his brother Valentine;
70 Mine uncle Capulet, his wife and daughters;
My fair niece Rosaline; Livia;
Signior Valentio and his cousin Tybalt;
Lucio and the lively Helena."
A fair assembly. Whither should they come?

75 SERVANT Up.

53 **broken** scratched   57 **God-den** good evening (good afternoon)   62 **if I know the letters and the language** i.e., if I already know what the writing says
63 **Rest you merry** may God keep you merry

ROMEO Whither? To supper?

SERVANT To our house.

ROMEO Whose house?

SERVANT My master's.

ROMEO Indeed I should have asked you that before.   80

SERVANT Now I'll tell you without asking. My master
  is the great rich Capulet; and if you be not of the
  house of Montagues, I pray come and crush a cup
  of wine. Rest you merry.   [*Exit.*]

BENVOLIO At this same ancient feast of Capulet's   85
  Sups the fair Rosaline whom thou so loves;
  With all the admirèd beauties of Verona.
  Go thither, and with unattainted eye
  Compare her face with some that I shall show,
  And I will make thee think thy swan a crow.   90

ROMEO When the devout religion of mine eye
    Maintains such falsehood, then turn tears to fires;
  And these, who, often drowned, could never die,
    Transparent heretics, be burnt for liars!
  One fairer than my love? The all-seeing sun   95
  Ne'er saw her match since first the world begun.

BENVOLIO Tut! you saw her fair, none else being by,
  Herself poised with herself in either eye;
  But in that crystal scales let there be weighed
  Your lady's love against some other maid   100
  That I will show you shining at this feast,
  And she shall scant show well that now seems best.

ROMEO I'll go along, no such sight to be shown,
  But to rejoice in splendor of mine own.   [*Exeunt.*]

---

83 **crush a cup** have a drink 85 **ancient** established by custom 88 **unattainted** impartial 94 **Transparent** obvious 98 **poised** balanced 99 **crystal
scales** i.e., Romeo's pair of eyes 102 **scant** scarcely 104 **splendor of mine
own** my own lady's splendor

[Scene III. *A room in Capulet's house.*]

Enter Capulet's Wife, and Nurse.

LADY CAPULET Nurse, where's my daughter? Call her
 forth to me.

NURSE Now, by my maidenhead at twelve year old,
 I bade her come. What, lamb! What, ladybird!
 God forbid, where's this girl? What, Juliet!

Enter Juliet.

JULIET How now? Who calls?

NURSE   Your mother.

5 JULIET   Madam, I am here.
 What is your will?

LADY CAPULET This is the matter—Nurse, give leave
 awhile;
 We must talk in secret. Nurse, come back again.
 I have rememb'red me; thou 's hear our counsel.
10 Thou knowest my daughter's of a pretty age.

NURSE Faith, I can tell her age unto an hour.

LADY CAPULET She's not fourteen.

NURSE   I'll lay fourteen of my teeth—
 And yet, to my teen be it spoken, I have but
 four—
 She's not fourteen. How long is it now
 To Lammastide?

15 LADY CAPULET A fortnight and odd days.

I.iii.3 **What** (an impatient call) 9 **thou 's** thou shalt 13 **teen** sorrow
15 **Lammastide** August 1

NURSE Even or odd, of all days in the year,
Come Lammas Eve at night shall she be fourteen.
Susan and she (God rest all Christian souls!)
Were of an age. Well, Susan is with God;
She was too good for me. But, as I said,   20
On Lammas Eve at night shall she be fourteen;
That shall she, marry; I remember it well.
'Tis since the earthquake now eleven years;
And she was weaned (I never shall forget it),
Of all the days of the year, upon that day;   25
For I had then laid wormwood to my dug,
Sitting in the sun under the dovehouse wall.
My lord and you were then at Mantua.
Nay, I do bear a brain. But, as I said,
When it did taste the wormwood on the nipple   30
Of my dug and felt it bitter, pretty fool,
To see it tetchy and fall out with the dug!
Shake, quoth the dovehouse! 'Twas no need, I
    trow,
To bid me trudge.
And since that time it is eleven years,   35
For then she could stand high-lone; nay, by th'
    rood,
She could have run and waddled all about;
For even the day before, she broke her brow;
And then my husband (God be with his soul!
'A was a merry man) took up the child.   40
"Yea," quoth he, "dost thou fall upon thy face?
Thou wilt fall backward when thou hast more wit;
Wilt thou not, Jule?" and, by my holidam,
The pretty wretch left crying and said, "Ay."
To see now how a jest shall come about!   45
I warrant, and I should live a thousand years,

19 **of an age** the same age   29 **I do bear a brain** i.e., my mind is still good
32 **tetchy** irritable   33 **Shake, quoth the dovehouse** i.e., the dovehouse (which
the Nurse personifies) began to tremble   33 **trow** believe   36 **high-lone** alone
36 **rood** cross   40 **'A** he   43 **holidam** holy thing, relic

I never should forget it. "Wilt thou not, Jule?"
    quoth he,
And, pretty fool, it stinted and said, "Ay."

LADY CAPULET Enough of this. I pray thee hold thy
    peace.

50 NURSE Yes, madam. Yet I cannot choose but laugh
To think it should leave crying and say, "Ay."
And yet, I warrant, it had upon it brow
A bump as big as a young cock'rel's stone;
A perilous knock; and it cried bitterly.
55 "Yea," quoth my husband, "fall'st upon thy face?
Thou wilt fall backward when thou comest to age,
Wilt thou not, Jule?" It stinted and said, "Ay."

JULIET And stint thou too, I pray thee, nurse, say I.

NURSE Peace, I have done. God mark thee to His
    grace!
60 Thou wast the prettiest babe that e'er I nursed.
And I might live to see thee married once,
I have my wish.

LADY CAPULET Marry, that "marry" is the very theme
I came to talk of. Tell me, daughter Juliet,
65 How stands your dispositions to be married?

JULIET It is an honor that I dream not of.

NURSE An honor? Were not I thine only nurse,
I would say thou hadst sucked wisdom from thy
    teat.

LADY CAPULET Well, think of marriage now. Younger
    than you,
70 Here in Verona, ladies of esteem,
Are made already mothers. By my count,
I was your mother much upon these years
That you are now a maid. Thus then in brief:
The valiant Paris seeks you for his love.

48 stinted stopped   52 it its   63 Marry indeed   72 much upon these years
the same length of time

NURSE A man, young lady! Lady, such a man   75
    As all the world— Why, he's a man of wax.

LADY CAPULET Verona's summer hath not such a
    flower.

NURSE Nay, he's a flower, in faith—a very flower.

LADY CAPULET What say you? Can you love the
    gentleman?
    This night you shall behold him at our feast.   80
    Read o'er the volume of young Paris' face,
    And find delight writ there with beauty's pen;
    Examine every married lineament,
    And see how one another lends content;
    And what obscured in this fair volume lies   85
    Find written in the margent of his eyes.
    This precious book of love, this unbound lover,
    To beautify him only lacks a cover.
    The fish lives in the sea, and 'tis much pride
    For fair without the fair within to hide.   90
    That book in many's eyes doth share the glory,
    That in gold clasps locks in the golden story;
    So shall you share all that he doth possess,
    By having him making yourself no less.

NURSE No less? Nay, bigger! Women grow by men.   95

LADY CAPULET Speak briefly, can you like of Paris'
    love?

JULIET I'll look to like, if looking liking move;
    But no more deep will I endart mine eye
    Than your consent gives strength to make it fly.

                    Enter Servingman.

SERVINGMAN Madam, the guests are come, supper   100

76 **man of wax** man of perfect figure   83 **married lineament** harmonious feature
84 **one another lends content** all enhance one another   86 **margent** marginal
commentary   87 **unbound** (1) without cover (2) uncaught   88 **only lacks a
cover** i.e., only a wife is lacking   89–90 **The fish … to hide** i.e., the fair sea is
made even fairer by hiding fair fish within it   96 **like of** be favorable to

served up, you called, my young lady asked for,
the nurse cursed in the pantry, and everything in
extremity. I must hence to wait. I beseech you
follow straight.   [*Exit*.]

LADY CAPULET We follow thee. Juliet, the County
105   stays.

NURSE Go, girl, seek happy nights to happy days.
                                                Exeunt.

[Scene IV. *A street*.]

*Enter Romeo, Mercutio, Benvolio, with five
or six other Maskers; Torchbearers*.

ROMEO What, shall this speech be spoke for our
       excuse?
Or shall we on without apology?

BENVOLIO The date is out of such prolixity.
We'll have no Cupid hoodwinked with a scarf,
5   Bearing a Tartar's painted bow of lath,
Scaring the ladies like a crowkeeper;
Nor no without-book prologue, faintly spoke
After the prompter, for our entrance;
But, let them measure us by what they will,
10   We'll measure them a measure and be gone.

ROMEO Give me a torch. I am not for this ambling.
Being but heavy, I will bear the light.

102 **the nurse cursed** i.e., because she is not helping 103 **to wait** to
serve 104 **straight** straightway 105 **the County stays** the Count is waiting
I.iv.1 **shall ... excuse** i.e., shall we introduce ourselves with the customary
prepared speech 3 **date ... prolixity** i.e., such wordiness is out of fashion
4 **hoodwinked** blindfolded 6 **crow-keeper** boy set to scare crows away
7 **without-book prologue** memorized speech 9 **measure** judge 10 **measure
them a measure** dance one dance with them

MERCUTIO Nay, gentle Romeo, we must have you
    dance.

ROMEO Not I, believe me. You have dancing shoes
    With nimble soles; I have a soul of lead   15
    So stakes me to the ground I cannot move.

MERCUTIO You are a lover. Borrow Cupid's wings
    And soar with them above a common bound.

ROMEO I am too sore enpiercèd with his shaft
    To soar with his light feathers; and so bound   20
    I cannot bound a pitch above dull woe.
    Under love's heavy burden do I sink.

MERCUTIO And, to sink in it, should you burden love—
    Too great oppression for a tender thing.

ROMEO Is love a tender thing? It is too rough,   25
    Too rude, too boist'rous, and it pricks like thorn.

MERCUTIO If love be rough with you, be rough with
    love;
    Prick love for pricking, and you beat love down.
    Give me a case to put my visage in.
    A visor for a visor! What care I   30
    What curious eye doth quote deformities?
    Here are the beetle brows shall blush for me.

BENVOLIO Come, knock and enter; and no sooner in
    But every man betake him to his legs.

ROMEO A torch for me! Let wantons light of heart   35
    Tickle the senseless rushes with their heels;
    For I am proverbed with a grandsire phrase,
    I'll be a candleholder and look on;

---

18 **bound** (1) leap (2) limit   21 **pitch** height (as in a falcon's soaring)   28 **Prick
love for pricking** i.e., give love the spur in return   29-31 **Give ... deformities**
i.e., give me a bag for my mask. A mask for a mask. What do I care who notices my
ugliness?   32 **beetle brows** bushy eyebrows (?)   32 **blush** be red, i.e., be
grotesque   34 **betake him to his legs** begin dancing   36 **rushes** (used for floor
covering)   37 **grandsire phrase** old saying   38 **candleholder** attendant

The game was ne'er so fair, and I am done.

MERCUTIO Tut! Dun's the mouse, the constable's own
40   word!
      If thou art Dun, we'll draw thee from the mire
      Of this sir-reverence love, wherein thou stickest
      Up to the ears. Come, we burn daylight, ho!

ROMEO Nay, that's not so.

MERCUTIO   I mean, sir, in delay
45   We waste our lights in vain, like lights by day.
      Take our good meaning, for our judgment sits
      Five times in that ere once in our five wits.

ROMEO And we mean well in going to this masque,
      But 'tis no wit to go.

MERCUTIO   Why, may one ask?

ROMEO I dreamt a dream tonight.

50 MERCUTIO   And so did I.

ROMEO Well, what was yours?

MERCUTIO   That dreamers often lie.

ROMEO In bed asleep, while they do dream things true.

MERCUTIO O, then I see Queen Mab hath been with
      you.
      She is the fairies' midwife, and she comes
55   In shape no bigger than an agate stone

39 **The game ... done** i.e., I'll give up dancing, now that I have enjoyed it as
much as I ever shall 40 **Dun's ... word** (Mercutio puns on Romeo's last clause,
saying in effect "You are not done [i.e., "dun": "dark," by extension, "silent"] but
the mouse is, and it's time to be quiet) 41 **Dun** (a common name for a horse,
used in an old game, "Dun is in the mire," in which the players try to haul a heavy
log) 42 **sir-reverence** save your reverence (an apologetic expression, used to
introduce indelicate expressions; here used humorously with the word "love")
43 **burn daylight** delay 45 **lights** (1) torches (2) mental faculties 47 **that** i.e.,
our good meaning 49 **'tis no wit** it shows no discretion 50 **tonight** last night
53 **Queen Mab** Fairy Queen (Celtic)

On the forefinger of an alderman,
Drawn with a team of little atomies
Over men's noses as they lie asleep;
Her wagon spokes made of long spinners' legs,
The cover, of the wings of grasshoppers;   60
Her traces, of the smallest spider web;
Her collars, of the moonshine's wat'ry beams;
Her whip, of cricket's bone; the lash, of film;
Her wagoner, a small gray-coated gnat,
Not half so big as a round little worm   65
Pricked from the lazy finger of a maid;
Her chariot is an empty hazelnut,
Made by the joiner squirrel or old grub,
Time out o' mind the fairies' coachmakers.
And in this state she gallops night by night   70
Through lovers' brains, and then they dream of
    love;
On courtiers' knees, that dream on curtsies straight;
O'er lawyers' fingers, who straight dream on fees;
O'er ladies' lips, who straight on kisses dream,
Which oft the angry Mab with blisters plagues,   75
Because their breath with sweetmeats tainted are.
Sometime she gallops o'er a courtier's nose,
And then dreams he of smelling out a suit;
And sometime comes she with a tithe pig's tail
Tickling a parson's nose as 'a lies asleep,   80
Then he dreams of another benefice.
Sometime she driveth o'er a soldier's neck,
And then dreams he of cutting foreign throats,
Of breaches, ambuscadoes, Spanish blades,
Of healths five fathom deep; and then anon   85
Drums in his ear, at which he starts and wakes,
And being thus frighted, swears a prayer or two

---

57 **atomies** tiny creatures   59 **spinners** spiders   63 **film** fine filament of some
kind   65–66 **worm ... maid** (lazy maids were said to have worms breeding in
their fingers)   68 **joiner squirrel or old grub** (both woodworkers and adept at
hollowing out nuts)   70 **state** stately array   78 **suit** i.e., a petitioner, who may be
induced to pay for the courtier's influence   79 **tithe pig** tenth pig (considered
part of the parson's tithe)   81 **benefice** income, "living"   85 **healths** toasts

And sleeps again. This is that very Mab
That plats the manes of horses in the night
90   And bakes the elflocks in foul sluttish hairs,
Which once untangled much misfortune bodes.
This is the hag, when maids lie on their backs,
That presses them and learns them first to bear,
Making them women of good carriage.
This is she—

95 ROMEO   Peace, peace, Mercutio, peace!
Thou talk'st of nothing.

MERCUTIO   True, I talk of dreams;
Which are the children of an idle brain,
Begot of nothing but vain fantasy;
Which is as thin of substance as the air,
100 And more inconstant than the wind, who woos
Even now the frozen bosom of the North
And, being angered, puffs away from thence,
Turning his side to the dew-dropping South.

BENVOLIO This wind you talk of blows us from ourselves.
105 Supper is done, and we shall come too late.

ROMEO I fear, too early; for my mind misgives
Some consequence yet hanging in the stars
Shall bitterly begin his fearful date
With this night's revels and expire the term
110 Of a despisèd life, closed in my breast,
By some vile forfeit of untimely death.
But he that hath the steerage of my course
Direct my sail! On, lusty gentlemen!

BENVOLIO Strike, drum.

They march about the stage, and
[*retire to one side*].

90 **elflocks** hair tangled by elves 92 **hag** nightmare or incubus 94 **carriage**
(1) posture (2) capacity for carrying children 98 **fantasy** fancy 107 **conse-**
quence future event 108 **date** duration (of the consequence or event)
109–11 **expire … death** (the event is personified here as one who deliberately
lends in expectation that the borrower will have to forfeit at great loss)

[Scene V. *A hall in Capulet's house.*]

Servingmen come forth with napkins.

FIRST SERVINGMAN Where's Potpan, that he helps not
to take away? He shift a trencher! He scrape a
trencher!

SECOND SERVINGMAN When good manners shall lie all
in one or two men's hands, and they unwashed too,   5
'tis a foul thing.

FIRST SERVINGMAN Away with the join-stools, remove
the court cupboard, look to the plate. Good thou,
save me a piece of marchpane, and, as thou loves
me, let the porter let in Susan Grindstone and Nell.   10
Anthony, and Potpan!

SECOND SERVINGMAN Ay, boy, ready.

FIRST SERVINGMAN You are looked for and called for,
asked for and sought for, in the great chamber.

THIRD SERVINGMAN We cannot be here and there too.   15
Cheerly, boys! Be brisk awhile, and the longer liver
take all.   *Exeunt.*

Enter [Capulet, his Wife, Juliet, Tybalt, Nurse, and]
all the Guests and Gentlewomen to the Maskers.

CAPULET Welcome, gentlemen! Ladies that have their
toes

I.v.s.d. (although for reference purposes this edition employs the conventional
post-Elizabethan divisions into scenes, the reader is reminded that they are merely
editorial; in the quarto this stage direction is part of the preceding one)
2 **trencher** wooden plate 7 **join-stools** stools fitted together by a joiner
8 **court cupboard** sideboard, displaying plate 9 **marchpane** marzipan, a
confection made of sugar and almonds

Unplagued with corns will walk a bout with you.
20   Ah, my mistresses, which of you all
Will now deny to dance? She that makes dainty,
She I'll swear hath corns. Am I come near ye now?
Welcome, gentlemen! I have seen the day
That I have worn a visor and could tell
25   A whispering tale in a fair lady's ear,
Such as would please. 'Tis gone, 'tis gone, 'tis gone.
You are welcome, gentlemen! Come, musicians, play.
                      Music plays, and they dance.
A hall, a hall! Give room! And foot it, girls.
More light, you knaves, and turn the tables up,
30   And quench the fire; the room is grown too hot.
Ah, sirrah, this unlooked-for sport comes well.
Nay, sit; nay, sit, good cousin Capulet;
For you and I are past our dancing days.
How long is't now since last yourself and I
Were in a mask?

35   SECOND CAPULET By'r Lady, thirty years.

CAPULET What, man? 'Tis not so much, 'tis not so
     much;
'Tis since the nuptial of Lucentio,
Come Pentecost as quickly as it will,
Some five-and-twenty years, and then we masked.

SECOND CAPULET 'Tis more, 'tis more. His son is elder,
40   sir;
His son is thirty.

CAPULET   Will you tell me that?
His son was but a ward two years ago.

ROMEO [*To a Servingman*] What lady's that which
     doth enrich the hand
Of yonder knight?

45   SERVINGMAN I know not, sir.

---

19 **walk a bout** dance a turn   21 **deny** refuse   21 **makes dainty** seems to hesitate
28 **A hall** clear the floor   31 **unlooked-for sport** (they had not expected
maskers)   42 **ward** minor

ROMEO O, she doth teach the torches to burn bright!
　　It seems she hangs upon the cheek of night
　　As a rich jewel in an Ethiop's ear—
　　Beauty too rich for use, for earth too dear!
　　So shows a snowy dove trooping with crows   50
　　As yonder lady o'er her fellows shows.
　　The measure done, I'll watch her place of stand
　　And, touching hers, make blessèd my rude hand.
　　Did my heart love till now? Forswear it, sight!
　　For I ne'er saw true beauty till this night.   55

TYBALT This, by his voice, should be a Montague.
　　Fetch me my rapier, boy. What! Dares the slave
　　Come hither, covered with an antic face,
　　To fleer and scorn at our solemnity?
　　Now, by the stock and honor of my kin,   60
　　To strike him dead I hold it not a sin.

CAPULET Why, how now, kinsman? Wherefore storm
　　you so?

TYBALT Uncle, this is a Montague, our foe,
　　A villain, that is hither come in spite
　　To scorn at our solemnity this night.   65

CAPULET Young Romeo is it?

TYBALT   'Tis he, that villain Romeo.

CAPULET Content thee, gentle coz, let him alone.
　　'A bears him like a portly gentleman,
　　And, to say truth, Verona brags of him
　　To be a virtuous and well-governed youth.   70
　　I would not for the wealth of all this town
　　Here in my house do him disparagement.
　　Therefore be patient; take no note of him.
　　It is my will, the which if thou respect,
　　Show a fair presence and put off these frowns,   75
　　An ill-beseeming semblance for a feast.

---

53 **rude** rough 58 **antic face** fantastic mask 59 **fleer** jeer 64 **in spite** insultingly 68 **portly** of good deportment

TYBALT It fits when such a villain is a guest.
   I'll not endure him.

CAPULET   He shall be endured.
   What, goodman boy! I say he shall. Go to!
80   Am I the master here, or you? Go to!
   You'll not endure him, God shall mend thy soul!
   You'll make a mutiny among my guests!
   You will set cock-a-hoop. You'll be the man!

TYBALT Why, uncle, 'tis a shame.

CAPULET   Go to, go to!
85   You are a saucy boy. Is't so, indeed?
   This trick may chance to scathe you. I know what.
   You must contrary me! Marry, 'tis time—
   Well said, my hearts!—You are a princox—go!
   Be quiet, or— More light, more light!—For shame!
90   I'll make you quiet. What!—Cheerly, my hearts!

TYBALT Patience perforce with willful choler meeting
   Makes my flesh tremble in their different greeting.
   I will withdraw; but this intrusion shall,
   Now seeming sweet, convert to bitt'rest gall.   *Exit.*

95 ROMEO If I profane with my unworthiest hand
   This holy shrine, the gentle sin is this:
   My lips, two blushing pilgrims, ready stand
   To smooth that rough touch with a tender kiss.

JULIET Good pilgrim, you do wrong your hand
     too much,
100   Which mannerly devotion shows in this;

---

79 **goodman** (a term applied to someone below the rank of gentleman) 79 **Go to** (impatient exclamation) 81 **God shall mend my soul** (roughly equivalent to our "Indeed") 82 **mutiny** disturbance 83 **set cock-a-hoop** be cock of the walk 86 **scathe** hurt, harm 88 **princox** impertinent youngster 91 **Patience perforce** enforced self-control 91 **choler** anger 95 **If** (here begins an English, or Shakespearean, sonnet) 96 **shrine** i.e., Juliet's hand 96 **the gentle sin is this** this is the sin of well-bred people

For saints have hands that pilgrims' hands do touch,
And palm to palm is holy palmers' kiss.

ROMEO Have not saints lips, and holy palmers too?

JULIET Ay, pilgrim, lips that they must use in prayer.

ROMEO O, then, dear saint, let lips do what hands do!   105
They pray; grant thou, lest faith turn to despair.

JULIET Saints do not move, though grant for prayers'
sake.

ROMEO Then move not while my prayer's effect I take.
Thus from my lips, by thine my sin is purged.
[*Kisses her.*]

JULIET Then have my lips the sin that they have took.   110

ROMEO Sin from my lips? O trespass sweetly urged!
Give me my sin again.   [*Kisses her.*]

JULIET   You kiss by th' book.

NURSE Madam, your mother craves a word with you.

ROMEO What is her mother?

NURSE   Marry, bachelor,
Her mother is the lady of the house,   115
And a good lady, and a wise and virtuous.
I nursed her daughter that you talked withal.
I tell you, he that can lay hold of her
Shall have the chinks.

ROMEO   Is she a Capulet?
O dear account! My life is my foe's debt.   120

BENVOLIO Away, be gone; the sport is at the best.

ROMEO Ay, so I fear; the more is my unrest.

---

102 **palmer** religious pilgrim (the term originally signified one who carried a palm
branch; here it is used as a pun meaning one who holds another's hand)   107 **do
not move** (1) do not initiate action (2) stand still   112 **kiss by th' book** i.e., you
take my words literally to get more kisses   117 **withal** with   119 **the chinks**
plenty of money   120 **my life is my foe's debt** my foe now owns my life

CAPULET Nay, gentlemen, prepare not to be gone;
        We have a trifling foolish banquet towards.
125   It is e'en so? Why then, I thank you all.
        I thank you, honest gentlemen. Good night.
        More torches here! Come on then; let's to bed.
        Ah, sirrah, by my fay, it waxes late;
        I'll to my rest.   [*Exeunt all but Juliet and Nurse.*]

130 JULIET Come hither, nurse. What is yond gentleman?

     NURSE The son and heir of old Tiberio.

     JULIET What's he that now is going out of door?

     NURSE Marry, that, I think, be young Petruchio.

     JULIET What's he that follows here, that would not
        dance?

135 NURSE I know not.

     JULIET Go ask his name.—If he is marrièd,
        My grave is like to be my wedding bed.

     NURSE His name is Romeo, and a Montague,
        The only son of your great enemy.

140 JULIET My only love, sprung from my only hate!
        Too early seen unknown, and known too late!
        Prodigious birth of love it is to me
        That I must love a loathèd enemy.

     NURSE What's this? What's this?

     JULIET   A rhyme I learnt even now
145   Of one I danced withal.   *One calls within,* "Juliet."

     NURSE   Anon, anon!
        Come, let's away; the strangers all are gone.
                                              Exeunt.

---

124 **towards** in preparation   125 **Is it e'en so?** (the maskers insist on leaving)
128 **fay** faith   142 **Prodigious** (1) monstrous (2) of evil portent   145 **Anon** at
once

[ACT II

Enter] Chorus.

CHORUS Now old desire doth in his deathbed lie,
    And young affection gapes to be his heir;
That fair for which love groaned for and would die,
    With tender Juliet matched, is now not fair.
Now Romeo is beloved and loves again,   5
    Alike bewitchèd by the charm of looks;
But to his foe supposed he must complain,
    And she steal love's sweet bait from fearful
        hooks.
Being held a foe, he may not have access
    To breathe such vows as lovers use to swear,   10
And she as much in love, her means much less
    To meet her new belovèd anywhere;
But passion lends them power, time means, to meet,
Temp'ring extremities with extreme sweet.   *[Exit.]*

II. Prologue   2 **young affection gapes** the new love is eager   3 **That fair** i.e.,
Rosaline   6 **Alike bewitched** i.e., both are bewitched   7 **complain** address his
lover's suit   10 **use to** customarily   14 **Temp'ring … sweet** softening difficul-
ties with extraordinary delights

[Scene I. *Near Capulet's orchard.*]

Enter Romeo alone.

ROMEO Can I go forward when my heart is here?
Turn back, dull earth, and find thy center out.

Enter Benvolio with Mercutio. [Romeo retires.]

BENVOLIO Romeo! My cousin Romeo! Romeo!

MERCUTIO   He is wise
And, on my life, hath stol'n him home to bed.

5 BENVOLIO He ran this way and leapt this orchard wall.
Call, good Mercutio.

MERCUTIO   Nay, I'll conjure too.
Romeo! Humors! Madman! Passion! Lover!
Appear thou in the likeness of a sigh;
Speak but one rhyme, and I am satisfied!
Cry but "Ay me!" pronounce but "love" and
10   "dove";
Speak to my gossip Venus one fair word,
One nickname for her purblind son and heir,
Young Abraham Cupid, he that shot so true
When King Cophetua loved the beggar maid!
15 He heareth not, he stirreth not, he moveth not;
The ape is dead, and I must conjure him.
I conjure thee by Rosaline's bright eyes,
By her high forehead and her scarlet lip,

II.i.1–2 **Can ... out** (Romeo refuses to pass Capulet's house, commanding his
body, or *earth*, to stop and join its proper soul, or *center*—i.e., Juliet)
11 **gossip** crony   12 **purblind** quite blind   13 **Abraham Cupid** (the phrase
may mean "ancient youth" or, since "abram man" was slang for "trickster,"
"rascally Cupid")   14 **King Cophetua ... maid** (reference to an old familiar
ballad)   16 **The ape is dead** i.e., Romeo plays dead, like a performing ape

By her fine foot, straight leg, and quivering thigh,
And the demesnes that there adjacent lie,   20
That in thy likeness thou appear to us!

BENVOLIO And if he hear thee, thou wilt anger him.

MERCUTIO This cannot anger him. 'Twould anger him
To raise a spirit in his mistress' circle
Of some strange nature, letting it there stand   25
Till she had laid it and conjured it down.
That were some spite; my invocation
Is fair and honest: in his mistress' name,
I conjure only but to raise up him.

BENVOLIO Come, he hath hid himself among these trees   30
To be consorted with the humorous night.
Blind is his love and best befits the dark.

MERCUTIO If love be blind, love cannot hit the mark.
Now will he sit under a medlar tree
And wish his mistress were that kind of fruit   35
As maids call medlars when they laugh alone.
O, Romeo, that she were, O that she were
An open *et cetera*, thou a pop'rin pear!
Romeo, good night. I'll to my truckle bed;
This field bed is too cold for me to sleep.   40
Come, shall we go?

BENVOLIO   Go then, for 'tis in vain
To seek him here that means not to be found.

Exit [with others].

---

20 demesnes domains   22 And if if   24 circle (conjurers worked within a magic
circle, but there is also a bawdy innuendo, as in *stand, laid, down, raise*)   27 spite
vexation   28 fair and honest respectable   31 consorted associated
31 humorous (1) damp (2) moody   36 medlars applelike fruit, eaten when
decayed (like pop'rin, in line 38, the word was often used to refer to sexual organs)
39 I'll to my truckle bed I'll go to my trundle bed, or baby bed (i.e., I'm
innocent in affairs of this kind)

[Scene II. *Capulet's orchard.*]

ROMEO [*Coming forward*] He jests at scars that never
   felt a wound.

[*Enter Juliet at a window.*]

But soft! What light through yonder window breaks?
It is the East, and Juliet is the sun!
Arise, fair sun, and kill the envious moon,
5   Who is already sick and pale with grief
That thou her maid art far more fair than she.
Be not her maid, since she is envious.
Her vestal livery is but sick and green,
And none but fools do wear it. Cast it off.
10   It is my lady! O, it is my love!
O, that she knew she were!
She speaks, yet she says nothing. What of that?
Her eye discourses; I will answer it.
I am too bold; 'tis not to me she speaks.
15   Two of the fairest stars in all the heaven,
Having some business, do entreat her eyes
To twinkle in their spheres till they return.
What if her eyes were there, they in her head?
The brightness of her cheek would shame those stars
20   As daylight doth a lamp; her eyes in heaven
Would through the airy region stream so bright
That birds would sing and think it were not night.
See how she leans her cheek upon her hand!
O, that I were a glove upon that hand,
That I might touch that cheek!

JULIET   Ay me!

II.ii.6 **her maid** (the moon is here thought of as Diana, goddess and patroness of
virgins)   8 **vestal livery** i.e., virginity   8 **sick and green** sickly, bearing the
characteristics of greensickness, the virgin's malady   17 **spheres** orbits

ROMEO   She speaks.   25
  O, speak again, bright angel, for thou art
  As glorious to this night, being o'er my head,
  As is a wingèd messenger of heaven
  Unto the white-upturnèd wond'ring eyes
  Of mortals that fall back to gaze on him   30
  When he bestrides the lazy puffing clouds
  And sails upon the bosom of the air.

JULIET O Romeo, Romeo! Wherefore art thou Romeo?
  Deny thy father and refuse thy name;
  Or, if thou wilt not, be but sworn my love,   35
  And I'll no longer be a Capulet.

ROMEO [*Aside*] Shall I hear more, or shall I speak
    at this?

JULIET 'Tis but thy name that is my enemy.
  Thou art thyself, though not a Montague.
  What's Montague? It is nor hand, nor foot,   40
  Nor arm, nor face. O, be some other name
  Belonging to a man.
  What's in a name? That which we call a rose
  By any other word would smell as sweet.
  So Romeo would, were he not Romeo called,   45
  Retain that dear perfection which he owes
  Without that title. Romeo, doff thy name;
  And for thy name, which is no part of thee,
  Take all myself.

ROMEO   I take thee at thy word.
  Call me but love, and I'll be new baptized;   50
  Henceforth I never will be Romeo.

JULIET What man art thou, that, thus bescreened in
    night,
  So stumblest on my counsel?

ROMEO   By a name
  I know not how to tell thee who I am.   55
  My name, dear saint, is hateful to myself

39 **though not** even if you were not   46 **owes** owns

Because it is an enemy to thee.
Had I it written, I would tear the word.

JULIET My ears have yet not drunk a hundred words
Of thy tongue's uttering, yet I know the sound.
60   Art thou not Romeo, and a Montague?

ROMEO Neither, fair maid, if either thee dislike.

JULIET How camest thou hither, tell me, and
        wherefore?
The orchard walls are high and hard to climb,
And the place death, considering who thou art,
65   If any of my kinsmen find thee here.

ROMEO With love's light wings did I o'erperch these
        walls;
For stony limits cannot hold love out,
And what love can do, that dares love attempt.
Therefore thy kinsmen are no stop to me.

70   JULIET If they do see thee, they will murder thee.

ROMEO Alack, there lies more peril in thine eye
Than twenty of their swords! Look thou but sweet,
And I am proof against their enmity.

JULIET I would not for the world they saw thee here.

75   ROMEO I have night's cloak to hide me from their eyes;
And but thou love me, let them find me here.
My life were better ended by their hate
Than death proroguèd, wanting of thy love.

JULIET By whose direction found'st thou out this place?

80   ROMEO By love, that first did prompt me to inquire.
He lent me counsel, and I lent him eyes.
I am no pilot; yet, wert thou as far
As that vast shore washed with the farthest sea,
I should adventure for such merchandise.

85   JULIET Thou knowest the mask of night is on my face;

61 **dislike** displeases   66 **o'erperch** fly over   73 **proof** protected   76 **but if**
only   78 **proroguèd** deferred   84 **adventure** risk the journey

430

Else would a maiden blush bepaint my cheek
For that which thou hast heard me speak tonight.
Fain would I dwell on form—fain, fain deny
What I have spoke; but farewell compliment!
Dost thou love me? I know thou wilt say "Ay";   90
And I will take thy word. Yet, if thou swear'st,
Thou mayst prove false. At lovers' perjuries,
They say Jove laughs. O gentle Romeo,
If thou dost love, pronounce it faithfully.
Or if thou thinkest I am too quickly won,   95
I'll frown and be perverse and say thee nay,
So thou wilt woo; but else, not for the world.
In truth, fair Montague, I am too fond,
And therefore thou mayst think my havior light;
But trust me, gentleman, I'll prove more true   100
Than those that have more cunning to be strange.
I should have been more strange, I must confess,
But that thou overheard'st, ere I was ware,
My truelove passion. Therefore pardon me,
And not impute this yielding to light love,   105
Which the dark night hath so discoverèd.

ROMEO Lady, by yonder blessèd moon I vow,
That tips with silver all these fruit-tree tops—

JULIET O, swear not by the moon, th' inconstant moon,
That monthly changes in her circle orb,   110
Lest that thy love prove likewise variable.

ROMEO What shall I swear by?

JULIET   Do not swear at all;
Or if thou wilt, swear by thy gracious self,
Which is the god of my idolatry,
And I'll believe thee.

ROMEO   If my heart's dear love—   115

JULIET Well, do not swear. Although I joy in thee,
I have no joy of this contract tonight.

89 **compliment** formal courtesy   98 **fond** (1) affectionate (2) foolishly tender
99 **havior** behavior   101 **strange** aloof   106 **discoverèd** revealed

It is too rash, too unadvised, too sudden;
Too like the lightning, which doth cease to be
120   Ere one can say it lightens. Sweet, good night!
This bud of love, by summer's ripening breath,
May prove a beauteous flow'r when next we meet.
Good night, good night! As sweet repose and rest
Come to thy heart as that within my breast!

125   ROMEO O, wilt thou leave me so unsatisfied?

JULIET What satisfaction canst thou have tonight?

ROMEO Th' exchange of thy love's faithful vow for
         mine.

JULIET I gave thee mine before thou didst request it;
And yet I would it were to give again.

ROMEO Wouldst thou withdraw it? For what purpose,
130   love?

JULIET But to be frank and give it thee again.
And yet I wish but for the thing I have.
My bounty is as boundless as the sea,
My love as deep; the more I give to thee,
135   The more I have, for both are infinite.
I hear some noise within. Dear love, adieu!
                              [Nurse calls within.]
Anon, good nurse! Sweet Montague, be true.
Stay but a little, I will come again.   [Exit.]

ROMEO O blessèd, blessèd night! I am afeard,
140   Being in night, all this is but a dream,
Too flattering-sweet to be substantial.

                    [Enter Juliet again.]

JULIET Three words, dear Romeo, and good night
         indeed.
If that thy bent of love be honorable,
Thy purpose marriage, send me word tomorrow,
145   By one that I'll procure to come to thee,
Where and what time thou wilt perform the rite;

131 frank generous   133 bounty capacity for giving   143 bent aim

And all my fortunes at thy foot I'll lay
And follow thee my lord throughout the world.

[*Nurse. Within*] Madam!

JULIET I come anon.—But if thou meanest not well,   150
I do beseech thee—

[*Nurse. Within*] Madam!

JULIET   By and by I come.—
To cease thy strife and leave me to my grief.
Tomorrow will I send.

ROMEO   So thrive my soul—

JULIET A thousand times good night!   [*Exit.*]

ROMEO A thousand times the worse, to want thy light!   155
Love goes toward love as schoolboys from their
    books;
But love from love, toward school with heavy looks.

Enter Juliet again.

JULIET Hist! Romeo, hist! O for a falc'ner's voice
To lure this tassel gentle back again!
Bondage is hoarse and may not speak aloud,   160
Else would I tear the cave where Echo lies
And make her airy tongue more hoarse than mine
With repetition of "My Romeo!"

ROMEO It is my soul that calls upon my name.
How silver-sweet sound lovers' tongues by night,   165
Like softest music to attending ears!

JULIET Romeo!

ROMEO   My sweet?

JULIET   What o'clock tomorrow
Shall I send to thee?

---

151 **By and by** at once   152 **strife** efforts   159 **tassel gentle** tercel gentle, male falcon   160 **Bondage is hoarse** i.e., being surrounded by "protectors," I cannot cry loudly   166 **attending** attentive

ROMEO   By the hour of nine.

JULIET I will not fail. 'Tis twenty year till then.
170   I have forgot why I did call thee back.

ROMEO Let me stand here till thou remember it.

JULIET I shall forget, to have thee still stand there,
        Rememb'ring how I love thy company.

ROMEO And I'll still stay, to have thee still forget,
175   Forgetting any other home but this.

JULIET 'Tis almost morning. I would have thee gone—
        And yet no farther than a wanton's bird,
        That lets it hop a little from his hand,
        Like a poor prisoner in his twisted gyves,
180   And with a silken thread plucks it back again,
        So loving-jealous of his liberty.

ROMEO I would I were thy bird.

JULIET   Sweet, so would I.
        Yet I should kill thee with much cherishing.
        Good night, good night! Parting is such sweet
          sorrow
185   That I shall say good night till it be morrow.
                                              [Exit.]

ROMEO Sleep dwell upon thine eyes, peace in thy
          breast!
        Would I were sleep and peace, so sweet to rest!
        Hence will I to my ghostly friar's close cell,
        His help to crave and my dear hap to tell.   Exit.

---

177 **wanton's** capricious child's 179 **gyves** fetters 185 **morrow** morning
187 **rest** (the four lines that follow in the quarto are here deleted because they are
virtually identical with the first four lines of the next scene. See Textual Note.
Apparently Shakespeare wrote them and then decided to use them at the start of
the next scene, but forgot to delete their first occurrence) 188 **ghostly friar**
spiritual father (i.e., confessor) 189 **dear hap** good fortune

[Scene III. *Friar Lawrence's cell.*]

Enter Friar [Lawrence] alone, with a basket.

FRIAR The gray-eyed morn smiles on the frowning
　　　night,
Check'ring the eastern clouds with streaks of light;
And fleckèd darkness like a drunkard reels
From forth day's path and Titan's burning wheels.
Now, ere the sun advance his burning eye　　　　　　5
The day to cheer and night's dank dew to dry,
I must upfill this osier cage of ours
With baleful weeds and precious-juicèd flowers.
The earth that's nature's mother is her tomb.
What is her burying grave, that is her womb;　　　　10
And from her womb children of divers kind
We sucking on her natural bosom find,
Many for many virtues excellent,
None but for some, and yet all different.
O, mickle is the powerful grace that lies　　　　　　15
In plants, herbs, stones, and their true qualities;
For naught so vile that on the earth doth live
But to the earth some special good doth give;
Nor aught so good but, strained from that fair use,
Revolts from true birth, stumbling on abuse.　　　　20
Virtue itself turns vice, being misapplied,
And vice sometime by action dignified.

Enter Romeo.

II.iii.3 **fleckèd** spotted　4 **Titan's burning wheels** wheels of the sun's chariot
7 **osier cage** willow basket　8 **baleful** (1) evil (2) poisonous　15 **mickle** much
19 **strained** diverted　20 **Revolts from true birth** falls away from its real
purpose　22 **dignified** made worthy　22s.d. **Enter Romeo** (the entry of Romeo
at this point, unseen by the Friar, emphasizes the appropriateness of the remaining
eight lines of the Friar's speech, not only to the flower but to Romeo)

Within the infant rind of this weak flower
Poison hath residence and medicine power;
For this, being smelt, with that part cheers each
25   part;
Being tasted, stays all senses with the heart.
Two such opposèd kings encamp them still
In man as well as herbs—grace and rude will;
And where the worser is predominant,
30   Full soon the canker death eats up that plant.

ROMEO Good morrow, father.

FRIAR   *Benedicite!*
What early tongue so sweet saluteth me?
Young son, it argues a distemperèd head
So soon to bid good morrow to thy bed.
35   Care keeps his watch in every old man's eye,
And where care lodges, sleep will never lie;
But where unbruisèd youth with unstuffed brain
Doth couch his limbs, there golden sleep doth reign.
Therefore thy earliness doth me assure
40   Thou art uproused with some distemp'rature;
Or if not so, then here I hit it right—
Our Romeo hath not been in bed tonight.

ROMEO That last is true. The sweeter rest was mine.

FRIAR God pardon sin! Wast thou with Rosaline?

45   ROMEO With Rosaline, my ghostly father? No.
I have forgot that name and that name's woe.

FRIAR That's my good son! But where hast thou been
    then?

ROMEO I'll tell thee ere thou ask it me again.
I have been feasting with mine enemy,
50   Where on a sudden one hath wounded me
That's by me wounded. Both our remedies

23 **infant rind** tender bark, skin   24 **medicine** medicinal   25 **For … part** i.e., being smelled, this flower stimulates every part of the body   27 **still** always 30 **canker** cankerworm, larva that feeds on leaves   31 **Benedicite** bless you 33 **distemperèd head** troubled mind   37 **unstuffed** untroubled

Within thy help and holy physic lies.
I bear no hatred, blessèd man, for, lo,
My intercession likewise steads my foe.

FRIAR Be plain, good son, and homely in thy drift.   55
Riddling confession finds but riddling shrift.

ROMEO Then plainly know my heart's dear love is set
On the fair daughter of rich Capulet;
As mine on hers, so hers is set on mine,
And all combined, save what thou must combine   60
By holy marriage. When and where and how
We met, we wooed, and made exchange of vow,
I'll tell thee as we pass; but this I pray,
That thou consent to marry us today.

FRIAR Holy Saint Francis! What a change is here!   65
Is Rosaline, that thou didst love so dear,
So soon forsaken? Young men's love then lies
Not truly in their hearts, but in their eyes.
Jesu Maria! What a deal of brine
Hath washed thy sallow cheeks for Rosaline!   70
How much salt water thrown away in waste
To season love, that of it doth not taste!
The sun not yet thy sighs from heaven clears,
Thy old groans ring yet in mine ancient ears.
Lo, here upon thy cheek the stain doth sit   75
Of an old tear that is not washed off yet.
If e'er thou wast thyself, and these woes thine,
Thou and these woes were all for Rosaline.
And art thou changed? Pronounce this sentence
  then:
Women may fall when there's no strength in men.   80

ROMEO Thou chidst me oft for loving Rosaline.

FRIAR For doting, not for loving, pupil mine.

---

52 **physic** medicine   54 **intercession** entreaty   54 **steads** helps   55 **homely
in thy drift** plain in your talk   56 **shrift** absolution   60 **combined** (1) brought
into unity (2) settled   72 **season** (1) preserve (2) flavor   80 **may fall** i.e., may be
expected to be fickle   80 **strength** constancy

ROMEO And badst me bury love.

FRIAR   Not in a grave
To lay one in, another out to have.

85 ROMEO I pray thee chide me not. Her I love now
Doth grace for grace and love for love allow.
The other did not so.

FRIAR   O, she knew well
Thy love did read by rote, that could not spell.
But come, young waverer, come go with me.
90 In one respect I'll thy assistant be;
For this alliance may so happy prove
To turn your households' rancor to pure love.

ROMEO O, let us hence! I stand on sudden haste.

FRIAR Wisely and slow. They stumble that run fast.
                                        Exeunt.

[Scene IV. *A street.*]

Enter Benvolio and Mercutio.

MERCUTIO Where the devil should this Romeo be?
Came he not home tonight?

BENVOLIO Not to his father's. I spoke with his man.

MERCUTIO Why, that same pale hardhearted wench,
that Rosaline,
5 Torments him so that he will sure run mad.

BENVOLIO Tybalt, the kinsman to old Capulet,
Hath sent a letter to his father's house.

MERCUTIO A challenge, on my life.

---

86 **grace** favor   88 **did read ... spell** i.e., said words without understanding
them   90 **In one respect** with respect to one particular   93 **stand on** insist on

BENVOLIO Romeo will answer it.

MERCUTIO Any man that can write may answer a letter.   10

BENVOLIO Nay, he will answer the letter's master, how he dares, being dared.

MERCUTIO Alas, poor Romeo, he is already dead: stabbed with a white wench's black eye; run through the ear with a love song; the very pin of his heart   15
cleft with the blind bow-boy's butt-shaft; and is he a man to encounter Tybalt?

BENVOLIO Why, what is Tybalt?

MERCUTIO More than Prince of Cats. O, he's the courageous captain of compliments. He fights as   20
you sing pricksong—keeps time, distance, and proportion; he rests his minim rests, one, two, and the third in your bosom! The very butcher of a silk button, a duelist, a duelist! A gentleman of the very first house, of the first and second cause.   25
Ah, the immortal *passado!* The *punto reverso!* The hay!

BENVOLIO The what?

MERCUTIO The pox of such antic, lisping, affecting fantasticoes—these new tuners of accent! "By   30
Jesu, a very good blade! A very tall man! A very good whore!" Why, is not this a lamentable thing, grandsir, that we should be thus afflicted with these

---

II.iv.15 **pin** center (of a target)   16 **blind bow-boy's butt-shaft** Cupid's blunt arrow   19 **Prince of Cats** (Tybalt's name, or some variant of it, was given to the cat in medieval stories of Reynard the Fox)   20 **compliments** formal courtesies   21 **sing pricksong** (1) sing from a text (2) sing with attention to accuracy   22 **he rests his minim rests** i.e., he scrupulously observes every formality (literally, he observes even the shortest rests in the notation)   24 **button** (on his opponent's shirt)   25 **first house** first rank   25 **first and second cause** (dueling terms, meaning formal grounds for taking offense and giving a challenge)   26 **passado** lunge   26 **punto reverso** backhanded stroke   27 **hay** home thrust (Italian *hai*)   30 **fantasticoes** fops   31 **tall** brave

35 strange flies, these fashionmongers, these pardon-
me's, who stand so much on the new form that
they cannot sit at ease on the old bench? O, their
bones, their bones!

Enter Romeo.

BENVOLIO Here comes Romeo! Here comes Romeo!

MERCUTIO Without his roe, like a dried herring. O
40 flesh, flesh, how art thou fishified! Now is he for
the numbers that Petrarch flowed in. Laura, to
his lady, was a kitchen wench (marry, she had a
better love to berhyme her), Dido a dowdy,
Cleopatra a gypsy, Helen and Hero hildings and
45 harlots, Thisbe a gray eye or so, but not to the
purpose. Signior Romeo, *bon jour!* There's a French
salutation to your French slop. You gave us the
counterfeit fairly last night.

ROMEO Good morrow to you both. What counterfeit
50 did I give you?

MERCUTIO The slip, sir, the slip. Can you not conceive?

ROMEO Pardon, good Mercutio. My business was
great, and in such a case as mine a man may strain
55 courtesy.

MERCUTIO That's as much as to say, such a case as
yours constrains a man to bow in the hams.

34–35 **pardon-me's** i.e., persons who affect foreign phrases (cf. Italian *perdona mi*)   35 **form** (1) fashion (2) bench   37 **bones** (pun on French *bon*)   39 **Without his roe** i.e., (1) emaciated like a fish that has spawned or (2) stripped of "Ro," leaving only "me-o" (a sigh)   41 **numbers** verses   41 **Laura** (Petrarch's beloved)   43 **Dido** (Queen of Carthage, enamored of Aeneas)   43 **dowdy** a drab woman   44 **gypsy** a deceitful woman (gypsies were commonly believed to be Egyptians)   44 **Helen and Hero** (beloved respectively of Paris and Leander)   44 **hildings** good-for-nothings   45 **Thisbe** (beloved of Pyramus in a story analogous to that of Romeo and Juliet)   45 **gray eye** i.e., gleam in the eye   47 **slop** loose breeches   51 **slip** (1) escape (2) counterfeit coin   56 **case** (1) situation (2) physical condition

ROMEO Meaning, to curtsy.

MERCUTIO Thou hast most kindly hit it.

ROMEO A most courteous exposition.   60

MERCUTIO Nay, I am the very pink of courtesy.

ROMEO Pink for flower.

MERCUTIO Right.

ROMEO Why, then is my pump well-flowered.

MERCUTIO Sure wit, follow me this jest now till thou   65
hast worn out thy pump, that, when the single sole
of it is worn, the jest may remain, after the wearing,
solely singular.

ROMEO O single-soled jest, solely singular for the
singleness!   70

MERCUTIO Come between us, good Benvolio! My wits
faints.

ROMEO Swits and spurs, swits and spurs; or I'll cry
a match.

MERCUTIO Nay, if our wits run the wild-goose chase,   75
I am done; for thou hast more of the wild goose in
one of thy wits than, I am sure, I have in my whole
five. Was I with you there for the goose?

ROMEO Thou wast never with me for anything when
thou wast not there for the goose.   80

MERCUTIO I will bite thee by the ear for that jest.

---

59 **most kindly hit** most politely interpreted   61 **pink** perfection (but Romeo
proceeds to exploit two other meanings: [1] flower [2] punches in an ornamental
design)   64 **pump** shoe   64 **well-flowered** ornamented with pinking (with pun
on "floored")   68 **solely singular** (1) single-soled (i.e., weak) (2) uniquely
remarkable (literally, "uniquely unique")   73 **Swits** switches   73-74 **cry a
match** claim a victory   75 **wild-goose chase** cross-country game of "follow the
leader" on horseback   78 **goose** end of the chase (i.e., end of the punning match)
80 **goose** prostitute

ROMEO Nay, good goose, bite not!

MERCUTIO Thy wit is a very bitter sweeting; it is a most sharp sauce.

85 ROMEO And is it not, then, well served in to a sweet goose?

MERCUTIO O, here's a wit of cheveril, that stretches from an inch narrow to an ell broad!

ROMEO I stretch it out for that word "broad," which
90 added to the goose, proves thee far and wide a broad goose.

MERCUTIO Why, is not this better now than groaning for love? Now art thou sociable, now art thou Romeo; now art thou what thou art, by art as well
95 as by nature. For this driveling love is like a great natural that runs lolling up and down to hide his bauble in a hole.

BENVOLIO Stop there, stop there!

MERCUTIO Thou desirest me to stop in my tale against
100 the hair.

BENVOLIO Thou wouldst else have made thy tale large.

MERCUTIO O, thou art deceived! I would have made it short; for I was come to the whole depth of my
105 tale, and meant indeed to occupy the argument no longer.

ROMEO Here's goodly gear!

---

82 **good goose, bite not** (proverbial for "Spare me!")   83 **bitter sweeting** tart kind of apple   85-86 **sweet goose** tender goose (here probably referring to Mercutio; but the expression "Sour sauce for sweet meat" was proverbial) 87 **cheveril** kid leather, easily stretched   88 **ell broad** forty-five inches wide 91 **broad** indecent (?)   96 **natural** idiot   96 **lolling** with tongue hanging out 97 **bauble** trinket (with ribald innuendo)   99-100 **against the hair** against my inclination   102 **large** indecent   105 **occupy the argument** discuss the matter 107 **gear** stuff

Enter Nurse and her Man [Peter].

A sail, a sail!

MERCUTIO Two, two! A shirt and a smock.

NURSE Peter! 110

PETER Anon.

NURSE My fan, Peter.

MERCUTIO Good Peter, to hide her face; for her fan's the fairer face.

NURSE God ye good morrow, gentlemen. 115

MERCUTIO God ye good-den, fair gentlewoman.

NURSE Is it good-den?

MERCUTIO 'Tis no less, I tell ye; for the bawdy hand of the dial is now upon the prick of noon.

NURSE Out upon you! What a man are you! 120

ROMEO One, gentlewoman, that God hath made, himself to mar.

NURSE By my troth, it is well said. "For himself to mar," quoth 'a? Gentlemen, can any of you tell me where I may find the young Romeo? 125

ROMEO I can tell you; but young Romeo will be older when you have found him than he was when you sought him. I am the youngest of that name, for fault of a worse.

NURSE You say well. 130

MERCUTIO Yea, is the worst well? Very well took, i' faith! Wisely, wisely.

NURSE If you be he, sir, I desire some confidence with you.

---

109 **A shirt and a smock** i.e., a man and a woman   116 **good-den** good evening (i.e., afternoon)   119 **prick** point on the dial of a clock (with bawdy innuendo)   124 **quoth 'a** indeed (literally, "said he")   128-29 **for fault of a worse** (mock-modestly parodying "for want of a better")   131 **took** understood   133 **confidence** conference (possibly a malapropism)

135 BENVOLIO She will endite him to some supper.

MERCUTIO A bawd, a bawd, a bawd! So ho!

ROMEO What hast thou found?

MERCUTIO No hare, sir; unless a hare, sir, in a lenten
pie, that is something stale and hoar ere it be
140 spent.

[*He walks by them and sings.*]

An old hare hoar,
And an old hare hoar,
Is very good meat in Lent;
But a hare that is hoar
145 Is too much for a score
When it hoars ere it be spent.

Romeo, will you come to your father's? We'll to
dinner thither.

ROMEO I will follow you.

150 MERCUTIO Farewell, ancient lady. Farewell, [*singing*]
"Lady, lady, lady."   *Exeunt* [*Mercutio, Benvolio*].

NURSE I pray you, sir, what saucy merchant was this
that was so full of his ropery?

ROMEO A gentleman, nurse, that loves to hear himself
155 talk and will speak more in a minute than he will
stand to in a month.

NURSE And 'a speak anything against me, I'll take him
down, and 'a were lustier than he is, and twenty
such Jacks; and if I cannot, I'll find those that shall.
160 Scurvy knave! I am none of his flirt-gills; I am

---

136 **endite** invite (Benvolio's intentional malapropism?) 136 **So ho!** (cry on
sighting a quarry) 138 **hare** prostitute 138–39 **lenten pie** rabbit pie (eaten
sparingly and hence stale) 139 **hoar** gray-haired, moldy (wordplay on "hare"
and "whore") 151 **Lady, lady, lady** (ballad refrain from "Chaste Susanna")
153 **ropery** rascally talk 160 **flirt-gills** flirting wenches

none of his skainsmates. And thou must stand
by too, and suffer every knave to use me at his
pleasure!

PETER I saw no man use you at his pleasure. If I had,
my weapon should quickly have been out, I warrant   165
you. I dare draw as soon as another man, if I see
occasion in a good quarrel, and the law on my side.

NURSE Now, afore God, I am so vexed that every part
about me quivers. Scurvy knave! Pray you, sir, a
word; and, as I told you, my young lady bid me   170
inquire you out. What she bid me say, I will keep
to myself; but first let me tell ye, if ye should lead
her in a fool's paradise, as they say, it was a very
gross kind of behavior, as they say; for the gentlewoman is young; and therefore, if you should deal   175
double with her, truly it were an ill thing to be
off'red to any gentlewoman, and very weak dealing.

ROMEO Nurse, commend me to thy lady and mistress.
I protest unto thee—

NURSE Good heart, and i' faith I will tell her as much.   180
Lord, Lord, she will be a joyful woman.

ROMEO What wilt thou tell her, nurse? Thou dost not
mark me.

NURSE I will tell her, sir, that you do protest, which,
as I take it, is a gentlemanlike offer.   185

ROMEO Bid her devise
Some means to come to shrift this afternoon;
And there she shall at Friar Lawrence' cell
Be shrived and married. Here is for thy pains.

NURSE No, truly, sir; not a penny.   190

ROMEO Go to! I say you shall.

NURSE This afternoon, sir? Well, she shall be there.

161 **skainsmates** harlots (?) daggers' mates (i.e., outlaws' mates)   173 **fool's paradise** seduction   177 **weak** unmanly, unscrupulous

ROMEO And stay, good nurse, behind the abbey wall.
Within this hour my man shall be with thee
195 And bring thee cords made like a tackled stair,
Which to the high topgallant of my joy
Must be my convoy in the secret night.
Farewell. Be trusty, and I'll quit thy pains.
Farewell. Commend me to thy mistress.

200 NURSE Now God in heaven bless thee! Hark you, sir.

ROMEO What say'st thou, my dear nurse?

NURSE Is your man secret? Did you ne'er hear say,
Two may keep counsel, putting one away?

ROMEO Warrant thee my man's as true as steel.

205 NURSE Well, sir, my mistress is the sweetest lady. Lord,
Lord! When 'twas a little prating thing— O, there is
a nobleman in town, one Paris, that would fain lay
knife aboard; but she, good soul, had as lieve see
a toad, a very toad, as see him. I anger her some-
210 times, and tell her that Paris is the properer man;
but I'll warrant you, when I say so, she looks as
pale as any clout in the versal world. Doth not
rosemary and Romeo begin both with a letter?

ROMEO Ay, nurse; what of that? Both with an *R*.

215 NURSE Ah, mocker! That's the dog's name. *R* is for
the— No; I know it begins with some other letter;
and she hath the prettiest sententious of it, of you
and rosemary, that it would do you good to hear it.

ROMEO Commend me to thy lady.

220 NURSE Ay, a thousand times. [*Exit Romeo.*] Peter!

PETER Anon.

NURSE Before, and apace.   *Exit* [*after Peter*].

195 **tackled stair** rope ladder   196 **topgallant** summit (mast above the topmast)
197 **convoy** conveyance   198 **quit** reward   207–08 **lay knife aboard** take a slice
208 **had as lieve** would rather   212 **clout** cloth   212 **versal world** universe
215 **dog's name** (the *R* sound suggests a dog's growl)   217 **sententious**
sentences, pithy sayings

[Scene V. *Capulet's orchard.*]

Enter Juliet.

JULIET The clock struck nine when I did send the
        nurse;
In half an hour she promised to return.
Perchance she cannot meet him. That's not so.
O, she is lame! Love's heralds should be thoughts,
Which ten times faster glides than the sun's beams   5
Driving back shadows over low'ring hills.
Therefore do nimble-pinioned doves draw Love,
And therefore hath the wind-swift Cupid wings.
Now is the sun upon the highmost hill
Of this day's journey, and from nine till twelve   10
Is three long hours; yet she is not come.
Had she affections and warm youthful blood,
She would be as swift in motion as a ball;
My words would bandy her to my sweet love,
And his to me.   15
But old folks, many feign as they were dead—
Unwieldy, slow, heavy and pale as lead.

Enter Nurse [and Peter].

O God, she comes! O honey nurse, what news?
Hast thou met with him? Send thy man away.

NURSE Peter, stay at the gate.   [*Exit Peter.*]   20

JULIET Now, good sweet nurse—O Lord, why lookest
        thou sad?
Though news be sad, yet tell them merrily;

II.v.7 nimble-pinioned doves swift-winged doves (sacred to Venus)   14 bandy
her speed her   16 old ... dead i.e., many old people move about as if they were
almost dead

If good, thou shamest the music of sweet news
By playing it to me with so sour a face.

25 NURSE I am aweary, give me leave awhile.
Fie, how my bones ache! What a jaunce have I!

JULIET I would thou hadst my bones, and I thy news.
Nay, come, I pray thee speak. Good, good nurse,
    speak.

NURSE Jesu, what haste! Can you not stay awhile?
30   Do you not see that I am out of breath?

JULIET How art thou out of breath when thou hast
    breath
To say to me that thou art out of breath?
The excuse that thou dost make in this delay
Is longer than the tale thou dost excuse.
35   Is thy news good or bad? Answer to that.
Say either, and I'll stay the circumstance.
Let me be satisfied, is't good or bad?

NURSE Well, you have made a simple choice; you
know not how to choose a man. Romeo? No, not
40   he. Though his face be better than any man's, yet
his leg excels all men's; and for a hand and a foot,
and a body, though they be not to be talked on,
yet they are past compare. He is not the flower of
courtesy, but, I'll warrant him, as gentle as a lamb.
45   Go thy ways, wench; serve God. What, have you
dined at home?

JULIET No, no. But all this did I know before.
What says he of our marriage? What of that?

NURSE Lord, how my head aches! What a head have I!
50   It beats as it would fall in twenty pieces.
My back a t' other side—ah, my back, my back!
Beshrew your heart for sending me about
To catch my death with jauncing up and down!

26 **jaunce** jaunt, fatiguing walk   29 **stay** wait   36 **stay the circumstance** wait
for the details   38 **simple** foolish   51 **a** on   52 **Beshrew** curse (in the sense of
"shame on")

JULIET I' faith, I am sorry that thou art not well.
  Sweet, sweet, sweet nurse, tell me, what says my
    love?   55

NURSE Your love says, like an honest gentleman, and
  a courteous, and a kind, and a handsome, and I
  warrant, a virtuous— Where is your mother?

JULIET Where is my mother? Why, she is within.
  Where should she be? How oddly thou repliest!   60
  "Your love says, like an honest gentleman,
  'Where is your mother?' "

NURSE   O God's Lady dear!
  Are you so hot? Marry come up, I trow.
  Is this the poultice for my aching bones?
  Henceforward do your messeges yourself.   65

JULIET Here's such a coil! Come, what says Romeo?

NURSE Have you got leave to go to shrift today?

JULIET I have.

NURSE Then hie you hence to Friar Lawrence' cell;
  There stays a husband to make you a wife.   70
  Now comes the wanton blood up in your cheeks:
  They'll be in scarlet straight at any news.
  Hie you to church; I must another way,
  To fetch a ladder, by the which your love
  Must climb a bird's nest soon when it is dark.   75
  I am the drudge, and toil in your delight;
  But you shall bear the burden soon at night.
  Go; I'll to dinner; hie you to the cell.

JULIET Hie to high fortune! Honest nurse, farewell.
                            Exeunt.

---

63 **hot** angry 63 **Marry ... trow** indeed, come now, by the Virgin 66 **coil**
disturbance 72 **straight** straightway

[Scene VI. *Friar Lawrence's cell.*]

Enter Friar [Lawrence] and Romeo.

FRIAR So smile the heavens upon this holy act
That afterhours with sorrow chide us not!

ROMEO Amen, amen! But come what sorrow can,
It cannot countervail the exchange of joy
5   That one short minute gives me in her sight.
Do thou but close our hands with holy words,
Then love-devouring death do what he dare—
It is enough I may but call her mine.

FRIAR These violent delights have violent ends
10   And in their triumph die, like fire and powder,
Which, as they kiss, consume. The sweetest honey
Is loathsome in his own deliciousness
And in the taste confounds the appetite.
Therefore love moderately: long love doth so;
15   Too swift arrives as tardy as too slow.

Enter Juliet.

Here comes the lady. O, so light a foot
Will ne'er wear out the everlasting flint.
A lover may bestride the gossamers
That idles in the wanton summer air,
20   And yet not fall; so light is vanity.

JULIET Good even to my ghostly confessor.

FRIAR Romeo shall thank thee, daughter, for us both.

II.vi.4 **countervail** equal   13 **confounds** destroys   17 **Will ... flint** i.e., Juliet's
feet are lighter than waterdrops, which are proverbially said to wear away stones
18 **gossamers** spiders' webs   19 **wanton** capricious   20 **vanity** a transitory
thing (an earthly lover and his love)

450

JULIET As much to him, else is his thanks too much.

ROMEO Ah, Juliet, if the measure of thy joy
    Be heaped like mine, and that thy skill be more   25
    To blazon it, then sweeten with thy breath
    This neighbor air, and let rich music's tongue
    Unfold the imagined happiness that both
    Receive in either by this dear encounter.

JULIET Conceit, more rich in matter than in words,   30
    Brags of his substance, not of ornament.
    They are but beggars that can count their worth;
    But my true love is grown to such excess
    I cannot sum up sum of half my wealth.

FRIAR Come, come with me, and we will make short
      work;   35
    For, by your leaves, you shall not stay alone
    Till Holy Church incorporate two in one.   [*Exeunt.*]

---

23 **As much to him** i.e., the same greeting to Romeo 25-26 **thy skill ... blazon it** you are better able to set it forth 30-31 **Conceit ... ornament** i.e., true understanding is its own proud manifestation and does not need words

[ACT III

Scene I. *A public place*.]

Enter Mercutio, Benvolio, and Men.

BENVOLIO I pray thee, good Mercutio, let's retire.
The day is hot, the Capels are abroad,
And, if we meet, we shall not 'scape a brawl,
For now, these hot days, is the mad blood stirring.

5 MERCUTIO Thou art like one of these fellows that,
when he enters the confines of a tavern, claps me
his sword upon the table and says, "God send me
no need of thee!" and by the operation of the
second cup draws him on the drawer, when indeed
10 there is no need.

BENVOLIO Am I like such a fellow?

MERCUTIO Come, come, thou art as hot a Jack in thy
mood as any in Italy; and as soon moved to be
moody, and as soon moody to be moved.

15 BENVOLIO And what to?

MERCUTIO Nay, and there were two such, we should
have none shortly, for one would kill the other.
Thou! Why, thou wilt quarrel with a man that hath

III.i.9 **draws him on the drawer** draws his sword on the waiter   14 **moody**
angry   14 **moody to be moved** quick-tempered

a hair more or a hair less in his beard than thou
hast. Thou wilt quarrel with a man for cracking   20
nuts, having no other reason but because thou hast
hazel eyes. What eye but such an eye would spy
out such a quarrel? Thy head is as full of quarrels
as an egg is full of meat; and yet thy head hath
been beaten as addle as an egg for quarreling. Thou   25
hast quarreled with a man for coughing in the street,
because he hath wakened thy dog that hath lain
asleep in the sun. Didst thou not fall out with a
tailor for wearing his new doublet before Easter?
With another for tying his new shoes with old   30
riband? And yet thou wilt tutor me from quarreling!

BENVOLIO And I were so apt to quarrel as thou art, any
man should buy the fee simple of my life for an
hour and a quarter.

MERCUTIO The fee simple? O simple!   35

> *Enter Tybalt, Petruchio, and others.*

BENVOLIO By my head, here comes the Capulets.

MERCUTIO By my heel, I care not.

TYBALT Follow me close, for I will speak to them.
Gentlemen, good-den. A word with one of you.

MERCUTIO And but one word with one of us? Couple   40
it with something; make it a word and a blow.

TYBALT You shall find me apt enough to that, sir, and
you will give me occasion.

MERCUTIO Could you not take some occasion without
giving?   45

TYBALT Mercutio, thou consortest with Romeo.

---

29 **doublet** jacket 31 **riband** ribbon 33 **fee simple** absolute possession
33–34 **for an hour and a quarter** i.e., the life expectancy of one with Mercutio's
penchant for quarreling 35 **O simple** O stupid 35 **Petruchio** (in I.v he was
one of Capulet's guests, but he has no lines) 39 **good-den** good evening (i.e.,
afternoon)

MERCUTIO Consort? What, dost thou make us minstrels? And thou make minstrels of us, look to hear
nothing but discords. Here's my fiddlestick; here's
50   that shall make you dance. Zounds, consort!

BENVOLIO We talk here in the public haunt of men.
Either withdraw unto some private place,
Or reason coldly of your grievances,
Or else depart. Here all eyes gaze on us.

MERCUTIO Men's eyes were made to look, and let them
55   gaze.
I will not budge for no man's pleasure, I.

Enter Romeo.

TYBALT Well, peace be with you, sir. Here comes my
man.

MERCUTIO But I'll be hanged, sir, if he wear your
livery.
Marry, go before to field, he'll be your follower!
60   Your worship in that sense may call him man.

TYBALT Romeo, the love I bear thee can afford
No better term than this: thou art a villain.

ROMEO Tybalt, the reason that I have to love thee
Doth much excuse the appertaining rage
65   To such a greeting. Villain am I none.
Therefore farewell. I see thou knowest me not.

TYBALT Boy, this shall not excuse the injuries
That thou hast done me; therefore turn and draw.

ROMEO I do protest I never injured thee,
70   But love thee better than thou canst devise
Till thou shalt know the reason of my love;
And so, good Capulet, which name I tender
As dearly as mine own, be satisfied.

---

47 **Consort** (1) to keep company with (2) company of musicians   49 **fiddlestick**
i.e., sword   50 **Zounds** by God's wounds   57 **man** (Mercutio takes this to mean
"manservant")   58 **livery** servant's uniform   59 **field** dueling field   62 **villain**
low fellow   64 **appertaining** appropriate   70 **devise** imagine   72 **tender** value

MERCUTIO O calm, dishonorable, vile submission!
   Alla stoccata carries it away.   *[Draws.]*   75
   Tybalt, you ratcatcher, will you walk?

TYBALT What wouldst thou have with me?

MERCUTIO Good King of Cats, nothing but one of your
   nine lives. That I mean to make bold withal, and,
   as you shall use me hereafter, dry-beat the rest of
   the eight. Will you pluck your sword out of his   80
   pilcher by the ears? Make haste, lest mice be about
   your ears ere it be out.

TYBALT I am for you.   *[Draws.]*

ROMEO Gentle Mercutio, put thy rapier up.   85

MERCUTIO Come, sir, your *passado!*   *[They fight.]*

ROMEO Draw, Benvolio; beat down their weapons.
   Gentlemen, for shame! Forbear this outrage!
   Tybalt, Mercutio, the Prince expressly hath
   Forbid this bandying in Verona streets.   90
   Hold, Tybalt! Good Mercutio!
              [Tybalt under Romeo's arm thrusts
                      Mercutio in, and flies.]

MERCUTIO   I am hurt.
   A plague a both houses! I am sped.
   Is he gone and hath nothing?

BENVOLIO   What, art thou hurt?

MERCUTIO Ay, ay, a scratch, a scratch. Marry, 'tis
   enough.
   Where is my page? Go, villain, fetch a surgeon.   95
                        [Exit Page.]

ROMEO Courage, man. The hurt cannot be much.

MERCUTIO No, 'tis not so deep as a well, nor so wide

---

75 **Alla stoccata** (a term in fencing, "At the thrust," which Mercutio uses
contemptuously as a nickname for Tybalt)   76 **walk** step aside   79 **make bold
withal** make bold with, take   80 **dry-beat** thrash   82 **pilcher** scabbard
86 **passado** lunge   90 **bandying** brawling   92 **a** on   92 **sped** wounded

as a church door; but 'tis enough, 'twill serve. Ask
for me tomorrow, and you shall find me a grave
100   man. I am peppered, I warrant, for this world. A
plague a both your houses! Zounds, a dog, a rat, a
mouse, a cat, to scratch a man to death! A braggart,
a rogue, a villain, that fights by the book of arithmetic! Why the devil came you between us? I was
105   hurt under your arm.

ROMEO I thought all for the best.

MERCUTIO Help me into some house, Benvolio,
Or I shall faint. A plague a both your houses!
They have made worms' meat of me. I have it,
110   And soundly too. Your houses!

Exit [Mercutio and Benvolio].

ROMEO This gentleman, the Prince's near ally,
My very friend, hath got this mortal hurt
In my behalf—my reputation stained
With Tybalt's slander—Tybalt, that an hour
115   Hath been my cousin. O sweet Juliet,
Thy beauty hath made me effeminate
And in my temper soft'ned valor's steel!

Enter Benvolio.

BENVOLIO O Romeo, Romeo, brave Mercutio is dead!
That gallant spirit hath aspired the clouds,
120   Which too untimely here did scorn the earth.

ROMEO This day's black fate on moe days doth
depend;
This but begins the woe others must end.

[Enter Tybalt.]

BENVOLIO Here comes the furious Tybalt back again.

---

99 **grave** (1) extremely serious (2) ready for the grave   100 **am peppered** have
been given a deathblow   103–04 **by the book of arithmetic** by formal rules
109 **I have it** i.e., I have received my deathblow   111 **ally** relative   112 **very**
true   117 **in … steel** softened the valorous part of my character   119 **aspired**
climbed to   121 **moe** more   121 **depend** hang over

ROMEO Alive in triumph, and Mercutio slain?
 Away to heaven respective lenity,   125
 And fire-eyed fury be my conduct now!
 Now, Tybalt, take the "villain" back again
 That late thou gavest me; for Mercutio's soul
 Is but a little way above our heads,
 Staying for thine to keep him company.   130
 Either thou or I, or both, most go with him.

TYBALT Thou, wretched boy, that didst consort him here,
 Shalt with him hence.

ROMEO   This shall determine that.
         They fight. Tybalt falls.

BENVOLIO Romeo, away, be gone!
 The citizens are up, and Tybalt slain.   135
 Stand not amazed. The Prince will doom thee death
 If thou art taken. Hence, be gone, away!

ROMEO O, I am fortune's fool!

BENVOLIO   Why dost thou stay?
         Exit Romeo.

Enter Citizens.

CITIZEN Which way ran he that killed Mercutio?
 Tybalt, that murderer, which way ran he?   140

BENVOLIO There lies that Tybalt.

CITIZEN   Up, sir, go with me.
 I charge thee in the Prince's name obey.

*Enter Prince, old Montague, Capulet, their Wives,
and all.*

PRINCE Where are the vile beginners of this fray?

BENVOLIO O noble Prince, I can discover all
 The unlucky manage of this fatal brawl.   145

125 **respective** **lenity** discriminating mercifulness 126 **conduct** guide
138 **fool** plaything, dupe 144 **discover** reveal 145 **manage** course

457

> There lies the man, slain by young Romeo,
> That slew thy kinsman, brave Mercutio.

LADY CAPULET Tybalt, my cousin! O my brother's child!
O Prince! O cousin! Husband! O, the blood is spilled
150   Of my dear kinsman! Prince, as thou art true,
For blood of ours shed blood of Montague.
O cousin, cousin!

PRINCE Benvolio, who began this bloody fray?

BENVOLIO Tybalt, here slain, whom Romeo's hand did
    slay.
155   Romeo, that spoke him fair, bid him bethink
How nice the quarrel was, and urged withal
Your high displeasure. All this—utterèd
With gentle breath, calm look, knees humbly
    bowed—
Could not take truce with the unruly spleen
160   Of Tybalt deaf to peace, but that he tilts
With piercing steel at bold Mercutio's breast;
Who, all as hot, turns deadly point to point,
And, with a martial scorn, with one hand beats
Cold death aside and with the other sends
165   It back to Tybalt, whose dexterity
Retorts it. Romeo he cries aloud,
"Hold, friends! Friends, part!" and swifter than his
    tongue,
His agile arm beats down their fatal points,
And 'twixt them rushes; underneath whose arm
170   An envious thrust from Tybalt hit the life
Of stout Mercutio, and then Tybalt fled;
But by and by come back to Romeo,
Who had but newly entertained revenge,
And to't they go like lightning; for, ere I
175   Could draw to part them, was stout Tybalt slain;
And, as he fell, did Romeo turn and fly.
This is the truth, or let Benvolio die.

---

156 **nice** trivial   156 **urged** mentioned   159 **spleen** ill nature   160 **tilts** thrusts
170 **envious** full of enmity   173 **entertained** contemplated

LADY CAPULET He is a kinsman to the Montague;
  Affection makes him false, he speaks not true.
  Some twenty of them fought in this black strife,   180
  And all those twenty could but kill one life.
  I beg for justice, which thou, Prince, must give.
  Romeo slew Tybalt; Romeo must not live.

PRINCE Romeo slew him; he slew Mercutio.
  Who now the price of his dear blood doth owe?   185

CAPULET Not Romeo, Prince; he was Mercutio's friend;
  His fault concludes but what the law should end,
  The life of Tybalt.

PRINCE   And for that offense
  Immediately we do exile him hence.
  I have an interest in your hate's proceeding,   190
  My blood for your rude brawls doth lie a-bleeding;
  But I'll amerce you with so strong a fine
  That you shall all repent the loss of mine.
  I will be deaf to pleading and excuses;
  Nor tears nor prayers shall purchase out abuses.   195
  Therefore use none. Let Romeo hence in haste,
  Else, when he is found, that hour is his last.
  Bear hence this body and attend our will.
  Mercy but murders, pardoning those that kill.
                       Exit [*with others*].

[Scene II. *Capulet's orchard.*]

Enter Juliet alone.

JULIET Gallop apace, you fiery-footed steeds,
  Towards Phoebus' lodging! Such a wagoner

191 **My blood** (Mercutio was the Prince's relative) 192 **amerce** punish by
fine 198 **attend our will** respect my decision III.ii.1 **fiery-footed steeds**
horses of the sun god, Phoebus 2 **Towards Phoebus' lodging** i.e., beneath the
horizon

As Phaëton would whip you to the west
And bring in cloudy night immediately.
5   Spread thy close curtain, love-performing night,
That runaways' eyes may wink, and Romeo
Leap to these arms untalked of and unseen.
Lovers can see to do their amorous rites,
And by their own beauties; or, if love be blind,
10   It best agrees with night. Come, civil night,
Thou sober-suited matron all in black,
And learn me how to lose a winning match,
Played for a pair of stainless maidenhoods.
Hood my unmanned blood, bating in my cheeks,
15   With thy black mantle till strange love grow bold,
Think true love acted simple modesty.
Come, night; come, Romeo; come, thou day in
        night;
For thou wilt lie upon the wings of night
Whiter than new snow upon a raven's back.
Come, gentle night; come, loving, black-browed
20   night;
Give me my Romeo; and, when I shall die,
Take him and cut him out in little stars,
And he will make the face of heaven so fine
That all the world will be in love with night
25   And pay no worship to the garish sun.
O, I have bought the mansion of a love,
But not possessed it; and though I am sold,
Not yet enjoyed. So tedious is this day
As is the night before some festival
30   To an impatient child that hath new robes
And may not wear them. O, here comes my nurse,

Enter Nurse, with cords.

And she brings news; and every tongue that speaks
But Romeo's name speaks heavenly eloquence.

---

3 **Phaëton** Phoebus' son, who mismanaged the horses and let them run away
6 **runaways'** of the horses (?)   6 **wink** shut   14 **Hood** i.e., cover with a hood, as
in falconry   14 **unmanned** (1) untamed (2) unmated   14 **bating** fluttering
15 **strange** unfamiliar

Now, nurse, what news? What hast thou there, the
  cords
That Romeo bid thee fetch?

NURSE   Ay, ay, the cords.   35

JULIET Ay me! What news? Why dost thou wring thy
  hands?

NURSE Ah, weraday! He's dead, he's dead, he's dead!
We are undone, lady, we are undone!
Alack the day! He's gone, he's killed, he's dead!

JULIET Can heaven be so envious?

NURSE   Romeo can,   40
Though heaven cannot. O Romeo, Romeo!
Who ever would have thought it? Romeo!

JULIET What devil art thou that dost torment me thus?
This torture should be roared in dismal hell.
Hath Romeo slain himself? Say thou but "Ay,"   45
And that bare vowel "I" shall poison more
Than the death-darting eye of cockatrice.
I am not I, if there be such an "Ay,"
Or those eyes' shot that makes thee answer "Ay."
If he be slain, say "Ay"; or if not, "No."   50
Brief sounds determine of my weal or woe.

NURSE I saw the wound, I saw it with mine eyes,
(God save the mark!) here on his manly breast.
A piteous corse, a bloody piteous corse;
Pale, pale as ashes, all bedaubed in blood,   55
All in gore-blood. I sounded at the sight.

JULIET O, break, my heart! Poor bankrout, break at
  once!
To prison, eyes; ne'er look on liberty!

---

37 **weraday** wellaway, alas 47 **cockatrice** basilisk (a serpent fabled to have a
killing glance) 48 **Ay** (1) I (2) eye 49 **eyes' shot** i.e., the Nurse's glance
53 **God save the mark** God avert the bad omen 54 **corse** corpse 56 **sounded**
swooned 57 **bankrout** bankrupt

Vile earth, to earth resign; end motion here,
60 And thou and Romeo press one heavy bier!

NURSE O Tybalt, Tybalt, the best friend I had!
O courteous Tybalt! Honest gentleman!
That ever I should live to see thee dead!

JULIET What storm is this that blows so contrary?
65 Is Romeo slaught'red, and is Tybalt dead?
My dearest cousin, and my dearer lord?
Then, dreadful trumpet, sound the general doom!
For who is living, if those two are gone?

NURSE Tybalt is gone, and Romeo banishèd;
70 Romeo that killed him, he is banishèd.

JULIET O God! Did Romeo's hand shed Tybalt's
blood?

NURSE It did, it did! Alas the day, it did!

JULIET O serpent heart, hid with a flow'ring face!
Did ever dragon keep so fair a cave?
75 Beautiful tyrant! Fiend angelical!
Dove-feathered raven! Wolvish-ravening lamb!
Despisèd substance of divinest show!
Just opposite to what thou justly seem'st—
A damnèd saint, an honorable villain!
80 O nature, what hadst thou to do in hell
When thou didst bower the spirit of a fiend
In mortal paradise of such sweet flesh?
Was ever book containing such vile matter
So fairly bound? O, that deceit should dwell
In such a gorgeous palace!

85 NURSE   There's no trust,
No faith, no honesty in men; all perjured,
All forsworn, all naught, all dissemblers.
Ah, where's my man? Give me some *aqua vitae*.
These griefs, these woes, these sorrows make me
old.

59 **vile earth** referring to her own body   59 **resign** return   67 **dreadful ...
doom** i.e., sound the trumpet of Doomsday   88 **aqua vitae** spirits

Shame come to Romeo!

JULIET   Blistered be thy tongue   90
For such a wish! He was not born to shame.
Upon his brow shame is ashamed to sit;
For 'tis a throne where honor may be crowned
Sole monarch of the universal earth.
O, what a beast was I to chide at him!   95

NURSE Will you speak well of him that killed your
   cousin?

JULIET Shall I speak ill of him that is my husband?
Ah, poor my lord, what tongue shall smooth thy
   name
When I, thy three-hours wife, have mangled it?
But wherefore, villain, didst thou kill my cousin?   100
That villain cousin would have killed my husband.
Back, foolish tears, back to your native spring!
Your tributary drops belong to woe,
Which you, mistaking, offer up to joy.
My husband lives, that Tybalt would have slain;   105
And Tybalt's dead, that would have slain my
   husband.
All this is comfort; wherefore weep I then?
Some word there was, worser than Tybalt's death,
That murd'red me. I would forget it fain;
But O, it presses to my memory   110
Like damnèd guilty deeds to sinners' minds!
"Tybalt is dead, and Romeo—banishèd."
That "banishèd," that one word "banishèd,"
Hath slain ten thousand Tybalts. Tybalt's death
Was woe enough, if it had ended there;   115
Or, if sour woe delights in fellowship
And needly will be ranked with other griefs,
Why followed not, when she said "Tybalt's dead,"
Thy father, or thy mother, nay, or both,
Which modern lamentation might have moved?   120

103 **tributary** contributed   117 **needly ... with** must be accompanied by
120 **modern** ordinary

But with a rearward following Tybalt's death,
"Romeo is banishèd"—to speak that word
Is father, mother, Tybalt, Romeo, Juliet,
All slain, all dead. "Romeo is banishèd"—
125 There is no end, no limit, measure, bound,
In that word's death; no words can that woe sound.
Where is my father and my mother, nurse?

NURSE Weeping and wailing over Tybalt's corse.
Will you go to them? I will bring you thither.

JULIET Wash they his wounds with tears? Mine shall be
130   spent,
When theirs are dry, for Romeo's banishment.
Take up those cords. Poor ropes, you are beguiled,
Both you and I, for Romeo is exiled.
He made you for a highway to my bed;
135 But I, a maid, die maiden-widowèd.
Come, cords; come, nurse. I'll to my wedding bed;
And death, not Romeo, take my maidenhead!

NURSE Hie to your chamber. I'll find Romeo
To comfort you. I wot well where he is.
140 Hark ye, your Romeo will be here at night.
I'll to him; he is hid at Lawrence' cell.

JULIET O, find him! Give this ring to my true knight
And bid him come to take his last farewell.
                                   Exit [*with Nurse*].

[Scene III. *Friar Lawrence's cell*.]

Enter Friar [*Lawrence*].

FRIAR Romeo, come forth; come forth, thou fearful
    man.
Affliction is enamored of thy parts,
And thou art wedded to calamity.

---

121 **rearward** rear guard 139 **wot** know III.iii.1 **fearful** frightened
2 **Affliction ... parts** affliction is in love with your attractive qualities

[Enter Romeo.]

ROMEO Father, what news? What is the Prince's doom?
What sorrow craves acquaintance at my hand
That I yet know not? 5

FRIAR Too familiar
Is my dear son with such sour company.
I bring thee tidings of the Prince's doom.

ROMEO What less than doomsday is the Prince's
doom?

FRIAR A gentler judgment vanished from his lips— 10
Not body's death, but body's banishment.

ROMEO Ha, banishment? Be merciful, say "death";
For exile hath more terror in his look,
Much more than death. Do not say "banishment."

FRIAR Here from Verona art thou banishèd. 15
Be patient, for the world is broad and wide.

ROMEO There is no world without Verona walls,
But purgatory, torture, hell itself.
Hence banishèd is banished from the world,
And world's exile is death. Then "banishèd"
Is death mistermed. Calling death "banishèd," 20
Thou cut'st my head off with a golden ax
And smilest upon the stroke that murders me.

FRIAR O deadly sin! O rude unthankfulness!
Thy fault our law calls death; but the kind Prince, 25
Taking thy part, hath rushed aside the law,
And turned that black word "death" to
"banishment."
This is dear mercy, and thou seest it not.

ROMEO 'Tis torture, and not mercy. Heaven is here,
Where Juliet lives; and every cat and dog 30
And little mouse, every unworthy thing,
Live here in heaven and may look on her;
But Romeo may not. More validity,

4 **doom** final decision   9 **doomsday** i.e., my death   10 **vanished** escaped
26 **rushed** pushed   33 **validity** value

More honorable state, more courtship lives
35 In carrion flies than Romeo. They may seize
On the white wonder of dear Juliet's hand
And steal immortal blessing from her lips,
Who, even in pure and vestal modesty,
Still blush, as thinking their own kisses sin;
40 But Romeo may not, he is banishèd.
Flies may do this but I from this must fly;
They are freemen, but I am banishèd.
And sayest thou yet that exile is not death?
Hadst thou no poison mixed, no sharp-ground
      knife,
45 No sudden mean of death, thou ne'er so mean,
But "banishèd" to kill me—"banishèd"?
O friar, the damnèd use that word in hell;
Howling attends it! How hast thou the heart,
Being a divine, a ghostly confessor,
A sin-absolver, and my friend professed,
50 To mangle me with that word "banishèd"?

FRIAR Thou fond mad man, hear me a little speak.

ROMEO O, thou wilt speak again of banishment.

FRIAR I'll give thee armor to keep off that word;
55 Adversity's sweet milk, philosophy,
To comfort thee, though thou art banishèd.

ROMEO Yet "banishèd"? Hang up philosophy!
Unless philosophy can make a Juliet,
Displant a town, reverse a prince's doom,
60 It helps not, it prevails not. Talk no more.

FRIAR O, then I see that madmen have no ears.

ROMEO How should they, when that wise men have
      no eyes?

FRIAR Let me dispute with thee of thy estate.

---

34 **courtship** opportunity for courting   38 **vestal** virgin   39 **their own kisses
sin** i.e., sin when they touch each other   45 **mean ... mean** method ... lowly
52 **fond** foolish   57 **Yet** still   63 **dispute** discuss   63 **estate** situation

ROMEO Thou canst not speak of that thou dost not feel.
  Wert thou as young as I, Juliet thy love,   65
  An hour but married, Tybalt murderèd,
  Doting like me, and like me banishèd,
  Then mightst thou speak, then mightst thou tear thy
    hair,
  And fall upon the ground, as I do now,
  Taking the measure of an unmade grave.   70
                      Enter Nurse and knock.

FRIAR Arise, one knocks. Good Romeo, hide thyself.

ROMEO Not I; unless the breath of heartsick groans
  Mistlike infold me from the search of eyes. [*Knock.*]

FRIAR Hark, how they knock! Who's there? Romeo,
  arise;
  Thou wilt be taken.—Stay awhile!—Stand up;   75
                          [*Knock.*]
  Run to my study.—By and by!—God's will,
  What simpleness is this.—I come, I come!   *Knock.*
  Who knocks so hard? Whence come you? What's
  your will?

                    Enter Nurse.

NURSE Let me come in, and you shall know my errand.
  I come from Lady Juliet.

FRIAR   Welcome then.   80

NURSE O holy friar, O, tell me, holy friar,
  Where is my lady's lord, where's Romeo?

FRIAR There on the ground, with his own tears made
  drunk.

NURSE O, he is even in my mistress' case,

---

70 **Taking the measure** i.e., measuring by my outstretched body   76 **By and by** in a moment (said to the person knocking)   77 **simpleness** silly behavior (Romeo refuses to rise)   84 **case** (with bawdy innuendo complementing "stand," "rise," etc. But the Nurse is unaware of this possible interpretation)

85   Just in her case! O woeful sympathy!
        Piteous predicament! Even so lies she,
        Blubb'ring and weeping, weeping and blubb'ring.
        Stand up, stand up! Stand, and you be a man.
        For Juliet's sake, for her sake, rise and stand!
90   Why should you fall into so deep an O?

ROMEO [*Rises.*] Nurse—

NURSE Ah sir, ah sir! Death's the end of all.

ROMEO Spakest thou of Juliet? How is it with her?
        Doth not she think me an old murderer,
95   Now I have stained the childhood of our joy
        With blood removed but little from her own?
        Where is she? And how doth she! And what says
        My concealed lady to our canceled love?

NURSE O, she says nothing, sir, but weeps and weeps;
100   And now falls on her bed, and then starts up,
        And Tybalt calls; and then on Romeo cries,
        And then down falls again.

ROMEO   As if that name,
        Shot from the deadly level of a gun,
        Did murder her; as that name's cursèd hand
105   Murdered her kinsman. O, tell me, friar, tell me,
        In what vile part of this anatomy
        Doth my name lodge? Tell me, that I may sack
        The hateful mansion.
                        [*He offers to stab himself, and Nurse
                        snatches the dagger away.*]

FRIAR   Hold thy desperate hand.
        Art thou a man? Thy form cries out thou art;
110   Thy tears are womanish, thy wild acts denote
        The unreasonable fury of a beast.
        Unseemly woman in a seeming man!

---

90 **so deep an O** such a fit of moaning   98 **canceled** invalidated   103 **level** aim
107 **sack** plunder   111 **unreasonable** irrational   112 **Unseemly** indecorous

And ill-beseeming beast in seeming both!
Thou hast amazed me. By my holy order,
I thought thy disposition better tempered.   115
Hast thou slain Tybalt? Wilt thou slay thyself?
And slay thy lady that in thy life lives,
By doing damnèd hate upon thyself?
Why railest thou on thy birth, the heaven, and
    earth?
Since birth and heaven and earth, all three do meet   120
In thee at once; which thou at once wouldst lose.
Fie, fie, thou shamest thy shape, thy love, thy wit,
Which, like a usurer, abound'st in all,
And usest none in that true use indeed
Which should bedeck thy shape, thy love, thy wit.   125
Thy noble shape is but a form of wax,
Digressing from the valor of a man;
Thy dear love sworn but hollow perjury,
Killing that love which thou hast vowed to cherish;
Thy wit, that ornament to shape and love,   130
Misshapen in the conduct of them both,
Like powder in a skilless soldier's flask,
Is set afire by thine own ignorance,
And thou dismemb'red with thine own defense.
What, rouse thee, man! Thy Juliet is alive,   135
For whose dear sake thou wast but lately dead.
There art thou happy. Tybalt would kill thee,
But thou slewest Tybalt. There art thou happy.
The law, that threat'ned death, becomes thy friend
And turns it to exile. There art thou happy.   140
A pack of blessings light upon thy back;
Happiness courts thee in her best array;
But, like a misbehaved and sullen wench,
Thou puts up thy fortune and thy love.

113 ill-beseeming ... both i.e., inappropriate even to a beast in being both man
and woman   120 birth and heaven and earth family origin, soul, and body
121 lose abandon   122 wit intellect   123 Which who   125 bedeck do honor to
127 valor of a man i.e., his manly qualities   131 conduct management
132 flask powder flask   134 dismemb'red ... defense (i.e., your intellect,
properly the defender of shape and love, is set off independently and destroys
all)   136 dead i.e., declaring yourself dead   137 happy fortunate

145 Take heed, take heed, for such die miserable.
Go get thee to thy love, as was decreed,
Ascend her chamber, hence and comfort her.
But look thou stay not till the watch be set,
For then thou canst not pass to Mantua,
150 Where thou shalt live till we can find a time
To blaze your marriage, reconcile your friends,
Beg pardon of the Prince, and call thee back
With twenty hundred thousand times more joy
Than thou went'st forth in lamentation.
155 Go before, nurse. Commend me to thy lady,
And bid her hasten all the house to bed,
Which heavy sorrow makes them apt unto.
Romeo is coming.

NURSE O Lord, I could have stayed here all the night
160 To hear good counsel. O, what learning is!
My lord, I'll tell my lady you will come.

ROMEO Do so, and bid my sweet prepare to chide.
                    [*Nurse offers to go in and turns again.*]

NURSE Here, sir, a ring she bid me give you, sir.
Hie you, make haste, for it grows very late.   [*Exit.*]

165 ROMEO How well my comfort is revived by this!

FRIAR Go hence; good night; and here stands all your
          state:
Either be gone before the watch be set,
Or by the break of day disguised from hence.
Sojourn in Mantua. I'll find out your man,
170 And he shall signify from time to time
Every good hap to you that chances here.
Give me thy hand. 'Tis late. Farewell; good night.

ROMEO But that a joy past joy calls out on me,
It were a grief so brief to part with thee.
175 Farewell.   *Exeunt.*

151 **blaze** announce publicly   166 **here ... state** this is your situation

[Scene IV. *A room in Capulet's house.*]

Enter old Capulet, his Wife, and Paris.

CAPULET Things have fall'n out, sir, so unluckily
That we have had no time to move our daughter.
Look you, she loved her kinsman Tybalt dearly,
And so did I. Well, we were born to die.
'Tis very late; she'll not come down tonight.   5
I promise you, but for your company,
I would have been abed an hour ago.

PARIS These times of woe afford no times to woo.
Madam, good night. Commend me to your daughter.

LADY I will, and know her mind early tomorrow;   10
Tonight she's mewed up to her heaviness.

CAPULET Sir Paris, I will make a desperate tender
Of my child's love. I think she will be ruled
In all respects by me; nay more, I doubt it not.
Wife, go you to her ere you go to bed;   15
Acquaint her here of my son Paris' love
And bid her (mark you me?) on Wednesday next—
But soft! What day is this?

PARIS   Monday, my lord.

CAPULET Monday! Ha, ha! Well, Wednesday is too
    soon.
A Thursday let it be—a Thursday, tell her,   20
She shall be married to this noble earl.
Will you be ready? Do you like this haste?
We'll keep no great ado—a friend or two;
For hark you, Tybalt being slain so late,

III.iv.2 **move** discuss the matter with 6 **promise** assure 11 **mewed** ...
heaviness shut up with her grief 12 **make** ... **tender** risk an offer 20 **A** on

471

25   It may be thought we held him carelessly,
        Being our kinsman, if we revel much.
        Therefore we'll have some half a dozen friends,
        And there an end. But what say you to Thursday?

    PARIS My lord, I would that Thursday were tomorrow.

30 CAPULET Well, get you gone. A Thursday be it then.
        Go you to Juliet ere you go to bed;
        Prepare her, wife, against this wedding day.
        Farewell, my lord.—Light to my chamber, ho!
        Afore me, it is so very late
35   That we may call it early by and by.
        Good night.   *Exeunt.*

                [Scene V. *Capulet's orchard.*]

                Enter Romeo and Juliet aloft.

    JULIET Wilt thou be gone? It is not yet near day.
        It was the nightingale, and not the lark,
        That pierced the fearful hollow of thine ear.
        Nightly she sings on yond pomegranate tree.
5   Believe me, love, it was the nightingale.

    ROMEO It was the lark, the herald of the morn;
        No nightingale. Look, love, what envious streaks
        Do lace the severing clouds in yonder East.
        Night's candles are burnt out, and jocund day
10   Stands tiptoe on the misty mountaintops.
        I must be gone and live, or stay and die.

    JULIET Yond light is not daylight; I know it, I.
        It is some meteor that the sun exhales
        To be to thee this night a torchbearer
15   And light thee on thy way to Mantua.

---

32 **against** in preparation for   34 **Afore me** indeed (a light oath)   35 **by and by**
soon   III.v.3 **fearful** fearing   13 **exhales** gives out

Therefore stay yet; thou need'st not to be gone.

ROMEO Let me be ta'en, let me be put to death.
I am content, so thou wilt have it so.
I'll say yon gray is not the morning's eye,
'Tis but the pale reflex of Cynthia's brow;   20
Nor that is not the lark whose notes do beat
The vaulty heaven so high above our heads.
I have more care to stay than will to go.
Come, death, and welcome! Juliet wills it so.
How is't, my soul? Let's talk; it is not day.   25

JULIET It is, it is! Hie hence, be gone, away!
It is the lark that sings so out of tune,
Straining harsh discords and unpleasing sharps.
Some say the lark makes sweet division;
This doth not so, for she divideth us.   30
Some say the lark and loathèd toad change eyes;
O, now I would they had changed voices too,
Since arm from arm that voice doth us affray,
Hunting thee hence with hunt's-up to the day.
O, now be gone! More light and light it grows.   35

ROMEO More light and light—more dark and dark
our woes.

Enter Nurse.

NURSE Madam!

JULIET Nurse?

NURSE Your lady mother is coming to your chamber.
The day is broke; be wary, look about.   [*Exit.*]   40

JULIET Then, window, let day in, and let life out.

ROMEO Farewell, farewell! One kiss, and I'll descend.
                                    [*He goeth down.*]

JULIET Art thou gone so, love-lord, ay husband-friend?

20 **reflex of Cynthia's brow** reflection of the edge of the moon   29 **division**
melody (i.e., a division of notes)   33 **affray** frighten   34 **hunt's-up** morning
song (for hunters)   43 **husband-friend** husband-lover

I must hear from thee every day in the hour,
45 For in a minute there are many days.
O, by this count I shall be much in years
Ere I again behold my Romeo!

ROMEO Farewell!
I will omit no opportunity
50 That may convey my greetings, love, to thee.

JULIET O, think'st thou we shall ever meet again?

ROMEO I doubt it not; and all these woes shall serve
For sweet discourses in our times to come.

JULIET O God, I have an ill-divining soul!
55 Methinks I see thee, now thou art so low,
As one dead in the bottom of a tomb.
Either my eyesight fails, or thou lookest pale.

ROMEO And trust me, love, in my eye so do you.
Dry sorrow drinks our blood. Adieu, adieu!   *Exit.*

60 JULIET O Fortune, Fortune! All men call thee fickle.
If thou art fickle, what dost thou with him
That is renowned for faith? Be fickle, Fortune,
For then I hope thou wilt not keep him long
But send him back.

Enter Mother.

65 LADY CAPULET Ho, daughter! Are you up?

JULIET Who is't that calls? It is my lady mother.
Is she not down so late, or up so early?
What unaccustomed cause procures her hither?

LADY CAPULET Why, how now, Juliet?

JULIET   Madam, I am not well.

LADY CAPULET Evermore weeping for your cousin's
70   death?

46 **much in years** much older   54 **ill-divining** foreseeing evil   59 **Dry** thirsty
(as grief was thought to be)   61 **what dost thou** what business have you   67 **not
down so late** so late getting to bed

What, wilt thou wash him from his grave with tears?
And if thou couldst, thou couldst not make him live.
Therefore have done. Some grief shows much of love;
But much of grief shows still some want of wit.

JULIET Yet let me weep for such a feeling loss.   75

LADY CAPULET So shall you feel the loss, but not the
    friend
Which you weep for.

JULIET   Feeling so the loss,
    I cannot choose but ever weep the friend.

LADY CAPULET Well, girl, thou weep'st not so much for
    his death
As that the villain lives which slaughtered him.   80

JULIET What villain, madam?

LADY CAPULET   That same villain Romeo.

JULIET [Aside] Villain and he be many miles asunder.—
    God pardon him! I do, with all my heart;
    And yet no man like he doth grieve my heart.

LADY CAPULET That is because the traitor murderer
    lives.   85

JULIET Ay, madam, from the reach of these my hands.
    Would none but I might venge my cousin's death!

LADY CAPULET We will have vengeance for it, fear
    thou not.
Then weep no more. I'll send to one in Mantua,
Where that same banished runagate doth live,   90
Shall give him such an unaccustomed dram
That he shall soon keep Tybalt company;
And then I hope thou wilt be satisfied.

JULIET Indeed I never shall be satisfied
    With Romeo till I behold him—dead—   95

---

75 **feeling loss** loss to be felt 90 **runagate** renegade 95 **dead** (Lady Capulet
takes this to refer to "him"; Juliet takes it to refer to "heart")

Is my poor heart so for a kinsman vexed.
Madam, if you could find out but a man
To bear a poison, I would temper it;
That Romeo should, upon receipt thereof,
100   Soon sleep in quiet. O, how my heart abhors
To hear him named and cannot come to him,
To wreak the love I bore my cousin
Upon his body that hath slaughtered him!

LADY CAPULET Find thou the means, and I'll find such
        a man.
105   But now I'll tell thee joyful tidings, girl.

JULIET And joy comes well in such a needy time.
What are they, beseech your ladyship?

LADY CAPULET Well, well, thou hast a careful father,
        child;
One who, to put thee from thy heaviness,
110   Hath sorted out a sudden day of joy
That thou expects not nor I looked not for.

JULIET Madam, in happy time! What day is that?

LADY CAPULET Marry, my child, early next Thursday
        morn
The gallant, young, and noble gentleman,
115   The County Paris, at Saint Peter's Church,
Shall happily make thee there a joyful bride.

JULIET Now by Saint Peter's Church, and Peter too,
He shall not make me there a joyful bride!
I wonder at this haste, that I must wed
120   Ere he that should be husband comes to woo.
I pray you tell my lord and father, madam,
I will not marry yet; and when I do, I swear
It shall be Romeo, whom you know I hate,
Rather than Paris. These are news indeed!

98 **temper** (1) mix (2) weaken   102 **wreak** (1) avenge (2) give expression to
108 **careful** solicitous   110 **sorted out** selected   112 **in happy time** most
opportunely

LADY CAPULET Here comes your father. Tell him so
    yourself,   125
    And see how he will take it at your hands.

Enter Capulet and Nurse.

CAPULET When the sun sets the earth doth drizzle dew,
    But for the sunset of my brother's son
    It rains downright.
    How now? A conduit, girl? What, still in tears?   130
    Evermore show'ring? In one little body
    Thou counterfeits a bark, a sea, a wind:
    For still thy eyes, which I may call the sea,
    Do ebb and flow with tears; the bark thy body is,
    Sailing in this salt flood; the winds, thy sighs,   135
    Who, raging with thy tears and they with them,
    Without a sudden calm will overset
    Thy tempest-tossèd body. How now, wife?
    Have you delivered to her our decree?

LADY CAPULET Ay, sir; but she will none, she gives
    you thanks.   140
    I would the fool were married to her grave!

CAPULET Soft! Take me with you, take me with you,
    wife.
    How? Will she none? Doth she not give us thanks?
    Is she not proud? Doth she not count her blest,
    Unworthy as she is, that we have wrought   145
    So worthy a gentleman to be her bride?

JULIET Not proud you have, but thankful that you have.
    Proud can I never be of what I hate,
    But thankful even for hate that is meant love.

CAPULET How, how, how, how, chopped-logic? What
    is this?   150

---

130 **conduit** water pipe   137 **sudden** unanticipated, immediate   140 **she gives you thanks** she'll have none of it, thank you   142 **Soft ... you** Wait! Help me to understand you   145 **wrought** arranged   147 **proud** highly pleased 150 **chopped-logic** chop logic, sophistry

"Proud"—and "I thank you"—and "I thank you
    not"—
And yet "not proud"? Mistress minion you,
Thank me no thankings, nor proud me no prouds,
But fettle your fine joints 'gainst Thursday next
155 To go with Paris to Saint Peter's Church,
Or I will drag thee on a hurdle thither.
Out, you greensickness carrion! Out, you baggage!
You tallow-face!

LADY CAPULET   Fie, fie! What, are you mad?

JULIET Good father, I beseech you on my knees,
160   Hear me with patience but to speak a word.

CAPULET Hang thee, young baggage! Disobedient
    wretch!
I tell thee what—get thee to church a Thursday
Or never after look me in the face.
Speak not, reply not, do not answer me!
165 My fingers itch. Wife, we scarce thought us blest
That God had lent us but this only child;
But now I see this one is one too much,
And that we have a curse in having her.
Out on her, hilding!

NURSE   God in heaven bless her!
170   You are to blame, my lord, to rate her so.

CAPULET And why, my Lady Wisdom? Hold your
    tongue,
Good Prudence. Smatter with your gossips, go!

NURSE I speak no treason.

CAPULET   O, God-i-god-en!

NURSE May not one speak?

---

152 **minion** minx   154 **fettle** make ready   156 **hurdle** sledge on which traitors
were taken to execution   157 **greensickness** anemic, after the fashion of young
girls   157 **baggage** strumpet   169 **hilding** worthless person   70 **rate** scold
172 **Smatter with your gossips** save your chatter for your cronies   173 **God-i-**
god-en God give you good even (here equivalent to "Get on with you!")

CAPULET   Peace, you mumbling fool!
  Utter your gravity o'er a gossip's bowl,   175
  For here we need it not.

LADY CAPULET   You are too hot.

CAPULET God's bread! It makes me mad.
  Day, night; hour, tide, time; work, play;
  Alone, in company; still my care hath been
  To have her matched; and having now provided   180
  A gentleman of noble parentage,
  Of fair demesnes, youthful, and nobly trained,
  Stuffed, as they say, with honorable parts,
  Proportioned as one's thought would wish a man—
  And then to have a wretched puling fool,   185
  A whining mammet, in her fortune's tender,
  To answer "I'll not wed, I cannot love;
  I am too young, I pray you pardon me"!
  But, and you will not wed, I'll pardon you!
  Graze where you will, you shall not house with me.   190
  Look to't, think on't; I do not use to jest.
  Thursday is near; lay hand on heart, advise:
  And you be mine, I'll give you to my friend;
  And you be not, hang, beg, starve, die in the streets,
  For, by my soul, I'll ne'er acknowledge thee,   195
  Nor what is mine shall never do thee good.
  Trust to't. Bethink you. I'll not be forsworn.   *Exit.*

JULIET Is there no pity sitting in the clouds
  That sees into the bottom of my grief?
  O sweet my mother, cast me not away!   200
  Delay this marriage for a month, a week;
  Or if you do not, make the bridal bed
  In that dim monument where Tybalt lies.

---

177 **God's bread** by the sacred host   182 **demesnes** domains   185 **puling** whining   186 **mammet** puppet   186 **in her fortune's tender** (1) on good fortune's offer (2) subject to fortuitous circumstance (?)   189 **I'll pardon you** i.e., in a way you don't expect   191 **do not use to jest** am not in the habit of joking   192 **advise** consider

LADY CAPULET Talk not to me, for I'll not speak a word.
205   Do as thou wilt, for I have done with thee.   *Exit.*

JULIET O God!—O nurse, how shall this be prevented?
         My husband is on earth, my faith in heaven.
         How shall that faith return again to earth
         Unless that husband send it me from heaven
210   By leaving earth? Comfort me, counsel me.
         Alack, alack, that heaven should practice stratagems
         Upon so soft a subject as myself!
         What say'st thou? Hast thou not a word of joy?
         Some comfort, nurse.

NURSE   Faith, here it is.
215   Romeo is banished; and all the world to nothing
         That he dares ne'er come back to challenge you;
         Or if he do, it needs must be by stealth.
         Then, since the case so stands as now it doth,
         I think it best you married with the County.
220   O, he's a lovely gentleman!
         Romeo's a dishclout to him. An eagle, madam,
         Hath not so green, so quick, so fair an eye
         As Paris hath. Beshrew my very heart,
         I think you are happy in this second match,
225   For it excels your first; or if it did not,
         Your first is dead—or 'twere as good he were
         As living here and you no use of him.

JULIET Speak'st thou from thy heart?

NURSE And from my soul too; else beshrew them both.

230 JULIET Amen!

NURSE What?

JULIET Well, thou hast comforted me marvelous much.
         Go in; and tell my lady I am gone,

---

207 **my faith in heaven** my vow is recorded in heaven   210 **By leaving earth**
i.e., by dying   215 **all the world to nothing** (the Nurse advises a safe bet)
221 **dishclout** dishcloth   223 **Beshrew** curse (used in light oaths)

Having displeased my father, to Lawrence' cell,
To make confession and to be absolved.   235

NURSE Marry, I will; and this is wisely done.   [*Exit.*]

JULIET Ancient damnation! O most wicked fiend!
Is it more sin to wish me thus forsworn,
Or to dispraise my lord with that same tongue
Which she hath praised him with above compare   240
So many thousand times? Go, counselor!
Thou and my bosom henceforth shall be twain.
I'll to the friar to know his remedy.
If all else fail, myself have power to die.   *Exit.*

---

237 **Ancient damnation** (1) damned old woman (2) ancient devil (note the term
"wicked fiend" immediately following)   238 **forsworn** guilty of breaking a vow
242 **Thou ... twain** i.e., you shall henceforth be separated from my trust

[ACT IV

Scene I. *Friar Lawrence's cell.*]

Enter Friar [Lawrence] and County Paris.

FRIAR On Thursday, sir? The time is very short.

PARIS My father Capulet will have it so,
And I am nothing slow to slack his haste.

FRIAR You say you do not know the lady's mind.
5   Uneven is the course; I like it not.

PARIS Immoderately she weeps for Tybalt's death,
And therefore have I little talked of love;
For Venus smiles not in a house of tears.
Now, sir, her father counts it dangerous
10   That she do give her sorrow so much sway,
And in his wisdom hastes our marriage
To stop the inundation of her tears,
Which, too much minded by herself alone,
May be put from her by society.
15   Now do you know the reason of this haste.

FRIAR [*Aside*] I would I knew not why it should be
          slowed.—
Look, sir, here comes the lady toward my cell.

IV.i.3 **I . . . haste** i.e., I shall not check his haste by being slow myself   5 **Uneven**
irregular   13 **minded** thought about   13 **by herself alone** when she is alone

482

Enter Juliet.

PARIS Happily met, my lady and my wife!

JULIET That may be, sir, when I may be a wife.

PARIS That "may be" must be, love, on Thursday next.   20

JULIET What must be shall be.

FRIAR   That's a certain text.

PARIS Come you to make confession to this father?

JULIET To answer that, I should confess to you.

PARIS Do not deny to him that you love me.

JULIET I will confess to you that I love him.   25

PARIS So will ye, I am sure, that you love me.

JULIET If I do so, it will be of more price,
Being spoke behind your back, than to your face.

PARIS Poor soul, thy face is much abused with tears.

JULIET The tears have got small victory by that,   30
For it was bad enough before their spite.

PARIS Thou wrong'st it more than tears with that
report.

JULIET That is no slander, sir, which is a truth;
And what I spake, I spake it to my face.

PARIS Thy face is mine, and thou hast sland'red it.   35

JULIET It may be so, for it is not mine own.
Are you at leisure, holy father, now,
Or shall I come to you at evening mass?

FRIAR My leisure serves me, pensive daughter, now.
My lord, we must entreat the time alone.   40

---

31 **before their spite** before they marred it 38 **evening mass** (evening mass was still said occasionally in Shakespeare's time) 40 **entreat the time alone** ask to have this time to ourselves

PARIS God shield I should disturb devotion!
    Juliet, on Thursday early will I rouse ye.
    Till then, adieu, and keep this holy kiss.   *Exit*.

JULIET O, shut the door, and when thou hast done so,
45   Come weep with me—past hope, past care, past help!

FRIAR O Juliet, I already know thy grief;
    It strains me past the compass of my wits.
    I hear thou must, and nothing may prorogue it,
    On Thursday next be married to this County.

50 JULIET Tell me not, friar, that thou hearest of this,
    Unless thou tell me how I may prevent it.
    If in thy wisdom thou canst give no help,
    Do thou but call my resolution wise
    And with this knife I'll help it presently.
55   God joined my heart and Romeo's, thou our hands;
    And ere this hand, by thee to Romeo's sealed,
    Shall be the label to another deed,
    Or my true heart with treacherous revolt
    Turn to another, this shall slay them both.
60   Therefore, out of thy long-experienced time,
    Give me some present counsel; or, behold,
    'Twixt my extremes and me this bloody knife
    Shall play the umpire, arbitrating that
    Which the commission of thy years and art
65   Could to no issue of true honor bring.
    Be not so long to speak. I long to die
    If what thou speak'st speak not of remedy.

FRIAR Hold, daughter. I do spy a kind of hope,
    Which craves as desperate an execution
70   As that is desperate which we would prevent.
    If, rather than to marry County Paris,
    Thou hast the strength of will to slay thyself,
    Then is it likely thou wilt undertake

41 **God shield** God forbid   48 **prorogue** delay   54 **presently** at once
57 **label** bearer of the seal   57 **deed** (1) act (2) legal document   64 **commission**
authority

A thing like death to chide away this shame,
That cop'st with death himself to scape from it;   75
And, if thou darest, I'll give thee remedy.

JULIET O, bid me leap, rather than marry Paris,
From off the battlements of any tower,
Or walk in thievish ways, or bid me lurk
Where serpents are; chain me with roaring bears,   80
Or hide me nightly in a charnel house,
O'ercovered quite with dead men's rattling bones,
With reeky shanks and yellow chapless skulls;
Or bid me go into a new-made grave
And hide me with a dead man in his shroud—   85
Things that, to hear them told, have made me
    tremble—
And I will do it without fear or doubt,
To live an unstained wife to my sweet love.

FRIAR Hold, then. Go home, be merry, give consent
To marry Paris. Wednesday is tomorrow.   90
Tomorrow night look that thou lie alone;
Let not the nurse lie with thee in thy chamber.
Take thou this vial, being then in bed,
And this distilling liquor drink thou off;
When presently through all thy veins shall run   95
A cold and drowsy humor; for no pulse
Shall keep his native progress, but surcease;
No warmth, no breath, shall testify thou livest;
The roses in thy lips and cheeks shall fade
To wanny ashes, thy eyes' windows fall   100
Like death when he shuts up the day of life;
Each part, deprived of supple government,
Shall, stiff and stark and cold, appear like death;
And in this borrowed likeness of shrunk death
Thou shalt continue two-and-forty hours,   105
And then awake as from a pleasant sleep.

---

75 **cop'st** negotiates   79 **thievish** infested with thieves   81 **charnel house** vault
for old bones   83 **reeky** damp   83 **chapless** jawless   94 **distilling** infusing
96 **humor** fluid   97 **native** natural   97 **surcease** stop   100 **wanny** pale
100 **windows** lids   102 **supple government** i.e., faculty for maintaining motion

Now, when the bridegroom in the morning comes
To rouse thee from thy bed, there art thou dead.
Then, as the manner of our country is,
110 In thy best robes uncovered on the bier
Thou shalt be borne to that same ancient vault
Where all the kindred of the Capulets lie.
In the meantime, against thou shalt awake,
Shall Romeo by my letters know our drift;
115 And hither shall he come; and he and I
Will watch thy waking, and that very night
Shall Romeo bear thee hence to Mantua.
And this shall free thee from this present shame,
If no inconstant toy nor womanish fear
120 Abate thy valor in the acting it.

JULIET Give me, give me! O, tell not me of fear!

FRIAR Hold! Get you gone, be strong and prosperous
In this resolve. I'll send a friar with speed
To Mantua, with my letters to thy lord.

JULIET Love give me strength, and strength shall help
125   afford.
Farewell, dear father.   *Exit [with Friar]*.

[Scene II. *Hall in Capulet's house*.]

*Enter Father Capulet, Mother, Nurse, and
Servingmen, two or three.*

CAPULET So many guests invite as here are writ.
                              [*Exit a Servingman*.]
Sirrah, go hire me twenty cunning cooks.

SERVINGMAN You shall have none ill, sir; for I'll try
if they can lick their fingers.

_____

113 **against** before 114 **drift** purpose 119 **inconstant toy** whim
IV.ii.2 **cunning** skillful   3 **try** test

CAPULET How canst thou try them so?   5

SERVINGMAN Marry, sir, 'tis an ill cook that cannot
  lick his own fingers. Therefore he that cannot lick
  his fingers goes not with me.

CAPULET Go, begone.   [*Exit Servingman.*]
  We shall be much unfurnished for this time.   10
  What, is my daughter gone to Friar Lawrence?

NURSE Ay, forsooth.

CAPULET Well, he may chance to do some good on her.
  A peevish self-willed harlotry it is.

Enter Juliet.

NURSE See where she comes from shrift with merry
  look.   15

CAPULET How now, my headstrong? Where have you
  been gadding?

JULIET Where I have learnt me to repent the sin
  Of disobedient opposition
  To you and your behests, and am enjoined
  By holy Lawrence to fall prostrate here   20
  To beg your pardon. Pardon, I beseech you!
  Henceforward I am ever ruled by you.

CAPULET Send for the County. Go tell him of this.
  I'll have this knot knit up tomorrow morning.

JULIET I met the youthful lord at Lawrence' cell   25
  And gave him what becomèd love I might,
  Not stepping o'er the bounds of modesty.

CAPULET Why, I am glad on't. This is well. Stand up.
  This is as't should be. Let me see the County.
  Ay, marry, go, I say, and fetch him hither.   30
  Now, afore God, this reverend holy friar,
  All our whole city is much bound to him.

6–7 **cannot lick his own fingers** i.e., cannot taste his own cooking   10 **unfurnished** unprovisioned   14 **A peevish self-willed harlotry it is** she's a silly
good-for-nothing   26 **becomèd** proper

JULIET Nurse, will you go with me into my closet
To help me sort such needful ornaments
35 As you think fit to furnish me tomorrow?

LADY CAPULET No, not till Thursday. There is time
enough.

CAPULET Go, nurse, go with her. We'll to church
tomorrow.   *Exeunt [Juliet and Nurse].*

LADY CAPULET We shall be short in our provision.
'Tis now near night.

CAPULET   Tush, I will stir about,
40 And all things shall be well, I warrant thee, wife.
Go thou to Juliet, help to deck up her.
I'll not to bed tonight; let me alone.
I'll play the housewife for this once. What, ho!
They are all forth; well, I will walk myself
45 To County Paris, to prepare up him
Against tomorrow. My heart is wondrous light,
Since this same wayward girl is so reclaimed.
                              Exit [with Mother].

[Scene III. *Juliet's chamber.*]

Enter Juliet and Nurse.

JULIET Ay, those attires are best; but, gentle nurse,
I pray thee leave me to myself tonight;
For I have need of many orisons
To move the heavens to smile upon my state,
5 Which, well thou knowest, is cross and full of sin.

Enter Mother.

LADY CAPULET What, are you busy, ho? Need you my
help?

33 **closet** private chamber   46 **Against** in anticipation of   IV.iii.3 **orisons** prayers
4 **state** condition   5 **cross** perverse

JULIET No, madam; we have culled such necessaries
    As are behoveful for our state tomorrow.
    So please you, let me now be left alone,
    And let the nurse this night sit up with you;   10
    For I am sure you have your hands full all
    In this so sudden business.

LADY CAPULET   Good night.
    Get thee to bed, and rest; for thou hast need.
                      Exeunt [*Mother and Nurse*].

JULIET Farewell! God knows when we shall meet again.
    I have a faint cold fear thrills through my veins   15
    That almost freezes up the heat of life.
    I'll call them back again to comfort me.
    Nurse!—What should she do here?
    My dismal scene I needs must act alone.
    Come, vial.   20
    What if this mixture do not work at all?
    Shall I be married then tomorrow morning?
    No, no! This shall forbid it. Lie thou there.
                  [*Lays down a dagger*.]
    What if it be a poison which the friar
    Subtly hath minist'red to have me dead,   25
    Lest in this marriage he should be dishonored
    Because he married me before to Romeo?
    I fear it is; and yet methinks it should not,
    For he hath still been tried a holy man.
    How if, when I am laid into the tomb,   30
    I wake before the time that Romeo
    Come to redeem me? There's a fearful point!
    Shall I not then be stifled in the vault,
    To whose foul mouth no healthsome air breathes in,
    And there die strangled ere my Romeo comes?   35
    Or, if I live, is it not very like
    The horrible conceit of death and night,
    Together with the terror of the place—
    As in a vault, an ancient receptacle

8 **behoveful** expedient   8 **state** pomp   15 **faint** causing faintness   25 **minist'red**
provided   29 **still** always   29 **tried** proved   37 **conceit** thought

40 Where for this many hundred years the bones
    Of all my buried ancestors are packed;
    Where bloody Tybalt, yet but green in earth,
    Lies fest'ring in his shroud; where, as they say,
    At some hours in the night spirits resort—
45 Alack, alack, is it not like that I,
    So early waking—what with loathsome smells,
    And shrieks like mandrakes torn out of the earth,
    That living mortals, hearing them, run mad—
    O, if I wake, shall I not be distraught,
50 Environèd with all these hideous fears,
    And madly play with my forefathers' joints,
    And pluck the mangled Tybalt from his shroud,
    And, in this rage, with some great kinsman's bone
    As with a club dash out my desp'rate brains?
55 O, look! Methinks I see my cousin's ghost
    Seeking out Romeo, that did spit his body
    Upon a rapier's point. Stay, Tybalt, stay!
    Romeo, Romeo, Romeo, I drink to thee.

                    [*She falls upon her bed within the curtains.*]

[Scene IV. *Hall in Capulet's house.*]

Enter Lady of the House and Nurse.

LADY CAPULET Hold, take these keys and fetch more
    spices, nurse.

NURSE They call for dates and quinces in the pastry.

                    Enter old Capulet.

CAPULET Come, stir, stir, stir! The second cock hath
    crowed,
    The curfew bell hath rung, 'tis three o' clock.

---

42 **green in earth** newly entombed   47 **mandrakes** plant with forked root,
resembling the human body (supposed to shriek when uprooted and drive the
hearer mad)   49 **distraught** driven mad   IV.iv.2 **pastry** pastry cook's room

Look to the baked meats, good Angelica;   5
Spare not for cost.

NURSE   Go, you cotquean, go,
Get you to bed! Faith, you'll be sick tomorrow
For this night's watching.

CAPULET No, not a whit. What, I have watched ere now
All night for lesser cause, and ne'er been sick.   10

LADY CAPULET Ay, you have been a mouse hunt in
    your time;
But I will watch you from such watching now.
                            Exit Lady and Nurse.

CAPULET A jealous hood, a jealous hood!

        *Enter three or four [Fellows] with spits and
                logs and baskets.*

                            Now, fellow,
What is there?

FIRST FELLOW Things for the cook, sir; but I know not
    what.   15

CAPULET Make haste, make haste.   [*Exit first Fellow.*]
Sirrah, fetch drier logs.
Call Peter; he will show thee where they are.

SECOND FELLOW I have a head, sir, that will find out
    logs
And never trouble Peter for the matter.

CAPULET Mass, and well said; a merry whoreson, ha!   20
Thou shalt be loggerhead.   [*Exit second Fellow, with
    the others.*] Good faith, 'tis day.
The County will be here with music straight,
For so he said he would.   *Play music.*

---

5 **baked meats** meat pies 5 **Angelica** (the Nurse's name) 6 **cotquean** man
who does woman's work 8 **watching** staying awake 11 **mouse hunt** night
prowler, woman chaser 13 **A jealous hood** i.e., you wear the cap of a jealous
person 18 **will find out logs** has an affinity for logs (i.e., is wooden also)
20 **Mass** by the Mass 20 **whoreson** rascal 21 **loggerhead** blockhead

                                    I hear him near.
          Nurse! Wife! What, ho! What, nurse, I say!

                          Enter Nurse.

25   Go waken Juliet; go and trim her up.
          I'll go and chat with Paris. Hie, make haste,
          Make haste! The bridegroom he is come already:
          Make haste, I say.   [*Exit.*]

                    [Scene V. *Juliet's chamber.*]

     NURSE Mistress! What, mistress! Juliet! Fast, I war-
               rant her, she.
            Why, lamb! Why, lady! Fie, you slugabed.
            Why, love, I say! Madam; Sweetheart! Why, bride!
            What, not a word? You take your pennyworths
               now;
5   Sleep for a week; for the next night, I warrant,
            The County Paris hath set up his rest
            That you shall rest but little. God forgive me!
            Marry, and amen. How sound is she asleep!
            I needs must wake her. Madam, madam, madam!
10   Ay, let the County take you in your bed;
            He'll fright you up, i' faith. Will it not be?
                                 [*Draws aside the curtains.*]
            What, dressed, and in your clothes, and down
               again?
            I must needs wake you. Lady! Lady! Lady!
            Alas, alas! Help, help! My lady's dead!

IV.v.1 **Nurse** (at the conclusion of the last scene the nurse presumably did not go offstage but remained on the forestage, and after Capulet's departure she now walks to the rear to open the curtains, revealing Juliet) 1 **Fast** fast asleep 2 **slugabed** sleepyhead   4 **pennyworths** small portions (i.e., short naps)   6 **set up his rest** firmly resolved (with bawdy suggestion of having a lance in readiness) 12 **down** gone back to bed

O weraday that ever I was born!   15
Some *aqua vitae*, ho! My lord! My lady!

[*Enter Mother.*]

LADY CAPULET What noise is here?

NURSE   O lamentable day!

LADY CAPULET What is the matter?

NURSE   Look, look! O heavy day!

LADY CAPULET O me, O me! My child, my only life!
Revive, look up, or I will die with thee!   20
Help, help! Call help.

Enter Father.

CAPULET For shame, bring Juliet forth; her lord is
come.

NURSE She's dead, deceased; she's dead, alack the day!

LADY CAPULET Alack the day, she's dead, she's dead,
she's dead!

CAPULET Ha! Let me see her. Out alas! She's cold,   25
Her blood is settled, and her joints are stiff;
Life and these lips have long been separated.
Death lies on her like an untimely frost
Upon the sweetest flower of all the field.

NURSE O lamentable day!

LADY CAPULET   O woeful time!   30

CAPULET Death, that hath ta'en her hence to make me
wail,
Ties up my tongue and will not let me speak.

*Enter Friar [Lawrence] and the County [Paris,
with Musicians].*

FRIAR Come, is the bride ready to go to church?

CAPULET Ready to go, but never to return.

15 **weraday** welladay, alas   16 **aqua vitae** spirits

493

35　　O son, the night before thy wedding day
　　　Hath Death lain with thy wife. There she lies,
　　　Flower as she was, deflowerèd by him.
　　　Death is my son-in-law, Death is my heir;
　　　My daughter he hath wedded. I will die
40　　And leave him all. Life, living, all is Death's.

PARIS　Have I thought, love, to see this morning's face,
　　　And doth it give me such a sight as this?

LADY CAPULET　Accursed, unhappy, wretched, hateful
　　　　day!
　　　Most miserable hour that e'er time saw
45　　In lasting labor of his pilgrimage!
　　　But one, poor one, one poor and loving child,
　　　But one thing to rejoice and solace in,
　　　And cruel Death hath catched it from my sight.

NURSE　O woe! O woeful, woeful, woeful day!
50　　Most lamentable day, most woeful day
　　　That ever ever I did yet behold!
　　　O day, O day, O day! O hateful day!
　　　Never was seen so black a day as this.
　　　O woeful day! O woeful day!

55　PARIS　Beguiled, divorcèd, wrongèd, spited, slain!
　　　Most detestable Death, by thee beguiled,
　　　By cruel, cruel thee quite overthrown.
　　　O love! O life!—not life, but love in death!

CAPULET　Despised, distressèd, hated, martyred, killed!
60　　Uncomfortable time, why cam'st thou now
　　　To murder, murder our solemnity?
　　　O child, O child! My soul, and not my child!
　　　Dead art thou—alack, my child is dead,
　　　And with my child my joys are burièd!

65　FRIAR　Peace, ho, for shame! Confusion's cure lives not
　　　In these confusions. Heaven and yourself
　　　Had part in this fair maid—now heaven hath all,
　　　And all the better is it for the maid.

60 Uncomfortable discomforting

Your part in her you could not keep from death,
But heaven keeps his part in eternal life.   70
The most you sought was her promotion,
For 'twas your heaven she should be advanced;
And weep ye now, seeing she is advanced
Above the clouds, as high as heaven itself?
O, in this love, you love your child so ill   75
That you run mad, seeing that she is well.
She's not well married that lives married long,
But she's best married that dies married young.
Dry up your tears and stick your rosemary
On this fair corse, and, as the custom is,   80
And in her best array bear her to church;
For though fond nature bids us all lament,
Yet nature's tears are reason's merriment.

CAPULET All things that we ordainèd festival
    Turn from their office to black funeral—   85
Our instruments to melancholy bells,
Our wedding cheer to a sad burial feast;
Our solemn hymns to sullen dirges change;
Our bridal flowers serve for a buried corse;
And all things change them to the contrary.   90

FRIAR Sir, go you in; and, madam, go with him;
    And go, Sir Paris. Everyone prepare
To follow this fair corse unto her grave.
The heavens do low'r upon you for some ill;
Move them no more by crossing their high will.   95

> *Exeunt [casting rosemary on her
> and shutting the curtains].
> Manet [the Nurse with Musicians].*

FIRST MUSICIAN Faith, we may put up our pipes and
    be gone.

NURSE Honest good fellows, ah, put up, put up!
    For well you know this is a pitiful case.   [*Exit.*]

76 **well** i.e., in blessed condition, in heaven 79 **rosemary** an evergreen,
signifying remembrance 82 **fond nature** foolish human nature 94 **low'r** frown
95s.d. **Manet** remains (Latin) 99 **case** (1) situation (2) instrument case

100 FIRST MUSICIAN Ay, by my troth, the case may be
     amended.

Enter [Peter].

PETER Musicians, O, musicians, "Heart's ease,"
     "Heart's ease"! O, and you will have me live, play
105 "Heart's ease."

FIRST MUSICIAN Why "Heart's ease"?

PETER O, musicians, because my heart itself plays
     "My heart is full." O, play me some merry dump
     to comfort me.

FIRST MUSICIAN Not a dump we! 'Tis no time to play
110 now.

PETER You will not then?

FIRST MUSICIAN No.

PETER I will then give it you soundly.

FIRST MUSICIAN What will you give us?

115 PETER No money, on my faith, but the gleek. I will
     give you the minstrel.

FIRST MUSICIAN Then will I give you the serving-
     creature.

PETER Then will I lay the serving-creature's dagger
120 on your pate. I will carry no crotchets. I'll *re*
     you, I'll *fa* you. Do you note me?

FIRST MUSICIAN And you *re* us and *fa* us, you note
     us.

SECOND MUSICIAN Pray you put up your dagger, and
125 put out your wit. Then have at you with my wit!

107 **dump** sad tune   115 **gleek** gibe   116 **give you** call you   120 **carry** endure
120 **crotchets** (1) whims (2) quarter notes   120–21 **re … fa** (musical notes, but
used perhaps with puns on "ray," or "bewray" ["befoul"], and "fay" ["polish"];
see H. Kökeritz, *Shakespeare's Pronunciation*, pp. 105–06)   121 **note** understand
122–23 **note us** set us to music   125 **put out** set out, display

PETER I will dry-beat you with an iron wit, and put
up my iron dagger. Answer me like men.

> "When griping grief the heart doth wound,
>   And doleful dumps the mind oppress,
> Then music with her silver sound"— 130

Why "silver sound"? Why "music with her silver
sound"? What say you, Simon Catling?

FIRST MUSICIAN Marry, sir, because silver hath a sweet
sound.

PETER Pretty! What say you, Hugh Rebeck? 135

SECOND MUSICIAN I say "silver sound" because musicians sound for silver.

PETER Pretty too! What say you, James Soundpost?

THIRD MUSICIAN Faith, I know not what to say.

PETER O, I cry you mercy, you are the singer. I will 140
say for you. It is "music with her silver sound" because musicians have no gold for sounding.

> "Then music with her silver sound
> With speedy help doth lend redress."   *Exit*.

FIRST MUSICIAN What a pestilent knave is this same! 145

SECOND MUSICIAN Hang him, Jack! Come, we'll in here,
tarry for the mourners, and stay dinner.
                                   Exit [*with others*].

128-30 **When ... sound** (the song is from Richard Edwards' "In Commendation
of Music," in *The Paradise of Dainty Devices*, 1576)   132 **Catling** catgut, a lute
string   135 **Rebeck** a three-stringed fiddle   138 **Soundpost** peg that gives
internal support to a violin   140 **cry you mercy** beg your pardon

[ACT V

Scene I. *Mantua. A street.*]

Enter Romeo.

ROMEO If I may trust the flattering truth of sleep,
My dreams presage some joyful news at hand.
My bosom's lord sits lightly in his throne,
And all this day an unaccustomed spirit
5   Lifts me above the ground with cheerful thoughts.
I dreamt my lady came and found me dead
(Strange dream that gives a dead man leave to think!)
And breathed such life with kisses in my lips
That I revived and was an emperor.
10   Ah me! How sweet is love itself possessed,
When but love's shadows are so rich in joy!

Enter Romeo's Man [Balthasar, booted].

News from Verona! How now, Balthasar?
Dost thou not bring me letters from the friar?
How doth my lady? Is my father well?
15   How fares my Juliet? That I ask again,
For nothing can be ill if she be well.

MAN Then she is well, and nothing can be ill.
Her body sleeps in Capel's monument,
And her immortal part with angels lives.

V.i.1 **flattering** illusory 3 **bosom's lord** i.e., heart 11 **shadows** dreams
18 **monument** tomb

I saw her laid low in her kindred's vault   20
And presently took post to tell it you.
O, pardon me for bringing these ill news,
Since you did leave it for my office, sir.

ROMEO Is it e'en so? Then I defy you, stars!
    Thou knowest my lodging. Get me ink and paper   25
    And hire post horses. I will hence tonight.

MAN I do beseech you, sir, have patience.
    Your looks are pale and wild and do import
    Some misadventure.

ROMEO   Tush, thou art deceived.
    Leave me and do the thing I bid thee do.   30
    Hast thou no letters to me from the friar?

MAN No, my good lord.

ROMEO   No matter. Get thee gone.
    And hire those horses. I'll be with thee straight.
                              Exit [Balthasar].
    Well, Juliet, I will lie with thee tonight.
    Let's see for means. O mischief, thou art swift   35
    To enter in the thoughts of desperate men!
    I do remember an apothecary,
    And hereabouts 'a dwells, which late I noted
    In tatt'red weeds, with overwhelming brows,
    Culling of simples. Meager were his looks,   40
    Sharp misery had worn him to the bones;
    And in his needy shop a tortoise hung,
    An alligator stuffed, and other skins
    Of ill-shaped fishes; and about his shelves
    A beggarly account of empty boxes,   45
    Green earthen pots, bladders, and musty seeds,
    Remnants of packthread, and old cakes of roses
    Were thinly scatterèd, to make up a show.
    Noting this penury, to myself I said,

21 **post** post horses 23 **office** duty 28 **import** suggest 39 **weeds** clothes
39 **overwhelming** overhanging 40 **Culling of simples** collecting medicinal
herbs 45 **account** number 47 **cakes of roses** pressed rose petals (for perfume)

50   "And if a man did need a poison now
        Whose sale is present death in Mantua,
        Here lives a caitiff wretch would sell it him."
        O, this same thought did but forerun my need,
        And this same needy man must sell it me.
55   As I remember, this should be the house.
        Being holiday, the beggar's shop is shut.
        What, ho! Apothecary!

                    [*Enter Apothecary.*]

APOTHECARY   Who calls so loud?

ROMEO Come hither, man. I see that thou art poor.
        Hold, there is forty ducats. Let me have
60   A dram of poison, such soon-speeding gear
        As will disperse itself through all the veins
        That the life-weary taker may fall dead,
        And that the trunk may be discharged of breath
        As violently as hasty powder fired
65   Doth hurry from the fatal cannon's womb.

APOTHECARY Such mortal drugs I have; but Mantua's
        law
        Is death to any he that utters them.

ROMEO Art thou so bare and full of wretchedness
        And fearest to die? Famine is in thy cheeks,
70   Need and oppression starveth in thy eyes,
        Contempt and beggary hangs upon thy back:
        The world is not thy friend, nor the world's law;
        The world affords no law to make thee rich;
        Then be not poor, but break it and take this.

75   APOTHECARY My poverty but not my will consents.

ROMEO I pay thy poverty and not thy will.

APOTHECARY Put this in any liquid thing you will
        And drink it off, and if you had the strength
        Of twenty men, it would dispatch you straight.

52 **caitiff** miserable   60 **soon-speeding gear** fast-working stuff   63 **trunk** body
67 **utters** dispenses   70 **starveth** stand starving

ROMEO There is thy gold—worse poison to men's   80
   souls,
   Doing more murder in this loathsome world,
   Than these poor compounds that thou mayst not
      sell.
   I sell thee poison; thou hast sold me none.
   Farewell. Buy food and get thyself in flesh.
   Come, cordial and not poison, go with me   85
   To Juliet's grave; for there must I use thee.

                                    Exeunt.

[Scene II. *Friar Lawrence's cell.*]

Enter Friar John to Friar Lawrence.

JOHN Holy Franciscan friar, brother, ho!

              Enter [Friar] Lawrence.

LAWRENCE This same should be the voice of Friar John.
   Welcome from Mantua. What says Romeo?
   Or, if his mind be writ, give me his letter.

JOHN Going to find a barefoot brother out,   5
   One of our order, to associate me
   Here in this city visiting the sick,
   And finding him, the searchers of the town,
   Suspecting that we both were in a house
   Where the infectious pestilence did reign,   10
   Sealed up the doors, and would not let us forth,
   So that my speed to Mantua there was stayed.

LAWRENCE Who bare my letter, then, to Romeo?

JOHN I could not send it—here it is again—
   Nor get a messenger to bring it thee,   15
   So fearful were they of infection.

---

85 **cordial** restorative   V.ii.6 **associate** accompany   8 **searchers** health officers

LAWRENCE Unhappy fortune! By my brotherhood,
　　　The letter was not nice, but full of charge,
　　　Of dear import; and the neglecting it
20　　May do much danger. Friar John, go hence,
　　　Get me an iron crow and bring it straight
　　　Unto my cell.

JOHN　　　　　Brother, I'll go and bring it thee.　*Exit.*

LAWRENCE Now must I to the monument alone.
　　　Within this three hours will fair Juliet wake.
25　　She will beshrew me much that Romeo
　　　Hath had no notice of these accidents;
　　　But I will write again to Mantua,
　　　And keep her at my cell till Romeo come—
　　　Poor living corse, closed in a dead man's tomb! *Exit.*

　　　　　　[Scene III. *A churchyard; in it a monument*
　　　　　　　　belonging to the Capulets.]

　　　　　　Enter Paris and his Page [*with flowers and*
　　　　　　　　sweet water].

PARIS Give me thy torch, boy. Hence, and stand aloof.
　　　Yet put it out, for I would not be seen.
　　　Under yond yew trees lay thee all along,
　　　Holding thy ear close to the hollow ground.
5　　So shall no foot upon the churchyard tread
　　　(Being loose, unfirm, with digging up of graves)
　　　But thou shalt hear it. Whistle then to me,
　　　As signal that thou hearest something approach.
　　　Give me those flowers. Do as I bid thee, go.

10　PAGE [*Aside*] I am almost afraid to stand alone

17 **brotherhood** religious order 18 **nice** trivial 18 **charge** importance
21 **crow** crowbar 25 **beshrew** blame 26 **accidents** happenings V.iii.3 **lay
thee all along** lie at full length

Here in the churchyard; yet I will adventure.

[Retires.]

PARIS Sweet flower, with flowers thy bridal bed I strew
    (O woe! thy canopy is dust and stones)
    Which with sweet water nightly I will dew;
      Or, wanting that, with tears distilled by moans.   15
    The obsequies that I for thee will keep
    Nightly shall be to strew thy grave and weep.

Whistle Boy.

    The boy gives warning something doth approach.
    What cursèd foot wanders this way tonight
    To cross my obsequies and true love's rite?   20
    What, with a torch? Muffle me, night, awhile.

[Retires.]

Enter Romeo, [and Balthasar with a torch, a mattock,
*   and a crow of iron].*

ROMEO Give me that mattock and the wrenching iron.
    Hold, take this letter. Early in the morning
    See thou deliver it to my lord and father.
    Give me the light. Upon thy life I charge thee,   25
    Whate'er thou hearest or seest, stand all aloof
    And do not interrupt me in my course.
    Why I descend into this bed of death
    Is partly to behold my lady's face,
    But chiefly to take thence from her dead finger   30
    A precious ring—a ring that I must use
    In dear employment. Therefore hence, be gone.
    But if thou, jealous, dost return to pry
    In what I farther shall intend to do,
    By heaven, I will tear thee joint by joint   35
    And strew this hungry churchyard with thy limbs.
    The time and my intents are savage-wild,
    More fierce and more inexorable far
    Than empty tigers or the roaring sea.

11 adventure risk it 14 sweet perfumed 20 cross interrupt 21 **Muffle** hide
32 dear employment important business 33 jealous curious

40 BALTHASAR I will be gone, sir, and not trouble ye.

ROMEO So shalt thou show me friendship. Take thou
  that.
Live, and be prosperous; and farewell, good fellow.

BALTHASAR [*Aside*] For all this same, I'll hide me here-
  about.
His looks I fear, and his intents I doubt. [*Retires.*]

45 ROMEO Thou detestable maw, thou womb of death,
Gorged with the dearest morsel of the earth,
Thus I enforce thy rotten jaws to open,
And in despite I'll cram thee with more food.
       [*Romeo opens the tomb.*]

PARIS This is that banished haughty Montague
50 That murd'red my love's cousin—with which grief
It is supposed the fair creature died—
And here is come to do some villainous shame
To the dead bodies. I will apprehend him.
Stop thy unhallowèd toil, vile Montague!
55 Can vengeance be pursued further than death?
Condemnèd villain, I do apprehend thee.
Obey, and go with me; for thou must die.

ROMEO I must indeed; and therefore came I hither.
Good gentle youth, tempt not a desp'rate man.
60 Fly hence and leave me. Think upon these gone;
Let them affright thee. I beseech thee, youth,
Put not another sin upon my head
By urging me to fury. O, be gone!
By heaven, I love thee better than myself,
65 For I come hither armed against myself.
Stay not, be gone. Live, and hereafter say
A madman's mercy bid thee run away.

PARIS I do defy thy conjurations.
And apprehend thee for a felon here.

70 ROMEO Wilt thou provoke me? Then have at thee, boy!
           [*They fight.*]

44 **doubt** suspect 45 **maw** stomach 48 **in despite** to spite you 68 **conjurations** solemn charges

PAGE O Lord, they fight! I will go call the watch.
                                    [*Exit. Paris falls.*]

PARIS O, I am slain! If thou be merciful,
    Open the tomb, lay me with Juliet.   [*Dies.*]

ROMEO In faith, I will. Let me peruse this face.
    Mercutio's kinsman, noble County Paris!   75
    What said my man when my betossèd soul
    Did not attend him as we rode? I think
    He told me Paris should have married Juliet.
    Said he not so, or did I dream it so?
    Or am I mad, hearing him talk of Juliet,   80
    To think it was so? O, give me thy hand,
    One writ with me in sour misfortune's book!
    I'll bury thee in a triumphant grave.
    A grave? O, no, a lanthorn, slaught'red youth,
    For here lies Juliet, and her beauty makes   85
    This vault a feasting presence full of light.
    Death, lie thou there, by a dead man interred.
                    [*Lays him in the tomb.*]
    How oft when men are at the point of death
    Have they been merry! Which their keepers call
    A lightning before death. O, how may I   90
    Call this a lightning? O my love, my wife!
    Death, that hath sucked the honey of thy breath,
    Hath had no power yet upon thy beauty.
    Thou art not conquered. Beauty's ensign yet
    Is crimson in thy lips and in thy cheeks,   95
    And death's pale flag is not advancèd there.
    Tybalt, liest thou there in thy bloody sheet?
    O, what more favor can I do to thee
    Than with that hand that cut thy youth in twain
    To sunder his that was thine enemy?   100
    Forgive me, cousin! Ah, dear Juliet,
    Why art thou yet so fair? Shall I believe
    That unsubstantial Death is amorous,

---

77 **attend** give attention to   84 **lanthorn** lantern (a windowed erection on the top
of a dome or room to admit light)   86 **feasting presence** festive presence chamber
89 **keepers** jailers   94 **ensign** banner

And that the lean abhorrèd monster keeps
105 Thee here in dark to be his paramour?
For fear of that I still will stay with thee
And never from this pallet of dim night
Depart again. Here, here will I remain
With worms that are thy chambermaids. O, here
110 Will I set up my everlasting rest
And shake the yoke of inauspicious stars
From this world-wearied flesh. Eyes, look your last!
Arms, take your last embrace! And, lips, O you
The doors of breath, seal with a righteous kiss
115 A dateless bargain to engrossing death!
Come, bitter conduct; come, unsavory guide!
Thou desperate pilot, now at once run on
The dashing rocks thy seasick weary bark!
Here's to my love! [*Drinks.*] O true apothecary!
120 Thy drugs are quick. Thus with a kiss I die. [*Falls.*]

Enter Friar [Lawrence], with lanthorn, crow,
and spade.

FRIAR Saint Francis be my speed! How oft tonight
Have my old feet stumbled at graves! Who's there?

BALTHASAR Here's one, a friend, and one that knows
you well.

FRIAR Bliss be upon you! Tell me, good my friend,
125 What torch is yond that vainly lends his light
To grubs and eyeless skulls? As I discern,
It burneth in the Capels' monument.

BALTHASAR It doth so, holy sir; and there's my master,
One that you love.

FRIAR   Who is it?

BALTHASAR   Romeo.

FRIAR How long hath he been there?

---

115 **dateless** eternal   115 **engrossing** all-buying, all-encompassing   116 **conduct**
guide   117 **desperate pilot** i.e., himself   121 **speed** help   122 **stumbled** (a
bad omen)

BALTHASAR   Full half an hour.   130

FRIAR Go with me to the vault.

BALTHASAR   I dare not, sir.
   My master knows not but I am gone hence,
   And fearfully did menace me with death
   If I did stay to look on his intents.

FRIAR Stay then; I'll go alone. Fear comes upon me.   135
   O, much I fear some ill unthrifty thing.

BALTHASAR As I did sleep under this yew tree here,
   I dreamt my master and another fought,
   And that my master slew him.

FRIAR   Romeo!
   Alack, alack, what blood is this which stains   140
   The stony entrance of this sepulcher?
   What mean these masterless and gory swords
   To lie discolored by this place of peace?
                                  [Enters the tomb.]
   Romeo! O, pale! Who else? What, Paris too?
   And steeped in blood? Ah, what an unkind hour   145
   Is guilty of this lamentable chance!
   The lady stirs.   [Juliet rises.]

JULIET O comfortable friar! Where is my lord?
   I do remember well where I should be,
   And there I am. Where is my Romeo?   150

FRIAR I hear some noise. Lady, come from that nest
   Of death, contagion, and unnatural sleep.
   A greater power than we can contradict
   Hath thwarted our intents. Come, come away.
   Thy husband in thy bosom there lies dead;   155
   And Paris too. Come, I'll dispose of thee
   Among a sisterhood of holy nuns.
   Stay not to question, for the watch is coming.
   Come, go, good Juliet. I dare no longer stay.

136 unthrifty unlucky   145 unkind unnatural   148 comfortable comforting

160 JULIET Go, get thee hence, for I will not away.

Exit [Friar].

What's here? A cup, closed in my truelove's hand?
Poison, I see, hath been his timeless end.
O churl! Drunk all, and left no friendly drop
To help me after? I will kiss thy lips.

165 Haply some poison yet doth hang on them
To make me die with a restorative.   [*Kisses him.*]
Thy lips are warm!

CHIEF WATCHMAN [*Within*] Lead, boy. Which way?

JULIET Yea, noise? Then I'll be brief. O happy
dagger!   [*Snatches Romeo's dagger.*]

170 This is thy sheath; there rust, and let me die.

[*She stabs herself and falls.*]

Enter [Paris'] Boy and Watch.

BOY This is the place. There, where the torch doth
burn.

CHIEF WATCHMAN The ground is bloody. Search about
the churchyard.
Go, some of you; whoe'er you find attach.

[*Exeunt some of the Watch.*]

Pitiful sight! Here lies the County slain;

175 And Juliet bleeding, warm, and newly dead,
Who here hath lain this two days burièd.
Go, tell the Prince; run to the Capulets;
Raise up the Montagues; some others search.

[*Exeunt others of the Watch.*]

We see the ground whereon these woes do lie,

180 But the true ground of all these piteous woes
We cannot without circumstance descry.

*Enter [some of the Watch, with] Romeo's Man
[Balthasar].*

SECOND WATCHMAN Here's Romeo's man. We found
him in the churchyard.

162 **timeless** untimely   163 **churl** rude fellow   169 **happy** opportune
180 **ground** cause   181 **circumstance** details

508

CHIEF WATCHMAN Hold him in safety till the Prince
    come hither.

Enter Friar [Lawrence] and another Watchman.

THIRD WATCHMAN Here is a friar that trembles, sighs,
    and weeps.
    We took this mattock and this spade from him   185
    As he was coming from this churchyard's side.

CHIEF WATCHMAN A great suspicion! Stay the friar too.

Enter the Prince [and Attendants].

PRINCE What misadventure is so early up,
    That calls our person from our morning rest?

Enter Capulet and his Wife [with others].

CAPULET What should it be, that is so shrieked abroad?   190

LADY CAPULET O, the people in the street cry "Romeo,"
    Some "Juliet," and some "Paris"; and all run
    With open outcry toward our monument.

PRINCE What fear is this which startles in your ears?

CHIEF WATCHMAN Sovereign, here lies the County Paris
    slain;   195
    And Romeo dead; and Juliet, dead before,
    Warm and new killed.

PRINCE Search, seek, and know how this foul murder
    comes.

CHIEF WATCHMAN Here is a friar, and slaughtered
    Romeo's man,
    With instruments upon them fit to open   200
    These dead men's tombs.

CAPULET O heavens! O wife, look how our daughter
    bleeds!
    This dagger hath mista'en, for, lo, his house
    Is empty on the back of Montague,
    And it missheathèd in my daughter's bosom!   205

203 his house its sheath

LADY CAPULET O me, this sight of death is as a bell
That warns my old age to a sepulcher.

Enter Montague [and others].

PRINCE Come, Montague; for thou art early up
To see thy son and heir more early down.

210 MONTAGUE Alas, my liege, my wife is dead tonight!
Grief of my son's exile hath stopped her breath.
What further woe conspires against mine age?

PRINCE Look, and thou shalt see.

MONTAGUE O thou untaught! What manners is in this,
215 To press before thy father to a grave?

PRINCE Seal up the mouth of outrage for a while,
Till we can clear these ambiguities
And know their spring, their head, their true
    descent;
And then will I be general of your woes
220 And lead you even to death. Meantime forbear,
And let mischance be slave to patience.
Bring forth the parties of suspicion.

FRIAR I am the greatest, able to do least,
Yet most suspected, as the time and place
225 Doth make against me, of this direful murder;
And here I stand, both to impeach and purge
Myself condemnèd and myself excused.

PRINCE Then say at once what thou dost know in this.

FRIAR I will be brief, for my short date of breath
230 Is not so long as is a tedious tale.
Romeo, there dead, was husband to that Juliet;
And she, there dead, that's Romeo's faithful wife.
I married them; and their stol'n marriage day
Was Tybalt's doomsday, whose untimely death
235 Banished the new-made bridegroom from this city;

216 **the mouth of outrage** these violent cries 219 **general of your woes** leader
in your sorrowing 226 **impeach and purge** make charges and exonerate
229 **date of breath** term of life

For whom, and not for Tybalt, Juliet pined.
You, to remove that siege of grief from her,
Betrothed and would have married her perforce
To County Paris. Then comes she to me
And with wild looks bid me devise some mean   240
To rid her from this second marriage,
Or in my cell there would she kill herself.
Then gave I her (so tutored by my art)
A sleeping potion; which so took effect
As I intended, for it wrought on her   245
The form of death. Meantime I writ to Romeo
That he should hither come as this dire night
To help to take her from her borrowed grave,
Being the time the potion's force should cease.
But he which bore my letter, Friar John,   250
Was stayed by accident, and yesternight
Returned my letter back. Then all alone
At the prefixèd hour of her waking
Came I to take her from her kindred's vault;
Meaning to keep her closely at my cell   255
Till I conveniently could send to Romeo.
But when I came, some minute ere the time
Of her awakening, here untimely lay
The noble Paris and true Romeo dead.
She wakes; and I entreated her come forth   260
And bear this work of heaven with patience;
But then a noise did scare me from the tomb,
And she, too desperate, would not go with me,
But, as it seems, did violence on herself.
All this I know, and to the marriage   265
Her nurse is privy; and if aught in this
Miscarried by my fault, let my old life
Be sacrificed some hour before his time
Unto the rigor of severest law.

PRINCE We still have known thee for a holy man.   270
          Where's Romeo's man? What can he say to this?

247 **as** on   255 **closely** hidden   266 **privy** accessory   270 **still** always

511

BALTHASAR I brought my master news of Juliet's death;
　　　　　And then in post he came from Mantua
　　　　　To this same place, to this same monument.
　　　　　This letter he early bid me give his father,
275　　　　And threat'ned me with death, going in the vault,
　　　　　If I departed not and left him there.

PRINCE Give me the letter. I will look on it.
　　　　　Where is the County's page that raised the watch?
280　　　　Sirrah, what made your master in this place?

BOY He came with flowers to strew his lady's grave;
　　　　　And bid me stand aloof, and so I did.
　　　　　Anon comes one with light to ope the tomb;
　　　　　And by and by my master drew on him;
285　　　　And then I ran away to call the watch.

PRINCE This letter doth make good the friar's words,
　　　　　Their course of love, the tidings of her death;
　　　　　And here he writes that he did buy a poison
　　　　　Of a poor pothecary and therewithal
290　　　　Came to this vault to die and lie with Juliet.
　　　　　Where be these enemies? Capulet, Montague,
　　　　　See what a scourge is laid upon your hate,
　　　　　That heaven finds means to kill your joys with love.
　　　　　And I, for winking at your discords too,
295　　　　Have lost a brace of kinsmen. All are punished.

CAPULET O brother Montague, give me thy hand.
　　　　　This is my daughter's jointure, for no more
　　　　　Can I demand.

MONTAGUE　　　　But I can give thee more;
　　　　　For I will raise her statue in pure gold,
300　　　　That whiles Verona by that name is known,
　　　　　There shall no figure at such rate be set
　　　　　As that of true and faithful Juliet.

---

280 **made your master** was your master doing 284 **by and by** soon
289 **therewithal** therewith 294 **winking at** closing eyes to 295 **brace** pair
(i.e., Mercutio and Paris) 297 **jointure** marriage settlement 301 **rate** value

CAPULET As rich shall Romeo's by his lady's lie—
  Poor sacrifices of our enmity!

PRINCE A glooming peace this morning with it brings.   305
    The sun for sorrow will not show his head.
  Go hence, to have more talk of these sad things;
    Some shall be pardoned, and some punishèd;
  For never was a story of more woe
  Than this of Juliet and her Romeo.   310

                                    [*Exeunt omnes.*]

                    FINIS

---

305 **glooming** cloudy

Textual Note

The First Quarto (Q1) of *Romeo and Juliet* was printed in 1597 without previous entry in the Stationers' Register. It bore the following title page: "An/ EXCELLENT/ conceited Tragedie/ OF/ Romeo and Iuliet./ As it hath been often (with great applause)/ plaid publiquely, by the right Ho-/ nourable the L. of *Hunsdon*/ his Seruants./ LONDON,/ Printed by Iohn Danter./ 1597." Until the present century, editors frequently assumed that this text, curtailed and manifestly corrupt, represented an early draft of the play. Most now agree that Q1, like the other "bad" Shakespeare quartos, is a memorial reconstruction; that is, a version which some of the actors (accusing fingers have been pointed at those who played Romeo and Peter) put together from memory and gave to the printer. The Second Quarto (Q2) was printed in 1599 with the following title page: "THE/ MOST/ EX-/ cellent and lamentable/ Tragedie, of Romeo/ and *Iuliet./ Newly corrected, augmented, and/ amended:* As it hath bene sundry times publiquely acted, by the/ right Honourable the Lord Chamberlaine/ his Seruants./ London/ Printed by Thomas Creede, for Cuthbert Burby, and are to/ be sold at his shop neare the Exchange./ 1599." Apparently Q2 derives directly from the same acting version that is imperfectly reflected in the memorially reconstructed Q1, but it is based on a written script of the play rather than on actors' memories. Q2, however, is the product of careless or hasty printing and does not inspire complete confidence. Lines that the author doubtless had canceled are sometimes printed along with the lines intended to replace them, and occasionally notes about staging appear which are probably the prompter's, or possibly Shakespeare's. Vexing matters like these, together with the fact that some speeches in Q2 are clearly based on Q1 (possibly the manuscript that provided the copy for most of Q2 was illegible in places), have caused editors to make at least limited use of Q1.

The other texts of *Romeo and Juliet* have no claim to authority. The Second Quarto provided the basis for a Third Quarto (1609), which in turn served as copy for an undated Fourth Quarto and for the text in the Folio of 1623. A Fifth Quarto, based on the Fourth, appeared in 1637.

None of these texts—including the Second Quarto, upon which the present edition is based—makes any real division of the play into acts and scenes. (The last third of Q1 does have a rough indication of scene division in the form of strips of ornamental border across the page, and the Folio has at the beginning *Actus Primus. Scena Prima*, but nothing further.) The division used here, like that in most modern texts, derives from the Globe edition, as do the *Dramatis Personae* and the various indications of place. Spelling and punctuation have been modernized, a number of stage directions have been added (in square brackets), and speech prefixes have been regularized. This last change will be regretted by those who feel, perhaps rightly, that at least some of the speech prefixes of Q2 show how Shakespeare thought of the character at each moment of the dialogue. Lady Capulet, for example, is variously designated in the speech prefixes of Q2 as *Wife*, *Lady*, and sometimes *Mother*; Capulet is occasionally referred to as *Father*, and Balthasar as *Peter*; the First Musician of our text (IV.v) is once called *Fidler* in Q2 and several times *Minstrel* or *Minstrels*. Other deviations (apart from obvious typographical errors) from Q2 are listed in the textual notes. There the adopted reading is given first, in bold, followed by a note in square brackets if the source of the reading is Q1; this is followed by the rejected reading in roman. Absence of a note in square brackets indicates that the adopted reading has been taken from some other source and represents guesswork at best. Apparently the editors of F as well as of Q3 and Q4 had no access to any authentic document.

In dealing with the troublesome stage direction at the end of I.iv, I have followed the solution adopted by H. R. Hoppe in his Crofts Classics edition (1947); and I

TEXTUAL NOTE

have adopted the reading of "eyes' shot" for the customary "eyes shut" at III.ii.49 from the Pelican edition of John E. Hankins (Penguin, 1960), which presents a good argument for retaining the reading of Q2 with the addition of an apostrophe.

I.i.29 in sense [Q1] sense   34 comes two [Q1] comes   65 swashing washing   123 drave driue   150 his is   156 sun same   182 well-seeming [Q1] welseeing   205 Bid a sick [Q1] A sicke   205 make [Q1] makes   206 Ah [Q1] A

I.ii.32 on one   65–73 Signior ... Helena [prose in Qq and F]   92 fires fier

I.iii.2–76 [Q2 prints Nurse's speeches in prose]   66, 67 honor [Q1] houre   99 make it [Q1] make

I.iv.7–8 Nor ... entrance [added from Q1]   23 Mercutio Horatio   39 done [Q1] dum   42 of this sir-reverence [Q1] or saue you reuerence   45 like lights   47 five fine   53–91 O ... bodes [verse from Q1; Q2 has prose]   57 atomies ottamie   63 film Philome   66 maid [Q1] man   113 sail [Q1] sute   114 s.d. They ... and [Q2 combines with s.d. used here at beginning of I.v]

I.v.s.d. [Q2 adds "Enter Romeo"]   1, 4, 7, 12 First Servingman ... Second Servingman ... First Servingman ... First Servingman [Q2 has "Ser.," "I.," "Ser.," and "Ser."]   97 ready [Q1] did readie   144 What's this? What's this? Whats tis? whats tis

II.i.9 one [Q1] on   10 pronounce [Q1] prouaunt   10 dove [Q1] day   12 heir [Q1] her   38 et cetera [Q1] or

II.ii.16 do to   20 eyes eye   45 were wene   83 washed washeth   99 havior [Q1] behauior   101 more cunning [Q1] coying   162 than mine then   167 sweet Neece   186 Romeo [Q1] Iu.   187–88 [between these lines Q2 has "The grey eyde morne smiles on the frowning night,/ Checkring the Easterne Clouds with streaks of light,/ And darknesse fleckted like a drunkard reeles,/ From forth daies pathway, made by *Tytans* wheeles," lines nearly identical with those given to the Friar at II.iii.1–4; presumably Shakespeare first wrote the lines for Romeo, then decided to use them in Friar Lawrence's next speech, but neglected to delete the first version, and the printer mistakenly printed it]

II.iii.2 Check'ring Checking   3 fleckèd [Q1] fleckeld   74 ring yet [Q1] yet ringing

II.iv.18 Benvolio [Q1] Ro.   30 fantasticoes [Q1] phantacies   215 Ah A

II.v.11 three there

II.vi.27 music's musicke

III.i.2 are [Q1; Q2 omits]   91s.d. Tybalt ... flies [Q1; Q2 has "Away Tybalt"]   110 soundly too. Your soundly, to your   124 Alive [Q1] He gan   126 eyed [Q1] end   168 agile [Q1] aged   190 hate's [Q1] hearts   194 I It

III.ii.51 determine of determine   60 one on   72–73 [Q2 gives line 72 to Juliet, line 73 to Nurse]   76 Dove-feathered Rauenous doue-featherd   79 damnèd dimme

III.iii.s.d. **Enter Friar** [Q1] Enter Frier and Romeo   40 **But ... banishèd** [in Q2 this line is preceded by one line, "This may flyes do, when I from this must flie," which is substantially the same as line 41, and by line 43, which is probably misplaced]   52 **Thou** [Q1] Then   61 **madmen** [Q1] mad man   73s.d. **Knock** They knocke   75s.d. **Knock** Slud knock   108s.d. **He ... away** [Q1; Q2 omits]   117 **lives** lies   143 **misbehaved** mishaued   162s.d. **Nurse ... again** [Q1; Q2 omits]   168 **disguised** disguise

III.v.13 **exhales** [Q1] exhale   36s.d. **Enter Nurse** [Q1] Enter Madame and Nurse   42 s.d. **He goeth down** [Q1; Q2 omits]   54 **Juliet** Ro.   83 **pardon him** padon   140 **gives** giue   182 **trained** [Q1] liand

IV.i.7 **talked** talke   72 **slay** [Q1] stay   83 **chapless** chapels   85 **his shroud** his   98 **breath** [Q1] breast   100 **wanny** many   110 **In** Is   110 [after this line Q2 has "Be borne to buriall in thy kindreds graue"; presumably as soon as Shakespeare wrote these words he decided he could do better, and expressed the gist of the idea in the next two lines, but the canceled line was erroneously printed]   111 **shalt** shall   116 **waking** walking

IV.iii.49 **wake** walke   58 **Romeo, I drink** [after "Romeo" Q2 has "heeres drinke," which is probably a stage direction printed in error]   58s.d. **She ... curtains** [Q1; Q2 omits]

IV.iv.21 **faith** [Q1] father

IV.v.65 **cure** care   82 **fond** some   95 s.d. **casting ... curtains** [Q1; Q2 omits]   101 **by** [Q1] my   101 **amended** amended.   Exit omnes   101s.d. **Peter** [Q2 has "Will Kemp," the name of the actor playing the role]   128 **grief** [Q1] griefes   129 **And ... oppress** [Q1; Q2 omits]   135, 138 **Pretty** [Q1] Prates

V.i.11s.d. **booted** [detail from Q1]   15 **fares my** [Q1] doth my Lady   24 **e'en** [Q1 "euen"] in   24 **defy** [Q1] denie   50 **And** An   76 **pay** [Q1] pray

V.iii.s.d. **with ... water** [Q1; Q2 omits]   3 **yew** [Q1] young   21s.d. **and Balthasar ... iron** [Q1; Q2 has "Enter Romeo and Peter," and gives lines 40 and 43 to Peter instead of to Balthasar]   48 s.d. **Romeo ... tomb** [Q1; Q2 omits]   68 **conjurations** [Q1] commiration   71 **Page** [Q2 omits this speech prefix]   102 **fair** [Q2 follows with "I will beleeue," presumably words that Shakespeare wrote, then rewrote in the next line, but neglected to delete]   108 **again. Here** [between these words Q2 has the following material, which Shakespeare apparently neglected to delete: "come lye thou in my arme,/ Heer's to thy health, where ere thou tumblest in./ O true Appothecarie/ Thy drugs are quicke. Thus with a kiss I die./ Depart againe"]   137 **yew** yong   187 **too** too too   189s.d. **Enter ... wife** [Q2 places after line 201, with "Enter Capels" at line 189]   190 **shrieked** [Q1] shrike   199 **slaughtered** Slaughter   209 **more early** [Q1] now earling

WILLIAM
SHAKESPEARE

A MIDSUMMER
NIGHT'S DREAM

Edited by Wolfgang Clemen

A MIDSUMMER
NIGHT'S DREAM

[ACT I

Scene I. *The palace of Theseus.*]

Enter Theseus, Hippolyta, [Philostrate,] with others.

THESEUS Now, fair Hippolyta, our nuptial hour
  Draws on apace. Four happy days bring in
  Another moon; but, O, methinks, how slow
  This old moon wanes! She lingers my desires,
  Like to a stepdame, or a dowager,   5
  Long withering out a young man's revenue.

HIPPOLYTA Four days will quickly steep themselves in
    night,
  Four nights will quickly dream away the time;
  And then the moon, like to a silver bow
  New-bent in heaven, shall behold the night   10
  Of our solemnities.

THESEUS   Go, Philostrate,
  Stir up the Athenian youth to merriments,
  Awake the pert and nimble spirit of mirth,
  Turn melancholy forth to funerals;

Text references are printed in **bold** type; the annotation follows in roman type.
I.i.4 **lingers** makes to linger, delays   6 **Long withering out a young man's
revenue** diminishing the young man's money (because she must be supported by
him)   13 **pert** lively

15   The pale companion is not for our pomp.

                                      [*Exit Philostrate.*]

         Hippolyta, I wooed thee with my sword,
         And won thy love, doing thee injuries;
         But I will wed thee in another key,
         With pomp, with triumph, and with reveling.

         Enter Egeus and his daughter Hermia, and Lysander,
                      and Demetrius.

20   EGEUS Happy be Theseus, our renownèd Duke!

     THESEUS Thanks, good Egeus. What's the news with
         thee?

     EGEUS Full of vexation come I, with complaint
         Against my child, my daughter Hermia.
         Stand forth, Demetrius. My noble lord,
25   This man hath my consent to marry her.
         Stand forth, Lysander. And, my gracious Duke
         This man hath bewitched the bosom of my child.
         Thou, thou, Lysander, thou hast given her rhymes,
         And interchanged love tokens with my child.
30   Thou hast by moonlight at her window sung,
         With feigning voice, verses of feigning love,
         And stol'n the impression of her fantasy
         With bracelets of thy hair, rings, gauds, conceits,
         Knacks, trifles, nosegays, sweetmeats, messengers
35   Of strong prevailment in unhardened youth.
         With cunning hast thou filched my daughter's heart,
         Turned her obedience, which is due to me,
         To stubborn harshness. And, my gracious Duke,
         Be it so she will not here before your Grace
40   Consent to marry with Demetrius,
         I beg the ancient privilege of Athens:

---

15 **companion** fellow (contemptuous)   15 **pomp** festive procession   16 **I
wooed thee with my sword** (Theseus had captured Hippolyta when he con-
quered the Amazons)   21 **Egeus** (pronounced "E-géus")   32 **stol'n the
impression of her fantasy** fraudulently impressed your image upon her
imagination   33-34 **gauds, conceits, Knacks** trinkets, cleverly devised tokens,
knickknacks

As she is mine, I may dispose of her,
Which shall be either to this gentleman
Or to her death, according to our law
Immediately provided in that case.   45

THESEUS What say you, Hermia? Be advised, fair
    maid.
To you your father should be as a god,
One that composed your beauties; yea, and one
To whom you are but as a form in wax
By him imprinted and within his power   50
To leave the figure or disfigure it.
Demetrius is a worthy gentleman.

HERMIA So is Lysander.

THESEUS   In himself he is;
But in this kind, wanting your father's voice,
The other must be held the worthier.   55

HERMIA I would my father looked but with my eyes.

THESEUS Rather your eyes must with his judgment
    look.

HERMIA I do entreat your Grace to pardon me.
I know not by what power I am made bold,
Nor how it may concern my modesty,   60
In such a presence here to plead my thoughts;
But I beseech your Grace that I may know
The worst that may befall me in this case,
If I refuse to wed Demetrius.

THESEUS Either to die the death, or to abjure   65
Forever the society of men.
Therefore, fair Hermia, question your desires;
Know of your youth, examine well your blood,
Whether, if you yield not to your father's choice,
You can endure the livery of a nun,   70
For aye to be in shady cloister mewed,
To live a barren sister all your life,

45 Immediately expressly   54 But in ... father's voice but in this particular
respect, lacking your father's approval   68 Know of ascertain from   68 blood
passions   71 mewed caged

Chanting faint hymns to the cold fruitless moon.
Thrice-blessèd they that master so their blood,
75   To undergo such maiden pilgrimage;
But earthlier happy is the rose distilled,
Than that which, withering on the virgin thorn,
Grows, lives, and dies in single blessedness.

HERMIA   So will I grow, so live, so die, my lord,
80   Ere I will yield my virgin patent up
Unto his lordship, whose unwished yoke
My soul consents not to give sovereignty.

THESEUS   Take time to pause; and, by the next new
      moon—
The sealing day betwixt my love and me,
85   For everlasting bond of fellowship—
Upon that day either prepare to die
For disobedience to your father's will,
Or else to wed Demetrius, as he would,
Or on Diana's altar to protest
90   For aye austerity and single life.

DEMETRIUS   Relent, sweet Hermia: and, Lysander,
      yield
Thy crazèd title to my certain right.

LYSANDER   You have her father's love, Demetrius;
Let me have Hermia's: do you marry him.

95   EGEUS   Scornful Lysander! True, he hath my love,
And what is mine my love shall render him.
And she is mine, and all my right of her
I do estate unto Demetrius.

LYSANDER   I am, my lord, as well derived as he,
100   As well possessed; my love is more than his;
My fortunes every way as fairly ranked
(If not with vantage) as Demetrius';
And, which is more than all these boasts can be,

73 moon i.e., Diana, goddess of chastity   76 distilled made into perfumes
80 patent privilege   92 crazèd title flawed claim   98 estate unto settle upon
100 As well possessed as rich   102 If not with vantage if not better

524

I am beloved of beauteous Hermia.
Why should not I then prosecute my right?   105
Demetrius, I'll avouch it to his head,
Made love to Nedar's daughter, Helena,
And won her soul; and she, sweet lady, dotes,
Devoutly dotes, dotes in idolatry,
Upon this spotted and inconstant man.   110

THESEUS I must confess that I have heard so much,
And with Demetrius thought to have spoke thereof;
But, being overfull of self-affairs,
My mind did lose it. But, Demetrius, come;
And come, Egeus. You shall go with me;   115
I have some private schooling for you both.
For you, fair Hermia, look you arm yourself
To fit your fancies to your father's will;
Or else the law of Athens yields you up—
Which by no means we may extenuate—   120
To death, or to a vow of single life.
Come, my Hippolyta. What cheer, my love?
Demetrius and Egeus, go along.
I must employ you in some business
Against our nuptial, and confer with you   125
Of something nearly that concerns yourselves.

EGEUS With duty and desire we follow you.
                    Exeunt [all but Lysander and Hermia].

LYSANDER How now, my love! Why is your cheek so
    pale?
How chance the roses there do fade so fast?

HERMIA Belike for want of rain, which I could well   130
Beteem them from the tempest of my eyes.

LYSANDER Ay me! For aught that I could ever read,
Could ever hear by tale or history,

---

106 **to his head** in his teeth   110 **spotted** i.e., morally stained   125 **Against** in
preparation for   126 **nearly** closely   129 **How chance** how does it come that
130 **Belike** perhaps   131 **Beteem** bring forth

The course of true love never did run smooth;
135   But, either it was different in blood—

HERMIA   O cross! Too high to be enthralled to low!

LYSANDER   Or else misgraffèd in respect of years—

HERMIA   O spite! Too old to be engaged to young!

LYSANDER   Or else it stood upon the choice of friends—

140   HERMIA   O hell! To choose love by another's eyes!

LYSANDER   Or, if there were a sympathy in choice,
War, death, or sickness did lay siege to it,
Making it momentany as a sound,
Swift as a shadow, short as any dream,
145   Brief as the lightning in the collied night,
That, in a spleen, unfolds both heaven and earth,
And ere a man hath power to say "Behold!"
The jaws of darkness do devour it up:
So quick bright things come to confusion.

150   HERMIA   If then true lovers have been ever crossed,
It stands as an edict in destiny:
Then let us teach our trial patience,
Because it is a customary cross,
As due to love as thoughts and dreams and sighs,
155   Wishes and tears, poor Fancy's followers.

LYSANDER   A good persuasion. Therefore, hear me,
    Hermia.
I have a widow aunt, a dowager
Of great revenue, and she hath no child.
From Athens is her house remote seven leagues,
160   And she respects me as her only son.
There, gentle Hermia, may I marry thee,
And to that place the sharp Athenian law
Cannot pursue us. If thou lovest me, then,

---

137 **misgraffèd** ill matched, misgrafted   143 **momentany** momentary, passing   145 **collied** blackened   146 **spleen** flash   152 **teach our trial patience** i.e., teach ourselves to be patient   155 **Fancy's** Love's   156 **persuasion** principle

Steal forth thy father's house tomorrow night;
And in the wood, a league without the town,   165
Where I did meet thee once with Helena,
To do observance to a morn of May,
There will I stay for thee.

HERMIA   My good Lysander!
I swear to thee, by Cupid's strongest bow,
By his best arrow with the golden head,   170
By the simplicity of Venus' doves,
By that which knitteth souls and prospers loves,
And by that fire which burned the Carthage
    queen,
When the false Troyan under sail was seen,
By all the vows that ever men have broke,   175
In number more than ever women spoke,
In that same place thou hast appointed me,
Tomorrow truly will I meet with thee.

LYSANDER Keep promise, love. Look, here comes
    Helena.

Enter Helena.

HERMIA God speed fair Helena! Whither away?   180

HELENA Call you me fair? That fair again unsay.
Demetrius loves your fair. O happy fair!
Your eyes are lodestars, and your tongue's
    sweet air
More tunable than lark to shepherd's ear,
When wheat is green, when hawthorn buds appear.   185
Sickness is catching. O, were favor so,
Yours would I catch, fair Hermia, ere I go;
My ear should catch your voice, my eye your eye,

---

170 **arrow with the golden head** (Cupid's gold-headed arrows caused love, the
leaden ones dislike)   173 **Carthage queen** Dido (who burned herself on a funeral
pyre when the Trojan Aeneas left her)   182 **fair** beauty   183 **lodestars** guiding
stars   183 **air** music   186 **favor** looks

My tongue should catch your tongue's sweet
   melody.
190   Were the world mine, Demetrius being bated,
The rest I'd give to be to you translated.
O, teach me how you look, and with what art
You sway the motion of Demetrius' heart!

HERMIA I frown upon him, yet he loves me still.

HELENA O that your frowns would teach my smiles
195   such skill!

HERMIA I give him curses, yet he gives me love.

HELENA O that my prayers could such affection move!

HERMIA The more I hate, the more he follows me.

HELENA The more I love, the more he hateth me.

200 HERMIA His folly, Helena, is no fault of mine.

HELENA None, but your beauty: would that fault were
   mine!

HERMIA Take comfort. He no more shall see my face;
Lysander and myself will fly this place.
Before the time I did Lysander see,
205   Seemed Athens as a paradise to me.
O, then, what graces in my love do dwell,
That he hath turned a heaven unto a hell!

LYSANDER Helen, to you our minds we will unfold.
Tomorrow night, when Phoebe doth behold
210   Her silver visage in the wat'ry glass,
Decking with liquid pearl the bladed grass,
A time that lovers' flights doth still conceal,
Through Athens' gates have we devised to steal.

HERMIA And in the wood, where often you and I
215   Upon faint primrose beds were wont to lie,
Emptying our bosoms of their counsel sweet,

190 **bated** excepted   191 **translated** transformed   209 **Phoebe** the moon
212 **still** always

There my Lysander and myself shall meet,
And thence from Athens turn away our eyes,
To seek new friends and stranger companies.
Farewell, sweet playfellow. Pray thou for us;   220
And good luck grant thee thy Demetrius!
Keep word, Lysander. We must starve our sight
From lovers' food till tomorrow deep midnight.

LYSANDER I will, my Hermia.   *Exit Hermia.*
                  Helena, adieu.
As you on him, Demetrius dote on you!   225
                        Exit Lysander.

HELENA How happy some o'er other some can be!
Through Athens I am thought as fair as she.
But what of that? Demetrius thinks not so;
He will not know what all but he do know.
And as he errs, doting on Hermia's eyes,   230
So I, admiring of his qualities.
Things base and vile, holding no quantity,
Love can transpose to form and dignity.
Love looks not with the eyes, but with the mind,
And therefore is winged Cupid painted blind.   235
Nor hath Love's mind of any judgment taste;
Wings, and no eyes, figure unheedy haste:
And therefore is Love said to be a child,
Because in choice he is so oft beguiled.
As waggish boys in game themselves forswear,   240
So the boy Love is perjured everywhere.
For ere Demetrius looked on Hermia's eyne,
He hailed down oaths that he was only mine;
And when this hail some heat from Hermia felt,
So he dissolved, and show'rs of oaths did melt.   245
I will go tell him of fair Hermia's flight.
Then to the wood will he tomorrow night
Pursue her; and for this intelligence

219 **stranger companies** the company of strangers   226 **some o'er other some**
some in comparison with others   232 **holding no quantity** having no proportion
(therefore unattractive)   237 **figure** symbolize   242 **eyne** eyes   248 **intelligence** piece of news

If I have thanks, it is a dear expense:
250 But herein mean I to enrich my pain,
To have his sight thither and back again.   *Exit.*

[Scene II. *Quince's house.*]

Enter Quince the Carpenter, and Snug the Joiner, and
Bottom the Weaver, and Flute the Bellows Mender, and
Snout the Tinker, and Starveling the Tailor.

QUINCE Is all our company here?

BOTTOM You were best to call them generally, man
by man, according to the scrip.

QUINCE Here is the scroll of every man's name,
5   which is thought fit, through all Athens, to play in
our interlude before the Duke and the Duchess,
on his wedding day at night.

BOTTOM First, good Peter Quince, say what the play
treats on; then read the names of the actors; and
10   so grow to a point.

QUINCE Marry, our play is, "The most lamentable
comedy, and most cruel death of Pyramus and
Thisby."

BOTTOM A very good piece of work, I assure you,

---

249 **dear expense** (1) expense gladly incurred (2) heavy cost (in Demetrius'
opinion) I.ii.s.d. (the names of the clowns suggest their trades. **Bottom** skein on
which the yarn is wound; **Quince** quines, blocks of wood used for building; **Snug**
close-fitting; **Flute** suggesting fluted bellows [for church organs]; **Snout** spout of a
kettle; **Starveling** an allusion to the proverbial thinness of tailors) 2 **generally**
(Bottom means "individually") 6 **interlude** dramatic entertainment 11 **Marry**
(an interjection, originally an oath, "By the Virgin Mary")

and a merry. Now, good Peter Quince, call forth   15
your actors by the scroll. Masters, spread yourselves.

QUINCE Answer as I call you. Nick Bottom, the
weaver.

BOTTOM Ready. Name what part I am for, and pro-   20
ceed.

QUINCE You, Nick Bottom, are set down for Pyramus.

BOTTOM What is Pyramus? A lover, or a tyrant?

QUINCE A lover that kills himself, most gallant, for
love.   25

BOTTOM That will ask some tears in the true performing of it: if I do it, let the audience look to
their eyes. I will move storms, I will condole in
some measure. To the rest: yet my chief humor
is for a tyrant. I could play Ercles rarely, or a   30
part to tear a cat in, to make all split.

> The raging rocks
> And shivering shocks
> Shall break the locks
>   Of prison gates;   35
> And Phibbus' car
> Shall shine from far,
> And make and mar
>   The foolish Fates.

This was lofty! Now name the rest of the players.   40
This is Ercles' vein, a tyrant's vein. A lover is
more condoling.

QUINCE Francis Flute, the bellows mender.

FLUTE Here, Peter Quince.

---

28 **condole** lament   29 **humor** disposition   30 **Ercles** Hercules (a part notorious for ranting)   36 **Phibbus' car** (mispronunciation for "Phoebus' car," or
chariot, i.e., the sun)

45   QUINCE Flute, you must take Thisby on you.

FLUTE What is Thisby? A wand'ring knight?

QUINCE It is the lady that Pyramus must love.

FLUTE Nay, faith, let not me play a woman. I have
a beard coming.

50   QUINCE That's all one. You shall play it in a mask,
and you may speak as small as you will.

BOTTOM An I may hide my face, let me play Thisby
too, I'll speak in a monstrous little voice, "Thisne,
Thisne!" "Ah Pyramus, my lover dear! Thy Thisby
55   dear, and lady dear!"

QUINCE No, no; you must play Pyramus: and, Flute,
you Thisby.

BOTTOM Well, proceed.

QUINCE Robin Starveling, the tailor.

60   STARVELING Here, Peter Quince.

QUINCE Robin Starveling, you must play Thisby's
mother. Tom Snout, the tinker.

SNOUT Here, Peter Quince.

QUINCE You, Pyramus' father: myself, Thisby's
65   father: Snug, the joiner; you, the lion's part. And
I hope here is a play fitted.

SNUG Have you the lion's part written? Pray you, if
it be, give it me, for I am slow of study.

QUINCE You may do it extempore, for it is nothing
70   but roaring.

BOTTOM Let me play the lion too. I will roar that I
will do any man's heart good to hear me. I will
roar, that I will make the Duke say, "Let him roar
again, let him roar again."

50 **That's all one** it makes no difference   51 **small** softly   52 **An** if   71 **that** so
that

QUINCE An you should do it too terribly, you would   75
fright the Duchess and the ladies, that they would
shriek; and that were enough to hang us all.

ALL That would hang us, every mother's son.

BOTTOM I grant you, friends, if you should fright the
ladies out of their wits, they would have no more   80
discretion but to hang us: but I will aggravate
my voice so that I will roar you as gently as any
sucking dove; I will roar you an 'twere any nightingale.

QUINCE You can play no part but Pyramus; for   85
Pyramus is a sweet-faced man; a proper man as
one shall see in a summer's day; a most lovely,
gentlemanlike man: therefore you must needs play
Pyramus.

BOTTOM Well, I will undertake it. What beard were   90
I best to play it in?

QUINCE Why, what you will.

BOTTOM I will discharge it in either your straw-color
beard, your orange-tawny beard, your purple-in-
grain beard, or your French-crown-color beard,   95
your perfit yellow.

QUINCE Some of your French crowns have no hair
at all, and then you will play barefaced. But, masters, here are your parts; and I am to entreat you,
request you, and desire you, to con them by to-   100
morrow night; and meet me in the palace wood, a
mile without the town, by moonlight. There will
we rehearse, for if we meet in the city, we shall be
dogged with company, and our devices known.

---

81 **aggravate** (Bottom means "moderate") 83 **an 'twere** as if it were
86 **proper** handsome 94-95 **purple-in-grain** dyed with a fast purple
95 **French-crown-color** color of French gold coin 96 **perfit** perfect
97 **crowns** (1) gold coins (2) heads bald from the French disease (syphilis)
98 **barefaced** (1) bald (2) brazen 100 **con** study 104 **devices** plans

105   In the meantime I will draw a bill of properties,
      such as our play wants. I pray you, fail me not.

      BOTTOM We will meet; and there we may rehearse
      most obscenely and courageously. Take pains; be
      perfit: adieu.

110   QUINCE At the Duke's Oak we meet.

      BOTTOM Enough; hold or cut bowstrings.   *Exeunt.*

---

105 **bill of properties** list of stage furnishings   108 **obscenely** (Bottom means
"seemly")   111 **hold or cut bowstrings** i.e., keep your word or give it up (?)

[ACT II

Scene I. *A wood near Athens.*]

Enter a Fairy at one door, and Robin Goodfellow
[Puck] at another.

PUCK How now, spirit! Whither wander you?

FAIRY Over hill, over dale,
    Thorough bush, thorough brier,
  Over park, over pale,
    Thorough flood, thorough fire,   5
I do wander everywhere,
Swifter than the moon's sphere;
And I serve the Fairy Queen,
To dew her orbs upon the green.
The cowslips tall her pensioners be: 10
In their gold coats spots you see;
Those be rubies, fairy favors,
In those freckles live their savors.
I must go seek some dewdrops here,
And hang a pearl in every cowslip's ear.   15

II.i.4 **pale** enclosed land, park 7 **moon's sphere** (according to the Ptolemaic system the moon was fixed in a hollow sphere that surrounded and revolved about the earth) 9 **orbs** fairy rings, i.e., circles of darker grass 10 **pensioners** bodyguards (referring to Elizabeth I's bodyguard of fifty splendid young noblemen) 12 **favors** gifts 13 **savors** perfumes

Farewell, thou lob of spirits; I'll be gone.
Our Queen and all her elves come here anon.

PUCK   The King doth keep his revels here tonight.
Take heed the Queen come not within his sight.
20 For Oberon is passing fell and wrath,
Because that she as her attendant hath
A lovely boy, stolen from an Indian king;
She never had so sweet a changeling.
And jealous Oberon would have the child
25 Knight of his train, to trace the forests wild.
But she perforce withholds the lovèd boy,
Crowns him with flowers, and makes him all her
    joy.
And now they never meet in grove or green,
By fountain clear, or spangled starlight sheen,
30 But they do square, that all their elves for fear
Creep into acorn cups and hide them there.

FAIRY   Either I mistake your shape and making quite,
Or else you are that shrewd and knavish sprite
Called Robin Goodfellow. Are not you he
35 That frights the maidens of the villagery,
Skim milk, and sometimes labor in the quern,
And bootless make the breathless housewife
    churn,
And sometime make the drink to bear no barm,
Mislead night wanderers, laughing at their harm?
40 Those that Hobgoblin call you, and sweet Puck,
You do their work, and they shall have good luck.
Are not you he?

PUCK   Thou speakest aright;
I am that merry wanderer of the night.
I jest to Oberon, and make him smile,

16 **lob** lubber, clumsy fellow   20 **passing fell and wrath** very fierce and angry
23 **changeling** (usually a child left behind by fairies in exchange for one stolen,
but here applied to the stolen child)   25 **trace** traverse   29 **starlight sheen**
brightly shining starlight   30 **square** clash, quarrel   35 **villagery** villagers
36 **quern** hand mill for grinding grain   37 **bootless** in vain   38 **barm** yeast,
froth

When I a fat and bean-fed horse beguile,   45
Neighing in likeness of a filly foal:
And sometime lurk I in a gossip's bowl,
In very likeness of a roasted crab;
And when she drinks, against her lips I bob
And on her withered dewlap pour the ale.   50
The wisest aunt, telling the saddest tale,
Sometime for three-foot stool mistaketh me;
Then slip I from her bum, down topples she,
And "tailor" cries, and falls into a cough;
And then the whole quire hold their hips and
  laugh,   55
And waxen in their mirth, and neeze, and swear
A merrier hour was never wasted there.
But, room, fairy! Here comes Oberon.

FAIRY And here my mistress. Would that he were
  gone!

*Enter [Oberon,] the King of Fairies, at one door, with his
train; and [Titania,] the Queen, at another, with hers.*

OBERON Ill met by moonlight, proud Titania.   60

TITANIA What, jealous Oberon! Fairy, skip hence.
I have forsworn his bed and company.

OBERON Tarry, rash wanton; am not I thy lord?

TITANIA Then I must be thy lady: but I know
When thou hast stolen away from fairy land   65
And in the shape of Corin sat all day,
Playing on pipes of corn, and versing love

---

47 **gossip's** old woman's   48 **crab** crab apple   50 **dewlap** fold of skin on the
throat   51 **saddest** most serious   54 **tailor** (suggesting the posture of a tailor
squatting; or a term of abuse: Middle English *taillard*, "thief")   55 **quire**
company, choir   56 **waxen** increase   56 **neeze** sneeze   57 **wasted** passed
63 **rash wanton** hasty willful creature   66 **Corin** (like **Phillida**, line 68, a
traditional name for a lover in pastoral poetry)   67 **pipes of corn** musical
instruments made of grain stalks

To amorous Phillida. Why art thou here,
Come from the farthest steep of India?
70 But that, forsooth, the bouncing Amazon,
Your buskined mistress and your warrior love,
To Theseus must be wedded, and you come
To give their bed joy and prosperity.

OBERON How canst thou thus for shame, Titania,
75 Glance at my credit with Hippolyta,
Knowing I know thy love to Theseus?
Didst not thou lead him through the glimmering
    night
From Perigenia, whom he ravishèd?
And make him with fair Aegles break his faith,
80 With Ariadne and Antiopa?

TITANIA These are the forgeries of jealousy:
And never, since the middle summer's spring,
Met we on hill, in dale, forest, or mead,
By pavèd fountain or by rushy brook,
85 Or in the beachèd margent of the sea,
To dance our ringlets to the whistling wind,
But with thy brawls thou hast disturbed our sport.
Therefore the winds, piping to us in vain,
As in revenge, have sucked up from the sea
90 Contagious fogs; which, falling in the land,
Hath every pelting river made so proud,
That they have overborne their continents.
The ox hath therefore stretched his yoke in vain,
The plowman lost his sweat, and the green corn
95 Hath rotted ere his youth attained a beard;
The fold stands empty in the drownèd field,
And crows are fatted with the murrion flock;

---

70 **bouncing** swaggering 71 **buskined** wearing a hunter's boot (buskin)
78–80 **Perigenia, Aegles, Ariadne, Antiopa** (girls Theseus loved and deserted)
82 **middle summer's spring** beginning of midsummer 84 **pavèd** i.e., with
pebbly bottom 85 **margent** margin, shore 90 **contagious** generating pestilence 91 **pelting** petty 92 **continents** containers (i.e., banks) 94 **corn** grain
97 **murrion flock** flock dead of cattle disease (murrain)

The nine men's morris is filled up with mud;
And the quaint mazes in the wanton green,
For lack of tread, are undistinguishable.   100
The human mortals want their winter here;
No night is now with hymn or carol blest.
Therefore the moon, the governess of floods,
Pale in her anger, washes all the air,
That rheumatic diseases do abound.   105
And thorough this distemperature we see
The seasons alter: hoary-headed frosts
Fall in the fresh lap of the crimson rose,
And on old Hiems' thin and icy crown
An odorous chaplet of sweet summer buds   110
Is, as in mockery, set. The spring, the summer,
The childing autumn, angry winter, change
Their wonted liveries; and the mazèd world,
By their increase, now knows not which is which.
And this same progeny of evils comes   115
From our debate, from our dissension;
We are their parents and original.

OBERON Do you amend it, then; it lies in you:
Why should Titania cross her Oberon?
I do but beg a little changeling boy,   120
To be my henchman.

TITANIA   Set your heart at rest.
The fairy land buys not the child of me.
His mother was a vot'ress of my order,
And, in the spicèd Indian air, by night,
Full often hath she gossiped by my side,   125
And sat with me on Neptune's yellow sands,

98 **nine men's morris** square cut in the turf (for a game in which each player has nine counters or "men") 99 **quaint mazes** intricate meandering paths on the grass (kept fresh by running along them) 99 **wanton green** grass growing without check 101 **Want their winter here** lack their usual winter festivities (?; some editors emend "here" to "cheer"). 106 **distemperature** disturbance in nature 109 **old Hiems'** the winter's 110 **chaplet** wreath 112 **childing** breeding, fruitful 113 **wonted liveries** accustomed apparel 113 **mazèd** bewildered 116 **debate** quarrel 121 **henchman** page 122 **The fairy land buys not** i.e., even your whole domain could not buy 123 **vot'ress** woman who has taken a vow

Marking th' embarkèd traders on the flood;
When we have laughed to see the sails conceive
And grow big-bellied with the wanton wind;
130   Which she, with pretty and with swimming gait
Following—her womb then rich with my young
        squire—
Would imitate, and sail upon the land,
To fetch me trifles, and return again,
As from a voyage, rich with merchandise.
135   But she, being mortal, of that boy did die;
And for her sake do I rear up her boy,
And for her sake I will not part with him.

OBERON How long within this wood intend you stay?

TITANIA Perchance till after Theseus' wedding day.
140   If you will patiently dance in our round,
And see our moonlight revels, go with us.
If not, shun me, and I will spare your haunts.

OBERON Give me that boy, and I will go with thee.

TITANIA Not for thy fairy kingdom. Fairies, away!
145   We shall chide downright, if I longer stay.
                        Exeunt [*Titania with her train*].

OBERON Well, go thy way. Thou shalt not from this
        grove
Till I torment thee for this injury.
My gentle Puck, come hither. Thou rememb'rest
Since once I sat upon a promontory,
150   And heard a mermaid, on a dolphin's back,
Uttering such dulcet and harmonious breath,
That the rude sea grew civil at her song,
And certain stars shot madly from their spheres,
To hear the sea maid's music.

PUCK   I remember.

155   OBERON That very time I saw, but thou couldst not,
Flying between the cold moon and the earth,

140 **round** circular dance 142 **spare** keep away from 149 **Since** when
152 **civil** well behaved

540

Cupid all armed. A certain aim he took
At a fair vestal thronèd by the west,
And loosed his love shaft smartly from his bow,
As it should pierce a hundred thousand hearts.   160
But I might see young Cupid's fiery shaft
Quenched in the chaste beams of the wat'ry moon,
And the imperial vot'ress passèd on,
In maiden meditation, fancy-free.
Yet marked I where the bolt of Cupid fell.   165
It fell upon a little western flower,
Before milk-white, now purple with love's wound,
And maidens call it love-in-idleness.
Fetch me that flow'r; the herb I showed thee once:
The juice of it on sleeping eyelids laid   170
Will make or man or woman madly dote
Upon the next live creature that it sees.
Fetch me this herb, and be thou here again
Ere the leviathan can swim a league.

PUCK I'll put a girdle round about the earth   175
In forty minutes.   [*Exit.*]

OBERON   Having once this juice,
I'll watch Titania when she is asleep,
And drop the liquor of it in her eyes.
The next thing then she waking looks upon,
Be it on lion, bear, or wolf, or bull,   180
On meddling monkey, or on busy ape,
She shall pursue it with the soul of love.
And ere I take this charm from off her sight,
As I can take it with another herb,
I'll make her render up her page to me.   185
But who comes here? I am invisible,
And I will overhear their conference.

Enter Demetrius, Helena following him.

158 vestal virgin (possibly an allusion to Elizabeth, the Virgin Queen)   160 **As it
should** as if it would   161 **might** could   164 **fancy-free** free from the power of
love   168 **love-in-idleness** pansy   171 **or man or woman** either man or
woman   174 **leviathan** sea monster, whale   181 **busy** meddlesome

DEMETRIUS I love thee not, therefore pursue me not.
Where is Lysander and fair Hermia?
190 The one I'll slay, the other slayeth me.
Thou told'st me they were stol'n unto this wood;
And here am I, and wood within this wood;
Because I cannot meet my Hermia.
Hence, get thee gone, and follow me no more!

195 HELENA You draw me, you hardhearted adamant;
But yet you draw not iron, for my heart
Is true as steel. Leave you your power to draw,
And I shall have no power to follow you.

DEMETRIUS Do I entice you? Do I speak you fair?
200 Or, rather, do I not in plainest truth
Tell you, I do not nor I cannot love you?

HELENA And even for that do I love you the more.
I am your spaniel; and, Demetrius,
The more you beat me, I will fawn on you.
205 Use me but as your spaniel, spurn me, strike me,
Neglect me, lose me; only give me leave,
Unworthy as I am, to follow you.
What worser place can I beg in your love—
And yet a place of high respect with me—
210 Than to be usèd as you use your dog?

DEMETRIUS Tempt not too much the hatred of my spirit,
For I am sick when I do look on thee.

HELENA And I am sick when I look not on you.

DEMETRIUS You do impeach your modesty too much,
215 To leave the city, and commit yourself
Into the hands of one that loves you not,
To trust the opportunity of night
And the ill counsel of a desert place
With the rich worth of your virginity.

---

192 **wood** out of my mind (with perhaps an additional pun on "wooed")
195 **adamant** (1) very hard gem (2) loadstone, magnet 199 **speak you fair**
speak kindly to you 214 **impeach** expose to reproach 218 **desert** deserted,
uninhabited

HELENA Your virtue is my privilege. For that   220
   It is not night when I do see your face,
   Therefore I think I am not in the night;
   Nor doth this wood lack worlds of company,
   For you in my respect are all the world.
   Then how can it be said I am alone,   225
   When all the world is here to look on me?

DEMETRIUS I'll run from thee and hide me in the
     brakes,
   And leave thee to the mercy of wild beasts.

HELENA The wildest hath not such a heart as you.
   Run when you will, the story shall be changed: 230
   Apollo flies, and Daphne holds the chase;
   The dove pursues the griffin; the mild hind
   Makes speed to catch the tiger; bootless speed,
   When cowardice pursues, and valor flies.

DEMETRIUS I will not stay thy questions. Let me go!   235
   Or, if thou follow me, do not believe
   But I shall do thee mischief in the wood.

HELENA Ay, in the temple, in the town, the field,
   You do me mischief. Fie, Demetrius!
   Your wrongs do set a scandal on my sex.   240
   We cannot fight for love, as men may do;
   We should be wooed, and were not made to woo.
                      [Exit Demetrius.]
   I'll follow thee, and make a heaven of hell,
   To die upon the hand I love so well.   *[Exit.]*

OBERON Fare thee well, nymph: ere he do leave this
     grove,   245
   Thou shalt fly him, and he shall seek thy love.

---

220 **Your virtue is my privilege** your inherent power is my warrant   224 **in my respect** in my opinion   227 **brakes** thickets   231 **Daphne** a nymph who fled from Apollo (at her prayer she was changed into a laurel tree)   232 **griffin** fabulous monster with an eagle's head and a lion's body   232 **hind** doe   235 **stay** wait for   224 **To die upon** dying by

Enter Puck.

Hast thou the flower there? Welcome, wanderer.

PUCK   Ay, there it is.

OBERON   I pray thee, give it me.
    I know a bank where the wild thyme blows,
250   Where oxlips and the nodding violet grows,
    Quite overcanopied with luscious woodbine,
    With sweet musk roses, and with eglantine.
    There sleeps Titania sometime of the night,
    Lulled in these flowers with dances and delight;
255   And there the snake throws her enameled skin,
    Weed wide enough to wrap a fairy in.
    And with the juice of this I'll streak her eyes,
    And make her full of hateful fantasies.
    Take thou some of it, and seek through this grove.
260   A sweet Athenian lady is in love
    With a disdainful youth. Anoint his eyes;
    But do it when the next thing he espies
    May be the lady. Thou shalt know the man
    By the Athenian garments he hath on.
265   Effect it with some care that he may prove
    More fond on her than she upon her love:
    And look thou meet me ere the first cock crow.

PUCK   Fear not, my lord, your servant shall do so.
                                      Exeunt.

[Scene II. *Another part of the wood.*]

Enter Titania, Queen of Fairies, with her train.

TITANIA   Come, now a roundel and a fairy song;
    Then, for the third part of a minute, hence;

255 **throws** casts off   256 **Weed** garment   266 **fond on her** foolishly in love
with her   II.ii.1 **roundel** dance in a ring

Some to kill cankers in the musk-rose buds,
Some war with reremice for their leathern wings
To make my small elves coats, and some keep back   5
The clamorous owl, that nightly hoots and wonders
At our quaint spirits. Sing me now asleep.
Then to your offices, and let me rest.

Fairies sing.

1ST   You spotted snakes with double tongue,
FAIRY   Thorny hedgehogs, be not seen;   10
          Newts and blindworms, do no wrong,
              Come not near our Fairy Queen.

CHORUS   Philomele, with melody
              Sing in our sweet lullaby;
          Lulla, lulla, lullaby, lulla, lulla, lullaby: 15
                  Never harm
                  Nor spell nor charm,
              Come our lovely lady nigh;
              So, good night, with lullaby.

1ST   Weaving spiders, come not here;   20
FAIRY   Hence, you long-legged spinners, hence!
          Beetles black, approach not near;
              Worm nor snail, do no offense.

CHORUS   Philomele, with melody, &c.

2ND   Hence, away! Now all is well.   25
FAIRY   One aloof stand sentinel.
                        [*Exeunt Fairies. Titania sleeps.*]

          *Enter Oberon [and squeezes the flower on
                  Titania's eyelids].*

OBERON   What thou seest when thou dost wake,
              Do it for thy truelove take;
              Love and languish for his sake.
              Be it ounce, or cat, or bear,   30

---

4 reremice bats   **7** quaint dainty   **11** blindworms small snakes   **13** **Philomele** nightingale   **30** ounce lynx

> Pard, or boar with bristled hair,
> In thy eye that shall appear
> When thou wak'st, it is thy dear.
> Wake when some vile thing is near.   [*Exit.*]

Enter Lysander and Hermia.

LYSANDER Fair love, you faint with wand'ring in the
35   wood;
And to speak troth, I have forgot our way.
We'll rest us, Hermia, if you think it good,
And tarry for the comfort of the day.

HERMIA Be't so, Lysander. Find you out a bed;
40   For I upon this bank will rest my head.

LYSANDER One turf shall serve as pillow for us both,
One heart, one bed, two bosoms, and one troth.

HERMIA Nay, good Lysander. For my sake, my dear,
Lie further off yet, do not lie so near.

45 LYSANDER O, take the sense, sweet, of my innocence!
Love takes the meaning in love's conference.
I mean, that my heart unto yours is knit,
So that but one heart we can make of it:
Two bosoms interchainèd with an oath;
50   So then two bosoms and a single troth.
Then by your side no bed-room me deny,
For lying so, Hermia, I do not lie.

HERMIA Lysander riddles very prettily.
Now much beshrew my manners and my pride,
55   If Hermia meant to say Lysander lied.
But, gentle friend, for love and courtesy
Lie further off, in human modesty.
Such separation as may well be said

---

31 **Pard** leopard   36 **troth** truth   45 **take the sense** understand the true meaning
46 **Love takes the meaning** lovers understand the true meaning of what they say
to each other   50 **troth** faithful love   52 **lie** be untrue   54 **beshrew** curse (but
commonly, as here, in a light sense)

546

Becomes a virtuous bachelor and a maid,
So far be distant; and, good night, sweet friend.   60
Thy love ne'er alter till thy sweet life end!

LYSANDER Amen, amen, to that fair prayer, say I,
And then end life when I end loyalty!
Here is my bed. Sleep give thee all his rest!

HERMIA With half that wish the wisher's eyes be   65
pressed!   [*They sleep.*]

Enter Puck.

PUCK Through the forest have I gone,
But Athenian found I none,
On whose eyes I might approve
This flower's force in stirring love.
Night and silence.—Who is here?   70
Weeds of Athens he doth wear:
This is he, my master said,
Despisèd the Athenian maid;
And here the maiden, sleeping sound,
On the dank and dirty ground.   75
Pretty soul! She durst not lie
Near this lack-love, this kill-courtesy.
Churl, upon thy eyes I throw
All the power this charm doth owe.
When thou wak'st, let love forbid   80
Sleep his seat on thy eyelid.
So awake when I am gone,
For I must now to Oberon.   *Exit.*

Enter Demetrius and Helena, running.

HELENA Stay, though thou kill me, sweet Demetrius.

DEMETRIUS I charge thee, hence, and do not haunt me
thus.   85

---

68 **approve** try   71 **Weeds** garments   78 **Churl** boorish fellow   79 **owe** possess

HELENA O, wilt thou darkling leave me? Do not so.

DEMETRIUS Stay, on thy peril! I alone will go.   [*Exit.*]

HELENA O, I am out of breath in this fond chase!
The more my prayer, the lesser is my grace.
90 Happy is Hermia, wheresoe'er she lies,
For she hath blessèd and attractive eyes.
How came her eyes so bright? Not with salt tears.
If so, my eyes are oft'ner washed than hers.
No, no, I am as ugly as a bear,
95 For beasts that meet me run away for fear.
Therefore no marvel though Demetrius
Do, as a monster, fly my presence thus.
What wicked and dissembling glass of mine
Made me compare with Hermia's sphery eyne?
100 But who is here? Lysander! On the ground!
Dead? Or asleep? I see no blood, no wound.
Lysander, if you live, good sir, awake.

LYSANDER [*Awaking*] And run through fire I will for
thy sweet sake.
Transparent Helena! Nature shows art,
105 That through thy bosom makes me see thy heart.
Where is Demetrius? O, how fit a word
Is that vile name to perish on my sword!

HELENA Do not say so, Lysander, say not so.
What though he love your Hermia? Lord, what
though?
110 Yet Hermia still loves you. Then be content.

LYSANDER Content with Hermia! No; I do repent
The tedious minutes I with her have spent.
Not Hermia but Helena I love:
Who will not change a raven for a dove?
115 The will of man is by his reason swayed
And reason says you are the worthier maid.
Things growing are not ripe until their season:

86 **darkling** in the dark   88 **fond** (1) doting (2) foolish   99 **sphery eyne** starry
eyes   104 **Transparent** bright   115 **will** desire

So I, being young, till now ripe not to reason.
And touching now the point of human skill,
Reason becomes the marshal to my will,   120
And leads me to your eyes, where I o'erlook
Love's stories, written in love's richest book.

HELENA Wherefore was I to this keen mockery born?
  When at your hands did I deserve this scorn?
  Is't not enough, is't not enough, young man,   125
  That I did never, no, nor never can,
  Deserve a sweet look from Demetrius' eye,
  But you must flout my insufficiency?
  Good troth, you do me wrong, good sooth, you do,
  In such disdainful manner me to woo.   130
  But fare you well. Perforce I must confess
  I thought you lord of more true gentleness.
  O, that a lady, of one man refused,
  Should of another therefore be abused!   *Exit*.

LYSANDER She sees not Hermia. Hermia, sleep thou
    there,   135
  And never mayst thou come Lysander near!
  For as a surfeit of the sweetest things
  The deepest loathing to the stomach brings,
  Or as the heresies that men do leave
  Are hated most of those they did deceive,   140
  So thou, my surfeit and my heresy,
  Of all be hated, but the most of me!
  And, all my powers, address your love and might
  To honor Helen and to be her knight!   *Exit*.

HERMIA [*Awaking*] Help me, Lysander, help me! Do
    thy best   145
  To pluck this crawling serpent from my breast!
  Ay me, for pity! What a dream was here!
  Lysander, look how I do quake with fear.

---

118 **ripe not** have not ripened   119 **touching now ... human skill** now
reaching the fulness of human reason   128 **flout** jeer at   129 **Good troth** indeed
(an expletive, like "good sooth")   132 **gentleness** noble character   143 **address**
apply

Methought a serpent eat my heart away,
150   And you sat smiling at his cruel prey.
Lysander! What, removed? Lysander! Lord!
What, out of hearing? Gone? No sound, no word?
Alack, where are you? Speak, an if you hear;
Speak, of all loves! I swoon almost with fear.
155   No? Then I well perceive you are not nigh.
Either death or you I'll find immediately.   *Exit.*

149 **eat** ate (pronounced "et")   150 **prey** act of preying   153 **an if** if   154 **of** for the sake of

[ACT III

Scene I. *The wood. Titania lying asleep.*]

Enter the clowns: [*Quince, Snug, Bottom, Flute, Snout, and Starveling*].

BOTTOM Are we all met?

QUINCE Pat, pat; and here's a marvail's convenient place for our rehearsal. This green plot shall be our stage, this hawthorn brake our tiring house, and we will do it in action as we will do it before   5
the Duke.

BOTTOM Peter Quince?

QUINCE What sayest thou, bully Bottom?

BOTTOM There are things in this comedy of Pyramus and Thisby that will never please. First, Pyramus   10
must draw a sword to kill himself; which the ladies cannot abide. How answer you that?

SNOUT By'r lakin, a parlous fear.

STARVELING I believe we must leave the killing out, when all is done.   15

III.i.2 **Pat** exactly, on the dot   2 **marvail's** (Quince means "marvelous") 4 **brake** thicket   4 **tiring house** attiring house, dressing room   8 **bully** good fellow   13 **By'r lakin** by our lady (ladykin = little lady)   13 **parlous** perilous, terrible

BOTTOM Not a whit. I have a device to make all well. Write me a prologue, and let the prologue seem to say, we will do no harm with our swords, and that Pyramus is not killed indeed; and, for the more better assurance, tell them that I Pyramus am not Pyramus, but Bottom the weaver. This will put them out of fear.

QUINCE Well, we will have such a prologue, and it shall be written in eight and six.

BOTTOM No, make it two more; let it be written in eight and eight.

SNOUT Will not the ladies be afeared of the lion?

STARVELING I fear it, I promise you.

BOTTOM Masters, you ought to consider with yourselves. To bring in—God shield us!—a lion among ladies, is a most dreadful thing. For there is not a more fearful wild fowl than your lion living; and we ought to look to't.

SNOUT Therefore another prologue must tell he is not a lion.

BOTTOM Nay, you must name his name, and half his face must be seen through the lion's neck, and he himself must speak through, saying thus, or to the same defect—"Ladies"—or, "Fair ladies—I would wish you"—or, "I would request you"—or, "I would entreat you—not to fear, not to tremble: my life for yours. If you think I come hither as a lion, it were pity of my life. No, I am no such thing. I am a man as other men are." And there indeed let him name his name, and tell them plainly, he is Snug the joiner.

QUINCE Well, it shall be so. But there is two hard things; that is, to bring the moonlight into a

24 **in eight and six** in alternate lines of eight and six syllables (ballad stanza)
43 **pity of my life** a bad thing for me

chamber; for, you know, Pyramus and Thisby
meet by moonlight. 50

SNOUT Doth the moon shine that night we play our
play?

BOTTOM A calendar, a calendar! Look in the almanac;
find out moonshine, find out moonshine.

QUINCE Yes, it doth shine that night. 55

BOTTOM Why, then may you leave a casement of the
great chamber window, where we play, open, and
the moon may shine in at the casement.

QUINCE Ay; or else one must come in with a bush of
thorns and a lantern, and say he comes to dis- 60
figure, or to present, the person of Moonshine.
Then, there is another thing: we must have a wall
in the great chamber; for Pyramus and Thisby,
says the story, did talk through the chink of a
wall. 65

SNOUT You can never bring in a wall. What say you,
Bottom?

BOTTOM Some man or other must present Wall: and
let him have some plaster, or some loam, or some
roughcast about him, to signify Wall; and let him 70
hold his fingers thus, and through that cranny shall
Pyramus and Thisby whisper.

QUINCE If that may be, then all is well. Come, sit
down, every mother's son, and rehearse your parts.
Pyramus, you begin. When you have spoken your 75
speech, enter into that brake; and so everyone according to his cue.

Enter Robin [Puck].

59-60 **bush of thorns** (legend held that the man in the moon had been placed
there for gathering firewood on Sunday) 60-61 **disfigure** (Quince means
"figure," "represent") 70 **roughcast** lime mixed with gravel to plaster outside
walls

PUCK What hempen homespuns have we swagg'ring
here,
So near the cradle of the Fairy Queen?
80   What, a play toward! I'll be an auditor;
An actor too perhaps, if I see cause.

QUINCE Speak, Pyramus. Thisby, stand forth.

PYRAMUS [*Bottom*] Thisby, the flowers of odious
savors sweet—

QUINCE Odors, odors.

85 PYRAMUS —odors savors sweet:
So hath thy breath, my dearest Thisby dear.
But hark, a voice! Stay thou but here awhile,
And by and by I will to thee appear.   *Exit.*

PUCK A stranger Pyramus than e'er played here!
[*Exit.*]

90 THISBY [*Flute*] Must I speak now?

QUINCE Ay, marry, must you. For you must understand he goes but to see a noise that he heard, and
is to come again.

THISBY Most radiant Pyramus, most lily-white of hue,
95   Of color like the red rose on triumphant brier,
Most brisky juvenal, and eke most lovely Jew,
As true as truest horse, that yet would never tire,
I'll meet thee, Pyramus, at Ninny's tomb.

QUINCE "Ninus' tomb," man. Why, you must not
100   speak that yet. That you answer to Pyramus. You
speak all your part at once, cues and all. Pyramus
enter. Your cue is past; it is "never tire."

THISBY O—as true as truest horse, that yet would
never tire.

---

78 **hempen homespuns** coarse fellows (clad in homespun cloth of hemp)
80 **toward** in preparation   88 **by and by** shortly   96 **juvenal** youth   96 **eke** also
98 **Ninny's** (blunder for "Ninus' "; Ninus was the legendary founder of Nineveh)

[Re-enter Puck, and Bottom with an ass's head.]

PYRAMUS If I were fair, Thisby, I were only thine.

QUINCE O monstrous! O strange! We are haunted. 105
Pray, masters! Fly, masters! Help!
[Exeunt all the clowns but Bottom.]

PUCK I'll follow you, I'll lead you about a round,
Through bog, through bush, through brake,
through brier.
Sometime a horse I'll be, sometime a hound; 110
A hog, a headless bear, sometime a fire;
And neigh, and bark, and grunt, and roar, and
burn,
Like horse, hound, hog, bear, fire, at every turn.
Exit.

BOTTOM Why do they run away? This is a knavery of
them to make me afeard.

Enter Snout.

SNOUT O Bottom, thou art changed! What do I see 115
on thee?

BOTTOM What do you see? You see an ass head of
your own, do you?   *[Exit Snout.]*

Enter Quince.

QUINCE Bless thee, Bottom! Bless thee! Thou art
translated.   *Exit.* 120

BOTTOM I see their knavery. This is to make an ass
of me; to fright me, if they could. But I will not
stir from this place, do what they can. I will walk
up and down here, and will sing, that they shall 125
hear I am not afraid.   *[Sings.]*

107 **about a round** roundabout   120 **translated** transformed

> The woosel cock so black of hue,
> With orange-tawny bill,
> The throstle with his note so true,
> The wren with little quill—

TITANIA [*Awaking*] What angel wakes me from my
130 flow'ry bed?

BOTTOM [*Sings*] The finch, the sparrow, and the lark,
> The plain-song cuckoo gray,
> Whose note full many a man doth
> mark,
> And dares not answer nay—

135 for, indeed, who would set his wit to so foolish
a bird? Who would give a bird the lie, though he
cry "cuckoo" never so?

TITANIA I pray thee, gentle mortal, sing again:
Mine ear is much enamored of thy note;
140 So is mine eye enthrallèd to thy shape;
And thy fair virtue's force perforce doth move me
On the first view to say, to swear, I love thee.

BOTTOM Methinks, mistress, you should have little
reason for that. And yet, to say the truth, reason
145 and love keep little company together nowadays;
the more the pity, that some honest neighbors will
not make them friends. Nay, I can gleek upon
occasion.

TITANIA Thou art as wise as thou art beautiful.

150 BOTTOM Not so, neither; but if I had wit enough to
get out of this wood, I have enough to serve mine
own turn.

TITANIA Out of this wood do not desire to go.

---

126 **woosel** ouzel, blackbird 129 **quill** (literally, "reed pipe"; here, "piping
voice") 132 **the plain-song cuckoo** the cuckoo, who sings a simple song
135 **set his wit** use his intelligence to answer 136 **give a bird the lie** contradict
a bird (the cuckoo's song supposedly tells a man he is a cuckold) 137 **never so**
ever so often 147 **gleek** make a satirical jest

Thou shalt remain here, whether thou wilt or no.
I am a spirit of no common rate.   155
The summer still doth tend upon my state;
And I do love thee. Therefore, go with me.
I'll give thee fairies to attend on thee,
And they shall fetch thee jewels from the deep,
And sing, while thou on pressèd flowers dost sleep: 160
And I will purge thy mortal grossness so,
That thou shalt like an airy spirit go.
Peaseblossom! Cobweb! Moth! And Mustardseed!

Enter four Fairies
[*Peaseblossom, Cobweb, Moth, and Mustardseed*].

PEASEBLOSSOM Ready.

COBWEB   And I.

MOTH   And I.

MUSTARDSEED   And I.

ALL   Where shall we go?

TITANIA Be kind and courteous to this gentleman;   165
Hop in his walks, and gambol in his eyes;
Feed him with apricocks and dewberries,
With purple grapes, green figs, and mulberries;
The honey bags steal from the humblebees,
And for night tapers crop their waxen thighs,   170
And light them at the fiery glowworm's eyes,
To have my love to bed and to arise;
And pluck the wings from painted butterflies,
To fan the moonbeams from his sleeping eyes.
Nod to him, elves, and do him courtesies.   175

PEASEBLOSSOM Hail, mortal!

COBWEB   Hail!

155 **rate** rank   156 **still doth tend** always waits upon   163 **Moth** (pronounced "mote," and probably a speck rather than an insect is denoted)   167 **apricocks and dewberries** apricots and blackberries   169 **humblebees** bumblebees

MOTH   Hail!

MUSTARDSEED   Hail!

BOTTOM I cry your worships mercy, heartily: I beseech your worship's name.

COBWEB Cobweb.

180   BOTTOM I shall desire you of more acquaintance,
good Master Cobweb: if I cut my finger, I shall
make bold with you. Your name, honest gentleman?

PEASEBLOSSOM Peaseblossom.

185   BOTTOM I pray you, commend me to Mistress Squash,
your mother, and to Master Peascod, your father.
Good Master Peaseblossom, I shall desire you of
more acquaintance too. Your name, I beseech you,
sir?

190   MUSTARDSEED Mustardseed.

BOTTOM Good Master Mustardseed, I know your patience well. That same cowardly, giantlike ox-beef
hath devoured many a gentleman of your house.
I promise you your kindred hath made my eyes
195   water ere now. I desire you of more acquaintance,
good Master Mustardseed.

TITANIA Come, wait upon him; lead him to my bower.
The moon methinks looks with a wat'ry eye;
And when she weeps, weeps every little flower,
200   Lamenting some enforcèd chastity.
Tie up my lover's tongue, bring him silently.
                          Exit [Titania with Bottom and Fairies].

177 I cry your worships mercy I beg pardon of your honors   180 I shall
desire you of more acquaintance I shall want to be better acquainted with you
181 if I cut my finger (cobweb was used for stanching blood)   185 Squash
unripe pea pod   193 devoured (because beef is often eaten with mustard)
200 enforcèd violated

[Scene II. *Another part of the wood.*]

Enter [Oberon,] King of Fairies, and Robin
Goodfellow [Puck].

OBERON I wonder if Titania be awaked;
Then, what it was that next came in her eye,
Which she must dote on in extremity.
Here comes my messenger. How now, mad spirit!
What night-rule now about this haunted grove?   5

PUCK My mistress with a monster is in love.
Near to her close and consecrated bower,
While she was in her dull and sleeping hour,
A crew of patches, rude mechanicals,
That work for bread upon Athenian stalls,   10
Were met together to rehearse a play,
Intended for great Theseus' nuptial day.
The shallowest thickskin of that barren sort,
Who Pyramus presented in their sport,
Forsook his scene, and entered in a brake.   15
When I did him at this advantage take,
An ass's nole I fixèd on his head.
Anon his Thisby must be answerèd,
And forth my mimic comes. When they him spy,
As wild geese that the creeping fowler eye,   20
Or russet-pated choughs, many in sort,
Rising and cawing at the gun's report,
Sever themselves and madly sweep the sky,
So, at his sight, away his fellows fly;

III.ii.3 **in extremity** to the extreme   5 **night-rule** happenings during the night
7 **close** private, secret   9 **patches** fools, clowns   9 **rude mechanicals** uneducated workingmen   13 **barren sort** stupid group   17 **nole** "noodle," head
18 **Anon** presently   21 **russet-pated ... in sort** gray-headed jackdaws, many in
a flock

25 And, at our stamp, here o'er and o'er one falls;
 He murder cries, and help from Athens calls.
 Their sense thus weak, lost with their fears thus
  strong,
 Made senseless things begin to do them wrong;
 For briers and thorns at their apparel snatch;
 Some sleeves, some hats, from yielders all things
30 catch.
 I led them on in this distracted fear,
 And left sweet Pyramus translated there:
 When in that moment, so it came to pass,
 Titania waked, and straightway loved an ass.

35 OBERON This falls out better than I could devise.
 But hast thou yet latched the Athenian's eyes
 With the love juice, as I bid thee do?

 PUCK I took him sleeping—that is finished too—
 And the Athenian woman by his side;
40 That, when he waked, of force she must be eyed.

Enter Demetrius and Hermia.

OBERON Stand close: this is the same Athenian.

PUCK This is the woman, but not this the man.

DEMETRIUS O, why rebuke you him that loves you so?
 Lay breath so bitter on your bitter foe.

45 HERMIA Now I but chide; but I should use thee worse,
 For thou, I fear, hast given me cause to curse.
 If thou hast slain Lysander in his sleep,
 Being o'er shoes in blood, plunge in the deep,
 And kill me too.
50 The sun was not so true unto the day
 As he to me. Would he have stolen away
 From sleeping Hermia? I'll believe as soon
 This whole earth may be bored, and that the moon

36 **latched** fastened (or possibly "moistened")   40 **of force** by necessity
41 **close** concealed   53 **whole** solid

May through the center creep, and so displease
Her brother's noontide with th' Antipodes.   55
It cannot be but thou hast murd'red him.
So should a murderer look, so dead, so grim.

DEMETRIUS So should the murdered look; and so
   should I.
Pierced through the heart with your stern cruelty.
Yet you, the murderer, look as bright, as clear,   60
As yonder Venus in her glimmering sphere.

HERMIA What's this to my Lysander? Where is he?
Ah, good Demetrius, wilt thou give him me?

DEMETRIUS I had rather give his carcass to my hounds.

HERMIA Out, dog! Out, cur! Thou driv'st me past the
   bounds   65
Of maiden's patience. Hast thou slain him, then?
Henceforth be never numb'red among men!
O, once tell true! Tell true, even for my sake!
Durst thou have looked upon him being awake?
And hast thou killed him sleeping? O brave touch!   70
Could not a worm, an adder, do so much?
An adder did it; for with doubler tongue
Than thine, thou serpent, never adder stung.

DEMETRIUS You spend your passion on a misprised
   mood:
I am not guilty of Lysander's blood;   75
Nor is he dead, for aught that I can tell.

HERMIA I pray thee, tell me then that he is well.

DEMETRIUS An if I could, what should I get therefore?

HERMIA A privilege, never to see me more.
And from thy hated presence part I so.   80
See me no more, whether he be dead or no.   *Exit.*

---

55 **Her brother's** i.e., the sun's   57 **dead** deadly pale   70 **brave touch** splendid
exploit (ironic)   74 **misprised mood** mistaken anger   78 **therefore** in return

DEMETRIUS There is no following her in this fierce vein.
Here therefore for a while I will remain.
So sorrow's heaviness doth heavier grow
85   For debt that bankrout sleep doth sorrow owe;
Which now in some slight measure it will pay,
If for his tender here I make some stay.
                                        Lie down [and sleep].

OBERON What hast thou done? Thou hast mistaken
        quite,
And laid the love juice on some truelove's sight.
90   Of thy misprision must perforce ensue
Some true love turned, and not a false turned true.

PUCK Then fate o'errules, that, one man holding troth,
A million fail, confounding oath on oath.

OBERON About the wood go swifter than the wind,
95   And Helena of Athens look thou find.
All fancy-sick she is and pale of cheer,
With sighs of love, that costs the fresh blood dear:
By some illusion see thou bring her here.
I'll charm his eyes against she do appear.

100   PUCK I go, I go; look how I go,
Swifter than arrow from the Tartar's bow.   [*Exit.*]

        OBERON Flower of this purple dye,
            Hit with Cupid's archery,
            Sink in apple of his eye.
105   When his love he doth espy,
            Let her shine as gloriously
            As the Venus of the sky.
            When thou wak'st, if she be by,
            Beg of her for remedy.

                            Enter Puck.

---

85 **For debt ... sorrow owe** because of the debt that bankrupt sleep owes to
sorrow 87 **tender** offer 90 **misprision** mistake 93 **confounding oath on
oath** breaking oath after oath 96 **fancy-sick** lovesick 96 **cheer** face 99 **against
she do appear** in preparation for her appearance

PUCK Captain of our fairy band,   110
   Helena is here at hand;
   And the youth, mistook by me,
   Pleading for a lover's fee.
   Shall we their fond pageant see?
   Lord, what fools these mortals be!   115

OBERON Stand aside. The noise they make
   Will cause Demetrius to awake.

PUCK Then will two at once woo one;
   That must needs be sport alone;
   And those things do best please me   120
   That befall prepost'rously.

Enter Lysander and Helena.

LYSANDER Why should you think that I should woo in
   scorn?
   Scorn and derision never come in tears:
Look, when I vow, I weep; and vows so born,
   In their nativity all truth appears.   125
How can these things in me seem scorn to you,
Bearing the badge of faith, to prove them true?

HELENA You do advance your cunning more and
   more.
   When truth kills truth, O devilish-holy fray!
These vows are Hermia's: will you give her o'er?   130
   Weigh oath with oath, and you will nothing
   weigh.
Your vows to her and me, put in two scales,
Will even weigh; and both as light as tales.

LYSANDER I had no judgment when to her I swore.

HELENA Nor none, in my mind, now you give her o'er.   135

LYSANDER Demetrius loves her, and he loves not you.

---

114 **fond pageant** foolish exhibition   119 **alone** unique, supreme   127 **badge of faith** (Lysander means his tears)   128 **advance** exhibit, display

DEMETRIUS [*Awaking*] O Helen, goddess, nymph, perfect, divine!
    To what, my love, shall I compare thine eyne?
    Crystal is muddy. O, how ripe in show
140   Thy lips, those kissing cherries, tempting grow!
    That pure congealèd white, high Taurus' snow,
    Fanned with the eastern wind, turns to a crow
    When thou hold'st up thy hand: O, let me kiss
    This princess of pure white, this seal of bliss!

145 HELENA O spite! O hell! I see you all are bent
    To set against me for your merriment:
    If you were civil and knew courtesy,
    You would not do me thus much injury.
    Can you not hate me, as I know you do,
150   But you must join in souls to mock me too?
    If you were men, as men you are in show,
    You would not use a gentle lady so;
    To vow, and swear, and superpraise my parts,
    When I am sure you hate me with your hearts.
155   You both are rivals, and love Hermia;
    And now both rivals to mock Helena:
    A trim exploit, a manly enterprise,
    To conjure tears up in a poor maid's eyes
    With your derision! None of noble sort
160   Would so offend a virgin, and extort
    A poor soul's patience, all to make you sport.

LYSANDER You are unkind, Demetrius. Be not so;
    For you love Hermia; this you know I know.
    And here, with all good will, with all my heart,
165   In Hermia's love I yield you up my part;
    And yours of Helena to me bequeath,
    Whom I do love, and will do till my death.

HELENA Never did mockers waste more idle breath.

DEMETRIUS Lysander, keep thy Hermia; I will none.

---

139 **show** appearance 141 **Taurus'** of the Taurus Mountains (in Turkey)
147 **civil** civilized 152 **gentle** well-born 153 **parts** qualities 157 **trim** splendid (ironical) 160 **extort** wear out by torturing 168 **idle** vain, futile

If e'er I loved her, all that love is gone. 170
My heart to her but as guestwise sojourned,
And now to Helen is it home returned,
There to remain.

LYSANDER   Helen, it is not so.

DEMETRIUS Disparage not the faith thou dost not
    know,
Lest, to thy peril, thou aby it dear. 175
Look, where thy love comes; yonder is thy dear.

Enter Hermia.

HERMIA Dark night, that from the eye his function
    takes,
The ear more quick of apprehension makes;
Wherein it doth impair the seeing sense,
It pays the hearing double recompense. 180
Thou art not by mine eye, Lysander, found;
Mine ear, I thank it, brought me to thy sound.
But why unkindly didst thou leave me so?

LYSANDER Why should he stay, whom love doth press
    to go?

HERMIA What love could press Lysander from my
    side? 185

LYSANDER Lysander's love, that would not let him
    bide,
Fair Helena, who more engilds the night
Than all yon fiery oes and eyes of light.
Why seek'st thou me? Could not this make thee
    know,
The hate I bare thee made me leave thee so? 190

HERMIA You speak not as you think: it cannot be.

HELENA Lo, she is one of this confederacy!
Now I perceive they have conjoined all three

175 **aby it dear** pay dearly for it   177 **his** its (the eye's)   188 **oes** orbs

To fashion this false sport, in spite of me.
195   Injurious Hermia! Most ungrateful maid!
Have you conspired, have you with these contrived
To bait me with this foul derision?
Is all the counsel that we two have shared,
The sister's vows, the hours that we have spent,
200   When we have chid the hasty-footed time
For parting us—O, is all forgot?
All school days friendship, childhood innocence?
We, Hermia, like two artificial gods,
Have with our needles created both one flower,
205   Both on one sampler, sitting on one cushion,
Both warbling of one song, both in one key;
As if our hands, our sides, voices, and minds,
Had been incorporate. So we grew together,
Like to a double cherry, seeming parted,
210   But yet an union in partition;
Two lovely berries molded on one stem;
So, with two seeming bodies, but one heart;
Two of the first, like coats in heraldry,
Due but to one, and crownèd with one crest.
215   And will you rent our ancient love asunder,
To join with men in scorning your poor friend?
It is not friendly, 'tis not maidenly.
Our sex, as well as I, may chide you for it,
Thou I alone do feel the injury.

220   HERMIA   I am amazèd at your passionate words.
I scorn you not. It seems that you scorn me.

HELENA   Have you not set Lysander, as in scorn,
To follow me and praise my eyes and face?
And made your other love, Demetrius
225   (Who even but now did spurn me with his foot),
To call me goddess, nymph, divine and rare,

---

195 **Injurious** insulting   196-97 **contrived To bait** plotted to assail   203 **artificial** skilled in art   205 **sampler** work of embroidery   208 **incorporate** one body 213-14 **Two of ... one crest** (Helena apparently envisages a shield on which the coat of arms appears twice but which has a single crest; Helena and Hermia have two bodies but a single heart)   215 **rent** rend, tear

Precious, celestial? Wherefore speaks he this
To her he hates? And wherefore doth Lysander
Deny your love, so rich within his soul,
And tender me (forsooth) affection,   230
But by your setting on, by your consent?
What though I be not so in grace as you,
So hung upon with love, so fortunate,
But miserable most, to love unloved?
This you should pity rather than despise.   235

HERMIA I understand not what you mean by this.

HELENA Ay, do! Persever, counterfeit sad looks,
Make mouths upon me when I turn my back;
Wink each at other; hold the sweet jest up.
This sport, well carried, shall be chronicled.   240
If you have any pity, grace, or manners,
You would not make me such an argument.
But fare ye well. 'Tis partly my own fault,
Which death or absence soon shall remedy.

LYSANDER Stay, gentle Helena; hear my excuse: 245
My love, my life, my soul, fair Helena!

HELENA O excellent!

HERMIA   Sweet, do not scorn her so.

DEMETRIUS If she cannot entreat, I can compel.

LYSANDER Thou canst compel no more than she en-
    treat.
Thy threats have no more strength than her weak
    prayers.   250
Helen, I love thee; by my life, I do!
I swear by that which I will lose for thee,
To prove him false that says I love thee not.

DEMETRIUS I say I love thee more than he can do.

---

229 **your love** his love for you   232 **in grace** in favor   237 **persever** persevere
(but accented on second syllable)   237 **sad** grave   238 **Make mouths** make
mocking faces   242 **argument** subject (of scorn)   248 **entreat** prevail by
entreating

255 LYSANDER If thou say so, withdraw and prove it too.

DEMETRIUS Quick, come!

HERMIA   Lysander, whereto tends all this?

LYSANDER Away, you Ethiope!

DEMETRIUS   No, no; he'll
    Seem to break loose; take on as you would follow,
    But yet come not: you are a tame man, go!

LYSANDER Hang off, thou cat, thou burr! Vile thing,
260   let loose,
    Or I will shake thee from me like a serpent!

HERMIA Why are you grown so rude! What change is
    this,
    Sweet love?

LYSANDER   Thy love! Out, tawny Tartar, out!
    Out, loathèd med'cine! O hated potion, hence!

HERMIA Do you not jest?

265 HELENA   Yes, sooth; and so do you.

LYSANDER Demetrius, I will keep my word with thee.

DEMETRIUS I would I had your bond, for I perceive
    A weak bond holds you. I'll not trust your word.

LYSANDER What, should I hurt her, strike her, kill
    her dead?
270   Although I hate her, I'll not harm her so.

HERMIA What, can you do me greater harm than
    hate?
    Hate me! Wherefore? O me! What news, my love!
    Am not I Hermia? Are not you Lysander?
    I am as fair now as I was erewhile.

---

257 **Ethiope** blackamoor (brunette) 258 **take on as** make a fuss as if
265 **sooth** truly 266 **my word** my promise to fight with you 274 **erewhile** a
little while ago

Since night you loved me; yet since night you left
    me.   275
Why, then you left me—O, the gods forbid!—
In earnest, shall I say?

LYSANDER   Ay, by my life!
And never did desire to see thee more.
Therefore be out of hope, of question, of doubt;
Be certain, nothing truer. 'Tis no jest   280
That I do hate thee, and love Helena.

HERMIA O me! You juggler! You canker blossom!
You thief of love! What, have you come by night
And stol'n my love's heart from him?

HELENA   Fine, i' faith!
Have you no modesty, no maiden shame,   285
No touch of bashfulness? What, will you tear
Impatient answers from my gentle tongue?
Fie, fie! You counterfeit, you puppet, you!

HERMIA Puppet? Why so? Ay, that way goes the
    game.
Now I perceive that she hath made compare   290
Between our statures; she hath urged her height,
And with her personage, her tall personage,
Her height, forsooth, she hath prevailed with him.
And are you grown so high in his esteem,
Because I am so dwarfish and so low?   295
How low am I, thou painted maypole? Speak!
How low am I? I am not yet so low
But that my nails can reach unto thine eyes.

HELENA I pray you, though you mock me, gentlemen,
Let her not hurt me. I was never curst;   300
I have no gift at all in shrewishness;
I am a right maid for my cowardice.
Let her not strike me. You perhaps may think,

---

275 **Since night** since the beginning of this night   282 **canker blossom** dog rose
(or possibly worm that cankers the blossom)   290 **compare** comparison
300 **curst** quarrelsome   302 **right maid** true young woman

Because she is something lower than myself,
That I can match her.

305 HERMIA   Lower! Hark, again!

HELENA Good Hermia, do not be so bitter with me.
I evermore did love you, Hermia,
Did ever keep your counsels, never wronged you;
Save that, in love unto Demetrius,
310 I told him of your stealth unto this wood.
He followed you; for love I followed him.
But he hath chid me hence, and threatened me
To strike me, spurn me, nay, to kill me too.
And now, so you will let me quiet go,
315 To Athens will I bear my folly back,
And follow you no further. Let me go.
You see how simple and how fond I am.

HERMIA Why, get you gone. Who is't that hinders you?

HELENA A foolish heart, that I leave here behind.

HERMIA What, with Lysander?

320 HELENA   With Demetrius.

LYSANDER Be not afraid. She shall not harm thee,
Helena.

DEMETRIUS No, sir, she shall not, though you take her
part.

HELENA O, when she's angry, she is keen and shrewd!
She was a vixen when she went to school;
325 And though she be but little, she is fierce.

HERMIA "Little" again! Nothing but "low" and "little"!
Why will you suffer her to flout me thus?
Let me come to her.

LYSANDER   Get you gone, you dwarf;
You minimus, of hind'ring knotgrass made;
You bead, you acorn!

317 fond foolish   323 keen and shrewd sharp-tongued and shrewish
329 minimus smallest thing   329 knotgrass (a weed that allegedly stunted one's
growth)

DEMETRIUS   You are too officious   330
  In her behalf that scorns your services.
  Let her alone. Speak not of Helena;
  Take not her part; for, if thou dost intend
  Never so little show of love to her,
  Thou shalt aby it.

LYSANDER   Now she holds me not.   335
  Now follow, if thou dar'st, to try whose right,
  Of thine or mine, is most in Helena.

DEMETRIUS Follow! Nay, I'll go with thee, cheek by
    jowl.   [*Exeunt Lysander and Demetrius.*]

HERMIA You, mistress, all this coil is 'long of you:
  Nay, go not back.

HELENA   I will not trust you, I,   340
  Nor longer stay in your curst company.
  Your hands than mine are quicker for a fray,
  My legs are longer though, to run away.

HERMIA I am amazed, and know not what to say.
                   Exeunt [*Helena and Hermia*].

OBERON This is thy negligence. Still thou mistak'st,   345
  Or else committ'st thy knaveries willfully.

PUCK Believe me, king of shadows, I mistook.
  Did not you tell me I should know the man
  By the Athenian garments he had on?
  And so far blameless proves my enterprise,   350
  That I have 'nointed an Athenian's eyes;
  And so far am I glad it so did sort,
  As this their jangling I esteem a sport.

OBERON Thou see'st these lovers seek a place to fight.
  Hie therefore, Robin, overcast the night.   355
  The starry welkin cover thou anon

---

333 intend give sign, direct (or possibly "pretend") 335 aby pay for 339 all
this coil is 'long of you all this turmoil is brought about by you 344 amazed in
confusion 352 sort turn out 356 welkin sky

With drooping fog, as black as Acheron;
And lead these testy rivals so astray,
As one come not within another's way.

360 Like to Lysander sometime frame thy tongue,
Then stir Demetrius up with bitter wrong;
And sometime rail thou like Demetrius.
And from each other look thou lead them thus,
Till o'er their brows death-counterfeiting sleep

365 With leaden legs and batty wings doth creep.
Then crush this herb into Lysander's eye,
Whose liquor hath this virtuous property,
To take from thence all error with his might,
And make his eyeballs roll with wonted sight.

370 When they next wake, all this derision
Shall seem a dream and fruitless vision,
And back to Athens shall the lovers wend,
With league whose date till death shall never end.
Whiles I in this affair do thee employ,

375 I'll to my queen and beg her Indian boy;
And then I will her charmèd eye release
From monster's view, and all things shall be peace.

PUCK My fairy lord, this must be done with haste,
For night's swift dragons cut the clouds full fast,

380 And yonder shines Aurora's harbinger;
At whose approach, ghosts, wand'ring here and
  there,
Troop home to churchyards: damnèd spirits all,
That in crossways and floods have burial,
Already to their wormy beds are gone.

385 For fear lest day should look their shames upon,
They willfully themselves exile from light,
And must for aye consort with black-browed night.

OBERON But we are spirits of another sort.

---

357 **Acheron** one of the rivers of the underworld   358 **testy** excited, angry
359 **As** that   361 **wrong** insult   365 **batty** bat-like   367 **virtuous** potent
370 **derision** i.e., ludicrous delusion   373 **With league whose date** in union
whose term   380 **Aurora's harbinger** dawn's herald (i.e., the morning star)

I with the Morning's love have oft made sport;
And, like a forester, the groves may tread,   390
Even till the eastern gate, all fiery-red,
Opening on Neptune with fair blessèd beams,
Turns into yellow gold his salt green streams.
But, notwithstanding, haste; make no delay.
We may effect this business yet ere day.   [*Exit.*] 395

PUCK   Up and down, up and down,
          I will lead them up and down:
          I am feared in field and town:
          Goblin, lead them up and down.
          Here comes one.   400

Enter Lysander.

LYSANDER Where art thou, proud Demetrius? Speak
      thou now.

PUCK Here, villain; drawn and ready. Where art
      thou?

LYSANDER I will be with thee straight.

PUCK   Follow me, then,
      To plainer ground.   [*Exit Lysander.*]

Enter Demetrius.

DEMETRIUS   Lysander! Speak again!
      Thou runaway, thou coward, art thou fled?   405
      Speak! In some bush? Where dost thou hide thy
      head?

PUCK Thou coward, art thou bragging to the stars,
      Telling the bushes that thou look'st for wars,
      And wilt not come? Come, recreant! Come, thou
      child!

389 **the Morning's love** Aurora (or possibly her lover Cephalus)   399 **Goblin**
Hobgoblin (one of Puck's names)   402 **drawn** with drawn sword   404 **plainer**
more level

410   I'll whip thee with a rod. He is defiled
      That draws a sword on thee.

DEMETRIUS   Yea, art thou there?

PUCK Follow my voice. We'll try no manhood here.
                                          Exeunt.

                  [*Enter Lysander.*]

LYSANDER He goes before me and still dares me on:
      When I come where he calls, then he is gone.
415   The villain is much lighter-heeled than I.
      I followed fast, but faster he did fly,
      That fallen am I in dark uneven way,
      And here will rest me. [*Lies down.*] Come, thou
         gentle day!
      For if but once thou show me thy gray light,
420   I'll find Demetrius, and revenge this spite.   [*Sleeps.*]

         [*Enter*] Robin [*Puck*] *and Demetrius.*

PUCK Ho, ho, ho! Coward, why com'st thou not?

DEMETRIUS Abide me, if thou dar'st; for well I wot
      Thou runn'st before me, shifting every place,
      And dar'st not stand, nor look me in the face.
      Where art thou now?

425   PUCK   Come hither. I am here.

DEMETRIUS Nay then, thou mock'st me. Thou shalt
         buy this dear,
      If ever I thy face by daylight see.
      Now, go thy way. Faintness constraineth me
      To measure out my length on this cold bed.
430   By day's approach look to be visited.
                          [*Lies down and sleeps.*]

---

412 **try no manhood** have no test of valor   422 **Abide me** wait for me
422 **wot** know   426 **buy this dear** pay dearly for this   430 **look to be visited**
be sure to be sought out

Enter Helena.

HELENA O weary night, O long and tedious night,
  Abate thy hours! Shine comforts from the east,
That I may back to Athens by daylight,
  From these that my poor company detest:
And sleep, that sometimes shuts up sorrow's eye, 435
Steal me awhile from mine own company. *Sleep.*

PUCK Yet but three? Come one more.
  Two of both kinds makes up four.
  Here she comes, curst and sad:
  Cupid is a knavish lad, 440
  Thus to make poor females mad.

[*Enter Hermia.*]

HERMIA Never so weary, never so in woe;
  Bedabbled with the dew and torn with briers,
I can no further crawl, no further go;
  My legs can keep no pace with my desires. 445
Here will I rest me till the break of day.
Heavens shield Lysander, if they mean a fray!
              [*Lies down and sleeps.*]

PUCK On the ground
  Sleep sound:
  I'll apply 450
  To your eye,
Gentle lover, remedy.
            [*Squeezing the juice on Lysander's eye*]
  When thou wak'st,
  Thou tak'st
  True delight 455
  In the sight
Of thy former lady's eye:
And the country proverb known,
That every man should take his own,

432 **Abate** make shorter   439 **curst** cross

460   In your waking shall be shown.
                 Jack shall have Jill;
                 Nought shall go ill;
         The man shall have his mare again, and all shall
                 be well.   [*Exit.*]

[ACT IV

Scene I. *The wood. Lysander, Demetrius, Helena,*
and Hermia, lying asleep.]

Enter [Titania,] Queen of Fairies, and [Bottom the]
Clown, and Fairies; and [Oberon,] the King, behind
them.

TITANIA Come, sit thee down upon this flow'ry bed,
    While I thy amiable cheeks do coy,
And stick musk roses in thy sleek smooth head,
    And kiss thy fair large ears, my gentle joy.

BOTTOM Where's Peaseblossom? 5

PEASEBLOSSOM Ready.

BOTTOM Scratch my head, Peaseblossom. Where's
Mounsieur Cobweb?

COBWEB Ready.

BOTTOM Mounsieur Cobweb, good mounsieur, get 10
you your weapons in your hand, and kill me a red-
hipped humblebee on the top of a thistle; and, good
mounsieur, bring me the honey bag. Do not fret
yourself too much in the action, mounsieur; and,
good mounsieur, have a care the honey bag break 15

IV.i.2 **While I ... do coy** while I caress your lovely cheeks

not; I would be loath to have you overflown with
a honey bag, signior. Where's Mounsieur Mustardseed?

MUSTARDSEED Ready.

20 BOTTOM Give me your neaf, Mounsieur Mustardseed. Pray you, leave your curtsy, good mounsieur.

MUSTARDSEED What's your will?

BOTTOM Nothing, good mounsieur, but to help Cava-
25 lery Cobweb to scratch. I must to the barber's,
mounsieur; for methinks I am marvail's hairy
about the face; and I am such a tender ass, if my
hair do but tickle me, I must scratch.

TITANIA What, wilt thou hear some music, my sweet
30   love?

BOTTOM I have a reasonable good ear in music. Let's
have the tongs and the bones.

TITANIA Or say, sweet love, what thou desirest to eat.

BOTTOM Truly, a peek of provender. I could munch
35   your good dry oats. Methinks I have a great desire
to a bottle of hay. Good hay, sweet hay, hath no
fellow.

TITANIA I have a venturous fairy that shall seek
The squirrel's hoard, and fetch thee new nuts.

40 BOTTOM I had rather have a handful or two of dried
peas. But, I pray you, let none of your people stir
me: I have an exposition of sleep come upon me.

---

20 **neaf** fist, hand   21 **leave your curtsy** i.e., stop bowing, leave your hat on (a
curtsy was any gesture of respect)   24-25 **Cavalery** i.e., Cavalier   26 **marvail's**
(Bottom means "marvelous")   32 **the tongs and the bones** rustic music, made
by tongs struck with metal and by bone clappers held between the fingers
36 **bottle** bundle   37 **fellow** equal   42 **exposition of** (Bottom means "disposition for")

TITANIA Sleep thou, and I will wind thee in my arms.
  Fairies, be gone, and be all ways away.

                          [*Exeunt Fairies.*]

  So doth the woodbine the sweet honeysuckle   45
  Gently entwist; the female ivy so
  Enrings the barky fingers of the elm.
  O, how I love thee! How I dote on thee!

                          [*They sleep.*]

          Enter Robin Goodfellow [*Puck*].

OBERON [*Advancing*] Welcome, good Robin. See'st
    thou this sweet sight?
  Her dotage now I do begin to pity: 50
  For, meeting her of late behind the wood,
  Seeking sweet favors for this hateful fool,
  I did upbraid her, and fall out with her.
  For she his hairy temples then had rounded
  With coronet of fresh and fragrant flowers;   55
  And that same dew, which sometime on the buds
  Was wont to swell, like round and orient pearls,
  Stood now within the pretty flouriets' eyes,
  Like tears, that did their own disgrace bewail.
  When I had at my pleasure taunted her,   60
  And she in mild terms begged my patience,
  I then did ask of her her changeling child;
  Which straight she gave me, and her fairy sent
  To bear him to my bower in fairy land.
  And now I have the boy, I will undo   65
  This hateful imperfection of her eyes:
  And, gentle Puck, take this transformèd scalp
  From off the head of this Athenian swain,
  That, he awaking when the other do,
  May all to Athens back again repair,   70
  And think no more of this night's accidents,

---

44 **all ways** in every direction   46 **female ivy** (called female because it clings to
the elm and is supported by it)   52 **favors** love tokens (probably flowers)
56 **sometime** formerly   57 **Was wont** used to   57 **orient** lustrous   58 **flouriets'** flowerets'   69 **other** others   71 **accidents** happenings

But as the fierce vexation of a dream.
But first I will release the Fairy Queen.
  Be as thou wast wont to be;
75 See as thou wast wont to see.
  Dian's bud o'er Cupid's flower
  Hath such force and blessèd power.
Now, my Titania, wake you, my sweet Queen.

TITANIA My Oberon, what visions have I seen!
80 Methought I was enamored of an ass.

OBERON There lies your love.

TITANIA   How came these things to pass?
  O, how mine eyes do loathe his visage now!

OBERON Silence awhile. Robin, take off this head.
  Titania, music call; and strike more dead
85 Than common sleep of all these five the sense.

TITANIA Music, ho, music! Such as charmeth sleep!

PUCK Now, when thou wak'st, with thine own fool's
  eyes peep.

OBERON Sound, music! [*Music*] Come, my Queen,
  take hands with me.
  And rock the ground whereon these sleepers be.
                                    [*Dance*]
90 Now thou and I are new in amity,
  And will tomorrow midnight solemnly
  Dance in Duke Theseus' house triumphantly,
  And bless it to all fair prosperity.
  There shall the pairs of faithful lovers be
95 Wedded, with Theseus, all in jollity.

PUCK   Fairy King, attend, and mark:
        I do hear the morning lark.

OBERON Then, my Queen, in silence sad,
        Trip we after night's shade.

91 **solemnly** ceremoniously 92 **triumphantly** in festive procession 98 **sad**
serious, solemn

We the globe can compass soon,   100
Swifter than the wand'ring moon.

TITANIA Come, my lord; and in our flight,
Tell me how it came this night,
That I sleeping here was found
With these mortals on the ground.   105

Exeunt.

Wind horn. Enter Theseus, and all his train;
[Hippolyta, Egeus].

THESEUS Go, one of you, find out the forester,
For now our observation is performed;
And since we have the vaward of the day,
My love shall hear the music of my hounds.
Uncouple in the western valley; let them go.   110
Dispatch, I say, and find the forester.

[Exit an Attendant.]

We will, fair Queen, up to the mountain's top,
And mark the musical confusion
Of hounds and echo in conjunction.

HIPPOLYTA I was with Hercules and Cadmus once,   115
When in a wood of Crete they bayed the bear
With hounds of Sparta. Never did I hear
Such gallant chiding; for, besides the groves,
The skies, the fountains, every region near
Seemed all one mutual cry. I never heard   120
So musical a discord, such sweet thunder.

THESEUS My hounds are bred out of the Spartan kind,
So flewed, so sanded; and their heads are hung
With ears that sweep away the morning dew;
Crook-kneed, and dew-lapped like Thessalian bulls; 125
Slow in pursuit, but matched in mouth like bells,

---

107 **observation** observance, i.e., of the rite of May (cf. I.i.167)   108 **vaward**
vanguard, i.e., morning   116 **bayed** brought to bay   123 **So flewed, so sanded**
i.e., like Spartan hounds, with hanging cheeks and of sandy color

Each under each. A cry more tunable
Was never holloed to, nor cheered with horn,
In Crete, in Sparta, nor in Thessaly.
Judge when you hear. But, soft! What nymphs
130 are these?

EGEUS My lord, this is my daughter here asleep;
And this, Lysander; this Demetrius is;
This Helena, old Nedar's Helena:
I wonder of their being here together.

135 THESEUS No doubt they rose up early to observe
The rite of May; and, hearing our intent,
Came here in grace of our solemnity.
But speak, Egeus. Is not this the day
That Hermia should give answer of her choice?

140 EGEUS It is, my lord.

THESEUS Go, bid the huntsmen wake them with their
horns.
                    Shout within. They all start up. Wind horns.
Good morrow, friends. Saint Valentine is past:
Begin these wood birds but to couple now?

LYSANDER Pardon, my lord.

THESEUS   I pray you all, stand up.
145 I know you two are rival enemies.
How comes this gentle concord in the world,
That hatred is so far from jealousy,
To sleep by hate, and fear no enmity?

LYSANDER My lord, I shall reply amazedly,
150 Half sleep, half waking: but as yet, I swear,
I cannot truly say how I came here.

---

127 **Each under each** of different tone (like the chime of bells)   127 **cry** pack of
hounds   130 **soft** stop   137 **in grace of our solemnity** in honor of our festival
143 **Begin these ... couple now** (it was supposed that birds began to mate on
February 14, St. Valentine's Day)   147 **jealousy** suspicion   149 **amazedly**
confusedly

But, as I think—for truly would I speak,
And now I do bethink me, so it is—
I came with Hermia hither. Our intent
Was to be gone from Athens, where we might,   155
Without the peril of the Athenian law—

EGEUS Enough, enough, my lord; you have enough.
I beg the law, the law, upon his head.
They would have stol'n away; they would,
    Demetrius,
Thereby to have defeated you and me,   160
You of your wife and me of my consent,
Of my consent that she should be your wife.

DEMETRIUS My lord, fair Helen told me of their
    stealth,
Of this their purpose hither to this wood,
And I in fury hither followed them,   165
Fair Helena in fancy following me.
But, my good lord, I wot not by what power—
But by some power it is—my love to Hermia,
Melted as the snow, seems to me now
As the remembrance of an idle gaud,   170
Which in my childhood I did dote upon;
And all the faith, the virtue of my heart,
The object and the pleasure of mine eye,
Is only Helena. To her, my lord,
Was I betrothed ere I saw Hermia: 175
But, like a sickness, did I loathe this food;
But, as in health, come to my natural taste,
Now I do wish it, love it, long for it,
And will for evermore be true to it.

THESEUS Fair lovers, you are fortunately met.   180
Of this discourse we more will hear anon.
Egeus, I will overbear your will,
For in the temple, by and by, with us

156 **Without** outside of   160 **defeated** deprived by fraud   163 **stealth** stealthy
flight   166 **in fancy** in love, doting   170 **idle gaud** worthless trinket   172 **virtue**
power   176 **like a sickness** like one who is sick   183 **by and by** shortly

These couples shall eternally be knit;
185 And, for the morning now is something worn,
Our purposed hunting shall be set aside.
Away with us to Athens! Three and three,
We'll hold a feast in great solemnity.
Come, Hippolyta.

[*Exeunt Theseus, Hippolyta, Egeus, and train.*]

DEMETRIUS These things seem small and undistin-
190   guishable,
Like far-off mountains turnèd into clouds.

HERMIA Methinks I see these things with parted eye,
When everything seems double.

HELENA   So methinks:
And I have found Demetrius like a jewel,
Mine own, and not mine own.

195 DEMETRIUS   Are you sure
That we are awake? It seems to me
That yet we sleep, we dream. Do not you think
The Duke was here, and bid us follow him?

HERMIA Yea, and my father.

HELENA   And Hippolyta.

200 LYSANDER And he did bid us follow to the temple.

DEMETRIUS Why, then, we are awake. Let's follow
     him,
And by the way let us recount our dreams.

[*Exeunt.*]

BOTTOM [*Awaking*] When my cue comes, call me,
and I will answer. My next is, "Most fair Pyramus."
205 Heigh-ho! Peter Quince? Flute, the bellows
mender? Snout, the tinker? Starveling? God's my
life, stol'n hence, and left me asleep? I have had
a most rare vision. I have had a dream, past the

---

185 **Something worn** somewhat spent   192 **with parted eye** i.e., with the eyes
out of focus   206-07 **God's my life** an oath (possibly from "God bless my life")

wit of man to say what dream it was. Man is but an ass, if he go about to expound this dream. 210
Methought I was—there is no man can tell what. Methought I was—and methought I had—but man is but a patched fool if he will offer to say what methought I had. The eye of man hath not heard, the ear of man hath not seen, man's hand is not 215
able to taste, his tongue to conceive, nor his heart to report, what my dream was. I will get Peter Quince to write a ballet of this dream. It shall be called "Bottom's Dream," because it hath no bottom; and I will sing it in the latter end of a 220
play, before the Duke. Peradventure to make it the more gracious, I shall sing it at her death.

[Exit.]

[Scene II. *Athens. Quince's house.*]

Enter Quince, Flute, Thisby and the rabble
[Snout, Starveling].

QUINCE Have you sent to Bottom's house? Is he come home yet?

STARVELING He cannot be heard of. Out of doubt he is transported.

FLUTE If he come not, then the play is marred. It 5
goes not forward, doth it?

QUINCE It is not possible. You have not a man in all Athens able to discharge Pyramus but he.

---

210 **go about** endeavor 213 **patched** (referring to the patchwork dress of jesters) 218 **ballet** ballad 222 **her death** i.e., Thisby's death in the play IV.ii.s.d. **Flute** (Shakespeare seems to have forgotten that Flute and Thisby are the same person) 4 **transported** carried off (by the fairies) 8 **discharge** play

FLUTE No, he hath simply the best wit of any handi-
10 craft man in Athens.

QUINCE Yea, and the best person too; and he is a
very paramour for a sweet voice.

FLUTE You must say "paragon." A paramour is, God
bless us, a thing of nought.

Enter Snug the Joiner.

15 SNUG Master, the Duke is coming from the temple,
and there is two or three lords and ladies more
married. If our sport had gone forward, we had
all been made men.

FLUTE O sweet bully Bottom! Thus hath he lost six-
20 pence a day during his life. He could not have
scaped sixpence a day. An the Duke had not given
him sixpence a day for playing Pyramus, I'll be
hanged. He would have deserved it. Sixpence a
day in Pyramus, or nothing.

Enter Bottom.

25 BOTTOM Where are these lads? Where are these
hearts?

QUINCE Bottom! O most courageous day! O most
happy hour!

BOTTOM Masters, I am to discourse wonders: but ask
30 me not what; for if I tell you, I am not true
Athenian. I will tell you everything, right as it fell
out.

QUINCE Let us hear, sweet Bottom.

---

14 **a thing of nought** a wicked thing   18 **made men** men whose fortunes are
made   19-20 **sixpence a day** (a pension)   27 **courageous** brave, splendid

BOTTOM Not a word of me. All that I will tell you
is, that the Duke hath dined. Get your apparel 35
together, good strings to your beards, new ribbons
to your pumps; meet presently at the palace; every
man look o'er his part; for the short and the long
is, our play is preferred. In any case, let Thisby
have clean linen; and let not him that plays the 40
lion pare his nails, for they shall hang out for the
lion's claws. And, most dear actors, eat no onions
nor garlic, for we are to utter sweet breath, and
I do not doubt but to hear them say it is a sweet
comedy. No more words. Away! Go, away! 45

[Exeunt.]

---

34 **of me** from me   37 **presently** immediately   39 **preferred** put forward,
recommended   43 **breath** (1) exhalation (2) words

[ACT V

Scene I. *Athens. The palace of Theseus.*]

*Enter Theseus, Hippolyta, and Philostrate, [Lords,
and Attendants].*

HIPPOLYTA 'Tis strange, my Theseus, that these lovers
speak of.

THESEUS More strange than true. I never may believe
These antique fables, nor these fairy toys.
Lovers and madmen have such seething brains,
5   Such shaping fantasies, that apprehend
More than cool reason ever comprehends.
The lunatic, the lover and the poet
Are of imagination all compact.
One sees more devils than vast hell can hold,
10   That is the madman. The lover, all as frantic,
Sees Helen's beauty in a brow of Egypt.
The poet's eye, in a fine frenzy rolling,
Doth glance from heaven to earth, from earth to
    heaven;
And as imagination bodies forth
15   The forms of things unknown, the poet's pen
Turns them to shapes, and gives to airy nothing
A local habitation and a name.

V.i.3 **antique** (1) ancient (2) grotesque (antic)   3 **fairy toys** trifles about fairies
5 **fantasies** imagination   8 **compact** composed   11 **brow of Egypt** face of a
gypsy

Such tricks hath strong imagination,
That, if it would but apprehend some joy,
It comprehends some bringer of that joy;   20
Or in the night, imagining some fear,
How easy is a bush supposed a bear!

HIPPOLYTA But all the story of the night told over,
And all their minds transfigured so together,
More witnesseth than fancy's images,   25
And grows to something of great constancy;
But, howsoever, strange and admirable.

Enter Lovers: Lysander, Demetrius, Hermia and
Helena.

THESEUS Here come the lovers, full of joy and mirth.
Joy, gentle friends! Joy and fresh days of love
Accompany your hearts!

LYSANDER   More than to us   30
Wait in your royal walks, your board, your bed!

THESEUS Come now, what masques, what dances
    shall we have,
To wear away this long age of three hours
Between our aftersupper and bedtime?
Where is our usual manager of mirth?   35
What revels are in hand? Is there no play,
To ease the anguish of a torturing hour?
Call Philostrate.

PHILOSTRATE   Here, mighty Theseus.

THESEUS Say, what abridgment have you for this
    evening?

20 **It comprehends ... that joy** it includes an imagined bringer of the joy
21 **fear** object of fear   26 **constancy** consistency (and reality)   27 **admirable**
wonderful   32 **masques** courtly entertainments with masked dancers   34 **aftersupper** refreshment served after early supper   39 **abridgment** entertainment (to
abridge or shorten the time)

40   What masque? What music? How shall we beguile
        The lazy time, if not with some delight?

PHILOSTRATE There is a brief how many sports are
            ripe:
        Make choice of which your Highness will see first.
                                          [*Giving a paper*]

THESEUS "The battle with the Centaurs, to be sung
45   By an Athenian eunuch to the harp."
        We'll none of that. That have I told my love,
        In glory of my kinsman Hercules.
        "The riot of the tipsy Bacchanals,
        Tearing the Thracian singer in their rage."
50   That is an old device; and it was played
        When I from Thebes came last a conqueror.
        "The thrice three Muses mourning for the death
        Of Learning, late deceased in beggary."
        That is some satire, keen and critical,
55   Not sorting with a nuptial ceremony.
        "A tedious brief scene of young Pyramus
        And his love Thisby; very tragical mirth."
        Merry and tragical? Tedious and brief?
        That is, hot ice and wondrous strange snow.
60   How shall we find the concord of this discord?

PHILOSTRATE A play there is, my lord, some ten words
            long,
        Which is as brief as I have known a play;
        But by ten words, my lord, it is too long,
        Which makes it tedious. For in all the play
65   There is not one word apt, one player fitted.
        And tragical, my noble lord, it is,
        For Pyramus therein doth kill himself.
        Which, when I saw rehearsed, I must confess,
        Made mine eyes water; but more merry tears
70   The passion of loud laughter never shed.

THESEUS What are they that do play it?

42 **brief** written list   42 **ripe** ready to be presented   49 **Thracian singer** Orpheus
50 **device** show   55 **sorting with** suited to   70 **passion** strong emotion

PHILOSTRATE Hard-handed men, that work in Athens
   here,
  Which never labored in their minds till now;
  And now have toiled their unbreathed memories
  With this same play, against your nuptial.   75

THESEUS And we will hear it.

PHILOSTRATE   No, my noble lord;
  It is not for you. I have heard it over,
  And it is nothing, nothing in the world;
  Unless you can find sport in their intents,
  Extremely stretched and conned with cruel pain,   80
  To do you service.

THESEUS   I will hear that play;
  For never anything can be amiss,
  When simpleness and duty tender it.
  Go, bring them in: and take your places, ladies.
                      [Exit Philostrate.]

HIPPOLYTA I love not to see wretchedness o'ercharged,   85
  And duty in his service perishing.

THESEUS Why, gentle sweet, you shall see no such
   thing.

HIPPOLYTA He says they can do nothing in this kind.

THESEUS The kinder we, to give them thanks for
   nothing.
  Our sport shall be to take what they mistake: 90
  And what poor duty cannot do, noble respect
  Takes it in might, not merit.
  Where I have come, great clerks have purposèd
  To greet me with premeditated welcomes;
  Where I have seen them shiver and look pale,   95
  Make periods in the midst of sentences,
  Throttle their practiced accent in their fears,

74 **unbreathed** unexercised   75 **against** in preparation for   85 **wretchedness
o'ercharged** lowly people overburdened   88 **in this kind** in this kind of thing
(i.e., acting)   92 **Takes it in might** considers the ability and effort made
93 **clerks** scholars

And, in conclusion, dumbly have broke off,
Not paying me a welcome. Trust me, sweet,
100 Out of this silence yet I picked a welcome;
And in the modesty of fearful duty
I read as much as from the rattling tongue
Of saucy and audacious eloquence.
Love, therefore, and tongue-tied simplicity
105 In least speak most, to my capacity.

[*Enter Philostrate.*]

PHILOSTRATE So please your Grace, the Prologue is
addressed.

THESEUS Let him approach.   [*Flourish trumpets.*]

Enter the Prologue [*Quince*].

PROLOGUE If we offend, it is with our good will.
That you should think, we come not to offend,
110 But with good will. To show our simple skill,
That is the true beginning of our end.
Consider, then, we come but in despite.
We do not come, as minding to content you,
Our true intent is. All for your delight,
We are not here. That you should here repent
115   you,
The actors are at hand; and, by their show,
You shall know all, that you are like to know.

THESEUS This fellow doth not stand upon points.

LYSANDER He hath rid his prologue like a rough colt;
120 he knows not the stop. A good moral, my lord:
it is not enough to speak, but to speak true.

---

105 **to my capacity** according to my understanding   106 **addressed** ready
111 **end** aim   116 **show** (probably referring to a kind of pantomime—"dumb
show"—that was to follow, in which the action of the play was acted without
words while the Prologue gave his account)   118 **stand upon points** (1) care
about punctuation (2) worry about niceties   120 **stop** (1) technical term for the
checking of a horse (2) mark of punctuation

HIPPOLYTA Indeed he hath played on this prologue
like a child on a recorder; a sound, but not in
government.

THESEUS His speech was like a tangled chain; noth-   125
ing impaired, but all disordered. Who is next?

*Enter Pyramus and Thisby and Wall and Moonshine
and Lion [as in dumbshow].*

PROLOGUE Gentles, perchance you wonder at this show;
   But wonder on, till truth make all things plain.
This man is Pyramus, if you would know;
   This beauteous lady Thisby is certain.   130
This man, with lime and roughcast, doth present
   Wall, that vile Wall which did these lovers
      sunder;
   And through Wall's chink, poor souls, they are
      content
   To whisper. At the which let no man wonder.
This man, with lantern, dog, and bush of thorn,   135
   Presenteth Moonshine; for, if you will know,
By moonshine did these lovers think no scorn
   To meet at Ninus' tomb, there, there to woo.
This grisly beast, which Lion hight by name,
   The trusty Thisby, coming first by night,   140
Did scare away, or rather did affright;
   And, as she fled, her mantle she did fall,
   Which Lion vile with bloody mouth did stain.
Anon comes Pyramus, sweet youth and tall,
   And finds his trusty Thisby's mantle slain: 145
Whereat, with blade, with bloody blameful blade,
   He bravely broached his boiling bloody breast;
And Thisby, tarrying in mulberry shade,
   His dagger drew, and died. For all the rest,

---

123 **recorder** flutelike instrument   124 **government** control   139 **hight** is called
142 **fall** let fall   144 **tall** brave   147 **bravely broached** gallantly stabbed

150   Let Lion, Moonshine, Wall, and lovers twain
           At large discourse, while here they do remain.

THESEUS I wonder if the lion be to speak.

DEMETRIUS No wonder, my lord. One lion may, when
many asses do.

           Exit Lion, Thisby and Moonshine.

155 WALL In this same interlude it doth befall
           That I, one Snout by name, present a wall;
           And such a wall, as I would have you think,
           That had in it a crannied hole or chink,
           Through which the lovers, Pyramus and Thisby,
160   Did whisper often very secretly.
           This loam, this roughcast, and this stone, doth
             show
           That I am that same wall; the truth is so;
           And this the cranny is, right and sinister,
           Through which the fearful lovers are to whisper.

165 THESEUS Would you desire lime and hair to speak
           better?

DEMETRIUS It is the wittiest partition that ever I
heard discourse, my lord.

THESEUS Pyramus draws near the wall. Silence!

PYRAMUS O grim-looked night! O night with hue so
170   black!
           O night, which ever art when day is not!
           O night, O night! Alack, alack, alack,
           I fear my Thisby's promise is forgot!
           And thou, O wall, O sweet, O lovely wall,
           That stand'st between her father's ground and
175   mine!
           Thou wall, O wall, O sweet and lovely wall,

151 **At large** at length 163 **right and sinister** i.e., running right and left,
horizontal 167 **wittiest partition** most intelligent wall (with a pun on "partition," a section of a book or of an oration)

Show me thy chink, to blink through with mine
    eyne!

[*Wall holds up his fingers.*]

Thanks, courteous wall. Jove shield thee well for
    this!
But what see I? No Thisby do I see.
O wicked wall, through whom I see no bliss!   180
    Cursed be thy stones for thus deceiving me!

THESEUS The wall, methinks, being sensible, should
curse again.

PYRAMUS No, in truth, sir, he should not. "Deceiving
me" is Thisby's cue. She is to enter now, and I   185
am to spy her through the wall. You shall see it
will fall pat as I told you. Yonder she comes.

Enter Thisby.

THISBY O wall, full often hast thou heard my moans,
    For parting my fair Pyramus and me!
My cherry lips have often kissed thy stones,   190
    Thy stones with lime and hair knit up in thee.

PYRAMUS I see a voice: now will I to the chink,
    To spy an I can hear my Thisby's face.
    Thisby!

THISBY My love thou art, my love I think.   195

PYRAMUS Think what thou wilt, I am thy lover's
    grace;
    And, like Limander, am I trusty still.

THISBY And I like Helen, till the Fates me kill.

PYRAMUS Not Shafalus to Procrus was so true.

---

182 **sensible** conscious   183 **again** in return   187 **pat** exactly   196 **thy lover's grace** thy gracious lover   197 **Limander** (Bottom means Leander, but blends him with Alexander)   198 **Helen** (Hero, beloved of Leander, is probably meant)   199 **Shafalus to Procrus** (Cephalus and Procris are meant, legendary lovers)

200   THISBY As Shafalus to Procrus, I to you.

PYRAMUS O kiss me through the hole of this vile wall!

THISBY I kiss the wall's hole, not your lips at all.

PYRAMUS Wilt thou at Ninny's tomb meet me straightway?

THISBY 'Tide life, 'tide death, I come without delay.
                              [*Exeunt Pyramus and Thisby.*]

205   WALL Thus have I, Wall, my part dischargèd so;
And, being done, thus wall away doth go.   [*Exit.*]

THESEUS Now is the moon used between the two
neighbors.

DEMETRIUS No remedy, my lord, when walls are so
210   willful to hear without warning.

HIPPOLYTA This is the silliest stuff that ever I heard.

THESEUS The best in this kind are but shadows; and
the worst are no worse, if imagination amend them.

HIPPOLYTA It must be your imagination then, and
215   not theirs.

THESEUS If we imagine no worse of them than they
of themselves, they may pass for excellent men.
Here come two noble beasts in, a man and a lion.

Enter Lion and Moonshine.

LION You, ladies, you, whose gentle hearts do fear
The smallest monstrous mouse that creeps on
220   floor,

---

204 'Tide life, 'tide death come (betide) life or death   207 moon used (the
quartos read thus, the Folio reads *morall downe*. Among suggested emendations are
"mural down," and "moon to see")   209-10 when walls ... without warning
i.e., when walls are so eager to listen without warning the parents (?)   212 in this
kind of this sort, i.e. plays (or players?)

May now perchance both quake and tremble here,
When lion rough in wildest rage doth roar.
Then know that I, as Snug the joiner, am
A lion fell, nor else no lion's dam;
For, if I should as lion come in strife   225
Into this place, 'twere pity on my life.

THESEUS A very gentle beast, and of a good conscience.

DEMETRIUS The very best at a beast, my lord, that
e'er I saw.   230

LYSANDER This lion is a very fox for his valor.

THESEUS True; and a goose for his discretion.

DEMETRIUS Not so, my lord; for his valor cannot
carry his discretion, and the fox carries the goose.

THESEUS His discretion, I am sure, cannot carry his   235
valor; for the goose carries not the fox. It is well.
Leave it to his discretion, and let us listen to the
moon.

MOONSHINE This lanthorn doth the hornèd moon
present—

DEMETRIUS He should have worn the horns on his
head.   240

THESEUS He is no crescent, and his horns are invisible
within the circumference.

MOONSHINE This lanthorn doth the hornèd moon
present;
Myself the man i' th' moon do seem to be.   245

THESEUS This is the greatest error of all the rest.

---

224 **lion fell** fierce lion (perhaps with a pun on *fell* = "skin") 226 **pity on my life** a dangerous thing for me 227 **gentle** gentlemanly, courteous 234 **carry** carry away 239 **lanthorn** (so spelled, and perhaps pronounced "lant-horn," because lanterns were commonly made of horn) 240 **horns on his head** (cuckolds were said to have horns)

The man should be put into the lanthorn. How is it else the man i' th' moon?

DEMETRIUS He dares not come there for the candle; for, you see, it is already in snuff.

250

HIPPOLYTA I am aweary of this moon. Would he would change!

THESEUS It appears, by his small light of discretion, that he is in the wane; but yet, in courtesy, in all reason, we must stay the time.

255

LYSANDER Proceed, Moon.

MOONSHINE All that I have to say is to tell you that the lanthorn is the moon; I, the man i' th' moon; this thorn bush, my thorn bush; and this dog, my dog.

260

DEMETRIUS Why, all these should be in the lanthorn; for all these are in the moon. But, silence! Here comes Thisby.

Enter Thisby.

THISBY This is old Ninny's tomb. Where is my love?

265 LION Oh—   [*The lion roars. Thisby runs off.*]

DEMETRIUS Well roared, Lion.

THESEUS Well run, Thisby.

HIPPOLYTA Well shone, Moon. Truly, the moon shines with a good grace.
            [*The Lion shakes Thisby's mantle, and exit.*]

270 THESEUS Well moused, Lion.

DEMETRIUS And then came Pyramus.

LYSANDER And so the lion vanished.

---

250 **in snuff** (1) in need of snuffing (2) resentful   270 **moused** shaken (like a mouse)

Enter Pyramus.

PYRAMUS Sweet Moon, I thank thee for thy sunny
   beams;
  I thank thee, Moon, for shining now so bright;
  For, by thy gracious, golden, glittering gleams,   275
      I trust to take of truest Thisby sight.
         But stay, O spite!
         But mark, poor knight,
    What dreadful dole is here!
         Eyes, do you see?   280
         How can it be?
    O dainty duck! O dear!
         Thy mantle good,
         What, stained with blood!
    Approach, ye Furies fell!   285
         O Fates, come, come,
         Cut thread and thrum;
    Quail, crush, conclude, and quell!

THESEUS This passion, and the death of a dear friend,
  would go near to make a man look sad.   290

HIPPOLYTA Beshrew my heart, but I pity the man.

PYRAMUS O wherefore, Nature, didst thou lions frame?
  Since lion vile hath here deflow'red my dear:
  Which is—no, no—which was the fairest dame
    That lived, that loved, that liked, that looked
      with cheer.   295
         Come, tears, confound;
         Out, sword, and wound
        The pap of Pyramus;
         Ay, that left pap,
         Where heart doth hop. [*Stabs himself.*]   300
        Thus die I, thus, thus, thus.
         Now am I dead,

---

277 **spite** vexation   279 **dole** sorrowful thing   289 **fell** fierce   287 **thread and thrum** i.e., everything (*thrum* = the end of the warp thread)   228 **Quail** destroy 288 **quell** kill   291 **Beshrew** curse (but a mild word)   295 **cheer** countenance

Now am I fled;
My soul is in the sky.
305   Tongue, lose thy light;
Moon, take thy flight.

[*Exit Moonshine.*]

Now die, die, die, die, die.   [*Dies.*]

DEMETRIUS No die, but an ace, for him; for he is but
one.

310 LYSANDER Less than an ace, man; for he is dead, he is
nothing.

THESEUS With the help of a surgeon he might yet recover, and yet prove an ass.

HIPPOLYTA How chance Moonshine is gone before
315   Thisby come back and finds her lover?

THESEUS She will find him by starlight. Here she comes;
and her passion ends the play.

[*Enter Thisby.*]

HIPPOLYTA Methinks she should not use a long one
for such a Pyramus. I hope she will be brief.

320 DEMETRIUS A mote will turn the balance, which Pyramus, which Thisby, is the better; he for a man,
God warr'nt us; she for a woman, God bless us!

LYSANDER She hath spied him already with those sweet
eyes.

325 DEMETRIUS And thus she means, videlicet:

THISBY Asleep, my love?
What, dead, my dove?
O Pyramus, arise!
Speak, speak. Quite dumb?
330   Dead, dead? A tomb

308 **No die, but an ace** not a die (singular of "dice"), but a one-spot on a die
314 **How chance** how does it come that   317 **passion** passionate speech
325 **means** laments

  Must cover thy sweet eyes.
   These lily lips,
   This cherry nose,
  These yellow cowslip cheeks,
   Are gone, are gone.   335
   Lovers, make moan.
  His eyes were green as leeks.
   O Sisters Three,
   Come, come to me,
  With hands as pale as milk;   340
   Lay them in gore,
   Since you have shore
  With shears his thread of silk.
   Tongue, not a word.
   Come, trusty sword,   345
  Come, blade, my breast imbrue!

           [Stabs herself.]

   And, farewell, friends.
   Thus Thisby ends.
  Adieu, adieu, adieu.   *[Dies.]*

THESEUS Moonshine and Lion are left to bury the 350
dead.

DEMETRIUS Ay, and Wall too.

BOTTOM [*Starting up*] No, I assure you; the wall is
down that parted their fathers. Will it please you
to see the epilogue, or to hear a Bergomask dance 355
between two of our company?

THESEUS No epilogue, I pray you; for your play needs
no excuse. Never excuse, for when the players are
all dead, there need none to be blamed. Marry, if
he that writ it had played Pyramus and hanged 360
himself in Thisby's garter, it would have been a
fine tragedy: and so it is, truly; and very notably
discharged. But, come, your Bergomask. Let your
epilogue alone.   *[A dance.]*

338 **Sisters Three** i.e., the three Fates 342 **shore** shorn 346 **imbrue** stain
with blood 355 **Bergomask dance** rustic dance

365 The iron tongue of midnight hath told twelve.
    Lovers, to bed; 'tis almost fairy time.
    I fear we shall outsleep the coming morn,
    As much as we this night have overwatched.
    This palpable-gross play hath well beguiled
370 The heavy gait of night. Sweet friends, to bed.
    A fortnight hold we this solemnity,
    In nightly revels and new jollity.   *Exeunt.*

              Enter Puck [with a broom].

    PUCK Now the hungry lion roars,
            And the wolf behowls the moon;
375   Whilst the heavy plowman snores,
            All with weary task fordone.
        Now the wasted brands do glow,
            Whilst the screech owl, screeching loud,
        Puts the wretch that lies in woe
380   In remembrance of a shroud.
        Now it is the time of night,
            That the graves, all gaping wide,
        Every one lets forth his sprite,
            In the churchway paths to glide:
385   And we fairies, that do run
            By the triple Hecate's team,
        From the presence of the sun,
            Following darkness like a dream,
        Now are frolic. Not a mouse
390   Shall disturb this hallowed house:
        I am sent, with broom, before,
        To sweep the dust behind the door.

---

365 **told** counted, tolled   369 **palpable-gross** obviously grotesque   376 **fordone** worn out   377 **wasted** used-up   386 **triple Hecate's team** i.e., because she had three names: Phoebe in Heaven, Diana on Earth, Hecate in Hades. (Like her chariot—drawn by black horses or dragons—the elves were abroad only at night; but III.ii.388-91 says differently)   389 **frolic** frolicsome   392 **behind the door** i.e., from behind the door (Puck traditionally helped with household chores)

Enter King and Queen of Fairies with all their train.

OBERON Through the house give glimmering light,
　　By the dead and drowsy fire:
　Every elf and fairy sprite   395
　　Hop as light as bird from brier;
　And this ditty, after me,
　Sing, and dance it trippingly.

TITANIA First, rehearse your song by rote,
　To each word a warbling note: 400
　Hand in hand, with fairy grace,
　Will we sing, and bless this place.

　　　　　　　　　　　　　　　　　　　　[Sing and dance.]

OBERON Now, until the break of day,
　Through this house each fairy stray.
　To the best bride-bed will we,   405
　Which by us shall blessèd be;
　And the issue there create
　Ever shall be fortunate.
　So shall all the couples three
　Ever true in loving be;   410
　And the blots of Nature's hand
　Shall not in their issue stand.
　Never mole, harelip, nor scar,
　Nor mark prodigious, such as are
　Despisèd in nativity,   415
　Shall upon their children be.
　With this field-dew consecrate,
　Every fairy take his gait,
　And each several chamber bless,
　Through this palace, with sweet peace,   420
　And the owner of it blest
　Ever shall in safety rest.
　Trip away; make no stay;
　Meet me all by break of day.

　　　　　　　　　　　　　　　　Exeunt [all but Puck].

---

407 **create** created　414 **mark prodigious** ominous birthmark　418 **take his gait** proceed　419 **several** individual

425 PUCK If we shadows have offended,
Think but this, and all is mended:
That you have but slumb'red here,
While these visions did appear.
And this weak and idle theme,
430 No more yielding but a dream,
Gentles, do not reprehend:
If you pardon, we will mend.
And, as I am an honest Puck,
If we have unearnèd luck
435 Now to scape the serpent's tongue,
We will make amends ere long;
Else the Puck a liar call:
So, good night unto you all.
Give me your hands, if we be friends,
440 And Robin shall restore amends.   [*Exit.*]

FINIS

429 **idle** foolish   430 **No more yielding but** yielding no more than   435 **to scape the serpent's tongue** i.e., to escape hisses from the audience   439 **Give me your hands** applaud   440 **restore amends** make amends

Textual Note

Our chief authority for the text of *A Midsummer Night's Dream* is the First Quarto of 1660 (Q1), possibly printed from Shakespeare's own manuscript. The Second Quarto of 1619 (Q2), fraudulently dated 1600, and the First Folio of 1623 (F) correct a few obvious mistakes of Q1 and add some new ones. The Folio introduces division into acts. The present text follows Q1 as closely as possible, but modernizes punctuation and spelling (and prints "and" as "an" when it means "if"), occasionally alters the lineation (e.g., prints as prose some lines that were mistakenly set as verse), expands and regularizes the speech prefixes, slightly alters the position of stage directions where necessary, and corrects obvious typographical errors. Other departures from Q1 are listed below, the adopted reading first in bold, and then Q1's reading in roman. If the adopted reading is derived from Q2 or from F, the fact is noted in a bracket following the reading.

I.i.4 **wanes** [Q2] waues   10 **New-bent** Now bent   19s.d., **Lysander** [F] Lysander and Helena   24 **Stand forth, Demetrius** [printed as s.d. in Q1, Q2, F]   26 **Stand forth, Lysander** [printed as s.d. in Q1, Q2, F]   102 **Demetrius'** Demetrius   136 **low** loue   187 **Yours would** Your words   191 **I'd** ile   216 **sweet** sweld   219 **stranger companies** strange companions

II.i.69 **steep** [Q2] steppe   79 **Aegles** Eagles   109 **thin** chinne   158 **the west** [F] west   190 **slay ... slayeth** stay ... stayeth   201 **not nor** [F] not not

II.ii.9, 13, 24 [speech prefixes added by editor]   39 **Be't** Bet it   47 **is** [Q2] it

III.i.13 **By'r lakin** Berlakin   29-30 **yourselves** [F] your selfe   56 **Bottom** [Q2] Cet   70 **and let** or let   84 **Odors, odors** [F] odours, odorous   89 **Puck** [F] Quin   164 **Peaseblossom ... All** [Q1, Q2, and F print as a single speech, attributed to "Fairies"]   176 **Peaseblossom ... Mustardseed. Hail** [Q1, Q2, and F print thus: 1 Fai. Haile mortall, haile./2. Fai. Haile./3. Fai. Haile]   195 **you of** you

III.ii.19 **mimic** [F] Minnick   80 **part I so** part I   85 **sleep** slippe   213 **first, like** first life   220 **passionate words** [F] words   250 **prayers** praise   299 **gentlemen** [Q2] gentleman   323 **she's** [Q2] she is   406 **Speak! In some bush?** Speake in some bush   426 **shalt** [Q2] shat   451 **To your eye** your eye

IV.i.76 **o'er** or   85 **sleep of all these five** sleepe: of all these, fine   120 **seemed** seeme   131 **this is my** [Q2] this my   175 **saw** see   202 **let us** [Q2] lets   210 **to expound** [Q2] expound   213 **a patched** [F] patcht a

IV.ii.3 **Starveling** [F] Flute

TEXTUAL NOTE

V.i.34 our [F] or   156 Snout [F] Flute   191 up in thee [F] now againe
275 gleams beams   320 mote moth   353 Bottom [F] Lion   373 lion Lyons
374 behowls beholds   421-22 And the owner ... rest [these two lines are
transposed in Q1, Q2 and F]

ABOUT THE INTRODUCER

TONY TANNER is Professor of English and American Literature in Cambridge University, and Fellow of King's College. Previous publications include *The Reign of Wonder*, *City of Words*, *Adultery and the Novel*, and *Venice Desired*. He has also published studies of Jane Austen, Henry James, Saul Bellow and Thomas Pynchon.

THE EVERYMAN SIGNET SHAKESPEARE

CHINUA ACHEBE
Things Fall Apart

THE ARABIAN NIGHTS
(tr. Husain Haddawy)

MARCUS AURELIUS
Meditations

JANE AUSTEN
Emma
Mansfield Park
Northanger Abbey
Persuasion
Pride and Prejudice
Sense and Sensibility

HONORÉ DE BALZAC
Cousin Bette
Eugénie Grandet
Old Goriot

SIMONE DE BEAUVOIR
The Second Sex

WILLIAM BLAKE
Poems and Prophecies

JORGE LUIS BORGES
Ficciones

JAMES BOSWELL
The Life of Samuel Johnson

CHARLOTTE BRONTË
Jane Eyre
Villette

EMILY BRONTË
Wuthering Heights

MIKHAIL BULGAKOV
The Master and Margarita

SAMUEL BUTLER
The Way of all Flesh

ITALO CALVINO
If on a winter's night a traveler

ALBERT CAMUS
The Stranger

WILLA CATHER
Death Comes for the Archbishop

MIGUEL DE CERVANTES
Don Quixote

GEOFFREY CHAUCER
Canterbury Tales

ANTON CHEKHOV
The Steppe and Other Stories
My Life and Other Stories

KATE CHOPIN
The Awakening

CARL VON CLAUSEWITZ
On War

SAMUEL TAYLOR COLERIDGE
Poems

WILKIE COLLINS
The Moonstone
The Woman in White

JOSEPH CONRAD
Heart of Darkness
Lord Jim
Nostromo
The Secret Agent
Typhoon and Other Stories
Under Western Eyes

DANTE ALIGHIERI
The Divine Comedy

DANIEL DEFOE
Moll Flanders
Robinson Crusoe

CHARLES DICKENS
Bleak House
David Copperfield
Dombey and Son
Great Expectations
Hard Times
Little Dorrit
Martin Chuzzlewit
Nicholas Nickleby
The Old Curiosity Shop
Oliver Twist
Our Mutual Friend
A Tale of Two Cities

DENIS DIDEROT
Memoirs of a Nun

JOHN DONNE
The Complete English Poems

FYODOR DOSTOEVSKY
The Brothers Karamazov
Crime and Punishment

W. E. B. DU BOIS
The Souls of Black Folk

GEORGE ELIOT
Adam Bede
Middlemarch
The Mill on the Floss
Silas Marner

HENRY FIELDING
Tom Jones

GUSTAVE FLAUBERT
Madame Bovary

FORD MADOX FORD
The Good Soldier
Parade's End

E. M. FORSTER
Howards End
A Passage to India

ELIZABETH GASKELL
Mary Barton

EDWARD GIBBON
The Decline and Fall of
the Roman Empire
Vols. 1 to 3: The Western Empire
Vols 4 to 6: The Eastern Empire

IVAN GONCHAROV
Oblomov

GÜNTER GRASS
The Tin Drum

GRAHAM GREENE
Brighton Rock
The Human Factor

THOMAS HARDY
Far From The Madding Crowd
Jude the Obscure
The Mayor of Casterbridge
The Return of the Native
Tess of the d'Urbervilles

JAROSLAV HAŠEK
The Good Soldier Švejk

NATHANIEL HAWTHORNE
The Scarlet Letter

GEORGE HERBERT
The Complete English Works

HINDU SCRIPTURES
(tr. R. C. Zaehner)

JAMES HOGG
Confessions of a Justified Sinner

HOMER
The Iliad
The Odyssey

HENRY JAMES
The Awkward Age
The Bostonians
The Golden Bowl
The Portrait of a Lady
The Princess Casamassima

JAMES JOYCE
Dubliners
A Portrait of the Artist as
a Young Man

FRANZ KAKFA
The Castle
The Trial
Collected Stories

JOHN KEATS
The Poems

SØREN KIERKEGAARD
Fear and Trembling
and The Book on Adler

RUDYARD KIPLING
Collected Stories
Kim

THE KORAN
(tr. Marmaduke Pickthall)

CHODERLOS DE LACLOS
Les Liaisons dangereuses

GIUSEPPE TOMASI DI
LAMPEDUSA
The Leopard